T0122619

Communications in Computer and Information Science   1013

Commenced Publication in 2007
Founding and Former Series Editors:
Phoebe Chen, Alfredo Cuzzocrea, Xiaoyong Du, Orhun Kara, Ting Liu,
Krishna M. Sivalingam, Dominik Ślęzak, Takashi Washio, and Xiaokang Yang

Editorial Board Members

More information about this series at http://www.springer.com/series/7899

Chuan-Yu Chang · Chien-Chou Lin ·
Horng-Horng Lin (Eds.)

New Trends in Computer Technologies and Applications

23rd International Computer Symposium, ICS 2018
Yunlin, Taiwan, December 20–22, 2018
Revised Selected Papers

 Springer

Editors
Chuan-Yu Chang
National Yunlin University
of Science and Technology
Douliu, Taiwan

Chien-Chou Lin
National Yunlin University
of Science and Technology
Douliu, Taiwan

Horng-Horng Lin
Southern Taiwan University
of Science and Technology
Tainan, Taiwan

ISSN 1865-0929   ISSN 1865-0937 (electronic)
Communications in Computer and Information Science
ISBN 978-981-13-9189-7   ISBN 978-981-13-9190-3 (eBook)
https://doi.org/10.1007/978-981-13-9190-3

This Springer imprint is published by the registered company Springer Nature Singapore Pte Ltd.
The registered company address is: 152 Beach Road, #21-01/04 Gateway East, Singapore 189721, Singapore

Preface

The present book includes extended and revised versions of papers presented at the 2018 International Computer Symposium (ICS 2018), held in Yunlin, Republic of China (Taiwan), during December 20–22, 2018.

The ICS 2018 was hosted by National Yunlin University of Science and Technology and technically co-sponsored by Ministry of Education (MOE), Taiwan, and the Ministry of Science and Technology (MOST), Taiwan. ICS 2018 was an excellent forum offering a great opportunity to share research experiences and to discuss potential new trends in the ICT industry. The conference aims mainly at promoting the development of computer technology and application, strengthening international academic cooperation and communication, and exchanging research ideas.

The conference program included invited talks delivered by four world renowned speakers, Professor Yi-Bing Lin from National Chiao Tung University, Taiwan, Dr. Raul Catena from IBM Research Zurich, Switzerland, Professor Reinhard Klette from Auckland University of Technology, New Zealand, and Professor Hitoshi Kiya from Tokyo Metropolitan University, Japan, as well as 20 oral sessions of 99 papers selected from 263 submissions from 11 countries. The topics of these papers range from machine learning, sensor devices and platforms, sensor networks, robotics, embedded systems, networks, operating systems, software system structures, database design and models, multimedia and multimodal retrieval, object detection, image processing, image compression, mobile and wireless security. This book contains 86 papers selected from the submissions to ICS 2018. We would like to thank the authors for contributing their novel ideas and visions that are recorded in this book.

December 2018

Chuan-Yu Chang
Chien-Chou Lin
Horng-Horng Lin

Organization

General Chairs

Pau-Choo Chung   National Cheng Kung University, Taiwan
Wen-Hui Liu   Ministry of Education, Taiwan
Chuan-Yu Chang   National Yunlin University of Science and Technology, Taiwan

International Board Chairs

Chein-I Chang   University of Maryland Baltimore County, USA
Gary Yen   Oklahoma State University, USA
You-Shun Wang   Nanyang Technological University, Singapore
Chia-Yen Chen   University of Auckland, New Zealand
Zhiping Lin   Nanyang Technological University, Singapore

Program Chairs

Ching-Lung Chang   National Yunlin University of Science and Technology, Taiwan
Sheng-Lung Peng   National Dong Hwa University, Taiwan
Sun-Yuan Hsieh   National Cheng Kung University, Taiwan

Publication Chairs

Chien-Chou Lin   National Yunlin University of Science and Technology, Taiwan
Horng-Horng Lin   Southern Taiwan University of Science and Technology

Finance Chair

Chian-Cheng Ho   National Yunlin University of Science and Technology, Taiwan

Local Arrangements Chair

Wen-Fong Wang   National Yunlin University of Science and Technology, Taiwan

Publicity Chairs

Chia-Hung Yeh	National Taiwan Normal University, Taiwan
Ching-Tsorng	TsaiTunghai University, Taiwan
Chung-Wen Hung	National Yunlin University of Science and Technology, Taiwan

Organizing Committee

Hsien-Huang P. Wu	National Yunlin University of Science and Technology, Taiwan
Dong-Her Shih	National Yunlin University of Science and Technology, Taiwan
Li-Wei Kang	National Yunlin University of Science and Technology, Taiwan
Shih-Yu Chen	National Yunlin University of Science and Technology, Taiwan
Wen-Chung Kuo	National Yunlin University of Science and Technology, Taiwan
Chung-Chian Hsu	National Yunlin University of Science and Technology, Taiwan
Der-Tsai Lee	National Taiwan University, Taiwan
Chang-Biau Yang	National Sun Yat-sen University, Taiwan
Hung-Lung Wang	National Taiwan Normal University, Taiwan
Hui-Huang Hsu	Tamkang University, Taiwan
Chin-Tsung Cheng	National Formosa University, Taiwan
Jen-Wei Huang	National Cheng Kung University, Taiwan
Chung-Ho Chen	National Cheng Kung University, Taiwan
Ming-Hwa Sheu	National Yunlin University of Science and Technology, Taiwan
Kun-Chih Chen	National Sun Yat-sen University, Taiwan
Rong-Guey Chang	National Chung Cheng University, Taiwan
Tsang-Ling Sheu	National Sun Yat-sen University, Taiwan
Jenq Muh Hsu	National Chiayi University, Taiwan
Chun-I Fan	National Sun Yat-sen University, Taiwan
Chih-Hung Wang	National Chiayi University, Taiwan
Hung-Min Sun	National Tsing Hua University
Yung-Jen Hsu	National Taiwan University, Taiwan
Yue-Shan Chang	National Taipei University, Taiwan
Jing-Doo Wang	Asia University
Pei-Yin Chen	National Cheng Kung University, Taiwan
Mong-Fong Horng	National Kaohsiung University of Applied Sciences, Taiwan
Mike Y. Chen	National Taiwan University, Taiwan
Kuo-Chin Fan	National Central University
Wen-Huang Cheng	Academia Sinica, Taiwan

Min-Chun Hu	National Cheng Kung University, Taiwan
Yi-Shun Wang	National Changhua University of Education, Taiwan
Wu-Yuin Hwang	National Central University, Taiwan
Wu Ting-Ting	National Yunlin University of Science and Technology, Taiwan
Yu-Chee Tseng	National Chiao Tung University
Chung-Nan Lee	National Sun Yat-sen University, Taiwan
Li-Hsing Yen	National Chiao Tung University, Taiwan
Jonathan Lee	National Taiwan University, Taiwan
Chien-Hung Liu	National Taipei University of Technology, Taiwan
Nien-Lin Hsueh	Feng Chia University, Taiwan
Jung-Hsien Chiang	National Cheng Kung University
Chien-Chuan Ko	National Chiayi University, Taiwan
Yung-Nien Sun	National Cheng Kung University, Taiwan
Jim-Min Lin	Feng Chia University, Taiwan
Ching-Yu Yang	National Penghu University of Science and Technology, Taiwan
Chin-Feng Lai	National Cheng Kung University, Taiwan

Contents

Computer Architecture, Embedded Systems, SoC and VLSI/EDA

Design of Instruction Analyzer with Semantic-Based Loop Unrolling
Mechanism in the Hyperscalar Architecture   3
   Yi-Xuan Lu, Jih-Ching Chiu, Shu-Jung Chao, and Yong-Bin Ye

Local Dimming Design for LCD Backlight   20
   Shih-Chang Hsia, Xin-Yan Jiang, and Shag-Kai Wang

Robot Localization Using Zigbee Nodes   28
   Shih-Chang Hsia, Xiang-Xuan Li, and Bo-Yung Wang

Speech-Based Interface for Embedded Systems.   35
   Yi-Chin Huang and Cheng-Hung Tsai

Computer Networks and Web Service/Technologies

Adaptive Linked-List Mechanism for Wi-Fi Wireless Network   49
   Tsung-Lin Lee, Jih-Ching Chiu, and Yueh-Lin Li

Design and Implementation of Tree Topology Algorithm for Power
Line Communication Network   62
   Guan-Jen Huang, Jih-Ching Chiu, and Yueh-Lin Li

Evolution of Advanced Persistent Threat (APT) Attacks and Actors   76
   Chia-Mei Chen, Gu-Hsin Lai, and Dan-Wei (Marian) Wen

The Impact of the Observation Period for Detecting P2P Botnets
on the Real Traffic Using BotCluster.   82
   Chun-Yu Wang, Jia-Hong Yap, Kuan-Chung Chen, Jyh-Biau Chang,
   and Ce-Kuen Shieh

**Digital Content, Digital Life, Human Computer
Interaction and Social Media**

Deep Residual Neural Network Design for Super-Resolution Imaging   95
   Wei-Ting Chen, Pei-Yin Chen, and Bo-Chen Lin

Markerless Indoor Augmented Reality Navigation Device Based
on Optical-Flow-Scene Indoor Positioning and Wall-Floor-Boundary
Image Registration   106
   Wen-Shan Lin and Chian C. Ho

An Adaptive Tai-Chi-Chuan AR Guiding System Based on Speed
Estimation of Movement   115
   Yi-Ping Hung, Peng-Yuan Kao, Yao-Fu Jan, Chun-Hsien Li,
   Chia-Hao Chang, and Ping-Hsuan Han

Multi-view Community Detection in Facebook Public Pages   131
   Zhige Xin, Chun-Ming Lai, Jon W. Chapman, George Barnett,
   and S. Felix Wu

Image Processing, Computer Graphics and Multimedia Technologies

Supervised Representation Hash Codes Learning.   141
   Huei-Fang Yang, Cheng-Hao Tu, and Chu-Song Chen

The Bread Recognition System with Logistic Regression   150
   Guo-Zhang Jian and Chuin-Mu Wang

Recognition and Counting of Motorcycles by Fusing Support Vector
Machine and Deep Learning.   157
   Tzung-Pei Hong, Yu-Chiao Yang, Ja-Hwung Su, and Shyue-Liang Wang

An Efficient Event Detection Through Background Subtraction and Deep
Convolutional Nets   163
   Kahlil Muchtar, Faris Rahman, Muhammad Rizky Munggaran,
   Alvin Prayuda Juniarta Dwiyantoro, Richard Dharmadi,
   Indra Nugraha, and Chuan-Yu Chang

Light-Weight DCNN for Face Tracking   168
   Jiali Song, Yunbo Rao, Puzhao Ji, Jiansu Pu, and Keyang Chen

3D Facade Reconstruction Using the Fusion of Images and LiDAR:
A Review   178
   Haotian Xu and Chia-Yen Chen

An Application of Detecting Cryptomeria Damage by Squirrels Using
Aerial Images   186
   Chien Shun Lo and Cheng Ssu Ho

Clothing Classification with Multi-attribute Using Convolutional
Neural Network   190
   Chaitawat Chenbunyanon and Ji-Han Jiang

Color Video and Convolutional Neural Networks Deep Learning Based
Real-Time Agtron Baking Level Estimation Method   197
   Qi-Hon Wu and Day-Fann Shen

Deep Virtual Try-on with Clothes Transform   207
   Szu-Ying Chen, Kin-Wa Tsoi, and Yung-Yu Chuang

Scene Recognition via Bi-enhanced Knowledge Space Learning   215
Jin Zhang, Bing-Kun Bao, and Changsheng Xu

Database, Data Mining, Big Data and Information Retrieval

A Hybrid Methodology of Effective Text-Similarity Evaluation   227
Shu-Kai Yang and Chien Chou

Research on Passenger Carrying Capacity of Taichung City Bus with
Big Data of Electronic Ticket Transactions: A Case Study of Route 151   238
Cheng-Yuan Ho and I-Hsuan Chiu

The Ridership Analysis on Inter-County/City Service for the Case
Study of Taichung City Bus System   250
Cheng-Yuan Ho and I-Hsuan Chiu

An Enhanced Pre-processing and Nonlinear Regression Based Approach
for Failure Detection of PV System   260
Chung-Chian Hsu, Jia-Long Li, Arthur Chang, and Yu-Sheng Chen

Evaluation of Performance Improvement by Cleaning on Photovoltaic
Systems   270
Chung-Chian Hsu, Shi-Mai Fang, Arthur Chang, and Yu-Sheng Chen

egoStellar: Visual Analysis of Anomalous Communication Behaviors
from Egocentric Perspective   280
*Mei Han, Qing Wang, Lirui Wei, Yuwei Zhang, Yunbo Cao,
and Jiansu Pu*

Visual Analysis for Online Communities Exploration Based on Social Data   291
*Lirui Wei, Qinghua Hu, Mei Han, Yuwei Zhang, Chao Fan, Yunbo Rao,
and Jiansu Pu*

Forecasting Monthly Average of Taiwan Stock Exchange Index   302
Wei-Ting Sun, Hsin-Ta Chiao, Yue-Shan Chang, and Shyan-Ming Yuan

Incorporating Prior Knowledge by Selective Context Features
to Enhance Topic Coherence   310
Chuen-Min Huang

Parallel, Peer-to-Peer, Distributed and Cloud Computing

Accelerated Parallel Based Distance Calculations for Live-Cell
Time-Lapse Images   321
Hui-Jun Cheng, Chun-Yuan Lin, and Chun-Chien Mao

Order Analysis for Translating NESL Programs into Efficient GPU Code . . .   330
   Ming-Yi Yan, Ming-Hsiang Huang, and Wuu Yang

Auto-scaling in Kubernetes-Based Fog Computing Platform   338
   Wei-Sheng Zheng and Li-Hsing Yen

Information Technology Innovation, Industrial Application and Internet of Things

A General Internet of Thing System with Person Emotion Detection
Function   349
   Wen-Pinn Fang, Wen-Chi Huang, and Yu-Chien Chang

A Biometric Entrance Guard Control System for Improving the Entrance
Security of Intelligent Rental Housing   358
   Jerry Chao-Lee Lin, Jim-Min Lin, and Vivien Yi-Chun Chen

Inception Network-Based Weather Image Classification with Pre-filtering
Process   368
   Li-Wei Kang, Tian-Zheng Feng, and Ru-Hong Fu

Defect Mapping of Lumber Surface by Image Processing for Automatic
Glue Fitting   376
   *Hsien-Huang Wu, Chung-Yuan Hung, Bo-jyun Zeng,
   and Ya-Yung Huang*

Software Testing Levels in Internet of Things (IoT) Architecture   385
   Teik-Boon Tan and Wai-Khuen Cheng

The Modeling of Path Planning for Fire Evacuation   391
   Ching-Lung Chang and Yi-Lin Tsai

Smart Automated Rubber Mixer System Implemented by Internet
of Things for Tire Manufacturing   399
   Yu-Chen Jhu and Chien-Chou Lin

Indoor Navigation Based on a Gait Recognition and Counting Scheme   406
   *Tin Chang, Tzu-Hsuan Chung, En-Wei Lin, Jun-Jie Lai, Xin-Hong Lai,
   Wen-Fong Wang, Chuan-Yu Chang, and Ching-Yu Yang*

Exploration on the Design of Sport Prescription and the Behavior
of College Students   415
   Li Yu-Chiang, Jun-Yi Lin, and Wen-Fong Wang

Algorithms and Computation Theory

A Diagonal-Based Algorithm for the Constrained Longest Common
Subsequence Problem 425
    Siang-Huai Hung, Chang-Biau Yang, and Kuo-Si Huang

Designing an Algorithm to Improve the Diameters of Completely
Independent Spanning Trees in Crossed Cubes 433
    Kung-Jui Pai

A Measure and Conquer Algorithm for the Minimum User
Spatial-Aware Interest Group Query Problem 440
    Chih-Yang Huang, Po-Chuan Chien, and Yen Hung Chen

A Minimum-First Algorithm for Dynamic Time Warping on Time Series ... 449
    Bo-Xian Chen, Kuo-Tsung Tseng, and Chang-Biau Yang

A Note on Metric 1-median Selection 457
    Ching-Lueh Chang

Accelerating Secret Sharing on GPU 460
    Shyong Jian Shyu and Ying Zhen Tsai

An $O(f)$ Bi-approximation for Weighted Capacitated Covering
with Hard Capacity 468
    Hai-Lun Tu, Mong-Jen Kao, and D. T. Lee

A Lyapunov Stability Based Adaptive Learning Rate of Recursive
Sinusoidal Function Neural Network for Identification of Elders
Fall Signal 476
    Chao-Ting Chu and Chian-Cheng Ho

Multi-recursive Wavelet Neural Network for Proximity Capacitive Gesture
Recognition Analysis and Implementation 485
    Chao-Ting Chu and Chian-Cheng Ho

Paired-Domination Problem on Distance Hereditary Graphs 495
    Ching-Chi Lin, Keng-Chu Ku, Gen-Huey Chen, and Chan-Hung Hsu

Rainbow Coloring of Bubble Sort Graphs 503
    Yung-Ling Lai and Jian-Wen He

The Multi-service Location Problems. 507
    Hung-I Yu, Mong-Jen Kao, and D. T. Lee

Total k-Domatic Partition and Weak Elimination Ordering 516
    Chuan-Min Lee

An Approximation Algorithm for Star p-Hub Routing Cost Problem   524
   Sun-Yuan Hsieh, Li-Hsuan Chen, and Wei Lu

Tube Inner Circumference State Classification Optimization by Using
Artificial Neural Networks, Random Forest and Support Vector
Machines Algorithms.   532
   Wei-Ting Li, Chung-Wen Hung, and Ching-Ju Chen

Cryptography and Information Security

A Secure User Authenticated Scheme in Intelligent Manufacturing System. . .   543
   *Ming-Te Chen, Hao-Yu Liu, Chien-Hung Lai, Wen-Shiang Wang,
   and Chao-Yang Huang*

On Delegatability of a Certificateless Strong Designated Verifier
Signature Scheme   550
   Han-Yu Lin, Chia-Hung Wu, and Yan-Ru Jiang

Dynamic Key Management Scheme in IoT.   559
   Po-Wen Chi and Ming-Hung Wang

Secure File Transfer Protocol for Named Data Networks Supporting
Homomorphic Computations   567
   Hsiang-Shian Fan, Cheng-Hsing Yang, and Chi-Yao Weng

A Weighted Threshold Visual Cryptography.   580
   Tai-Yuan Tu, Tzung-Her Chen, Ji-min Yang, and Chih-Hung Wang

Enhancement of FTP-NDN Supporting Nondesignated Receivers   590
   Arijit Karati, Chun-I Fan, and Ruei-Hau Hsu

Flexible Hierarchical Key Assignment Scheme with Time-Based Assured
Deletion for Cloud Storage.   599
   Ping-Kun Hsu, Mu-Ting Lin, and Iuon-Chang Lin

Malware Detection Method Based on CNN   608
   Wen-Chung Kuo and Yu-Pin Lin

Uncovering Internal Threats Based on Open-Source Intelligence   618
   *Meng-Han Tsai, Ming-Hung Wang, Wei-Chieh Yang,
   and Chin-Laung Lei*

Artificial Intelligence and Fuzzy Systems

A Comparison of Transfer Learning Techniques, Deep Convolutional
Neural Network and Multilayer Neural Network Methods
for the Diagnosis of Glaucomatous Optic Neuropathy 627
  Mohammad Norouzifard, Ali Nemati, Anmar Abdul-Rahman,
  Hamid GholamHosseini, and Reinhard Klette

Analysis of Voice Styles Using i-Vector Features 636
  Wen-Hung Liao, Wen-Tsung Kao, and Yi-Chieh Wu

Applying Deep Convolutional Neural Network to Cursive Chinese
Calligraphy Recognition. 646
  Liang Jung and Wen-Hung Liao

Grassmannian Clustering for Multivariate Time Sequences 654
  Beom-Seok Oh, Andrew Beng Jin Teoh, Kar-Ann Toh, and Zhiping Lin

Inflammatory Cells Detection in H&E Staining Histology Images Using
Deep Convolutional Neural Network with Distance Transformation 665
  Chao-Ting Li, Pau-Choo Chung, Hung-Wen Tsai,
  Nan-Haw Chow, and Kuo-Sheng Cheng

Machine Learning Techniques for Recognizing IoT Devices. 673
  Yu Chien Lin and Farn Wang

Scale Invariant Multi-view Depth Estimation Network with cGAN
Refinement. 681
  Chia-Hung Yeh, Yao-Pao Huang, and Mei-Juan Chen

Tracking of Load Handling Forklift Trucks and of Pedestrians
in Warehouses 688
  Syeda Fouzia, Mark Bell, and Reinhard Klette

UAV Path Planning and Collaborative Searching for Air Pollution
Source Using the Particle Swarm Optimization 698
  Yerra Prathyusha and Chung-Nan Lee

Software Engineering and Programming Languages

A Framework for Design Pattern Testing 713
  Nien Lin Hsueh

Supporting Java Array Data Type in Constraint-Based Test Case
Generation for Black-Box Method-Level Unit Testing 721
  Chien-Lung Wang and Nai-Wei Lin

Cost-Driven Cloud Service Recommendation for Building
E-Commerce Websites.   732
   Chia-Ying Wang, Shang-Pin Ma, and Shou-Hong Dai

Healthcare and Bioinformatics

A Computer-Aided-Grading System of Breast Carcinoma:
Pleomorphism, and Mitotic Count.   745
   Chien-Chaun Ko, Chi-Yang Chen, and Jun-Hong Lin

Cateye: A Hint-Enabled Search Engine Framework for Biomedical
Classification Systems.   758
   Chia-Jung Yang and Jung-Hsien Chiang

Wearable Ear Recognition Smartglasses Based on Arc Mask Superposition
Operator Ear Detection and Coherent Point Drift Feature Extraction   764
   Wen-Shan Lin and Chian C. Ho

Automatic Finger Tendon Segmentation from Ultrasound Images
Using Deep Learning.   778
   Chan-Pang Kuok, Bo-Siang Tsai, Tai-Hua Yang, Fong-Chin Su,
   I-Ming Jou, and Yung-Nien Sun

Two-Dimensional TRUS Image and Three-Dimensional MRI Prostate
Image Fusion System   785
   Chuan-Yu Chang, Chih-An Wang, and Yuh-Shyan Tsai

Author Index   793

Computer Architecture, Embedded Systems, SoC and VLSI/EDA

Design of Instruction Analyzer
with Semantic-Based Loop Unrolling
Mechanism in the Hyperscalar Architecture

Yi-Xuan Lu, Jih-Ching Chiu$^{(\boxtimes)}$, Shu-Jung Chao, and Yong-Bin Ye

Department of Electric Engineering, National Sun Yat-Sen University,
Kaohsiung, Taiwan
b013011012@gmail.com, chiujihc@mail.ee.nsysu.edu.tw,
windy55367@gmail.com, zsefbvcx75321@gmail.com,

Abstract. Nowadays ILP processors can't analyze the semantic information of instruction thread to change instruction series automatically for increasing ILP degree. High performance required programs such as image processing or machine learning contain a lot of loop structure. Loop structure will be bounded with the instruction number of one basic block. That cause processors are hard to enhance the computing efficiency. The characteristics of the loop structure in the program are as follows: (1) Instruction will be fetched from cache and be decoded repeatedly. (2) The issued instructions are bounded by the loop body. (3) There is data dependence between iterations. These factors will get worse the poor ILP in the loop codes. In this paper, we propose an architecture called semantic-based dynamic loop unrolling mechanism. The proposed architecture can buffer the instruction series of nested loop, unroll it automatically by analyzing the instruction flow to find the loop body with the semantic of loop instructions, store them to the instruction buffer, and dispatch them to target the processor cores. The proposed architecture consists of three units: loop detect unit (LDU), unrolling control unit (UCU) and loop unrolling unit (LUU). LDU will parse the semantic of instructions to find the closed interval of the loop body instructions. UCU will control LUU in the whole process. LUU will unroll the loop based on the information collected by LDU. Loop controller will handle the complementation overhead for branch miss prediction and the loop finish-up codes. The verifications use ARM instructions generated by *Keil μVision5* compiler. The results show that eliminating iteration dependence can improve ILP by 140% to 180%.

Keywords: ILP of loop · Semantic of loop · Loop unrolling · Hyperscalar · Nested loop

1 Introduction

Loop structures are the main portion of program [1]. The characteristics of the loop structure are as follows: (1) Instruction will be fetched from cache and be decoded again and again. (2) The repeat dependence of instructions in the loop body. (3) The dependence relations between iterations. These factors will cause poor ILP in the

© Springer Nature Singapore Pte Ltd. 2019
C.-Y. Chang et al. (Eds.): ICS 2018, CCIS 1013, pp. 3–19, 2019.
https://doi.org/10.1007/978-981-13-9190-3_1

implementation of the loop for the super-scalar architecture. To improve the computing efficiency of super-scalar architecture, and combine the characteristic of it. In this paper, we propose an approach, called semantic analyzer for loop unrolling, which can increase ILP of loops by parsing the semantics of instructions for collecting the required information of loop unrolling. Loop structure has a specific ordering pattern in machine codes, which produced by compiling it, by formulating the semantic of the loop with the observations of this pattern, we can find the section of loop.

In this paper, we build a semantic-based dynamic loop unrolling mechanism on the instruction analyzer in hyper-scalar architecture, we exploit the ILP for loop structures by unrolling and eliminating iteration of the loop. The characteristics of the semantic-based dynamic loop unrolling mechanism are as follows: (1) Parsing the semantic of instructions to find the closed interval of the loop body instructions. (2) Promote the ILP of loop instructions by eliminating its iteration dependence with an immediate operation. (3) Analyzing the situation during loop unrolling and the relationship between loops to achieve unrolling of a nested loop. (4) Update the data dependence tag of instructions when the branch instruction is taken. (5) Flush the instructions which should not be executed when the branch instruction taken happened. The concepts of proposed architecture are shown in Fig. 1.

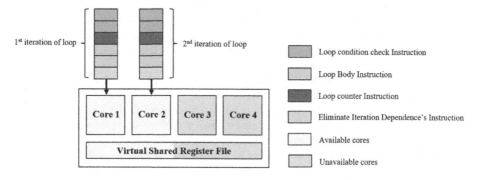

Fig. 1. Concepts of semantic-based dynamic loop unrolling mechanism

2   Related Work

In Hyper-scalar architecture [2–6], it allows the multi-core system to allocate the cores in the system into a single processor system to accelerate of one program. The characteristics of Hyper-scalar architecture are as follows: 1. It can group cores in processor dynamically. 2. its architecture is high flexibility and scalability, 3. It can accelerate single-threaded performance with several cores.

The instructions in Hyper-scalar architecture can be divided into two types as follows by the dependence between them: 1. Intra-Dependence. 2. Inter-Dependence. Hyper-scalar architecture solves Inter-Dependence by analyzing the dependence between instructions dynamically and establishing a distributed system to exchange information between cores.

Figure 2 shows the architecture of Hyper-scalar. The Hyper-scalar architecture dispatch instructions into cores based on the current hardware resources. To exchange information from cores, Hyper-scalar architecture finds the data dependence of instructions clearly by analyzing the relationship between instructions. In order to communicate the information required by the instructions to each core correctly, Hyper-scalar architecture proposed a distributed exchanging information system. It adds information processing unit in each core, the unit is built to deal with the data request from other cores and dispatch the request of the core itself to each core. By connecting cores in the processor, an information exchanging network is built.

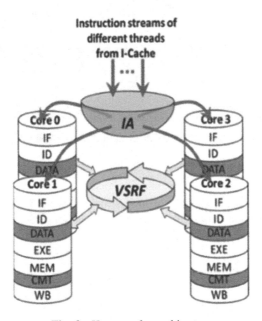

Fig. 2. Hyper-scalar architecture

Hyper-scalar architecture analyzes the dependence of instructions by instruction analyzer (IA). IA analyzes the relationship between instructions and generates the dependence tag of instructions. Virtual shared register files (VSRF) deals with the information exchanging between cores by dependence tag.

Comparing Hyper-scalar architecture and super-scalar architecture, both of them can analyze the dependence of instructions, and dispatch the instruction which data are prepared. By building an information exchanging system of cores, Hyper-scalar architecture has a better performance than super-scalar architecture, but it still has a poor performance when facing loop structure [7–10].

3 Dynamic Loop Unrolling Mechanism

This paper proposed the dynamic loop unrolling mechanism based on semantic analysis of nested loop can analyze the semantic information of instructions and find the interval of a loop. It can also unroll loop and dispatch to each core to improve the ILP as Fig. 3 shows.

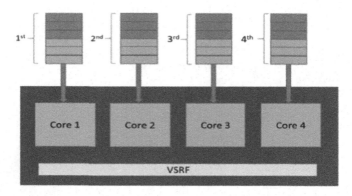

Fig. 3. Loop unrolling

To represent the instruction flow of loop structure, we define six types of nodes: Jump node, Normal node, Counting times node, Flag set node, Branch node, Initial time node, shown as Fig. 4.

Fig. 4. Six types of node

Observe instruction flow of loop, will find the law of compiler, shows as Fig. 5. With the law, we can collect the information in each layer of loop.

3.1 System Architecture

The system architecture proposed by this paper shows as Fig. 6. It can be divided into three parts:

3.1.1 Loop Detect Unit (LDU)

Loop detect unit located in the IA, it analyzes the information came from Pre-Decoder to find the instruction interval of loop. When finding the interval of loop, it will record the Loop Address Information into Loop Buffer inside itself. Loop detect unit compares the instruction which was caught from Instruction Cache with detected loop interval, if

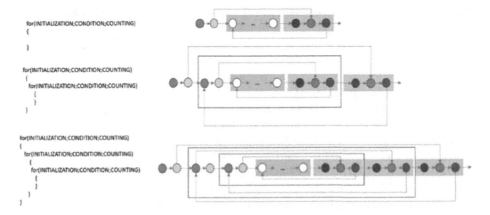

Fig. 5. The instructions of loop after compiled

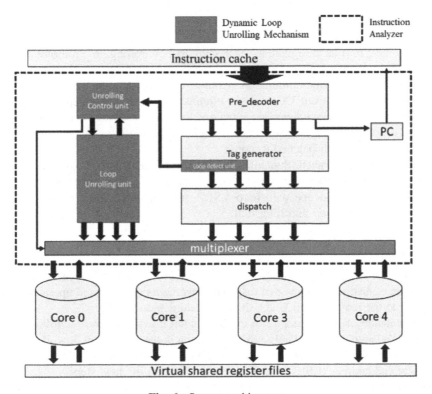

Fig. 6. System architecture

the address is in the interval, it will record the instruction and its operand frame from Pre-Decoder into Loop Instruction Table and Parsing Table.

When Loop Address Information was collected completely, loop-detect-unit will compare the information with other loop's address information to find nested loop structure in the instruction flow. Loop detect unit also record the relationship between loops. After all information in the loop interval in the instruction flow is collected completely, it will send a signal to unrolling control unit (UCU) and dispatch the instruction and its operand frame to UCU according to its request.

3.1.2 Unrolling Control Unit (UCU)

Unrolling control unit is designed to deal with unrolling nested loop. It sends a data request to loop detect unit to get instructions and its operand frame from Loop Instruction Table and Parsing Table and dispatches to loop unrolling unit (LUU) before start unrolling. The dynamic loop unrolling mechanism proposed by this paper divided nested loop structure into inner layer loop and outer layer loop. Dynamic loop unrolling mechanism unrolls the outer layer loop first to get the number of executions of outer layer loop, then unrolls the inner layer loop continuously until the completed times of unrolling equals to the number of executions of outer layer loop. Unrolling control unit decides the number of unrolling loop according to the relationship between loops and the unrolling condition.

3.1.3 Loop Unrolling Unit (LUU)

Loop unrolling unit is designed to deal with loop unrolling, it promotes ILP by eliminating the iteration dependence. Loop unrolling unit detects and eliminates the iteration dependence with eliminating iteration dependence unit, when getting the parsed operand frame from UCU. After eliminating the iteration dependence, loop unrolling unit will generate dependence tag and loop tag to record the execution times of loop. The generated tag and instruction will be pushed into the instruction dispatch queue, and wait to be dispatched to cores.

If unrolling is completed, dynamic loop unrolling mechanism needs to update the data dependence of VSRF mapping table and memory tag mapping table in IA. It updates the data dependence with loop VSRF mapping table and loop memory tag mapping table in the loop unrolling unit.

3.2 Loop Detect Unit

Loop detect unit finds the loop interval in instruction flow by analyzing the semantic information of instruction flow, and dispatches instructions and parsed operand frames according to the request from UCU, the architecture shows as Fig. 7.

The semantic of loop structure in the instruction flow is detected as follow:

Step 1: When detect absolutely jump instruction in the instruction flow, then record the jump address (JA) as loop start address (LS) and its jump target address (JTA) as loop body end address (LBE), shows as Fig. 8. Get into the next step.

Step 2: When detect branch instruction in the instruction flow, then record the branch address (BA) as loop end address (LE) and branch target address (BTA) as loop body start address (LBS), shows as Fig. 9. Get into the next step.

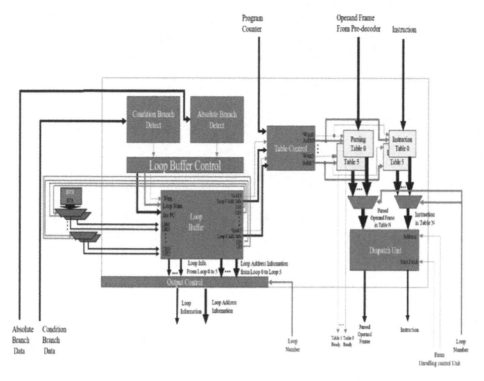

Fig. 7. Architecture of LDU

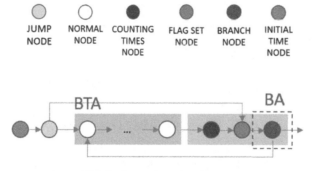

Fig. 8. Loop detecting-Step 1

Step 3: If the information satisfies following conditions: JA < BTA < JTA < BA and BTA = JA + 1. The interval between JTA and BTA is defined as a loop body, shown as Fig. 10.

Each Loop Buffer contains two tables to store the instruction and its parsed operand frame in the interval of the loop. (1). Loop Instruction Table:Record the machine code of the instructions in the interval of loop. (2). Loop Parsing Table:Record the parsed operand frame of the instructions in the interval of loop, shows as Fig. 11.

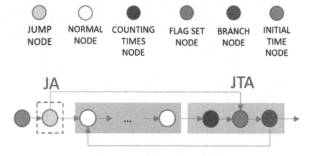

Fig. 9. Loop detecting-Step 2

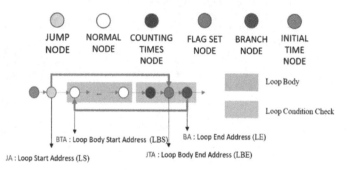

Fig. 10. The interval of loop

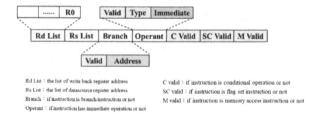

Fig. 11. The format in loop parsing table

3.3 Unrolling Control Unit

Unrolling control unit decides the number of loop by analyzing the signals from LDU and the relationship between loops in unrolling table, the architecture shows as Fig. 12.

The dynamic loop unrolling mechanism proposed by this paper divides the nested loop into outer layer and inner layer when unrolling it as Fig. 13 shows. Dynamic loop unrolling mechanism unrolls the outer layer loop first to get the number of executions of outer layer loop, then unrolls the inner layer loop continuously until the completed times of unrolling equals to the number of executions of outer layer loop. Unrolling the outer layer loop is for getting the number of executions. Therefore, UCU has to deal with the information which will be dispatched to LUU.

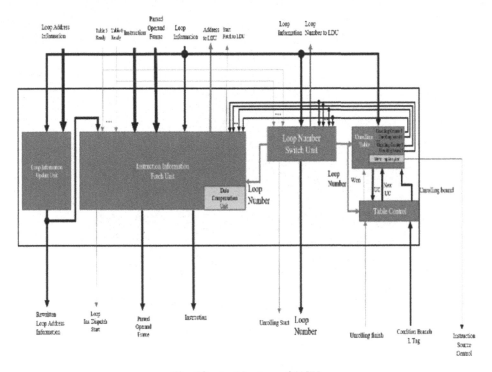

Fig. 12. Architecture of UCU

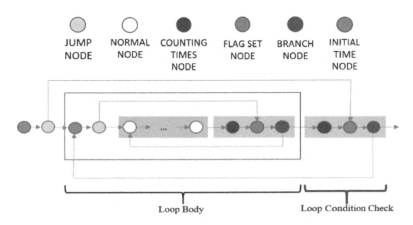

Fig. 13. The structure of nested loop

Take a two-layer nested loop, for example, its loop body contains a single loop. Unrolling the interval of loop condition check to get the number of executions of outer layer loop. To get the correct interval and loop information, when finding the loop in the loop buffer is nested loop, change the loop body start address of outer layer loop into the start address of its loop condition check as Fig. 14 shows.

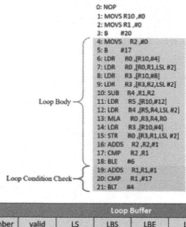

```
0: NOP
1: MOVS R10 ,#0
2: MOVS R1 ,#0
3: B      #20
4: MOVS   R2 ,#0
5: B      #17
6: LDR    R0 ,[R10,#4]
7: LDR    R0 ,[R0,R1,LSL #2]
8: LDR    R3 ,[R10,#8]
9: LDR    R3 ,[R3,R2,LSL #2]
10: SUB   R4 ,R1,R2
11: LDR   R5 ,[R10,#12]
12: LDR   R4 ,[R5,R4,LSL #2]
13: MLA   R0 ,R3,R4,R0
14: LDR   R3 ,[R10,#4]
15: STR   R0 ,[R3,R1,LSL #2]
16: ADDS  R2 ,R2,#1
17: CMP   R2 ,R1
18: BLE   #6
19: ADDS  R1,R1,#1
20: CMP   R1 ,#17
21: BLT   #4
```

Loop Body — lines 4–18

Loop Condition Check — lines 19–21

Loop Buffer							
Number	valid	LS	LBS	LBE	LE	LIN	MLF
0	1	3	19	20	21	1	1
1	1	5	6	17	18	-	-
2	-	-	-	-	-	-	-

Loop Buffer							
Number	valid	LS	LBS	LBE	LE	LIN	MLF
0	1	3	4	20	21	1	1
1	1	5	6	17	18	-	-
2	-	-	-	-	-	-	-

Fig. 14. The correction of nested loop

Unrolling table is inside UCU, it records the unrolling process. Unrolling table records the number of executions of outer layer loop as unrolling bound and records the times of unrolling complete of inner layer loop as unrolling counter.

When the outer layer loop unrolls completely, UCU records the execution times in the unrolling table by its LIN in the loop buffer. When inner layer loop unrolls completely, UCU records the times in the unrolling counter of unrolling table by its own loop number, as Fig. 15 shows.

Loop Buffer							
Number	valid	LS	LBS	LBE	LE	LIN	MLF
0	1	3	19	20	21	1	1
1	1	5	6	17	18		-
2	-	-	-	-	-		-

Unrolling Table		
Number	Unrolling Counter	Unrolling Bound
0		
1		
2		

Fig. 15. Data updating in unrolling table

3.4 Loop Unrolling Unit

Loop unrolling unit (LUU) decides the times of loop unrolling by available core numbers. LUU generates the dependence tag of instructions and the dependence eliminated iteration with immediate operation by the information collected after unrolling finish. It also generates mapping tables to compensate for the dependence of some instructions been aborted. Rearrange dispatch order of these instructions before dispatch, the architecture shows as Fig. 16.

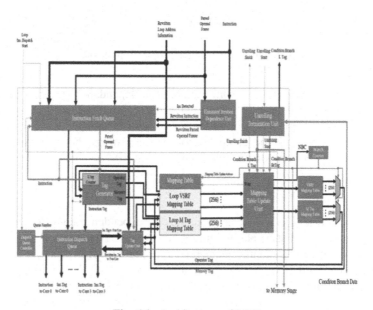

Fig. 16. Architecture of LUU

LUU deals with the data dependence between iterations by register renaming. The RAW hazard of instructions in the internal loop might cause to get the incorrect data dependence in this renaming method, example shows as Fig. 17.

4	AND	R0, R3, #1	I_L0		4	AND	R16, R3, #1	I_L0
5	CBZ	R0, #8	I_L1		5	CBZ	(R0) #8	I_L1
6	ADD	R6, R6, R4	I_L2		6	ADD	R17, R6, R4	I_L2
7	B	#9	I_L3	Renaming Rd of 1st iteration	7	B	#9	I_L3
8	ADD	R7, R7, R4	I_L4	and Rs of 2nd interation	8	ADD	R18, R7, R4	I_L4
9	ADDS	R4, R4, #1	I_L5		9	ADDS	R19, R4, #1	I_L5
4	AND	R0, R3, #1	I_L0		4	AND	R0, R19, #1	I_L0
5	CBZ	R0, #8	I_L1		5	CBZ	(R16) #8	I_L1
6	ADD	R6, R6, R4	I_L2	Renaming Rd of n iteration	6	ADD	R6, R17, R19	I_L2
7	B	#9	I_L3	and Rs of n+1 interation	7	B	#9	I_L3
8	ADD	R7, R7, R4	I_L4		8	ADD	R7, R18, R19	I_L4
9	ADDS	R4, R4, #1	I_L5		9	ADDS	R4, R19, #1	I_L5

Fig. 17. Register renaming between iterations

To deal with it, LUU find out those instructions with the RAW hazard of internal loop and rename them later, shows as Fig. 18.

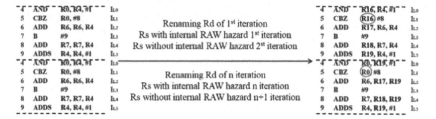

Fig. 18. Register renaming between iterations

There are some situations may cause wrong data dependence mapping or memory get the wrong data, hen unrolling loop. This paper proposed an architecture with compensation mechanism to make sure the accuracy of data dependence mapping and data writing into memory. The compensation mechanism has been divided into two parts to deal with two situations which shown in Fig. 19.

1. The exceeding of loop execution times
2. Specific instruction flush

Since some instructions will be aborted, the data dependence tag of the instructions after the instructions which be aborted might be wrong. To deal with it, we record the data dependence mapping situation demarcated by the branch instruction. Those data dependences are recorded in compensation tables such as Loop VSRF Mapping Table, Loop M Tag Mapping Table and Specific Instruction Flush Table by adding the basic value in Up-to-date Mapping Table to the offset tag of those tables which generated by LUU, shows as Fig. 20.

The L tag records the iteration times of instructions. When the exceeding of loop execution occurs, the mapping tables of IA will be updated by L tag before returning dispatch right to IA.

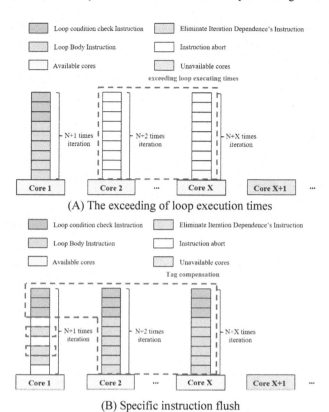

(A) The exceeding of loop execution times

(B) Specific instruction flush

Fig. 19. Compensation mechanism

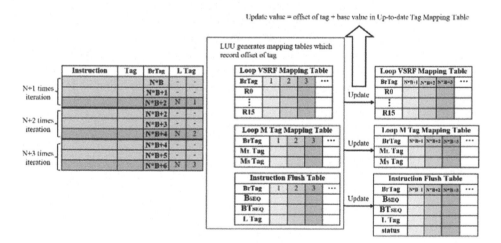

Fig. 20. Compensation tables

Memory Access Delay Buffer is designed to make sure memory data accuracy, shows as Fig. 21. When memory load occurs, it will be searched first, and then get data from memory if there is no data in it. The memory data will store data to Memory Access Delay Buffer first and then store back to memory according to L tag when the unrolling is done.

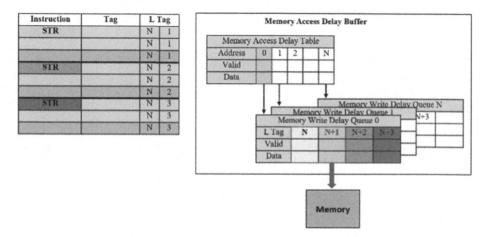

Fig. 21. Memory access delay buffer

4   Simulation and Results

Simulation use C language to build a software simulation model to verify the implementation of semantic-based dynamic loop unrolling mechanism in the Hyper-scalar architecture. The parameter of the simulation model is as shown in Table 1. And the test programs generated by Keil-μVision-5 compiler are as shown in Fig. 22.

The results of instruction flow simulation shown in Fig. 23. The results show that eliminating iteration dependence can improve ILP by 140% to 180%, because of the redundant instructions generated during unrolling, performance improved 50% to 100%.

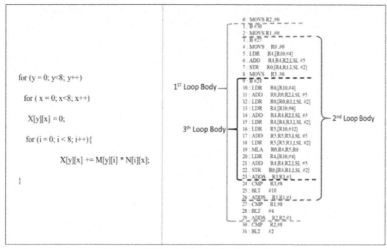

(A) Matrix multiplication

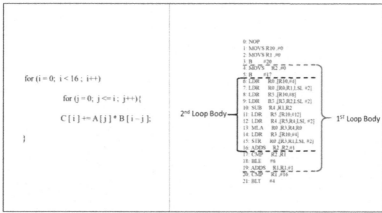

(B) Convolution

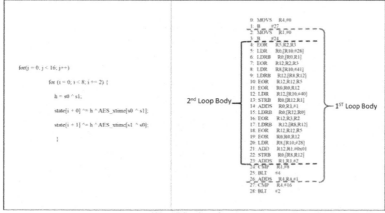

(C) AES-mix column

Fig. 22. The test program

	With unrolling mechanism	Without unrolling mechanism
instructions	5027	3140
cycles	1257	2062
ILP	1.570381	0.591049

(A) Convolution

	With unrolling mechanism	Without unrolling mechanism
instructions	4621	3108
cycles	1123	1640
ILP	1.607916	0.698312

(B) AES-mix column

	With unrolling mechanism	Without unrolling mechanism
instructions	21757	14408
cycles	5703	11323
ILP	1.748356	0.621463

(C) Matrix multiplication

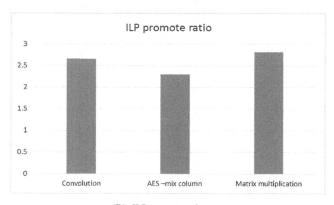

(D) ILP promote ratio

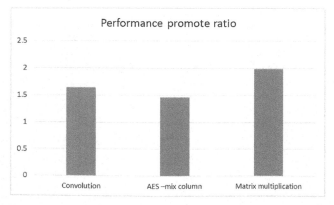

(E) Performance promote ratio

Fig. 23. Simulation results

5 Conclusion and Future Work

This paper proposes the semantic-based dynamic loop unrolling mechanism which is based on the hyper-scalar architecture, it can detect and unroll the loop automatically. It can also decide the unrolling time by core resource.

By eliminating iteration dependence and specific instruction flush can promote ILP of loop. It also makes sure the accuracy of data dependence compensation mechanism. By the result of software simulation, we know that the semantic-based dynamic loop unrolling mechanism can increase the performance while executing loop. When facing the unfixed repeated times of loop and the iteration with the branch instruction, this architecture can also make sure the accuracy of data. In this mechanism, we unroll the loops only according to how many cores resources there are. It may cause the redundant instructions generated during unrolling. We must release the core resources dynamically [11], so that its unrolling time will depend on how many times it used to execute to increase the efficiency of the processors.

References

1. Rotenberg, S.B., Smith, J.E.: Trace cache: a low latency approach to high bandwidth instruction fetching. In: Proceedings of the 29th Annual IEEE/ACM International Symposium on Microarchitecture, MICRO-29, pp. 24–34 (1996)
2. Chou, Y.-L.: Study of the hyperscalar multi-core architecture, Department of Electrical Engineering National Sun Yat-Sen University (2011)
3. Su, D.-S.: Design of the execution-driven simulation environment for hyper-scalar architecture, Department of Electrical Engineering National Sun Yat-Sen University (2008)
4. Chiu, J.-C., Chou, Y.-L., Chen, P.-K., Ding-Siang, S.: A unitable computing architecture for chip multiprocessors. Comput. J. **54**(12), 2033–2052 (2011)
5. Chen, P.-K.: ESL model of the hyper-scalar processor on a chip, Department of Electrical Engineering National Sun Yat-Sen University (2007)
6. Chiu, J.-C., Huang, Y.-J., Ye, Y.-L.: Design of the optimized group management unit by detecting thread parallelism on the hyperscalar architecture, National Computer Symposium, December 2013
7. Yeh, T.Y., Marr, D.T., Patt, Y.N.: Increasing the instruction fetch rate via multiple branch prediction and a branch address cache. In: 7th International Conference on Supercomputing, pp. 67–76, July 1993
8. Dennis, J.B., Misunas, D.P.: A preliminary architecture for a basic data-flow processor. In: Proceedings of the 2nd Annual Symposium on Computer Architecture, Houston, TX, pp. 126–131, January 1975
9. Lerner, E.J.: Data-flow architecture. IEEE Spectr., 57–62 (1984)
10. Fisher, J.A., Faraboschi, P., Young, C.: Embedded Computing, A VLIW Approach to Architecture, Compilers and Tools. Elsevier (2005)
11. Huang, Y.-J.: Design of the optimized group management unit by detecting thread parallelism on the hyperscalar architecture, Department of Electrical Engineering National Sun Yat-Sen University (2013)

Local Dimming Design for LCD Backlight

Shih-Chang Hsia$^{(\boxtimes)}$, Xin-Yan Jiang, and Shag-Kai Wang

National Yunlin University of Science and Technology/Electronic,
Douliu, Taiwan
hsia@yuntech.edu.tw

Abstract. The local-dimming backlight has recently been presented for use in LCD TVs. However, the image resolution is low, particularly at weak edges. In this work, a local-dimming backlight is developed to improve the image contrast and reduce power dissipation. The algorithm enhances low-level edge information to improve the perceived image resolution. Based on the algorithm, a 42-in. backlight module with white LED (Light-Emitting Diode) devices was driven by a local dimming control core. The block-wise register approach substantially reduced the number of required line-buffers and shortened the latency time. The measurements made in the laboratory indicate that the backlight system reduces power dissipation by an average of 48 percents and exhibits no visible distortion compared relative to the fixed backlighting system. The system was successfully demonstrated in a 42-in. LCD TV, and the contrast ratio was greatly improved by a factor of 100.

Keywords: Backlight · Local-dimming · LCD · LED · Image

1 Introduction

Conventional LCD utilizes a fixed backlight to illuminate the LCD panel uniformly. This method consumes much power and causes light leakage from the liquid crystals in the black areas. Recently, the local-dimming backlight was proposed to overcome this drawback [1–5]. The lighting level of the backlight follows the local features in the image. It is dynamically adjusted by the content of the image blocks for local-dimming control. When an image block is bright, the lighting level of the backlight turns high also. Oppositely, the backlighting level is adjusted to low in a black region. This arrangement reduces power dissipation and light leakage from the LCD, increasing the image contrast on the display.

2 Design Methodology

The local dimming method can turn the lighting level low in the black regions, to reduce power dissipation and improve the image contrast. When an image is displayed on an LCD, the most important information is at the edge. However, if the edge is in a low-brightness region, then the estimated level of the backlight is relatively low, and the system turns the level of backlighting to low in this region. Unfortunately, a weak edge is missed and the details of the image may not be perceived, and the resolution is then low.

© Springer Nature Singapore Pte Ltd. 2019
C.-Y. Chang et al. (Eds.): ICS 2018, CCIS 1013, pp. 20–27, 2019.
https://doi.org/10.1007/978-981-13-9190-3_2

To solve this problem, an efficient algorithm was developed to improve the edge information a weakly lit region. Figure 1 presents the proposed local dimming scheme. An image is divided into M × N blocks, and each of which corresponds to one lighting source in the backlight. If the block contains edges, then the lighting level is enhanced to make them more visible on the LCD. Generally, an edge block exhibits a high variance in an image. The mean variance can be used to find the edge blocks. The local block mean-variance (BMV) can be calculated from

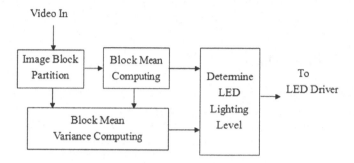

Fig. 1. The proposed local dimming diagram.

$$BMV = \sum_{j=0}^{m} \sum_{k=0}^{n} |F_{jk} - Block_{Mean}|, \tag{1}$$

$$Block_{Mean} = \frac{1}{m \times n} \sum_{j=0}^{m} \sum_{k=0}^{n} F_{jk}. \tag{2}$$

Wherein F_{jk} is the gray-level luminance value of the (j, k)th pixel in a block, and the block size is m × n. If *BMV* is high, then the block contains edge information. Firstly, the maximum BMV value (BMV_{max}) of the image is determined from the estimated frame. The enhancement factor (*Ef*) is defined by

$$Ef = \frac{BMV_{current}}{BMV_{max}} \times \alpha, \tag{3}$$

where $BMV_{current}$ is estimated from the currently processed block, and α is an constant factor. If *Ef* > 1, then let *Ef* = 1. The block backlighting can be calculated by

$$Block_{light} = (1 - Ef) \times Block_{meanlight} + Ef \times Block_{max\,light}, \tag{4}$$

where $Block_{meanlight} = \beta \times Block_{mean}$.

$Block_{maxlight}$ is the maximum lighting level on backlight, which corresponds to the highest gray level of the image. $Block_{meanlight}$ is the mean level lighting that is mapped to the estimated block mean with Eq. (2) by the β. The β value is used to control the brightness of the display. If β is set to high, then the average of backlight level becomes high and the power saving is reduced. When the current block contains edge information, the enhanced factor is increased. From Eq. (4), the block lighting can be raised to improve the perceived resolution of the weak edges on an LCD panel. To reduce one multiplication, the Eq. (4) can be reformed to

$$Block_{light} = Block_{meanlight} + Ef \times (Block_{max\,light} - Block_{meanlight}) \tag{5}$$

If $Ef = 1$, then the backlighting is maximal. If $Ef = 0$, then the backlighting is at its average level.

3   Processing Flowchart

Figure 2 presents the processing flowchart. The color video RGB is converted to YUV using a linear matrix [15]. The Y-signal is used to calculate the lighting level for a white LED backlight. Y-image is divided into M × N blocks, and each of which corresponds to one LED module. Each module contains several LED components. The local-dimming algorithm can compute the LED PWM (Pulse Width Modulation) duty cycle to control the lighting in a manner consistent with image brightness. Since the LED is a discrete light source, multi-layered optical diffuse films are necessary to smooth the LED lighting to make the illumination uniform. The multi-layered optical diffuse films were simulated using multiple-time recursive 7 × 7 low-pass filters [15]. The implemented system uses common diffuse films over the isolated blocks. Figure 3(a) shows the original local-dimming backlight. Figure 3(b) shows the smoothing result after the recursive low-pass filters have been applied 100 times to reduce the LED blocky effect. The low-pass filter effectively simulates the function of the optical diffuse films, which is to make the LED lighting more uniform.

The final image is composed of the original image and the backlight brightness. Each pixel of a displaying image is given by

$$Y_{ij} = \left(\frac{F_{jk} \times B_{jk}}{B_{max}}\right), \tag{7}$$

where F_{jk} is the original pixel and B_{ik} is the backlighting level at the (j, k)th pixel. One local-dimming block has the same backlighting level that is estimated from (5), which can be given by

$$B_{jk}^P = Block_{light}^P, for\ j = 0\ to\ n-1, and\ for\ k = 0\ to\ m-1 \tag{8}$$

when the block size is n × m. B_{jk}^P and $Block_{light}^P$ denote the backlighting for the (j, k)th pixel at the P-th block and the P-th block, respectively. B_{max} is the maximum brightness of the backlight in the estimated frame. If $B_{jk}^P = B_{max}$, then $Y_{jk} = F_{jk}$. The image can be completely reconstructed. When the backlighting is zero, the pixel output Y_{jk} is zero and so the pixel appears a black dot on display.

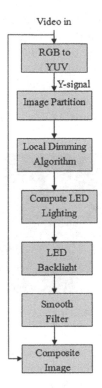

Fig. 2. The flowchart of simulation for local-dimming algorithm

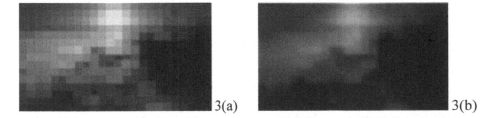

Fig. 3. The original and its filtering image

4   Simulations and Comparisons

Now, various local-dimming algorithms are simulated by C-programming, according to the processing flowchart above. The backlight is designed for a large LCD panel, such as 42-in. Full HD (high-definition) with 1920 × 1080 pixels. It is divided into 24 × 15 blocks for local-dimming control. Each block contains a 2 × 2 LED array, and each block illuminates 5760 pixels. Figure 4 shows the original test image. Figures 5(a), (b), (c) and (d) shows the local dimming backlighting realized using the average, the maximum, the reference [6] and our proposed methods, respectively. In the simulations, our proposed algorithm enhances the backlight level at the low-level edges with $\alpha = 1.25$ in Eq. (3) and $\beta = 1$ in Eq. (4) in simulations. Figures 11(a), (b), (c) and (d) shown the reconstructed images on the LCD obtained using the average, the maximum, the reference [6] and our proposed methods, respectively. The average and the maximum methods can not capture the details of the low-level edges. The reference method [6] improves the detail of the most of the edges. The proposed algorithm further improves the quality of weak edges.

Fig. 4. Original image.

The error values are calculated as the absolute difference between the original image and that of the reconstructed image obtained using each algorithm. Figures 12 (a), (b), (c) and (d) show the error images of the average, the maximum, reference [6] and our proposed methods, respectively. Obviously, the average and maximum methods have large errors. The error in Chen's method [12] is largely reduced. The proposed algorithm can almost exactly reproduce the original image with a very small error.

Next, the parameters are evaluated on various video sequences. Table 1 shows the results with PSNR (peak signal to noise ratio) values and error values. The PSNR values are low in the results of the average and the maximum methods. The reference method [6] has much better 10 to 20 dB than those of the average and maximum methods. Our proposed algorithm yields PSNRs that are further improved by 4 to 5 dB over that of the reference method [6]. The error values are the sum of the absolute errors of one frame in various video sequences. Clearly, the proposed algorithm achieves a lower error than the other local-dimming algorithms (Fig. 6).

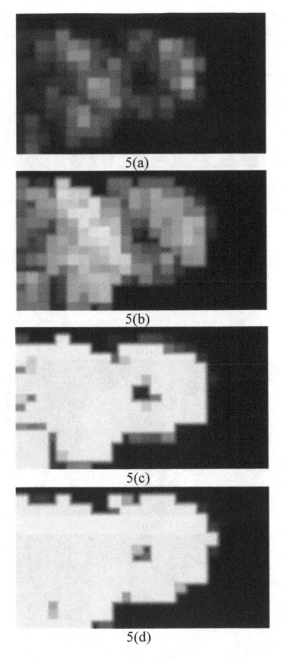

5(a)

5(b)

5(c)

5(d)

Fig. 5. (a), (b), (c) and (d) local dimming backlight with the average, the maximum, the reference [6] and our proposed methods, respectively.

6(a)

6(b)

6(c)

6(d)

Fig. 6. (a), (b), (c) and (d) the reconstructed image as backlight with the average, the maximum, the reference [6] and our proposed methods, respectively.

5 Conclusion

This work presents a high-performance local-dimming algorithm to enhance weak edges and thereby improve the perceived image resolution. Unlike other local-dimming algorithms, the proposed method reproduces images on a LCD without visible distortion. The difference between the fixed and the proposed backlight was almost imperceptible.

References

1. Chen, C.-C., Wu, C.-Y., Wu, T.-F.: LED back-light driving system for LCD panels. In: Proceedings of Applied Power Electronics Conference, pp. 381–385 (2006)
2. Lin, F.C., Liao, C.Y., Liao, L.Y., Huang, Y.P., Shieh, H.P.D.: Inverse of mapping function method for image quality enhancement of high dynamic range LCD TVs. SID Symp. Dig. Tech Papers **38**, 1343–1346 (2007)
3. Lee, T.W., Lee, J.-H., Kim, C.G., Kang, S.H.: An optical feedback system for local dimming backlight with RGB LEDs. IEEE Trans. Consum. Electron. **55**(4), 2178–2183 (2009)
4. Liao, L.Y., Chen, C.W., Huang, Y.P.: Local blinking HDR LCD systems for fast MPRT with high brightness LCDs. J. Disp. Tech. **6**(5), 178–183 (2010)
5. Lai, C.-C., Tsai, C.-C.: Backlight power reduction and image contrast enhancement using adaptive dimming for global backlight applications. IEEE Trans. Consum. Electron. **54**(2), 669–674 (2008)
6. Chen, H., Sung, J., Ha, T., Park, Y., Hong, C.: Backlight local dimming algorithm for high contrast LCD-TV. In: Proceedings of ASID 2006, New Delhi, pp. 168–171, October 2006

Robot Localization Using Zigbee Nodes

Shih-Chang Hsia[✉], Xiang-Xuan Li, and Bo-Yung Wang

National Yunlin University of Science and Technology/Electronic,
Douliu, Taiwan
hsia@yuntech.edu.tw

Abstract. This study, we present a novel robot localization system based on Zigbee nodes. The Zig-Bee locator can provide relative indoor position information. Based on the Zigbee locator, the computer calculates the sensing data and its results are sent to the micro-controller to control motors, to enable make robot walking on the middle of the passageway. The system is successfully implemented and demonstrated in real environment.

Keywords: Robot · Zig-Bee locator · Navigation · Localization

1 Introduction

In the past, many researches studied about the positioning and navigation for robot control in indoor [1–15]. The imaging vision methods are used to record the environmental images and then to recognize them for robot navigation [2–5]. Visual techniques had been applied by many feedback control laws and modeling methods. Generally, the processing of huge image data causes to slow-down for the control speed. Sensor-based approaches [6, 7], such as ultrasonic Sensors and Laser scanning rangefinder, are presented. The former only detect the distance of one direction between robot and obstacle, which is difficult to create the environmental path for positioning. The latter can be used to create 2D path with wide angles to construct the environmental information. The wireless-based with RSSI signal is used to detect the location of robot possible [8–10]. This approach calculates the RSSI signal strengths of all transmitters to determine the robot's position by wireless network sensing. First, we install sensor module within a desired area, and then to sort the strong RF signals to find the short-distance between robot and wireless module. The fuzzy method [13–15] is also used to improve the accuracy of positioning.

In this study, we present auto navigation and positioning system for robot control based on Zig-bee networking. The Zig-bee networking is used to construct global path and positioning point for robot. The rest of this paper is organized as follows. The Zig-bee networking for global positioning is presented in Sect. 2. The implementation and experiments are described in Sect. 3. The conclusions are marked in Sect. 4.

© Springer Nature Singapore Pte Ltd. 2019
C.-Y. Chang et al. (Eds.): ICS 2018, CCIS 1013, pp. 28–34, 2019.
https://doi.org/10.1007/978-981-13-9190-3_3

2 Proposed Global Planning Algorithm Based on Zigbee

The global planning is to guide the robot go to the destination. To design navigation system, the five points of destinations are marked as A ~ E, where C is laboratory inside; D is at the elevator; E is at the door outside of laboratory; A is at the middle of channel; B is a crossing point between channel and elevator. Figure 1 shows the top view for robot navigation, which can guide the robot from elevator (D) to laboratory (C) or alternatively. Each destination set one Zigbee transmitter as a location reference node. ZigBee locator can provide relative indoor position information. The robot has one Zigbee receiver that receives the Received Signal Strength Indication (RSSI) of Zigbee signal. According to RSSI, we can compute the position of robot in the plane immediately.

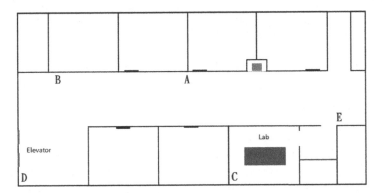

Fig. 1. The top view for robot navigation with five destinations A ~ E.

Figure 2 shows the robot locator using RSSI of zigbee. If the C > E and RSSI > 50, the robot confirms in the laboratory. Otherwise, If the E > C and 20 < RSSI < 50, the robot may near to the door inside of laboratory. If E > A and E > C and RSSI > 50, the robot confirm at the door outside of laboratory. If A > B and A > E and E > B and, the robot locates on the channel between A and E when the signal level is 20 < RSSI < 50. When the signal level is RSSI > 50, the robot is on the middle of channel near to the point A. If B > A and 20 < RSSI < 50, the robot locates on the channel between A and B. RSSI > 50, when the robot near to the point of B. If D > B and 20 < RSSI < 50, the robot now goes to the channel of elevator. When the signal becomes RSSI > 50, the robot now had arrived at the elevator.

The robot navigation combined with global and local planning. First, we set the destination of robot, and read the signal of zigbee and electronic compass to identify the location of the current robot. We check the robot whether located at the crossing points B and E. If it is at E or B, the robot moving direction should be rotated to laboratory or elevator. According to the destination and the current location, we can decide the robot moving forward or backward. If backward moving, the robot rotates 180 degree that let the head of robot at the front of moving direction. Next, we read the histogram of LSR and image to search the best way for robot moving. The controller can send PWM signals to control the motor of robot to go to the destination.

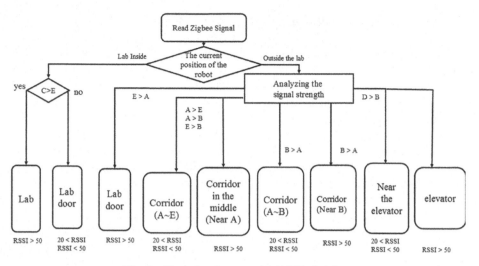

Fig. 2. The robot locator with RSSI of zigbee.

3 System Integration and Experiments

We integrate multi sensors and controller for robot navigation to the specified destination. Figure 3 shows the system control diagram of robot control. In the local control of robot, we used one PIC processor to read compass information and to control PWM of motors. Besides, we employed a flat PC to read the information of zigbee, LSR and camera. The control algorithms are implemented by C programming. The results of computing are sent to PIC through blue tooth for robot motion control.

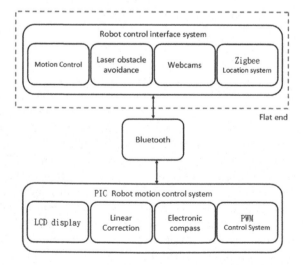

Fig. 3. The system control diagram of robot control.

For real-time robot control, the computer program used multithreading approach that can execute sub-routines in parallel. The robot motion is determined by the sensing signals of LSR, compass, zigbee and camera. We read these sensors using four threads. The information of sensor is processed with one thread for real-time control. Users can select direct motion control mode or patrol mode. Direct motion control mode is to control robot speed, direction, forward or backward by users' command from remote computer. The patrol mode is auto navigation for robot according to sensing information and map. First users set patrol destination, and then robot move following to navigation route. The computer calculates the location according to zigbee RSSI signal, and to find the best way with LSR and camera, and to turn direction with compass sensing.

To verify this system, we design a robot, as shown in Fig. 4. The robot consists of two motors. By speed control of two motors, we can control the moving direction of robot using the differential of motor speed. The flat computer also had been carried on the robot to implement the navigation algorithms, for interactive control of user. The information of zigbee is from its coordinator to computer though Bluetooth networking. We construct a map of routing for robot on a computer. The present robot position can be marked with "red" point on the map to check whether it moving to our expection. We can send a command to robot through Bluetooth to where going. Then robot can move to our predict location. Now we demonstrate the robot navigation system. The starting point of the robot locates on the way between A and B, as shown in Fig. 5(a). If the destination is set to laboratory in the point of C, the navigation system guides the robot move forward to the points A and E. The robot will stop at the point of E that is great gate of laboratory. Then the robot turns its direction to the gate according to compass information, as shown in Fig. 5(b). Then the robot enters to the great gate of laboratory and going the small gate of laboratory C, as shown in Fig. 5(c).

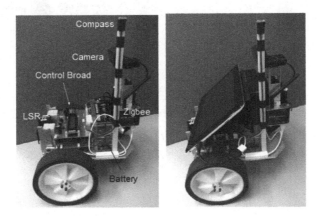

Fig. 4. The prototype of our proposed robot.

32   S.-C. Hsia et al.

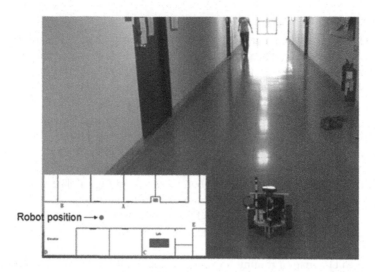

Fig. 5(a). The robot navigation on the way between the location A and B. (Color figure online)

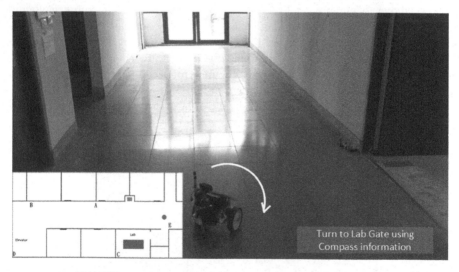

Fig. 5(b). Control robot turn to Lab. gate by compass sensing.

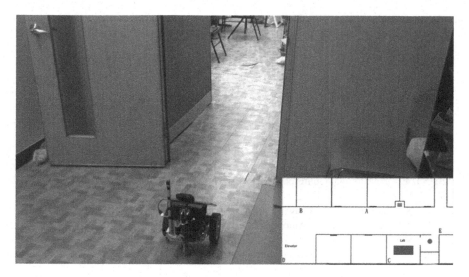

Fig. 5(c). Robot enter to Lab.

4 Conclusions

In this study, we presented a navigation system of robot using multi-sensors. The RSSI signals of zigbee are used to calculate the location of robot. We employ LSR information with double scanning method to find the best channel for robot passing. Besides, camera is used as an auxiliary of LSR when the robot faces thin obstacle. The compass sensor is used when the robot require to turn its direction at a specified location. The prototype of robot is successfully realized, which consists of a flat computer, control board, two motors and multi-sensors. The navigation algorithms had been developed and integrated into robot system. Both of the user mode and patrol mode for robot control are effectively implemented. Results demonstrate that the navigation system of our robot can be guided the robot to its destination by a remote computer when the patrol mode is set.

References

1. Hamid, M., Adom, A., Rahim, N., Rahiman, M.: Navigation of mobile robot using global positioning system (GPS) and obstacle avoidance system with commanded loop daisy chaining application method. In: 2009 5th International Colloquium on Signal Processing & Its Applications (CSPA), pp. 176–181 (2009)
2. Wang, C., Fu, Z.: A new way to detect the position and orientation of the wheeled mobile robot on the image plane. In: 2014 IEEE International Conference on Robotics and Biomimetics, pp. 2158–2162 (2104)
3. Chen, C.-J., Huang, W.S.-W., Song, K.-T.: Image tracking of laparoscopic instrument using spiking neural networks. In: 2013 13th IEEE International Conference on Control, Automation and Systems (ICCAS), pp. 951–955 (2013)

4. Mardiyanto, R., Anggoro, J., Budiman, F.: 2D map creator for robot navigation by utilizing Kinect and rotary encoder. In: 2015 IEEE International Seminar on Intelligent Technology and Its Applications, pp. 81–84 (2015)
5. Li, L., Liu, Y.-H., Wang, K., Fang, M.: Estimating position of mobile robots from omnidirectional vision using an adaptive algorithm. IEEE Trans. Cybern. **45**(8), 1633–1646 (2015)
6. Luo, C., Gao, J., Li, X., Mo, H., Jiang, Q.: Sensor-based autonomous robot navigation under unknown environments with grid map representation. In: 2014 IEEE Symposium on Swarm Intelligence (SIS), pp. 1–7 (2014)
7. Lim, J., Lee, S., Tewolde, G., Kwon, J.: Indoor localization and navigation for a mobile robot equipped with rotating ultrasonic sensors using a smartphone as the robot's brain. In: 2015 IEEE International Conference on Electro/Information Technology (EIT), pp. 621–625 (2015)
8. Zhou, N., Zhao, X., Tan, M.: RSSI-based mobile robot navigation in grid-pattern wireless sensor network. In: Chinese Automation Congress (CAC), pp. 497–501 (2013)
9. Miah, M.S., Gueaieb, W.: Indoor robot navigation through intelligent processing of RFID signal measurements. In: 2010 International Conference on Autonomous and Intelligent Systems (AIS), pp. 1–6 (2010)
10. Chang, C.L., Jhu, J.H.: Zigbee-assisted mobile robot gardener. In: 2013 International Automatic Control Conference (CACS), pp. 41–46 (2013)
11. Li, W., Wu, H., Chen, Y., Cheng, L.: Autonomous navigation experiment for mobile robot based on IHDR algorithm. In: The 5th Annual IEEE International Conference on Cyber Technology in Automation, Control and Intelligent Systems, pp. 572–576 (2015)
12. Choi, S., Lee, J.-Y., Yu, W.: uRON v1.5: a device-independent and reconfigurable robot navigation library. In: 2010 IEEE Workshop on Advanced Robotics and its Social Impacts, pp. 170–175 (2010)
13. Chinag, C.-H., Ding, C.: Robot navigation in dynamic environments using fuzzy logic and trajectory prediction table. In: 2014 International Conference on Fuzzy Theory and Its Applications (iFUZZY2014), pp. 99–104 (2014)
14. Faisal, M., Al-Mutib, K., Hedjar, R., Mathkour, H., Alsulaiman, M., Mattar, E.: Multi modules fuzzy logic for mobile robots navigation and obstacle avoidance in unknown indoor dynamic environment. In: 2013 International Conference on Systems, Control and Informatic, pp. 371–379 (2013)
15. Nazari, M., Amiryan, J., Nazemi, E.: Improvement of robot navigation using fuzzy method. In: 2013 3rd Joint Conference of AI & Robotics and 5th RoboCup Iran Open International Symposium (RIOS), pp. 1–5 (2013)

Speech-Based Interface for Embedded Systems

Yi-Chin Huang[1(✉)] and Cheng-Hung Tsai[2]

[1] National Pingtung University, Pingtung, Taiwan
ychuangnptu@mail.nptu.edu.tw
[2] Institute for Information Industry, Taipei, Taiwan

Abstract. In recent years, there is a rising interest in aiding people with computer technologies. One of the possible research ways is the use of speech interface for the low resource device such as mobile phones or PDAs. In this paper, we proposed a systematic way to construct a speech interface for the mobile device such as an Android phone. First, an automatic speech recognition system is built based on the Hidden Markov Model (HMM) framework. In order to understand the utterance from user in daily life, the spontaneous speech recognition is implemented. For speech generation, a personalized speech synthesis system is also included for the proposed system. Experimental results have shown that the performance of the speech recognition and synthesis achieve good performance. Therefore, the proposed speech interface could be applied to other system such as computer vision system in order to help people to perceive the environment and interact with other people in daily life.

Keywords: Embedded system · Speech interface · Speech recognition · Speech synthesis

1 Introduction

According to estimates by the World Health Organization (WHO), there are about 285 million people suffered from visual impairments or blindness [1]. Without visual information, people will have difficulties with their daily life such ad reading, finding objects and etc. Therefore, we would like to proposed a speech interface system as a bridge to communicate with other system, such as a dialog management System, in order to let user to intuitively interact with the system. However, the computation power of the mobile devices usually not as powerful as the personal computer. Therefore, a small footprint speech interface is required for such device in order to respond to user in real time. The statistical-based speech interface would be helpful since it only requires the constructed model and the underlying model framework such as Hidden Markov Model.

The proposed speech interface system consists of two sub-systems as Fig. 1 shows. The user utters the speech command, *Utt*, to the first sub-system, which is a speech recognition system. The proposed speech recognition system is implemented with the

C.-Y. Chang et al. (Eds.): ICS 2018, CCIS 1013, pp. 35–45, 2019.
https://doi.org/10.1007/978-981-13-9190-3_4

focus on the spontaneous speech uttered by user. Therefore, the occurrence of the syllable-construction is critical to deal with. The output of the first sub-system, W_Q, is the word sequence of the recognized speech commands. The backend system should be able to capture the key information of the input command and then provide the suitable feedback of the command. In the scope of this paper, we will not address the implementation of the backend system. In a typical applicable situation, the backend system could be a computer vision system which could identify the objects captured by the wearable equipment. The recognized command then processed by the backend system and give the answer for the user command. Finally, the pre-trained speech synthesis model is adopted to generate speech output for the answer, W_A, from the backend system. Here, the framework of the speech synthesis system is based on the HMM-based acoustic model. In order to generated fluent speech, the prosodic command-based system [2] is used here.

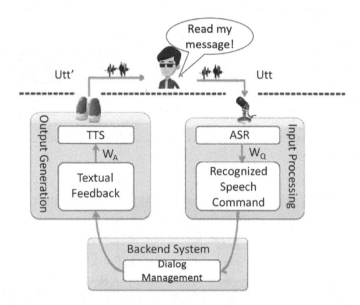

Fig. 1. Illustration of the proposed speech interface system for user on a mobile device.

The rest of the paper is organized as follows. In Sect. 2, the proposed speech recognition system is introduced. In Sect. 3, the fluent speech generation sub-system is introduced. In Sect. 4, evaluation of sub-systems are addressed. Finally, the conclusion remarks are discussed in Sect. 5.

2   Speech Recognition Sub-system

Automatic speech recognition (ASR) is a field in human-computer interaction in which the speaker's utterances are transcribed to a string of word. Moreover, ASR enables a computer to receive input speech through speech. The challenge in the proposed speech recognition sub-system consists of transcribing a speaker's utterance U in to a word sequence W. This is described by the fundamental equation of speech recognition Mathematically as follow:

$$
\begin{aligned}
\mathbf{W}_t^* &= \arg\max_w P(\mathbf{W}|U_t) \\
&= \arg\max_w \frac{P(U_t|\mathbf{W})P(\mathbf{W})}{P(U_t)} \\
&\propto \arg\max_w P_{AM}(U_t|\mathbf{W})P_{LM}^{\alpha}(\mathbf{W})
\end{aligned}
\tag{1}
$$

Given an utterance U, ASR determines the word sequence W_t^* that maximize the probability $P_{AM}(W|U_t)$ and thus is most likely to be spoken. This leads to three general components: *(1)* Acoustic Modeling: calculating the conditional probability $P_{AM}(U_t|W)$ of yielding utterance U given the word sequence W; *(2)* Language Modeling: estimating the probability of the word sequence $P_{LM}(W)$ in language; *(3)* Decoder: efficiently estimate the best word sequence W_t^* that maximize the product of acoustic model and language model. In process of speech recognition, a word sequence is further into basic phonetic units from the word-level units. The acoustic model (AM) provides an estimation on the phonetic layer, while the language model (LM) describes the sequence of words. This process is linked by the pronunciation lexicon, mapping phonetic units to words. Furthermore, a signal processing is employed to extract features from the input utterance.

AMs can be created from a corpus and represented as hidden Markov models (HMMs). For LM, commonly used statistical models, n-gram, are flexible and are able to easily cope with ungrammatical utterances as found in spontaneous speech. Similar to the acoustic models they need a great deal of training data, which does not necessarily need to stem from a gathered training set.

2.1   Pronunciation Variation

Pronunciation variation (PV) is a key factor contributing the high error rate of current ASR techniques. In Mandarin, PV can be categorized into several various types [3]: Prolong, Assimilation, Syllable Construction, Nasalization, Inappropriate pronunciation. Syllable contraction (SC) is the dominant PV among all PVs; thus, this work focuses on PVs caused by syllable contraction.

For the phonological factor, SC can be explained using edge-in theory [4],

$$
C_1 V X_1 + C_2 V X_2 \rightarrow C_1 V X_2
\tag{2}
$$

where the initial part C_1 of the first syllable and ends with the final part X_2 of the second syllable in Mandarin speech. For the morphological factor, the morphological distribution influence characteristics of SC and more than one contraction forms for a given sequence of syllables can be obtained. These words are mostly function words. As addressed in [5], most frequent words with reduced pronunciation are also the most frequent words in the Switchboard corpus.

A two-pass strategy for spontaneous speech recognition with meta-information is adopted in this paper. For example, an utterance with transcription is "喔(oh)這樣 (zheyang)子(tz)." However, "這樣/zheyang/" was a syllable contracted word and pronounced as "/jiang/," which is regarded as a PV. For first-pass, a conventional ASR with an expanded dictionary which a dictionary entry can comprise multiple pronunciations is utilized to generate the initial N-best list.

In second-pass, the meta-information is employed to re-score the N-best list to obtain the optimal word sequence, W^*, as the final recognition result. Therefore, in the proposed system, the acoustic-level score in Eq. (1) is rescored by the meta-information E and further broken into two terms.

$$
\begin{aligned}
P_{AM}(U_t|W) &= \sum_E P(U_t, E|W) \\
&= \sum_E P(U_t|E)P(E|W) \\
&\propto \max_E P_D(U_t|E)P_T(E|W)
\end{aligned}
\tag{3}
$$

where the terms $P_D(U_t|E)$ and $P_T(E|W)$ are introduced as duration score and transformation score.

For the transformation score training, first, forced-alignment is employed to obtain the training targets for k-th SC word SC^k. Then, ASR process these speech segments and output J-best candidates. Next, each candidate $c_{i,j}$ of the i-th instance is assigned a weight value

$$
W(c_{i,j}) = J - j + 1
\tag{4}
$$

where $W(\bullet)$ is a simple weighting function. For example, the weight value of candidate $c_{i,2}$ in 5-best candidates is $5 - 2 + 1 = 4$. Moreover, M unique token types are sorted over all $I \times M$ candidates in which I is the size of training set.

Figure 2 illustrates the motivation and flowchart for duration score training. In dynamic programming, when state sequences of HMMs are well trained from a corresponding utterance, an aligned path appears in the diagonal as the alignment example (Fig. 2(a)). Either the features of a SC-word are aligned to states of the normal word or the SC case will match the cases (Fig. 2(b) and (c)), where most frames are assigned to one state, such that alignment paths appear in the upper-right or lower-left regions. Here, we adopted the eigen-codeword method proposed in our previous work [6] for generating the duration score. By re-scoring the N-best results of the original recognition, we could obtained the optimal word sequences considering the syllable contraction occurrence.

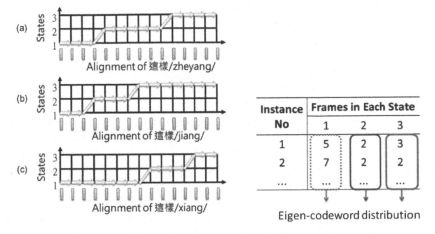

Fig. 2. Illustration of duration score and modeling.

3   Speech Synthesis Sub-system

In this sub-system, we combined the HMM-based Mandarin speech synthesis system with a novel method that selecting natural prosodic unit sequence by pitch pattern retrieval, which is called "Hierarchical prosodic unit selection" in the paper. Subsequently, the prosodic sequence is applied as the feature vector of F_0, together with spectral feature vector and duration information to regenerate synthesized speech with natural pitch contour.

The details of the proposed hierarchical prosodic unit selection are described in the following. pitch patterns are consists of two components, namely the prosodic phrase (PP) and prosodic word (PW). As described by previous researches, each prosodic units has its contribution of observed pitch contour. From the corpus analysis, each PW in Mandarin speech usually consists of one to three syllables, and a PP is composed of more than one PW. The length of an utterance is approximately 1 to 25 syllables, which usually consists of 1 to 5 PPs. This phenomenon is consistent with the description in the previous study [7]. Based on this observation, syllable is regarded as the basic unit, PW is regarded as the higher-level unit, and PP is the highest-level unit in the prosodic structure of one utterance, respectively. Thus, in this study, each prosodic unit is modeled to fully regenerate original pitch contour.

Since Mandarin is a tonal language, which means pitch contour of each syllable can be modulated by its tone. So, a two-level pitch pattern clustering is applied to both prosodic units. For each PW, it is categorized by its linguistic information, such as number of syllable in the PW, duration of PW, and it tone combination. Subsequently, in the same linguistic category, an iterative K-means clustering applied based on its shape of the interpolated pitch contour is adopted. Finally, each resultant cluster is called "PW-codeword" for the clustered similar pitch patterns. For PP case, since PP is more related to its position of utterance, in the first level clustering, its position is used as the clustering criterion. The same k-means clustering based on its shape is adopted.

Finally, "PP-codeword" can be obtained. For the second level clustering, spline interpolation is adopted to fill the unvoiced part of each syllable. The PW and PP codewords are used to calculate the statistical distribution of training corpus and synthesized corpus.

For pitch patterns of the same codeword cluster, its pitch contour and duration have to be stored to regenerate it original pitch contour. However, in conventional way, each pitch value of pitch contour is stored and used directly to concatenate a desired pitch contour. This method causes the need of large storage and discontinuity problem between unit boundaries. Here, we adopted a well-known Fujisaki model [8] to deal with these two problems. Fujisaki model is designed to generate pitch contour by the sum of three components. The first one is Low Frequency Component (LFC), which represents the global movement of input pitch contour, is modeled by phrase command. The second one is High Frequency Component (HFC), which represents the subtle, local variation of the input pitch contour, is modeled by accent/tone command. The last on is Base Frequency (Fb), which represents the basis frequency value of the input pitch contour. Figure 3 shows an example of original pitch contour and three Fujisaki components. In our study, we modified the original Fujisaki model in some aspects to fit our hierarchical prosodic units. Figure 4 shows the modified Fujisaki commands. First, the positive and negative commands are adopted in the tone component to simulate rising and falling tone more accurately, and the tone command sequence of each PW codeword is calculated. Second, for each PP, we calculated phrase command sequence of each PP in the utterance, instead of calculating phrase command of entire utterance in order to model detailed pitch con-tour of each PP.

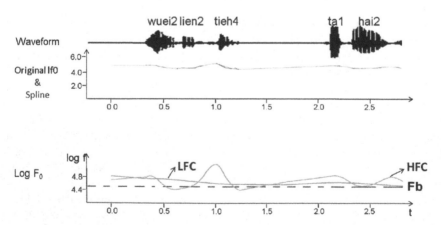

Fig. 3. Example of waveform and its high frequency component (HFC) low frequency component (LFC) generated by modified Fujisaki model.

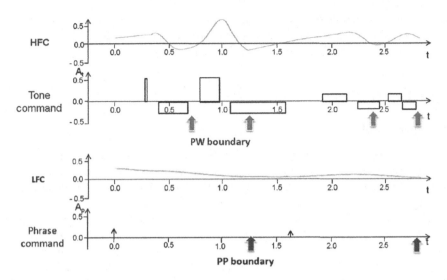

Fig. 4. Tone command of PW and phrase command of PP of the modified Fujisaki model.

Here, we used a codeword vector to represent the query of each input utterance. The vector representation of PW and PP codeword sequence is generated, respectively. The same vector representation is adopted for the synthesized corpus. The cosine measure is applied to rank each utterance of the synthesized corpus based on the similarity of vector representation of input utterance.

After ranking all utterances in the synthesized corpus, the candidate synthesized codewords are selected based on their ranking, respectively. The codeword mapping procedure is then adopted to map each synthesized codeword to its corresponding real codeword occurred in the same utterance of training corpus. In this way, the real codewords can be selected to expend the candidate codewords. With candidate codewords of each PW and PP of the input utterance, a codeword language model is used to find the most suitable codeword sequence for PW and PP. Note that the codeword language model is trained based on real-PW and real-PP codewords, so the optimal codeword sequence becomes more similar to the pitch pattern of real pitch contour. The optimal codeword sequence is selected based on the following equation.

$$\hat{c}_1^L = \arg\max_{c_1^L}\left\{Lan(c_1^L, u_1^L)\right\}$$

$$Lan(c_1^L, u_1^L) = \sum_{i=1}^{L} Uni(i_i, c_i) + \sum_{i=2}^{L} Bi(c_{i-1}, c_i)$$

(5)

and $Uni(u_i, c_i)$ is the unigram probability of codeword c and $Bi(c_{i-1}, c_i)$ is the bigram probability of (c_{i-1}, c_i).

After the optimal codeword sequences is selected, the pitch con-tour regeneration is achieved by selecting suitable pitch pattern of each selected codeword cluster. Since each pitch pattern is stored as command, the pitch contour can be regenerated by applying filter function of the Fujisaki model. The suitable pitch pattern of each codeword is selected based on the continuity of boundary of nearby pitch contour, and a trivial smoothing criterion between trajectory is applied here.

4   System Evaluation

4.1   Speech Data

For the both speech recognition and synthesis systems, a parallel corpus from a native Mandarin male speaker was collected. This phonetically balanced small parallel speech corpus, containing read speech and spontaneous speech with syllable contraction, was designed and collected. An acoustician verified the accuracy of the expressed syllable contraction in each spontaneous speech utterance and tagged the syllabic boundaries.

The textual sentences of the parallel sub-corpora were collected from daily conversations, gossip, chatting, and similar forms of everyday verbal communication. Of the more than 300 collected textual sentences, only a few sentences (containing words with syllable contraction) were selected for recording by the speaker. The speaker recorded all parallel speech utterances of the same sentences in reading and spontaneous styles.

The recorded speech in a spontaneous style was collected by asking the speaker to utter the designed sentences naturally in a spontaneous style. Some speech sentences, which were mispronounced, and the utterances with low quality or high background noise were removed. Finally, 200 sentences satisfying the above requirements were remained. The average duration of a syllable in spontaneous speech is much shorter.

4.2   Implementation of Speech Recognizer and Performance

For speech recognition, an Hidden Markov model Toolkit (HTK)-based speech recognition system [9] was constructed to transcribe the speech data. Each of 411 Mandarin base syllables can be decomposed into an Initial/Final format very similar to the consonant/vowel relations in other language. The acoustic models in our ASR system include 115 right-context-dependent Initial models, 38 context-independent Final models. There are 47 syllable-level models for hyper-articulated speech (also the most frequent SC-word) are included into our ASR system.

For training, non-skipping 3-state HMMs for the Initials, 5-state HMMs for the Finals, 7-state HMMs for the contracted Di-syllable, and 10-state HMMs for the contracted Tri-syllable with no more than 32 Gaussian mixtures per state, are used in our system. The speech feature vector consists of the 12 Mel-frequency cepstral coefficients (MFCCs) and the log energy, enhanced by the delta and acceleration features for a frame size of 32 ms with a frame shift of 10 ms. For the real-world data with a variety of speakers, a reliable acoustic model is needed. Hence, seed acoustic model set trained by the TCC-300 Mandarin read-speech corpus [10] is adapted by the evaluation data via maximum-likelihood linear regression (MLLR). A bi-gram language model is estimated by the SRILM [11] toolkit and adapted by the evaluation data.

Table 1 shows the recognition results at syllable level. The row captioned as Baseline demonstrates the recognition performance of baseline ASR. For the case **+Duration**, the transformation score is set to equal value; where the duration score is set to equal value for the case **+Transform**. The last row captioned as **+Both** demonstrates the speech recognition performance of proposed approach. As shown in the results, the meta-information can be employed to improve the recognition performance.

Table 1. Average recognition results at syllable level.

Set	Accuracy (%)
Baseline	76.28
+Duration	78.46
+Transform	79.15
+Both	80.46

4.3   Implementation of Speech Synthesizer and Performance

For speech synthesis sub-system, the pitch pattern clustering, the stopping criterion is that the number of pitch pattern should be no less than 10 in each cluster. The resultant number of the PW and PP codeword is 4,206 and 1,856 for the synthesized corpus. The number of codeword for the training corpus is 4532 and 1902 for PW and PP, respectively.

In order to compare with the conventional HMM-based method, we integrated the proposed method with a HMM-based Mandarin TTS system, as proposed in our previous work [2]. The generated pitch contour is aligned to pitch contour of HMM-based model based on the prosodic boundary and then is scaled to match the duration of syllables of the synthesized speech.

The 5-point Mean Opinion Score (MOS) test is held to evaluate the effectiveness of the proposed method. 20 synthesized speech generated by the proposed method and HMM-based method were presented to 10 native participants in a random order. The synthesized utterances were not included in the training corpus, and were selected from the daily newspapers. The participants were asked to score speech quality of each utterance. The ABX preference test is also held to compare the speaker similarity of both methods. Participants listened to some utterances of training corpus as the reference of the target voice, and then a pair of synthesize utterances is presented, which were generated by both methods. Participants were asked to chose which one is more similar to voice of training corpus, especially in terms of pitch variation.

The results of MOS test showed in the upper plot of Fig. 5. The proposed method achieved similar score to that of HMM-based method, and the speech quality of reference real speech achieved highest score (which was scored by participants using 10 training utterances). As the results showed, the speech quality of the pro-posed method, which basically modified the pitch contour of the synthesized speech of the HMM-based method, did not decrease the speech quality of the synthesized speech. The lower plot of Fig. 5 showed the results of ABX test. The generated speech of the pro-posed method is perceived more like the voice of the training corpus than that of HMM-based method.

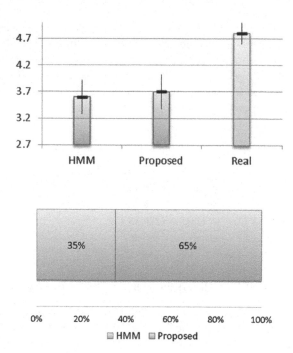

Fig. 5. Upper plot: speech quality comparison results of MOS test. Lower plot: Speaker similarity results of ABX test.

5   Discussion and Concluding Remarks

In this paper, we proposed a systematic way to construct a speech interface for an embedded system such as mobile phone and also able to generate intelligible synthesized speech. First, an automatic speech recognition system is built based on the Hidden Markov Model (HMM) framework. In order to understand the utterance from user in daily life, the spontaneous speech recognition is implemented. For speech generation, a personalized speech synthesis system is also included for the proposed system. The hierarchical prosodic unit selection method for generating natural pitch contour for TTS system is proposed. With a modified Fujisaki model, pitch contour can be regenerated by hierarchical prosodic commands without storing the whole pitch contour.

The proposed prosodic codeword retrieval is useful for selecting more suitable prosodic patterns than the conventional HMM-based method. Experimental results have shown that the performance of the speech recognition and synthesis achieve good performance. Therefore, the proposed speech interface could have applied to other system such as computer vision system in order to help visual impaired people to perceive the environment and interact with other people in daily life.

Acknowledgements. This study is conducted under the "III system-of-systems driven emerging service business development Project" of the Institute for Information Industry which is subsidized by the Ministry of Economic Affairs of the Republic of China.

References

1. WHO Media Centre: Visual impairment and blindness. http://www.who.int/mediacentre/factsheets/fs282/en/. Accessed 25 Aug 2018
2. Huang, Y.-C., Wu, C.-H., Weng, S.-T.: Improving mandarin prosody generation using alternative smoothing techniques. IEEE/ACM Trans. Audio Speech Lang. Processing **24**(11), 1897–1907 (2016)
3. Tseng, S.-C., Liu, Y.-F.: Annotation manual of mandarin conversational dialogue corpus. Technical report 02-01, Chinese Knowledge Information Processing Group, Academia Sinica. Taiwan, (2002)
4. Chung, R.-F.: Syllable contraction in Chinese. In: Chinese Languages and Linguistics III. Morphology and Lexicon. Symposium Series of the Institute of History and Philology, pp. 199–235 (1997)
5. Jurafsky, D., Bell, A., Gregory, M., Raymond, W.D.: The effect of language model probability on pronunciation reduction. In: International Conference on Acoustic, Speech, and Signal Processing (ICASSP 2001), pp. 801–804 (2001)
6. Huang, Y.-C., Wu, C.-H., Chao, Y.-T.: Personalized spectral and prosody conversion using frame-based codeword distribution and adaptive CRF. IEEE Trans. Audio Speech Lang. Process. **21**(1), 51–62 (2013)
7. Liu, F., Jia, H., Tao, J.: A maximum entropy based hierarchical model for automatic prosodic boundary labeling in mandarin. In: The 6th International Symposium on Chinese Spoken Language Processing (ISCSLP 2008), pp. 1–4 (2008)
8. Fujisaki, H., Kawai, H.: Realization of linguistic information in the voice fundamental frequency contour of the spoken Japanese. In: International Conference on Acoustics, Speech, and Signal Processing (ICASSP-88), pp. 663–666 (1988)
9. Young, S.J., Kershaw, D., Odell, J., Ollason, D., Valtchev, V., Woodland, P.: The HTK Book. 3.4 edn. Cambridge University Press (2006)
10. Brief Introduction to TCC-300 Corpus. http://www.aclclp.org.tw/use_mat.php#tcc300edu. Accessed 25 Aug 2018
11. Stolcke, A.: SRILM - an extensible language modeling toolkit. In: International Conference on Spoken Language Processing (ICSLP), pp. 901–904 (2002)

Computer Networks and Web Service/Technologies

Adaptive Linked-List Mechanism for Wi-Fi Wireless Network

Tsung-Lin Lee[✉], Jih-Ching Chiu, and Yueh-Lin Li

Department of Electronic Engineering, National Sun Yat-sen University, Kaohsiung, Taiwan
{m053010050,m063010112}@student.nsysu.edu.tw,
chiujihc@ee.nsysu.edu.tw

Abstract. In response to the concept of Smart City and Internet of Things (IoT) being prevailed in recent years, networking requirements for various devices have increased significantly, however, many related problems have arisen. To solve the problems and shortcomings of the existing IoT wireless networking technologies, for example, the data rate of ZigBee is slow and the wireless networking technologies which uses star topology like NB-IoT and LoRa is rely on the signal of base station, if the node is at communication deadzone, it will not be able to successfully transmit data. Therefore, this paper proposes an Adaptive Linked-List Mechanism For Wi-Fi Wireless Network, this algorithm takes advantage of the low-collision of the linked-list architecture and solves the problem that multiple nodes cannot be started at the same time, moreover, the nodes are able to use signal strength as the basis for constructing a linked-list network that ensure that the nodes within the signal coverage can be stably connected, and the entire system will not be interrupted due to a problem with a few nodes. The algorithm also modifies the linked-list network construction and broken node recovery process, and adds the packet signal strength queue mechanism, so that multiple nodes can quickly construct the network chain. Furthermore, we design a Wi-Fi control board which is based on CC3220MODA and implement our algorithm on it, finally, after testing in different environment, we offer two objective function for two important arguments. We hope to take advantage of this wireless linked-list network in data collection network in the future, and then solve the multi-device networking requirements, and build a stable, reliable and high-speed data collection network for IoT.

Keywords: Linked-list network · Data collection network · IoT · Wireless network · Wi-Fi

1 Introduction

In recent years, the Internet of Things has become more and more prosperous, and many Internet-related wireless technologies have been developed. More and more applications such as smart cities, smart factories, sensing networks, and remote monitoring are becoming constructed, however, there also has many problems. For example, the number of nodes that IPv4 can support is also close to saturation. Once a

© Springer Nature Singapore Pte Ltd. 2019
C.-Y. Chang et al. (Eds.): ICS 2018, CCIS 1013, pp. 49–61, 2019.
https://doi.org/10.1007/978-981-13-9190-3_5

large number of nodes are connected, IPv4 will not be able to be working. How to manage it efficiently after node connecting to the cloud must also be considered. When a large number of nodes are connected through the wireless network, it will inevitably affect the whole environment. [5] Chiu and Wang proposed a wormhole linked-list wireless network algorithm that creates a low-collision network system with a simple routing table with only upper and lower node information and an easy-to-maintain linked-list topology. However, although the linked-list wireless network algorithm is simple in the process of network construction and can reduce the probability of packet collision, it must be actually tested and adjusted related mechanisms and processes in order to make the entire network system become more robust and applied to the Internet of Things.

The purpose of this paper is to design a Wi-Fi linked-list network suitable for IoT data collection. It attempts to use the linked-list wireless network to make information simple and easy to maintain and use Wi-Fi to transmit packets based on the current linked-list wireless network topology. The high speed feature of Wi-Fi has reduced the large delay effect of linked-list topology and applies it to IoT data collection network system. The linked-list network system in the Internet of Things is designed to smoothly deliver data and commands to the destination. The pursuit of the stability of the entire system, as long as the data can be collected, even if the purpose is achieved, however, we must design various mechanisms and processes, such as linked-list net- work construction, data transmission, and node failure response, to cope with the problem in actual implementation of the entire linked-list network data collection system in the wireless environment. As long as the nodes in the entire Wi-Fi linked-list network to be powered on, they can construct a linked-list network and automatically maintain the route without the intervention of the user, the user can simply access information and control all nodes in the entire network chain through the master.

At the same time, in order to verify the feasibility of the Wi-Fi linked-list network applicable to IoT data collection proposed in this paper, we also designed the data monitoring circuit control board and actually tested it in the selected field. Finally, we also offered objective functions of some important parameters for setting the parameters of the linked-list network for data collection in the future.

2   Related Works

2.1   Link-Listed Wireless Routing Algorithm

[5] Chiu and Wang proposed a wireless linked-list routing algorithm. Figure 1 shows the architecture of the linked-list routing wireless network. There are one data collector (Master) and several wireless sensor nodes, these nodes may build the linked-list network by the algorithm with the only two routing information, the preview node address and the next node address. Because of the convenient routing table in the nodes, we can establish the linked-list network quickly and maintain it easily without wasting the resource in the network. The Master can send the only command, which goes through the all nodes in the network according to the direction of linked-list topology path and finally reaches the final node, to avoid the packet's collision. Each

node can receive the command and do the corresponding work, and if the command is the data collecting command like Gather, the node which receives the command finally may initiate a data returning packet. As the data returning packet travels back from the final node to data collector, it fuses each node data along the path. If the size of data reaches the limit of packet, it travel back to data collector through wormhole path and informs that the second data can begin collecting.

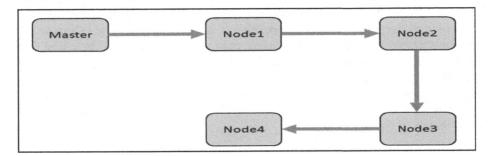

Fig. 1. Linked-list network architecture

Although the algorithm presents a new solution of the wireless data collecting system, the current linked-list network still has some problems which make the network system unstable. Although the linked-list architecture make the network's establish and maintain more conveniently and quickly, the simple routing table in the node may cause the incorrect linked sequence and make the whole linked-list network system crashed. Besides, the high delay time of the command packet transmission in the network chain also causes the linked-list network inefficient. Based on above, the linked-list architecture still needs to overcome some problems such as the data rate of the network system and the improvement of linked-list network construction and maintenance to build a stable data collecting system for IoT (Fig. 2).

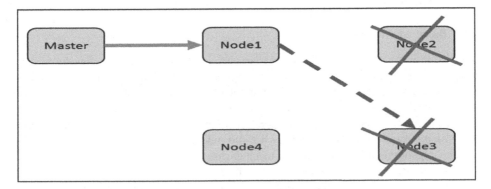

Fig. 2. Linked-list network problems – incorrect linked sequence

2.2 Current IoT-Related Wireless Technologies

The IoT-related wireless technologies introduced in this chapter are currently used by a certain percentage of vendors or countries, and these technologies are mainly used in applications such as sensing networks, data collection, environmental detection, smart homes and smart cities. Some of these technologies operate on licensed spectrum, like NB-IoT, so they have less interference and better communication quality, while those technologies operating in unlicensed spectrum can be classified as 2.4 GHz and Sub-1G bands, these are all that do not require authorization and only require output power to comply with regulations. ZigBee operating at 2.4 GHz band may be in a crowded, high-interference frequency band, causing transmission to be easily interfered and because it is a high-frequency signal, so the valid transmission distance is also low, and the related technology working in Sub-1G band, although the interference in its working environment is relatively small, the valid transmission distance is large, however the actual application may still affect by the signal coverage rate due to the environment or buildings (Table 1).

Table 1. Comparison of the current wireless technologies

Comparison of the current wireless technologies						
Type	NB-IoT	Sigfox	LoRa	ZigBee	Thread	Wi-SUN
Topology	Star	Star	Star	Star, mesh, tree	mesh	mesh
Working frequency	Sub-1G	Sub-1G	Sub-1G	2.4G, Sub-1G	2.4G, Sub-1G	Sub-1G
Data Rate	50 kbps	100 bps	50 kbps	250 kbps	250 kbps	300 kbps
Transmission distance	15 km	50 km	15 km	70 M	70 M	1 km

3 Adaptive Linked-List Mechanism for Wi-Fi Wireless Network

3.1 Basic Architecture

Due to the instruction of the linked-list network in the section II, we can know that using low rate wireless technology like ZigBee to construct a linked-list wireless network will make the system inefficient and get high delay time. Connecting multiple Wi-Fi nodes in series to form a linked-list wireless network, and let the packets pass through the network chain one by one, because of the high data rate of Wi-Fi makes the delay of the entire linked-list topology not too much.

The algorithm proposes different mechanisms and process for the three parts of network construction, transmission and rescuing, and considers the problems that may be encountered when the actual deployment is applied to the IoT data collection system, and give solutions to construct a a stable and reliable linked-list wireless network system (Fig. 3).

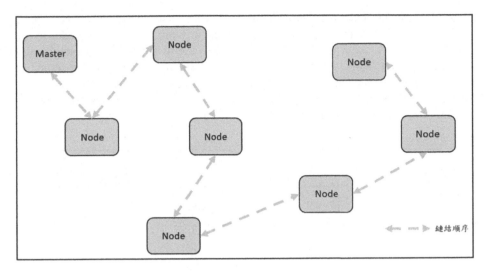

Fig. 3. Basic architecture

3.2 Network Construction Mechanism

When during the linked-list network construction, if the node and the node are unconditionally linked after receiving the first network-construction-related packet, the entire linked-list network chain will be relatively unstable. For example, two nodes are at the edge of their respective signal coverage, so that although they can be smoothly linked, the transmission range of each node at different times is highly related to environmental conditions. Assume that the two nodes are now passing packets, at the time, the valid transmission range may be slightly reduced due to environmental interference, which may give rise to the two nodes disconnected temporarily (Fig. 4).

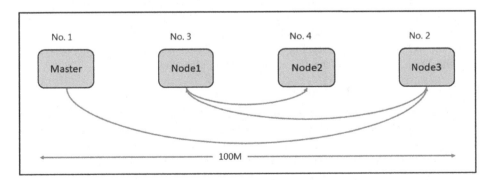

Fig. 4. Unconditionally construction

After the node is powered on, the network construction process without the signal strength queue mechanism is executed, that is, the packet with the strongest signal strength is not selected for a period of time, but the first received network request packet replied whether the signal strength is strong or weak. The order of nodes in the linked-list network chain is not built according to the distance, but unconditionally constructing the network. As far as the network construction results are concerned, it may be because the interference in the current environment of the network is very low, but the transmission coverage of the device is not always fixed, the transmission distance may sometimes be changed due to some external factors (Fig. 5).

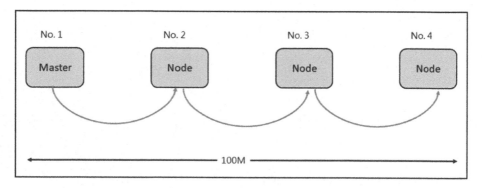

Fig. 5. Ideal construction

- **Multiple Node Simultaneous Insertion Mechanism**

  After the Master initializes, the Lock Flag status is False, indicating that it can respond to the network-construction-related packet, and then waits to receive the network request packet sent by the Node. Once the network request packet is received, the Lock Flag status is set to True, indicating it can't respond to the network-construction-related packets, then, it responds to the Join Reply packet (Join_R) with its own address to the Node, and then waits for the Node to return the changed address packet(Join08) with the Node address, which needs to change its own routing table after receiving, and the Unlock packet is sent to inform the Node to change the Lock Flag state to False, but the Lock Flag state of the Master itself remains True, therefore, only the Lock Flag state of the last node will be False (Fig. 6).

- **Single Node Insertion Mechanism**

  When a new node is to be added after the completion of the network construction, there is a slightly difference between the single node insertion network construction process and the multiple node simultaneous insertion network construction process. The single node insertion network construction handshake diagram is as shown in Fig. 7, compared to the multiple node simultaneous insertion process. There is one more Join0A packet to be transmitted to the next node with its own address.

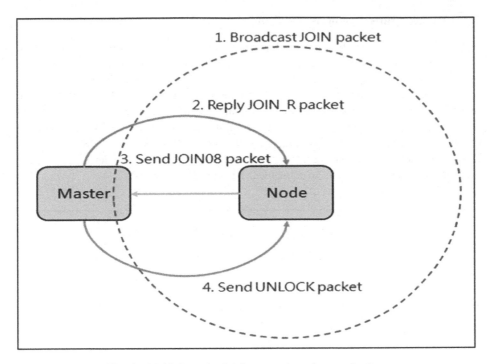

Fig. 6. Multiple node simultaneous insertion mechanism

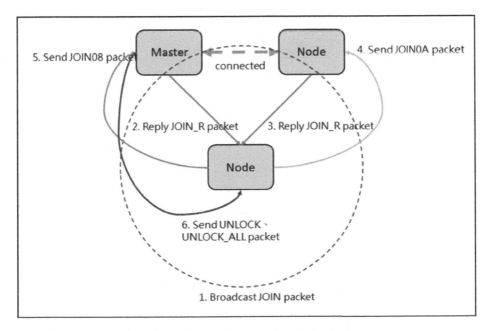

Fig. 7. Single node insertion mechanism

3.3 Packet Transmission Mechanism

When the node has already retransmitted the packet too many times or does not receive a response, it will need to find a new path; therefore, node will start to periodically broadcast the Find Next (Prev) packet with the original forward (backward) node's address. When a packet is transmitted in the network chain, the transmission path is interrupted at a certain point in the network chain because of a node or other factors. At this time, in order to continue the transmission, the packet must be detoured. After the node resending several times, if it still does not receive the response ACK, we will be able to determine that the transmission path is temporarily unable to transmit, and must find another path to continue to transmit the packet (Fig. 8).

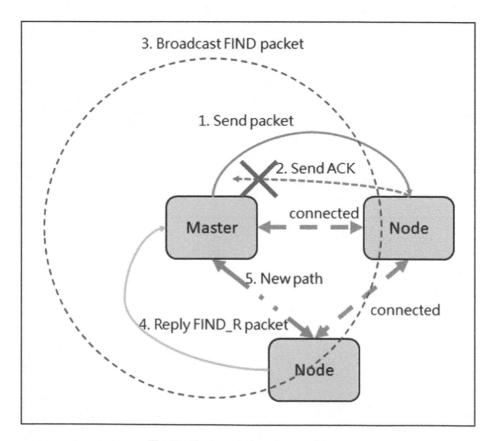

Fig. 8. Single node insertion mechanism

Adaptive Linked-List Mechanism For Wi-Fi Wireless Network is designed to collect data stably for IoT network system. The ultra-low latency is not so important. Therefore, when the packet does not receive a response, it needs to be resent. The time interval will increase with the number of resends; when the first resend or the response is not received, the short-term interference in the current environment may be severe, so the second retransmission timeout will become twice of the first retransmission time-out, the third time is three times the time of the first retransmission, and so on. Although the total time will be a little longer than the fixed retransmission interval under the same number of retransmissions, if you spend more time, you may be able to avoid having the node re-execute the network construction process. This is a trade-off between increase transmission latency and the time that node re-execute the network construction process. The time spent resending is still lower than the time required for the node to rebuild the network. It is worthwhile for the stability of the entire chain network system.

In the various types of packets of the Wi-Fi linked-list network, there are two priority orders, as long as the packets related to the network construction or have the opportunity to change to the address in the routing table are Critical CMD (command), and the data collect relevant packets, such as: Modbus CMD (command), Gather, Scatter, Keep Alive packets, the priority order is Normal CMD (command); When a packet is transmitted in the network chain, if a node is required to find a new path or a node is to perform an insert network, when the above process has started, it will determine the priority of the packet while receiving packets. If it is Normal CMD, it will be backed up first and then processed and responded to the Critical CMD, then it will process the Normal CMD that has just backed up. If the packet does not distinguish the priority order, it will cause the packet to be confused during the packet transmission because of the change of the routing table, and even cause the entire system to be disabled.

3.4   Rescuing Mechanism

The Keep Alive mechanism is to keep nodes in the network chain alive, because when a node does not receive a particular type of packet for a period of time, it will determine itself as an isolated node and need to go back to the network chain. In addition to transmitting data collection instructions, the Master will also periodically transmit Keep Alive command packets through the linked-list network chain. In order to prevent the Active Time timer on each node in the network chain from timing out, which will cause the node to re-execute the network construction process, the Keep Alive command packet is transmitted periodically by the master to inform each node in the network chain to update the Active Time timer. In addition to the Keep Alive packet, which updates the node's Active Time timer, the Modbus packet and the data collection-related packet from the Master can also be used to update the node's Active Time timer. In other words, the Keep Alive command timer on the Master is also updated by the other related commands described above. The Keep Alive packet is transmitted when the timer expires and no relevant command packet needs to be transmitted, which is also to reduce the chance of the Master transmitting unnecessary commands. After finishing the network construction process, the node will know that it has successfully joined the network because it has obtained the information of the routing table and received the Unlock packet transmitted by other nodes, however, if the node is unable to receive the packet transmitted by other nodes, then the Active Time Timer will expire because the node does not periodically receive a specific packet, that means the node is no longer a member of the linked-list network chain.

4   Implementation

In this chapter, based on the measured results, the objective function is proposed for the parameters in the linked-list network system, as a reference for the construction and setting of the whole system in the future. The part of the measured results will propose the lost ratio of the entire system, and analyze the data transmission time and compare it with the time spent by the AODV algorithm.

4.1   Lost Ratio and Objective Function

The part of the measured results will propose the loss rate of the entire system, and analyze the node transmission time and compare it with the time spent by the AODV algorithm.

Here we first define the Lost Ratio in this algorithm. The loss rate is composed of the total number of times the Master sends the Keep Alive packet and the sent Keep Alive packet returns the result to the Master. When the Master sends the Keep Alive packet, the nodes on the network chain will forward them in the direction of the end nodes of the network after receiving the Keep Alive packet. When the last node is reached, each node will attach its own ID and MAC address into the packet and transmit in the direction of the master.

When the Master receives the reply packet, it will know that how many nodes are there in the current network chain. If the number does not match the actual number of modules, it means that some node is not currently in the network chain. At this time, the Keep Alive packet sent by the Master should be marked as a lost packet. Otherwise, if the number of nodes included in the reply packet is consistent with the actual number, it is marked as an ALL packet (Table 2).

Table 2. The lost ratio of multiple nodes

The lost ratio of multiple nodes			
7 nodes	8 nodes	9 nodes	10 nodes
3.24%	2.7%	3.9%	3.85%

$$\text{Lost Ratio} = \frac{the\ numbers\ of\ Lost\ packet}{the\ numbers\ of\ Keep\ Alive\ packet} \times 100\%$$

After testing multiple numbers of node and obtaining the loss rate, in the test of the loss ratio, the long-term transmission test is performed from the total number of nodes 7 to 10 and measured loss ratio. It is found that the amount of the loss rate is related to the environmental factors. It can be found from the results that the number of nodes and the rate of loss are positively correlated. The more the number of nodes, the higher the rate of loss will be. However, if the number of nodes is not large, the impact of the environment is rather obvious.

The Keep Alive interval is the Master's Keep Alive mechanism, in order to allow each node in the network chain to update the Active Time timer to prevent it from being determined to have left the network chain and need to re-execute the network construction process again. The value obtained by the objective function is the minimum value that can be set for the Keep Alive time interval. At the same time, this value is also the minimum interval that the Master send any data collection related command packets. The following equation is the objective function provided by this algorithm.

$$\text{Keep Alive Interval}$$
$$> (\text{module react time} + \text{packet transmission time}$$
$$+ \text{resend delay time}) \times (N - 1) \times 2$$

4.2   Comparison of End-To-End Dalay with AODV

In this part, the End To End Delay time of both the Wi-Fi linked-list network algorithm and the AODV protocol applied to the Internet of Things data collection is compared in the actual measurement without any retransmission.

First of all, we measured the end to end delay time of the number of nodes is increased from 3 to 10, when the End To End Delay time is measured, we used the trend of the data just measured to predict the data of 30 nodes. When there are 10 nodes, the End-To-End Delay time is about 12.7 ms, and the estimated End-To-End Delay time of 30 nodes is about 41 ms. At this time, the packet length is 500 bytes (Fig. 9).

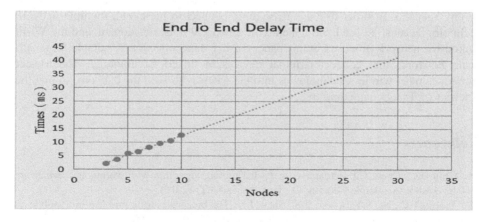

Fig. 9. End To End Delay time

Next, we compare the result with AODV, we can find out that the Adaptive Linked-list Mechanism For Wi-Fi Wireless Network has lower latency than AODV while transmitting data (Table 3).

Table 3. The comparison of linked-list network and AODV

Nodes	Adaptive linked-list mechanism for Wi-Fi wireless network	AODV
10	12.7 ms	27.9 ms
30	41 ms	44 ms

5 Conclusion and Future Works

This paper retains the advantages of simple routing information and easy maintenance and low environmental interference in the linked-list network topology, and presents a Wi-Fi linked-list network which is suitable for IoT data collection and has been continuously tested.

In the process of network construction, in order to make the linked-list network link more stable, a signal strength Queue mechanism is proposed to select a path between the node and the node based on the received signal strength, rather than the random use of the first received packet to establish the link.

The Keep Alive mechanism and the Active Time timeout mechanism are proposed to update the network chain through the Keep Alive packet sent by the Master periodically. If the node's Active Time timer expires, it means that the node is out of the network and is not in the network chain. The network construction process must be re-executed by the node to make itself back to the network chain; These two parameters are factors that affect the performance and stability of the entire linked-list network system. Therefore, this paper proposes an objective function for these two parameters provides a reference for setting the parameters of the linked-list network for data collection in the future.

In today's IoT-related wireless network technology, no technology can be applied to any scenario. In order to make everything connect to the cloud, multiple network technologies must be used and a hierarchical concept must be adopted, and the Wi-Fi linked-list network proposed in this paper for IoT data collection is suitable for small-scale networks that connect terminal devices in linked-list topology. The Master integrates other wireless technologies into the gateway to send the data out, so that the Internet of Things can come true.

References

1. Chiu, J.C., Chen, C.L.: Adaptive linked-list routing algorithm with wormhole mechanism. In: Taiwan Academic Network Conference (TANET) (2015)
2. Tseng, Y.C., Ni, S.Y., Chen, Y.S., Sheu, J.P.: The broadcast storm problem in a mobile ad hoc network. Comput. Sci. Wireless Netw. **8**(2–3), 153–167 (2002)
3. Malek, A.G., Chunlin, L.I., Li, L.: Improving ZigBee AODV mesh routing algorithm topology and simulation analysis. Ind. J. Electr. Eng. Comput. Sci. **12**(2), 1528–1535 (2014)
4. Sornin, N.: LoRaWAN™ Specifications. LoRa™ Alliance (2015)
5. Chiu, J.C., Wang, W.S.: Linked list routing algorithm with wormhole mechanism for data collecting wireless network. In: 2014 International Computer Symposium (ICS) (2014)
6. LORA Alliance. https://www.lora-alliance.org/

7. ZigBee Alliance. http://www.zigbee.org/
8. Sigfox. https://www.sigfox.com/en
9. Thread. https://www.threadgroup.org/
10. Wi-SUN. https://www.wi-sun.org/
11. IEEE Std 802.11-2016
12. Baker, N.: ZigBee and Bluetooth strengths and weaknesses for industrial applications. Comput. Control Eng. J. **16**(2), 20–25 (2005)
13. Chiu, J.C., Yang, K.M., Huang, Y.C., Wu, M.S.: Dynamic multi-channel multi-path routing protocol for smart grid. In: The 3rd FTRA International Conference on Computer Science and its Applications (CSA 2011) at Korea, December 2011
14. Chavan, A.A., Kurule, D.S., Dere, P.U.: Performance analysis of AODV and DSDV routing protocol in MANET and modifications in AODV against black hole attack. Procedia Comput. Sci. **79**, 835–844 (2016). https://doi.org/10.1016/j.procs.2016.03.108
15. Chatzimisios, P., Boucouvalas, A.C., Vitsas, V.:. IEEE 802.11 packet delay -a finite retry limit analysis. In: GLOBECOM, pp. 950–954. IEEE (2003)
16. Texas Instruments.: CC3220 SimpleLink™ Wi-Fi® Wireless and Internet-of-Things Solution, a Single-Chip Wireless MCU, February 2017. http://www.ti.com/lit/ds/swas035a/swas035a.pdf

Design and Implementation of Tree Topology Algorithm for Power Line Communication Network

Guan-Jen Huang$^{(\boxtimes)}$, Jih-Ching Chiu, and Yueh-Lin Li

Department of Electronic Engineering, National Sun Yat-sen University,
Kaohsiung, Taiwan
{m053010049, chiujihc}@ee.nsysu.edu.tw,
m063010112@student.nsysu.edu.tw

Abstract. The concept of smart grid has been proposed for years. Many countries, such as United State, England and Japan, have been replacing traditional electric meters with smart electric meters in recent years. There are lots of communication methods used in smart grid, power line communication (PLC) is an important one among them. G3-PLC is a widely-used specification for long-distance PLC, however, PLC is sensitive to old power lines and the interference caused by large electric current flowing through the power line. Moreover, although G3-PLC has stable performance of communication, the AODV routing protocol and the complex startup procedures results in taking long time for G3-PLC devices to finish the whole startup procedures.

To reduce the time to finish the startup procedures in G3-PLC, in this paper, a tree topology algorithm is proposed. In the tree topology algorithm, a simple startup procedure is provided, by setting up the parent-child relationship between nodes, the routes for nodes in networks are simplified. Furthermore, a maintain procedure is also provide in the algorithm, in the maintain procedure, the nodes in networks can use Check Alive mechanism to check the connection between their parent nodes and child nodes, when a broken connection is found by a node, the node will use Recovery mechanism to rescue the isolated nodes.

In this paper, the feasibility of the tree topology algorithm is verified by NS-3 platform, and suggestions of the suitable value of the parameters in the algorithm are proposed. In addition, the algorithm is implemented on Atmel SAM4CP16C evolution kits, the measurement results show that the time for PLC devices to finish the startup procedures of the tree topology algorithm is at least 6.7 times less than G3-PLC specification.

Keywords: PLC · Tree topology · Startup procedure · Maintain procedure

1 Introduction

THE Smart Grid works by establishing the Advanced Metering Infrastructure(AMI). As shown in Fig. 1, AMI includes Meter Data Management System (MDMS), Smart Meter, Communication systems and Power supply-consumption management [1]. There are lots of communication methods used in smart grid, however, considering the

© Springer Nature Singapore Pte Ltd. 2019
C.-Y. Chang et al. (Eds.): ICS 2018, CCIS 1013, pp. 62–75, 2019.
https://doi.org/10.1007/978-981-13-9190-3_6

wide establishment of Smart Meters in the future, how to arrange transmission lines for Smart Meters appropriately is important. To adapt different geographic environments and to consider the economic benefit, power line communication (PLC) is an appropriate way for communication of Smart Grid because the new arrangement of power line is needless. G3-PLC is a widely-used specification for long-distance PLC, however, although G3-PLC has stable performance of communication, the AODV routing protocol and the complex startup procedures results in taking long time for G3-PLC devices to finish the whole startup procedures. To reduce the time to finish the startup procedures in G3-PLC, in this paper, a tree topology algorithm is proposed. In the tree topology algorithm, a simple startup procedure and a maintain procedure are provided.

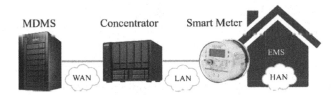

Fig. 1. Structure of AMI

2   Background Knowledge

According to the frequency of carrier used in PLC technology, there are broadband PLC and narrowband PLC. The carrier frequency of narrowband PLC ranges from tens of kHz to hundreds of kHz, and the lower carrier frequency results in the longer transmission distance. G3-PLC [2] and PRIME [3] are the widely-used narrowband PLC specification nowadays, both specifications use OFDM as the signal modulation method in physical layer [4–7] because OFDM provides low interrupt between subcarriers and increases bandwidth usage rate which can improve the low transmission quality of old power line. In addition, every subcarrier uses PSK to modulate digital signal to analog signal, although both specifications use OFDM and PSK as modulation methods, different encode way between them makes G3-PLC have better bit error rate BER) than PRIME [8–10]. The OSI model of G3-PLC is shown in Fig. 2, IEEE 802.15.4 protocol [11] is used in MAC layer, and 6LoWPAN protocol is used in Adaption sublayer to connect IEEE802.15.4 with IPv6.

To compare the startup procedure and routing way of G3-PLC with the tree topology algorithm proposed in this paper, the introduction of the startup procedure and routing protocol of G3-PLC are as follows.

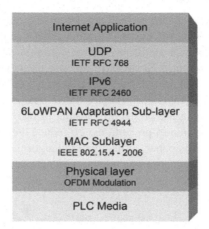

Fig. 2. OSI model of G3-PLC

2.1 Startup Procedure: LoWPAN Bootstrapping Protocol

The LoWPAN Bootstrapping Protocol (LBP) [12] defines the startup procedure of every 6LoWPAN device. There are three proper nouns in LBP, include LoWPAN BootStrapping Device (LBD) which represent the device that not yet join a PAN, LoWPAN BootStrapping Server (LBS) is the coordinator of PAN which in charge of all devices, and LoWPAN BootStrapping Agent (LBA) which represent the device that already join a PAN. Every device has its unique EUI-64 which is the MAC Address defined in IEEE 802.15.4, in addition, LBAs need to help LBDs or LBS transfer data. The following steps are the startup procedure of G3-PLC.

1. LBD starts and resets.
2. LBD checks if there is any devices nearby, so broadcasts "Beacon request" during active scan, any LBS or LBA receive this frame needs to reply "Beacon".
3. LBD starts processing LBP. LBD broadcast "LBA Solicitation Message" to find LBA who can help it transfer data to LBS.
4. After receiving "LBA Advertisement" from LBAs or LBS, LBD chooses a best LBA(LBS) among them. The way to choose the best LBA is as following: (1) If there is LBS who reply "LBA Advertisement", LBS is the one to choose, (2) the LBA that has the smallest hops from LBD to LBS is the one to choose.
5. LBD and LBS starts to exchange some frames through the LBA chosen in step 4. The sequence chart is shown in Fig. 3. "Joining" represents the frame transmitted from LBD to LBS, and "Challenge" represents the frame transmitted from LBS to LBD, and "Accept" is the frame that LBS decides to accept this LBD join this PAN. Every LBD needs at least three back and forth data exchange between itself and LBS to finish joining a PAN.

Furthermore, every G3-PLC device has a Neighbor Table which contains the connection situation between itself and other devices.

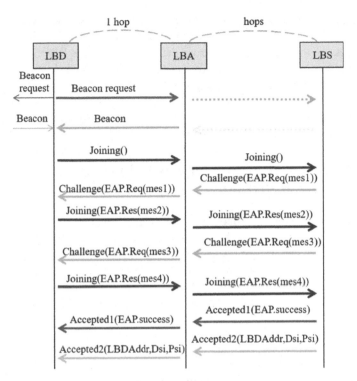

Fig. 3. Sequence chart of LBD to register

2.2 Routing Protocol: 6LoWPAN Ad Hoc On-Demand Distance Vector Routing

G3-PLC uses 6LoWPAN Ad Hoc On-Demand Distance Vector Routing (LOAD) [13, 14] as its routing protocol. A registered node will process LOAD before its data transmission to find the route between itself and the destination node. The following steps are the routing protocol of G3-PLC.

1. Source node broadcast "Route Request (RREQ)" which contains the information of the destination node.
2. A relay node that receives RREQ adds the source node's information to its "Routing Request Table", meaning itself is now helping the source node to find routes to destination node. And then this relay node also adds the source node's information to its "Routing Table", helping the source node to find routes by broadcast RREQ.
3. Until the destination node receives the RREQ of the source node from any relay nodes and updates its Routing Table, it replies "Route reply (RREP)" to the source node through reply nodes.

LOAD not only can establish routes but repair routes. The repair mechanism will process when any relay node in a route is off. The upstream node of the offline node broadcasts RREQ again to find a new route to the destination node, besides, the frame that failed to transmit will be save for next try after new route established. If new route failed to build, the upstream node of the offline node will transmit "Local Repair and Route Error (RRER)" to the source node, when the source node receives RRER, a new routing process of the destination node will start by broadcasts RREQ.

From what has been discussed above, G3-PLC not only needs long time to register and many frames exchange in startup procedure but using the LOAD as its routing protocol results in many frame collisions. To improve those problem, the tree topology algorithm is proposed in this paper. The tree topology could establish simple routes between each node to reduce the frame collision.

3 Tree Topology Algorithm for Power Line Communication Network

The tree topology algorithm proposed in this paper contains startup procedure and maintain procedure, and it's suitable for tree topology, besides, the Modbus transfer protocol is used for data transfer after the startup procedure. In tree topology, every node has their own parent node and child nodes. The names of the characters used in this algorithm are as following: Coordinator oversees a PAN, Device is a node that wants to join a PAN, and Agent is a node that already join a PAN, in addition, Agent also helps Coordinator and Devices to transfer messages if needed.

To build a tree topology, the routing tables are needed, so in this algorithm, there are three tables for Coordinators, they are Registered Node's MAC Address Table, Registered Node's last Agent Node's MAC Address Table, and Registered Node's Modbus Address Table, furthermore, there are four tables for Device, they are Parent Node's MAC Address Table, Child Node's MAC Address Table, Multilevel-Child Node's MAC Address Table, and Multilevel-Child Node's last Agent Node's MAC Address Table. The introduction of startup procedure and maintain procedure are as following sections.

3.1 Startup Procedure

In this section, bold font represents the name of frame used in startup procedure, and bottom line represents the name of tables. The illustration of startup procedure is shown in Fig. 4. The details of Startup Procedure in Fig. 4 is as following steps:

1. Device2 broadcasts **Routing Request** following the "Resend Mechanism of Routing Request" to look for replies from any registered devices nearby.
2. Device1 receives Routing Request from Device2, and it's already registered, so it transmits **Routing Reply** to Device2. After Device2 receives Routing Reply, it can start to transmit the register-related frame through Device1.
3. Device2 transmits **Direct Register Request** to Device1, since Device1 is not Coordinator, Device1 needs to add Device2 to its Child Node's MAC Address Table and form **Indirect Register Request** which includes the information of Device2 and transmit to its parent node. "Direct" here means a device wants to join a PAN is accepted directly from Coordinator, not other devices. After Coordinator receives **Indirect Register Request** which includes the information of Device2, it adds Device2 to its Registered Node's MAC Address Table, meaning it accepts Device2 to join this PAN.

4. Coordinator then transmits **Indirect Register Reply** to the last Agent Node of Device2-Device1, and Device1 add Device2 to its <u>Child Node's MAC Address Table</u>. When Device2 receives **Indirect Register Reply**, it adds Device1 to its <u>Parent Node's MAC Address Table</u>, and the register procedure of Device2 is finished.

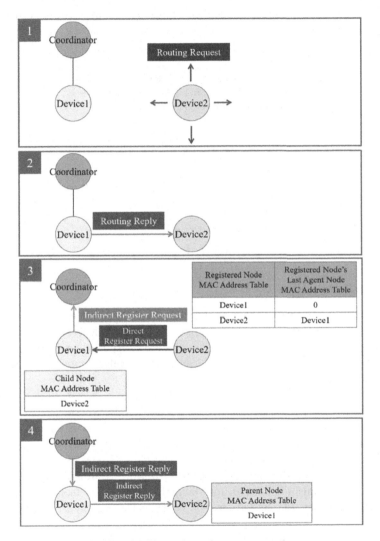

Fig. 4. The illustration of startup procedure

3.2   Resend Mechanism of Routing Request

In startup procedure, when a not-registered device broadcasts Routing Request but doesn't get any reply, the register procedure fails, that is, the not-registered node needs to restart the register procedure. The Resend Mechanism is proposed in this section to make sure every device can register successfully. The illustration of the Resend Mechanism is shown in Fig. 5. A check period is the product of Duration of check receiving Routing Reply (t) and Times of check receiving Routing Reply (p). At the beginning of a check period, device which wants to register will check whether itself received **Routing Reply** or not, if not, it will resend **Routing Request** or do nothing until next inspection time. After p times inspection, the device will check itself registered or not, if not, it will resend Routing Request and restart a new check period or stop the Resend Mechanism. How to choose the value of t and p will be discussed in chapter IV.

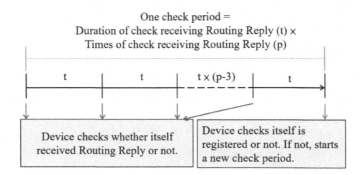

Fig. 5. Illustration of Resend Mechanism of Routing Request

3.3   Maintain Procedure

Since power line is sensitive to ambient interference, how to maintain a network build with power line is also important. In this algorithm, a Maintain Procedure is proposed. The procedure has Check Alive Mechanism and Recovery Mechanism respectively to periodic check the connection between itself and its related nodes and rescue the isolated nodes.

The definition of the characters in Maintain Procedure is shown in Fig. 6. There are three new defined character, they are Missing Child Node, Missing Parent Node and Isolated Child Node. The left side diagram in Fig. 6, when Device1 Finds that one of its child nodes-Device2 is disconnect, Device2 is called Missing Child Node, in addition, Device3 and Device4 are called Isolated Child Node. Since Device2 is disconnected, Device3 and Device4 are disconnected with Coordinator, too, that's why the Recovery Mechanism is needed, for Device1 to rescue the Isolated Child Nodes. Furthermore, the other side diagram in Fig. 6, when Device2 finds its parent node is disconnected, it uses the Recovery Mechanism to seek for a new parent node, in order to connect to coordinator again.

The details of Maintain Procedure will be introduced from the viewpoint of Parent Node and Child point individually. The illustration of the viewpoint of Parent Node is shown in Figs. 7 and 8, and the details are as following steps. The bold fonts represent name of frames, the bottom line represent name of tables, and the italics font represent parameters.

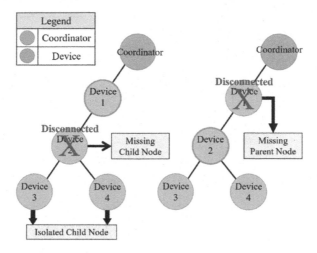

Fig. 6. Definition of the characters in Maintain Procedure

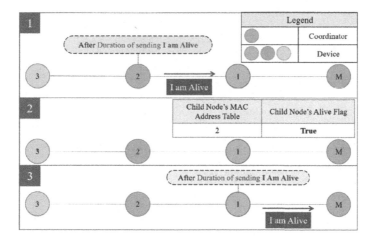

Fig. 7. Illustration of Maintain Procedure by viewpoint of Parent Node (1)

1. Every Child Node of Device1 transmit **I am Alive** to its Parent Node when its timer counts to *Duration of sending I am Alive.*
2. When Device1 receives **I am Alive** from Device2, it updates the *Child Node's Alive Flag* in Child Node's MAC Address Table to True.
3. After the timer of Device1 counts to *Duration of sending I am Alive*, it transmits **I am Alive** to its Parent Node-Coordinator.
4. And then Device1 Check the *Child Node's Alive Flag* of its Child Node's MAC Address Table with the yellow table in step 4 of Fig. 8.
5. If the *Times of Child Node is Not Alive* has counted to the *Child Node Not Alive Value*, it means that Device1 considered Device2 is disconnect, and need to start the Recovery Mechanism to rescue the isolated Child Node.

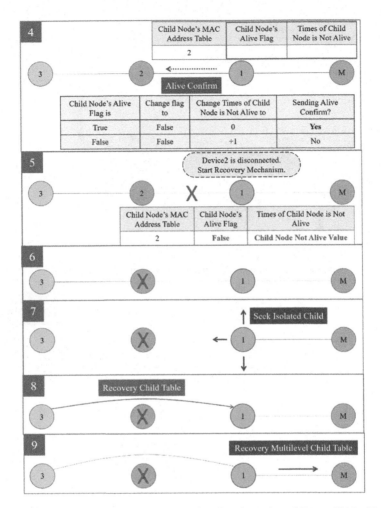

Fig. 8. Illustration of Maintain Procedure by viewpoint of Parent Node (2)

6. Device2 has been considered disconnect by Device1.
7. The Recovery Mechanism starts, Device1 broadcasts **Seek Isolated Child** to seek for replies from isolated child nodes.
8. If Device3 is able to receive **Seek Isolated Child**, it replies **Recovery Child Table** with all the information of its Child Nodes and its Multilevel Child Node, in order to inform Device1 to update the Child Node's MAC Address Table.
9. After updating its Child Node's MAC Address Table, Device1 transmits **Recovery Multilevel Child Table** to its Parent Node, informing its Parent Node to update Multilevel-Child Node's MAC Address Table, and then the Recovery Mechanism is finished.

On the other hand, the illustration of the viewpoint of Child Node is shown in, and the details are as following steps.

1. When Device2 receives **Alive Confirm** from Device1, it updates the *Parent Node's Alive Flag* in Parent Node's MAC Address Table to True, and after the timer of Device1 counts to *Duration of sending I am Alive*, it transmits **I am Alive** to its Parent Node-Device1.

2. Then Device2 Check the *Parent Node's Alive Flag* of its Parent Node's MAC Address Table with the yellow table in step 2 of Fig. 9.

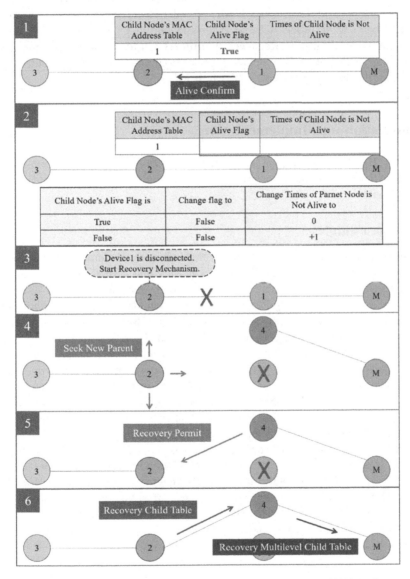

Fig. 9. Illustration of Maintain Procedure by viewpoint of Child Node

3. If the *Times of Parent Node is Not Alive* has counted to the *Parent Node Not Alive Value*, it means that Device2 considered Device1 is disconnect, and need to start the Recovery Mechanism to find a new Parent Node.
4. The Recovery Mechanism starts, Device2 broadcasts **Seek New Parent** to seek for replies from other registered nodes.
5. If Device4 is able to receive **Seek New Parent**, it replies **Recovery Permit** to Device2 telling Device2 that I'm your new Parent Node.
6. Then, Device2 replies **Recovery Child Table** with all the information of its Child Nodes and its Multilevel Child Node, in order to inform Device4 to update the Child Node's MAC Address Table. After updating its Child Node's MAC Address Table, Device4 transmits **Recovery Multilevel Child Table** to its Parent Node, informing its Parent Node to update Multilevel-Child Node's MAC Address Table, and then the Recovery Mechanism is finished.

4 Simulation and Implementation

This Tree Topology Algorithm is verified with NS-3 [15, 16] platform, and the appropriate value of parameters is proposed, and this algorithm is also implemented on evolution module of G3-PLC.

4.1 Verified with NS-3

The following discussion is about the factor that influence the duration of whole startup procedure. The verification uses different value of t and p of Resend Mechanism of Routing Request, and there is some conclusion about those tests. The most important factor is the times of Resending Routing Request. There are some reasons about a node has to resend. First, the node who is able to receive the Routing Request from the node wants to register is not yet registered, so it can't transfer frame for the node wants to register, results in the node want to register has to resend Routing Request. Second, the node wants to register already received Routing Reply, but the following register-related frames lost in progress, so it's needed to restart the register procedure.

Besides, the tree level of the topology doesn't influence the duration of a single node to finish to Startup Procedure, the factor that influence the most is the position of Agent node and the workload of the Agent load.

Moreover, the value of t and p is also an important factor. After many tests, p = 2 and p = 3 is better than other value of p. So the following tests of different value of t are under p = 2 and p = 3. Figure 10 shows the diagram of recommend value of t vs. duration of Startup Procedure, the node numbers of simulations are from 10 to 80 nodes, and the curve of duration of Startup Procedure with different node number is linear, furthermore, the recommended value of t is stuck in 3200 ms after the node number is over 40 nodes. From this relation diagram, the duration of 80 nodes is 208 s. The equation of the curve of recommended value of t is shown as Eq. (1).

$$t = \begin{cases} 800 + 70 \times (\text{node number} - 10) \text{ ms}, & 10 \le \text{node number} < 40 \\ 3200 & \text{ms}, \ \text{node number} \ge 40 \end{cases} \tag{1}$$

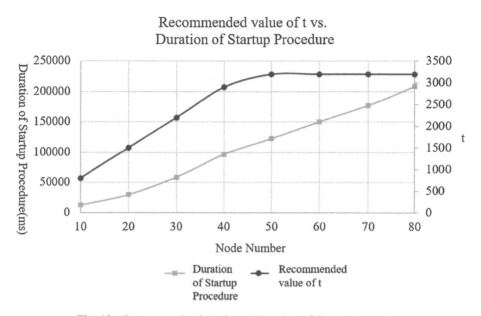

Fig. 10. Recommend value of t vs. Duration of Startup Procedure

4.2 Implementation on Atmel SAM4CP16C-EK [17]

This algorithm is also implemented on Atmel SAM4CP16C-EK. To test the feasibility of the algorithm, using 1 node to 6 nodes, each node executes Startup Procedure. To verify the recommended value of t and p mentioned last section, four different values of t and p are used, from No. 1 to No. 4, the values of p and t are 3/800 ms, 1/800 ms, 3/1200 ms, 3/2000 ms. The values of No. 3 is match with the recommended values mentioned last section. The test results of the duration of Startup procedure are shown in Fig. 11. The results show that the duration which used the recommended value of t and p have the smallest duration of the Startup Procedure. The recommended values are verified.

Furthermore, the comparison result of the tree topology and G3-PLC is in Fig. 12. The duration of this tree topology algorithm is at least 6.7 times less than G3-PLC specification.

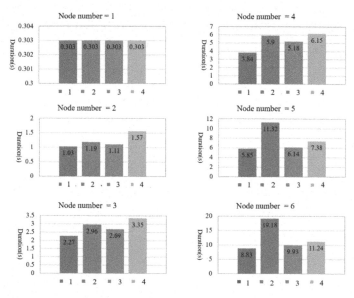

Fig. 11. Tests results of different values of t and p

Duration of Startup procedure (s)	Node = 1	Node = 2	Node = 3	Node = 4	Node = 5	Node = 6
Tree Topology Algorithm	0.303	1.03	2.27	3.84	5.85	8.83
G3-PLC	15	20	26	33	47	60

Fig. 12. The results of implementation

5   Conclusion

The tree topology algorithm is proposed in this paper, by exchanging frames between nodes, a tree topology and routing table is established. And a Maintain Procedure is also proposed to prevent the network from broken connection. The verification and the recommended values of parameters are proposed, and the results of implementation is also proposed, the results show that the duration of this tree topology algorithm is at least 6.7 times less than G3-PLC specification.

References

1. Author, F.: Article title. Journal **2**(5), 99–110 (2016)
2. Author, F., Author, S.: Title of a proceedings paper. In: Editor, F., Editor, S. (eds.) Conference 2016, LNCS, vol. 9999, pp. 1–13. Springer, Heidelberg (2016)
3. Author, F., Author, S., Author, T.: Book title, 2nd edn. Publisher, Location (1999)

4. Author, F.: Contribution title. In: 9th International Proceedings on Proceedings, pp. 1–2. Publisher, Location (2010)
5. LNCS Homepage. http://www.springer.com/lncs. Accessed 21 Nov 2016
6. Kabalci, Y.: A survey on smart metering and smart grid communication. Renew. Sustain. Energy Rev. **57**, 302–318 (2016)
7. G3-PLC Alliance. http://www.g3-plc.com/home/
8. PRIME Alliance. http://www.prime-alliance.org/
9. PLC G3 Physical Layer Specification, Électricité de France S.A. https://www.edf.fr/en/meta-home
10. Specification for PoweRline Intelligent Metering Evolution, PRIME Alliance Technical Working Group. http://www.prime-alliance.org/
11. Narrowband orthogonal frequency division multiplexing power line communication transceivers – Power spectral density specification, ITU-T G.9901, Telecommunication Standardization sector of ITU. https://www.itu.int/en/pages/default.aspx
12. Narrowband orthogonal frequency division multiplexing power line communication transceivers for G3-PLC networks, ITU-T G.9903, Telecommunication Standardization Sector of ITU. https://www.itu.int/en/pages/default.aspx
13. Hoch, M.: Comparison of PLC G3 and PRIME. Presented at IEEE International Symposium on Power Line Communications and Its Applications, Udine, Italy, April 2011
14. Matanza, J., Alexandres, S., Rodriguez-Morcillo, C.: Performance evaluation of two narrowband PLC systems: PRIME and G3. Comput. Stand. Interfaces **36**(1), 198–208 (2013)
15. Sadowski, Z.: Comparison of PLC-PRIME and PLC-G3 protocols. Presented at International School on Nonsinusoidal Currents and Compensation (ISNCC), Lagow, Poland, June 2015
16. IEEE Computer Society, IEEE 802.15.4-2006: Wireless Medium Access Control (MAC) and Physical Layer (PHY) Specifications for Low-Rate Wireless Personal Area Networks (WPANs). http://www.ieee802.org/15/pub/TG4.html
17. Network Working Group of IETF, Commissioning in 6LoWPAN. https://www.ietf.org/
18. Network Working Group of IETF, 6LoWPAN Ad Hoc On-Demand Distance Vector Routing (LOAD). https://www.ietf.org/
19. Ramírez, D.F., Céspedes, S.: Routing in neighborhood area networks: a survey in the context of AMI communications. J. Netw. Comput. Appl. **55**, 68–80 (2015)
20. Network Simulator-3. https://www.nsnam.org/
21. Low-Rate Wireless Personal Area Network (LR-WPAN).https://www.nsnam.org/docs/models/html/lr-wpan.html
22. Microchip, Microchip_G3-PLC Firmware Stack User Guide. http://www.microchip.com/design-centers/smart-energy-products/power-line-communications/g3-based-plc-solutions

Evolution of Advanced Persistent Threat (APT) Attacks and Actors

Chia-Mei Chen[1], Gu-Hsin Lai[2], and Dan-Wei (Marian) Wen[1(✉)] (iD)

[1] National Sun Yat-sen, Kaohsiung 80424, Taiwan
marian.wen@gmail.com
[2] Taiwan Police College, Taipei 11696, Taiwan

Abstract. Advanced Persistent Threat (APT) has become one of the most complicated and intractable cyber attack over the last decade. As APT attacks are conducted through series of actions that comprise social engineering, phishing, command and control servers, and remote desktop control, conventional anti-virus mechanisms become insufficient because they were designed to cope with traditional stand-alone malware attacks. Furthermore, data transmission from the compromised network to the APT actors is usually well disguised and embedded in normal transmission, exacerbating the detection of APT attacks to the point that even major anti-virus firms are not sure about the ratio of discovered APT attacks against real attacks. To make things worse, APT actors tend to be well-organized and potentially government-funded groups of hackers and professionals who are capable of developing and maintaining malware specifically made for their own purposes and interpret the stolen data. While most efforts in defending against APT attacks focus on related technologies, this research argues the importance of constructing a holistic understanding by analyzing the behaviors and changes of ATP attacks and actors. This research aims to understand the evolution of technologies and malware on the one hand and the behavioral changes of attacking groups. By doing so, this research is expected to contribute to constructing a clearer roadmap of APT attacks and actors that cyber security providers can use as reference.

Keywords: Advanced Persistent Threat · APT · Evolution · Behavior analysis

1 Introduction

Advanced Persistent Threat (APT) is an emerging cyber attack that is used in cyber espionage [1–4]. This new form of attack is baffling for network administrators, largely due to its complexity and discrepancies from traditional cyber attacks in the following aspects: (1) Organizing: purpose – APT actors are well-organized teams that appear to be directly or indirectly supported by governments, making them more resourceful and organized than traditional actors. (2) Sophistication: APTs are implemented through a series of properly plotted activities, from spear phishing, malware injection, data transmission to trace clearance. The multiplicity of attack channels and mechanisms significantly increased the success rate of compromise (3) Concealment: actors lurk in the target network and disguise activities as normal ones, and could update the malware without being noticed. (4) Purpose: traditional actors typically pursuit financial gains

© Springer Nature Singapore Pte Ltd. 2019
C.-Y. Chang et al. (Eds.): ICS 2018, CCIS 1013, pp. 76–81, 2019.
https://doi.org/10.1007/978-981-13-9190-3_7

from victims, but APTs aim at confidential information in the firms or government agencies. Because of aforementioned characters, APTs are trickier and more difficult to defend against.

Since the revealing of APT groups in early 2010's, researchers have been looking for methods and mechanisms to detect and defend against APTs [5]. However, the distinctiveness of APTs from traditional attacks imply that the behavior analysis needs to be extended form traditional malware-level to incorporate the related series of activities and pay attention to strategic changes of the attack groups. Efforts from both academia and cyber security firms are devoted to learning more about APT attacks and actors. With the growing number of reports and profiles, more is known about the techniques, tactics, and procedures the APT actors adopt to compromise organizations and government agencies. As pointed out by Lemay and colleague [1] that cyber security firms have better access to real data and accumulate large volume of APT attack instance so that they provide more in-depth reports than academic researchers, analyses of these reports can construct a holistic picture of APT attacks and actors [1, 4]. Following the work of Ussath [4] and Lemay [1] that organized the 39 APT groups of actors identified in publicly available industry reports, this research aims to push the frontier a little bit further because there is a lack of related studies delving into the behavioral changes of these attacking groups. Furthermore, as APT groups update their tools and techniques periodically, an integrated investigation into the evolution of these tools and techniques is equally essential in constructing the holistic understanding of APT attacks and actors.

In this vein, this paper analyzes the publically available APT reports provided by FireEye to extract technical and behavioral changes of APT groups. As an initiation of the project, this research chooses APT1 the case group. The major reasons are that there are very through reports on the persona, background, techniques and tools used [3] and that there are follow-up on-line reports about the developments.

The rich information provided by FireEye allows this research to analyze APT attacks and actors from the evolutionary view used in organization studies [6]. In order to understand the evolution of attack technologies and actor behaviors, this research follows the comprehensive review by Lemay [1] and Ussath [4] to use manual classification of collected information.

This paper is organized as follows: Sect. 2 discusses the related work on APT attacks and actors. Section 3 provides the overview of the analyzed evolution in techniques and behavior. Finally, Sect. 4 concludes the work and proposes future work.

2 Related Work

Starting from early 2000's, Advanced Persistent Threat (APT) has emerged to be an important method of cyber espionage [1–3]. This new form of attacks is baffling for network administrators and cyber defense firms, due to its complexity and discrepancies from the traditional cyber attacks in the following aspects: (1) Organizing: the attackers are well-organized and well-skilled teams that are directly or indirectly supported by governments, making them more resourceful and organized than traditional attackers. (2) Sophistication: APT attacks are implemented through a series of properly plotted activities, from spear phishing, malware injection, data transmission to trace clearance. The multiplicity of attack channels and mechanisms significantly increase the success rate of compromising the target network (3) Concealment: attackers lurk in the target network and disguise their behaviors as normal ones, and could update the malware without being noticed. According to survey, it takes financial firms 98 days and retailers 197 days on average to detect a data breach [7]. (4) Purpose: the traditional attackers typically pursuit financial gains from victims, but the APT groups aim at confidential information from target firms or government agencies. In a word, APT attacks are trickier and more difficult to defend against.

Based on the aforementioned characteristics of the APT groups, they are "organizations" that can compete with the cyber defense service providers and bring changes to the cyber security industry. According to the comprehensive survey by Lemay and colleague [1], at least 39 APT organizations can be identified that differ in organizational history, strategies and resources. The emergence of the malicious competitors has caused much attention from the cyber defense firms. In order to enhance detection and defend against APT organizations, cyber defense firms (e.g., FireEye and Symantec) and academia seek to find feasible solutions to detect and prevent advanced attack methods, such as Portable Executable Injection and Dynamic-Link Library injection.

2.1 APT Techniques, Tactics, and Procedures Analysis

In order to accomplish these complex steps, APT actors need to establish ample techniques, tactics and procedures [8] to penetrate a network, compromise a first system, stay in the network without being noticed [7], collecting target information, and clear the trace of their existence after completing the task [2].

With respect to techniques, APT actors are capable of developing distinctive malware that serve their specific purposes. Also, they typically use spear phishing when trying to lure victims, then control the victim or update the malware through command and control (C2) servers. Remote control is used during data collection phase [1, 2, 4].

APT attacks tend to aim for highly valuable information, such as intellectual properties of firms [9]. To accomplish the task, APT actors carefully plan and execute their tactics and procedures. According to an interviewee who runs a mass-malware campaign that targets at stealing banking and other credentials from millions of computers, there are seven necessary steps: (1) Gain exposure, (2) Acquire capabilities, (3) Establish a delivery network, (4) Exploit the target, (5) Install malware, (6) Establish command and control, and (7) Perform actions on objectives [9]. More systematically, the targeted attack lifecycle is proposed to decompose APT intrusion into steps as: initial reconnaissance, initial compromise, establish foothold, escalate privileges, internal reconnaissance, move laterally, maintain presence, and complete mission [8].

3 Overview of the Analyzed Evolution

3.1 Data Collection and Analysis Method

As APT attacks are very sophisticated and involve series of actions, current on-hand resources may fall short in capturing the activities of APTs, this research uses publically available reports of APT groups as the source data. The comprehensive work by

Lemay and colleague [1] provides clear guidance to locate the wealth of reports from major anti-virus companies and organizations. Although there are different names for the same APT group from various anti-virus firms and organizations, Lemay and colleague [1] has devoted much effort in mapping them so that further analyses can target at APT groups. Therefore, in order to generate insights about the behaviors of different APTs, collecting available reports is considered more practical and suitable for this proposed research.

3.2   Contact Author Information

Shown as the growing number of victims in Fig. 1, APT1 gets more adept in accomplishing its task of penetrating target networks. It is observed that APT1 is capable of stealing huge amount of data from a single victim: 6.5 Terabytes over 10 months [3], indicating APT1's capability of lurking and stay undetected for at least 10 months, and can partition huge data into small data packets so that the transferring from the victim network to the C2 server can blend in normal network traffic.

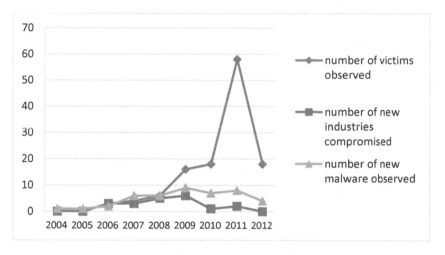

Fig. 1. Evolution of APT1 (Source: Mandiant 2013)

As the oldest tailored malware, WEBC2 backdoor family evolved over the years. The original version was designed to retrieve a web page containing special HTML tags from C2 servers and to interpret the tags as commands. Initially, WEBC2 backdoor could read HTML comments. Over the years of development, newer version can read data contained within other types of tags and make more functions as depicted in Table 1 below.

Table 1. Evolution of the WEBC2 backdoor family.

Year	Name	Function
2004	WEBC2-KT3	searches for a comment in the format of <!--aHR0cAXXXXXX -->
2007	WEBC2-Y21K	searches for Base64 encoded commands within HTML comments, and make below functions: (1) establish connection; (2)set sleep interval; (3) download and execute file from specified URL
	WEBC2-UGX	
2008	WEBC2-AUSOV	a downloader that looks for HTML
	WEBC2-CLOVER	perform a GET request searches the response for the strings <form and /form>
2009	WEBC2-RAVE	look for commands embedded in HTML comments ("<-- ->") Once decoded the malware expects one of the following commands: (1) Set sleep interval; (2) Download and execute file; (3) Interactive command shell
	WEBC2-ADSPACE	attempt to connect to the C2 server at a specified time
	WEBC2-HEAD	communicates over HTTPS, using the system's SSL implementation to encrypt all communications with the C2 server.
	WEBC2-TOCK	search a web page for these strings: · <!---[<if IE 5>]id="all" · <!---[<if IE 5>]id="%COMPUTERNAME%" · <![<endif>]--->
2010	WEBC2-YAHOO	enters a loop where every ten minutes it attempts to download a web page that may contain an encoded URL of a file to download and execute.
	WEBC2-CSON	perform a GET request in the following format. The malware generates 10 random alphabetical characters for each connection
	WEBC2-QBP	searches for two strings, "<!--<2010QBP " followed by " 2010QBP//-->", in a HTML comment. a DES-encrypted string is placed inside these tags.
2011	WEBC2-DIV	searches for the strings "<div safe:" and " balance>" to delimit encoded C2 information
2012	WEBC2-TABLE	issues an initial GET request. The malware expects the decoded background data to be the hostname of the infected system.
	WEBC2-BOLID	performs a GET request

4 Conclusion and Future Work

The growing sophistication of cyber attack, APTs in particular, has made successful security very challenging. Just as the authors are working on analyzing the seminal FireEye report, FireEye releases another new APT group in late March [10], just a few months from the release of previous group, indicating the urgency to defend against the growing number of APT groups. As pointed out by Lemay and colleague [1], more knowledge in the APT groups themselves can facilitate finding more effective ways of protecting organizational information. This research illustrates an initial analysis into the changes of techniques, tactics, and procedures in APT1 from FireEye reports.

As a seminal research, broader investigations are needed to provide more insights for cyber security against APT attacks. For the first thing, a full-range analysis into publically available reports [1] is essential. For the second, advanced big data analytics [11, 12] should be employed to build holistic and insightful trends of APT actors.

References

1. Lemay, A., Calvet, J., Menet, F., Fernandez, J.M.: Survey of publicly available reports on advanced persistent threat actors. Comput. Secur. **72**, 26–59 (2018)
2. Li, F., Lai, A., Ddl, D.: Evidence of Advanced Persistent Threat: A case study of malware for political espionage. In: 6th International Conference on Malicious and Unwanted Software, pp. 102–109 (2011)
3. Mandiant: APT1: Exposing One of China's Cyber Espionage Units (2013). https://www.fireeye.com/content/dam/fireeye-www/services/pdfs/mandiant-apt1-report.pdf. Accessed 1 Mar 2018
4. Ussath, M., Jaeger, D., Feng, C., Meinel, C.: Advanced persistent threats: behind the scenes. In: 2016 Annual Conference on Information Science and Systems (CISS), pp. 181–186 (2016)
5. Marchetti, M., Pierazzi, F., Colajanni, M., Guido, A.: Analysis of high volumes of network traffic for Advanced Persistent Threat detection. Comput. Netw. **109**, 127–141 (2016)
6. Nelson, R.R., Winter, S.: An Evolution Theory of Economic. Change Press (1982)
7. Osborne, C.: Most companies take over six months to detect data breaches. https://www.zdnet.com/article/businesses-take-over-six-months-to-detect-data-breaches/. Accessed 20 Feb 2018
8. Aldridge, J.: Remediating Targeted-threat Intrusions (2018). https://media.blackhat.com/bh-us-12/Briefings/Aldridge/BH_US_12_Aldridge_Targeted_Intrustion_WP.pdf. Accessed 20 May 2018
9. Guido, D.: A case study of intelligence-driven defense. IEEE Secur. Priv. **9**, 67–70 (2011)
10. FireEye: APT37: The Overlooked North Korean Actor (2018). https://www2.fireeye.com/rs/848-DID-242/images/rpt_APT37.pdf. Accessed 1 Mar 2018
11. Blazquez, D., Domenech, J.: Big data sources and methods for social and economic analyses. Technol. Forecast. Soc. Change **130**, 99–113 (2018)
12. Wang, Y., Xu, W.: Leveraging deep learning with LDA-based text analytics to detect automobile insurance fraud. Decis. Support Syst. **105**, 87–95 (2018)

The Impact of the Observation Period for Detecting P2P Botnets on the Real Traffic Using BotCluster

Chun-Yu Wang[1](✉), Jia-Hong Yap[1], Kuan-Chung Chen[1],
Jyh-Biau Chang[3], and Ce-Kuen Shieh[1,2]

[1] Institute of Computer and Communication Engineering,
Department of Electrical Engineering,
National Cheng Kung University, Tainan, Taiwan
wicanr2@gmail.com, yapjiahong@gmail.com,
j8456784@gmail.com, shieh@ee.ncku.edu.tw
[2] National Center for High-Performance Computing, Hsinchu, Taiwan
[3] Department of Digital Applications, University of Kang Ning, Tainan, Taiwan
andrew@ukn.edu.tw

Abstract. In recent years, many studies on peer-to-peer (P2P) botnet detection have exhibited the excellent detection precision on synthetic logs collected from the testbed. However, most of them do not evaluate their effectiveness on real traffic. In this paper, we use our BotCluster to analyze real traffic from April 2nd to April 15th, 2017, collected as Netflow format, with three time-scopes for detecting P2P botnet activities in two campuses (National Cheng Kung University (NCKU) and National Chung Cheng University (CCU)). Three time-scopes including single-day, three-day, and weekly observation period applied to the same traffic logs for revealing the influence of the observation period on P2P botnet detection. The experiments show that with the weekly observation period, the precision can increase 10% from 84% to 94% on the combined traffic logs of two campuses.

Keywords: P2P botnet detection · NetFlow · Network security · BotCluster

1 Introduction

Along with the peer-to-peer applications on Internet are raised rapidly, such as Bit-torrent, Bitcoin; meanwhile, potential threats are also appearing upon them. P2P bot-nets are consisting of a lot of compromised machine, controlled by botmaster, and been used for various cybercrime purposes including phishing, spam, distributed denial of service (DDoS). For example, the recently Mirai botnet, which can intrude many off-the-shelf routers and acquire the root access, had been reported by anti-virus

The authors are grateful to the Ministry of Science and Technology, Taiwan for the financial support (This research funded by contract MOST-103-2221-E-006-144-MY3), National Center for High-Performance Computing, Taiwan for providing NetFlow log and VirusTotal for contributing the malicious IP checking.

© Springer Nature Singapore Pte Ltd. 2019
C.-Y. Chang et al. (Eds.): ICS 2018, CCIS 1013, pp. 82–92, 2019.
https://doi.org/10.1007/978-981-13-9190-3_8

companies. Mirai also generates DDoS attacks for paralyzing several leading service platforms such as GitHub, Twitter and Minecraft server. The typical P2P botnets, like Mirai, use comprised peers to form a P2P network for exchanging command directly. Other advanced P2P botnets, e.g., Zeus, Kelihos, have improved for the robustness by adding rendezvous points in their network structure. Moreover, both the typical or advanced P2P botnets own the ability to avoid the single point of failure (SPOF) problem, which makes themselves are more difficult to detect in contrast to traditional centralized command and control botnets.

Previous studies [2–22] use the supervised-based learning or signature-based approach to identify malware activities and have very high precision on particular botnets. However, some deficiencies have existed among those studies. First, supervised-based learning can only detect already-known botnets, as opposed to the mutated version of the same codebase malware, e.g., Kelihos, such that the performance perhaps degrade due to the behavior pattern had changed. Second, the signature-based approach requires examining the content of packets or infected executable file for digging out the malware execution flow; it may spend a lot of pre-training time for analyzing the malware behaviors and may cause privacy concerns because of the inevitable investigating on payloads in the detecting phase. Third, most research uses synthetic logs, which collected from the testbed in the short-term period, for evaluating their performance. They are not verified on the real traffic and may impractical especially in facing the rapidly mutated botnets.

In this paper, we use our BotCluster [1] to give the discussions of the observation period on botnet detection between the short-term and long-term duration. The testing traffic logs as Netflow format are collected from two campuses in Taiwan, (National Cheng Kung University (NCKU) and National Chung Cheng University (CCU)) upon TWAREN [24] (Taiwan Advanced Research and Education Network). We analyze the traffic logs of two campuses in the same duration between April 2nd to April 15th, 2017, accompanied with three time-scopes including single-day, three-day, and weekly observation period for presenting their importance on detecting the activities of P2P botnets. The contributions of our work are as follows:

- We use BotCluster to analyze the activities of P2P botnets on the real traffic.
- The precision was evaluated using public blacklist service VirusTotal [23] to ensure detection results feasible and reliable.
- We present three time-scopes including single-day, three-day and weekly observation period for proving that has a significant influence on the P2P botnet detection.
- We also show that even botnets stay in stealth communication, the detected results aggregated by BotCluster, can grow dramatically either in the long-term observing or using combined traffic logs from different campuses, e.g., NCKU and CCU.

The rest of this paper is organized as follows: Sect. 2 presents the related work. Section 3 gives a brief of BotCluster. Section 4 presents experiments and discussions. Finally, the conclusion and future work are illustrated in Sect. 5.

2 Related Work

Yan et al. [15] are tracking P2P botnet activities over 6 months to recognize the super peers, normal peers, and their statistical characterization within one AS (Autonomous System) scope. Their main contribution is to give a proof that the botnet communication pattern would eventually appear on long-term observation.

Sun et al. [6] traces the network behavior of compromised hosts to discover malicious domains. It consists of two central procedures for the feature extraction and domain classifier. The first phase runs on the MapReduce used to construct the Process-Domain Bipartite-Graph from the training dataset for explaining the connection between the domain and the process. Every domain will be labeled malicious or benign using blacklist and whitelist, and then it will mark each process as infected or good accompanied with at least two different malicious domains. After labeling, each domain will extract a process behavior feature proposed to represent as its feature vector. In the classifier phase, they use Spark to build the random forest model for identifying the unknown domain as malicious or benign. The experiment uses the ROC to evaluate the precision and the false positive rate of itself with two enterprises traffic log in gigabyte level and the malicious IP provided by the VirusTotal.

Qiu et al. [8] use the Chow-Liu Bayesian Network, Gaussian Mixture, and logistic regression to form an active learning framework with human-in-the-loop for modeling traffic behavior as a feature set. They extract the first ten packets of each flow after the handshake of the connection and make a distribution accompanying with the sequence of directions and packet sizes of them. Next, they use Gaussian Mixture Model to derive the feature vector; those vectors then applied to a regression model for building a classifier model. Experiments, using the traffic comprised of the LBNL background traffic, VRT Zeus, and the ISOT Zeus, show that the ROC and AUC of the proposed framework has better performance than other feature set CSET11 and TNNLS16.

Yang et al. [9] implements a two-stage algorithm for detecting P2P botnets on the SCADA system, the first stage removes the hosts without P2P network traffic, and the second stage uses Affinity Propagation to identify the bots. A self-organizing map (SOM) introduced in [10] is applied to recognize the botnets. It is based on two datasets, ISOT and CTU13, with three plans for model training. The experiment shows that the classifier under given full knowledge can achieve the best performance up to 99% on traffic classification. The Generic Algorithm (GA) on [11] is used to resolve the appropriate features on the initial set of 19 characteristics for training the C4.5 model. Their experiments adopt the two datasets, ISOT and ISCX, and use the GA to obtain the best combination of the features for detecting a particular botnet activity. The results show that with the optimal feature vector, the detection rate can boost up dramatically, and they conclude that feature selection is an important impact factor on the botnet detection.

Mai and Park [12] use ISOT dataset to evaluate the performance of the three unsupervised clustering K-means, DBSCAN and Mean Shift and construct decision trees using clustering results for traffic classification. Their experiments show that when the number of traffic data is small, the K-means gets the poor performance, but it achieves the best detection rate at the traffic volume is enormous enough. Moreover, there is no significant improvement for others while the amount of traffic was growing up. However, the proper size K of the cluster in the K-means is hard to determine in the real traffic, and it may lead to the low accuracy against variants of the botnets. Gavrilut et al. [13] presents a DGA-based botnet detection using traffic log between hosts and DNS services. They observe the domain name resolving among 18 botnets to construct the composition rules of them and create a query distribution. Chebyshev's inequality then applied to the distribution for detecting the unusual fraction of DNS traffic to identify botnets. Our BotCluster is based on unsupervised-based learning and can detect P2P botnet activities on real traffic with the non-prior knowledge required in contrast to [2–22].

3   Introduction to BotCluster

BotCluster [1] is a generic P2P botnet detection system. It can identify P2P botnets using the similar behavior in Netflow traces. In this section, we introduce each stage of BotCluster including Session Extraction, Filter and Grouping to give an overview of our previous work. Figure 1 shows the workflow of BotCluster. The implementation of Session Extraction, Filter and Grouping stages are using Hadoop's MapReduce.

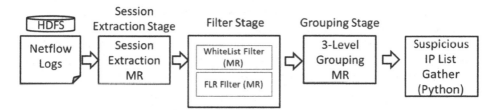

Fig. 1. The workflow of BotCluster.

3.1   Session Extraction

In Session Extraction stage, it constructs sessions and extracts features from unidirectional flows in the Netflow. Netflow's features are including the source and destination endpoints (IP addresses), communication ports and its protocol, and the number of incoming and outgoing of bytes and packets. For aggregating sessions from unidirectional flows between the two endpoints, we collect continuous flows within a timeout threshold into a session. In other words, any two flows that their inter-arrival time is less than a timeout threshold would be merged into the same session. Every session also accompanies with a feature vector consist of the number of packets, the number of bytes, the maximal, minimal and average packet length, the ratio of the incoming and outgoing bytes, session duration and the flow loss-response ratio (FLR). FLR ratio is a proportion of the requests to corresponding reverse directional response.

3.2   Filter

In Filter Stage, it decreases the input size for reducing the computing overhead. We use the whitelist to filter safety network transactions and utilize FLR to remove unassociated sessions which their endpoints have lower likelihood in P2P traffic for decreasing the total amount of volume in the dataset. Filter Stage is composed of two phase including the whitelist filter and the FLR filter. Whitelist filter would eliminate sessions that their endpoint is on the whitelist including public DNS servers or validate websites. Next, remaining sessions with low FLR would be excluded from the FLR filter. A session has a lower FLR also means that it unlikely participates any P2P networks.

3.3   Grouping

In the Grouping phase, a mutant DBScan-like algorithm [1] was used to cluster sessions with a like behavior hierarchically. It consists of three-level subgrouping for aggregating similar behaviors by measuring the similarity in their feature vectors with different target correspondingly at each level as shown in Fig. 2. The first subgrouping applied to collect similar sessions with the same endpoints to form Super-Sessions. Next, it merged similar Super-Sessions of the same source endpoint to construct the Session-Groups. Finally, we examine the behavior similarity among the Session-Groups to consolidate them as Behavior-Groups. Hosts inside a Behavior-Group can be considered them belong to the same P2P network with most likely behaviors. Besides, the similarity measurement is based on Euclidean distance. After performing the three-level grouping, we use a Python script for reversing lookup the correlated IP address within each Behavior-Group to generate a suspicious IP list.

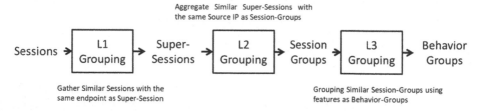

Fig. 2. 3-level grouping workflow in BotCluster

4   Experiments

4.1   Environment

Our experiments run on Braavos [25] at the National Center for High-Performance Computing (NCHC) in Taiwan. It has 256 nodes, total 4096 cores and 16.38 TB memory, and its Hadoop version is YARN 2.7.2 with 1.5 PB storage space in HDFS. Each node had installed the operating system CentOS 6.7 and equipped with dual eight-core Xeon CPU E5-2630 up to 2.4 GHz and 128 GB DDR3 memory.

4.2   Netflow Dataset and Parameter Setting

The Netflow traffic logs, provided by NCHC (National Center for High-Performance Computing), are collected between April 2nd to April 15th, 2017 at the two campuses in Taiwan (National Cheng Kung University (NCKU) and National Chung Cheng University (CCU)) upon the TWAREN (Taiwan Advanced Research and Education Network). All statistics of our collected logs had shown in Table 1. The column "IPs" is the number of IP address, "Size" is the file size in gigabytes and "Flows" is the number of record in Netflow log. The total number of unique IP address is about 1.29 million and 0.67 million for NCKU and CCU. Moreover, the total size and total flows are about 39.5 GB and 23.8 GB, and 342 million and 206 million for NCKU and CCU correspondingly. The FLR Threshold set as 0.225 adopted from our previous work setting [1]; the minimal points (MinPts) and the distance threshold in grouping stage of BotCluster set as 5 and 1.5 respectively.

Table 1. Netflow statistics for NCKU and CCU between April 2nd to 15th 2017.

Campus	NCKU			CCU		
Date	Size	IPs	Flows	Size	IPs	Flows
2017/4/2	1.8 GB	46330	15611350	0.9 GB	31088	7994485
2017/4/3	1.9 GB	56793	16824650	1 GB	36815	8836488
2017/4/4	3.0 GB	64672	25847407	5.4 GB	77342	46790383
2017/4/5	2.9 GB	101814	24694844	1.4 GB	46995	12543183
2017/4/6	3.2 GB	167463	27747846	1.6 GB	50185	13828164
2017/4/7	3.1 GB	114596	26709460	1.8 GB	54395	15568044
2017/4/8	2.7 GB	102683	23467483	1.6 GB	36388	13696158
2017/4/9	2.4 GB	53740	20913070	1.6 GB	33929	13457701
2017/4/10	2.9 GB	78745	25413952	1.6 GB	46046	14042519
2017/4/11	3.2 GB	81230	28085449	1.7 GB	48758	14472257
2017/4/12	3.4 GB	117904	29408179	1.5 GB	58686	13401049
2017/4/13	3.2 GB	118096	27733224	1.4 GB	57494	11902365
2017/4/14	3.0 GB	108450	26221063	1.2 GB	53846	10231447
2017/4/15	2.8 GB	85602	23843488	1.1 GB	42042	9285028
Total	39.5 GB	1298118	342 million	23.8 GB	674009	206 million

4.3   Precision

Due to the nature of the stealth and evading communication of P2P botnets, only using the blacklist cannot reveal the complete malicious activities. Therefore, we use the blacklist from VirusTotal for inferring infected IP from our detection results. We use the inference rule in [1] to identify malicious IP. The inference rule is that if the numbers of IP in a group are more than 5 or over 50% directly recording on VirusTotal, then all IPs in the same group would be considered as malicious IPs, because only similar behavioral sessions with a strong association would be aggregated into the same group. The precision verification also adopts from BotCluster as a ratio of CIP to

DIP. "Detected IPs" (DIP) is the total number of IPs detected by BotCluster. "Detected Mal. IPs" (DMIP) is the total number of malicious IPs found by BotCluster and directed reported on VirusTotal; "Correct IPs" (CIP) is the number of correct IPs, as inferred by the verification rule; and "Wrong IPs (WIP)" is the number of improperly identified IPs, as WIP = DIP – CIP.

4.4   Experiments

Experiment 1–The Impact of the Observation Period on the Traffic in NCKU

In this experiment, we analyze the Netflow logs on the NCKU from April 2nd to April 15th, 2017, and traffic logs were merged according to three time-scopes including the single-day (1D), three-day (3D) and weekly (1W) observation period respectively. The purpose of this experiment was to observe the influence of different time-scopes on the precision. All duplicated IPs are erased for ensuring the accuracy of the detection results. The statistical average detection results had shown in Table 2. The experimental results show that the number of detected malicious IPs (DIP) on the NCKU using the single-day observation period has only 6809 at the beginning. However, as more daily traffic logs merged, the detected results grow up to 8277 and 8826 corresponding to three-day (3D) and weekly (1W) observation period. Detected malicious IP on VirusTotal (DMIP) also increased from 313 to 377, and the precision climbed up from 88% to 92% compared to the single-day observation period.

Table 2. Detection results for NCKU with three observation periods.

Time-scopes	DIP	DMIP	CIP	WIP	Precision
1D	6809	313	6024	785	88.47%
3D	8277	365	7536	741	91.04%
1W	8826	377	8192	634	92.81%

Experiment 2–The Impact of the Observation Period on the Traffic in CCU

We also analyze the P2P botnet activities of CCU between April 2nd to April 15th, 2017. The experimental results were demonstrated in Table 3. It seems that the botnet activities of CCU are more silence compared to NCKU because their amount of detected malicious IPs (DMIP) is far less than NCKU, i.e., for single-day (1D) observation period has found only 61 DMIP in CCU contrast to 313 DMIP in NCKU. The precision corresponding to three time-scopes including single-day (1D), three-day (3D) and weekly (1W) observation period are about 60%, 77%, and 83%. However, even CCU has more silence botnet activities as opposed to NCKU, the detected malicious IPs on VirusTotal (DMIP) still increased about 42% following time-scope extending from single-day (1D) observation period to weekly (1W) observation period. It also shows that as a time-scope extending, more the traffic logs merged, more the invisible sessions can dig out by BotCluster.

Table 3. Detection results for CCU with three observation periods.

Time-scopes	DIP	DMIP	CIP	WIP	Precision
1D	2356	61	1404	952	59.36%
3D	2804	89	2172	632	77.46%
1W	3299	105	2692	607	83.36%

Experiment 3–The Impact of the Observation Period on the Combined Traffic

Finally, we merge the Netflow traffic logs of NCKU and CCU in Experiment 3 to observe the influence of the combined logs in botnet detection. The results are summarized in Table 4; we can see that the number of detected IPs is not equal to the sum of individual's DIP because some of them have appeared on both campuses. i.e., the detected IP (DIP) of single-day (1D) observation period is 9136, which is higher than individual detected IP, which is 6809 and 2356, in NCKU and CCU. Moreover, the precision has significant increment from 85% to 95%. The detected malicious IP on VirusTotal (DMIP) also had extended from 378 in single-day (1D) observation period to 490 in weekly (1W) observation period (which increased by 29%). The experiment result also indicates that there is some connection of P2P botnet may both exist between NCKU and CCU, and use the combined logs can provide a more comprehensive viewpoint in botnet detection.

Table 4. Detection results for the combined logs of NCKU and CCU with three observation periods.

Time-scopes	DIP	DMIP	CIP	WIP	Precision
1D	9136	378	7849	1287	85.91%
3D	11130	444	10298	832	92.52%
1W	12079	490	11475	604	94.99%

In P2P botnet, the rendezvous points or super-peers are used to exchange the botmaster commands and to ensure the connectivity; meanwhile, the normal peer periodically communicates with super-peers. Table 5 showed the statistics of the number of detected intersection IP and detected malicious intersection IP in the NCKU and CCU. There were 24 DMIP existed on both NCKU and CCU under the single-day observation period. We believe that those DMIP can be treated as the super-peers in the P2P botnets. Besides, the number of detected malicious intersection IP had grown up about 58% (increased by 14) from 24 DMIP in the single-day observation period to 38 DMIP in the weekly observation period. The detected intersection IP had also risen by expanding the observation period. Moreover, this experimental result represents an evidence that some rendezvous points had been utilized to exchange message for peers on both campuses NCKU and CCU.

Table 6 shows the new additional detected results of DIP and DMIP in combined traffic logs. The definition of the new additional DIP or DMIP is that a detected IP or a detected malicious IP has never been found in the individual traffic logs of NCKU and

Table 5. The statistics of the number of intersection DIP and DMIP for the traffic logs of NCKU and CCU with three observation periods.

Time-scopes	DIP intersection in NCKU and CCU	DMIP intersection in NCKU and CCU
1D	661	24
3D	738	35
1W	794	38

CCU, but it had been detected on the combined traffic logs. The experimental results show that the additional DMIP had risen upward from 48 in the single-day observation period to 79 in the weekly observation period (which increased by 64%). Also, the new additional DIP is growing from 933 in 1D time-scope to 1256 in 1W time-scope (which increased by 35%). We further examine the new additional DMIP and find that there are some of them may act as OpenCandy servers for installing PUP (potentially unwanted programs) purpose. Further, this experimental result also presents the fact, that analyzing the combined logs can provide more insight into the botnet activities.

Table 6. The statistics of the number of the new additional DIP and DMIP for the combined logs of NCKU and CCU with three observation periods.

Time-scopes	The new additional DIP	The new additional DMIP
1D	933	48
3D	1157	59
1W	1256	79

The above experiments verify the fact that even Bots communicate with each other in the stealth way, time-scope extending will improve the opportunity for detecting malicious behaviors. We also demonstrate that the detection results are getting more accurate with incremental observation period on the same traffic logs. Furthermore, these experimental results also tell us that the botnets may invisible in the short-term period, but they can be caught in the long-term observing.

5 Conclusion

In this paper, we use BotCluster [1] on two campuses NCUK and CCU to analyze the impact of the observation period to P2P botnet detection in real traffic. As time-scope extending, more maliciously sessions had been revealed, and the precision is getting better in long-term observing opposed to short-term observing. Moreover, using combined traffic logs and the weekly observation period can improve the precision from 84% to 94%, and obtain more malicious IP compared to the single-day and the three-day observation period. Experiments also proved that the long-term observation is necessary for discovering botnet activities. Our future work will focus on integrating more campuses traffic log to dig out the long-term P2P botnet activities.

References

1. Wang, C.-Y., et al.: BotCluster: a session-based P2P botnet clustering system on NetFlow. Comput. Netw. **145**, 175–189 (2018)
2. Wang, P., Wang, F., Lin, F., Cao, Z.-Z., et al.: Identifying peer-to-peer botnets through periodicity behavior analysis. In: 12th IEEE International Conference On Big Data Science And Engineering (TrustCom/BigDataSE) (2018)
3. Saad, S., et al.: Detecting P2P botnets through network behavior analysis and machine learning. In: 9th Annual International Conference on Privacy Security and Trust (PST), pp. 174–180 (2011)
4. Sengar, B., Padmavathi, B.: P2P bot detection system based on mapreduce. In: 2017 International Conference on Computing Methodologies and Communication (ICCMC) (2017)
5. Mane, Y.D.: Detect and deactivate P2P Zeus bot. In: 2017 8th International Conference on Computing, Communication and Networking Technologies (ICCCNT) (2017)
6. Sun, J.-H., Jeng, T.-H., Chen, C.-C., Huang, H.-C., Chou, K.-S.: MD-Miner: behavior-based tracking of network traffic for malware-control domain detection. In: IEEE Third International Conference on Big Data Computing Service and Applications (BigDataScrvice), pp. 96–105 (2017)
7. Almutairi, S., Mahfoudh, S., Alowibdi, J.S.: Peer to peer botnet detection based on network traffic analysis, new technologies. In: 2016 8th IFIP International Conference on Mobility and Security (NTMS), pp. 1–4 (2016)
8. Qiu, Z., Miller, D.J., Kesidis, G.: Flow based botnet detection through semi-supervised active learning. In: IEEE International Conference on Acoustics, Speech and Signal Processing (ICASSP), pp. 2387–2391 (2017)
9. Yang, H., Cheng, L., Chuah, M.-C.: Detecting peer-to-peer botnets in SCADA systems. In: GlobeCom Workshops (2016)
10. Le, D.C., Zincir-Heywood, A.N., Heywood, M.I.: Data analytics on network traffic flows for botnet behavior detection. In: IEEE Symposium Series on Computational Intelligence (SSCI), pp. 1–7 (2016)
11. Alejandre, F.V., Cortés, N.C., Anaya, E.A.: Feature selection to detect botnets using machine learning algorithms. In: International Conference on Electronics, Communications and Computers (CONIELECOMP), pp. 1–7 (2017)
12. Mai, L., Park, M.: A comparison of clustering algorithms for botnet detection based on network flow. In: 8th International Conference on Ubiquitous and Future Networks (ICUFN), pp. 667–669 (2016)
13. Gavrilut, D.T., Popoiu, G., Benchea, R.: Identifying DGA-based botnets using network anomaly detection. In: 18th International Symposium on Symbolic and Numeric Algorithms for Scientific Computing (SYNASC), pp. 292–299 (2016)
14. Zhuang, D., Chang, J.M.: PeerHunter: detecting peer-to-peer botnets through community behavior analysis. In: 2017 IEEE Conference on Dependable and Secure Computing (2017)
15. Yan, J., Ying, L., Yang, Y., Su, P., Feng, D.: Long term tracking and characterization of P2P botnet. In: IEEE TrustCom, pp. 244–251 (2014)
16. Yahyazadeh, M., Abadi, M.: BotOnus: an online unsupervised method for botnet detection. ISC Int. J. Inf. Secur. (ISeCure) **4**(1), 51–62 (2012)
17. Khodadadi, R., Akbari, B.: Ichnaea: Effective P2P botnet detection approach based on analysis of network flows. In: 7th International Symposium on Telecommunications (IST), pp. 934–940 (2014)

18. Zhang, J.-J., Perdisci, R., Lee, W.-K., Luo, X.-P., Sarfraz, U.: Building a scalable system for stealthy P2P-botnet detection. IEEE Trans. Inf. Forensics and Secur. **9**(1), 27–38 (2014)
19. Narang, P., Ray, S., Hota, C, Venkatakrishnan, V.: Peershark: detecting peer-to-peer botnets by tracking conversations. In: Security and Privacy Workshops (SPW) (2014)
20. Ye, W., Cho, K.: P2P and P2P botnet traffic classification in two stages. Soft Comput. J. **21**, 1–12 (2015)
21. Garg, S., Peddoju, K., Sarje, A.: Scalable P2P bot detection system based on network data stream. Peer-to-Peer Networking Appl. **9**, 1–16 (2016)
22. Thangapandiyan, M., Anand, P.M.R.: An efficient botnet detection system for P2P botnet. In: International Conference on Wireless Communications, Signal Processing and Networking (WiSPNET), pp. 1217–1221 (2016)
23. VirusTotal. https://www.virustotal.com/
24. TaiWan Advanced Research and Education Network (TWAREN). http://www.twaren.net/
25. Braavos. https://www.nchc.org.tw/

Digital Content, Digital Life, Human Computer Interaction and Social Media

Deep Residual Neural Network Design for Super-Resolution Imaging

Wei-Ting Chen$^{(\boxtimes)}$ (ID), Pei-Yin Chen$^{(\boxtimes)}$, and Bo-Chen Lin$^{(\boxtimes)}$

Department of Computer Science and Information Engineering,
National Cheng Kung University, Tainan, Taiwan, R.O.C.
weiting84610@gmail.com, pychen@mail.ncku.edu.tw,
alan19942002@hotmail.com

Abstract. Convolution neural network recently confirmed the high-quality reconstruction for single-image super-resolution (SR). In this paper we present a Deep Level Residual Network (DLNR), a low-memory effective neural network to reconstruct super-resolution images. This neural network also has the following characteristics. (1) Ability to perform different convolution size operations on the image which can achieve more comprehensive feature extraction effects. (2) Using residual learning to expand the depth of the network and increase the capacity of learning. (3) Taking the skill of parameter sharing between the network module to reduce the number of parameters. After the experiment, we find that DLNR can achieve 37.78 in PSNR and 0.975 in SSIM when using Manga109 as testing set for $2\times$ SR.

Keywords: Super-resolution · Neural network · Residual learning · PSNR · SSIM

1 Introduction

At the moment when broadcast media is prevalent, the consumer's demanding of high image quality also increased. The resolution of the image can affect the quality of image directly. The higher resolution it is, the more information can be displayed on the image, and the more delicate details are. As a result, the discussion and research on image resolution improvement is a topic undergoing intense study. However, under the challenges of ultra-high resolution, the traditional image processing technology has been slightly fatigued. Therefore, several papers have presented the methods with neural networks to enhance the resolution of images recently.

Single-image super-resolution (SR) aims to reconstruct high-resolution (HR) images from single low-resolution (LR) input images. Including interpolation such as bicubic interpolation [1], bilinear interpolation [2] as mentioned in the previous methods. Recently, the method of machine learning is widely used to simulate the mapping from LR to SR, such as using sparse coding to implement Sparse Dictionary Learning [2, 4], Random Forest [5] and Convolution Neural Network (CNN) [6]. All of these methods are widely discussed and applied for super-resolution in recent years.

© Springer Nature Singapore Pte Ltd. 2019
C.-Y. Chang et al. (Eds.): ICS 2018, CCIS 1013, pp. 95–105, 2019.
https://doi.org/10.1007/978-981-13-9190-3_9

Convolution Neural Networks have been widely used in image processing and analysis, such as Object Recognition [7], Denoising [8], Optical Flow [9] and Super-Resolution, etc. As for the application of super-resolution, the Super-Resolution Convolution Neural Network (SRCNN) [6], which is proposed by C. Dong et al., learns the non-linear LR-to-HR mapping functions. The architecture of this network has been studied and extended several times, such as sparse coding models [9], increases the depth of networks VDSR [10] or applied in the recursive layer (DRCN) [11]. All of these models are capable of generating high resolution images, but there are still several issues needed to be addressed.

First, before the networks predict the details of images, these methods take the previously defined image scaling operations (e.g. bicubic interpolation) to amplify the input low-resolution images to the desired resolution. This pre-sampling step increases the unnecessary computational costs. In addition, some algorithms extract features directly from the input low-resolution images and replace the magnification of pre-sampled images with deconvolution [12], which uses a relatively small network.

For these reasons, we propose a Deep Level Residual Network (DLRN) which consists of one detail feature extraction, one local information feature extraction branch and one image reconstruction branch. The residual learning method makes the training process easier to converge, effectively solve the problem of gradient vanishing and gradient exploding. The result shows that DLRN reconstructs the high-resolution images in a progressive way, which can achieve not only the better quality of reconstructed images than the papers presented above, but also use the lowest memory space. The detail of DLRN will be presented in the following subsection.

2   Related Work

2.1   Single-Image Super-Resolution

Super-Resolution Convolutional Neural Network (SRCNN) [6] proves that SR can get high quality from end-to-end convolutional networks. As shown in Fig. 2, the SRCNN refers to the Sparse-Coding-Based architecture to establish this network model. The SRCNN neural network architecture can be divided into three main parts:

- **Patch Extraction and Representation**
  Relying on n_1 convolutional filters to extract features of input images, it is important to note that before the image input SRCNN, a pre-sampling (Bicubic interpolation) is required. It enlarges the original LR images to the same size as the SR images you want to achieve, and then enters it into the neural network. The formula is $F_1(Y) = \max(0, W_1 * Y + B_1)$ where Y is the image after bicubic interpolation (LR), W_1 denotes n_1 filters which size are $c \times f_1 \times f_1$ (c is the number of channel and f_1 is the convolution size of filters), B_1 indicates the Bias, * indicates the convolution operation, and max represents the activation function RELU.
- **Non-Linear Mapping**
  After patch extraction and representation, converting n_1 dimension to n_2 dimension. The formula is as follow:

$$F_2(Y) = \max\left(0, W_2 * F_1(Y) + B_2\right). \tag{1}$$

- **Reconstruction**

It is considered whether the value of each pixel is similar to the value of SR images. This step can be illustrated as taking an average among a plurality of related high-dimensional feature vectors, so that a convolution performed here is able to reconstructed. This behavior is similar to the average processing of traditional methods. The formula is as follow:

$$F_3(Y) = \max\left(0, W_3 * F_2(Y) + B_3\right). \tag{2}$$

2.2 Residual Neural Network

Recently, in order to achieve powerful performance, the architecture of neural networks is getting more complicated. In our design, we will also increase the number of hidden layers to learn extra feature information and reconstruction methods. However, if we simply increase the depth of neural networks, it may encounter several problems like gradients vanishing and gradient exploding. When the gradient is back-propagated to the upper layer, the infinite multiplication may cause the gradient to become infinitely small or infinite, so its performance will gradually become saturated and even begin to decline. Therefore, the ResNet [13] is proposed to solve this problem.

The feature of ResNet [13] is that the hidden layers in the architecture only learn the residuals between next one layer, where only focus on the difference between output and input. With this method, it makes the training more precise and simple, the principle of residual learning is showed in Fig. 1 where the input is x and the output is Y, then we can get the formula (3) where σ is the activity function ReLU and Wn represents the weight of each hidden layer. We can also find the output function in formula (4) where $F(x, \{W\})$ is exactly the residual function. To simplify the formula, the bias isn't shown in the figure. In the formula, we can easily find that residual function just needs to fit $Y - x$ which is easier to achieve than fit Y.

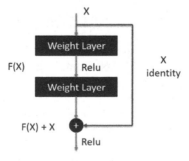

Fig. 1. The residual learning model proposed in ResNet [12]

$$F(x) = W_2 * \sigma(W_1 * x) \qquad (3)$$

$$Y = F(x, \{W\}) + x \qquad (4)$$

2.3   VDSR

VDSR [10] is a modified convolution neural network of residual network, the difference is that VDSR does the residual learning between input LR and output SR. With residual learning, we can increase learning rate of VDSR and get converge faster. The number of hidden layers are 20 in VDSR, which is much more than SRCNN (only three hidden layers). Figure 2 shows the comparison among ResNet, VDSR and DLNR.

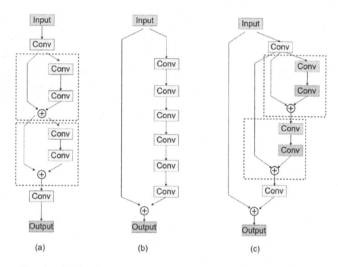

Fig. 2.   (a) ResNet [13] (b) VDSR [10] (c) DLNR (Proposed)

2.4   Laplacian Pyramid

Laplacian Pyramid is a method widely used for image processing, including image compacting [14], semantic segmentation [15], edge-aware [16], etc. Denton et al. established the Laplacian Pyramid in a machine learning model [17]. They built a generative adversarial network (LAPGAN) framework to generate realistic and completed images based on Laplacian Pyramid. Lai et al. proposed LapSRN [18] which extracts features from LR images space and gets the SR images at the end of each level. LapSRN adjusts the network weight coefficient by means of feedback at each level. With the network design which is similar to Laplacian pyramid, SR images are predicted. We also use this architecture and take a local information feature extraction branch to extract more features of different regions.

3 Proposed Method

3.1 Proposed Network

We propose a SR network named DLRN, the architecture is showed in Fig. 3. The input is a LR image then we predict L-level images, where L is based on log_2n, n is the scaling ratio ($2\times$, $4\times$, $8\times$). There are three branches in our network including Detail Feature Extraction, Local Information Feature Extraction Branch and Image Reconstruction Branch.

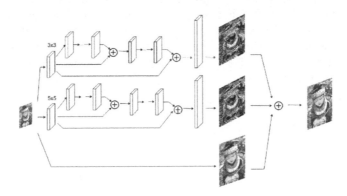

Fig. 3. The one level network architecture ($2\times$ SR)

- **Detail Feature Extraction Branch**
  This branch takes filters with 3*3 spatial region to extract images, Fig. 4 shows two levels network ($4\times$ SR) of this branch, in each level, it consists of some convolution layers for feature mapping, one de-convolution layer and one convolution layer for predicting residuals of reconstructed image. There are **B** sets of residual units in the feature mapping (Fig. 4 red dotted block is a set of residual units) and there are d_1 convolution layers in each residual unit, which are used to process non-linear high-dimension feature mapping.

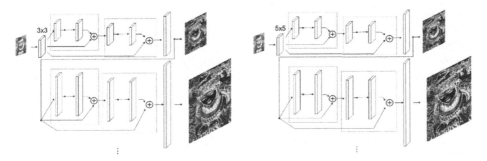

Fig. 4. The detail extraction branch of two levels (B = 2)

Fig. 5. The local information extraction branch of two levels (B = 2)

- **Local Information Feature Extraction Branch**

  To complement the detail feature extraction branch without considering image information of the local block. Figure 5 shows two levels network (4× SR) of this branch. In this branch, we hope to refer to Local image information as the basis for feature extraction. The filters' size in this branch is 5*5 and there are **B** sets of residual units in each level. Each unit consists of d_2 convolution layers for feature mapping of high-dimensional nonlinearity and a convolutional layer for predicting reconstructed image residuals.

- **Image Reconstruction**

  In each level, the input images of image reconstruction branch is upsampled 2× by a de-convolution layer. In this branch, we take filters with 4*4 spatial region and use bilinear kernel to initialize it. Finally, the SR images of this level are generated by element-wise summation of the upsampled images and the prediction residual images of the above two feature extraction branches. The operation process is shown in Fig. 6.

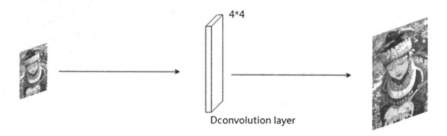

4*4

Dconvolution layer

Fig. 6. The one level image reconstruction

3.2 Architecture Optimization

While increasing the quality of SR images, we also need to pay attention to the execution time and the amount of memory usage. In DLNR, we take two optimization methods residual learning and parameter sharing, respectively. The detail will be presented in the following.

- **Residual Learning**

  When the architecture design goes deeper, to avoid gradients vanishing and gradient exploding, we let the identity mapping of each residual unit block. The branch input is the result of the convolution operation, which is the input of the identity mapping branch of each residual unit is the same, as shown in Fig. 7 and the formula shown in (5) where H^0 represents the initial result after convolution operation, H^{b-1} and H^b are the input and output of bth residual block.

$$H^b = F\left(H^{b-1}, W^b\right) + H^0 \tag{5}$$

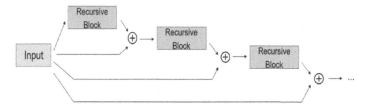

Fig. 7. Residual learning of blocks

- **Parameter Sharing**

  In order to minimize the memory, DLNR takes two oriented-parameter sharing, the parameters sharing among different levels and sharing parameters in each residual unit. The former shares parameters of hidden layers on the feature extraction branch, parameters of upsample network and parameters of convolution layers used to predict residuals of reconstructed images. The latter uses a recursive layer to extend the architecture of network. In other words, each residual unit is composed of the same convolution layers.

3.3   Multi-scale

Since the architecture of DLNR is similar to Laplacian Pyramid, the input images are scaling level by level. DLNR takes $2\times$ scaling in each level, so the images will get $4\times$ scaling if repeating sub-level of DLNR, and so on; $8\times$ or $16\times$ images is generated. By this method, DLNR can reconstruct $2\times$, $4\times$, $8\times$ SR images at the same time. It is an effective practice for devices limited by hardware resources. We only need to put the trained DLRN model into the device, using the same set of weight parameters to apply different magnification of scaling.

4   Experiments and Comparisons

We take 291 images as training sets, 91 of which were used by Yang et al. [19] and the other 200 were implemented by Berkeley Segmentation Datasets [20]. As for the testing sets, we use five widely used standard data sets as testing sets, Set5 [21] (5 images), Set14 [4] (14 images), BSD100 [20] (100 images), Urban100 [22] (100 images), and MANGA109 [25] (109 images), respectively. First, we compare the number of parameter and the testing time with SRCNN [6], FSRCNN [12], VDSR

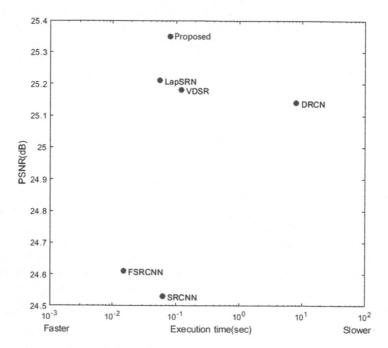

Fig. 8. Execution time comparison

Table 1. Parameters comparison

	[10]	[11]	[18]	Proposed
Parameters	650 K	1800 K	838 K	439 K
PSNR	25.18	25.14	25.21	25.35

[10], DRCN [11] and LapSRN [18] and the result is shown in Fig. 8. The PSNR of DLNR is the best and because the convolution layers are stacked in multiple layers, the average time to test an image is slightly worse than LapSRN [17]. As for the comparison result of parameters in whole network shown in Table 1, and due to parameter sharing, the DLNR needs the fewest parameters.

Finally, we compare the image quality of SR generated from DLNR with those from several famous papers that also study SR. Figure 9 shows the SR generated by each network.

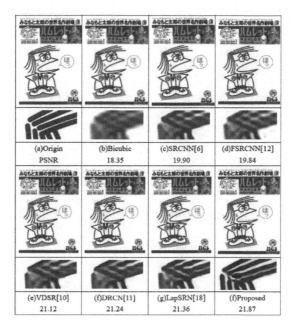

Fig. 9. $8\times$ SR testing images of Manga109-Hamlet.png

5 Conclusion and Future Work

We proposed a convolution neural network named Deep Level Residual Network (DLNR), which is applied to super-resolution image scaling. DLNR can let images $2\times$, $4\times$ and $8\times$ SR without excessive distortion and maintain high image quality. Using two feature extraction branches and one image reconstruction branch to let reconstructed SR images get higher similarity to original images. Laplacian pyramid is also adopted by DLNR which provides multiple rate SR. Compare with the results, $4\times$ and $8\times$ SR images have higher quality than those applying several methods proposed before. In terms of performance optimization, we take parameters sharing to compress initial model and also enhance the inference efficiency. The time of SR processing is only 0.04 s when taking Urban100 as testing set [22] (HD). In the future, we will focus on improving training preference and deepening the number of hidden layers in case of parameters quantity, expecting a shorter training time for a better SR images (Fig. 10).

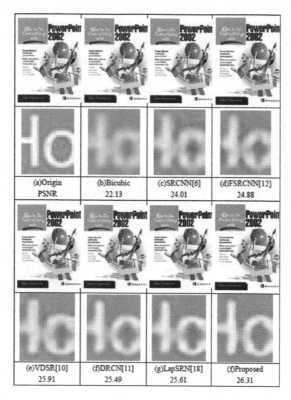

Fig. 10. 4× SR testing images of Set14-ppt3.png

References

1. Keys, R.: Cubic convolution interpolation for digital image processing. IEEE Trans. Acoust. Speech Signal Process. **29**(6), 1153–1160 (1981). https://doi.org/10.1109/TASSP.1981.1163711
2. Numerical Recipes in C. Cambridge University Press, pp. 123–128 (1988–92). ISBN 0-521-43108-5
3. Yang, J., Wright, J., Huang, T., Ma, Y.: Image super-resolution as sparse representation of raw image patches. In: IEEE Conference on Computer Vision and Pattern Recognition (2008)
4. Zeyde, R., Elad, M., Protter, M.: On single image scale-up using sparse-representations. In: Boissonnat, J.-D., et al. (eds.) Curves and Surfaces 2010. LNCS, vol. 6920, pp. 711–730. Springer, Heidelberg (2012). https://doi.org/10.1007/978-3-642-27413-8_47
5. Schulter, S., Leistner, C., Bischof, H.: Fast and accurate image upscaling with super-resolution forests. In: CVPR (2015)
6. Dong, C., Loy, C.C., He, K., Tang, X.: Image super-resolution using deep convolutional networks. IEEE Trans. Pattern Anal. Mach. Intell. **38**(2), 295–307 (2015)
7. He, K., Zhang, X.,. Ren, S., Sun, J.: Deep residual learning for image recognition. In: IEEE Conference on Computer Vision and Pattern Recognition (2016)

8. Jain, V., Seung, H.S.: Natural image denoising with convolutional networks. In: Advances in Neural Information Processing Systems 21 (NIPS 2008). MIT Press (2008)
9. Wang, Z., Liu, D., Yang, J., Han, W., Huang, T.: Deep networks for image super-resolution with sparse prior. In: IEEE International Conference on Computer Vision (2015)
10. Kim, J., Lee, J.K., Lee, K.M.: Accurate image super-resolution using very deep convolutional networks. In: IEEE Conference on Computer Vision and Pattern Recognition (2016)
11. Kim, J., Lee, J.K., Lee, K.M.: Deeply-recursive convolutional network for image super-resolution. In: IEEE Conference on Computer Vision and Pattern Recognition (2016)
12. Dong, C., Loy, C.C., Tang, X.: Accelerating the super-resolution convolutional neural network. In: Leibe, B., Matas, J., Sebe, N., Welling, M. (eds.) ECCV 2016. LNCS, vol. 9906, pp. 391–407. Springer, Cham (2016). https://doi.org/10.1007/978-3-319-46475-6_25
13. He, K., Zhang, X., Ren, S., Sun, J.: Deep residual learning for image recognition. In: CVPR (2016)
14. Burt, P.J., Adelson, E.H.: The Laplacian pyramid as a compact image code. IEEE Trans. Commun. 31(4), 532–540 (1983)
15. Ghiasi, G., Fowlkes, C.C.: Laplacian pyramid reconstruction and refinement for semantic segmentation. In: Leibe, B., Matas, J., Sebe, N., Welling, M. (eds.) ECCV 2016. LNCS, vol. 9907, pp. 519–534. Springer, Cham (2016). https://doi.org/10.1007/978-3-319-46487-9_32
16. Paris, S., Hasinoff, S.W., Kautz, J.: Local laplacian filters: edge-aware image processing with a laplacian pyramid. ACM Trans. Graph. 30(4), 68 (2011). (Proceedings of SIGGRAPH)
17. Denton, E.L., Chintala, S., Fergus, R.: Deep generative image models using a laplacian pyramid of adversarial networks. In: Neural Information Processing Systems (2015)
18. Lai, W.-S., Huang, J.-B., Ahuja, N., Yang, M.-H.: Deep laplacian pyramid networks for fast and accurate super-resolution. In: IEEE Conference on Computer Vision and Pattern Recognition (2017)
19. Yang, J., Wright, J., Huang, T., Ma, Y.: Image super-resolution via sparse representation. IEEE Trans. Image Process. 19(11), 2861–2873 (2010)
20. Martin, D., Fowlkes, C., Tal, D., Malik, J.: A database of human segmented natural images and its application to evaluating segmentation algorithms and measuring ecological statistics. In: ICCV (2001)
21. Bevilacqua, M., Roumy, A., Guillemot, C., Alberi Morel, M.L.: Low complexity single-image super-resolution based on nonnegative neighbor embedding. In: BMVC (2012)
22. Huang, J.-B., Singh, A., Ahuja, N.: Single image super resolution from transformed self-exemplars. In: CVPR (2015)

Markerless Indoor Augmented Reality Navigation Device Based on Optical-Flow-Scene Indoor Positioning and Wall-Floor-Boundary Image Registration

Wen-Shan Lin[1] and Chian C. Ho[2(✉)]

[1] Graduate School of Vocation and Technological Education, National Yunlin University of Science and Technology, Douliou, Yunlin County 64002, Taiwan
[2] Department of Electrical Engineering, National Yunlin University of Science and Technology, Douliou, Yunlin County 64002, Taiwan
futureho@yuntech.edu.tw

Abstract. For markerless indoor Augmented Reality Navigation (ARN) technology, camera pose is inevitably the fundamental argument of positioning estimation and pose estimation, and floor plane is indispensably the fiducial target of image registration. This paper proposes optical-flow-scene indoor positioning and wall-floor-boundary image registration to make ARN more precise, reliable, and instantaneous. Experimental results show both optical-flow-scene indoor positioning and wall-floor-boundary image registration have higher accuracy and less latency than conventional well-known ARN methods. On the other hand, these proposed two methods are seamlessly implemented on the handheld Android embedded platform and are smoothly verified to work well on the handheld indoor augmented reality navigation device.

Keywords: Augmented reality · Indoor positioning · Image registration · Navigation

1 Introduction

With the rapid development and wide deployment of emerging technologies in ubiquitous computing field, personal navigation system that can accommodate to perform well outdoors and indoors have drawn more and more interest. This is because personal navigation device offering personal destination awareness anywhere and anytime is essential to versatile ubiquitous computing applications, like outdoor and indoor path directions, outdoor and indoor information guide, outdoor and indoor marketing advertisement, outdoor and indoor social networking, and so on.

However, conventional 2D (birdview) or 3D (overlook) virtual-model navigation devices are not intuitive enough to guarantee the proper perception alignment between virtual-model navigation scenario and real-world navigation situation. Besides, conventional 2D or 3D virtual model navigation devices fail to be evolved into the ever-

© Springer Nature Singapore Pte Ltd. 2019
C.-Y. Chang et al. (Eds.): ICS 2018, CCIS 1013, pp. 106–114, 2019.
https://doi.org/10.1007/978-981-13-9190-3_10

growing wearable see-through devices, like eyeglasses, helmet, or goggles. Even worse, staring at 2D or 3D virtual model navigation devices on driving or on foot might cause careless accidents or dangerous occurrences.

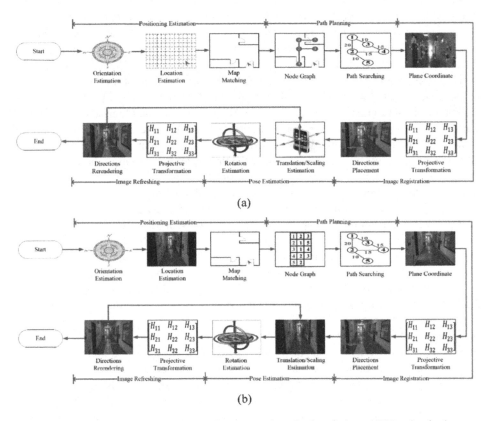

Fig. 1. Flowchart of (a) typical and (b) proposed markerless indoor ARN technologies.

Augmented Reality Navigation (ARN) technology is the best alternative choice and becomes more and more fascinating in ubiquitous computing applications since it can lay real-world navigation directions over what users are actually seeing in front of themselves in the true world [1–8]. In general, according to the object-tracking principles, ARN technologies can be divided into three main categories: (1) marker, (2) markerless, and (3) positioning. The marker ARN technology is the most reliable one tracking the registered objects and projects the computer graphics onto the registered objects based on distinctive markers or landmarks [1, 2]. Nevertheless, a large amount of deployment of distinctive markers or landmarks for marker ARN technology are very expensive and unrealistic. The markerless ARN technology simply on the cost-effective basis of natural or plain features, like points, lines, corners, textures, is actually recognized as the most practical but difficult one [3–5]. The positioning ARN technology is the most common and used one depending only upon the available location coordinate from outdoor Global Positioning System (GPS) or specific indoor Wireless Sensor Networking (WSN) infrastructure [6–8].

Due to the markerless characteristic of main playground of outdoor and indoor real-world environments, most of recent research activities and interests in ARN technologies focuses on markerless issue, especially for indoor scenarios [9–11]. Figure 1 (a) shows the algorithm flowchart of typical markerless indoor ARN device. In Fig. 1 (a), first of all, the indoor ARN device has to finish the estimation of location coordinate through external radio positioning infrastructure (e.g., WiFi, Bluetooth LE, RFID) or internal inertial positioning unit at the step of location estimation, in the stage of positioning estimation. Meanwhile, the indoor ARN device also finishes the estimation of orientation angle through fusion of digital compass and Inertial Measurement Unit (IMU) sensors at the step of orientation estimation, in the stage of positioning estimation. Then, the indoor ARN device matches the estimated location coordinate and orientation angle of the targeted device onto the built 2D map at the step of map matching, in the stage of positioning estimation. Next, the indoor ARN device has to build the critical nodes on the built 2D map at the step of node graph, in the stage of path planning, and has to finish the shortest or fastest navigation path evaluation to the destination on the built 2D map at the step of path searching, in the stage of path planning. After accomplishing the floor plane registration (including camera pose initialization) at the step of plane coordinate, in the stage of image registration, and Homography-based 2D-to-3D projective transformation of the map and navigation path at the step of projective transformation, in the stage of image registration, the indoor ARN device can accurately project the ARN path directions onto the markerless real-world floor plane through elaborate floor region segmentation at the step of directions placement, in the stage of image registration. Afterward, when the camera (viewing) pose of the indoor ARN device varies, the translation/scaling and rotation variations of camera (viewing) coordinate in real-world coordinate can be properly evaluated at the steps of translation/scaling estimation and rotation estimation, respectively, in the stage of pose estimation. Finally, the ARN path directions on the screen of the indoor ARN device can be rotated and deformed properly in object (image) coordinate at the step of projective transformation, in the stage of image refreshing, so as to be closely stuck onto the markerless real-world floor plane through elaborate camera pose estimation at the step of directions rerendering, in the stage of image refreshing.

Among stages of the algorithm flowchart of the typical markerless indoor ARN device in Fig. 1(a), the accuracy and reality of the ARN path directions is actually sensitive and vulnerable to these three stages of positioning estimation, pose estimation, and image registration, especially to these three steps of location estimation, translation/scaling estimation, and plane coordinate. For markerless indoor ARN technology, camera pose is inevitably the fundamental argument of positioning estimation and pose estimation, and floor plane is indispensably the fiducial target of image registration. Thus this paper concentrates to address on issues of camera pose estimation and floor plane registration in the subsequent sessions.

This paper is organized as follows. Section 2 reviews pros and cons of conventional well-known camera pose estimation methods for the markerless indoor ARN device, like frame-to-frame planar homographies and feature-based optical flow. In addition, Sect. 2 also reviews pros and cons of conventional well-known floor plane registration methods for the markerless indoor ARN device, like Otsu binarization floor plane registration and moving-average binarization floor plane registration. Section 3 presents optical-flow-scene indoor positioning and wall-floor-boundary image registration to improve the accuracy and reality of the ARN path directions. Section 4 compares the experimental results between these proposed two methods and conventional well-known methods. Section 5 demonstrates the implementation results of Android-based portable indoor ARN device based on proposed optical-flow-scene indoor positioning and wall-floor-boundary image registration. Finally, Sect. 6 draws brief conclusions.

2   Conventional Methods

There are many conventional camera pose estimation methods and floor plane registration methods applied to for the indoor ARN device in the past 10 years. But these conventional methods are rightly the dominant factors to degrade the accuracy and reality of markerless indoor ARN technologies.

2.1   Conventional Camera Pose Estimation Methods

Single planar homography can thoroughly interpret the relation between a real plane in 3D real-world coordinate and its projective plane on the 2D image coordinate, so frame-to-frame planar homographies [10, 12–15] can estimate the camera pose variation and some depth information when the camera is rotated or translated. It is the most popular and reliable method for camera pose estimation. However, the accuracy and reliability of camera pose estimation of frame-to-frame planar homographies depends deeply upon the accuracy and reliability of feature detection of the fiducial projection planar surface, e.g. floor plane. In addition, it is difficult to guarantee to detect correct and enough distinctive features on the fiducial projection planar surface frame by frame when the camera is sometimes rotated or translated dramatically.

Another widely-used camera pose estimation method is feature-based optical flow. Feature-based optical flow is more efficient and effective to track the distinctive features and estimate the pose variation, but it can not estimate the depth information and viewpoint rotation [10, 13, 15].

2.2   Conventional Floor Plane Registration Methods

All conventional floor plane detection or floor plane segmentation methods can be sorted into 2 main categories: (1) Otsu binarization floor detection and (2) moving-average binarization floor detection [15–18].

The binarization threshold of Otsu binarization floor detection is decided by the illumination statistical distribution result of the scene. It can perform well and readily on low-contrast scenes, but not on high-contrast scenes. Because the illumination of the floor plane under high-contrast scenes is almost deeply dark.

On the other hand, the binarization threshold of moving-average binarization floor plane detection is determined by a series of averages of different lines on the full-scale scenes. Although it can perform better on high-contrast scenes than Otsu binarization floor detection, its computation complexity is too high to meet the real-time requirement, especially on complicated-background scenes.

3 Proposed Methods

This paper proposes optical-flow-scene indoor positioning and wall-floor-boundary image registration to improve these three stages of positioning estimation, pose estimation, and image registration of typical markerless indoor ARN technologies, especially to improve these three steps of location estimation, translation/scaling estimation, and plane coordinate, illustrated in Fig. 1(b).

3.1 Proposed Optical-Flow-Scene Indoor Positioning Method

Optical-flow-scene indoor positioning method with only monocular RGB camera can solve the location estimation and translation/scaling estimation effectively and efficiently. Figure 2 illustrates the transformation model of camera pose estimation from 2D image-plane coordinate onto 3D real-world coordinate in proposed optical-flow-scene indoor positioning method, and how to work out the camera pose estimation issue. In Fig. 2, C means the known location of the faraway wall or obstacle, along Yr axis of 3D real-world coordinate. h represents the height difference between some real-world pixel and the middle point of real-world field, along Zr axis of 3D real-world coordinate. V and V' are the present and displaced real- world location of the camera, along Yr axis of 3D real-world coordinate, respectively. f implies the focal length of the camera. w denotes the height difference between some optical flow pixel P and the middle point of optical flow field on the present image plane, and w' denotes the height difference between some optical flow pixel P' and the middle point of optical flow field

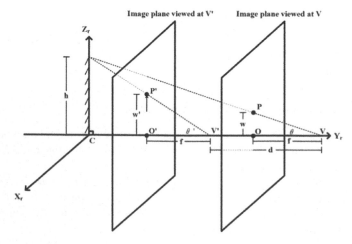

Fig. 2. Transformation model of camera pose estimation of proposed optical-flow-scene indoor positioning method.

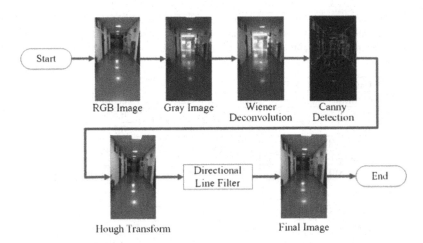

Fig. 3. Flowchart of proposed wall-floor-boundary image registration method.

on the displaced image plane, along Yi axis of 2D image-plane coordinate. d indicates the real-world displaced distance of the camera, that is the location difference between V and V′, along Yr axis of 3D real-world coordinate. The unit of all variables above is centimeter.

Therefore, the real-world forward/backward displaced distance of the camera can be elaborately evaluated by (1)–(3), along Yr axis of 3D real-world coordinate, while (V − C) is given from the difference between known locations of the faraway wall (or obstacle) and the present camera on the real-world map.

$$\frac{(V-C)}{h} = \frac{f}{w} = \; > h = \frac{w(V-C)}{f} \tag{1}$$

$$\frac{V'-C}{h} = \frac{f}{w'} = \; > V' = C + \frac{hf}{w'} \tag{2}$$

$$d = V - V' = (V-C) - \frac{hf}{w'} = (V-C) - (\frac{f}{w'})(\frac{(V-C)}{f})w = (V-C)(1-\frac{w}{w'}) \tag{3}$$

As for the real-world horizontal or slightly vertical displaced distance of the camera can be proportional and reversely evaluated by the horizontal or slightly vertical displaced distance of some optical flow pixels on the image plane.

3.2 Proposed Wall-Floor-Boundary Image Registration Method

Figure 3 illustrates the algorithm flowchart of proposed wall-floor-boundary image registration. The detailed descriptions on Fig. 3 will be explained step-by-step as follows. Wiener Deconvolution filter is a key preprocessing method for floor detection, because it can blur and simplify the background details. Then, strong features of edges or contours can be preserved inherently.

Table 1. Localization error and execution time comparison between proposed optical-flow-scene indoor positioning and conventional camera pose estimation methods under various indoor spaces of (a) laboratory, (b) corridor, and (c) lobby.

(a)

Laboratory (11m)		
Method	Localization error	Execution time
RFID	0.972 m	0.524 sec
Wi-Fi	0.712 m	0.372 sec
Feature-Tracking Optical Flow	0.773 m	0.209 sec
Optical Flow Field	**0.463 m**	**0.124 sec**

(b)

Corridor (14m)		
Method	Localization error	Execution time
RFID	0.532 m	0.481 sec
Wi-Fi	0.698 m	0.371 sec
Feature-Tracking Optical Flow	0.721 m	0.198 sec
Optical Flow Field	**0.526 m**	**0.112 sec**

(c)

Lobby (21m)		
Method	Localization error	Execution time
RFID	0.482 m	0.453 sec
Wi-Fi	0.643 m	0.312 sec
Feature-Tracking Optical Flow	0.877 m	0.203 sec
Optical Flow Field	**0.441 m**	**0.113 sec**

Table 2. Accuracy and execution comparison between various floor plane detection methods.

Floor detection methods	Coverage accuracy	Execution performance
Otsu binarization	40%	7.19 fps
Moving-average binarization	65%	2.85 fps
Wall-floor-boundary	**88%**	**6.22 fps**

Because the floor plane usually has fewer edges or contours than the furniture or the wall decorations, edge detector or contour detector can extract non-floor regions smoothly and easily. Hough transform stands for Probabilistic Hough Line Transform. It is an efficient and effective way to detect the extremes of edge-lines. In order to detect the representative edge-line features, Directional Line filter is intended to reduce a number of noisy points or unconnected lines in a curve that is approximated by a series of points. After acquiring the end dots (extremes) of edge-lines exactly, the contours connected by every end dots are rightly the border of floor segmentation.

4 Experimental Results

Table 1 shows Localization error and execution time comparison between conventional RFID indoor positioning, conventional WiFi indoor positioning, conventional feature-based optical flow indoor positioning, and proposed optical-flow-scene indoor positioning, under various indoor spaces of (a) laboratory, (b) corridor, and (c) lobby. From Table 1, it is evident that proposed optical-flow-scene indoor positioning has much higher localization accuracy and less execution latency than conventional camera pose estimation methods, especially under high-obstructed environments.

Table 2 shows the coverage accuracy and execution time comparison between conventional Otsu binarization floor detection, conventional moving-average binarization floor detection, and proposed wall-floor-boundary detection. From Table 2, it is obvious that proposed wall-floor-boundary detection has much higher coverage accuracy and less execution latency than conventional floor detection registration methods, especially under high-contrast environments.

5 Android Implementation

Android embedded platform with rich HW/SW features is the best choice to implement and verify the portable markerless indoor ARN device. The proposed optical-flow-scene indoor positioning and wall-floor-boundary image registration methods are smoothly integrated into the portable markerless indoor ARN device and are certainly verified to work well.

6 Conclusions

Although Visual Simultaneous Localization And Mapping (VSLAM) also can improve the issues of positioning estimation, pose estimation, and image registration, this paper proposes and implements two more effective and efficient methods, optical-flow-scene indoor positioning and wall-floor-boundary image registration, to make markerless indoor ARN device more precise, reliable, and instantaneous.

Acknowledgments. This work was supported in part by Ministry of Science and Technology, Taiwan, under Grant MOST 106-2221-E-224-053.

References

1. Kim, J., Jun, H.: Vision-based location positioning using augmented reality for indoor navigation. IEEE Trans. Consum. Electron. **54**(3), 954–962 (2008)
2. Mohareri, O., Rad, A.B.: Autonomous humanoid robot navigation using augmented reality technique. In: Proceedings of 2011 IEEE International Conference on Mechatronics (ICM), pp. 463–468, April 2011
3. DiVerdi, S., Hollerer, T.: Heads up and camera down: a vision-based tracking modality for mobile mixed reality. IEEE Trans. Visual. Comput. Graphics **14**(3), 500–512 (2008)

4. Hile, H., Borriello, G.: Positioning and orientation in indoor environments using camera phones. IEEE Comput. Graph. Appl. **28**(4), 32–39 (2008)
5. Oskiper, T., Sizintsev, M., Branzoi, V., Samarasekera, S., Kumar, R.: Augmented reality binoculars. IEEE Trans. Visual. Comput. Graphics **21**(5), 611–623 (2015)
6. Cheok, A.D., Yue, L.: A novel light-sensor-based information transmission system for indoor positioning and navigation. IEEE Trans. Instrum. Meas. **60**(1), 290–299 (2011)
7. Hervas, R., Bravo, J., Fontecha, J.: An assistive navigation system based on augmented reality and context awareness for people with mild cognitive impairments. IEEE J. Biomed. Health Inform. **18**(1), 368–374 (2014)
8. Thomas, B.H., Sandor, C.: What wearable augmented reality can do for you. IEEE Pervasive Comput. **8**(2), 8–11 (2009)
9. Comport, A.I., Marchand, E., Pressigout, M., Chaumette, F.: Real-time markerless tracking for augmented reality: the virtual visual servoing framework. IEEE Trans. Visual. Comput. Graphics **12**(4), 615–628 (2006)
10. Lee, T., Hollerer, T.: Multithreaded hybrid feature tracking for markerless augmented reality. IEEE Trans. Visual. Comput. Graphics **15**(3), 355–368 (2009)
11. Kim, Y.-G., Kim, W.-J.: Implementation of augmented reality system for smartphone advertisements. Int. J. Multimed. Ubiquitous Eng. **9**(2), 385–392 (2014)
12. Simon, G., Berger, M.-O.: Pose estimation for planar structures. IEEE Comput. Graph. Appl. **22**(6), 46–53 (2002)
13. Prince, S.J.D., Xu, K., Cheok, A.D.: Augmented reality camera tracking with homographies. IEEE Comput. Graph. Appl. **22**(6), 39–45 (2002)
14. Maidi, M., Preda, M., Le, V.H.: Markerless tracking for mobile augmented reality. In: Proceedings of IEEE International Conference on Signal and Image Processing Applications, pp. 301–306, November 2011
15. Barcelo, G.C., Panahandeh, G., Jansson, M.: Image-based floor segmentation in visual inertial navigation. In: Proceedings of IEEE International Instrumentation and Measurement Technology Conference (I2MTC), pp. 1402–1407, May 2013
16. Ling, M., Jianming, W., Bo, Z., Shengbei, W.: Automatic floor segmentation for indoor robot navigation. In: Proceedings of International Conference on Signal Processing Systems (ICSPS), vol. 1, pp. V1-684–V1-689, July 2010
17. Posada, L.F., Narayanan, K.K., Hoffmann, F., Bertram, T.: Floor segmentation of omnidirectional images for mobile robot visual navigation. In: Proceedings of IEEE/RSJ International Conference on Intelligent Robots and Systems (IROS), pp. 804–809, October 2010
18. Rodriguez-Telles, F.G., Abril Torres-Mendez, L., Martinez-Garcia, E.A.: A fast floor segmentation algorithm for visual-based robot navigation. In: Proceedings of International Conference on Computer and Robot Vision (CRV), pp. 167–173, May 2013

An Adaptive Tai-Chi-Chuan AR Guiding System Based on Speed Estimation of Movement

Yi-Ping Hung[1,2,3]($\boxtimes$), Peng-Yuan Kao[2], Yao-Fu Jan[4],
Chun-Hsien Li[3], Chia-Hao Chang[2], and Ping-Hsuan Han[2]

[1] Graduate Institute of Animation and Film Art,
Tainan National University of the Arts, Tainan, Taiwan
hung@csie.ntu.edu.tw
[2] Graduate Institute of Networking and Multimedia,
National Taiwan University, Taipei, Taiwan
[3] Department of Computer Science and Information Engineering,
National Taiwan University, Taipei, Taiwan
[4] Department of Computer Science,
National Chengchi University, Taipei, Taiwan

Abstract. Augmented Reality (AR) headsets has become a potential device as an auxiliary tool for practicing physical activities such like Tai-Chi Chuan (TCC). Although some learning systems can display the virtual coach movement in AR headsets, the playing speed cannot be adjusted appropriately just like a real coach stand next to you. In most of the learning system, the common approach is using controller to control the playback system under a specific speed. Once user want to speed up or speed down, he has to do these commands via a controller. In this work, we propose a TCC learning system which will real time detect the delay time between current action of user and virtual coach. After obtaining the delay time, our learning system will adjust speed of virtual coach automatically. With real time speed adjustment, learners can practice TCC with their own pace and virtual coach will slow down or speed up to follow learners' movement.

Keywords: Real-time speed estimation · Physical activity learning ·
Mixed reality · Tai-Chi Chuan

1 Introduction

In the processing of learning Tai-Chi Chuan, users are asked to perform a sequence of body movements with highly accurate position. According to the learner is familiar with the movement or not, learner might practice in different speed. In addition, learner may not only start practicing at the first movement but also a specific movement. The way to control playback system can be generally grouped into several categories: controller, camera, voice command and wearable based. First of all, controller-based learning systems usually use hands to control system via touch the screen, push the buttons, and using other input device, e.g., mouse or keyboard [1]. However, controller-based approach will cause some problem. Once user would like to adjust the

© Springer Nature Singapore Pte Ltd. 2019
C.-Y. Chang et al. (Eds.): ICS 2018, CCIS 1013, pp. 115–130, 2019.
https://doi.org/10.1007/978-981-13-9190-3_11

speed faster or slower, he should suspend the current movement to control the learning system. These pausing will make the practicing incoherent and inefficient, we called it practice interrupt problem. Second, camera-based learning systems [2, 3] overcome the practice interrupt problem. This approach use camera as additional sensor to detect user's gesture, but it will cause another problem that user should face to the camera with specific direction. The third approach, voice command, uses speech recognizer to control the playback system [4], and it has no problem which users are limited to specific position and direction. Nevertheless, it leads to another problem that speech recognizer not always detect the correct word successfully.

In this work, we propose a TCC learning system which will real time detect the delay time between current action of user and virtual coach. After obtaining the delay time, our learning system will adjust speed of virtual coach automatically. With real time speed adjustment, learners can practice TCC with their own pace and virtual coach will slow down or speed up to follow learners' movement.

2   Related Work

In Around Me [3], they developed a learning system with a movable robot which contains computer, monitor and camera. The robot could dynamically change the position based on user's position. Swimoid [5] support system also provides a movable robot in water, it shows user's swim posture real-time on monitor of robot. These two system both use movable robot to carry monitor, so users still need to face the display of robot although these robots would follow users automatically.

Some of these researches don't provide any way to control learning system, users can only play the whole movements from the beginning to the end. MotionMA [1] is a system that provide body movement and current speed information, it doesn't allow users make the system play faster or slower. In [6] and [7], they also focus on learning steps of dancing, but don't provide an interactive learning system for dancing learner. However, people do exercise would have different speed, the fixed speed definitely not suit for everyone.

Several researches control learning system by using gesture recognition technology. YouMove [2] is one of the interactive learning system that use Kinect to recognize user's skeleton and track the hand position to control system. However, this approach would cause practice interrupt problem, users may not have good practicing experience if they should stop current movement to control learning system. Around Me [3] is a learning system that combine gesture recognition and vision-based approach, it used gesture to send movable robot remote instructions and use camera to track user's position to follow him. Joggobot [8] and Flying Sports Assistant [9] are also using a drone as a movable robot to encourage and guide users. These approaches also cause the practice interrupt problem as mention before. My Tai-Chi coaches [4] is an interactive TCC learning system using finger gesture and voice command to control system. Finger gesture doesn't overcome the practice interrupt problem because users still need to stop and do finger gesture. Although voice command doesn't have this problem, speech recognition approach isn't work well in every environment such like noisy place. If the number of command growth, recognize correct keyword will also be more difficult.

3   Speed Estimation of Movement

When learning process of general exercise, there is always a delay between learner and coach. According to the difficulty of actions, the delay time will be different. The more difficult or unfamiliar the movement is, the more delay will be caused. In this chapter, we propose a method to estimate the delay time of movements between the learner and the virtual coach, and to estimate the speed difference between the coach and the learner by the known delay. At the end of this chapter, we designed an experiment to verify the accuracy of the algorithm and the efficiency of execution.

3.1   Problem Definition

In this system, we except that leaner will follow the movements of the virtual coach to practice TCC. But when the user moves much more slowly than the virtual coach, the learner usually forgets what the coach was doing, and will skip to the current action of the virtual coach. So, we constraint the range of the delay time, and set the maximum delay time to 5 s. For those who have some experience of TCC, their speed of playing TCC might be faster than the virtual coach, so we have set a maximum of 5 s for the time which is faster than the virtual coach.

As you can see from formula 1, where a_u is current action of user and a_c is action of virtual coach. In our learning system, *fps* equals to 35 which means data receive rate is thirty-five frames per second. We can notify that when Δt is positive, it means that the movement of the learner is slower than the virtual coach. When Δt is negative, it means that the movement of the learner is faster than the virtual coach.

$$\Delta t = \frac{a_u - a_c}{fps} \tag{1}$$

The constraint for Δt is as following:

$$-5 \le \Delta t \le 5 \tag{2}$$

3.2   Movement Acquisition

Before making an estimate of speed, we must get the movement of virtual coaches and the learner first. The movement of virtual coaches are obtained in advance, and we import the movement file into unity, then set the virtual coach to play TCC which based on the movement file. So, the learner can see each detail of the movement through the AR headsets from TCC coach. We can estimate the delay time between virtual coaches and the learner by comparing the information which obtained by wrist wearable device for both of them.

3.2.1   Standard Movement Acquisition

While getting the standard movements, we used the Vicon Motion Capture System in order to record the movement which obtain high accuracy. We have invited a coach who has more than 10 years of TCC experience and we use many infrared Vicon cameras to record the movement of the coach (Fig. 1).

Fig. 1. Using Vicon cameras to record coach movement

3.2.2 Learner Movement Acquisition

In the process of practicing TCC, we ask learners to wear the smart bracelet which has built-in nine axis IMU. So, we can obtain the information of the wrist movements from the user through Bluetooth to the mobile device.

3.3 Algorithm

We propose an effective and accurate algorithm. First of all, we take the current action of the virtual coach as the center of search space. We will crop the data from the previous five seconds to the next five seconds from the center. This segment of whole data is the search space. When searching the data, we use a sliding window with size $fps \times 5$ s, and the sliding window stride equals to $fps \times 0.5$ s.

After cropping the search space, we will move sliding window through search space with every 0.5 s and the end of sliding window start from $t - 5$ s to $t + 5$ s. When we find the end of sliding window, we can take this sliding window which starts from 5 s ago as a feature (Fig. 2). Take Fig. 2 as an example, when the current point we search is at $t - 5$ s, the data which start previous 5 s than the point to $t - 10$ s will be regarded as a feature. As for learner movement, we regard data obtained from learner from five seconds previous than current action as a feature (Fig. 3).

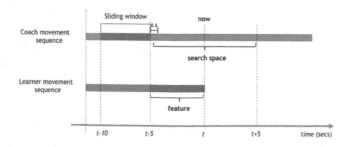

Fig. 2. Illustration of algorithm

```
                    Function SpeedEstimation()

Input:    C – a TimeSeries of coach movement with length |C|
          U – a TimeSeries of user movement with length |U|
          Mc – coach current movement
Output:   time interval between user current movement and coach current
          movement

  1|   // Crop user movement data to let |U| equal to fps × 5(seconds)
  2|   U = crop_data_with_length( user_movement, length = fps × 5 )
  3|
  4|   // Set sliding window width and sliding window stride
  5|   sliding_window_width = fps × 5
  6|   sliding_window_stride = fps × 0.5
  7|
  8|   // Let Mc be the center and compute signal similarity between each sliding
  9|   // window data which is in search space and U
 10|   // Record the smallest DTW distance happened in which sliding window
 11|   min_distance = MAX_INFINITE
 12|   sliding_window_index = -1
 13|   FOR( each sliding window data Ci in search space)
 14|   {
 15|       dist, path = fastDTW( U, Ci )
 16|       IF( dist < min_distance )
 17|       {
 18|          min_distance = dist
 19|          sliding_window_index = i
 20|       }
 21|   }
 22|
 23|   // Use the last frame of sliding_window_index^th sliding window data and
 25|   // Mc to calculate Δt
 26|   last_frame_index = last_frame_in_sliding_window( C, index =
 27|                          sliding_window_index)
 28|
 29|   deltaT = ( last_frame_index - Mc) / fps
 30|
 31|   RETURN deltaT
```

Fig. 3. Pseudocode of algorithm

After obtaining the feature of learner and virtual coach, we will calculate signal similarity between these two features. When find out all of sliding windows under search space, we will have an estimation result which has highest similarity with learner current action. We can estimate Δt by dividing the frame number between learner current action and the last frame of sliding window which has highest similarity with learner movement by fps which equals to 35 in our system.

3.4   Details of Implementation

In this chapter, we will illustrate some details of our implementation of this algorithm. This contain the pre-processing after receiving data and the implementation details of comparing the similarity for two signals.

3.4.1   Space Correspondence Alignment

After collecting information from both hands of the learner and the virtual coach, we have to align the coordinate axis of the data of the left and the right hand first. We can compare the data after corresponding the coordinate axis. The corresponding coordinate axis for smart bracelet and the wrist of the virtual coach is shown in the following table (Fig. 4) (Table 1):

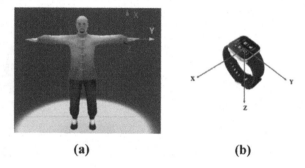

(a)   **(b)**

Fig. 4. (a) Space correspondence of virtual (b) Space correspondence of Sony SmartWatch3

Table 1. Corresponding coordinate axis

Coach movement axis	Sony SmartWatch3 axis
X	−Z
Y	−X
Z	Y

3.4.2   Signal Similarity

In our algorithm, we use dynamic time warping (DTW) to compute the distance between two signals. People usually use DTW to compute the similarity of two 1D-signals. However, we consider that both of left wrist and right wrist at the same time, so we concatenate the acceleration of both wrists and the dimension of input data when computing DTW have become 6D. Suppose there are two time series R and Q, and the acceleration of ith point in R can be expressed as $(acceR_x^i, acceR_y^i, acceR_z^i)$, and the acceleration of jth point in Q can be expressed as $(acceQ_x^j, acceQ_y^j, acceQ_z^j)$ We can derive the distance $Dist(i,j)$ between R_i and Q_j by following formula:

$$Dist(i,j) = \sqrt{(acceR_{lx}^i - acceQ_{lx}^j)^2 + (acceR_{ly}^i - acceQ_{ly}^j)^2 + (acceR_{lz}^i - acceQ_{lz}^j)^2} + \\ \sqrt{(acceR_{rx}^i - acceQ_{rx}^j)^2 + (acceR_{ry}^i - acceQ_{ry}^j)^2 + (acceR_{rz}^i - acceQ_{rz}^j)^2} \tag{3}$$

3.4.3 Computing Efficiency Improvement

In order to give users real-time feedback, computing efficiency of the algorithm is also an important consideration. To improve computing efficiency, we use FastDTW [10] in our TCC learning system instead of DTW. FastDTW uses a multilevel approach that recursively projects a solution from a coarse resolution and refines the projected solution. By using FastDTW, time complexity and space complexity can be reduced to linear time.

3.5 Sliding Window Size Selection

The size of sliding window is an important part of our algorithm. As sliding window size too small, we only can view little part of whole signal. When there is no significant feature or some significant features which are divided into two segments, learning system will misjudge the matching feature and cause bizarre speed adjustment. When sliding window size is big enough, it can reduce the influence of misjudgment caused by incomplete feature. However, sliding window size is not the bigger the better. When sliding window size is too big, it will significantly reduce the computing efficiency. To design a real-time interactive learning system, we must make a tradeoff between accuracy and computing efficiency.

To select an appropriate sliding window size, we design an experiment. We invited four TCC coaches who have experience of TCC for several years. Two of them have more than 10 years' experience and one of coaches has more than 6 years' experience and the other coach has more than 4 years' experience. We ask coaches to wear smart bracelets on both wrists and wear AR HEADSETS. We choose a TCC movement which is consist of eight key postures (Fig. 5) and ask coaches to follow the virtual coach. Each coach practiced this movement for five times.

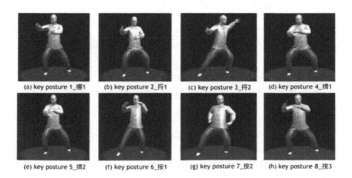

(a) key posture 1_搠1   (b) key posture 2_挤1   (c) key posture 3_挤2   (d) key posture 4_挤1

(e) key posture 5_挤2   (f) key posture 6_按1   (g) key posture 7_按2   (h) key posture 8_按3

Fig. 5. Eight key postures in one TCC movement

When coaches practicing this movement, we record the coach's movement with a camera at the same time. After practicing, we label the timestamps of each key posture occurs in coach's movement manually.

We defined the ground truth of delay time difference of ith key posture Δt_g^i as timestamps of ith key posture labelled manually minus timestamps of ith key posture virtual coach played. And We defined estimation delay time difference of ith key posture Δt_e^i as timestamps of ith key posture estimated by our algorithm minus timestamps of ith key posture virtual coach played. After deriving ground truth and estimation of delay time difference, we can calculate average estimation error of each coach by formula 4. Then we can get total average estimation error by calculating the average of four average estimation error of coaches.

$$Error_{avg} = \frac{\sum_{n=1}^{5} \sum_{i=1}^{8} |\Delta t_{g,n}^i - \Delta t_{e,n}^i|}{5 \times 8} \tag{4}$$

We defined $\Delta t_{g,n}^i$ as delay time difference of ith key posture Δt_g^i as timestamps of ith key posture labelled manually minus timestamps of ith key posture virtual coach played at nth times coach playing this movement.

In this experiment, we limit the sliding window size to multiple of fps which equals to 35 in our learning system and constraint the multiple from 1 to 10. We will record the accuracy and total computing time of different sliding window size using in our algorithm. We found that when sliding window size equals to $fps \times 5$, the algorithm had lowest estimation error and the total computing time is acceptable. So, we use

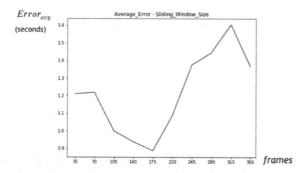

Fig. 6. Average estimation error with different sliding window sizes

$fps \times 5$ as sliding window size in our algorithm (Fig. 6).

3.6   Evaluation

We design an experiment to evaluate our algorithm. We invited four TCC coaches who have experience of TCC for several years. Two of them have more than 10 years' experience and one of coaches has more than 6 years' experience and the other coach has more than 4 years' experience. We ask coaches to wear smart bracelets on both wrists and wear AR headsets. We choose a TCC movement which is consist of eight key postures (Fig. 5) and ask coaches to follow the virtual coach practicing this movement for five times and we record the coach's movement with a camera at the same time. After deriving ground truth and estimation of delay time difference, we can calculate average estimation error equals to 0.8875 s and cost 0.05 s for each estimation.

There is estimation error distribution of each key posture (Fig. 7). We can find that the estimation error of key posture 1 is lowest and key posture 6, 7, 8 will cause higher

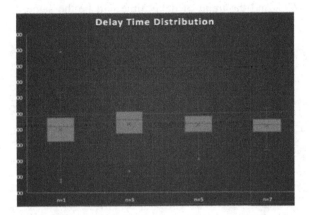

Fig. 7. Algorithm estimation error distribution

estimation error and the range of estimation error is wider, because each coach has different habits when practicing this movement.

4 Delay Time Normalization

In real life, when the speed of the user is not able to keep up with the coach, the coach will stop or slow down to wait for the student to follow. And we propose a method to adjust the speed of the virtual coach by using the algorithm described in previous chapter. After calculating the time difference between virtual coach and the learner, we can estimate the difference of speed between learner and virtual coach. When the learner is slower than the virtual coach, the virtual coach will slow down. Whereas when the speed of the learner is faster than the virtual coach, the virtual coach will speed up.

4.1 Delay Time Distribution

We hope to understand the distribution of delay time for each key posture of both leaner and the coach. After knowing the time difference between coach and learner, we hope to design a TTC learning system to shorten the delay between the novice and the coach, so we designed an experiment. We Invited four coaches with many years of TCC experience and five novices without TCC experience. We asked the learner to wear smart bracelet and head-mounted monitor and follow the virtual coach in the head-mounted monitor to do one style with eight key postures of TTC movements (Fig. 5). We will use camera to record the movements and analyze the distribution of Δt_g.

We can find three things from the following figure. First, when the delta t (Formula 1) is less than 0, it means that the speed of the user is much faster than the virtual coach. Due to the coach is more familiar with the movement, the average of a lot of key posture appear earlier than the coach. Second, the delay time of the coach is more concentrated, and due to the reason that novice is not familiar to the movements, so the delay time is more dispersed. Third, there will be a delay time whether it is coach or novice playing TCC, and the trend of delay time will be the same. For example, the

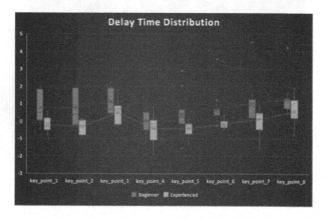

Fig. 8. Delay time distribution

movement of the user will be much slower than the virtual coach when the key posture 2 moves to key posture 3. And the movement of the user will be faster when key posture 3 moves to key posture 4 (Fig. 8).

4.2 Delay Time Normalization Implementation

When we get the Δt from calculating algorithm, the delta t will be a consistent value ideally. However, in reality, there will have different delay time delta Δt^k at different time k. We propose a method that we will add the delay time Δt^k which obtained at the timing t^k to the next n seconds. In other words, we change to play the film of n seconds to $n + \Delta t^k$ after t^k (Fig. 9). The updated speed $speed_{adjust}$ is calculated as follows:

$$speed_{adjust}^k = speed_{normal} \times \frac{n}{n + \Delta t_e^{k-1}} \tag{5}$$

We can see that when Δt^k is a positive, it means that the movement of the user is slower than the virtual coach, so speed adjust will be a value less than 1. On the other

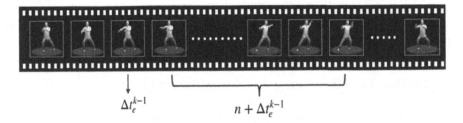

$$\Delta t_e^{k-1} \qquad\qquad n + \Delta t_e^{k-1}$$

Fig. 9. Delay time normalization

hand, when Δt^k is a negative, it means the movement of the user is faster than the virtual coach, so *speed_{adjust}* will be a value more than 1.

4.3 Experiment

Before using Δt^k to adjust the speed of virtual coach, we need to determine the value of n first. In order to find out the best n value for users, we design an experiment. In this experiment, we limit n to 1, 3, 5, 7. We invited two TCC coaches who have experience of TCC for several years and two beginners. We ask participants to wear smart bracelets on both wrists and wear AR HEADSETS. We choose a TCC movement which is consist of eight key postures (Fig. 5) and ask participants to follow the virtual coach practicing TCC for three times under each mode with different n. When participants practicing this movement, we record their movement with a camera at the same time.

As the following result (Fig. 10), we can find that when n is equal to 7, average delay time between learner and virtual coach almost equal to zero. Although average delay time is almost zero when n is equal to 1, the distribution of delay time is very divergence. Because when n equals to 1, learning system is too sensitive for adjusting the speed of virtual coach. When the speed of virtual coach is changed intensely,

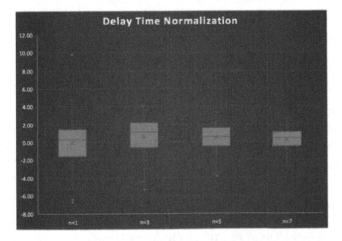

Fig. 10. Delay time normalization

learners cannot follow the virtual coach movement. According to the result, we choose the value of n as seven and normalize the speed of virtual coach in our TCC learning system.

5 Adaptive Tai-Chi-Chuan Learning System

In this chapter, we will introduce the intelligent TCC learning system. We can know how to calculate the delay time of the current action between user and virtual coach in this system, and we will use the result to adjust playback speed of the virtual coach.

5.1 System Overview

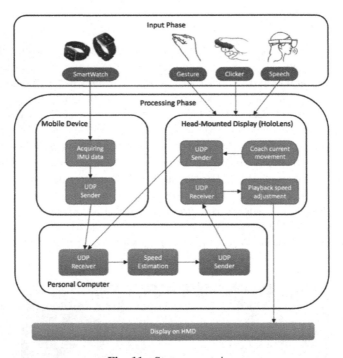

Fig. 11. System overview

Our TCC learning system can be separated into three phases (Fig. 11). First, this TCC learning system needs a control module to interact with the system. We can use Gesture, Clicker and Speech to achieve this goal. Besides, in order to acquire user's wrist rotation information, we have two smart bracelets in our input module.

In processing phase, the IMU in smart bracelet will transfer information to mobile device through Bluetooth. After receiving data, mobile device will transfer information through UDP to PC. At the same time, AR HEADSETS will transfer the current action of the coach through UDP to PC. When obtain the information from the wrist of the user and the current action of the coach, PC will calculate delta t by the algorithm in the third chapter. PC will calculate the updated speed after calculating Δt, and then transfer the updated speed through UDP to AR headsets.

5.2   Hardware Configuration

5.2.1   Head-Mounted Display

(a)   (b)

Fig. 12. Hardware devices (a) Microsoft HoloLens (b) Sony SmartWatch3

The TCC learning system in this research was developed on an augmented reality device, Microsoft HoloLens shown in Fig. 12(a). HoloLens is a see-through head-mounted display worn over the user's eyes because the eye-piece component is transparent.

5.2.2   Smart Bracelet

The smart bracelet that we use is Sony SmartWatch3 which has built-in nine-axis IMU shown in Fig. 12(b). After Sony SmartWatch3 receive information from the wrist of the user, it will transfer the IMU information through Bluetooth to mobile device. When we receive the information from the current action of the user, we can determine the time discrepancy between the user and the virtual coach immediately.

5.3   Speed-Adaptive Mode

In Speed-Adaptive Mode, the learning system will calculate the delay time Δt of the user and the coach immediately. According the result in the fourth chapter, our learning system will add Δt to next seven seconds and normalize the playing speed of virtual coach. When the learning system detect the difference of playing speed between the learner and the virtual coach. When the learner is slower than virtual coach, learning system will slow down the playing speed.

5.4   Waiting Mode

We also consider about another teaching scenario in reality. Once learners in class are slower too much than the coach, instead of playing slow down and moving on next action, the coach may stop at some important pose and let learners to capture more details. For this scenario, we design the Waiting Mode. In Waiting Mode, if the learner is slower than the virtual coach more than 3 s, the virtual coach will stop at current action and wait for the learner until the learner is also stop at the same action.

6 User Study

We designed a user study to compare the efficiency of Speed Adjustment Mode and Waiting Mode. We invited two TCC coaches who have experience of TCC for several years and two beginners to wear smart bracelets on both wrists and wear AR headsets. We ask participants to follow AR headsets virtual coach and practice a TCC movement which is consist of eight key postures (Fig. 5) and play under three modes which are Without Speed-Guided Mode, Speed-Adaptive Mode and Waiting Mode. Participants were asked to practice five times of each mode. We will use camera to record the movement and calculate the average delay time. After deriving ground truth and estimation of delay time difference, we analysis the distribution of delay time under these three modes.

As we can see the figure below, we can find that if learners practice TCC with Speed-Adaptive Mode, their delay time will be closer to zero which means the movement of learners is more similar with the virtual coach. However, when learners practice TCC under Waiting Mode, delay time will be bigger than Without Speed-Guided Mode. Because when the virtual coach stop, learners cannot detect immediately.

After ANOVA analysis, we obtain that there is a significant difference between Without Speed-Guided Mode and Speed-Adaptive Mode in the group of beginners. It means that Speed-Adaptive Mode is significantly helpful for beginners to decrease the delay time toward the virtual coach. However, for those who already have several years' experience of TCC, there is no significantly difference under Speed-Adaptive

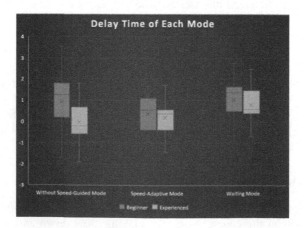

Fig. 13. System overview

Mode. As the analysis result, there is no significant difference between Without Speed-

Guided Mode and Waiting Mode. In our opinion, Waiting-Mode is more appropriate to practice one static action and Speed-Adaptive Mode is more appropriate to practice a serial of sequential movements (Fig. 13).

7 Conclusions and Future Works

In this work, we propose a TCC learning system which will real time detect the delay time between current action of user and virtual coach. After obtaining the delay time, our learning system will adjust speed of virtual coach automatically. With real time speed adjustment, learners can practice TCC with their own pace and virtual coach will slow down or speed up to follow learners' movement. With this learning system, users can learn TCC better and more efficiency.

In the future, we will try to combine the techniques of deep learning. Consider about processing efficiency, we may try SSD or YOLO. Use an image as input data and find out the wrists position at real time. By acquiring this additional information, we expect that we can increase the accuracy of movement recognition. Once the accuracy of movement recognition is increased, we can modify our learning system to become better and help those who want to learn Tai-Chi Chuan.

Acknowledgements. This study is partially supported by Ministry of Science and Technology, Taiwan (R.O.C.), under grant MOST 107-2221-E-369 -001 -MY2 and supported by the "III Innovative and Prospective Technologies Project" of the Institute for Information Industry which is subsidized by the Ministry of Economy Affairs of the Republic of China.

References

1. Velloso, E., Bulling, A., Gellersen, H.: MotionMA: motion modelling and analysis by demonstration. In: Proceedings of the SIGCHI Conference on Human Factors in Computing Systems, pp. 1309–1318. ACM, April 2013
2. Anderson, F., Grossman, T., Matejka, J., Fitzmaurice, G.: YouMove: enhancing movement training with an augmented reality mirror. In: Proceedings of the 26th Annual ACM Symposium on User Interface Software and Technology, pp. 311–320. ACM, October 2013
3. Tominaga, J., Kawauchi, K., Rekimoto, J.: Around me: a system with an escort robot providing a sports player's self-images. In: Proceedings of the 5th Augmented Human International Conference, p. 43. ACM, March 2014
4. Han, P.H., Chen, Y.S., Zhong, Y., Wang, H.L., Hung, Y.P.: My Tai-Chi coaches: an augmented-learning tool for practicing Tai-Chi Chuan. In: Proceedings of the 8th Augmented Human International Conference, p. 25. ACM, March 2017
5. Ukai, Y., Rekimoto, J.: Swimoid: a swim support system using an underwater buddy robot. In: Proceedings of the 4th Augmented Human International Conference, pp. 170–177. ACM, March 2013
6. Drobny, D., Borchers, J.: Learning basic dance choreographies with different augmented feedback modalities. In: CHI 2010 Extended Abstracts on Human Factors in Computing Systems, pp. 3793–3798. ACM, April 2010
7. Chan, J.C., Leung, H., Tang, J.K., Komura, T.: A virtual reality dance training system using motion capture technology. IEEE Trans. Learn. Technol. **4**(2), 187–195 (2011)

8. Graether, E., Mueller, F.: Joggobot: a flying robot as jogging companion. In: CHI 2012 Extended Abstracts on Human Factors in Computing Systems, pp. 1063–1066. ACM, May 2012

9. Higuchi, K., Shimada, T., Rekimoto, J.: Flying sports assistant: external visual imagery representation for sports training. In: Proceedings of the 2nd Augmented Human International Conference, p. 7. ACM, March 2011

10. Salvador, S., Chan, P.: FastDTW: toward accurate dynamic time warping in linear time and space. Intell. Data Anal. **11**(5), 561–580 (2007). ISBN:978-1-4503-0000-0/18/06

Multi-view Community Detection in Facebook Public Pages

Zhige Xin[✉], Chun-Ming Lai, Jon W. Chapman, George Barnett, and S. Felix Wu

University of California, Davis, CA 95616, USA
{zxin,cmlai,jwchapman,gabarnett,sfwu}@ucdavis.edu

Abstract. Community detection in social networks is widely studied because of its importance in uncovering how people connect and interact. However, little attention has been given to community structure in Facebook public pages. In this study, we investigate the community detection problem in Facebook newsgroup pages. In particular, to deal with the diversity of user activities, we apply multi-view clustering to integrate different views, for example, likes on posts and likes on comments. In this study, we explore the community structure in Facebook public pages. The results show that our method can effectively reduce isolates and improve the quality of community structure.

Keywords: Community detection · Multi-view clustering · Modularity

1 Introduction

In the last decade, the rapid growth and adoption of online social networks, such as Facebook, Twitter, Linkedin, has fundamentally changed the way people interact with each other. There are many people who would rather spend more time on these social networking sites than traditional media. With this trend, a great deal of data has been generated from the increasing number of online social networking users. Therefore, it is important to study the structure of social networks, which can provide meaningful insight to Sociology, Communications, Economics, Marketing or even Epidemiology.

One important type of structure of social networks is how the entities are divided into different groups. Basically, there is no formal definition of community, but it is believed that entities are densely connected inside each community with less links between different communities [16]. This community structure plays a significant role in visualization [9], dynamic community detection [13], opinion mining [15], and behavior prediction [12].

Previous research work on community detection generally dealt with the single-view setting. Views are independent data sources or datasets. One classic example is the web-page classification [3], in which one view is the content of web-page, and the other is comprised of the hyperlinks pointing to it. In

© Springer Nature Singapore Pte Ltd. 2019
C.-Y. Chang et al. (Eds.): ICS 2018, CCIS 1013, pp. 131–138, 2019.
https://doi.org/10.1007/978-981-13-9190-3_12

social networks, such as YouTube and Flickr, the interactions between users are complex [14]. Similarly, on Facebook, users like, comment and share content, and interact with each other through these activities. Specifically, in the same page, the activities on posts and those on comments can form two views. From each view, we can generate features and construct a graph to find community structures within a given page.

In this paper, we propose to model Facebook page as a weighted graph that is generated by two views (posts and comments). Then we examine the community structure of the CBS News and The New Times Facebook pages in last week of 2012. In addition, the community structure for common users across multiple pages is studied. Our findings show that combining different views can remarkably reduce the number of isolates in a single-view and make the community structure more cohesive in networks because both views can mutually benefit from each other.

2 Issues of Single-View Community Detection

In the traditional research of community detection in the single-view setting, the procedure is the following: first construct a graph based on the connection between users and then apply some algorithm to partition the graph. However, in real social networks, the interaction between users are complex. For example, users can like or comment a post so it is hard to use only one graph to represent different interactions between users.

For the CBS News page, we extract 205 sample users from our database and construct two graphs based on the interactions of different content: posts and comments. The definition is shown in the next section. Then, we apply the multi-level algorithm [2,6,8] to find the community structure in the two graphs. The connected nodes with the same color belong to the same community.

It is clear that there are a number of isolates in the post graph in Fig. 1a but few in Fig. 1b. Therefore, the issue is that single-view or one graph, can't best represent the interactions between users. In particular, in this example, the users that are considered as isolates in the post graph actually have connections with others in the comment graph.

3 Multi-view Community Detection

3.1 Problem Formulation

Before we formulate the problem, it is necessary to mention the terminology in this paper. We consider networks as graphs, where a node represents a Facebook user and an edge represents interaction between a pair of nodes. Community and cluster are interchangeable as well.

A multi-view dataset can be represented by $\mathbf{m}$ graphs that have the same set of nodes but with a different set of edges. Formally, given m graphs $\mathcal{G}1 = (\mathcal{V}1, \mathcal{E}1), \mathcal{G}2 = (\mathcal{V}2, \mathcal{E}2), ..., \mathcal{G}m = (\mathcal{V}m, \mathcal{E}m)$ and the number of communities $\mathbf{k}$, our goal is to find a vector $\mathbf{v} = (v_1, v_2, ..., v_n)$ such that $\mathbf{v}$ gives an optimal community structure for all graphs, where v_i represents that node i belongs to community v_i and $1 \leq i \leq n$, $1 \leq v_i \leq \mathbf{k}$. In this paper, we focus on two views (activities on posts and comments) in Facebook public pages. Thus, $\mathbf{k} = 2$.

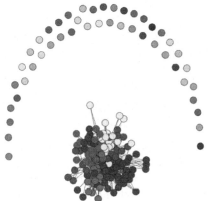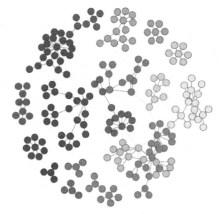

(a) Community structure of post graph for CBS News

(b) Community structure of comment graph for CBS News

Fig. 1. Community structure for the CBS News graph

3.2 Multi-view Community Detection via Weighted Graphs

To some extent, community detection is a graph partitioning problem. So, it is important to define the appropriate graph for our purpose. In Facebook, users have three basic types of actions: comment, like and share. Specifically, in newsgroup pages, post and comment are the basic blocks in which users interact with each other.

In data clustering, a matrix is used to represent and analyze a graph. Here we use adjacency matrices to represent our social interaction graphs.

If a pair of users i and j concurrently like a post, then we put 1 in the cell (i, j) of the matrix. And we call this the post graph. The adjacency matrix 1 for post view/graph is defined as follows:

$$A_{ij} = \begin{cases} 1 \text{ if } i \text{ and } j \text{ concurrently like the same post} \\ 0 \text{ otherwise} \end{cases} \quad (1)$$

The other adjacency matrix 2 for the comment view/graph is defined by likes on comment. And we call this comment graph. If user i likes the comment of user j or vice versa or they concurrently like a comment, we assign the weight B_{ij} to be 1, otherwise 0.

$$B_{ij} = \begin{cases} 1 \text{ if } i \text{ likes } j\text{'s comment or vice versa or} \\ \quad i \text{ and } j \text{ concurrently like a comment} \\ 0 \text{ otherwise} \end{cases} \quad (2)$$

Then we define our weighted graph by combining the two graphs into one and assigning each graph a weight based on importance factor. Moreover, it can be easily extended to multiple views. Its formal definition is as follows:

$$W = \sum_{i=1}^{n} \alpha_i X_i \tag{3}$$

where n is the number of views/graphs, $0 \leq \alpha \leq 1$ and $\sum_{i=1}^{n} \alpha_i = 1$. And when $n = 2$, it becomes the adjacency matrix for two views 4.

$$W = \alpha X_1 + (1 - \alpha)X_2 \tag{4}$$

It turns out when $\alpha = 0$ or $\alpha = 1$, it is reduced to single-view.

Algorithm for Multi-view Community Detection via Weighted Graphs. To learn the optimal parameter in Eq. 4, modularity [10] is introduced. Modularity 5 is a measurement that evaluates how apposite community structure is for any given network. It ranges from -1 to 1 inclusively and the larger it is, the better the community structure is. From the definition, modularity essentially is the value that the real weight of an edge minus the probability of generating it and sum them all.

$$Q = \frac{1}{2m} \sum_{ij} \left[W_{ij} - \frac{d_i d_j}{2m} \right] \delta(c_i, c_j) \tag{5}$$

$$\delta(c_i, c_j) = \begin{cases} 1 \text{ if } i \text{ and } j \text{ are in the same community} \\ 0 \text{ otherwise} \end{cases} \tag{6}$$

where m is the number of edges, W is the adjacency matrix, d_i, d_j are the degree of node i and j respectively.

Our algorithm borrows the idea of modularity maximization [4]. First, we generate a set of parameters and calculate the modularity for each network's structure. Then, we pick the largest modularity value and its corresponding community structure as the result. The details can be seen in Algorithm 1.

Algorithm 1. Multi-View Community Detection via Weighted Graphs
---

Input: Adjacency matrices X_i, and its parameter α_i, where
    $\sum_{i=1}^{n} \alpha_i = 1, 0 < \alpha_i < 1$ and $1 \leq i \leq n$
Output: Indicator vector v

1 Initialize an empty vector set V ;
2 **foreach** *possible combination of α_i* **do**
3   generate the unified similarity matrix W_j by 3; compute community structure v_j using matrix W_j ;
4   put v_j into V ;
5 **end**
6 pick the v in V with largest modularity value as the final indicator vector ;

The time complexity of Algorithm 1 is based on two aspects. The first is to construct the adjacency matrix, which takes $O(n^2)$ time theoretically, but this can be reduced to $O(m)$ because most social networks are sparse ($m \ll n^2$), where n and m are the number of nodes and edges of the network. In addition, the second is to run the core community detection algorithm [2] k times that takes $O(km)$, where k is the number of parameters. In total, the time complexity of our algorithm is $O(m + k * m)$, which is $O(m)$ since $k \ll m$.

4 Empirical Study

4.1 Data Collection

We collected two datasets from the CBS News and The New York Times in the last week of 2012. The statistics of the two datasets are listed in Table 1.

Table 1. Statistics of Facebook newsgroups

Category	CBS	NY Times
Users	11,610	42,001
Posts	42	57
Comments	5,488	3,244
Likes	15,000	64,104

According to previous work [5,7], most variables in internet or social networks display power-law/long tail distributions. To verify this, we plot the users distribution with the number of activities in Facebook public pages, where the x-axis is the number of likes of users on comments or posts and the y-axis is the number of users. Figure 2a and b reveal the users distributions with likes on posts and on comments respectively for the CBS News page. And Fig. 2c plots the distributions of users with comments. It can be seen that with the increase in number of likes, the number of users drops significantly, approximately power distributions. Most Facebook users in the two pages have less than 10 likes and 10 comments in a week.

4.2 Parameter Tuning

After defining the graphs, we study how the parameter affects the community structure of pages. Comment graphs show less density than post graphs, which implies that users are inclined to like posts rather than like comments. Moreover, the number of clusters decrease tens of times in Table 2 and hundreds of times in Table 3 for each page, which shows our algorithm can effectively reduce isolates and uncover a more cohesive structure of networks. View 1 and View 2 represent post graph and comment graph respectively. Merged represents the weighted

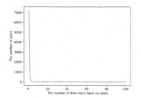 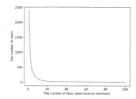 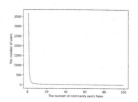

(a) User distribution with likes on posts for CBS News

(b) User distribution with likes on comments for CBS News

(c) User distribution with comments for CBS News

Fig. 2. User distribution for CBS News

Table 2. Statistics of the CBS News graph

Category	View 1	View 2	Merged
Users	10,535	10,535	10,535
Edges	2,448,338	28,208	2,475,896
Clusters	3,338	6,821	**120**
Isolates	3,321	6,647	**4**
Modularity	0.8334	**0.9135**	0.8350

graph from the two views. On the other hand, we observe that modularity is not a perfect measurement especially for networks with a number of isolates because the more isolates are, the larger modularity is.

In order to find the optimal parameter, we generate a set of parameters as the candidates, {0.0, 0.2, 0.4, 0.6, 0.8, 1.0}. Then we run Algorithm 1 repetitively for each parameter and calculate the corresponding modularity. We plot the relation between the parameters and their modularity in Fig. 3 for both CBS News and The New York Times.

Also we examine how the parameter affects the number of communities. Table 4 shows the relation between the parameters and their number of communities for the two pages. The results demonstrate the parameter does not change the modularity value and the number of communities. In this study,

Table 3. Statistics of The New York Times graph

Category	View 1	View 2	Merged
Users	41,252	41,252	41,252
Edges	106,115,374	213,746	106,296,974
Clusters	3,395	36,340	**31**
Isolates	3,383	36,279	**0**
Modularity	0.6054	**0.8057**	0.6050

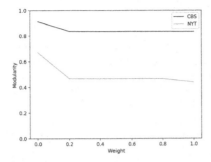

Fig. 3. Relation between weight and modularity for CBS News and The New York Times

the parameter value is to set to be 0.5. It is worth noting that the parameter improves the modularity of the post graph and it makes the both graphs denser. Modularity is inclined to increase with more isolates for the same set of users, which can explain why it reaches the maximum value when the parameter is 0.

Table 4. Relation between parameter and number of communities for CBS News and The New York Times

Parameter	CBS	NY Times
0	6,821	36,340
0.2	120	31
0.4	120	31
0.6	120	31
0.8	120	31
1	3,338	3,395

5 Conclusion

Prior research provided innovative theories, algorithms, and applications. However little work has been done with regards to exploring community structure in Facebook public pages. In this work, we propose a weighted multi-view community detection method and apply it to the Facebook newsgroup pages, CBS News, and The New York Times, etc. The results reveal three advantages of our method: (1) it can alleviate the isolates issue in the sparse networks. For example, in the CBS News page (last week of 2012), the isolates are decreased from 3, 321 and 6, 647 to 4. (2) more cohesive community structure can be found during the process, take the New York Times page (last week of 2012) as an example, the number of communities becomes 31 from 3, 395 and 36, 340.

References

1. Aslam, S.: Facebook by the numbers: stats, demographics and fun facts, January 2018. https://www.omnicoreagency.com/facebook-statistics/
2. Blondel, V.D., Guillaume, J.L., Lambiotte, R., Lefebvre, E.: Fast unfolding of communities in large networks. J. Stat. Mech. Theor. Exp. **2008**(10), P10008 (2008). http://stacks.iop.org/1742-5468/2008/i=10/a=P10008
3. Blum, A., Mitchell, T.: Combining labeled and unlabeled data with co-training. In: Proceedings of the Eleventh Annual Conference on Computational Learning Theory, pp. 92–100. ACM (1998)
4. Chen, M., Kuzmin, K., Szymanski, B.K.: Community detection via maximization of modularity and its variants. IEEE Trans. Comput. Soc. Syst. **1**(1), 46–65 (2014)
5. Clauset, A., Shalizi, C.R., Newman, M.E.: Power-law distributions in empirical data. SIAM Rev. **51**(4), 661–703 (2009)
6. Csardi, G., Nepusz, T.: The igraph software package for complex network research. InterJournal Complex Sys. **1695**(5), 1–9 (2006)
7. Faloutsos, M., Faloutsos, P., Faloutsos, C.: On power-law relationships of the internet topology. In: ACM SIGCOMM Computer Communication Review, vol. 29, pp. 251–262. ACM (1999)
8. Hagberg, A., Swart, P., Chult, D.S.: Exploring network structure, dynamics, and function using networkx. Technical report, Los Alamos National Lab. (LANL), Los Alamos, NM (United States) (2008)
9. Kang, H., Getoor, L., Singh, L.: Visual analysis of dynamic group membership in temporal social networks. ACM SIGKDD Explor. Newsl. **9**(2), 13–21 (2007)
10. Newman, M.E.J.: Modularity and community structure in networks. Proc. Nat. Acad. Sci. **103**(23), 8577–8582 (2006). https://doi.org/10.1073/pnas.0601602103. http://www.pnas.org/content/103/23/8577.abstract
11. Statista: Number of monthly active facebook users worldwide, April 2018. https://www.statista.com/statistics/264810/number-of-monthly-active-facebook-users-worldwide/
12. Tang, L., Liu, H.: Scalable learning of collective behavior based on sparse social dimensions. In: Proceedings of the 18th ACM Conference on Information and Knowledge Management, pp. 1107–1116. ACM (2009)
13. Tang, L., Liu, H., Zhang, J., Nazeri, Z.: Community evolution in dynamic multimode networks. In: Proceedings of the 14th ACM SIGKDD International Conference on Knowledge Discovery and Data Mining, pp. 677–685. ACM (2008)
14. Tang, L., Wang, X., Liu, H.: Uncovering groups via heterogeneous interaction analysis. In: Ninth IEEE International Conference on Data Mining, ICDM 2009, pp. 503–512. IEEE (2009)
15. Wang, T., Wang, K.C., Erlandsson, F., Wu, S.F., Faris, R.: The influence of feedback with different opinions on continued user participation in online newsgroups. In: 2013 IEEE/ACM International Conference on Advances in Social Networks Analysis and Mining (ASONAM), pp. 388–395. IEEE (2013)
16. Wasserman, S., Faust, K.: Social Network Analysis: Methods and Applications, vol. 8. Cambridge University Press, Cambridge (1994)

Image Processing, Computer Graphics
and Multimedia Technologies

Supervised Representation Hash Codes Learning

Huei-Fang Yang[1]([⊠]) [iD], Cheng-Hao Tu[2] [iD], and Chu-Song Chen[2,3] [iD]

[1] Department of Computer Science and Information Engineering,
National University of Kaohsiung, Kaohsiung, Taiwan
`hfyang@nuk.edu.tw`
[2] Institute of Information Science, Academia Sinica, Taipei, Taiwan
`{andytu28,song}@iis.sinica.edu.tw`
[3] MOST Joint Research Center for AI Technology and All Vista Healthcare,
Taipei, Taiwan

Abstract. Learning-based hashing has been widely employed for large-scale similarity retrieval due to its efficient computation and compressed storage. In this paper, we propose ResHash, a deep representation hash code learning approach to learning compact and discriminative binary codes. In ResHash, we assume that each semantic label has its own representation codeword and these codewords guide hash coding. The codewords are attractors that attract semantically similar images and are also repulsors that repel semantically dissimilar ones. Furthermore, ResHash jointly learns compact binary codes and discover representation codewords from data by a simple margin ranking loss, making it easily realizable and avoiding the need to hand-craft the codewords beforehand. Experimental results on standard benchmark datasets show the effectiveness of ResHash.

Keywords: Image retrieval · Binary codes · Deep learning

1 Introduction

Recent years have witnessed learning-based hash becoming an active research topic for efficient large-scale image search [2, 11, 19]. The learning-based hashing aims to learn a mapping from high-dimensional image data to low-dimensional binary codes from training samples such that images of similar content have similar codes. Once learned, similarity image retrieval can be performed in Hamming space, thereby achieving computational efficiency and storage reduction. To learn similarity-preserving binary codes, many hashing approaches have been proposed to enhance the discrimination power of learned codes. These approaches range from earlier studies using shallow architectures [6, 8, 12, 14, 17] to more recent

---

This work is supported in part by the Ministry of Science and Technology of Taiwan under contract MOST 107-2634-F-001-004 and MOST 107-2218-E-390-006-MY2.

© Springer Nature Singapore Pte Ltd. 2019
C.-Y. Chang et al. (Eds.): ICS 2018, CCIS 1013, pp. 141–149, 2019.
https://doi.org/10.1007/978-981-13-9190-3_13

deep hashing approaches [9–11,19,22] using deep neural networks. Deep networks enable end-to-end, joint learning of image representations and hash codes directly from raw images via well-designed objectives, and hence great strides in retrieval performance have been made.

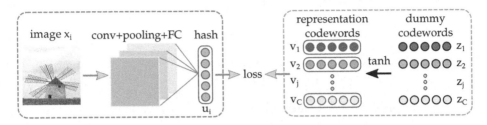

Fig. 1. The proposed deep representation hash code (ResHash) learning. ResHash is designed based on the assumption that there is a set of C representation codewords $\{v_j\}$, each of which represents a particular concept (or semantic category), and hash coding is guided by these codewords. Each codeword attracts images of similar content to the concept it represents and repulses images of dissimilar content to the concept it represents. That is, the compact image representation u_i of an image x_i moves toward (away from) v_j when x_i and v_j share a (no) common concept. As such, similar images have similar hash codes and dissimilar images have different codes. The representation codewords $\{v_j\}$ are generated by applying a soft sign function (tanh) to dummy representations $\{z_j\}$, the input to the right-hand-side network, where $\{z_j\}$ serve as free parameters to be learned. One nice characteristic of ResHash is that it is able to learn similarity-preserving hash codes and discover the representation codewords simultaneously during the learning process, therefore requiring no prior knowledge about the codewords. conv+pooling+FC denotes a network that consists of convolutional layers, max-pooling layers and fully connected layers.

The design philosophy of deep hashing approaches lies in allowing the networks to discover the mapping from images to a low-dimensional embedding of binary codes during network training without any additional cues. A typical difficulty arises in this process is that we do not have the respective target codewords for the semantic categories. To address this issue, some approach (e.g., CNNH [18]) decomposes the pairwised similarity matrix of data into binary submatrices to establish the target hash codes beforehand. Such a method enforces a two-stage procedure and the target codes cannot be trained or refined later.

This paper introduces ResHash, a simple yet effective deep approach to representation hash code learning. We assume that each semantic label has its own representation codeword and these codewords are driving force behind hash coding. The codewords serve as attractors that attract images of semantically similar contents and repulsors that keep dissimilar images apart. ResHash employs a learning criterion of drawing the semantically similar samples closer in the codeword space, i.e., centralizing them to the representation code, and simultaneously de-centralizing the semantically dissimilar samples. Through the guidance of codewords, similarity-preserving binary codes can be learned. Unlike CNNH,

ResHash need not design the codewords beforehand. They are directly expressed as part of the "inputs" of a network. When the training data are provided as the other part of network input, the network learns the mapping and the representation codewords are jointly recovered via back-propagation. Employing input as part of the parameters for training has been utilized for visualizations [15], image style transfer [5], and optimizing the latent space of generative models [1]. We exploit this idea for hash codes establishment to afford an explicit representation of binary codeword per semantic category. An illustration of ResHash is shown in Fig. 1.

The main contributions of this paper are as follows. (1) A novel idea that explores the representation codewords of semantic categories as the unknown inputs to deep models is introduced. (2) Our approach can learn similarity-preserving hash codes and discover the representation codewords simultaneously during the learning process, therefore requiring no prior knowledge or biased assumptions about the codewords.

2 Related Work

Learning-based hashing approaches can be classified into three categories: unsupervised, semi-supervised, and supervised hashing. Unsupervised hashing approaches use unlabeled samples to learn hash functions with a learning criterion that preserves similarity between data points in the original space (e.g., SH [17]) or minimizes quantization error (e.g., ITQ [6]). Semi-supervised hashing uses both unlabeled and labeled samples (e.g., SSH [16]). Supervised hashing exploits supervised information provided in the data, such as pairwise similarity relations or class labels (e.g., ITQ-CCA [6]).

The traditional methods learn hash functions from hand-crafted features that may not be optimal for hash coding. Recently, deep hashing approaches have shown superior performance thanks to the ability to learn discriminative features need for the tasks in an end-to-end manner. CNNH [18] employs a two-stage approach in which the first stage learns approximate hash codes and the second uses a deep network to learn a mapping from images to hash codes. The drawback is that hash code learning and image representation learning cannot benefit each other. Hence, DNNH [9] proposes to learn hash codes and feature representations within one network so hash functions and image representations are jointly optimized. Later, much of the work has been proposed. DSRH [21] utilizes a ranking-based loss to improve the retrieval performance of multi-label images. DHN [22] and DPSH [10] leverage pairwise label similarity to optimize cross-entropy loss. Assuming that classification depends on a set of *on* and *off* attributes, [11] learns binary codes that preserve label semantics. DVSQ [2] learns a visual-semantic embedding by a two-stream network, one taking as input the image labels and the other the images. HashNet [3] aims to learn exactly binary codes by starting from a smoothed objective function to more non-smooth one during training. More recently, SSDH [19] treats binary codes as hidden concepts that govern classification and learns discriminative codes complying with semantic labels.

Prior approaches do not provide representative codes for semantic categories. Instead, our ResHash does. The introduction of codewords also leads to a simpler network that learns in a pointwise manner, avoiding the need to use complex networks that take pairs or triplets of training samples.

3   Deep Representation Hash Code Learning

Let $X = \{x_i\}_{i=1}^{N} \in \mathbb{R}^{D \times N}$ denote a training set of N images, each represented by a D-dimensional vector. The goal of learning to hash is to learn a mapping $\Omega :$ $X \rightarrow \{-1, 1\}^{K \times N}$ that encodes an image x_i into a K-bit binary code $h_i = \Omega(x_i)$. The learned binary codes are expected to preserve the similarity relationship among images: Similar images have similar codes and dissimilar images have different codes.

We leverage a deep neural network to learn the projection of images onto binary codes. In doing so, we introduce a hash layer with tanh functions on top of the deepest image representation layer of a network. The binary code h_i of an image x_i is obtained by quantizing the activations u_i of the hash layer, which is:

$$h_i = \text{sgn}(\mathcal{F}(x_i, \mathcal{W})) = \text{sgn}(u_i), \tag{1}$$

where $\mathcal{F}(x_i, \mathcal{W})$ is a composition of non-linear projection functions with parameter $\mathcal{W}$ that projects an image onto u_i, and $\text{sgn}(u) = 1$ if $u > 0$ and -1 otherwise. $\text{sgn}(\cdot)$ is an element-wise operator for a matrix or a vector.

3.1   Model Formulation

ResHash utilizes the representation codewords to guide the hash coding process. Assume that there exist C representation codewords, $B = \{b_j\}_{j=1}^{C} \in \{-1, 1\}^{K \times C}$, where b_j denotes a representative K-bit binary codeword and C is the number of semantic categories. Each semantic category has one codeword, The representation codewords serve as both attractors and repulsors to guide the hash coding process. The learning objective is to make the binary code h_i of an image x_i and a codeword b_j close if image x_i and the codeword belong to a same semantic category c_j, and at the same keep h_i and b_j as apart as possible if they are in different categories.

When the representation codewords are known beforehand, one can directly treat the representation codewords as the learning goal and optimize a loss based on the fixed, given representation codewords. However, without any prior knowledge about the underlying data distribution, it is unlikely to obtain representation codewords that well partition the feature space. To avoid the need to hand-craft the representation codewords, we treats the codewords as part of the network parameters to be learned. Specifically, we assume that the codewords B are directly drived from a set of dummy variables $Z = \{z_j\}_{j=1}^{C} \in \mathbb{R}^{K \times C}$ that are unknown and to be learned. These z_j's are the inputs directly to the network with tanh activations as shown in Fig. 1. Then binary codeword b_j can be obtained by binarizing the activations of z_j, which is

$$b_j = \text{sgn}(\tanh(z_j)) = \text{sgn}(v_j). \tag{2}$$

Hence, ResHash aims to learn the hash coding $\mathcal{F}(x_i, \mathcal{W})$ and the codewords Z simultaneously. During learning, the codewords are adjusted along with the network updates based on the given image data. Because the codewords are also learned from data, they are expected to better capture the underlying data structure than hand-crafted ones.

3.2 Learning Objective

The closeness between a pair of binary codes h_i and b_j is determined by their Hamming distance: $\text{dist}_H(h_i, b_j) = \frac{1}{2}(K - \langle h_i, b_j \rangle)$, where $\langle \cdot, \cdot \rangle$ is the inner product. A larger value of the inner product between two binary codes leads to a smaller Hamming distance. Hence, the inner product can be used as a closeness measure between binary codes. As we apply a continuous relaxation on the discrete constraint by using $\tanh(\cdot)$ activations in the hash layer and the representation codewordes, the similarity instead is measured by the real-valued hash codes u_i and codewords v_j and is given as $u_i^T v_j$.

To enable similarity-preserving learning, we first define a similarity matrix that indicates the pairwise similarity between images and the categories that codewords represent. Let $S = \{s_{ij}\}$ be the similarity matrix, with $s_{ij} = 1$ denoting image x_i belongs to category c_j, and $s_{ij} = 0$ otherwise. Given one such similarity matrix, we adopt a margin ranking loss based on the similarity between hash code u_i and codeword v_j in order for ResHash to learn to produce larger inner products between the binary codes and codewordes when they share a common category than those when they are of different categories. The loss for N training samples is defined as

$$\min_{\mathcal{W}, Z} L(\mathcal{W}, Z) = \sum_{i=1}^{N} \sum_{s_{ij}=1} \max(0, m - u_i^T v_j + \max(u_i^T v_t [s_{it} \neq 1])), \tag{3}$$

where m is the margin that defines the inner product of a similar image-codeword pair should be at least m larger than the least dissimilar image-codeword pair, v_t denotes the codeword that does not contain the label of the image, and Iverson bracket indicator function $[s_{ij} \neq 1]$ evaluates to 1 when $s_{ij} \neq 1$ and 0 otherwise.

Finally, because tanh functions are used to constrain the binary codes, the codewords generated are in the range $[-1, 1]$. One may introduce a quantization error in the learning objective as in [19], so that the elements of the learned codewords are better binarized (approaching to either 0 or 1). To simplify our study, we opt for a simpler learning objective that considers only preserving the similarity between samples, and have not added such quantization loss terms yet. Besides, several studies (such as [11]) have achieved good performance without considering the quantization error. ResHash is a general framework and can incorporate it easily.

3.3   Retrieval

Once trained, the learned binary codes of an image x can be efficiently obtained by propaging the image through the network and quantizing the activations of the hash layer, i.e., $h = \text{sgn}(u)$.

4   Experiments

4.1   Datasets and Experimental Settings

Datasets. CIFAR-10 is a single-label dataset that comprises 60,000 32×32 color images in 10 classes, with 6,000 images per class. NUS-WIDE is a collection of about 270,000 flickr images. Following the given URLs, we were able to collect only about 230,000 images due to the reason that the other images have been removed by the owners. NUS-WIDE is a multi-label dataset, in which each image is associated with one or multiple labels in 81 concept tags. In accordance with in the previous studies [9,18], a subset of 162,289 images in the 21 most frequent concepts are used. Each concept contains at least 5,000 images.

The supervised setting follows that in [19]. In CIFAR-10, we use 10,000 images (1,000 images per class) as the query set and use the remaining images to train the network and to form the retrieval database. In NUS-WIDE, 2,100 images (100 images per concept) are randomly selected to construct the query set, and the rest are used as training images as well as the retrieval database.

We determine the relevance between images and codewords by image labels. Each image label has its own representation codeword. An image and a codeword are considered similar if the image is associated with the label the codeword represents. Otherwise, an image and a codeword are deemed dissimilar.

Evaluation Metrics. We evaluate the retrieval performance using mean average precision (mAP). It is defined as the mean of the average precision (AP) of all the queries, that is, $\text{mAP} = \frac{1}{N} \sum_i^N \text{AP}_i$, with N the number of query images. The AP_i of a query image i is given as $\text{AP}_i = \frac{1}{M} \sum_{r=1}^R \text{prec}(r) \odot \text{rel}(r)$, where M is the number of relevant images in the returned list, $\text{prec}(r)$ denotes the precision at the top r returned images, and $\text{rel}(r)$ indicates whether the rth retrieved image is relevant to the query or not. $\text{rel}(r) = 1$ means the returned image is a relevance of the query and 0 otherwise.

We use image labels to determine the relevance between images. When two images share at least one common label, they are considered relevant.

Implementation Details. We implement ResHash using Keras with a Tensorflow backend and choose CNN-F [4] as the network model for hash coding. We consider CNN-F a proper choice for a fair comparison with other studies that use the same network or AlexNet [7] that is similar to CNN-F. CNN-F consists of 5 convolutional, 2 fully-connected and one output layers. We remove the output classification layer and add in a hash layer of K nodes with tanh activations. The weights of the first 7 layers are initialized with those pre-trained on ImageNet [13] and the weights of the hash layer are initialized by a Xavier uniform.

Besides image inputs, the other inputs to ResHash are dummy codewords for the learning representation codewords of semantic categories. Codeword learning is similar to word embeddings in natural language processing where words are mapped to real-valued vectors, and hence can be easily implemented by the Embedding layer originally provided in Keras. The Embedding layer starts with random weights. The entire ResHash network is optimized via backpropagation using mini-batch stochastic gradient descent (SGD) with Nesterov momentum.

4.2   Results on CIFAR-10

ResHash is compared to several deep learning-based approaches, including SSDH [19], DPSH [10], DRSCH [20], DSCH [20], DSRH [21], CNNH [18], DNNH [9], DHN [22], and DVSQ [2]. As reported in Table 1, ResHash provides significantly better retrieval performance than the other approaches, demonstrating that the idea driven by employing representation codewords to guide hash coding is effec-

Table 1. The mAP scores of different hashing approaches on CIFAR-10

Method	24 bits	32 bits	48 bits
ResHash	**0.930**	**0.946**	**0.934**
SSDH	0.919	0.914	0.914
DPSH	0.781	0.795	0.807
DVSQ	—	0.730	0.733
DRSCH	0.622	0.629	0.631
DSCH	0.613	0.617	0.620
DSRH	0.611	0.617	0.618
DHN	0.594	0.603	0.621
DNNH	0.566	0.558	0.581
CNNH	0.511	0.509	0.522

Table 2. The mAP scores of different hashing approaches on NUS-WIDE. The mAP is calculated based on top 50,000 returned images

Method	24 bits	32 bits	48 bits
ResHash	0.758	**0.769**	**0.800**
SSDH	**0.787**	0.750	0.782
DPSH	0.722	0.736	0.741
DRSCH	0.622	0.623	0.628
DSCH	0.597	0.611	0.609
DSRH	0.618	0.621	0.631

tive because the representation codewords are the underlying driving force that makes semantically relevant images close and keeps irrelevant images apart.

4.3   Results on NUS-WIDE

Like the evaluation done on CIFAR-10, ResHash is compared to several deep supervised hashing approaches, and the comparison is reported in Table 2. As can be seen, ResHash performs more favorably against most of the other approaches at all bits, except for SSDH that achieves better mAP scores at lower bits.

In sum, the results on CIFAR-10 and NUS-WIDE suggest that ResHash is a general framework that can deal with single-label and multi-label images.

5   Conclusions

We have presented ResHash, a novel deep hashing approach that learns representation hash codes for image search. In ResHash, we assume that there exists a set of representation codewords that guide the learning process. The codewords act as attractors that make similar images have similar binary codes as well as repulsors that make dissimilar images have different codes. ResHash learns compact binary codes and can find the codewords simultaneously. Experimental results have shown that ResHash performs favorably against other approaches.

References

1. Bojanowski, P., Joulin, A., Lopez-Paz, D., Szlam, A.: Optimizing the latent space of generative networks. CoRR **abs/1707.05776** (2017)
2. Cao, Y., Long, M., Wang, J., Liu, S.: Deep visual-semantic quantization for efficient image retrieval. In: CVPR (2017)
3. Cao, Z., Long, M., Wang, J., Yu, P.S.: HashNet: deep learning to hash by continuation. In: ICCV (2017)
4. Chatfield, K., Simonyan, K., Vedaldi, A., Zisserman, A.: Return of the devil in the details: delving deep into convolutional nets. In: BMVC (2014)
5. Gatys, L.A., Ecker, A.S., Bethge, M.: Image style transfer using convolutional neural networks. In: CVPR, pp. 2414–2423 (2016)
6. Gong, Y., Lazebnik, S., Gordo, A., Perronnin, F.: Iterative quantization: a procrustean approach to learning binary codes for large-scale image retrieval. IEEE Trans. Pattern Anal. Mach. Intell. **35**(12), 2916–2929 (2013)
7. Krizhevsky, A., Sutskever, I., Hinton, G.E.: ImageNet classification with deep convolutional neural networks. In: NIPS, pp. 1106–1114 (2012)
8. Kulis, B., Darrell, T.: Learning to hash with binary reconstructive embeddings. In: NIPS, pp. 1042–1050 (2009)
9. Lai, H., Pan, Y., Liu, Y., Yan, S.: Simultaneous feature learning and hash coding with deep neural networks. In: CVPR, pp. 3270–3278 (2015)
10. Li, W., Wang, S., Kang, W.: Feature learning based deep supervised hashing with pairwise labels. In: IJCAI, pp. 1711–1717 (2016)
11. Lin, K., Yang, H.F., Hsiao, J.H., Chen, C.S.: Deep learning of binary hash codes for fast image retrieval. In: CVPRW on Deep Vision, pp. 27–35 (2015)

12. Norouzi, M., Fleet, D.J.: Minimal loss hashing for compact binary codes. In: ICML, pp. 353–360 (2011)
13. Russakovsky, O., et al.: ImageNet large scale visual recognition challenge. Int. J. Comput. Vis. **115**, 211–252 (2015)
14. Shen, F., Shen, C., Liu, W., Shen, H.T.: Supervised discrete hashing. In: CVPR, pp. 37–45 (2015)
15. Simonyan, K., Vedaldi, A., Zisserman, A.: Deep inside convolutional networks: visualising image classification models and saliency maps. CoRR **abs/1312.6034** (2013)
16. Wang, J., Kumar, S., Chang, S.: Semi-supervised hashing for large-scale search. IEEE Trans. Pattern Anal. Mach. Intell. **34**(12), 2393–2406 (2012)
17. Weiss, Y., Torralba, A., Fergus, R.: Spectral hashing. In: NIPS, pp. 1753–1760 (2008)
18. Xia, R., Pan, Y., Lai, H., Liu, C., Yan, S.: Supervised hashing for image retreieval via image representation learning. In: AAAI, pp. 2156–2162 (2014)
19. Yang, H.F., Lin, K., Chen, C.S.: Supervised learning of semantics-preserving hash via deep convolutional neural networks. IEEE Trans. Pattern Anal. Mach. Intell. **40**(2), 437–451 (2018)
20. Zhang, R., Lin, L., Zhang, R., Zuo, W., Zhang, L.: Bit-scalable deep hashing with regularized similarity learning for image retrieval and person re-identification. IEEE Trans. Image Process. **24**(12), 4766–4779 (2015)
21. Zhao, F., Huang, Y., Wang, L., Tan, T.: Deep semantic ranking based hashash for multi-label image retreieval. In: CVPR, pp. 1556–1564 (2015)
22. Zhu, H., Long, M., Wang, J., Cao, Y.: Deep hashing network for efficient similarity retrieval. In: AAAI, pp. 2415–2421 (2016)

The Bread Recognition System with Logistic Regression

Guo-Zhang Jian and Chuin-Mu Wang$^{(\boxtimes)}$

Department of Computer Science and Information Engineering,
National Chin-Yi University of Technology, No. 57, Sec. 2, Zhongshan Rd.,
Taiping District, Taichung 41170, Taiwan (R.O.C.)
s3A417068@student.ncut.edu.tw, cmwang@ncut.edu.tw

Abstract. With the advancement of technology, image processing has become very common and widely used in the field of detection and recognition. This paper uses the digital image processing method to capture the feature of breads and recognize them. The experimental results: First detect the bread and then capture the image features. Finally, using Logistic Regression to classify them. The highest score as the recognition result. Through the above we can achieve effective and outstanding results.

Keywords: Machine learning · Bread recognition · Hu moments · GLCM · Object detection · Feature extraction

1 Introduction

In many bakeries, there are a lot of breads to sell in a single day, which is a tough task to remember all because the bread is changing every day. Therefore, in a bakery, it is necessary to reduce the workload and increase efficiency in checkout.

In order to solve this problem, we propose an automatic bread recognition system [1]. The system recognizes the bread portion, first detects the bread position, and performs feature extraction on the detected bread. It mainly captures the shape feature, color feature and texture feature in the image.

2 Object Recognition System

2.1 Extraction Object Region

Before the feature is captured, the image is pre-processed, and the image is processed by edge detection, erosion expansion, filter, etc., and the position of the bread is finally detected, as shown in Figs. 1 and 2:

© Springer Nature Singapore Pte Ltd. 2019
C.-Y. Chang et al. (Eds.): ICS 2018, CCIS 1013, pp. 150–156, 2019.
https://doi.org/10.1007/978-981-13-9190-3_14

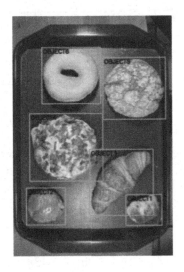

Fig. 1. Detecting a result of a bread.

Fig. 2. Detecting a result of multiple breads

2.2 Feature Extraction

In the system, we took the following features: After inputting the image, we took the shape, color and texture features of each bread. In this paper, we call these features "conventional features."

2.3 Shape Features

Using Hu moments [2] to describe the shape of a numerical image of an object is an important feature. This method is an image after rotating zoom or pan, the value of its new features with the original chart won't be affected, if the pixel errors into consideration, it has shown the gap is very small, it is an important feature as the image recognition. Assuming that the image size is M × N, the pixel position (x, y), and the color value is f(x, y), the moment of the qth order in the pth order and the y-axis direction in the x-axis direction, as in the formula (1) shown:

$$m_{pq} = \sum_{x=0}^{M} \sum_{y=0}^{N} x^p y^q f(x, y) \tag{1}$$

Let the center point coordinate, then normalize center moment, as shown in Eq. (1):

$$\eta_{pq} = \frac{\left[\sum\limits_{x=0}^{M} \sum\limits_{y=0}^{N} (x - \hat{x})^p (y - \hat{y})^q f(x,y) \right]}{\left[\sum\limits_{x=0}^{M} \sum\limits_{y=0}^{N} f(x,y) \right]^{[(p+q)/2+1]}} \tag{2}$$

The seven values we use to represent the shape of the object represent different meanings, respectively, defined as follows, the symbol is ϕ_1, ϕ_2, ϕ_3, ϕ_4, ϕ_5, ϕ_6, ϕ_7, as shown in Eq. (3):

$$
\begin{aligned}
\phi_1 &= \eta_{20} + \eta_{02}, \\
\phi_2 &= (\eta_{20} + \eta_{02})^2 + 4\eta_{11}^2, \\
\phi_3 &= (\eta_{30} - 3\eta_{12})^2 + (3\eta_{21} - \eta_{32})^2, \\
\phi_4 &= (\eta_{30} + \eta_{12})^2 + (\eta_{21} + \eta_{32})^2, \\
\phi_5 &= (\eta_{30} - 3\eta_{12})(\eta_{30} + \eta_{12})[(\eta_{30} + \eta_{12})^2 - 3(\eta_{21} + \eta_{03})^2] \\
&\quad + (3\eta_{21} - \eta_{03})(\eta_{21} - \eta_{03})[3(\eta_{30} + \eta_{12})^2 - (\eta_{21} + \eta_{03})^2], \\
\phi_6 &= (\eta_{20} + \eta_{02})[(\eta_{30} + \eta_{12})^2 - (\eta_{21} + \eta_{03})^2] \\
&\quad + 4\eta_{11}^2(\eta_{30} + \eta_{12})(\eta_{21} + \eta_{32})^2, \\
\phi_7 &= (\eta_{21} - 3\eta_{03})(\eta_{30} + \eta_{12})[(\eta_{30} + \eta_{12})^2 - 3(\eta_{21} + \eta_{03})^2] \\
&\quad + (\eta_{30} - 3\eta_{21})(\eta_{21} + \eta_{03})[3(\eta_{30} + \eta_{12})^2 - (\eta_{21} + \eta_{03})^2].
\end{aligned}
\tag{3}
$$

We can use these seven values to evaluate the shape and difference of the object. The method is as follows: Assume that there are two different shapes of objects O_1 and O_2, which represent the momentum constant values of the object shape, $\phi_1^{o_1}, \ldots, \phi_7^{o_1}$ and $\phi_1^{o_2}, \ldots, \phi_7^{o_2}$ the O_1 and O_5 shapes are different. As shown in formula (4):

$$\Delta_M(O_1, O_2) = \sqrt{\sum_{i=1}^{7} (\phi_i^{o_1}, -\phi_i^{o_2})^2}. \tag{4}$$

2.4   Color Features

After color space is separated by color space, the average and variation are calculated separately, and these values are used as features to describe their color [4].

2.5   Texture Features

Using Haralick texture to describe the texture on the surface of the object, we need to quantify or compare the touch, texture, and pattern of the surface of the texture, so we use this method to describe the texture features. In fact, it is a kind of pattern shape that appear repeatedly. When such images are converted into gray scales, their gray scales will show repeated changes. With this feature, it will be found that there are certain pixels between any two pixels at a certain distance. The relationship of proportions. The Haralick texture [3] used in this topic is derived from the grey-level co-occurrence matrix (GLCM), a second-order statistical method that uses the results of the moving window method to count each pair of possible grayscale values. The frequency appears in a specific correlation position. The statistical method calculates four sets of GLCM based on four different directions. The GLCM of each group can calculate the value of Haralick texture, as shown in Fig. 3.

- GLCM quantification method:

The GLCM matrix provides information on the spatial distribution of grayscale values in an image, but it is still necessary to further quantify the information into a single numerical form for direct analysis by the computer. There are many ways to quantify textures. Haralick (1973) has suggested 14 kinds of statistics that can be used to quantify GLCM matrices. This topic selects six kinds of texture values that are often used. The formula is (5), (6), (7), (8), (9), (10):

(i) Contrast

$$\sum_i \sum_j (i-j)^2 \times P_\delta(i,j) \tag{5}$$

Contrast is used to measure the intensity of contrast in an image, and its value is proportional to the contrast intensity.
In the P_δ image, the gray scales i and j appear in the relative probability value of the relative position, and δ represents the directivity.

(ii) Energy

$$\sum_i \sum_j P_\delta^2(i,j). \tag{6}$$

The energy value, also known as the Angular Second Moment (ASM), is used to measure the consistency of the texture.

(iii) Entropy

$$-\sum_i \sum_j P_\delta(i,j) \times Log P_\delta(i,j) \tag{7}$$

The nature of entropy is exactly the opposite of the energy value and is used to measure the degree of clutter in the texture.

(iv) Homogeneity

$$\sum_i \sum_j P_\delta(i,j) / \left(1 + (i-j)^2\right) \tag{8}$$

Homogeneity is used to measure the uniformity of an image.

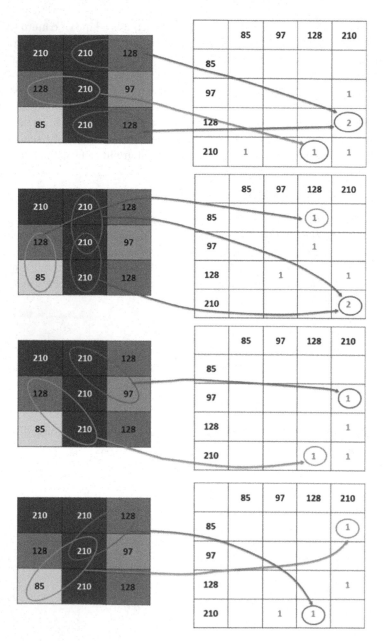

Fig. 3. The above is a schematic diagram of calculating GLCM

(v) Dissimilarity

$$\sum_i \sum_j P_\delta(i,j) \times |i-j| \qquad (9)$$

Dissimilarity is a measure of the degree of dissimilarity of grayscale values in an image. It is sensitive to the arrangement of grayscale values in space or the hue of an image.

(vi) Correlation

$$\sum_{ij} P_\delta(i,j) - \mu_x\mu_y/(\sigma_x\sigma_y) \tag{10}$$

Correlation is used to distinguish whether two objects have mutual correlations in shape and other features, and then use correlation value (Correlation Value) to determine the characteristics of the object to be found to find the location of the object.

3 Training Model – Logistic Regression

Using the method of multiple Logistic Regression model [5], as shown in Fig. 4, the features of each bread in each captured image are converted into an array, as the input of the model, and each input feature parameter is multiplied by a corresponding one weight. The sum of all the results, after Softmax [6] calculate which type of bread has the highest probability. The highest probability as the result of bread recognition.

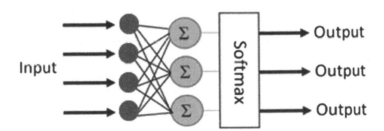

Fig. 4. The above is logistic regression architecture.

4 Conclusions

At present, only methods of digital image processing are used, and it is hoped that artificial intelligence can be added in the future to make the entire system intelligent and improve the accuracy.

This paper only recognizes bread. In the future, this paper method can be used not only to recognize bread, but also to recognize other foods that are not easily labeled after delivery. It can also reduce the workload of each store and increase the checkout speed.

References

1. Morimoto, M., Higasa, A.: A bread recognition system using RGB-D sensor. In: 2015 International Conference on Informatics, Electronics & Vision (ICIEV), pp. 1–4. IEEE, June 2015
2. Hu, M.K.: Visual pattern recognition by moment invariants. IRE Trans. Inf. Theory **8**(2), 179–187 (1962)
3. Mohanaiah, P., Sathyanarayana, P., GuruKumar, L.: Image texture feature extraction using GLCM approach. Int. J. Sci. Res. Publ. **3**(5), 1 (2013)
4. Smith, J.R., Chang, S.F.: Single color extraction and image query. In: 1995 Proceedings of International Conference on Image Processing, vol. 3, pp. 528–531. IEEE, October 1995
5. Nasrabadi, N.M.: Pattern recognition and machine learning. J. Electron. Imaging **16**(4), 049901 (2007)
6. Chong, W., Blei, D., Li, F.F.: Simultaneous image classification and annotation. In: IEEE Conference on Computer Vision and Pattern Recognition. CVPR 2009, pp. 1903–1910. IEEE, June 2009

Recognition and Counting of Motorcycles by Fusing Support Vector Machine and Deep Learning

Tzung-Pei Hong[1,2]([⊠]), Yu-Chiao Yang[1], Ja-Hwung Su[3], and Shyue-Liang Wang[4]

[1] Department of Computer Science and Information Engineering, National University of Kaohsiung, Kaohsiung, Taiwan
tphong@nuk.edu.tw
[2] Department of Computer Science and Engineering, National Sun Yat-Sen University, Kaohsiung, Taiwan
[3] Department of Information Management, Cheng Shiu University, Kaohsiung, Taiwan
[4] Department of Information Management, National University of Kaohsiung, Kaohsiung, Taiwan

Abstract. In recent years, rapid growth of motorcycles enables a large number of traffic accidents. Hence, how to manage the traffic flow has been a hot topic. In this paper, we propose a method for recognizing and counting the motorcycles by integrating the support vector machine (SVM) and convolutional neural network (CNN). In this work, the CNN is first adopted to generate the implicit features, and then the SVM is trained based on the implicit features and tested for unknown images. The experimental results reveal the proposed method can achieve low error rates in counting motorcycles.

Keywords: Convolutional neural network · Support vector machine · Motorcycle counting · Motorcycle recognition

1 Introduction

An important reason leading to traffic accidents is that the lanes on a road are usually not wide enough, such that many motorcycles and cars congest on the lanes. Therefore, how to make an effective management of traffic flow has been a challenging issue. Currently, there have been many researches in car detection and they achieve good performances. Compared with car detection, motorcycles are more difficult to detect because there are different numbers of people on motorcycles, and their shapes are not as regular as cars. In this paper, we propose a method that recognizes and counts the motorcycles automatically. First, the motorcycle images are used to train the Convolutional Neural Network (CNN) for building a classification model. This process can extract implicit features of motorcycle by the CNN model. Next, the Support Vector Machine is performed to recognize and count the motorcycles using the implicit features. The experimental results show that, our proposed method is very effective on recognizing and counting the motorcycles in terms of error rate. The remaining of this

© Springer Nature Singapore Pte Ltd. 2019
C.-Y. Chang et al. (Eds.): ICS 2018, CCIS 1013, pp. 157–162, 2019.
https://doi.org/10.1007/978-981-13-9190-3_15

paper is organized as follows: the previous work on is briefly reviewed in Sect. 2. Section 3 presents the proposed method on how to recognize and count of motorcycles in detail. The empirical study on a real dataset is shown in Sect. 4 and conclusions are mentioned in Sect. 5.

2 Related Work

Although there are many approaches about vehicle detecting, these approaches still encounter some problems. First, the induction loop approach buries a metal loop detector under the road surface [3]. When the vehicle passes, the traffic flow of the lane can be measured by the change of the electromagnetic field. Through two loop detectors, the length and speed of the vehicle are obtained by using the time difference. Then the category of the vehicle is judged. The setup of this type approaches needs to close the lane for a long time. It cannot be used in a hard traffic environment. In addition to induction loop, the ultrasonic vehicle detector uses the ultrasonic sensors to erect above the road [5]. The difference of ultrasonic reflection time can be used to detect the traffic flow of the lane. However, the equipment of the ultrasonic sensor is hard to maintain and the cost is very high. Another well-known method is Global Positioning System (GPS). GPS can get the position of the vehicle on the road immediately. Some applications, such as Google Maps use GPS to get real time traffic information. However, there is no GPS in most of vehicles. Also GPS may not detect vehicles very accurately on the road. And, privacy issue may appear in the GPS. That is, most people do not share their traces without authorized. To solve the above problems, in this paper, we propose an auto-counting method by integrating Deep Learning and SVM. The Convolutional Neural Networks (CNN) is a kind of Deep Learning. A CNN consists of convolution layers, pooling layers and fully-connected layers [6]. CNN is employed in many applications, such as speech recognition [10], and image recognition [4]. This is why we adopt CNN as the base of the proposed method. Another machine learning method adopted in this paper is SVM, which is shown to be successful in many fields [7, 8] of object recognition.

3 Proposed Method

In this paper, we propose a method for auto-counting of motorcycles to reach the goal of effective auto-management of traffic flow. In this method, the implicit features are first extracted by CNN and then the SVM is performed to train the classification model. SVM is used to classify each region by the features extracted by the last Convolutional layer. The framework of the proposed approach is described in Fig. 1, which can be divided into two phases including offline training and online counting. For offline training, it can be viewed as two-stage learning. In the first stage, we use the standard CNN model with convolution layers, pooling layers, and fully-connected networks to train the classification model of a single motorcycle. The images of single motorcycle for training the model came from the datasets collected by California Institute of Technology [1] and surveillance video in the Ho Chi Minh City [2]. Each image in the dataset is resized into the input size for the adopted CNN. The adopted CNN model, which includes 6 convolution layers, 3 max-pooling layers and a fully-connected layer with 3 hidden layers.

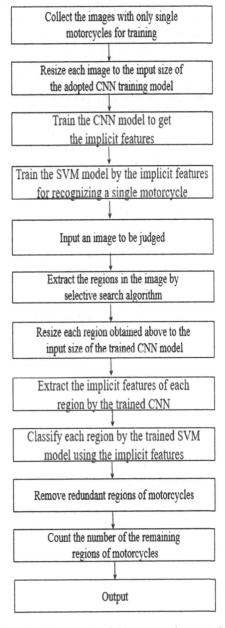

Fig. 1. Framework of the proposed approach.

Each two convolution layers are accompanied with a pooling layer. There are two final output nodes at the end of the CNN. One represents the true class if containing a motorcycle and the other denotes the false class if no motorcycle is contained. After the training, the outputs in the last pooling layer are extracted as the feature sets. Next, the implicit features are extracted by the last pooling layer. The size of the last pooling layer is m × n × p, which is then transformed into a one-dimension vector, acting as the input of the SVM. Then, the SVM model is constructed by the images with the implicit features for recognizing a single motorcycle.

For online counting, first, we use the selective search algorithm [9] to generate the regions from an image. Each region represents an object in the image. We can use these regions in an image to determine whether they are motorcycles or not. Second, resize each region to the input size of the trained CNN model. Third, extract the implicit features using the trained CNN model. Fourth, classify each region with the trained SVM using the implicit features. Fifth, remove redundant regions of motorcycles. Note that, since the regions may overlap when we use the rectangle boxes to represent objects, a motorcycle may be located in more than one bounding boxes. Thus, the redundant bounding boxes are necessary to be removed for incorrect counting. We use the intersection over union (IoU) to measure the overlap degree of two regions. The IoU value is denoted in Eq. (1), where A and B denote two different regions:

$$IoU(A, B) = \frac{A \cap B}{A \cup B} \tag{1}$$

If the measure value of two regions is larger than the overlapping threshold, then the two regions are recognized as redundant ones and the one with the smaller CNN output score is removed.

4 Experiments

4.1 Experimental Settings

There are two datasets used in the experiments. The first dataset was collected by students at California Institute of Technology from the Web [1]. The dataset contains 826 images of a single motorcycle from the side. The second dataset was generated by a six-minute surveillance video in the Ho Chi Minh City [2], which is one of the cities with high motorcycle density in the world. 1500 image frames were extracted from the videos and each image is setting as the original size of 1706*959. From each original image, we cut and got a sub-image of size 500*250. Therefore 700 motorcycle sub-images were determined finally. Then, 700 images were labeled a number of the motorcycles quantity, where the number is viewed as a category in CNN and SVM. In the experiments, one of the evaluation measures is error-rate in motorcycle counting, which is defined as:

$$\text{error rate} = \begin{cases} \frac{|A-P|}{A}, & \text{if } A \neq 0 \\ P, & \text{if } A = 0 \end{cases}, \tag{2}$$

Where P is the predicted number of the motorcycles and A is the actual number of motorcycles.

4.2   Experimental Results

In the evaluation, the error rate under different IoU thresholds is shown in Fig. 2. From Fig. 2, we can know that the best result for error rate is 0.17, which says that the proposed method can achieve an acceptable error rate on recognition and counting of motorcycles.

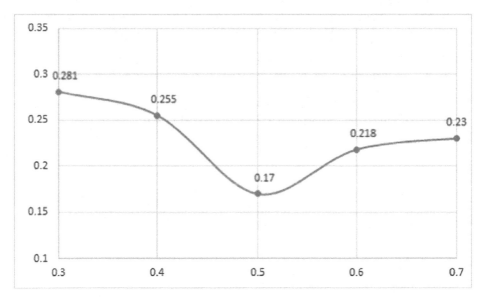

Fig. 2.   The counting error rate with different IoU thresholds.

5   Conclusions and Future Work

The goal of this paper is to achieve an effective method for auto-counting of motorcycles. To reach this goal, in this paper, the CNN are used to generate the conceptual features and thereupon the SVM is performed to recognize and count motorcycles automatically. To reveal the effectiveness of the proposed method, two measures including error rate and accuracy are employed. From the experimental results, we can obtain that, the CNN model provide SVM with a good support in motorcycle counting. In the future, we will apply the proposed approach to real applications in different environments such as weather and illumination (day or night).

References

1. http://www.vision.caltech.edu/html-files/archive.html
2. https://www.youtube.com/watch?v=Op1hdgzmhXM
3. https://en.wikipedia.org/w/index.php?title=Induction_loop&oldid=826349762
4. Connie, T., Al-Shabi, M., Cheah, W.P., Goh, M.: Facial expression recognition using a hybrid CNN–SIFT aggregator. In: Phon-Amnuaisuk, S., Ang, S.-P., Lee, S.-Y. (eds.) MIWAI 2017. LNCS (LNAI), vol. 10607, pp. 139–149. Springer, Cham (2017). https://doi.org/10.1007/978-3-319-69456-6_12
5. Hu, Y., Huber, A., Anumula, J., Liu, S.: Overcoming the vanishing gradient problem in plain recurrent networks. In: Proceedings of 6th International Conference on Learning Representations (2018)
6. Krizhevsky, A., Sutskever, I., Hinton, G.E.: Imagenet classification with deep convolutional neural networks. In: Proceedings of the 25th International Conference on Neural Information Processing Systems (2012)
7. Mukhtar, A., Tang, T.B.: Vision based motorcycle detection using hog features. In: Proceeding of 2015 IEEE International Conference on Signal and Image Processing Applications (2015)
8. Silva, R., Aires, K., Santos, T., Abdala, K., Veras, R., Soares, A.: Automatic detection of motorcyclists without helmet. In: Proceeding of 2013 XXXIX Latin American Computing Conference (2013)
9. Uijlings, J.R.R., van de Sande, K.E.A., Gevers, T., Smeulders, A.W.M.: Selective search for object recognition. Int. J. Comput. Vis. **104**(2), 154–171 (2013)
10. Zhang, Y., et al.: Towards end-to-end speech recognition with deep convolutional neural networks. Interspeech, pp. 410–414 (2016)

An Efficient Event Detection Through Background Subtraction and Deep Convolutional Nets

Kahlil Muchtar[1,2]([email]), Faris Rahman[1],
Muhammad Rizky Munggaran[1], Alvin Prayuda Juniarta Dwiyantoro[1],
Richard Dharmadi[1], Indra Nugraha[1], and Chuan-Yu Chang[3]

[1] Nodeflux, Jakarta, Indonesia
kahlil@nodeflux.io
[2] Department of Electrical and Computer Engineering,
Syiah Kuala University, Banda Acch, Aceh, Indonesia
[3] Department of Computer Science and Information Engineering,
National Yunlin University of Science and Technology, Yunlin, Taiwan

Abstract. The smart transportation system is one of the most essential parts in a smart city roadmap. The smart transportation applications are equipped with CCTV to recognize a region of interest through automated object detection methods. Usually, such methods require high-complexity image classification techniques and advanced hardware specification. Therefore, the design of low-complexity automated object detection algorithms becomes an important topic in this area. A novel technique is proposed to detect a moving object from the surveillance videos based on CPU (central processing units). We use this method to determine the area of the moving object(s). Furthermore, the area will be processed through a deep convolutional nets-based image classification in GPU (graphics processing units) in order to ensure high efficiency and accuracy. It cannot only help to detect object rapidly and accurately, but also can reduce big data volume needed to be stored in smart transportation systems.

Keywords: Background subtraction · Deep convolutional nets · Smart city

1 Introduction

In practice, the cloud computing based smart transportation applications face significant challenges. Although they require real-time object detection, transferring the massive amount of raw full frame data to cloud centers not only leads to uncertainty in timing but also poses extra workload to the communication networks [1, 2].

Related to this problem, this research aims to accelerate this process by comprehensively considering both algorithm design and implementation. For algorithm design, a block texture-based approach is chosen for the determination of moving object areas. For algorithm implementation, a deep convolutional nets is parallelized on modern graphics processing units (GPU) to improve the recognition efficiency.

C.-Y. Chang et al. (Eds.): ICS 2018, CCIS 1013, pp. 163–167, 2019.
https://doi.org/10.1007/978-981-13-9190-3_16

The most relevant related work is proposed by Kim et al. [3] which introduces a hybrid framework to detect the moving person rapidly. The method utilizes a GMM background subtraction to find the region of interest (ROI) [4]. However, the GMM is prone to noise and very sensitive to illumination changes. In our preliminary work, we aim to leverage a block texture-based foreground extraction as a new ROI extractor. Finally, the obtained ROI will feed the deep convolutional nets to classify objects more efficient and accurate. Our proposed system might be useful as a surveillance system, which has a strict hardware and network specification in the end-user side.

2 Proposed Method

2.1 ROI Extractor

Our proposed model is based on the model uses a non-overlapping block to extract the foreground (FG) [5]. The initial step is to divide the current frame into n x n non-overlapping blocks. The process converts each block into a binary bitmap. When a new observed bitmap, BM_{obs}, comes in, it will be compared against the several numbers of weights BG model BM_{mod}, where the total number of weights is set as parameter K in the algorithm. From [5], we only perform the 1-bit mode due to its efficiency.

$$Dist(BM_{obs}, BM_{mod}) = \sum_{i=1}^{n} \sum_{j=1}^{n} (b_{ij}^{obs} \oplus b_{ij}^{mod}) \tag{1}$$

The corresponding frame rate for original GMM (before post-processing) [4] and 1-bit mode [5] are about 30 and 62 frames/second, respectively. For clarity purposes, we draw the detailed step of ROI generation in Fig. 1.

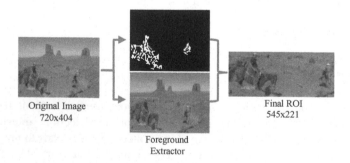

Original Image
720x404

Foreground
Extractor

Final ROI
545x221

Fig. 1. Illustration of ROI generation

2.2 Deep Detector

To achieve our goal to design a real-time unified technique, we select YOLO as a deep detector. YOLO [6, 7], a state-of-the-art detection method, which first divides an image into grid cells. It then performs the prediction of the coordinates of bounding boxes and the probabilities of each cell. Every bounding boxes have their own confidence score, which is calculated by aggregating the probabilities. Therefore, a smaller number of grid cells of an incoming frame, faster detection will be (Fig. 2).

Fig. 2. The complete proposed workflow system

3 Experimental Results

In this section, we discuss a public datasets in order to evaluate the entire proposed system. The dataset is UCF-Sports dataset [8, 9] that provides several sports actions, for example, people riding a horse, walking, diving, etc.

3.1 UCF-Sports Dataset: Riding-Horse and Walk-Front

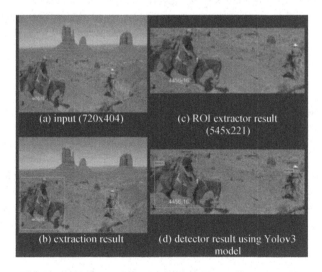

Fig. 3. UCF-Sports Dataset: Riding-Horse (frame no: 23)

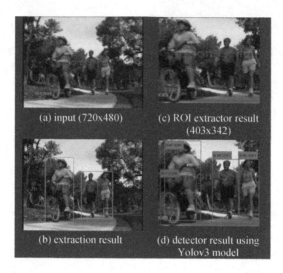

Fig. 4. UCF-Sports Dataset: Walk-Front (frame no: 49)

3.2 Frame Rate and Confidence Scores

In Table 1, we provide confidence scores for all tested videos. The detection uses a common Yolov3 model, which is publicly available [6]. As depicted below, the scores represent the corresponding bounding boxes from Figs. 3 and 4. In Table 2, we evaluate the frame rate comparison. In [3], Kim et al. tested 64 × 64 pixels of the input frame, and the entire framework achieved 15 fps on an NVIDIA Tesla M40. Our workflow yields a significant improvement in terms of frame rate that achieve ∼16,62 fps for relatively higher input size on an NVIDIA GTX 1050 Ti. Both devices are equipped with 12 GB memory size.

Table 1. Confidence scores of Figs. 3 and 4.

Frame no.	Datasets	Confidence scores using Yolov3 model
23	UCF-Sports (riding-horse)	horse: 97%, person: 93%, horse: 53%, person: 96%
49	UCF-Sports (walk-front)	bicycle: 99%, person: 100%, person: 100%, person: 100%

Table 2. Representative frame rate comparison.

	Yolov3 model (80 object classes)	Our vehicle model (24 object classes)
Entire-frame detection	14,74 frames/sec	22,02 frames/sec
ROI-based event detection	**16,62** frames/sec	**24,57** frames/sec

4 Conclusions

In this paper, we introduced an approach for low-cost smart transportation application. It was thoroughly evaluated that incorporating an ROI robust extractor and efficient deep learning is beneficial for a light and real-time smart system.

References

1. Xu, R., et al.: Real-time human objects tracking for smart surveillance at the edge. In: IEEE International Conference on Communications (ICC) 2018, Kansas City, MO, USA (2018)
2. Zheng, R., Yao, C., Jin, H., Zhu, L., Zhang, Q., Deng, W.: Parallel key frame extraction for surveillance video service in a smart city. PLoS ONE **10**, e0135694 (2015)
3. Kim, C., Lee, J., Han, T., Kim, Y.-M.: A hybrid framework combining background subtraction and deep neural networks for rapid person detection. J. Big Data **5**, 22 (2018)
4. Stauffer, C., Grimson, W.E.L.: Adaptive background mixture models for real-time tracking. In: IEEE Computer Society Conference on Computer Vision and Pattern Recognition, New York, pp. 246–252 (1999)
5. Yeh, C.-H., Lin, C.-Y., Muchtar, K., Kang, L.-W.: Real-time background modeling based on a multi-level texture description. Inf. Sci. **269**, 106–127 (2014)
6. Redmon, J., Farhadi, A.: YOLO9000: better, faster, stronger. In: IEEE Conference on Computer Vision and Pattern Recognition (CVPR) 2017, Honolulu, HI, USA, pp. 6517–6525 (2017)
7. Redmon, J., Divvala, S., Girshick, R., Farhadi, A.: You only look once: unified, real-time object detection. In: IEEE Conference on Computer Vision and Pattern Recognition (CVPR), Las Vegas, NV, USA, pp. 779–788 (2016)
8. Rodriguez, M.D., Ahmed, J., Shah, M.: Action MACH: a spatio-temporal maximum average correlation height filter for action recognition. In: IEEE Conference on Computer Vision and Pattern Recognition (CVPR 2008), Anchorage, AK, USA (2008)
9. Soomro, K., Zamir, A.R.: Action recognition in realistic sports videos. In: Moeslund, T.B., Thomas, G., Hilton, A. (eds.) Computer Vision in Sports. ACVPR, pp. 181–208. Springer, Cham (2014). https://doi.org/10.1007/978-3-319-09396-3_9

Light-Weight DCNN for Face Tracking

Jiali Song[1], Yunbo Rao[1(✉)], Puzhao Ji[1], Jiansu Pu[2], and Keyang Chen[3]

[1] School of Information and Software Engineering,
University of Electronic Science and Technology of China,
Chengdu, China
uestc2008@126.com

[2] School of Computer Science and Engineering,
University of Electronic Science and Technology of China, Chengdu, China
jiansu.pu@uestc.edu.cn

[3] School of Computer Science and Telecommunications Engineering,
Jianshu University, Zhenjiang, China
kycheng@ujs.edu.cn

Abstract. Face tracking methods are increasingly critical for many expression mapping analysis applications, along its research track, deep convolutional neural network (DCNN-based) search techniques have attracted broad interests due to their high efficiency in 3D feature points. In this paper, we focus on the problem of 3D feature point's extraction and expression mapping using a light-weight deep convolutional neural network (LW-DCNN) search and data conversion model, respectively. Specifically, we proposed novel light-weight deep convolutional neural network for 3D feature point's extraction to solve the great initial shape errors in regression cascaded framework and the slow processing speed in traditional CNN. Furthermore, an effective data conversion model is proposed to generate the deformation coefficient to realize the expression mapping. Extensive experiments on several benchmark image databases validate the superiority of the proposed approaches.

Keywords: LW-DCNN · Face tracking · Expression mapping ·
3D feature extraction

1 Introduction

The face tracking technology is a quite active research field in the area of computer graphics, which is a process of mapping the expression of a face to another faces. With the gradual maturity of the hardware device processing capabilities, face tracking technology began to be used in many areas [1], such as internet

Supported by the Fundamental Research Funds for the Central Universities of China (No. A03013023001050, No. ZYGX2016J095). Natural Science Foundation of Sichuan (No. 2017JY0229). CERNET Innovation Project (NGII20170805). National Natural Science Foundation of China (Grant Nos. 61502083 and 61872066).

© Springer Nature Singapore Pte Ltd. 2019
C.-Y. Chang et al. (Eds.): ICS 2018, CCIS 1013, pp. 168–177, 2019.
https://doi.org/10.1007/978-981-13-9190-3_17

social scenes, the virtual avatar modeling, and the film-making, etc. Face tracking technology mainly contains two aspects: facial feature point's extraction, expression mapping. However, the current feature extraction algorithm is difficult to balance the accuracy and speed, especially 3D feature, for instance, handling with deflection angles faces. This paper aims at improving the 3D feature extraction of complex faces to achieve the tracking effect of subtle expressions.

The accuracy of extracted feature points directly affects the authenticity of subsequent facial expression mapping. Dollár [2] presented a traditional conventional cascaded regression, it constructs an initial shape, and then gradually optimizing the initial shape by training several weak repressors, the framework is highly dependent on the initial shape. If the initial shape and the target shape differ greatly, the subsequent optimization of the regressor will also result in large positioning deviations. To solve this problem, Lai et al. [3] designed a network structure which consists of a global layer and multi-stage local layers, the global layer estimates the initial shape through the global image features, then refining the estimated shape by local layers. Compared with the conventional cascade regression, it decreases the prediction bias indeed, but cannot avoid the deviation that the initial shape estimation may bring. Besides, deep learning is effective method for facial feature extraction. In order to enhance the accuracy of extraction results, the traditional convolutional neural networks focus on building deeper and more complex networks, which results in excessive model size and slow running speed [4]. To improve these limitations, we propose a lightweight non-linear convolutional deep neural network to achieve the 3D feature extraction. The proposed network based on the Depthwise Separable Convolution (DSC) structure [5] which decomposes the convolution kernel of the standard convolutional network into a deep convolution and a point convolution to compress the model size and improves the speed and accuracy.

Due to the rich and complexity of facial expression, the difficulty of mapping from faces to avatars is enhanced, where the exactitude of facial data process directly affects the authenticity of the final results. Stoiber et al. [6] presented a method that combines the parameter-based animation method and the performance-based animation method to realize an animation system, but the system just simply animated so that the expression mapping result is lack of authenticity. Parakash et al. [7] developed a 3D facial animation system, it reflects the expression of a 2D image on a 3D facial avatar by facial feature points, and however, these feature points are manually marked by users and cannot reflect the facial expression adequately. To solve these problems, we mark the feature points by a light-weight DCNN algorithms and process the points to deformation coefficient by an effective data conversion method to control the expression change of avatars. In this paper, we propose a high-efficiency face tracking method based on 3D feature point's extraction and expression mapping. In summary, our paper makes the following contributions:

(1) Our network structure focus on DSC to realize the 3D feature extraction which improves the operate speed, reduces the model size and guarantees the feature accuracy of deflection angles faces. Meanwhile, in order to avoid the reliance on the initial shape, entire face images are used as input images.

(2) An effective data conversion method is used to generate correspond defor-
    mation coefficient that the avatars can discern, and realize the expression
    tracking.

2   The Proposed Method

In this paper, we present an effective face expression tracking method based on
the DCS structure to realize the expression mapping from users to the avatars.
Our Light-weight DCNN is used for 3D feature extraction. Then, the expression
mapping method will be described for face tracking. The whole process is as
follows: inputting a face through the webcam and extracting the 3D face feature points by our trained network, then converting the extracted 3D feature
to deformation coefficient by our data conversion model and last applying the
coefficient to avatar. The overview of our method is shown in Fig. 1.

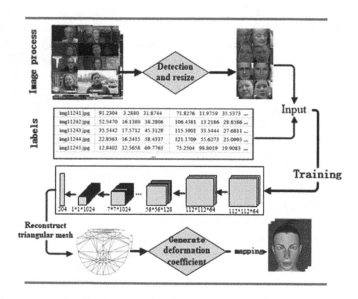

Fig. 1. The overview of our algorithm

2.1   The Depthwise Separable Convolution

Traditional face alignment mostly adopts the cascade regression algorithm [8].
First, an initial shape needs to be constructed, and then the initial face gradually
approximates the real face shape by several weak regressors of linear combination. The main drawback of this algorithm is that once the initial shape is greatly
different with the ground truth, the subsequent work will produce a huge deviation. Common convolution neural network has a good performance in this field,
however, its huge size and slow running speed make it difficult to be used in
mobile devices.

The DSC structure is very popular by its high running speed and high precision [5], as shown in Fig. 2, it decomposes the standard convolution into a depth wise convolution which applies each convolution kernel to each channel and a dot convolution (1 * 1 convolution kernel) which combines the output of the channel convolution. This decomposition can reduce the complexity of model effectively. Assuming M is the number of input channels, N is the number of output channels, and DF is the spatial width and height of a square input feature map. The time complexity of standard convolution is $D_k \cdot D_k \cdot M \cdot N \cdot D_F \cdot D_F$, and the decomposed convolution is $D_k \cdot D_k \cdot M \cdot D_F \cdot D_F + M \cdot N \cdot D_F \cdot D_F$. And then, it can be described as Eq. (1) that the DSC structure can greatly reduce the computational time complexity.

$$\frac{D_k \cdot D_k \cdot M \cdot D_F \cdot D_F + M \cdot N \cdot D_F \cdot D_F}{D_k \cdot D_k \cdot M \cdot N \cdot D_F \cdot D_F} = \frac{1}{N} + \frac{1}{D_K^2} \tag{1}$$

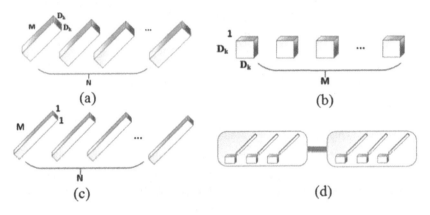

Fig. 2. The standard convolutional filters [5] in (a) are replaced by two layers: depth wise convolution in (b) and point wise convolution in (c), (d) is the final convolutional filters.

2.2 Light-Weight DCNN for 3D Feature Extraction

Since our final goal is to achieve the expression mapping from face to 3D avatar, this paper we proposed a new face alignment method based on light-weight deep convolution neural network framework. The key points is that we applied the DSC structure to our network to locate the 3D feature points, the experimental result proves our method is much faster under the premise of guaranteeing accuracy.

Our network body architecture is shown in Fig. 3. Assuming input a face image I with a height of h and a width w. The first layer is a standard convolution with 64 convolution kernel which convolves I to $(h/2) \times (w/2) \times 64$ feature size with stride 2. The second layer is a combination of depth wise convolution and a dot convolution, iterating 11 layers to make the feature maps more precise

Type / Stride	Filter Shape	Input Size	Type / Stride	Filter Shape	Input Size
Conv / s2	3×3×5×64	224×224×3	Conv / s1	1×1×256×256	28×28×256
Conv dw / s1	3×3×64 dw	112×112×64	Conv dw/ s2	3×3×256 dw	28×28×256
Conv / s1	1×1×64×64	112×112×64	Conv / s1	1×1×256×512	14×14×256
Conv dw / s2	3×3×64 dw	112×112×64	5 × Conv dw/ s1	3×3×512 dw	14×14×512
Conv / s1	1×1×64×128	56×56×64	Conv / s1	1×1×512×512	14×14×512
Conv dw / s1	3×3×128 dw	56×56×128	Conv dw/ s2	3×3×512 dw	14×14×512
Conv / s1	1×1×128×128	56×56×128	Conv / s1	1×1×512×1024	7×7×512
Conv dw / s1	3×3×128 dw	56×56×128	Avg Pool / s1	Pool 7×7	7×7×1024
Conv / s1	1×1×128×256	28×28×128	FC / s1	1024×204	1×1×1024
Conv dw / s2	3×3×256 dw	28×28×256	Softmax / s1	Classifier	1×1×204

Fig. 3. Our network body architecture

as $(h/32) \times (w/32) \times 1024$. Next, an average pooling layer compress the feature maps to 111024 with stride m to extract the primary features. To extract the 3D coordinate of 68 face points, we set the neurons number of the full connection (FC) layer to 204, finally, the FC layer and a Softmax layer realize the classification and output of 68 3D feature points.

Considering the speed of reading and processing pictures, and the accuracy of feature extraction, a bounding box is detect for each images before inputting it into the network, then the bounding box is resized as 48×48. Meanwhile, the dataset is handled accordingly, z is unchanged, x and y coordinates are reduced proportionately as follows Eqs. (2) and (3):

$$h\_r = 48/h, \quad w\_r = 48/w \tag{2}$$

$$new\_x = x * h, \quad new\_y = y * w\_r \tag{3}$$

Where h_r refers to the compression ratio of image height, w_r refers to the compression ratio of width, new_x and new_y refer to the compressed x and y respectively.

To evaluate the error between the output coordinates and the ground truth, this paper adopts the smooth L1 function as the loss function, as follows:

$$loss\,(x_i, y_i) = \begin{cases} \frac{1}{2}\,(x_i - y_i)^2, if\,|x_i - y_i| < 1 \\ |x_i - y_i| - \frac{1}{2}, otherwise \end{cases} \tag{4}$$

The function error is square loss on $(-1, 1)$, and the other case is L1 loss. After training a large number of data, the model effectively completes the extraction of 68 3D feature points.

2.3 Expression Mapping for Face Tracking

After extracting the 3D facial feature points, it is time to map the data to avatars. In this paper, we achieve map by an effective data conversion model which transfer the common 3D data to deformation coefficient.

We adopt a feed forward neural network to complete the conversion, which is inspired by Kim's method [9]. The network uses the Euclidean distances between

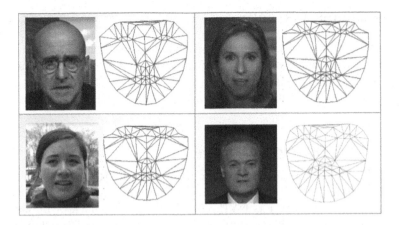

Fig. 4. The extracted feature points location and the corresponding delaunay triangulation

the vertices in the triangular mesh constructed by S as input data, where S is the collection of 68 3D feature points extracted from our light-weight DNN. To generate the input data, as shown in Fig. 4, we improved **Delaunay** triangulation algorithm to reconstruct a face into a triangular mesh, the process is described as follows:

Algorithm 1 The construction of triangular mesh

Step1: construct the triangle T which containing all points,
$S = \{s1, s2, \ldots sn\}, 1 \leq n \leq 68$
Step2:for i=1 to 68,do(Insert(T(s1,s2,s3,...,si-1),si)),remove the common side of T;
Step3: optimizing the triangles, return T (s1, s2, s3, s68).

Next, it's time to compute the Euclidean distances between these vertices in M. Since our vertices are 3D coordinates, the formula is as (5). Calculating the distances between the adjacent vertices in M iteratively to get the input dataset.

$$\rho = \sqrt{(x_i - x_j)^2 + (y_i - y_j)^2 + (z_i - z_j)^2}, 0 \leq i, j \leq 68 \qquad (5)$$

Where i, j are two adjacent vertices numbers in M, xi, yi, zi and xj, yj, zj are the 3D coordinates of vertices si and sj respectively.

Ultimately, inputting the **dataset** to the feed forward neural network, through a hidden layer and a linear output layer to generate the blendshape coefficient. Meanwhile, we complete the expression mapping process by reading the coefficient files.

3   Experimental Results

In this section, a face tracking method was implemented on a PC with an Intel Core i7-6700 CPU and a webcam as input device (recording 640480 images at 30 fps). We will analysis light-weight DCNN-based for face tracking method from two aspect: 3D feature point's extraction and expression mapping of face tracking.

3.1   3D Feature Extraction Analysis

We train the network under the Pytorch framework [10] which provides the Tensor **supporting** CPU and GPU that can greatly accelerate computation, and the graphics card driver is NVIDIA 387. Due to the lack of published 3D face dataset, we make 3D face dataset for our experiment. About generating the 3D coordinates, we compared several methods, then choose a method called Open face [11] which is more accurate than current methods. Ultimately, we download 100 videos containing human faces on YouTuBe and mark the 3D feature coordinates of the faces in videos, meanwhile, cutting the videos into a single picture per frame by Opencv, the 3D coordinates are divided by frame as well. At last, tens of thousands pictures and their corresponding labels are obtained. Figure 5 is the partial faces display of our dataset. This paper selects people of different ages from different nations in different scenes, and the facial expression in the videos are rich enough so that the trained network has strong robustness.

Fig. 5. Partial faces display of the dataset

In the training stage, to enhance the effect of network training, we first detect the bounding boxes of every training image by the Funnel-Structured Cascade(FuSt) face detector [12]. The detector contains three layers: fast LAB cascade, coarse MLP cascade, and fine MLP cascade, which detects face fast and accuracy, as shown in Fig. 6.

Fig. 6. Partial faces display of the dataset

Besides, this paper divides dataset to training set and validation set according to the ratio of 7:3, more than 20 thousand images and their labels are used to train our network. Due to the large amount of data, all training samples is divided into 512 every batch, each training the epoch value is set to 20 and every 5 epoch saves one model. After several training cycles, multiple models would be generated, we validate each model generated by validation set, then adjusting parameters, training and validating model once again until the optimal model is obtained, where weight decay is adjusted to 1e-4, learning rate is 1e-3, learning rate decay is 0.95.

Different from most of the CNN models with large model size, our model size is lower than 10M, which is very suitable for mobile devices. Besides, the FPS value of our method is around 200. We compute the Normalized Error (NE) of our method, the result is shown as Fig. 7, the X-axis is the normalized error value, and the Y-axis refers to the ratio of feature points which are less than the NE, it can clearly be seen that the NE value of 80% frontal faces points are lower than 45%, the value of 80% slight defected faces points are lower than 55%, and the proportion of half-definition faces whose NE value lower than 50% is 62%, the ratio of large deflection angle faces whose NE value lower than 50% is 59%.

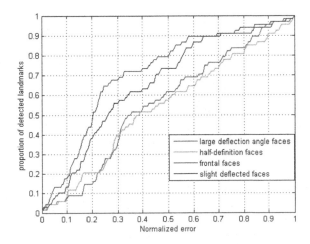

Fig. 7. The NE of four pose groups for our method

3.2   Expression Mapping Analysis

After the model is trained well, inputting a face by webcam into the model we can get the precise 3D feature points. Then, we realize the transformation from 3D coordinates to deformation coefficient, and putting the generated coefficient to achieve the mapping from common faces to avatars, as shown in Fig. 8, our method can even handle very subtle expressions.

According to the experimental results, our method enables the users to control the avatars' expression easily and the expression of avatars are authentic enough. The proposed method can be used for various application such as games, film production, office and social scene. Besides, our method can be used as an interface for other system invokes, such as intelligent dialogue system, telepresence system.

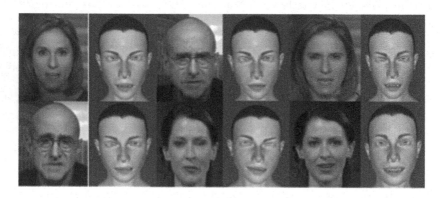

Fig. 8. The expression mapping results

4   Conclusion

To avoid the initial shape errors and the problem of model size and running speed, meanwhile solving the problem of 3D feature extraction, this paper we propose a light-weight DCNN network to extract the 3D feature points, obviously, we gain excellent results. Furthermore, we realize the face mapping process by data conversion model, which effectively transfer the expression data to avatars. In the future, we will focus on the gaze and head tracking.

References

1. Lee, Y.J., Lee, Y.J.: Face tracking for augmented reality game interface and brand placement. In: Kim, T., Adeli, H., Robles, R.J., Balitanas, M. (eds.) UCMA 2011. CCIS, vol. 151, pp. 72–78. Springer, Heidelberg (2011). https://doi.org/10.1007/978-3-642-20998-7_10
2. Dollár, P., Welinder, P., Perona, P.: Cascaded pose regression. In: IEEE Conference on Computer Vision and Pattern Recognition (CVPR), San Francisco, pp. 1078–1085 (2010)

3. Lai, H., Xiao, S., Cui, Z., Pan, Y., Xu, C.Y., Yan, S.C.: Deep cascaded regression for face alignment. arXiv:1510.09083v2 (2015)
4. Sun, Y., Wang, X., Tang, X.: Deep convolutional network cascade for facial point detection. In IEEE Conference on Computer Vision and Pattern Recognition (CVPR), Portland, pp. 3476–3483 (2013)
5. Chollet, F.: Xception: deep learning with depthwise separable convolutions. In: IEEE Conference on Computer Vision and Pattern Recognition (CVPR), Las Vegas, pp. 1800–1807 (2016)
6. Stoiber, N., Seguier, R., Breton, G.: Facial animation retargeting and control based on a human apperance space. Comput. Animation Virtual Worlds **21**, 39–54 (2010)
7. Parakash, K.G., Balasubramanian, S.: Facial animation retargeting and control based on a human appearance space. Comput. Animation Virtual Worlds **21**, 1–7 (2010)
8. Lee, D., Park, H., Chang, D.Y.: Face alignment using cascade Gaussian process regression trees. In: IEEE Conference on Computer Vision and Pattern Recognition (CVPR), Boston, pp. 4204–4212 (2015)
9. Kim, E., Moritz, C.: Enhancing the communication spectrum in collaborative virtual environments. In: Bebis, G., et al. (eds.) ISVC 2016. LNCS, vol. 10072, pp. 681–690. Springer, Cham (2016). https://doi.org/10.1007/978-3-319-50835-1_61
10. Paszke, A., Gross, S., Chintala, S.: Automatic differentiation in PyTorch. In: Advances in Neural Information Processing Systems, pp. 1–4 (2017)
11. Baltrusaitis, T., Robinson, P., Morency, L.P.: OpenFace: an open source facial behavior analysis toolkit. In: IEEE Winter Conference on Application of Computer Vision, pp. 1–10 (2016)
12. Kan, M., Shan, S.: Funnel-structured cascade for multi-view face detection with alignment-awareness. Neurocomputing, 138–145 (2017)

3D Facade Reconstruction Using the Fusion of Images and LiDAR: A Review

Haotian Xu$^{(\boxtimes)}$ (ID) and Chia-Yen Chen (ID)

Department of Computer Science, The University of Auckland,
Auckland 1010, New Zealand
hxu454@aucklanduni.ac.nz

Abstract. Three-dimensional (3D) urban reconstruction becomes increasingly crucial in many application areas, such as entertainment, urban planning, digital mapping. To achieve photorealistic 3D urban reconstruction, the detailed reconstruction of building facades is the key. Light Detection and Ranging (LiDAR) point clouds and images are the two most important data types for 3D urban reconstruction, which are complementary regarding data characteristic. LiDAR scans are sparse and noisy but contain the precise depth data, whereas images can offer the color and high-resolution data but no depth information. In recent years, an increasing number of studies show that the fusion of LiDAR point clouds and images can attain better 3D reconstruction results than a single data type. In this paper, we aim to provide a systematic review of the research in the area of the 3D facade reconstruction based on the fusion of LiDAR and images. The reviewed studies are classified by the different usage of images in the reconstruction process. We hope that this research could help future researchers have a more clear understanding of how existing studies leverage the data in LiDAR scans and images and promote more innovations in this area.

Keywords: Data fusion · Point cloud · Optical image · LiDAR · Urban reconstruction · Facade reconstruction · 3D reconstruction · Registration · Sensor fusion · Laser scanning

1 Introduction

Three-dimensional (3D) urban reconstruction is a significant topic with commercial and intellectual values [13], which has a great diversity of applications, such as traffic planning, visualization for navigation, virtual tours, utility management, civil engineering, and crisis management [2]. Therefore, in recent years, there is an increasing demand for the 3D reconstruction of photorealistic urban building models [21]. As building facades are the essential part of urban buildings, the detailed facade reconstruction is especially crucial for photorealistic 3D urban reconstruction.

© Springer Nature Singapore Pte Ltd. 2019
C.-Y. Chang et al. (Eds.): ICS 2018, CCIS 1013, pp. 178–185, 2019.
https://doi.org/10.1007/978-981-13-9190-3_18

Light Detection and Ranging (LiDAR) point clouds and images are the two main kinds of data used for 3D reconstruction. Many studies which aim at the automatic generation of 3D models based on LiDAR and photographs have been conducted in computer vision, photogrammetry, and computer graphics communities [20]. Nevertheless, images have a long history and are usually captured by different kinds of cameras, while the LiDAR point cloud is a new 3D data type [25]. LiDAR devices acquire the range data of target objects through the time-of-flight of lasers [4]. In general, LiDAR devices can be classified by resolution level. High-resolution LiDAR can generate dense point clouds but are slow and have small working volumes, while the low-resolution LiDAR is fast and easy to use but usually generate noisy and sparse data points [9]. In the last two decades, most of the studies for facade reconstruction are based on either of these two data types, including image-based methods [12,22,23], and LiDAR-based methods [5,15,18]. Typically, images have high resolution and color information but lack 3D data, while LiDAR point clouds have the demerits like noise, sparsity, and the lack of color information but naturally contain precise 3D data [20]. Thus, the characteristics of LiDAR point clouds and images are complementary. Moreover, an increasing number of researchers recently reported that the fusion of LiDAR scans and photographs could have a better performance in many different kinds of applications than a single data type [25].

There have already been a few surveys related to 3D urban reconstruction [3,7,13,19,20]. However, the systematic review for the studies on the facade reconstruction using the fusion of LiDAR data and images is still rare. Therefore, this paper aims to fill this research gap. In all the studies that we reviewed, we found that LiDAR point clouds are only used to reconstruct facade structures, but images can be used for different purposes. Therefore, we classify these studies into two groups by the different application purposes of images. The first category only uses images to texture the 3D model generated from LiDAR point clouds, while the second category uses images not only for texturing 3D facade models but also for assisting the reconstruction of facade structures in point clouds. In Tables 1 and 2, we provide a quick reference to the relevant studies of the two categories. In the rest of this paper, we will introduce the two classes of methods respectively.

Table 1. Methods only using 2D images for texturing.

Study	Reconstruction scale	Features used for 2D-3D registration
[16]	Individual building	Sets of 2D and 3D linear features
[17]	Individual building	Clusters of 3D and 2D linear features
[10]	Individual building	3D rectangular parallelepipeds and 2D rectangles
[11]	Individual building	2D and 3D linear features
[26]	City	Geo-referenced information
[6]	City	Pre-calibration of 2D and 3D sensors

Table 2. Using 2D images for texturing based on 2D-3D registration.

Study	Reconstruction scale	Approach to assisting the reconstruction of 3D facade structures
[24]	Individual building	Combining 2D and 3D facade linear features in 3D space
[14]	Individual building	Combining 2D and 3D facade linear features in 2D space and projecting the refined 2D linear feature back to 3D space
[9]	Individual building	Fusing 2D and 3D data to detect the main planes with different depth of facades
[1]	Individual building	Using 2D data to reconstruct 3D window crossbars
[8]	City	Fusing 2D and 3D data to determine the shape grammar of facades

2 Using Images Only for Texturing Process

In this group of studies, usually 3D facade structures are first generated from only the point cloud captured by LiDAR, and then the texture is mainly produced by the registration of 2D images and 3D point clouds. Usually, this kind of approaches utilizes high-resolution LiDAR to collect the depth data as LiDAR is the only data source used for reconstructing facade structures. This group of methods can be divided into two classes. The first category has no requirement that the relative position and orientation of the camera and LiDAR should be fixed, while the second category has such a requirement.

Both classes of methods have advantages and disadvantages. The first category of methods has the complete flexibility for capturing 2D and 3D data, which makes the captured data more complete in comparison with the second category of methods when the placement of 2D and 3D sensors are constrained by geographical conditions. However, this kind of methods may require different 2D-3D registration methods depending on different facade structure, which makes it relatively difficult to be applied to large-scale urban reconstruction. Therefore, the first kind of methods usually focuses on the reconstruction of individual buildings [10,11,16,17]. In contrast, since the relative position and orientation of 2D and 3D sensors are fixed, and 2D and 3D sensors are pre-calibrated, the registration of 2D and 3D data are quite easy for the second kind of methods. Thus, the second one is proper for large-scale urban reconstruction [6,26]. Nevertheless, for this kind of methods, the flexibility of the data capturing process and the completeness of data are sacrificed in some particular situations [11]. In the rest of this section, we will introduce the two classes of methods respectively.

2.1 Methods Using LiDAR and Cameras with Unfixed Relative Position and Orientation

[16] first proposes a method for the photorealistic reconstruction of urban buildings using unfixed LiDAR and cameras. The method mainly utilizes the corresponding linear features detected in both 2D and 3D data for 2D-3D registration. 3D linear features are extracted from the intersection of the planar regions segmented from point clouds, and 2D linear features are extracted by edge detection in images. Based on the registration result, 3D building models are textured by using 2D images. The authors then proposed another slightly different registration approach based on the clusters of 3D and 2D lines instead of the sets of 3D and 2D lines [17].

Based on the previous work [17], some updates were then made in [10]. One of the critical updates is that the clusters of the higher-level 3D and 2D features, i.e., the vertical or horizontal 3D rectangular parallelepipeds extracted from 3D point clouds and the 2D rectangles acquired from 2D images, are used for 2D-3D registration. The authors stated that the use of such higher-level features is because of the large search space which makes the matching of 3D individual lines and 2D individual lines almost impossible, and the inexistence of the corresponding 2D lines of some 3D lines in 2D data or the inexistence of some corresponding 3D lines of 2D lines in 3D data. However, the authors then proposed a new method for 2D-3D registration which utilizes only linear features instead of clusters of significantly grouped linear features [11]. This approach employs a more efficient algorithm for achieving the faster matching process of linear features.

2.2 Methods Using LiDAR and Cameras with Fixed Relative Position and Orientation

There are relatively few papers using rigidly mounted cameras and LiDAR for urban reconstruction. This kind of methods often is used for large-scale urban reconstruction. Generally, the methods use a car with rigidly mounted LiDAR and cameras to collect a large number of 2D and 3D data of urban environment. 3D facade models usually are first reconstructed by 3D point clouds. Then, the 3D models are textured by using geo-referenced information [26] or the pre-calibration of 2D and 3D sensors [6].

3 Using 2D Images for both Texturing Process and Assisting the Reconstruction of 3D Facade Structures

As mentioned before, the point clouds produced by LiDAR generally have problems including sparsity, noisiness, and missing data. Therefore, some other papers about the building facade reconstruction based on the fusion of LiDAR and images utilize 2D images to enhance 3D point clouds. Accurate facade features, like linear features, can be extracted from images and then used to consolidate the structure of 3D facade models [9,14,24]. Besides, images can provide the detailed information of facade elements which LiDAR can hardly capture, such as the crossbar of windows [1]. In addition, 2D images can also be used for texturing 3D facade models.

Linear features are the most significant component in the facade structure of many different kinds of buildings and can be relatively easily extracted from 2D images. [24] proposes a 3D reconstruction method for the building facade whose structure is mainly composed of straight lines. First, the pre-processing of the 3D point cloud and 2D image are executed for filtering the noise and outliers of the 3D data points, detecting the target building, and registering 3D point clouds and 2D images. Then, straight lines existing in facade structures are extracted from the 2D space of photographs and projected to the 3D space of LiDAR point clouds. Finally, these projected 3D lines are employed for consolidating the corresponding feature lines extracted in point clouds.

In [14], a similar method which also employs the linear features extracted from 2D images to refine the 3D facade model produced from LiDAR data is introduced. The main difference regarding the approach to 2D-3D fusion between the paper and [24] is the space used for matching and enhancing the linear features of facade structures. In [24], 2D linear features are projected to the 3D space to directly enhance the 3D linear features of the point cloud, whereas this approach projects 3D linear features to the 2D space for the matching and consolidation process. Thus, once the projected linear features are improved in the 2D space, they will be projected back to the 3D space for completing the 3D model.

Fig. 1. The generated depth-layers of a building facade (differently colored) [9].

2D images can enhance not only the linear features of 3D point clouds but also planar features. An approach to reconstructing the building facade with large-scale repetitions is introduced in [9]. The decomposition of the planes with different depths (depth-layers) of building facades in 2D images (Fig. 1) is the core of this method. This is achieved by assigning the depth values obtained from each part of facades in 3D point clouds to the corresponding part of facades in images. Once the depth-layers in 2D images are extracted, the self-symmetries in facade structures can be recognized and used for model texturing and handling the missing data in point clouds.

Furthermore, 2D images can be used to capture elements which may be missed out by the LiDAR since images usually have higher resolutions. In [1], terrestrial LiDAR scans and photographs are used to reconstruct the different levels of details of building facades. Since it is hard to capture the accurately detailed structure inside windows by using LiDAR, images are used for reconstructing the small structures inside windows like windows frames and windows crossbars.

Moreover, the fusion of images and LiDAR can be used for assisting the determination of a specific kind of facade style. This is another way to use images for assisting the reconstruction of facade structures. In [8], a workflow used for the automatic reconstruction of the 80% of buildings in the city of Graz, Austria is introduced. As Graz has plenty of different kinds of complex building styles, many grammar templates of building styles are pre-generated for guiding the feature detection. First, the fusion of images and LiDAR data are used to generate the grammar representation of facades. Then, the corresponding grammar template of a facade is found by matching its grammar representation against all the templates. In this research, the key to reconstructing building facades is to get the corresponding shape grammars by processing the combination of the detected features from orthophotos, the segmented plane regions from depth images, and the corresponding shape grammar template.

4 Conclusion

This paper presents a comprehensive systematic review of the research on the 3D facade reconstruction based on the fusion of LiDAR and images. It can be seen from our review that the fusion 2D and 3D sensors is able to reconstruct high-quality textured 3D building facade models. Also, most of the studies in the early stage of this area only utilize images for texturing purpose. However, most of the subsequent studies focus on using images for both the refinement of facade structures in 3D point clouds and the texturing process. We believe that this trend is reasonable and promising for the photorealistic 3D reconstruction of building facades.

Currently, most of the studies in this areas aim to reconstruct the building facades with regular or straightforward structures, such as the one mainly composed of straight line and planes. However, if the building facade which needs to be reconstructed contains more complicated structures, like the highly decorated neo-classical facades in [8], such direct reconstruction based on refinement and texturing would be quite challenging. Shape grammar is a potential solution for this kind of situation. However, this method is not efficient and generic, especially in the case that there are a large number of various elaborate building facades to be reconstructed. Hence, the primary challenge for this research area is how to leverage the rich color information in 2D images and the precise depth information in 3D LiDAR point clouds for achieving the balance between the quality and the efficiency of 3D facade reconstruction.

We hope that this paper can boost the future research on 3D facade reconstruction from different communities including remote sensing, computer vision, and computer graphics. Most of the challenges in this research area would be resolved by the improvement of both algorithms and hardware. Finally, with the increasing number of the applications of 3D urban reconstruction, we believe that this area will be increasingly crucial.

References

1. Becker, S., Haala, N.: Refinement of building fassades by integrated processing of LIDAR and image data. Int. Arch. Photogrammetry Remote Sens. Spat. Inf. Sci. **36**, 7–12 (2007)
2. Biljecki, F., Stoter, J., Ledoux, H., Zlatanova, S., Çöltekin, A.: Applications of 3D city models: state of the art review. ISPRS Int. J. Geo-Inf. **4**(4), 2842–2889 (2015). https://doi.org/10.3390/ijgi4042842
3. Brenner, C.: Building reconstruction from images and laser scanning. Int. J. Appl. Earth Obs. Geoinf. **6**(3), 187–198 (2005). https://doi.org/10.1016/j.jag.2004.10.006
4. Campbell, J.B., Wynne, R.H.: Introduction to Remote Sensing. Guilford Press, New York (2011)
5. Edum-Fotwe, K., Shepherd, P., Brown, M., Harper, D., Dinnis, R.: Fast, accurate and sparse, automatic facade reconstruction from unstructured ground laser-scans. In: ACM SIGGRAPH 2016 Posters, SIGGRAPH 2016, pp. 45:1–45:2. ACM, New York (2016). https://doi.org/10.1145/2945078.2945123
6. Fruh, C., Zakhor, A.: 3D model generation for cities using aerial photographs and ground level laser scans. In: Proceedings of the 2001 IEEE Computer Society Conference on Computer Vision and Pattern Recognition, CVPR 2001, vol. 2, p. II, December 2001. https://doi.org/10.1109/CVPR.2001.990921
7. Haala, N., Kada, M.: An update on automatic 3D building reconstruction. ISPRS J. Photogrammetry Remote Sens. **65**(6), 570–580 (2010). https://doi.org/10.1016/j.isprsjprs.2010.09.006
8. Hohmann, B., Krispel, U., Havemann, S., Fellner, D.: Cityfit-high-quality urban reconstructions by fitting shape grammars to images and derived textured point clouds. In: Proceedings of the 3rd ISPRS International Workshop 3D-ARCH, vol. 2009, p. 3D (2009)
9. Li, Y., Zheng, Q., Sharf, A., Cohen-Or, D., Chen, B., Mitra, N.J.: 2D–3D fusion for layer decomposition of urban facades. In: 2011 International Conference on Computer Vision, pp. 882–889, November 2011. https://doi.org/10.1109/ICCV.2011.6126329
10. Liu, L., Stamos, I.: Automatic 3D to 2D registration for the photorealistic rendering of urban scenes. In: 2005 IEEE Computer Society Conference on Computer Vision and Pattern Recognition (CVPR 2005), vol. 2, pp. 137–143, June 2005. https://doi.org/10.1109/CVPR.2005.80
11. Liu, L., Stamos, I.: A systematic approach for 2D-image to 3D-range registration in urban environments. In: 2007 IEEE 11th International Conference on Computer Vision, pp. 1–8, October 2007. https://doi.org/10.1109/ICCV.2007.4409215

12. Müller, P., Zeng, G., Wonka, P., Van Gool, L.: Image-based procedural modeling of facades. In: ACM SIGGRAPH 2007 Papers, SIGGRAPH 2007. ACM, New York (2007). https://doi.org/10.1145/1275808.1276484
13. Musialski, P., Wonka, P., Aliaga, D.G., Wimmer, M., Gool, L., Purgathofer, W.: A survey of urban reconstruction. Comput. Graph. Forum **32**(6), 146–177 (2013). https://doi.org/10.1111/cgf.12077
14. Pu, S., Vosselman, G.: Building facade reconstruction by fusing terrestrial laser points and images. Sensors **9**(6), 4525–4542 (2009). https://doi.org/10.3390/s90604525
15. Sadeghi, F., Arefi, H., Fallah, A., Hahn, M.: 3D building Façade reconstruction using handheld laser scanning data. Int. Arch. Photogrammetry Remote Sens. Spat. Inf. Sci. **40** (2015). https://doi.org/10.5194/isprsarchives-XL-1-W5-625-2015
16. Stamos, I., Allen, P.K.: 3-D model construction using range and image data. In: CVPR, p. 1531. IEEE (2000). https://doi.org/10.1109/CVPR.2000.855865
17. Stamos, I., Allen, P.K.: Automatic registration of 2-D with 3-D imagery in urban environments. In: Proceedings Eighth IEEE International Conference on Computer Vision, ICCV 2001, vol. 2, pp. 731–736, July 2001. https://doi.org/10.1109/ICCV.2001.937699
18. Wang, J., et al.: Automatic modeling of urban facades from raw lidar point data. Comput. Graph. Forum **35**(7), 269–278 (2016). https://doi.org/10.1111/cgf.13024
19. Wang, R., Peethambaran, J., Chen, D.: Lidar point clouds to 3-D urban models: a review. IEEE J. Sel. Top. Appl. Earth Obs. Remote Sens. **11**(2), 606–627 (2018). https://doi.org/10.1109/JSTARS.2017.2781132
20. Wang, R.: 3D building modeling using images and lidar: a review. Int. J. Image Data Fusion **4**(4), 273–292 (2013). https://doi.org/10.1080/19479832.2013.811124
21. Wang, R., Bach, J., Ferrie, F.P.: Window detection from mobile LIDAR data. In: 2011 IEEE Workshop on Applications of Computer Vision (WACV), pp. 58–65. IEEE (2011)
22. Xiao, J., Fang, T., Tan, P., Zhao, P., Ofek, E., Quan, L.: Image-based Façade modeling. ACM Trans. Graph. **27**(5), 161:1–161:10 (2008). https://doi.org/10.1145/1457515.1409114
23. Xiao, J., Fang, T., Zhao, P., Lhuillier, M., Quan, L.: Image-based street-side city modeling. ACM Trans. Graph. **28**(5), 114:1–114:12 (2009). https://doi.org/10.1145/1661412.1618460
24. Yang, L., Sheng, Y., Wang, B.: 3D reconstruction of building facade with fused data of terrestrial LIDAR data and optical image. Optik - Int. J. Light Electron Opt. **127**(4), 2165–2168 (2016). https://doi.org/10.1016/j.ijleo.2015.11.147
25. Zhang, J., Lin, X.: Advances in fusion of optical imagery and LiDAR point cloud applied to photogrammetry and remote sensing. Int. J. Image Data Fusion **8**(1), 1–31 (2017). https://doi.org/10.1080/19479832.2016.1160960
26. Zhao, H., Shibasaki, R.: Reconstructing a textured cad model of an urban environment using vehicle-borne laser range scanners and line cameras. Mach. Vis. Appl. **14**(1), 35–41 (2003). https://doi.org/10.1007/s00138-002-0099-5

An Application of Detecting Cryptomeria Damage by Squirrels Using Aerial Images

Chien Shun Lo[1]([⋈]) and Cheng Ssu Ho[2]

[1] Department of Multimedia Design, National Formosa University,
Hu-Wei, Yunlin, Taiwan
cslo@nfu.edu.tw
[2] Graduate Institute of Digital Content and Creative Industries,
National Formosa University, Hu-Wei, Yunlin, Taiwan

Abstract. The study proposed an application to detect cryptomeria trees which had been damaged by squirrels from an aerial image. Each pixel of the aerial image is classified into damaged tree pixels or healthy pixels by super vector machine (SVM) developed in this paper. The application achieves about 82.24% true positive rate (TPR) in detecting damaged trees and about 1.30% false positive rate (FPR). It is a smart tool for monitoring smart forests.

Keywords: Aerial images · Cryptomeria squirrel damage · Image classification

1 Introduction

Xitou is a forest area in the center of Taiwan which is managed by Taiwan University. The area of Xitou is about 2500 ha. The altitude of Xitou is between 600 and 2000 m high. There are a lot of valuable plant's in Xitou, including a lot of Cryptomeria. However, the bark of the cryptomeria is often eaten by Formosan Giant Flying Squirrel or Callosciurus erythraeus. Cryptomeria bark is not a natural part of the diet of the Formosan Giant Flying Squirrel. However, the population of squirrels in the area has exceeded the natural food supply due to excess feeding by tourists. As they lack natural food sources they have started to eat the Cryptomeria bark. When the bark of the Cryptomeria is eaten by the squirrel, the top canopy of the trees displays a green to pink color change in the leaves, and in latter stages turn white. The pink or white canopy is the target detected in this study. Burges [1] analyses that SVM has been used for pattern recognition many different fields. Especially, aerial image become great important for earth observation [2], recently. This study follows a suggestion from a previous study to use Super Vector Machine (SVM) to identify target trees from the aerial image take in Xitou.

© Springer Nature Singapore Pte Ltd. 2019
C.-Y. Chang et al. (Eds.): ICS 2018, CCIS 1013, pp. 186–189, 2019.
https://doi.org/10.1007/978-981-13-9190-3_19

2 Methods

2.1 Supervised Learning

A support vector machine (SVM) is a supervised learning algorithm. It constructs an optimal hyperplane as a decision surface such that the margin of separation between the two classes in the data is maximized. In this study, pixels selected from RGB images are 3-dimensional feature space for the input data. Two classes of training data are selected. One is the pixels from the damaged trees which are the target pixels, the other is healthy pixels. These training data is processed to find the optimal decision surface as the classifier. Figure 1 shows two test sample images with the resolution 400 × 400 pixels. Each one image contains several damaged areas in the upper canopy. In this study, SVM training using linear kernel. The training result obtained 8 × 3 support vectors and other parameters shown in the appendix.

(a)   (b)

Fig. 1. Two test sample images.

2.2 Classifications

Figure 2 shows the detected target pixels shown on the two right hand images. Pixels transformed by using the SVM classifier into a rage of negative to positive values. The transformed pixels with a positive value are considered as target pixels, these target pixels are shown colored yellow.

3 Experimental Results

3.1 Sub Samples Testing

There are two images used for classification. Each image with 400 × 400 pixel size. Tables 1 and 2 shows the experimental results. Total number of pixels for each image are 160,000 pixels. Each pixel is classified as a target pixel or a non-target pixel. The true positive (TP) number achieves 18,574 and 10,642 pixels for image no. 1 and 2 respectively. The true positive rate achieves 87.14% and 77.34%.

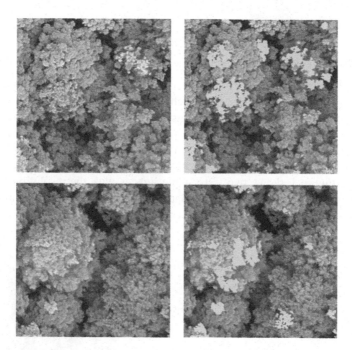

Fig. 2. Two SVM resulted images, the left two images are the original images and the right two images are corresponding SVM resulted images. (Color figure online)

The average rate is 82.24%. The true negative rate (TNR) achieves 98.44% and 98.97%, the average rate is 98.70%.

Table 1. The detected pixel counts.

Image no	Positive pixels	Negative pixels	TP	TN	FP	FN
1	21314	138686	18574	136521	2165	2740
2	13760	146240	10642	144735	1505	3118

Table 2. The precision of detecting rate.

Image no	TPR	TNR	FPR	FNR
1	87.14%	98.44%	1.56%	12.86%
2	77.34%	98.97%	1.03%	22.66%
Average	82.24%	98.70%	1.30%	17.76%

3.2   Whole Image

The whole image is processed by SVM is shown in Fig. 3b.

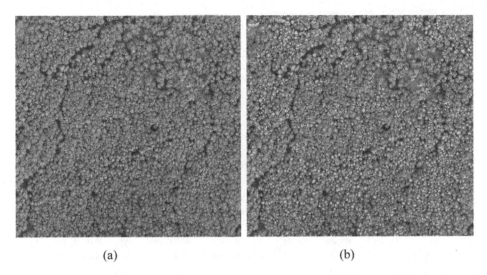

(a)   (b)

Fig. 3. The whole image classification. (a) is the original image. (b) is the SVM transformed image.

4   Conclusions and Discussions

SVM is a good choice for the classification and identification of squirrel damaged cryptomeria using an aerial image. The red to white colors of damaged cryptomeria provides a stark contrast with its healthy green color. Therefore, SVM is easily used to identify individual damaged trees in the forest. The aerial image is obtained at a lower cost and higher resolution then a satellite image. It is a smart tool for forest management.

References

1. Burges, C.J.C.: A tutorial on support vector machines for pattern recognition. Data Min. Knowl. Disc. **2**, 121–167 (1998)
2. Lu, X., Yuan, Y, Fang, J.: JM-Net and cluster-SVM for aerial scene classification. In: 26th International Joint Conference on Artificial Intelligence, pp. 2386–2392. IJCAI Press (2017). https://doi.org/10.24963/ijcai.2017/332

Clothing Classification with Multi-attribute Using Convolutional Neural Network

Chaitawat Chenbunyanon and Ji-Han Jiang[✉]

Department of Computer Science and Information Engineering,
National Formosa University, Yunlin County, Taiwan
chaitawat.che@gmail.com, jhjiang@nfu.edu.tw

Abstract. Convolutional Neural Network (CNN) has demonstrated great efficiency in image classification tasks. In this paper, CNN is used with multi-label classification to extract features from clothing images and classify clothing types and colors. In our method, we first develop a neural network for types and colors separately then combine into a multi-output model to identify them. The experimental results show that the proposed method achieves practical performance in classify precision.

Keywords: Convolutional Neural Network · Image classification · Multi-label classification

1 Introduction

This research is aimed at the capability of identifying clothing types and colors from pictures using deep learning. We create our dataset by collecting from Google Images and applying data augmentation to add more image data. As described in papers [2, 3], they show advantages of data augmentation in image classification. This paper focuses on a deep neural network based approaches using the convolutional neural network which has become a powerful technique in the field of deep learning [1].

The dataset consists of 5,609 clothing images with 2 attributes: types and colors. At the beginning of this study, we choose clothes because they are often found in daily life and we want to know the capabilities of machine learning perform in classify them.

In the area of clothing types and colors classification, Neural Networks was applied and gained good results [4]. Another paper [5] they proposed the method for clothing classification using image features. Rachmadi et al. [6] trained CNN to recognize the color of the vehicle. In [7], a big clothing dataset, Fashion-MNIST, was used with Convolutional Neural Networks that have obtained good performance.

The most popular deep learning method for image processing tasks is the convolutional neural networks or CNNs [13]. It is applied in many applications like Object recognition, Natural language processing, Recommender Systems and more.

In this research, we apply a convolution neural network algorithm with the combination of multi-label classification [9] and multiple output model to identify clothing types and colors. And then we compare differences between predicting 1 attribute and 2

© Springer Nature Singapore Pte Ltd. 2019
C.-Y. Chang et al. (Eds.): ICS 2018, CCIS 1013, pp. 190–196, 2019.
https://doi.org/10.1007/978-981-13-9190-3_20

attributes. In these papers [8, 10, 15] present how well can multi-label classification perform with deep learning.

2   Materials and Method

2.1   Dataset

We build the dataset for experiments by gathering Google Images. Google Images is the powerful search engine which can help to quickly and easily gather image data for our deep learning models. We choose some clothing types and colors randomly then use it as the query term then download relevant results. After collecting all clothing images, they were scaled down to 100 × 100 pixels. Some of the sample images have been shown in Fig. 1.

(a) Shirts in red color   (b) Trousers in blue color

(c) Dress in green color   (d) Shoes in black color

Fig. 1. Examples of clothing type and color images from our dataset. (Color figure online)

But the image results are too small, so the data augmentation techniques are used to enlarge our dataset. We use some techniques like flipping, adding noise, and blurring as shown in Fig. 2.

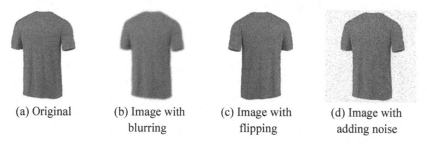

| (a) Original | (b) Image with blurring | (c) Image with flipping | (d) Image with adding noise |

Fig. 2. Examples of original image and image with some data augmentation techniques.

Finally, our resulted dataset contains 4 clothing types and 4 colors with about 5,609 images. The labels were spread across types and colors as shown in Table 1.

Table 1. The number of images for each label in each clothing types and colors.

Labels of clothing types	Labels of colors			
	Black	Red	Blue	Green
Shirt	0	620	0	639
Trouser	528	0	528	0
Shoes	867	0	0	756
Dress	0	885	786	0

2.2   Method

CNN model is a multilayer neural network and consists of 3 operation layers.

First, the convolutional layers (Conv) perform a function to extract and learn the feature representations of input. To realize the features of the picture, we need the network to recognize. The previous output of convolution layer will be the input of another convolution layer.

During the convolution layers, it needs to contain a nonlinear layer (or activation layer) to increase non-linearity to a system that has been computing linear operations during the convolution layers. Rectified Linear Units layer, ReLU [14], is used to apply activation function by this equation.

$$\text{ReLU}(x) = \max(0, x) \tag{1}$$

After a convolution operation, pooling layers (Pool) operate to reduce the spatial dimensions of the input and overfitting.

Finally, the fully connected layers (FC) interpret the input features into classes based on the training dataset.

This paper is focused on using a multi-output model to predict multiple outputs. In the multi-output classification model, we can utilize more than one fully-connected heads and each head is responsible for performing a specific classification task. The picture of the structure model and the example of input and output are shown in Figs. 3 and 4.

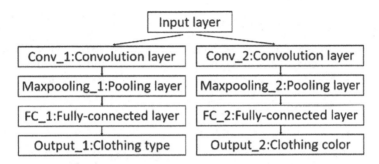

Fig. 3. The CNN with multi-output model adopted in the experiment.

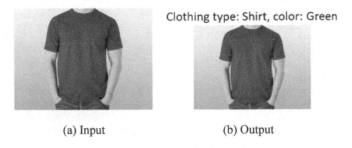

(a) Input   (b) Output

Fig. 4. Examples of input and output image in the experiment. (Color figure online)

In order to set up our CNN model, we used Keras library [11]. It provides the package that is a high-level neural networks API developed with a focus on enabling fast experimentation and the functional API to build model more complex or custom your own input and output and can be trained with your model. We develop multi-output models that is one of the functional API in Keras [12]. For our model, we define a model that used to classify two different types of outputs. After passing the input layer, we split our network into 2 subnetworks: one is responsible for classifying the clothing types. and the other for classifying the color of the clothing.

3   Experimental Results

In this part, the dataset is split into 2 parts: the training data contains 4,767 images and testing data contains 842 images. All clothing images are normalized to 20×20 pixels. For the classification results, we also use precision and recall metrics to evaluate our models.

3.1   Experiment I – Predict 1 Attribute

The models are trained to identify clothing types with CNN. Our CNN structure includes 5 layers: 2 convolutional layers, 2 pooling layers, and 1 full-connected layer. Tables 2 and 3 show the model structure and the results for the model.

Clothing type : Dress , color : Blue   Clothing type : Shirt , color : Red

Fig. 5. Examples of image results in the experiment. (Color figure online)

Table 2. The structure of clothing type model

Layer	Shape	Filter
Convolution_1	3×3	32
Convolution_2	3×3	16
Max pooling_1	2×2	-
Fully connected	-	4

Table 3. Experiment results of clothing type model

Attribute	Accuracy (%)	Precision (%)	Recall (%)
Type	91.09	91.34	90.64

Each convolutional layer is applied to ReLU activation function. The last layer predicts the clothing type by using a fully-connected layer with softmax activations from 4 clothing type classes.

Our CNN architecture consists of layers: 5 convolutional layers, 3 pooling layers, and 1 full-connected layer. We also use a ReLU activation for every convolution layer and a softmax to predict the output. Results and structure of this model are shown in Tables 4 and 5.

Table 4. The structure of clothing color model.

Layer	Shape	Filter
Convolution_1	3×3	32
Max pooling_1	3×3	-
Convolution_2	3×3	64
Convolution_3	3×3	64
Max pooling_2	3×3	-
Convolution_4	3×3	64
Convolution_5	3×3	128
Max pooling_3	2×2	-
Fully connected	-	4

Table 5. Experiment results of clothing color model.

Attribute	Accuracy (%)	Precision (%)	Recall (%)
Color	92.52	92.93	92.69

3.2 Experiment II – Predict 2 Attributes

We merge 2 models from the experiment I into a multi-output model then perform this model. The results for our experiment are given in Table 6 and Fig. 5.

Table 6. Experiment results of clothing type and color model.

Attribute	Accuracy (%)	Precision (%)	Recall (%)
Type	92.87	93.13	93.35
Color	93.23	92.59	93.29

4 Conclusion

In this project, we successfully construct our own dataset which is enlarged with data augmentation techniques and train the CNN model. Our networks achieved accuracy, precision and recall with 2 attributes around 90% which can be considered good for classification and prediction problem.

In the future research, we plan to apply this method in larger scale dataset by expanding more attributes and we want to include dataset in other related topics.

References

1. Schmidhuber, J.: Deep learning in neural networks: an overview. Neural Networks **61**, 85–117 (2015)
2. Mikołajczyk, A., Grochowski, M.: Data augmentation for improving deep learning in image classification problem, International Interdisciplinary Ph.D. Workshop (IIPhDW), pp. 117–122 (2018)
3. Perez, L., Wang, J.: The Effectiveness of Data Augmentation in Image Classification Using Deep Learning, arXiv preprint arXiv:1712.04621 (2017)
4. Fengxin, L., Yueping, L., Xiaofeng, Z.: A novel approach to cloth classification through deep neural networks. In: International Conference on Security, Pattern Analysis, and Cybernetics (SPAC), pp. 368–371 (2017)
5. Yamazaki, K., Inaba, M.: Clothing classification using image features derived from clothing fabrics, wrinkles and cloth overlaps. In: IEEE/RSJ International Conference on Intelligent Robots and Systems, pp. 2710–2717 (2013)
6. Rachmadi, R.F., Ketut Eddy Purnama, I.: Vehicle Color Recognition using Convolutional Neural Network, arXiv preprint arXiv:1510.07391 (2015)
7. Bhatnagar, S., Ghosal, D., Kolekar, M.H.: Classification of fashion article images using convolutional neural networks. In: Fourth International Conference on Image Information Processing (ICIIP), pp. 357–362 (2017)
8. Zeggada, A., Melgani, F.: Multilabel classification of UAV images with Convolutional Neural Networks. In: IEEE International Geoscience and Remote Sensing Symposium (IGARSS), pp. 5083–5086 (2016)
9. Wei, Y., et al.: CNN: Single-label to Multi-label. arXiv:1406.5726v3 (2014)
10. Zhang, P.-F., Wu, H.-Y., Xu, X.-S.: A dual-CNN model for multi-label classification by leveraging co-occurrence dependencies between labels. In: Advances in Multimedia Information Processing – PCM 2017, pp. 315–324 (2017)
11. Keras. https://keras.io/. Accessed 30 Sept 2018
12. Keras functional API. https://keras.io/getting-started/functional-api-guide/. Accessed 30 Sept 2018
13. Simonyan, K., Zisserman, A.: Very deep convolutional networks for large-scale image recognition. Computer Science. arXiv:1409.1556v6 (2014)
14. Ide, H., Kurita, T.: Improvement of learning for CNN with ReLU activation by sparse regularization. In: International Joint Conference on Neural Networks (IJCNN), pp. 2684–2691 (2017)
15. Gong, Y., Jia, Y., Leung, T., Toshev, A., Ioffe, S.: Deep Convolutional Ranking for Multilabel Image Annotation, arXiv preprint arXiv:1312.4894v2 (2013)

Color Video and Convolutional Neural Networks Deep Learning Based Real-Time Agtron Baking Level Estimation Method

Qi-Hon Wu[✉] and Day-Fann Shen[✉]

Department of Electrical Engineering,
National Yunlin University of Science and Technology, Douliu, Taiwan
gimmy4268@gmail.com, shendf@yuntech.edu.tw

Abstract. This paper examines different methods of producing real-time Agtron index outputs for coffee bean baking. The goal is to provide an optimal roasting output based on the required profile, increasing baking accuracy over the commonly used time-temperature method. Although the Agtron baking degree is based on the caramel infrared index, it is also highly correlated with color and shape information. Experimentally, a baking color was sub-divided into ten categories (grades), images were taken with a common color camera, then a deep learning convolutional neural network performed analysis. Based on the LenNet architecture and parameters, this study develops a "convolution neural network for coffee bean baking identification" and develops a time-sequential binary classification model (TSBC) based on the time-decreasing characteristics of baking. The resultant system correctly determines the baking grades.

Keywords: Agtron baking degree · Baking degree estimation ·
Convolutional neural network · Deep learning · Time sequential

1 Introduction

Coffee is one of the most popular natural drink in the world. Drinking coffee is refreshing and comes in a wide variety of different coffee baking flavors. Taiwan imported 25,558 tons of raw beans in 2016, making it the second largest import in terms of value, after oil.] Currently, the coffee bean baking degree is primarily dependent on the baker's continuous observation during the process. Considering the variance within the SCAA baking degree color card, judging the exact status of the beans being baked is very complicated and every second counts. When the coffee beans are cooled, the value of the baking index is measured offline by the Agtron near-infrared caramel analyzer. This value extracted is on a scale of 100-0, representing the degree of baking from the shallowest to the deepest.

Although the Agtron near-infrared caramel analyzer is the most authoritative coffee baking measurement instrument in the industry, it cannot meet the real-time requirements because infrared is easily affected by high temperatures. During the baking process, the sampling spoon of the coffee baker is continuously sampled manually, and

© Springer Nature Singapore Pte Ltd. 2019
C.-Y. Chang et al. (Eds.): ICS 2018, CCIS 1013, pp. 197–206, 2019.
https://doi.org/10.1007/978-981-13-9190-3_21

the eight baking degree colors in the "SCAA coffee color card" are compared by the human eye. This allows for instant assessment, but it is complicated and time consuming. Furthermore, the process is subject to human error, ambient light environment and other forms of interference.

Therefore, this study develops a technique for estimating the Agtron baking degree by a general color camera combined with a convolutional neural network (CNN). The expected impacts are: (1) Instantly transfer the baking degree and related information to the baker during the baking process, (a) reduce the workload of professional bakers who need to otherwise continually observe the progress and remove possible human error. (b) allow the general amateur produce professional-grade coffee beans. (2) Provide a time-baking degree curve that more directly reflects the degree of baking than the traditionally widely used time-temperature curve, and more accurately grasp the degree of coffee baking. (3) Make a fundamental improvement in the immediate control of the large-scale coffee industry core technology.

2   Literature Review

The existing coffee baking technology available today depends heavily on users and free market adoption of ideas, rather than journal publications. Some sources are available and the following is a review of data available on coffee baking generally, color matching, and CNN.

In 2016, Virgen-Navarroa et al. [1] proposed that the image brightness (L*), the distance from the target baking degree (ΔE), and the browning-index input to the fuzzy neural network can be used to determine the water content of coffee beans as the water content is related to the degree of baking. In this study, we use the L*a*b* color space, and the browning index obtained by the formula, as well as the Euclidean distance from the American commercial beans. The structure of the image taken through this system can provide clear and unaffected data. However, it can only calculate the Euclidean distance with one baking degree. 2017, Nasution et al. [2] proposed with the use of a Gray Level Co-Occurrence Matrix (GLCM) combined with Back Propagation (BP) in a neural network to determine the baking degree. The baking degree of here is divided into 16 degrees, and the final output can be obtained with an accuracy of 97%, but this is for a single coffee bean and impossible to estimate a whole batch of coffee beans during baking.

With regard to CNNs, in 2012, Krizhevsky et al. [3] won the 2012 ILSVRC (ImageNet Large Scale Visual Recognition Competition) using a deep convolutional network. ILSVRC is an annual large-scale visual identity challenge operated by a globally renowned company. The academic community regards winning this prize as the highest honor. This particular architecture is called AlexNet, and has a Top-5 error rate of 15.4%, a gap of more than 10% over other competitors, it goes on to become the first SVM machine learning technology used by the Xerox team, and since then has been applied in various innovative neural networks. In 2015, Rachmadi et al. [4] used CNNs to identify vehicle colors and compared the accuracy of RGB, HSV, CIE LAB, and CIE YUV color spaces. Unexpectedly, the result was 94.47% of the RGB color space. This paper uses LeNet [7] as a reference to adjust the architecture for coffee baking.

3 Neural Networks Deep Learning Based Real-Time Agtron Baking Level Estimation Method

The system experiment software and hardware environment and system usage flow of this paper were as follows:

3.1 Experimental Environment

The black cubic object in Fig. 1, is a baking machine. There will be a half-open space or small hole in the baker, which allows the camera to take the image of the coffee beans while they are inside. It allows for an external light source if desired or can make the experimental environment free from external light. The camera has wireless transmission function, which can transfer the captured image or video to the computer (mobile phone) for image processing and then use the convolutional neural network to identify baking degrees, there will be an cooler next to the baker, which can cool the baked coffee beans.

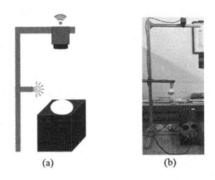

Fig. 1. Experimental hardware environment (a) schematic and (b) entity diagram

3.2 Possible Use of the System

This flow chart in Fig. 2 is used to provide the user (baker) with real-time baking information during coffee baking progress. This means that the baking degree can be used instead of time/temperature for automatic coffee baking control. The users can input their target baking degree, whereupon the computer will estimate the degree of baking that it detects in the image it is given. The system can also report the estimated degree of baking per second (frequency adjustable). Once the preset target baking degree is reached, the system will send a message "Target baking degree achieved" to the user, allowing the user to stop baking and pour out the coffee beans.

Procedure:
Gather equipment from Fig. 1(a), assemble as seen in (b). Turn on the camera and aim it at the baker. Turn on the baker and allow it to warm up. Set the target roast level in the user interface (this paper offers 9 preset baking levels).

Insert the green (un-roasted) beans and begin the video stream. For highest accuracy it is best to start the video at the same time as putting in the beans.

The system automatically transmits the baking video and the estimated bake level to the computer (or mobile phone) for classification and identification of the baking progress, depending on the preset frequency. The camera will take a sample frame every second and transmit this for analysis. Select the region of interest as the image frame may not be able to contain all the beans, thus it is necessary to select 50×50 square blocks containing only coffee beans, as shown in Fig. 3.

Use the CNN to classify the baking degree. The trained CNN was used to identify 10 classes (9, plus raw beans), as shown in Fig. 4. On the left side are the 10 levels of bake used for training, and the right side, for comparison, are the 8 industry standard levels. The system recognizes and estimates the current bake rate once per second. When the CNN classification output class (class 2–10) reaches the user-set level, the system will issue "Agtron xx degrees of target xx bake".

When complete, stop baking immediately and cool the beans to avoid any residual heat within the beans continuing to bake.

4   Temporal Sequential Binary Classifier Baking Degree Identification Method

The actual Agtron baking degree should be reduced over time when the coffee beans are actually baked. If the current class of bake is class k, then the next must be the k + 1 class. This chapter proposes the "Temporal Sequential Binary Classifier

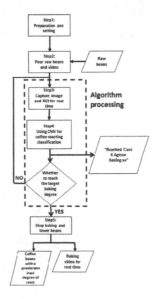

Fig. 2. System flow chart

Fig. 3. Taking a 50 × 50 coffee bean area as a region of interest (ROI)

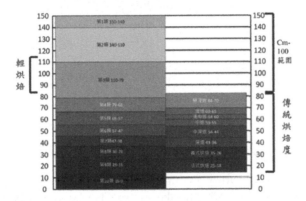

Fig. 4. Agtron spectrum. Left: 10 classes in this paper; Right: 8 classes popular in market.

(TSBC)". If the total number of categories is $\mathbb{K}$, the model is composed of a $\mathbb{K} - 1$ binary Classifier. The P_k binary Classifier classifies only the k and k + 1 classes, $\mathbb{P} = \{P_1, P_2, \ldots, P_{\mathbb{K}-1}\}$. Because it is divided into two categories at a time, its accuracy and computational cost are expected to be greatly improved, and results will not cause a violation of the order of baking. The remaining problem to be solved is when the model P_k is converted to the P_{k+1} mechanism, that is, when the P_k model is classified into the k + 1 class for consecutive T times. When this occurs, the system will send a message "The current baking degree is in the k + 1 class" to the baker and switch to the P_{k+1} Classifier (Fig. 5).

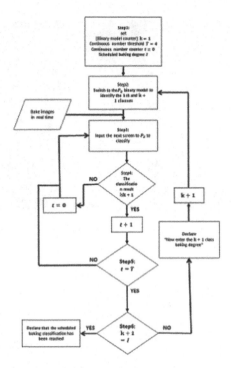

Fig. 5. TSBC flow chart

4.1 Making an Image Training Set

Figure 6 shows the flow chart of the image training set. Here we divide the baking degree into 10 categories (including raw beans), so 9 batches of raw beans are baked to obtain the sample data required for the convolutional network training and testing. The corresponding Agtron roast information is acquired: (1) 10 types of sample coffee beans (including raw beans), (2) its corresponding Agtron baking degree, (3) 9 types of sample coffee beans baking process RGB video (class 1 is Raw beans, not baked), to generate the RGB image training set required for training, and to adjust convolutional neural network architecture parameters.

The goal of preparing sample coffee beans is to obtain ten different degrees of baking ($\mathbb{K} = 10$) classification for convolutional neural network training. Except for the first class (raw beans), the acquired information on each type of baking training sample is divided into two parts: one is to control the coffee bean baking machine, the timer and the coffee bean processing; the second is to control the camera to obtain the relevant process video, and the final result will be obtained (1) the kth sample coffee bean and its Agtron Value as a base line for (2) The k-th sample coffee bean baking video, this video will be made into the image training set and test.

The image training set is to bake the kth sample of coffee beans, take the last 50 frames to make the image training set B. B represents the heating of the baking, the number of each type of training image is 50 frames, but it can reflect the heating of the baking. Though the actual coffee bean color, the smoke condition, and the increase the number of images, the image training set BA can be obtained.

Using established data augmentation [8] techniques, each 100×100 training image is rotated by 90°, 3 times (90°, 180°, 270°) to expand into four 100×100 images (x4)., as shown in Fig. 8(a). Each image is then cropped into 9 sub-images (x9), as shown in Fig. 8(c). The next step is to flip horizontally and flip the input image horizontally (left and right) (x2), as shown in Fig. 8(b). The above rotation and cutting steps are repeated, so that it can be expanded to a 72 ($4 \times 9 \times 2$) 50×50 sub-image. Therefore, 50 100×100 images obtained can be upgraded to 3600 (50×72) by data Augmentation technology, which is called image training set BA.

4.2 Training TSBC

Because TSBC is composed of multiple binary classifiers, $\mathbb{P} = \{P_1, P_2, \ldots, P_{\mathbb{K}-1}\}$. If the total number of categories is $\mathbb{K}$, it is operated by $\mathbb{K} - 1$ binary classification models. The input of the P_k model training process is that the k-th image training set belongs to the kth and k + 1th training images, the output is the P_k model, and so on, repeating the above steps until $k = \mathbb{K} - 1$, the TSBC can be obtained. The model is given by $\mathbb{P} = \{P_1, P_2, \ldots, P_{\mathbb{K}-1}\}$.

4.3 Convolutional Neural Network Model for Coffee Bean Baking Identification

In the literature review and discussion, it is discovered that (1) the design of the general CNN architecture is mainly based on geometric information of an object, however coffee baking identification in this paper is highly correlated with color information. Therefore, color data is relatively important. (2) The design of the general CNN architecture is mainly applied to the identification of a huge image database, so the architecture will be relatively large, and this paper only distinguishes 10 types of baking, which is relatively simple. Based on the above observations, the remainder of this chapter will test and adjust based on the general CNN architecture and the parameters to develop a "convolutional neural network for coffee bean baking identification".

In 2017, Mishkin et al. [5] also mentioned that an additional layer of convolutional layer can be added after the input of the image, because this convolutional layer does not have a coined term, it is referred to as an "adaptive pre-processing convolutional layer" in this paper. It functions similarly to a CNN, learning the color space itself to achieve the best accuracy. In addition to the adaptive pre-processing convolutional layer, there is also a change in the color space of the input image, as well as an attempt to change the convolution kernel, the excitation function, the size of the pooling layer, and the stride, and finally the "applicable to the coffee bean baking degree identification. The convolutional neural network model, as shown in Table 1 (Fig. 7).

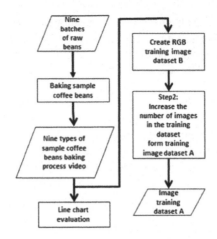

Fig. 6. Flow chart of making image training set

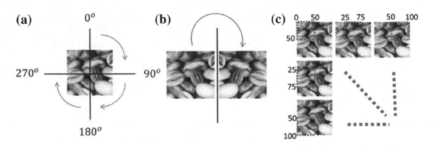

Fig. 7. Data Augmentation of the image training set (a) rotation (x4) (b) horizontal flip (x2) (c) crop (x9)

Table 1. Convolutional neural network model parameters for coffee bean baking identification

	Convolutional neural network model parameters for coffee bean baking identification
Input	50 × 50 pixels, RGB image
Color space	YCrCb
Adaptive preprocessing convolutional layer	1 × 1 × 10 (no activation function)
Convolutional layer	7 × 7 × 64 (hard sigmoid)
Pooling layer	3 × 3, strides: 3
Convolutional layer	7 × 7 × 64 (hard sigmoid)
Pooling layer	3 × 3, strides: 3
Flatten	
Fully connected layer	512 (hard sigmoid)
Fully connected layer	512 (hard sigmoid)
Fully connected layer	512 (hard sigmoid)
Fully connected layer	10 (softmax)

4.4   TSBC Test Results

To test TSBC's ability to identify samples, enter the k-th sample coffee beans baking video to the system, set identification of baking degree at a frequency to once per second, and record the results of each estimation in a line chart (as shown in Figs. 8, 9 and 10). The vertical axis of the line graph is the Agtron baking degree, and the horizontal axis is the baking time in seconds.

Figure 8 shows beans starting from raw, and after some period of time, jumping into the first class, and then the second class, indicating that the degree of roast is changing. Finally, it will stop in the second class, indicating that the coffee beans have completely changed into the second class. This was the second set experimented with, and confirmed that the classification method was functioning as required.

Fig. 8. The second class of sample coffee bean baking video line chart

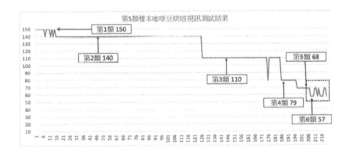

Fig. 9. The fifth class of sample coffee bean baking video line chart

In order to increase the stability of the TSBC output, it is necessary to identify the P_k model as k + 1 class for T times, then determine that it actually enters the k + 1 class and switches to the P_{k+1} model. In the Fig. 9 (class 5), although the last is in the 5th and 6th jumps (dashed box), but the number of the sixth class does not reach the continuous number threshold, it is still recognized as the fifth class.

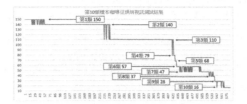

Fig. 10. The tenth class of sample coffee bean baking video line chart

5 Conclusion

In this paper, a general color camera's visible light detection property and a CNN are combined to estimate an authoritative index of Agtron bakes for coffee beans. Because Agtron baking degrees are highly correlated with color information, the general CNN architecture is adjusted. The parameters are used to develop the "convolutional neural network for coffee bean baking identification", and also to develop a time-order binary classification model (TSBC) based on the characteristics of baked coffee beans, which resulted in satisfactory results and also met. The system is capable of instant bake level data delivery to bakers, reducing the workload for professionals, and allowing amateur bakers to produce higher quality beans.

Further research can still be done to uncover the effects of decreasing the frame frequency below one second, to see if this affects classification.

References

1. Virgen-Navarro, L., Herrera-Lopez, E.J., Corona-Gonzalez, R.I., Arriola-Guevara, E., Guatemala-Morales, G.M.: Neuro-fuzzy model based on digital images for the monitoring of coffee bean color during baking in a spouted bed. Expert Syst. Appl. **54**, 162–169 (2016)
2. Nasution, T., Andayani, U.: Recognition of baked coffee bean levels using image processing and neural network. In: IOP Conference Series: Materials Science and Engineering, vol. 180, no. 1, p. 012059. IOP Publishing (2017)
3. Krizhevsky, A., Sutskever, I., Hinton, G. E.: ImageNet classification with deep convolutional neural networks. In: Advances in Neural Information Processing Systems, pp. 1097–1105 (2012)
4. Rachmadi, R.F., Purnama, I.: Vehicle color recognition using convolutional neural network. arXiv preprint arXiv:1510.07391 (2015)
5. Mishkin, D., Sergievskiy, N., Matas, J.: Systematic evaluation of convolution neural network advances on the imagenet. Comput. Vis. Image Underst. **161**, 11–19 (2017)
6. Thoma, M.: Analysis and optimization of convolutional neural network architectures. arXiv preprint arXiv:1707.09725 (2017)
7. LeCun, Y., Bottou, L., Bengio, Y., Haffner, P.: Gradient-based learning applied to document recognition. Proc. IEEE **86**(11), 2278–2324 (1998)
8. Banerjee, A., Iyer, V.: Cs231n project report-tiny imageNet challenge

Deep Virtual Try-on with Clothes Transform

Szu-Ying Chen[✉], Kin-Wa Tsoi[✉], and Yung-Yu Chuang[✉]

Computer Science and Information Engineering, National Taiwan University,
Taipei, Taiwan
{clairecat,rance1108}@cmlab.csie.ntu.edu.tw, cyy@csie.ntu.edu.tw

Abstract. The goal of this work is to enable users to try on clothes by photos. When users providing their own photo and photo of intended clothes, we can generate the result photo of themselves wearing the clothes. Other virtual try-on methods are focused on the front-view of the person and the clothes. Meanwhile, our method can handle front and slightly turned-view directions. The details of the clothes are clearer. In the user study, about 90% of the cases, respondents chose our results over others.

Keywords: Convolutional neural network · Virtual try-on · Perceptual loss

1 Introduction

In recent years, the demand for online shopping has been increased dramatically, one of the best-selling commodities is clothes. However, the problem of online purchasing clothes is people cannot try the clothes and see if they are suitable for them until they buy them. Therefore, it is very convenient for consumers to try on clothes virtually.

There are some researches on image-based virtual try-on. However, most of them focus on front-view clothes and people. We want to expand the clothes and people to different viewing angles.

Therefore, we want to develop a system that uses images for virtual try-on, which allows trying on clothes without limiting the view direction of people and target clothes. In this way, consumers can try on clothes more easily which promotes desire to purchase and keep the cost down for clothes stores.

2 Related Work

Recently, plenty of researches have been conducted on fashion-related works. Virtual try-on is the more challenging task among them, which should preserve more details of a target clothes as output. Two papers have been conducted on this task for the recent two years, VITON [3] and CAGAN [4], which deliver good results on image-based virtual try-on with aids of deep learning.

© Springer Nature Singapore Pte Ltd. 2019
C.-Y. Chang et al. (Eds.): ICS 2018, CCIS 1013, pp. 207–214, 2019.
https://doi.org/10.1007/978-981-13-9190-3_22

2.1   VITON

VITON consists of two stages. In the encoder-decoder generator stage, the network generates a coarse result. While in the refinement stage, target clothes is warped with the mask by estimating a thin plate spline (TPS) transformation with shape context matching [1]. After warping, a network composites the coarse image with the warped clothes and generates a final output.

However, VITON requires accurate poses and segmentations, which needs manually fine tuning and are difficult to be obtained.

2.2   CAGAN

Conditional Analogy Generative Adversarial Network (CAGAN) is based on Conditional GAN (CGAN) [6]. Given a person image and a target clothes image, CAGAN can output an image with the target clothes worn by the person. Moreover, CAGAN can also learn a segmentation mask of difference between the input and output person image without labeling data.

However, the output from CAGAN is blurry and preserves less details than the target clothes.

3   Methodology

3.1   Data Collection

Since we require different viewing directions of clothes, we select the MVC dataset [5] as our training data, which is used in clothing retrieval and clothing style recognition. It contains 161260 images in 9 categories. Since our task is focused in upper-body clothes, images of followed three categories are selected from the dataset, *Shirts and Tops, Sweaters and Cardigans, Coats and Outerwear.* Meanwhile, the datasets include 4 different viewing directions of people wearing the same clothes and 3 of them are used in our task (front, left, and right views).

3.2   The Proposed Approach

Our proposed method contains four steps. Firstly, given a person image and a target clothes image, CAGAN is used to generate a preliminary result and a binary mask of where to change. Secondly, a transform network is used to extract the clothes only. Meanwhile, the mask and output from previous step are used in segmentation step for a better mask to indicate where the clothes should be transformed to. Next, the mask is used to transform the target clothes. Lastly, the transformed clothes and the output from CAGAN are combined which becomes our final output. Figure 1 shows our overall architecture.

Figure 2 shows the generator and discriminator of CAGAN. Given a person image x_i and a clothes image y_j as inputs, it gives a intermediate output x'' and a alpha mask M'. Then the input person x_i and the intermediate output x''_j are merged according to the mask M' and generate the final output of that person wearing the clothes x'_j.

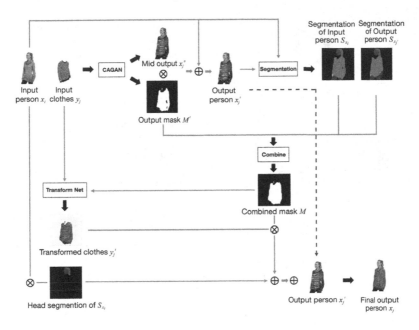

Fig. 1. Overall architecture of our method

CAGAN [4] is trained with our own dataset to suit our task. During training, image from the generator is used to fool the discriminator while discriminator try to discriminate it. Which can result in an improvement of the generated image.

The loss of CAGAN is defined as:

$$\min_{G}\max_{D}\mathcal{L}_{cGAN}(G,D) + \gamma_i\mathcal{L}_{id}(G) + \gamma_c\mathcal{L}_{cyc}(G), \tag{1}$$

where consists of three terms: the adversarial loss of CAGAN, the regularization of generator and the cycle loss of generator, which is weighted by γ_i and γ_c.

The adversarial loss of CAGAN is different from typical GAN as the discriminator have to discriminate both the rationality of the image and the correctness of the changed clothes, as shown in Fig. 2b. The regularization term restricts the output mask from the generator from getting much difference compared with the original image. The cycle loss of the generator keeps the other parts remain unchanged except the clothing part.

Segmentation. Since the output masks of CAGAN are often shattered, It is difficult to transform the target clothes into masks. To solve this problem, modification of the mask is needed to improve the integrality of it.

The clothing part of the person image is the mask region. A state-of-the-art human parser, LIP-SSL [2] is used to capture the clothes worn by people. The human parser network is used to obtain a segmentation map with 19 human parts with clothes.

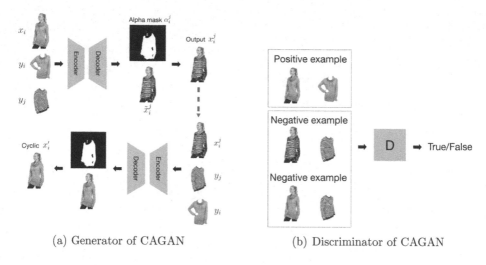

(a) Generator of CAGAN　　　　　　(b) Discriminator of CAGAN

Fig. 2. Network of CAGAN

The final combined mask M is then calculated by:

$$M = (S_{x_i}(clothes) \cup S_{x'_j}(clothes) \cup M') - S_{x_i}(head) - S_{x'_j}(hands). \quad (2)$$

Where S_{x_i} and $S_{x'_j}$ are the segmentation maps from the original image x_i and CAGAN x'_j respectively.

Figure 3 shows some results of our map is cleaner and more integral.

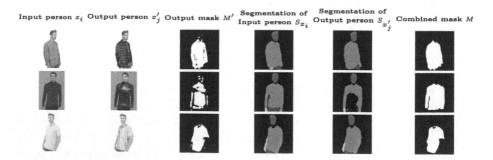

Fig. 3. Results of the segmentation step

Transform. The combined mask M is then used for transformation. The target clothes y_j and the mask M act as an input for the Transform Net, which gives an output of transformed clothes y'_j.

The architecture of the Transform Net is based on U-net, with skip connections to directly share information between layers.

Supervised learning is used to train the Transform Net. Two clothes with different viewing directions and a binary mask of one of the clothes are needed. Let $\hat{y}$ be the ground truth of the clothes image, y be the output of the Transform Net, and $\phi_j(y)$ be the feature map from the jth layer of the network VGG16 [7] for the input y. So is for $\hat{y}$. The loss function is defined as:

$$\mathcal{L}_T = \lambda_p \|\phi_j(\hat{y}) - \phi_j(y)\|_2^2 + \lambda_m \|\hat{y} - y\|_2^2, \tag{3}$$

where is weighted by λ_p and λ_m. Since perceptual loss is computed on higher frequency information, the details and patterns of the inputs are preserved in the output image. While MSE loss requires lower frequency information, which results in blurry output but preserving more correct color.

Combination. The outputs from the Transform Net and CAGAN are combined in this step.

Let $\otimes$ denotes element-wise product, $\oplus$ denotes combining the contents. As above, with the input person image x_i, the transformed clothes y'_j, the head part of the input image $S_{x_i}(head)$, the combined mask M, the output from CAGAN x'_j. Then the final output with changed clothes x_j can be solved as follows:

$$x_j = (x_i \otimes S_{x_i}(head)) \oplus (y'_j \otimes M) \oplus ((1 - S_{x_i}(head) - M) \otimes x'_j). \tag{4}$$

Figure 4 shows some results of the above-mentioned steps.

3.3   Experiments

Implementation Details. CAGAN and the Transform Net are implemented on Keras with Tensorflow backend. Parameters used for training CAGAN are the same as original paper, where the learning rate and batch size is set at 0.0002 and 16 respectively and it is trained with our 18573 image pairs. 15000 training steps are used rather than 10000 steps from the original paper, as a better results can be obtained in theory.

The learning rate and batch size is set at 0.0001 and 4 respectively for the Transform Net and it is trained for 30 epochs with 14858 image pairs while validating with 3715 image pairs. The weights of loss equation 3 are $\lambda_p = 0.9999$ and $\lambda_m = 0.0001$ respectively. Fifth layer of VGG16 ($j = 5$) is used.

4   Evaluation

4.1   Qualitative Evaluation

Comparison with VITON and CAGAN. Since VITON [3] also contains a procedure of warping clothes to the mask, it is used to compare with our proposed method in terms of warping stage performance.

VITON [3] uses shape context matching. With our unclean masks, estimation errors are occurred and the warping results from it may not fully match the mask.

Input person x_i Input clothes y_j CAGAN result x'_j Combined mask M Transformed clothes y'_j Final result x_j

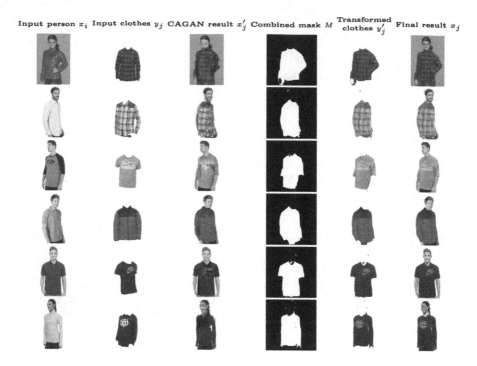

Fig. 4. Results of our proposed method

On the other hand, VITON [3] aims to warp clothes in the front-view. Masks of other viewing angles besides front-view will result in error of transforming the correct shape and details of the clothes by VITON [3].

Meanwhile, since our proposed method is based on CAGAN [4], comparison with CAGAN [4] is provided which showed that ours gives more details on the clothes than CAGAN [4] does. Comparison results are showed in Fig. 5.

4.2   User Study

29 volunteers were participated in our user study. CAGAN [4] is regarded as our baseline. 499 clothes is picked from our dataset for testing.

Two different versions of questionnaire are made. Each questionnaire contains 60 pairs images which were randomly sampled from the testing dataset. The questionnaires are showing two generated results, one from CAGAN [4] and one from ours, and asking respondents which one do they prefer.

Statistical results are presented in Table 1. 88.3%, 92.5% and 90.3% of the votes are in favor of our results in questionnaire A, questionnaire B and on average respectively. That is, in about 90% cases the respondents prefer our results over the results from CAGAN [4].

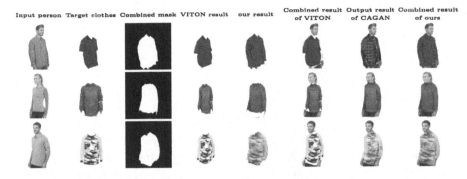

Fig. 5. Comparison with VITON [3] and CAGAN [4]

Table 1. Statistical results of user study

	Q_A	Q_B	Mean
Samples	15	14	
Our votes (%)	88.3	92.5	90.3

Input person x_i Target clothes y_j CAGAN mask M' Combined mask M Final result x_j

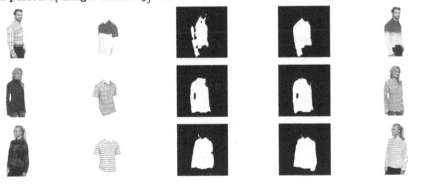

Fig. 6. Failure cases

5   Conclusion

5.1   Conclusion

We proposed an image-based virtual try-on system, which is able to change a clothes on a person image to another with multiple view directions, while preserving the details on clothes. Our system is consists of four steps:

i Use CAGAN to get a preliminary result and a mask.
ii Modify the mask with segmentation of input person and output person from CAGAN.
iii Transform the target clothes to the modified mask with Transform Net.

iv Combine the transformed clothes with the preliminary result from CAGAN.

In the user study, in about 90% cases, our results are preferred over CAGAN [4].

5.2 Discussion

The masks generated from CAGAN [4] are not completely correct. Since the places they represented have changed, if the input person wears a long-sleeves shirt while the target clothes is in short-sleeves, the mask will wrongly transformed with the arms part which does not belongs to the clothes part and resulting in the following failure examples shown in Fig. 6. To solve this issue, our future work aims to get a correct mask.

References

1. Belongie, S., Malik, J., Puzicha, J.: Shape matching and object recognition using shape contexts. IEEE Trans. Pattern Anal. Mach. Intell. **24**(4), 509–522 (2002)
2. Gong, K., Liang, X., Zhang, D., Shen, X., Lin, L.: Look into person: self-supervised structure-sensitive learning and a new benchmark for human parsing. In: The IEEE Conference on Computer Vision and Pattern Recognition (CVPR), July 2017
3. Han, X., Wu, Z., Wu, Z., Yu, R., Davis, L.S.: VITON: an image-based virtual try-on network. In: Proceedings of IEEE Conference on Computer Vision and Pattern Recognition (CVPR) (2018)
4. Jetchev, N., Bergmann, U.: The conditional analogy GAN: swapping fashion articles on people images. In: The IEEE International Conference on Computer Vision (ICCV) Workshops, October 2017
5. Kuan-Hsien, L., Ting-Yen, C., Chu-Song, C.: MVC: a dataset for view-invariant clothing retrieval and attribute prediction. In: ACM International Conference on Multimedia Retrieval, ICMR (2016)
6. Mirza, M., Osindero, S.: Conditional generative adversarial nets. CoRR, abs/1411.1784 (2014)
7. Simonyan, K., Zisserman, A.: Very deep convolutional networks for large-scale image recognition. CoRR, abs/1409.1556 (2014)

Scene Recognition via Bi-enhanced Knowledge Space Learning

Jin Zhang[1], Bing-Kun Bao[2,3]([✉]), and Changsheng Xu[1,3]

[1] Hefei University of Technology, Hefei, China
jin_zhang@duckj.cn
[2] Nanjing University of Posts and Telecommunications, Nanjing, China
bingkunbao@njupt.edu.cn
[3] National Lab of Pattern Recognition, Institute of Automation, Beijing, China
csxu@nlpr.ia.ac.cn

Abstract. Scene recognition is one of the hallmark tasks in computer vision, as it provides rich information beyond object recognition and action recognition. It is easy to accept that scene images from the same class always include the same essential objects and relations, for example, scene images of "wedding" usually have bridegroom and bride next to him. Following this observation, we introduce a novel idea to boost the accuracy of scene recognition by mining essential scene sub-graph and learning a bi-enhanced knowledge space. The essential scene sub-graph describes the essential objects and their relations for each scene class. The learned knowledge space is bi-enhanced by global representation on the entire image and local representation on the corresponding essential scene sub-graph. Experimental results on the constructed dataset called Scene 30 demonstrate the effectiveness of our proposed method.

Keywords: Scene recognition · Sub-graph mining · Bi-enhanced

1 Introduction

Scene recognition is one of the most challenging tasks in image classification and various scene recognition methods have been proposed over the past decades [3,12,15,21–23,25,26,29]. To deal with large intra-class variance caused by nuisance factors such as pose, viewpoint and occlusion, it normally requires two stages for a scene recognition solution, that is, scene representation and scene classification.

Scene representation aims to fully use all the information of scene images to extract discriminative features. It explores not only the generalized characteristics in the same category but also the distinctive characteristics among different categories. The representation methods can be mainly classified into two categories, hand-crafted and deeply-learned representations. In early studies, hand-crafted representation was popular due to its simplicity and low computational cost. These methods only capture low-level information, such as texture and

C.-Y. Chang et al. (Eds.): ICS 2018, CCIS 1013, pp. 215–223, 2019.
https://doi.org/10.1007/978-981-13-9190-3_23

structure of the information. In recent works, deeply-learned feature extraction methods exploit high-level semantic information in scene images by using Convolutional Neural Networks (CNNs).

In this paper, we propose an effective scene recognition framework, which firstly extracts the essential scene sub-graph for each scene class, then learns a classifier to distinguish different scene classes by learning a bi-enhanced knowledge space. The whole work is based on the scene images and their corresponding scene graphs. The main contributions of our work are summarized as follows:

- We propose a novel framework to extract discriminative representation from both entire image and essential scene sub-graph for scene recognition. The learned bi-enhanced knowledge space is proved to be useful for classification.
- This work explores a pioneer study on learning knowledge graph, i.e. essential scene sub-graph, for scene recognition. The proposed approach has great potential for other categorization tasks, while enables people to think about how knowledge graph can better drive current tasks.

The rest of the paper is organized as follows. Section 2 briefly reviews related work. The proposed framework including the essential scene sub-graph mining and the bi-enhanced knowledge space learning is described in Sect. 3. Experimental results are reported and discussed in Sect. 4, followed by the conclusion in Sect. 5.

2   Related Work

In this section, we briefly review the related work on scene representation and scene classification.

Scene representation is the most important step in scene recognition task, which aims to extract discriminative features from scene images. GIST [15], which is one of hand-crafted global features, lexicographically converts an entire scene image into a high-dimensional feature vector, but fails to exploit local structure information in scenes, especially the indoor scenes with complex spatial layouts. Methods focusing on local features, such as OTC [14] and CEN-TRIST [22], firstly describe the structure pattern of each local patch and then combine the statistics of all patches into a concatenated feature vector. Recently, as Convolutional Neural Networks (CNNs) have made remarkable progress on image recognition, deeply-learned methods have been widely adopted. Gong *et al.* [7] proposed a multi-scale orderless pooling (MOP) method to extract fully-connected features on image local patches. While these methods have achieved encouraging performance, a largely overlooked aspect is the role of the scale and its relation with the feature extractor in a multi-scale scenario. Herranz *et al.* [8] adapted the feature extractor to each particular scale, which combined ImageNet-CNNs [17] and Places-CNNs [29] to improve classification performance. However, the essential objects and their relations are still not fully utilized, while much information extracted from patches is redundant. Furthermore, most of the recent methods need to produce the proposal of each objects, which push the computational costs too high when dealing with large scale dataset.

Over the past decades, many methods have been proposed for scene classification [2,6,16,19,20,27,28] and can be categorized into two groups: generative models and discriminative models. Generative models usually adopt hierarchical Bayesian to express various relations in a complex scene, such as Markov random fields (MRF) [6], hidden Markov model (HMM) [19] and latent Dirichlet allocation (LDA) [1]. However, these models need to build complex probabilistic graph model and require high computational cost. The discriminative models extract feature descriptors from images and then encode them into a fixed length vector for classification. The typical classifiers include logistic regression and support vector machine (SVM) [2]. Especially, the SVM classifier has been widely used for scene classification. Object bank (OB) [13] and deformable part based model (DPM) [5] are representative examples of training a feature classifier for scene classification. Unlike the generative models, the parameters of discriminative models are easy to learn for feature classification.

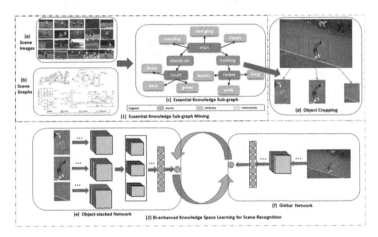

Fig. 1. Overview of proposed framework. The model consists of: (1) essential scene sub-graph mining; (2) bi-enhanced knowledge space learning for scene recognition.

3   Our Approach

Our proposed framework is illustrated in Fig. 1, which contains two key stages: essential scene sub-graph mining and bi-enhanced knowledge space learning. Firstly, we adopt a statistical method to mine the essential scene sub-graph for each scene class. Next, the bi-enhanced knowledge space is sought for scene image recognition by iteratively learning representations from essential scene sub-graph and entire image. In this section, we present the details of the proposed framework.

3.1   Essential Scene Sub-graph Mining

The scene graph is a graph of each scene image to describe all the objects, attributes and inter-object relations. Our approach attempts to mine the essential scene sub-graph by using the similarity between the scene graphs from the same class.

For essential scene sub-graph mining, we statistically analyze the frequencies of objects for each scene. Firstly, we count the occurring frequencies of all object sets for each scene class. Next, we choose object sets with the highest frequencies and size varying from 1 to 6 for each scene class. Lastly, we calculate the percentages of images including all the objects in above selected object sets for each scene class, and then the average of them for all the scene classes. Taking the scene of "tennis game" as an example, after counting the occurring frequencies of all object sets in all "tennis game" scene images, we obtain that *tennis player* surfacing out when object set size is 1 and 98.5% of images include it. Similarly, *tennis player, tennis court* is selected when object set size is 2, with 76.4% of images include them. More details on essential scene sub-graph mining are shown in Algorithm 1.

Algorithm 1. Essential Scene Sub-graph Mining

Input: Image set C_j in the j-th scene class.
Output: Essential scene sub-graph(objects set $\hat{O}_j$ that contains relations) for the j-th scene class
1: Initiate $k[m][m] = 0$ and a empty dictionary D_j
2: **for** $i = 0$ to $N(C_j)$ **do**
3:     **while** c_i has *object* **do**
4:         $S_i.add(object)$
5:     **end while**
6:     **for** object in S_i **do**
7:         **if** *object* not in D_j.Keys() **then**
8:             $D_j[object] = D_j[object] + 1$
9:         **else**
10:             $D_j[object] = 1$
11:        **end if**
12:    **end for**
13: **end for**
14: pick $O_m = \{o_1, o_2, , , o_m\}$ from the top of D_j
15: **for** $n = 0$ to $N(C_j)$, $i = 0$ to m, $l = 0$ to m **do**
16:     **if** (o_i, o_j) has edge **then**
17:         $k[i][l] = k[i][l] + 1$
18:     **end if**
19: **end for**
20: **if** $set(i, l, p, q) == 3$ **then**
21:     return $\hat{O}_j = (o_1, o_2, o_3)$, ($o_2$ is the repeat object)
22: **else**
23:     return $\hat{O}_j = (o_i, o_j, o_p)$
24: **end if**

3.2   Bi-enhanced Knowledge Space Learning

This section aims to illustrate the learning of a knowledge space that saves useful and discriminative features from entire images and essential scene sub-graph. The structure of the whole model is shown in Fig. 2. It includes three parts: (1) object-stacked network, which learns features from essential scene

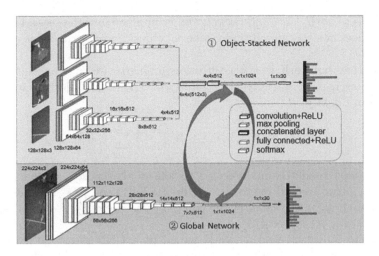

Fig. 2. Illustration of the bi-enhanced knowledge space learning. ① is the object-stacked network and ② describes the global network. The whole figure demonstrates an iterative process for knowledge space learning.

sub-graph enhanced by global representation, (2) global scene network, which learns features from the entire image enhanced by object-stacked representation, and (3) bi-enhanced knowledge space optimization, which iteratively seeks the knowledge space from both object-stacked representation learning and global representation learning.

Inspired by Huang *et al.* [9] and considering the structure of essential scene sub-graph, we adopt an object-stacked network to process three objects and the relations in essential scene sub-graph as shown in Fig. 2. The object-stacked network contains three separate convolutional blocks, a concentrated layer which is adopted to combine the three-stream features, a 1×1 convolutional layer which is to reduce dimension, and a fully-connected layer which is utilized to build a knowledge space. The objective function is in Eq. (1):

$$\min_{W,b} \sum_{i=1}^{m} (||f(o_{i_1}, o_{i_2}, o_{i_3}) - h(c_i)||) + \lambda||W||^2 \tag{1}$$

where W and b are the weight and bias of the layers in network, respectively, m is the number of all the scene images, $f(\cdot)$ is the output of the first fully-connected layer $f6$ from object-stacked network, $h(c_i)$ is the global representation of image c_i which is learned from global network. $o_{i_1}, o_{i_2}, o_{i_3}$ are the objects of essential scene sub-graph cropped from image c_i and $h(\cdot)$ is the output of the first fully-connected layer from global scene network, $\lambda||W||^2$ is regularization term. Note that the object o_{i_2} which has relations to other two objects o_{i_1}, o_{i_3} is fed into the second stream. For example, for the scene of "tennis game", the essential objects are *man, court* and *racket*. The relations from essential scene sub-graph are *the man holding the racket* and *the man stands on the court*. Obviously, *man* has the relations to both *court* and *racket*, and is inputted into the second stream. If the image does not contain all three essential objects, we set the value of missing object as 0.

Recall that our task is a classification problem, we add another 2 fully-connected layers and softmax layer after fc6. The final objective function is expressed in Eq. (2)

$$\min_{W,b} \gamma \sum_{i=1}^{m} ||f(o_{i_1}, o_{i_2}, o_{i_3}) - h(c_i)|| + \xi\lambda||W||^2 - \delta \sum_{i=1}^{m} (y_i \log(T(o_{i_1}, o_{i_2}, o_{i_3})) \quad (2)$$

where ξ is used to determine whether to join regularization, γ and δ are the parameters introduced to reduce the difference between the two losses that we set 0.01 and 1. y_i is the label of image c_i, $T(\cdot)$ is the output of final softmax layer in object-stacked network.

Similar to object-stacked network, we adopt a CNN model to learn global representation as shown in Fig. 2. It contains five convolutional blocks, two fully-connected layers and a softmax layer for classification. The dimension of the first fully-connected layer is equal to the dimension of representation from object-stacked network. The objective function is shown in Eq. (3):

$$\min_{W,b} \alpha \sum_{i=1}^{m} ||h(c_i) - f(o_{i_1}, o_{i_2}, o_{i_3})|| + \mu\lambda||W||^2 - \beta \sum_{i=1}^{m} (y_i \log(H(c_i)) \quad (3)$$

where $H(\cdot)$ is the output of final softmax layer in global scene network. The parameters α and β are utilized to balance these two losses, and μ controls whether to use regularization term. The meaning of the remaining parameters is the same as before. We use mini-batch stochastic gradient descent (SGD) to optimize Eq. (3). When Eq. (3) reaches an optima, we obtain the global representation enhanced by object-stacked representation.

Based on the above mentioned two networks, an iterative process between them is adopted. The iterative process is initiated by object-stacked network with cross-entropy cost function instead of global representations. Next, at each iteration, we update object-stacked representations by optimizing Eq. (2) which is enhanced with global representations, and then adjust global representations by optimizing Eq. (3) which is enhanced with object-stacked representations. The knowledge space is optimized iteratively until convergence. For test, we only employ the trained global network to predict the scene class.

4   Experiments

This section demonstrates the effectiveness of the learned bi-enhanced knowledge space on Scene 30.

4.1   Datasets and Implementation

To better demonstrate the proposed method in large scale dataset, we construct Scene 30 from Visual Genome [10]. The constructed Scene 30 contains 4608 color images of 30 different scenes including both indoor and outdoor scenes. The number of images varies across categories with at least 50 images per category. Each image has a corresponding scene graph. There are 10,034 objects and 30,000 types of relations in total in Scene 30. We split 85% of each class from the entire dataset for training and the rest as test set. The object-stacked network and global scene network are implemented using the open-source package Keras [4]. We adopt the VGG-16 model pre-trained in ImageNet [18]. In object-stacked network, the cropped object patches are resized to 128 × 128, and the input of global scene network are warped to a 224 × 224. The features of scene and object-stacked network are extracted from the layer of $fc6$.

4.2 Result and Comparison

Table 1 shows the comparison results. From the table, we can see that the accuracy of the classification increased from 82.51% to 88.29% after two iteration cycles. Moreover, through the bi-enhanced knowledge space learning, global network and object-stacked network capture more meaningful and discriminative information. The accuracy of the classification in object-stacked network increased from 89.60% to 90.32%. Similarly, the accuracy of the global network also increased from 82.51% to 86.71% and then to 88.29% under the supervision of local essential objects features.

Table 1. Recognition performance comparisons in different iterations

Methods	Accuracy
VGG-16 [18]	82.51%
OSN-iter1	89.60%
OSN-iter2	90.32%
OSN-iter2 fc6 + SVM	87.57%
GN-iter1	86.71%
GN-iter2 + SVM	87.43%
GN-iter2	88.29%

Table 2. Recognition performance comparisons on Scene 30

Methods	Accuracy
AlexNet [11]	72.40%
VGG-16 [18]	82.51%
PlaceNet205 (AlexNet) [29]	72.19%
PlaceNet365 (AlexNet) [24]	76.56%
PlaceNet205 (VGG-16) [29]	86.77%
PlaceNet365 (VGG-16) [24]	86.67%
HybridNet (AlexNet) [29]	73.54%
HybridNet (VGG-16) [24]	87.08%
Our fc6 + SVM	87.43%
Ours	**88.29%**

We then evaluate our proposed methods on Scene 30 and compare it with several recent CNN based methods. Table 2 records the recognition accuracy of our approach and other methods where we achieve the highest recognition rate. The method named "Our $fc6$ + SVM" extracts the feature in $fc6$ and trains a SVM for classification. The method named "Ours" directly utilizes the global network to predict the scene class. From the table, we have following 3 observations. (1) VGG-16 outperforms AlexNet. For example, VGG-16 in PlaceNet 365 is 10.11% higher than AlexNet. Therefore, we choose VGG-16 as a basic model. (2) the essential scene sub-graph is beneficial to scene recognition. The accuracy of our approach is 1.52% higher than PlaceNet 365 (VGG-16) and 1.21% higher than HybridNet 1365 (VGG-16). (3) The logistic regression is better than SVM for scene classification. We analyze that our model is an end to end framework for testing, while the SVM extracts the $fc6$ feature and then is optimized for classification.

5 Conclusion

In this paper, we propose a novel framework to learn the discriminative representations from both entire scene image and essential scene sub-graph. In future work, we will focus on utilizing the probability graph model to mine the essential scene sub-graph, such as Markov random fields (MRF [6]), and build a more accurate relationship between the scene image and objects.

Acknowledgement. This work is supported by the National Key Research & Development Plan of China (No. 2017YFB1002800), by the National Natural Science Foundation of China under Grant 61872424, 61572503, 61720106006, 61432019, and by NUPTSF (No. NY218001), also supported by the Key Research Program of Frontier Sciences, CAS, Grant NO. QYZDJ-SSW-JSC039, and the K.C. Wong Education Foundation.

References

1. Blei, D.M., Ng, A.Y., Jordan, M.I.: Latent Dirichlet allocation. J. Mach. Learn. Res. **3**, 993–1022 (2003)
2. Chen, P.H., Lin, C.J., Schölkopf, B.: A tutorial on-support vector machines. Appl. Stoch. Models Bus. Ind. **21**(2), 111–136 (2005)
3. Cheng, X., Lu, J., Feng, J., Yuan, B., Zhou, J.: Scene recognition with objectness. Pattern Recogn. **74**, 474–487 (2018)
4. Chollet, F., et al.: Keras (2015). https://github.com/keras-team/keras
5. Felzenszwalb, P.F., Girshick, R.B., McAllester, D., Ramanan, D.: Object detection-with discriminatively trained part-based models. PAMI **32**(9), 1627–1645 (2010)
6. Geman, S., Graffigne, C.: Markov random field image models and their applications to computer vision. In: Proceedings of the International Congress of Mathematicians, vol. 1, p. 2 (1986)
7. Gong, Y., Wang, L., Guo, R., Lazebnik, S.: Multi-scale orderless pooling of deep convolutional activation features. In: Fleet, D., Pajdla, T., Schiele, B., Tuytelaars, T. (eds.) ECCV 2014. LNCS, vol. 8695, pp. 392–407. Springer, Cham (2014). https://doi.org/10.1007/978-3-319-10584-0_26
8. Herranz, L., Jiang, S., Li, X.: Scene recognition with CNNs: objects, scales and dataset bias. In: CVPR, pp. 571–579 (2016)
9. Huang, S., Xu, Z., Tao, D., Zhang, Y.: Part-stacked CNN for fine-grained visual categorization. In: CVPR, pp. 1173–1182 (2016)
10. Krishna, R., et al.: Visual genome: connecting language and vision using crowd-sourced dense image annotations. IJCV **123**(1), 32–73 (2017)

11. Krizhevsky, A., Sutskever, I., Hinton, G.E.: ImageNet classification with deep convolutional neural networks. In: Advances in Neural Information Processing Systems, pp. 1097–1105 (2012)
12. Bao, B.-K., Zhu, G., Shen, J., Yan, S.: Robust image analysis with sparse representation on quantized visual features. IEEE Trans. Image Process. **22**(3), 860–871 (2013)
13. Li, L.J., Su, H., Fei-Fei, L., Xing, E.P.: Object bank: A high-level image representation for scene classification and semantic feature sparsification. In: Advances in Neural Information Processing Systems, pp. 1378–1386 (2010)
14. Margolin, R., Zelnik-Manor, L., Tal, A.: OTC: a novel local descriptor for scene classification. In: Fleet, D., Pajdla, T., Schiele, B., Tuytelaars, T. (eds.) ECCV 2014. LNCS, vol. 8695, pp. 377–391. Springer, Cham (2014). https://doi.org/10.1007/978-3-319-10584-0_25
15. Oliva, A., Torralba, A.: Modeling the shape of the scene: a holistic representation of the spatial envelope. IJCV **42**(3), 145–175 (2001)
16. Parizi, S.N., Oberlin, J.G., Felzenszwalb, P.F.: Reconfigurable models for scene recognition. In: CVPR 2012, pp. 2775–2782. IEEE (2012)
17. Russakovsky, O., et al.: Imagenet large scale visual recognition challenge. IJCV **115**(3), 211–252 (2015)
18. Simonyan, K., Zisserman, A.: Very deep convolutional networks for large-scale image recognition. arXiv preprint arXiv:1409.1556 (2014)
19. Stamp, M., Professor, A.: A revealing introduction to hidden Markov models. IEEE ASSP Magruine **1**(24), 258–261 (2004)
20. Sudderth, E.B., Torralba, A., Freeman, W.T., Willsky, A.S.: Learning hierarchical models of scenes, objects, and parts. In: ICCV 2005, vol. 2, pp. 1331–1338. IEEE (2005)
21. Wang, Z., Wang, L., Wang, Y., Zhang, B., Qiao, Y.: Weakly supervised patchnets: describing and aggregating local patches for scene recognition. TIP **26**(4), 2028–2041 (2017)
22. Wu, J., Rehg, J.M.: Centrist: a visual descriptor for scene categorization. PAMI **33**(8), 1489–1501 (2011)
23. Xie, G.S., Zhang, X.Y., Yan, S., Liu, C.L.: Hybrid CNN and dictionary-based models for scene recognition and domain adaptation. IEEE Trans. Circuits Syst. Video Technol. **27**(6), 1263–1274 (2017)
24. Zhou, B., Lapedriza, A., Khosla, A., Oliva, A., Torralba, A.: Places: a 10 million image database for scene recognition. PAMI **40**, 1452–1464 (2017)
25. Bao, B.-K., Liu, G., Changsheng, X., Yan, S.: Inductive robust principal component analysis. IEEE Trans. Image Process. **21**(8), 3794–3800 (2012)
26. Bao, B.-K., Min, W., Li, T., Changsheng, X.: Joint local and global consistency on interdocument and interword relationships for co-clustering. IEEE Trans. Cybern. **45**(1), 15–28 (2015)
27. Min, W., Bao, B.-K., Mei, S., Zhu, Y., Rui, Y., Jiang, S.: You are what you eat: exploring rich recipe information for cross-region food analysis. IEEE Trans. Multimed. **20**(4), 950–964 (2018)
28. Bao, B.-K., Changsheng, X., Min, W., Hossain, M.S.: Cross-platform emerging topic detection and elaboration from multimedia streams. TOMCCAP **11**(4), 54 (2015)
29. Zhou, B., Lapedriza, A., Xiao, J., Torralba, A., Oliva, A.: Learning deep features for scene recognition using places database. In: Advances in Neural Information Processing Systems, pp. 487–495 (2014)

Database, Data Mining, Big Data and Information Retrieval

A Hybrid Methodology of Effective Text-Similarity Evaluation

Shu-Kai Yang[(✉)] and Chien Chou

National Chiao-Tung University,
No. 1001, Daxue Rd., Hsinchu 300, Taiwan (R.O.C.)
skyang@csie.nctu.edu.tw, cchou@mail.nctu.edu.tw

Abstract. In this paper, an effective methodology which hybridizes a LCS finding algorithm and SimHash computation is presented for evaluating the text-similarity of articles. It reduces the time-space scale needed by the LCS algorithm by breaking the articles into word subsequences of sentences, managing and pairing them by SimHash comparisons, and reaching the goal of evaluating long-length articles rapidly, with the similar parts and similarity score of compared articles figured out exactly.

Keywords: Text similarity · LCS · LSH · SimHash · Plagiarism detection

1 Introduction

The evaluation of text similarity is a classic problem in computer science. It is widely used in paraphrasing evaluation, plagiarism detection, version control, and the duplication checking of documents or web pages. The mainstream methodology of text-similarity evaluation is based on the longest common subsequence (LCS) finding algorithms [1]. If we treat an article as a sequence of words and punctuation marks, the problem of figuring out the similar parts of two articles is equal to finding the longest common subsequence of the two sequences. For example, here are two text sequences:

"that words is that words words that"
"is words that words that is"

The longest common subsequence (LCS) is

"is that words that"

In the six words of the second text sequence, there are four words in common with the first text sequence. We can say that the sequence has the 66% similarity with the first one. As shown above, exploiting a LCS finding algorithm in text-similarity not only evaluates the score but also figures out the similar parts of the text. But the disadvantage is, a LCS finding algorithm always takes squared complexity in both space and time. This makes the algorithm hard to evaluate long-length articles.

In this paper, presented an effective methodology that hybridizes Myers' LCS finding algorithm [2] and Similarity hash (SimHash) [3] computation, and develops the brand new framework to reduce the time-space scale needed by a LCS finding algorithm, and perform fast text-similarity evaluations to long-length articles. Similarity

© Springer Nature Singapore Pte Ltd. 2019
C.-Y. Chang et al. (Eds.): ICS 2018, CCIS 1013, pp. 227–237, 2019.
https://doi.org/10.1007/978-981-13-9190-3_24

hashing (SimHash) is the way to compute the "fingerprints" of articles. It completely ignores the literal meaning of text data. It only emphasizes and gathers the statistics of the characteristics of bit patterns of the words in the text. With the SimHash computations and comparisons, it is easy to find similar articles in a text library, just like telling people by fingerprints. But SimHash cannot figure out the similarity score and similar parts of evaluated articles.

In the presented methodology, first parse the original and to-be-compared text, and get two sequences of words and punctuation marks. Then separate each sequence into the subsequences of sentences. Compute the SimHash of each subsequence, and find the most similar pairs between the subsequences of the original and to-be-compared text by checking the hamming distance of their SimHash values. Finally apply a LCS finding to the paired subsequences to figure out the similar parts and compute the similarity score of the whole text.

2 Previous Works

The most well-known algorithm used in text-similarity evaluation is Myers' algorithm and its variations [4]. Instead of iterative string comparisons, the algorithm transforms the subsequence finding problem into a path-finding problem on an edit graph as shown in Fig. 1. Considering the example text A and B to be evaluated, the goal of Myers' algorithm is to find the shortest path to change A to B.

A: *"that words is that words words that"*
B: *"is words that words that is"*

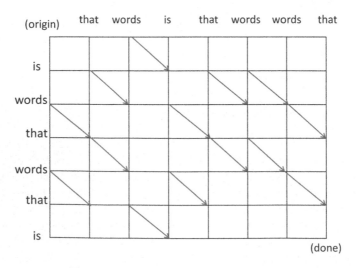

Fig. 1. The edit graph of the compared text

As shown in Fig. 1, the original text A is laid out as the horizontal dimension, the destination text B is laid out as the vertical dimension of the graph. In the graph, since the origin (0, 0) at the upper left corner, a horizontal step is equal to delete a word of A, a vertical step is equal to add a word of B. For example, the sub-path that moves from (0, 0) to (1, 1) go one step horizontally from (0, 0) to (1, 0), and one step vertically from (1, 0) to (1,1). The sub-path means that deleting "that" and adding "in" when changing text A to B.

Myers' algorithm also develops an optimized method for finding the shortest path since the origin to the lower right corner [5]. When the shortest path is found, the steps of changing A to B is known, the path is also called "edit script" from A to B, and the passed diagonal lines is exactly the "longest common subsequence (LCS)" of A and B.

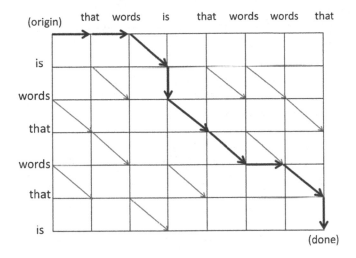

Fig. 2. The path found by Myers' algorithm.

Myers' path finding is basically a breadth-first-search (BFS). When growing the path of depth d to d + 1, the branches with the longer length are prior to the others. Passing the diagonal lines does not increase the depth but increases the length of current path. The shortest path found by Myers' algorithm is shown in Fig. 2, and we know the longest common subsequence (LCS) of A and B is:

"is that words that"

Although Myers' algorithm helps to skip some branches of searching, finding the shortest path is basically a squared complexity task in both space and time. If we are going to evaluate two articles of 10,000 words, we still have to prepare a grid graph with 100,000,000 cells, and lots of CPU time for the computation. Because a LCS finding algorithm like this detects the "subsequence" of text, plagiarism may evade the detection by swapping the order of sentences and paragraphs.

Similarity hashing (SimHash) is a counter-intuitive method of text-similarity evaluation [3]. Instead of traversing the text, it invents a rapid method compares the composition of articles. The main idea of SimHash methodology is assuming the articles that talk about the same keywords with the same frequencies should be similar or equivalent articles, hence the SimHash computation tries to transform the words and their frequencies of occurrence to something like integer values or bit patterns for rapid comparisons.

Hash functions are the standard functions that map the inputted values to wide ranges evenly [6]. The mapped values always have the fixed length of data, even the length of the inputted data varies. For example, a typical hash function maps ASCII strings to 32-bit integers. A well-defined hash function has the characteristics:

1. A hash function maps a close value set to a wide range. A little change of the inputted value causes a very different hash value outputted by the hash function.
2. The hash values outputted by a hash function have the fixed data-length, such as 32 bits or 64 bits.
3. A hash function is not invertible. You cannot guess the inputted data according to its hash value.

Hash function are usually implemented as the shifting and XORing of the bits of the inputted byte stream. The original paper of SimHash has told us, you can apply any hash function that fits in with the described definitions when calculating the SimHash of an article. In the implementation of this paper, a 64-bit SDBM hash function is used.

For an article to calculate its SimHash, the hash values of every word in the article are calculated first. As shown in Fig. 3, we gather the statistics of each bit of the word hash values, and form the requested SimHash. For each i-th bit of the requested SimHash, it is 1 if all the i-th bits of word hash values have more 1 than 0, otherwise the i-th bit of SimHash is 0.

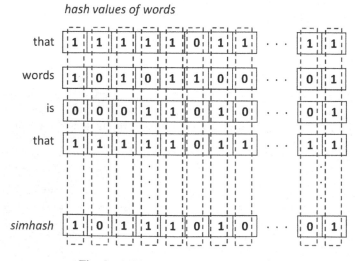

Fig. 3. A SimHash calculation example.

After the statistics shown in Fig. 3, each i-th bit of the result SimHash tells the characteristics of the article: how many words whose hash values have their i-th bits 1 or 0. If two compared articles have their SimHash values having more equal bits, the more similar those articles are. The SimHash calculation is one kind of local sensitive hashing (LSH), meaning that each bit of the hash value reflects a local change of the inputted source data. One 64-bit SimHash value remembers 64 characteristics of the article, and calculating the hamming distance (how many bits differ) of two SimHash tells the similarity of the two compared articles.

The SimHash methodology is very efficient to verify the similarity of two articles, so it is widely exploited in searching the plagiarism papers in the academic library, and in finding similar or duplicated web pages in a web-cache database. In the database, stored are the fixed-length SimHash values of articles, and we can rapidly find the plagiarized source by checking the hamming distance of the SimHash of the compared article and the SimHash values stored in the database without traversing the text.

Although the SimHash methodology is very efficient for long-length articles, the hamming distances neither tell the percentages of similarity nor figure out the similar parts of compared articles. In this paper, we hybridize the advantages of the LCS-based and SimHash-based algorithms, without their disadvantages.

3   The Hybrid Methodology

Considering the architecture of an article, sentences and paragraphs are swappable without changing the meaning of the original article, and the words inside a sentence are not swappable. The presented methodology therefore breaks the LCS-based text-similarity evaluation into three stages. In the first stage, the article is segmented into sentences. In the second stage, hash and pair the similar sentences by SimHash calculations. And in the third stage, LCS and edit scripts of the paired sentences are evaluated, and the similarity score of entire article can be calculated. The shortest edit script (SES) that scribes how to rewire the original text as the compared one is also acquired.

As shown in Fig. 4, for the two evaluated text A and B, they are parsed into sequences of words and punctuation marks, and the sequences are segmented in to subsequences, hashed, paired, and evaluated. Finally, the similarity of A and B is summed up by collecting the results of subsequences.

3.1   The Segmentation Stage

For further hashing and longest common subsequence (LCS) finding, the inputted text is parsed into sequences of words and punctuation marks. In the parsed punctuation marks, some are the separators of sentences, depending on languages. For example, English sentences are separated by periods, exclamatory marks, and question marks. And Chinese sentences are separated by comma and periods. After segmentation, one sequence of the inputted text is separated into subsequences of sentences.

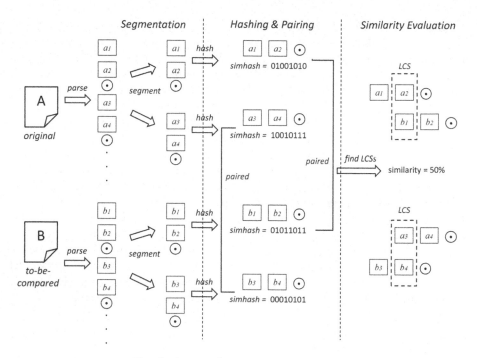

Fig. 4. Stages of the hybrid methodology.

3.2 The Hashing and Pairing Stage

For each word in the subsequences of sentences, compute their hash values by a 64-bit SDBM hash function, and form the similarity hash (SimHash) value of the sentence by the calculation introduced in [3]. As shown in Fig. 4, the hamming distances of the SimHash values of the sentences in A and B tells how similar there are. [3] has told us, if the hamming distance of two 32-bit SimHash values is greater than 3, they are not similar. In our implementation, if the hamming distance of two 64-bit SimHash values of a sentence in A and another sentence in B is greater than the threshold 12, they are determined completely different.

SimHash computation is a statisties-based methodology. Longer articles lead the results close to the expectations. [3] recommended the threshold value 3 for 32-bit SimHash values, so 6 can be a proper threshold for 64-bit SimHash values according to the bucketing principle. We take a doubled value 12 for handling short articles well.

For each sentence b in B, find the most similar sentence a in A by finding the minimal hamming distance to the SimHash values of b, and these two sentences a and b are paired for finding LCS in the next stage. If there is no such sentence a in A whose SimHash value has a hamming distance less than 12 to b, there is no similar sentence in A for the sentence b in B.

3.3   The Similarity Evaluation Stage

For every paired sentences *a* and *b*, find their longest common subsequence (LCS) by Myers' Algorithm [2]. Sum up the length of found LCS, and divide it by the total of words in the to-be-compared text B, we get the similarity of A and B. It is so intuitive that the score tells the percentage of B is plagiarized from A. The presented definition of similarity is

similarity (A, B) = sum of length of LCS/total words of B

where A is the original text and B is the to-be-compared paraphrase. The presented methodology has reduced the time-space complexity of LCS finding from the square of full-length of the text to the square of sentence length by breaking the task into three stages. It makes the methodology efficient enough to process long-length articles. It keeps the advantages of LCS finding that exactly finds the similar parts and the shortest edit Scripts (SES) of the compared text.

3.4   The Shortest Edit Script

A shortest edit script (SES) is a valuable by-product of Myers' Algorithm [2]. As shown in Fig. 2, the algorithm transforms the LCS finding problem to a shortest-path finding problem on an edit graph. Each horizontal or vertical step on an edit graph denotes a word deletion of adding, so that when the shortest path is found, the minimal steps to rewrite the original text A to the compared paraphrase B is also found. The minimal steps to rewrite the text are named the shortest edit scripts (SES) from A to B. See the mentioned example:

A: *"that words is that words words that"*
B: *"is words that words that is"*
LCS: *"is that words that"*

The shortest path on Fig. 2 is also the SES:

"~~that words~~ is +(words) that words ~~words~~ that +(is)"

In the presented methodology, it also collects the SES data of paired sentences, and tells the way to rewrite the original text to the compared one. The function is very useful in the paraphrasing practices of literature writing lessons.

3.5   Extending to Non-english Text

The presented methodology not only works well on English text, but also works on other languages. Here is the tip to make it applicable. One word in English is composed of multiple alphabets, but one word in another language, such as Chinese, is a single character, and a single character does not form a distinguished hash value in any hash function. For these cases, multiple words have to be grouped together for a hash value, and the rest parts of the presented methodology works fine. That is why we select 64-bit SDBM as the built-in hash function. It shifts the most bits of the inputted byte stream, and the fewest grouped characters are needed to form a distinguished hash value. In Chinese, it needs only four characters. This tip makes the presented methodology works well on Chinese, and Chinese-English mixed articles.

4   Implementation and Results

We have implemented the presented methodology as a.NET class library. It is applicable to both PC and web-based applications. The demonstrated is the results of the app processing the written text examples provided by Princeton University [7]. The original text is from the pages of an old book talking about Shakespeare. Here are some paraphrases detected different similarities. As shown in Fig. 5, the app shows the comparison sheets of the original text and the paraphrase, emphasizes the similar parts, and calculates the similarity score by counting the percentage of common words.

In Fig. 5(c) is the most similar paraphrase, and in Fig. 5(d) is the shortest edit script that rewrites the original text to the paraphrase. The app also saves to evaluation results as HTML pages with built-in JavaScript code. When you click on a similar sentence of the compared paraphrase, the window of original text scrolls to and highlights the sentence where the clicked sentence is plagiarized from.

The demonstration in Fig. 6 shows that the presented methodology also works well on non-English text. The written text examples provided by National Taiwan University [8]. As shown in Fig. 6, inserting some redundancy words in sentences does not avoid the detection of text similarity.

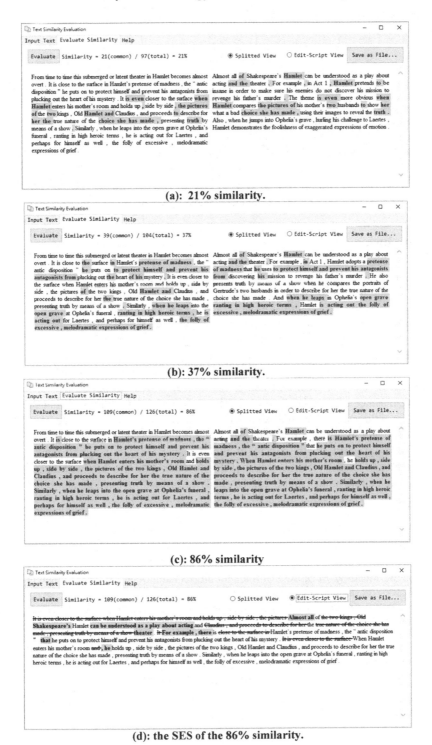

(a): 21% similarity.

(b): 37% similarity.

(c): 86% similarity

(d): the SES of the 86% similarity.

Fig. 5. The paraphrase detected 21%, 37%, and 86% similarity.

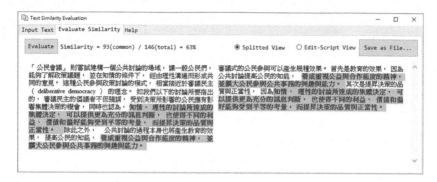

Fig. 6. The demonstration in Chinese.

5 Conclusion

We present a hybrid methodology of text similarity evaluation that keeps the advantages of LCS finding algorithm and SimHash calculation. It is effective for long-length text, and is keeping the rich information of detected similar parts, percentage of similarity, and the shortest path to rewrite the compared text. It is very applicable for the plagiarism detection, version control and duplication checking of documents, and for literature writing lessons. In the presented methodology, long-length articles are segmented into the subsequences of words and punctuation marks of sentences. The subsequences of the original text and to-be-compared text are paired by the minimal hamming distance of SimHash values. Then perform LCS finding in the subsequence pairs, the similar parts of paired sentences are found, and the percentage of text similarity is also acquired. The presented methodology has reduced the time-space complexity of LCS-based to the square of the sentence length. If works well on both English and non-English text. The cost of the methodology is so low that it can be used on PC or web applications, and it can be easily integrated in a text database for further applications.

References

1. Hunt, J.W., MacIlroy, M.D.: An algorithm for differential file comparison. Computing science technical report, #41, Bell Laboratories (1976)
2. Myers, E.W.: An O(ND) difference algorithm and its variations. Algorithmica **1**(1–4), 251–266 (1986)
3. Sadowski, C., Levin, G.: SimHash: Hash-based similarity detection. Technical report UCSC-SOE-11-07, University of California, Santa Cruz, February 2011
4. Indu, P., et al.: A comparative study of different longest common subsequence algorithms. Int. J. Recent Res. Aspects **3**(2), 65–69 (2016). ISSN 2349-7688

5. Hertel, M.: An O(ND) Difference Algorithm for C# (2006). https://www.mathertel.de/Diff/
6. Partow, A.: General Purpose Hash Function Algorithms. http://www.partow.net/programming/hashfunctions/
7. Examples of Plagiarism: Princeton University. https://pr.princeton.edu/pub/integrity/pages/plagiarism/
8. Lin, K.-M.: What is Plagiarism? Examples and Explanations. https://www.facebook.com/notes/657936507563326/

Research on Passenger Carrying Capacity of Taichung City Bus with Big Data of Electronic Ticket Transactions: A Case Study of Route 151

Cheng-Yuan Ho[1,2,3(✉)] and I-Hsuan Chiu[4]

[1] Department of Computer Science and Information Engineering,
Asia University, Taichung City, Taiwan
tommyho@asia.edu.tw
[2] Big Data Research Center, Asia University, Taichung City, Taiwan
[3] Taichung City Smart Transportation Big Data Research Center,
Asia University, Taichung City, Taiwan
[4] Department of Civil Engineering, National Chiao Tung University,
Hsinchu City, Taiwan
sherry52168@g2.nctu.edu.tw

Abstract. In order to find passengers' behaviors when the passengers take buses, 456 thousand and 82 million records of electronic ticket transactions of route 151 and Taichung City Bus in 2015 are respectively analyzed in this article. There are three statistical/analytic results. First, about 5.26 million electronic ticket users received benefits from Taichung City Government's policy for a free bus ride within 10 km with an electronic ticket; however, less than 0.5% users still used cash. Second, The passengers usually got on and off route 151 at THSR Taichung Station no matter which direction. Other bus stops for passengers usually getting on and off were T.P.C.C., Wufeng Agr. Ind. Senior High School, Wufeng, and Wufeng Post Office. Finally, on Friday and the day before holidays, many passengers changed their behaviors to take route 151 from Wufeng District to THSR Taichung Station. This change was that the passengers took another bus route to the station near the start station of route 151 to increase the probability to get on the route 151.

Keywords: Intelligent transport system · Smart Transportation ·
Passenger carrying capacity · Big Data · Electronic ticket transaction ·
Bus passenger · Taichung bus · Taiwan High Speed Rail · Hot spot distribution

1 Introduction

With the development of high-speed public transportation and the rapid economic development of Taiwan, in recent years, passengers for intercity travels, especially for business travels, are notably increased. In other words, a lot of passengers arrive, depart, and transfer in high-speed rail stations, railway stations, passenger transport stations, bus stations and so on [1]. The original designs of the connecting lines may

© Springer Nature Singapore Pte Ltd. 2019
C.-Y. Chang et al. (Eds.): ICS 2018, CCIS 1013, pp. 238–249, 2019.
https://doi.org/10.1007/978-981-13-9190-3_25

not be appropriate for the new travel needs and the increasing traffic flow has triggered traffic jams around such external traffic hubs.

Furthermore, Developed countries not only develop public transportation systems (PTSs) but also integrate related transportation systems. This is because PTSs are also shared transport services; providing energy saving, reductions air pollution and traffic congestion, and enhanced convenience, while at the same time tackling the deteriorating traffic of private transportation. In order to make public transportation the major transport for people, PTSs have to be seamlessly integrated, and thus improve people's willingness to use them. Consequently, in order to establish a comprehensive public transport network and increase the service coverage ratio, Taichung City Government has aggressively enhanced its smart transport services and promoted the policy of a free bus ride within 10 km with an electronic ticket [2].

In the past, it was difficult to collect passengers' thoughts and feedback through telephone interviews, roadside interviews, simple surveys, or household visits. These methods were not only costly but also had biasing problems and there was a large gap between research and the real world. Fortunately, with the progress of science and technology, the charging system has been changed from coin-based to an electronic ticket-based system. In the future, the charging system may include third party payments and mobile payments. Currently, all buses in Taiwan are equipped with electronic ticket readers in support of electronic ticket payment. In addition, according to the statistics from EasyCard Corporation (2000–2016) [3], the number of EasyCards in March 2012 exceeded 30 million, and by April 2016, the number of EasyCards exceeded 60 million in Taiwan. Similarly, according to the statistics from iPASS Corporation (2008–2017) [4], the number of iPass in 2014 exceeded 5 million, and by 2017, the number of iPass had risen to over 12 million. The statistics from these two corporations show that the use of electronic tickets is gradually increasing every year.

The electronic ticket itself implies the identity of a user, such as general/full-fare, student, preferential/half-fare, senior, and concessionaire; while a transaction record of an electronic ticket used for public transport implies the user's boarding record. The information may include the type of transportation used, route number, boarding or alighting station (depending on the charging method), etc. More information can be obtained through statistical analysis, such as the number of passengers getting on and off the bus/train, and the type of passengers in terms of electronic ticket used. These are valuable data for developing traffic and city management policies. Therefore, this has become an important focus of research in recent years.

Route 151 is a very important bus service for people living in Wufeng District because it is the only one bus service connecting to Taiwan High Speed Rail (abbreviated THSR) at Wuri District. In fact, as shown in Fig. 1, route 151 starts from Chaoyang University of Technology (labeled 1 and abbreviated CYUT) at Wufeng, passes through the THSR (labeled 17), and ends to Taichung City Council (labeled 25 and abbreviated TCC) at Xitun, and vice versa. Lots passengers, especially businessmen, travelers, and students, take route 151 for their major tools from THSR to Wufeng or Xitun, and vice versa. In this article, to understand the ridership of route 151 and the electronic ticket usages of Taichung City Bus, the electronic ticket transaction records of 2015 used in route 151 and Taichung City Bus, totaling 456,747 and 82,820,553 records, are analyzed, respectively.

The remainder of this article is organized as follows. Section 2 briefs the background of Wufeng District, Taiwan High Speed Rail, Taichung City Bus, and the classification of electronic tickets. Literature review is presented in Sect. 3. Section 4 shows the case study and analytic results of passengers' patterns of route 151. Finally, Sect. 5 concludes the article with a brief summary.

Fig. 1. Route path and stops of route 151.

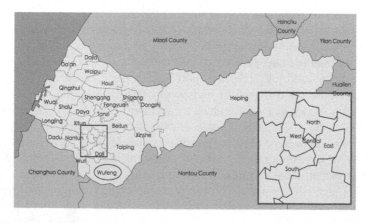

Fig. 2. Taichung City and its administrative regions.

2 Background

2.1 Wufeng District

Wufeng District is a suburban district in southernmost Taichung City, Taiwan, as shown in Fig. 2. It is an important traffic hub of Taichung City since it has the complete highway system, like Freeway No. 3 and No. 6, and Provincial Highway 3, 63, and 74. Wufeng District is a mainly agricultural town, but it was a very early development zone in central Taiwan and Wufeng Lin Family, one of five major families of Taiwan under Japanese rule, located here. Moreover, Wufeng District is one of the birthplaces of democratization in Taiwan, is rich in many cultural and arts facilities, and has two major geographical features, (1) the Wu Xi (or Wu River), which forms the Wufeng's southern border, and (2) Xiangbi Shan (or Elephant Trunk Mountain), which lies in the eastern part of the township.

2.2 Taiwan High Speed Rail and Taichung Station

THSR is a high-speed rail line, approximately 349.5 km (217 mi) along the west coast of Taiwan, from the national capital Taipei to the southern city of Kaohsiung. The maximum speed of a train on the THSR can reach about 300 km/h (186 mph) and a passenger can only spend about 105 min taking the train from the northernmost station, Nangang, to the southernmost station, Zuoying.

THSR opened for service on January 5th, 2007. In the first few months of operation, the ridership was few, about 25,000 to 36,000 passengers per day. Today, after ten years, the ridership grows to about 152,000 to 175,000 passengers per day. This is because in the first two years of operation, THSR Corporation (THSRC) accumulated debt by high depreciation charges and interest. In 2009, THSRC negotiated with the government to vary the method of depreciation from depending on concessions on rights to ridership. At the same time, the government also started to help refinance THSRC's loans. With the government's help, THSR carried its first 100 million passengers by August 2010, and respectively over 200 and 400 million passengers by December 2012 and December 2016.

Most intermediate stations on the high-speed rail line locate outside the cities; however, the passengers can choose a variety of transfer options. For example, if the passengers have their own private transportations, they may take their cars, motorcycles, and electric vehicles. Otherwise, they will take the public transportations, such as shuttle buses, city buses, conventional rails, light rails, metros, subways, and ferries.

Taichung station, as labeled 17 in Fig. 1, is located in Wuri District of Taichung City and it has the biggest space of all THSR stations. It opened for service on October 24th, 2006. The architectural image of the Taichung Station integrates the regional transit through middle Taiwan and is a gateway to Taichung. Therefore, the development includes the High Speed Railway Station, Taiwan Railway Station, bus transit, parking lots, public squares, supporting facilities, and the road system for the adjacent areas. Unlike some of the other THSR stations, the surrounding areas of Taichung station are not as commercially vigorous. Instead, noted chain restaurants and souvenir stores stationed inside the station attract crowds who are actually not here to commute on their day-offs.

2.3 Taichung City Bus

Taichung City Bus, managed by the Transportation Bureau of Taichung City Government in Taichung City, Taiwan, includes at least 200 bus routes, which are numbered from route 1 to route 999 and operated by different 15 bus companies. Furthermore, Taichung City Bus provides major services in downtown area and for residents in rural or remote areas in Taichung City, and supplies minor services to connect different counties, such as Changhua and Nantou Counties, which are south on Taichung, and Miaoli County, which is north on Taichung.

The bus fare is calculated by mileage per ride. The basic fare is NT$20 for 8 km, and the extended fare is calculated by NT$2.431*(1 + 5% tax included) per km and round to the nearest integer. Due to the policy of Taichung City Government, from July 1st, 2015 to date, a passenger with an electronic ticket (i.e., either an EasyCard or an iPass) can take buses for free below 10 km when the route numbers of buses are between route 1 and route 999.

2.4   Classification of Electronic Tickets

There are five types of electronic tickets in "Taichung City Smart Transportation Big Data Database" which is provided by the Bureau of Transportation. The electronic ticket types and their owners' qualifications are as follows.

- Taichung City Senior Card: (1) The person who aged 65 and over establishes his/her household registration in Taichung and (2) The Taiwanese aborigine who aged 55 and over establishes his/her household registration in Taichung.
- Other City/County Senior Card: The senior card was not issued by the Taichung City Government. This means the person/Taiwanese aborigine aged 65/55 and over, but he/she established his/her household registration in other city/county, not in Taichung.
- Half-fare Card: (1) Children whose ages are between 6 and 12 years old, (2) Elderly whose age is over 65 years old and does not have a Senior Card, and (3) The person with a disability and his/her one of companions.
- Full-fare Card: The person does not meet the qualifications of above descriptions.
- Token: The passenger takes a bus with cash, i.e., without using an electronic ticket. In practice, when the passenger gets on the bus, the driver will issue a token to the passenger. When the passenger wants to get off the bus, he/she needs to check the fare by tapping the token to the electronic ticket reader, then pays the fare by cash, and returns the token to the driver.

3   Literature Review

This section will introduce relevant researches on the application of electronic ticket data in public transport.

Bagchi and White [5] used the origin and destination records in the electronic ticket data to adjust the transportation service and so increased the performance and improved the quality of the transportation service. Chapleau and Chu [6] used electronic ticket data to analyze variation in the number of passengers and thus determine changes in passenger carrying capacity on specific routes. Furthermore, Chu and Chapleau [7] conducted a study on smart card boarding transactions and revealed the transfer patterns of travellers in their studies on transit demand modeling. Seaborn et al. [8] developed a method based on the maximum elapsed time to explain the transfer behaviors of passengers traveling on London public transport. This transfer behavior was divided into pure transfer, incidental activity transfer, and non-transfer. Wang et al. [9] used an Automatic Data Collection System (ADCS) to collect electronic ticket data to deduce passengers' destinations and analyze transfer service information, such as the transfer waiting time. Pelletier et al. [10] divided the use of electronic ticket data in public transport into three levels: (1) strategic level: setting a long-term plan; (2) tactical level: dynamically arranging the most suitable shifts to improve the quality of service; and (3) operational level: estimating various indicators of the public transport network. Alsger et al. [11] used South East Queensland (SEQ) data to study the effect of different data sample sizes on the accuracy level of the generated public transport O-D matrices and to quantify the sample size required for a certain level of accuracy. Agard et al. [12] divided the public transport users into four behavioral patterns according to the similar trip habits of travellers using K-mean clustering and Hierarchical Ascending Clustering (HAC) method on the boarding records. Medina [13] recognized the weekly mobility patterns by clustering a 14-dimension vector composed by start time and duration of mobility during 7 days in a week. Kieu et al. [14] proposed a new algorithm to detect the spatial travel pattern according to the number of repeated journeys from smart card data. Zhong et al. [15] measured the variability of mobility patterns using multiday smart card data and found out that mobility patterns varies from day to day.

4 Case Study

In this Section, 456,747 and 82,260,553 electronic ticket transaction records of route 151 and Taichung City Bus in 2015 are analyzed, respectively, and discussed by the number and utilization of electronic ticket type, the top 10 hot bus stops for passengers with different directions and the passengers' special patterns on Friday and the day before holidays.

4.1 Statistics of the Type of Electronic Ticket

By classifying the number of tickets (i.e., no matter how many times an electronic ticket is used), it can be found that the preferential policy for the free 10 km with an electronic ticket supplied by the Bureau of Transportation, Taichung City Government has been achieved a certain result. As shown in Fig. 3, there are about 5.26 million electronic ticket cards and nearly 99.57% of passengers use electronic tickets to take buses and only 0.43% of passengers use cash. There are three major reasons: (1) the balance of the electronic ticket has been negative, (2) the electronic ticket does not belong to any series of Easy Card and iPass, and (3) the passenger is the first time to take a bus in Taichung City and he/she does not have any electronic ticket.

According to the electronic ticket type utilization, as shown in Fig. 4, it can be found that the utilization of the full-fare card is about 89.17% of the total number of utilizations, equaling to 73.85 million rides. It is interesting to note that the Taichung

City Senior Card loses Other City/County Senior Card in the number of electronic tickets, but the utilization of Taichung City Senior Card is much higher than that of Other City/County Senior Card. This means the seniors who have established their household registrations in Taichung have more locomotion abilities than other seniors.

Similar to 151, by classifying the number of tickets, it can be found that, as shown in Fig. 5, in 456,747 electronic ticket transactions, there are 115,069 electronic ticket cards and nearly 99.67% of passengers use electronic tickets to take buses and only 0.33% of passengers use cash. On the other hand, according to the electronic ticket type utilization, as shown in Fig. 6, it can be found that the utilization of the full-fare card is about 87.48% of the total number of utilizations, equaling to 399,573 rides.

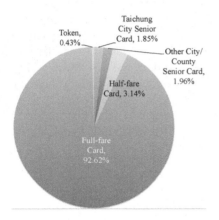

Fig. 3. Number of electronic ticket type.

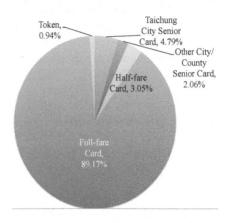

Fig. 4. Electronic ticket type utilization.

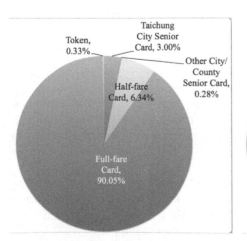

Fig. 5. Number of electronic ticket type of 151.

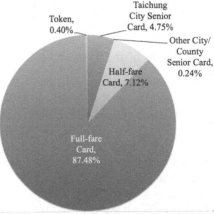

Fig. 6. Electronic ticket type utilization of 151.

4.2 Top 10 Hot Bus Stops

In this subsection, top 10 hot boarding and alighting bus stops of route 151 for different directions are discussed since route 151 only has 25 bus stops. From Tables 1 and 2, it can be found that THSR Taichung Station is the top one hot bus stop no matter which direction is and whether passengers board or alight the bus stop. Furthermore, the numbers of passengers of THSR Taichung Station are about 1.80, 1.19, 2.11, and 1.96 times greater than those of the top 2 hot bus stops (i.e., Shin Kong Mitsukoshi Department Store and T.P.C.C. in Table 1, and T.P.C.C. and Shin Kong Mitsukoshi Department Store in Table 2), respectively. In addition, four bus stops, T.P.C.C., Wufeng Agr. Ind. Senior High School, Wufeng, and Wufeng Post Office, come out on top in both two tables as THSR Taichung Station does. This means that, except THSR Taichung Station, the passengers who usually get route 151 on and off at these four bus stops may live, study, or work here or nearby. In the future, if a new route or service is created, these bus stops should be considered as the main bus stops.

Table 1. Top 10 hot bus stops of route 151 from TCC to CYUT.

Hop-on		Hop-off	
Count	Bus stop name	Count	Bus stop name
61,527	THSR Taichung Station	42,912	THSR Taichung Station
34,137	Shin Kong Mitsukoshi Department Store	36,096	T.P.C.C.
18,793	T.P.C.C.	15,662	Wufeng
17,638	Chaoma	13,342	Wufeng Post Office
16,838	Taichung City Police Bureau	11,406	Wu Feng Elementary School
16,752	Maple Garden (Chaoyang Bridge)	10,837	Zhongzheng-Caohu Intersection
7,129	Wufeng Agr. Ind. Senior High School	8,772	Wufeng Agr. Ind. Senior High School
6,783	Wufeng	7,943	Jiayin
5,552	Taichung City Hall	5,342	Ministry of Education
5,179	Wufeng Post Office	3,343	Maple Garden (Chaoyang Bridge)

Table 2. Top 10 hot bus stops of route 151 from CYUT to TCC.

Hop-on		Hop-off	
Count	Bus stop name	Count	Bus stop name
59,022	THSR Taichung Station	65,755	THSR Taichung Station
27,943	T.P.C.C.	33,618	Shin Kong Mitsukoshi Department Store
14,986	Wufeng Post Office	18,166	Maple Garden (Chaoyang Bridge)
14,384	Wufeng	16,257	Taichung City Police Bureau

(continued)

Table 2. (*continued*)

Hop-on		Hop-off	
9,706	Zhongzheng-Caohu Intersection	15,600	Wufeng Agr. Ind. Senior High School
9,354	Wufeng Agr. Ind. Senior High School	15,330	Chaoma
7,014	Ministry of Education	10,801	Wufeng Post Office
5,949	Jiayin	10,675	Wufeng
3,062	Shin Kong Mitsukoshi Department Store	9,853	Taichung City Hall
2,976	Wu Feng Elementary School	8,749	T.P.C.C.

4.3   Passengers' Special Patterns on Friday

On Friday and the day before holidays, many passengers changed their behaviors to take route 151 from Wufeng District (and/or Xitun District) to THSR Taichung Station. This was because when the route 151 arrived its maximum passenger carrying capacity, the driver would pass the remaining bus stations unless someone got off the route 151. Besides, a passenger with an electronic ticket can take bus journeys for free below 10 km. Hence, many passengers would take another bus route to the station near the start station of route 151 to increase the probability to get on the route 151. Tables 3 and 4 respectively show the numbers of passengers getting on the Top 10 hot bus stops of route 151 from CYUT to TCC and from TCC to CYUT by weekday. Two things can be found from tables. One is that the numbers of passengers on Friday are much larger

Table 3. Number of passengers getting on the Top 10 hot bus stops of route 151 from CYUT to TCC by weekday.

Bus stop name	Sun.	Mon.	Tue.	Wed.	Thur.	Fri.	Sat.
THSR Taichung Station	10,295	9,603	8,541	8,654	8,936	11,913	10,833
T.P.C.C.	3,654	3,779	3,902	4,300	4,918	7,559	4,142
Wufeng Post Office	2,301	2,372	2,210	2,180	2,508	3,494	2,483
Wufeng	2,688	2,504	2,187	2,056	2,266	3,040	2,455
Zhongzheng-Caohu Intersection	1,584	1,344	1,230	1,382	1,587	2,672	1,671
Wufeng Agr. Ind. Senior High School	624	1,800	1,919	1,840	1,824	1,828	928
Ministry of Education	677	1,247	1,290	1,196	1,399	1,724	652
Jiayin	1,032	994	774	955	1,013	1,262	986
Shin Kong Mitsukoshi Department Store	564	454	450	415	492	591	660
Wu Feng Elementary School	439	508	446	486	461	704	449

than those on Thursday at some specific bus stops, such as T.P.C.C., Zhongzheng-Caohu Intersection, Wufeng Post Office, and so on. The other is that when the station is nearer the start station, there are more passengers getting on the route 151. For example, Zhongzheng-Caohu Intersection station and T.P.C.C. station are the most increasing rate of passengers getting on the route 151 (about 168% and 139%, respectively) in Tables 3 and 4.

Table 4. Number of passengers getting on the Top 10 hot bus stops of route 151 from TCC to CYUT by weekday.

Bus stop name	Sun.	Mon.	Tue.	Wed.	Thur.	Fri.	Sat.
THSR Taichung Station	10,655	10,794	7,846	7,200	8,054	10,397	8,093
Shin Kong Mitsukoshi Department Store	6,179	4,897	4,772	5,182	5,277	6,112	6,875
T.P.C.C.	5,211	5,211	3,817	3,536	3,485	4,853	3,762
Chaoma	1,877	2,888	2,620	2,569	2,925	2,980	1,779
Taichung City Police Bureau	2,176	2,871	2,958	2,747	2,713	3,368	2,436
Maple Garden (Chaoyang Bridge)	2,991	2,991	2,552	2,806	2,790	3,570	2,565
Wufeng Agr. Ind. Senior High School	196	1,361	1,473	1,367	1,406	1,193	300
Wufeng	592	1,145	1,159	1,153	1,172	1,145	778
Taichung City Hall	759	972	851	957	970	1,092	952
Wufeng Post Office	386	857	835	813	913	1,032	532

5 Conclusions

In this article, more than 456 thousand and 82 million records of electronic ticket transactions of route 151 and Taichung City Bus in 2015 are respectively analyzed. The analytic results are as follows. (1) About 5.26 million electronic ticket users received benefits from Taichung City Government's policy; however, less than 0.5% users still used cash. The electronic ticket usage percentage of route 151 was similar to the whole case. (2) The passengers usually got on and off route 151 at THSR Taichung Station no matter which direction. Other bus stops for passengers usually getting on and off were T.P.C.C., Wufeng Agr. Ind. Senior High School, Wufeng, and Wufeng Post Office. (3) On Friday and the day before holidays, many passengers changed their behaviors to take route 151 from Wufeng District to THSR Taichung Station. This change was that the passengers took another bus route to the station near the start station of route 151 to increase the probability to get on the route 151. After Sep. 2016, the routing path of route 151 was changed to Fig. 7, so in the next step, it is necessary to compare the difference between two routing paths and use more electronic ticket transaction data of Taichung City Bus to create more value and relevant applications for smart city.

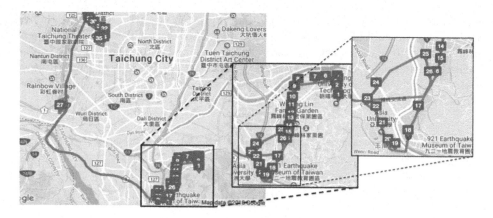

Fig. 7. New routing path of route 151.

References

1. Hai, X., Zhang, R., Zhao, C., Gao, B., Peng, J.: Hierarchical dividing of train station in passenger dedicated line based on self-organizing map. J. Convergence Inf. Technol. **7**(10), 265–271 (2012)
2. Official Website of the Bureau of Transportation, Taichung City Government. World Wide Web. http://www.traffic.taichung.gov.tw/index.asp. Accessed 28 Jan 2019
3. Official Website of EasyCard Corporation's Milestones. World Wide Web. https://www.easycard.com.tw/about/milestone.asp. Accessed 28 Jan 2019
4. Official Website of iPASS Corporation's Operations. World Wide Web. https://www.i-pass.com.tw/About/Operating. Accessed 28 Jan 2019
5. Bagchi, M., White, P.R.: The potential of public transport smart card data. Transp. Policy **12**(5), 464–474 (2005)
6. Chapleau, R., Chu, K.K.A.: Modeling transit travel patterns from location-stamped smart card data using a disaggregate approach. Presented at the 11th World Conference on Transportation Research, Berkeley, California (2007)
7. Chu, K.K.A., Chapleau, R.: Enriching archived smart card transaction data for transit demand modeling. Transp. Res. Rec. **2063**, 63–72 (2008)
8. Seaborn, C., Attanucci, J.P., Wilson, N.H.M.: Analyzing multimodal public transport journeys in London with smart card fare payment data. Transp. Res. Rec.: J. Transp. Res. Board **2121**, 55–62 (2009)
9. Wang, W., Attanucci, J.P., Wilson, N.H.M.: Bus passenger origin-destination estimation and related analyses using automated data collection systems. J. Public Transp. **14**(4), 131–150 (2011)
10. Pelletier, M.-P., Martin, T., Morency, C.: Smart card data use in public transit: a literature review. Transp. Res. Part C: Emerg. Technol. **19**(4), 557–568 (2011)
11. Alsger, A.M., Mesbah, M., Ferreira, L., Safi, H.: Public transport origin-destination estimation using smart card fare data. In: Transportation Research Board 94th Annual Meeting, no. 15–0801 (2015)
12. Agard, B., Morency, C., Trépanier, M.: Mining public transport user behaviour from smart card data. IFAC Proc. Volumes **39**(3), 399–404 (2006)

13. Medina, S.A.O.: Inferring weekly primary mobility patterns using public transport smart card data and a household travel survey. Travel Behav. Soc. **12**, 93–101 (2016)
14. Kieu, L.-M., Bhaskar, A., Chung, E.: A modified density-based scanning algorithm with noise for spatial travel pattern analysis from smart card AFC data. Transp. Res. C: Emerg. Technol. **58**, 193–207 (2015)
15. Zhong, C., Manley, E., Arisona, S.M., Batty, M., Schmitt, G.: Measuring variability of mobility patterns from multiday smart-card data. J. Comput. Sci. **9**, 125–130 (2015)

The Ridership Analysis on Inter-County/City Service for the Case Study of Taichung City Bus System

Cheng-Yuan Ho[1,2,3]([✉]) and I-Hsuan Chiu[4]

[1] Department of Computer Science and Information Engineering,
Asia University, Taichung City, Taiwan
tommyho@asia.edu.tw
[2] Big Data Research Center, Asia University, Taichung City, Taiwan
[3] Taichung City Smart Transportation Big Data Research Center,
Asia University, Taichung City, Taiwan
[4] Department of Civil Engineering,
National Chiao Tung University, Hsinchu City, Taiwan
sherry52168@g2.nctu.edu.tw

Abstract. In order to find passengers' behaviors when the passengers take buses, more than 82 million records of electronic ticket transactions of Taichung City Bus in 2015 and 8 inter-county/city bus routers are analyzed in this article. There are three statistical/analytic results. First, about 5.26 million electronic ticket users received benefits from Taichung City Government's policy; however, less than 0.5% users still used cash. The situations of 8 inter-county/city bus services in adjacent counties were little similar to that of Taichung City. Second, route 208 was the major route took by most people between Taichung City and Miaoli County among the routes supported by Taichung City Government. Routes 108 and 101 were the major routes connecting Nantou County and Taichung City, and Changhua County and Taichung City, respectively. Finally, in three adjacent counties, the names of top 5 bus stops for each county are almost same, but the order of top 5 bus stops for each county are quite different.

Keywords: Intelligent transport system · Smart Transportation · Big Data · Electronic ticket · Bus passenger · Ridership · Taichung bus · Inter-county · Inter-city

1 Introduction

Developed countries effectively not only develop public transportation systems (PTSs) but also integrate related transportation systems. This is because the PTSs are so-called shared transport services providing energy saving, air pollution reduction, traffic congestion reduction, and convenience enhancement in some place, and tackling deteriorating traffic by the private transportation. In order to make the public transportation to be the major transport for people, the PTSs have to be seamless integration and improve people's willingness to take them. For example, in order to establish a comprehensive public transport network and increase the service coverage ratio,

© Springer Nature Singapore Pte Ltd. 2019
C.-Y. Chang et al. (Eds.): ICS 2018, CCIS 1013, pp. 250–259, 2019.
https://doi.org/10.1007/978-981-13-9190-3_26

Taichung City Government aggressively enhances the smart transport services and promotes the policy for a free bus ride within 10 km with an electronic ticket [1].

In the past, it was difficult to collect the passengers' thoughts and feedbacks by telephones, roadside interviews, simple surveys, and household visits. Moreover, this method was not only costly but also had bias problem and a large gap between research and realistic world. Fortunately, with the advancement and development of science and technology, the charging system has been changed from coin-based to electronic ticket-based system. In the future, it may include the third party payment and mobile payment. Currently, all buses in Taiwan equip with electronic ticket readers to support electronic ticket payment. In addition, according to the statistics from EasyCard Corporation (2000–2017) [2], the number of Easy Card in March 2012 exceeded 30 million, and in 2017, the number of Easy Card exceeded 73 million. Similarly, according to the statistics from iPASS Corporation (2008–2017) [3], the number of iPass in 2014 exceeded 5 million, and in 2017, the number of iPass was close to 15 million. The statistics of these two corporations show that the electronic tickets are increasing gradually and are popularly used every year.

The electronic ticket itself implies the identity of a user, such as general/full-fare, student, preferential/half-fare, senior, and concessionaire, while a transaction record of an electronic ticket in the public transport implies the user's boarding record. For example, the information may include the type of transportation tool, route number, boarding or alighting station (depending on the charging method) and so on. Through the statistic and analysis methods, more information can be obtained, such as the number of passengers getting on and off the bus/train and the type of passengers. This is a great and valuable reference to the traffic and city management and policy. Therefore, it is extremely important to study in a lot of research areas in recent years. In this article, to understand the electronic ticket usages of Taichung City Bus and the ridership on inter-county/city service by Taichung City Bus system from Taichung City to adjacent county/city, and vice versa, the electronic ticket transaction records of 2015 used in Taichung City Bus, totaling 82,820,553 records, and 8 inter-county/city bus routers are analyzed.

The remainder of this article is organized as follows. Section 2 briefs the background of Taichung City, Taichung City Bus, and the classification of electronic tickets. Literature review is presented in Sect. 3. Section 4 shows the case study and analytic results of electronic ticket usages and the ridership. Finally, Sect. 5 concludes the article with a brief summary.

2 Background

2.1 Taichung City

Taichung City is a special municipality located in center-western Taiwan. In fact, it is located in the Taichung Basin along the main western coastal plain that stretches along the west coast from northern Taiwan almost to the southern tip. The adjacent countries/cities of Taichung City, as shown in Fig. 1, are Miaoli County, Hsinchu County, Yilan County, Hualien County, Nantou County, and Changhua County.

The Central Mountain Range lies just to the east of Taichung City. Lower, rolling hills run to the north leading to Miaoli County. Flat coastal plains dominate the landscape to the south leading to Changhua County and the Taiwan Strait to the west.

Since July 2017, Taichung City has been officially ranked as Taiwan's second most populous city because of its population of approximately 2.79 million people. One of the possible reasons is that Taichung City has not only a warm humid subtropical climate but also a suitable humidity. Furthermore, Taichung City has an average annual temperature of 23.3 °C (73.9 °F) with the highest temperature of the year occurring in July and August, while the lowest temperature occurs in January and February. Day-time temperatures remain warm to hot year-round, though night time temperatures during the winter months are significantly cooler than those during the summer and the warm daytime temperature. The average annual rainfall is just above 1,700 mm (67 in) and the average humidity is around 75%.

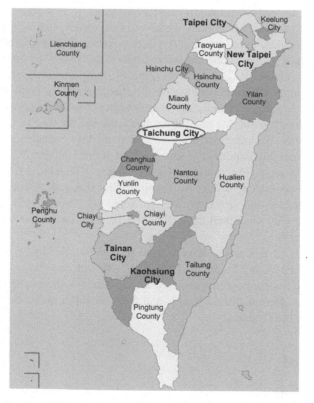

Fig. 1. Taiwan map, location of Taichung City and adjacent counties.

2.2   Taichung City Bus

Taichung City Bus, managed by the Transportation Bureau of Taichung City Government in Taichung City, Taiwan, includes at least 200 bus routes, which are numbered from route 1 to route 999 and operated by different 15 bus companies. Furthermore, Taichung City Bus provides major services in downtown area and for residents in rural or remote areas in Taichung City, and supplies minor services to connect different counties, such as Changhua and Nantou Counties, which are south on Taichung, and Miaoli County, which is north on Taichung.

The bus fare is calculated by mileage per ride. The basic fare is NT$20 for 8 km, and the extended fare is calculated by NT$2.431*(1 + 5% tax included) per km and round to the nearest integer. Due to the policy of Taichung City Government, from July 1st, 2015 to date, a passenger with an electronic ticket (i.e., either an EasyCard or an iPass) can take buses for free below 10 km when the route numbers of buses are between route 1 and route 999.

2.3   Classification of Electronic Tickets

There are five types of electronic tickets in "Taichung City Smart Transportation Big Data Database" which is provided by the Bureau of Transportation. The electronic ticket types and their owners' qualifications are as follows.

- Taichung City Senior Card: (1) The person who aged 65 and over establishes his/her household registration in Taichung and (2) The Taiwanese aborigine who aged 55 and over establishes his/her household registration in Taichung.
- Other City/County Senior Card: The senior card was not issued by the Taichung City Government. This means the person/Taiwanese aborigine aged 65/55 and over, but he/she established his/her household registration in other city/county, not in Taichung.
- Half-fare Card: (1) Children whose ages are between 6 and 12 years old, (2) Elderly whose age is over 65 years old and does not have a Senior Card, and (3) The person with a disability and his/her one of companions.
- Full-fare Card: The person does not meet the qualifications of above descriptions.
- Token: The passenger takes a bus with cash, i.e., without using an electronic ticket. In practice, when the passenger gets on the bus, the driver will issue a token to the passenger. When the passenger wants to get off the bus, he/she needs to check the fare by tapping the token to the electronic ticket reader, then pays the fare by cash, and returns the token to the driver.

3   Literature Review

This section will introduce relevant researches on the application of electronic ticket data in public transport.

Bagchi and White [4] used the origin and destination records in the electronic ticket data to adjust the transportation service that increased the performance and improved the quality of the transportation service. Chapleau and Chu [5] observed the changes in passenger carrying capacity on the specific routes by analyzing variation of the number of passenger in electronic ticket data. Seaborn et al. [6] developed a method based on the maximum elapsed time to explain the transfer behaviors of passengers traveling on the London public transport and divided the transfer behaviors into pure transfer, incidental activity transfer, and non-transfer. Wang et al. [7] used the Automatic Data Collection System (ADCS) to collect electronic ticket data and tried to deduce passengers' destinations and analyze the transfer service information, such as the transfer waiting time. Pelletier et al. [8] divided the use of electronic ticket data in public transport into three levels: (1) strategical level: setting a long-term plan; (2) tactical level: dynamically arranging the most suitable shifts to improve the quality of service; and (3) operational level: estimating various indicators of the public transport network. Alsger et al. [9] used the South East Queensland (SEQ) data to study the effect of different data sample sizes on the accuracy level of the generated public transport O-D matrices and to quantify the sample size required for a certain level of accuracy.

4   Case Study

In this Section, 82,260,553 electronic ticket transaction records of Taichung City Bus in 2015 and 8 inter-county/city bus routers are analyzed and discussed by the number and utilization of electronic ticket type, and passengers' behaviors for boarding and alighting bus stops at adjacent county/city of Taichung City.

4.1   Statistics of Type of Electronic Ticket for Taichung City

By classifying the number of tickets (i.e., no matter how many times an electronic ticket is used), it can be found that the preferential policy for the free 10 km with an electronic ticket supplied by the Bureau of Transportation, Taichung City Government has been achieved a certain result. As shown in Fig. 2, there are about 5.26 million electronic ticket cards and nearly 99.57% of passengers use electronic tickets to take buses and only 0.43% of passengers use cash. There are three most possible reasons for using cash: (1) the balance of the electronic ticket has been negative, (2) the electronic ticket does not belong to any series of Easy Card and iPass, and (3) the passenger is the first time to take a bus in Taichung City and he/she does not have any electronic ticket.

According to the electronic ticket type utilization, as shown in Fig. 3, it can be found that the utilization of the full-fare card is about 89.17% of the total number of utilizations, equaling to 73.85 million rides. It is interesting to note that the Taichung City Senior Card loses Other City/County Senior Card in the number of electronic tickets, but the utilization of Taichung City Senior Card is much higher than that of Other City/County Senior Card. This means the seniors who established their household registrations in Taichung have more locomotion abilities than other seniors.

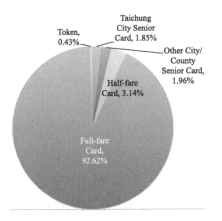

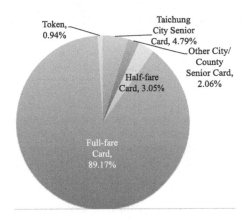

Fig. 2. Number of electronic ticket type.   **Fig. 3.** Electronic ticket type utilization.

4.2 Inter-County/City Bus Service and Routes

There are 8 inter-county/city bus services in Taichung City Bus system: (1) Taichung City ← → Miaoli County: routes 97, 181, 208, 253, and 258; (2) Taichung City ← → Nantou County: route 108; and (3) Taichung City ← → Changhua County: routes 101 and 180. The monthly passenger carrying capacities of these 8 bus routes are described in Table 1. From Table 1, it can be found that every route omits some data except routes 97 and 180. The possible reasons are as follows. (1) Bus companies forgot to upload the electronic ticket transaction records to Bureau of Transportation, Taichung City Government in some month, such as Aug. and Oct. of route 181, Mar., Jun., Jul., Aug., and Sep. of both routes 108 and 180. (2) After the format of records was modified, one party (either the bus company or Bureau of Transportation) did not follow the changes that resulted in data loss during automatic data format conversion. For example, the passenger carrying capacity data of routes 208, 253, and 258 is missing after Jun. 2015.

According to the data in Table 1, it can be inferred that route 208 is the major route took by most people between Taichung City and Miaoli County among the routes supported by Taichung City Government. Moreover, the passenger carrying capacity of route 208 is about 4 times larger than that of the second place, route 181. The possible reason is that the population and liveliness of Fengyuan District where route 208 connected to Miaoli County are higher than those of Dajia District where route 181 connected to Miaoli County.

The possible reasons for routes 108 and 101 with huge passenger carrying capacities are that route 108 passes through lots of schools, including high schools and universities, traditional markets, and Taichung Railway Station, and drives along the main roads of Taichung while route 101 passes through less schools and traditional markets, but it crosses two main traffic concentrations, Taichung Railway Station and Taiwan High Speed Rail Taichung Station.

Table 1. Passenger carrying capacities of 8 inter-county/city bus routes for every month in 2015.

County	Route	Jan.	Feb.	Mar.	Apr.	May	Jun.	Jul.	Aug.	Sep.	Oct.	Nov.	Dec.
Miaoli	97	3,642	3,163	3,373	3,458	3,229	3,317	3,532	3,065	3,483	4,069	3,909	3,979
	181	14,426	8,926	15,473	14,770	15,388	13,884	11,816	—	13,876	—	14,317	14,765
	208	64,367	34,719	51,825	49,240	49,551	—	—	—	—	—	—	—
	253	7,365	3,547	5,884	5,661	5,809	—	—	—	—	—	—	—
	258	5,015	3,354	3,353	3,244	3,310	—	—	—	—	—	—	—
Nantou	108	79,372	60,841	—	79,346	81,799	—	—	—	—	93,302	89,298	93,793
Changhua	101	69,606	56,531	—	74,484	79,726	—	—	—	—	78,718	80,801	84,938
	180	7,474	4,588	8,729	8,104	8,130	7,522	5,660	3,991	6,200	6,582	8,710	8,813

Figure 4(a) classifies the 1,663,162 electronic ticket transaction records of 8 inter-county/city bus routers in Table 1 by the electronic ticket type utilization. According to Fig. 4(a), it can be found that the utilization of the full-fare card is about 82.88% of total number of utilizations, equaling to 1,378,350 rides. It is interesting to note that the percentage of Taichung City Senior Card and Other City/County Senior Card rise from 4.79% and 2.06% to 8.07% and 5.26%, respectively. This may mean that the senior citizens take inter-county/city routes more frequently. Furthermore, Figs. 4(b) and (c) respectively show the electronic ticket type utilization results with passengers boarding and alighting buses in adjacent counties. The numbers of transaction records in Figs. 4(b) and (c) are 186,901 and 157,681, respectively. From both Figs. 4(b) and (c), it can be observed that the percentages of full-fare card are less than that in Fig. 4 (a), about 80.35% and 74.41%, respectively. On the other hand, the percentages of Other City/County Senior Card are increased, especially with passengers alighting buses in adjacent counties. The possible reason is the senior citizens live and establish their household registrations in adjacent counties, so they naturally take buses by the Other City/County Senior Cards. Figure 4(d) shows the electronic ticket type utilization result with passengers both boarding and alighting buses in adjacent counties. The number of transaction records in Fig. 4(d) is 39,132. It can be found that the proportional allocation is quite different from that in Fig. 3 and guessed that the passengers' activity ranges may be within adjacent counties.

4.3 Top 5 Hot Bus Stops in Adjacent Counties

Tables 2, 3 and 4 present the top 5 hot hop-on and off bus stops in Miaoli, Nantou, and Changhua Counties, respectively. From three tables, it can be found that, in three counties, the names of top 5 bus stops for each county are almost same, but the order of top 5 bus stops for each county are quite different. For example, in Miaoli County, the orders between hop-on and hop-off bus stops are almost same except Jiuzhan and Xizhou bus stops. However, in Nantou County, the variations in the order of hop-on and hop-off bus stops are very large. As for the orders of hop-on and hop-off bus stops in Changhua County, it seems that the third top bus stop is a boundary line to separate the first and second top bus stops to be a group and the fourth and fifth top bus stops to be another group.

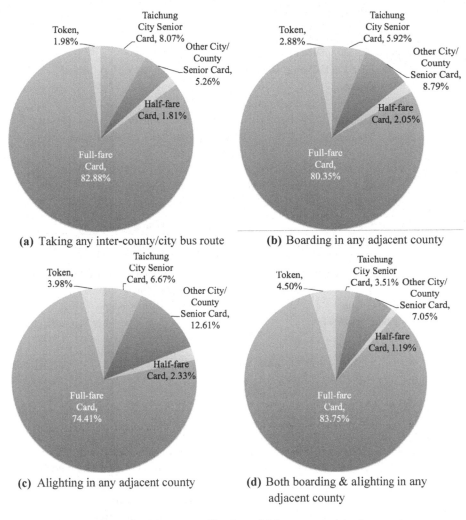

(a) Taking any inter-county/city bus route

(b) Boarding in any adjacent county

(c) Alighting in any adjacent county

(d) Both boarding & alighting in any adjacent county

Fig. 4. Electronic ticket type utilization of 8 inter-county/city bus services.

Table 2. Top 5 hot hop-on/off bus stops in Miaoli county.

Hop-on		Hop-off	
Count	Bus stop name	Count	Bus stop name
20,911	Zhongjie	27,277	Zhongjie
4,595	Zhuolan	3,281	Zhuolan
3,599	Jiuzhan	1,559	Toll Station
852	Toll Station	940	Xizhou
626	Post Office	833	Post Office

Table 3. Top 5 hot hop-on/off bus stops in Nantou county.

Hop-on		Hop-off	
Count	Bus stop name	Count	Bus stop name
29,190	First Bank Caotun Branch	2,774	Tongder Voca.High School
7,671	Daguan	1,929	Xinfeng
7,309	Tongder Voca.High School	1,919	Nanan
5,250	Xinfeng	1,269	Yushi Village
5,245	Yushi Village	1,181	First Bank Caotun Branch

Table 4. Top 5 hot hop-on/off bus stops in Changhua county.

Hop-on		Hop-off	
Count	Bus stop name	Count	Bus stop name
15,191	Changhua County Yuanzhumin Shenghuoguan	16,684	Changhua Station
13,791	Changhua Station	14,730	Changhua County Yuanzhumin Shenghuoguan
11,490	Hediao Village	10,370	Hediao Village
5,450	Irrigation Association	8,848	Chang-Hua Girls Senior High School
2,984	Zhongzhuangzi	8,225	Irrigation Association

5 Conclusions

In this article, more than 82 million records of electronic ticket transactions of Taichung City Bus in 2015 and 8 inter-county/city bus routers are analyzed. The analytic results are as follows. (1) About 5.26 million electronic ticket users received benefits from Taichung City Government's policy; however, less than 0.5% users still used cash. The situations of 8 inter-county/city bus services in adjacent counties were little similar to that of Taichung City. (2) Route 208 was the major route took by most people between Taichung City and Miaoli County among the routes supported by Taichung City Government. Routes 108 and 101 were the major routes connecting Nantou County and Taichung City, and Changhua County and Taichung City, respectively. (3) In three adjacent counties, the names of top 5 bus stops for each county are almost same, but the order of top 5 bus stops for each county are quite different. In the next step, the electronic ticket transaction data of Taichung City Bus within a specific application, district, area, or bus route will be analyzed to create more value and relevant applications for smart city.

Acknowledgments. The database used in this article is called "Taichung City Smart Transportation Big Data Database" which is provided by the Bureau of Transportation, Taichung City Government. We would like to give special thanks to Taichung City Government, Asia University, and Tableau for their immense supports.

References

1. Official Website of the Bureau of Transportation, Taichung City Government. World Wide Web. http://www.traffic.taichung.gov.tw/index.asp. Accessed 28 Jan 2019
2. Official Website of EasyCard Corporation's Milestones. World Wide Web. https://www.easycard.com.tw/about/milestone.asp. Accessed 28 Jan 2019
3. Official Website of iPASS Corporation's Operations. World Wide Web. https://www.i-pass.com.tw/About/Operating. Accessed 28 Jan 2019
4. Bagchi, M., White, P.R.: The potential of public transport smart card data. Transp. Policy 12(5), 464–474 (2005)
5. Chapleau, R., Chu, K.K.A.: Modeling transit travel patterns from location-stamped smart card data using a disaggregate approach. Presented at the 11th World Conference on Transportation Research, Berkeley, California (2007)
6. Seaborn, C., Attanucci, J.P., Wilson, N.H.M.: Analyzing multimodal public transport journeys in London with smart card fare payment data. Transp. Res. Rec.: J. Transp. Res. Board 2121, 55–62 (2009)
7. Wang, W., Attanucci, J.P., Wilson, N.H.M.: Bus passenger origin-destination estimation and related analyses using automated data collection systems. J. Public Transp. 14(4), 131–150 (2011)
8. Pelletier, M.-P., Martin, T., Morency, C.: Smart card data use in public transit: a literature review. Transp. Res. Part C: Emerg. Technol. 19(4), 557–568 (2011)
9. Alsger, A.M., Mesbah, M., Ferreira, L., Safi, H.: Public transport origin-destination estimation using smart card fare data. In: Transportation Research Board 94th Annual Meeting, no. 15–0801 (2015)

An Enhanced Pre-processing and Nonlinear Regression Based Approach for Failure Detection of PV System

Chung-Chian Hsu[1(✉)], Jia-Long Li[1], Arthur Chang[1], and Yu-Sheng Chen[2]

[1] Big Data Research Center, National Yunlin University of Science and Technology, Yunlin, Taiwan
hsucc@yuntech.edu.tw
[2] Reforecast Co., Ltd., Taipei, Taiwan
anson@reforecast.com.tw

Abstract. The solar energy is getting popular due to the awareness of the environmental issues. Multiple module strings are set up in a solar-power plant to increase power production which is sold to electricity company via connected grid. Inevitably, devices can break, leading to loss of power production. To minimize the loss, it is important to be able to detect faulty devices as soon as possible for maintenance. In this paper, an approach relying on careful data pre-processing is proposed and compares with an existing approach.

Keywords: Solar energy · Fault detection · Machine learning · k-nearest neighbors

1 Introduction

The photovoltaic (PV) power plants have grown rapidly in the last decade due to large demand on solar energy, which becomes an indispensable resource of human culture [1, 2]. All around the world, corporations as well as governments are exploiting solar energy market [3]. In order to respond to ever increased demand on energy consumption, many countries began to address the problem of energy production. As a result, the green energy has attracted attention from many governments. Green energy includes the wind power, the tidal power, solar energy, etc.

Various aspects of PV systems have been explored as discussed in a number of review papers [4–6, 10], including fault detection, diagnosis, prediction and degradation. Despite PV arrays have protective arrangement, there may still undetected faults occurring on devices [9]. To prevent from continuous loss of power production, it is important to detect faulty devices as soon as possible so that maintenance can take place.

Many methods have been proposed to detect faulty devices, and yet they usually took lots of time and required high-quality data. For instance, a fault detection and diagnosis of a grid-connected PV system approach based on PNN classifier was presented by Garoudja et al. in [4]. The fault detection of PV systems based on local outlier factor was proposed by Ding et al. in [5]. They preprocessed data and identified

© Springer Nature Singapore Pte Ltd. 2019
C.-Y. Chang et al. (Eds.): ICS 2018, CCIS 1013, pp. 260–269, 2019.
https://doi.org/10.1007/978-981-13-9190-3_27

normal and faulty data before constructing models. Various approaches based on the K-Nearest-Neighbor technique have been proposed in recent papers like [6, 7], which compared real-time data read from the device in the solar-power plant with similar historical data. This approach can fail when historical data themselves are abnormal due to long-time faulty devices or rainy days.

PR is an important indicator of production performance of PV modules [8], which measures efficiency of solar power production within a certain time period. In contrast, array ratio (RA) is an instant indicator which measures production performance in real-time. In this study, we intend to detect faulty devices as soon as possible. Therefore, RA is adopted. For normal devices, RA values shall be stable. However, several factors such as module brand, module degradation, bad weather, faulty modules in a string, cloud, etc. can affect the values more or less. As a result, the RA value threshold setting for judging whether a solar device is faulty or not becomes a non-trivial issue.

In this paper, we propose a fault detection approach which exploits statistics median and nonlinear regression based on the plant-owned data collected from individual solar-power plants. In such a way, each plant has its own threshold which is adapted to the plant's conditions. In particular, the RA values of all devices are calculated and sorted. To avoid affecting by faulty devices, only a certain range around the median of the RAs is considered. Then, we use nonlinear regression on training, historical data to obtain the upper and the lower boundary of the RA for a device to be considered normal. Devices continuously have RA values out of the range are claimed faulty once detected.

2 Data Acquisition of PV Systems

The PV data were collected from several solar power plants located in central Taiwan. Data used in the analysis of this study include date, time, irradiance, power, current, voltage, and capacity of individual module strings. Irradiance, current, voltage, and power were sampled every five minutes. One pyrheliometer was installed in each plant for measuring irradiance. The angle of the pyrheliometer is horizontal in some plants and the same with the angle of panels along the roof in the others. The period of historical data analyzed in this study was between 2018/08/01 and 2018/09/10. The capacity of individual strings varies. Therefore, when calculating power production efficiency of the strings, the capacity shall be taken into consideration.

3 Method

The proposed approach is based on the idea that normal RA values shall fall in a certain range under normal conditions. However, many unexpected factors can lead to abnormal RA values which can prevent us from estimating the proper range of normal RAs. To tackle the problems, enhanced preprocessing is suggested and the nonlinear regression algorithm is used to estimate the RA range. The devices which RAs exceed the range are considered faulty. The architecture of the proposed method is showed in Fig. 1.

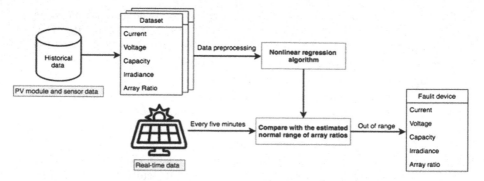

Fig. 1. Architecture of the fault detection system.

3.1   PV Module Formula

Many studies used one diode model (ODM) as shown in Fig. 2 to simulate the power production of the PV system. In this model, the output current is given by Eq. (1). As shown, the output estimation requires several parameters which may not be obtained easily.

$$I_{PV} = I_{ph} - I_0 \underbrace{\left(exp\left(\frac{q(V_{pv}+R_sI_{pv})}{nK_BT}\right) - 1\right)}_{I_d} - \underbrace{\frac{V_{pv}+R_sI_{pv}}{R_{sh}}}_{I_{sh}} \tag{1}$$

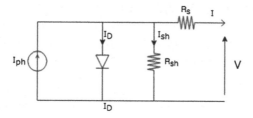

Fig. 2. Include new data and old data about Irradiance distribution of a day.

In the study, we evaluate the performance of PV modules by array ratio or RA, which is expressed as in Eq. (2).

$$Array\ Ratio = \frac{P_{DC}/P_0}{G_1/G_0} \tag{2}$$

where P_{DC} and P_0 divides to real-time of power and system rated of power; G_1 and G_0 divides to project plane of radiance and standard strong of irradiance. In this work, array ratio is for references to evaluate device that is normal or faulty device.

3.2   Data Pre-processing

The RA value is very sensitive to dramatic change of irradiance. Therefore, the pre-processing includes two steps: First, the removal of data points which have a dramatic change of irradiance at the times. Second, the removal of data points which production efficiency is abnormal, much higher or lower than most of the rest devices. We divide the data points into those collected in the morning and those in the afternoon, respectively.

As can be seen in Fig. 3, an abrupt drop in irradiance can yield extremely high RA. To avoid this, we replace the points with smooth points.

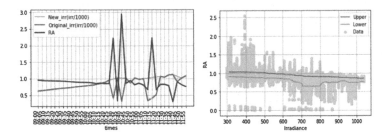

Fig. 3. Abnormal irradiances in the left diagram are smoothed by neighbor normal points and RA outliers shown in the right diagram can occur occasionally.

In addition, RA outliers can occur due to malfunction of solar devices. To address this problem, we sort RA values of all the devices and consider only the second and the third quartile of the RAs. Not only eliminating abnormal data, it might eliminate normal data at the same time. In the next section, we use nonlinear regression method with some tolerance to avoid deleting too many normal data points.

3.3   Nonlinear Regression Algorithm

To find out the range for detecting faulty devices, the regression on the RAs with respect to various irradiances is used. The polynomial regression algorithm is one of the regression analysis methods in which independent variable x and the dependent variable y are modelled as an nth degree polynomial in x, as expressed in Eq. (3). In our case, the dependent variable is the RA and the independent is the irradiance.

$$y_i = \alpha_0 + \alpha_1 x + \alpha_2 x^2 + \ldots + \alpha_n x^n + \varepsilon \tag{3}$$

To avoid eliminating too many normal data points, tolerance shall be added to the regression result. According to empirical results, the new upper and lower bounds is determined by the equations shown in (4) and (5).

$$New(upper_i) = upper_i + (Upper_i - y_i) \tag{4}$$

$$New(lower_i) = lower_i - (y_i - lower_i) \tag{5}$$

3.4 Evaluation

Confusion matrix is used to evaluate the results by comparing to the K-nearest neighbor algorithm. The matrix has four indicators of a true positive (TP), a false negative (FN), a false positive (FP) and a true negative (TN), respectively. Classification accuracy, precision, and recall can be calculated based on those four indicators as shown in Eq. (6)–(8).

$$Classfication\ accuracy = (TP+TN)/(TP+FN+FP+TN) \tag{6}$$

$$Precision = TP/(TP+FP) \tag{7}$$

$$Recall = TP/(TP+FN) \tag{8}$$

4 Experiments

We first present the result of data preprocessing and the result of model construction. Then we compare the proposed approach with the K-Nearest-Neighbor approach [7] on accuracy of diagnosing PV string fault.

4.1 Results of the Data Pre-processing

Table 1. The number of training and test data in the three PV plants

		PV plant 1	PV plant 2	PV plant 3
Training data	Morning	129,652	106,370	41,158
	Afternoon	131,546	98,098	39,068
Test data	Morning	2,548	2,100	1,000
	Afternoon	3,774	3,108	1,200

The training data came from data acquisition of PV between 2018/08/17 and 2018/10/08. The test data were collected on 2018/10/03 as shown in Table 1. As can be seen in Fig. 4, malfunction of the devices can result in outliers which have extreme values, even become zero.

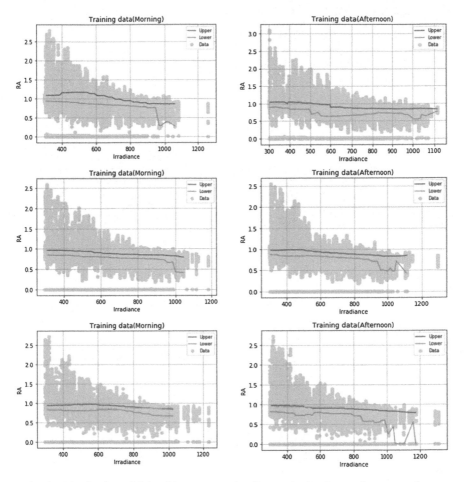

Fig. 4. Distribution of RA with respect to irradiances in the three solar power plants.

4.2 Results of Nonlinear Regression Algorithm

Figure 5 shows the regression result of the training data. According to data distribution, the quadratic regression was chosen. In each diagram, the green and the red dash line indicate the range of RAs considered acceptable. Those outside the boundaries are considered abnormal.

Figure 6 shows the distribution from the test data. The results demonstrated the most of the abnormal data points can be detected based on the boundaries estimated from the training data. Some points which might be normal were out of the boundary, such as those in the second row (Plant 2). However, the later stage which require three consecutive abnormal points for a device to be taken as faulty can avoid misclassification in those cases.

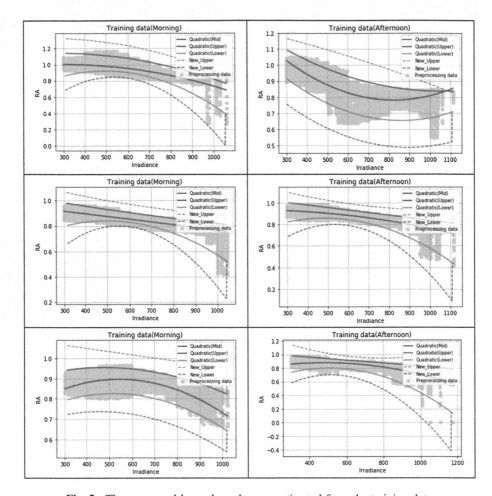

Fig. 5. The upper and lower bounds were estimated from the training data.

4.3   Results of Fault Detection and Diagnosis

To verify the performance, we compare the proposed method with the KNN approach [7] which estimated the power production by the average of the ten nearest neighbors found from the data collected in the past seven days. If the measured power is lower than the estimated by the threshold, 25% used in this study according to experimental results for three consecutive points, the device is thus considered faulty.

Table 2 shows the numbers of individual abnormal data points detected by the nonlinear regression approach is much larger than those by the KNN. Furthermore, the KNN took 2.14 min while the NLR took 0.42 min. We require the number of the consecutive abnormal points must at least be three to avoid false positive alarms. The right part of Table 2 shows the number of the points, representing the number of faulty devices, after merging consecutive points and eliminating the merged points which did not contain more than two consecutive points.

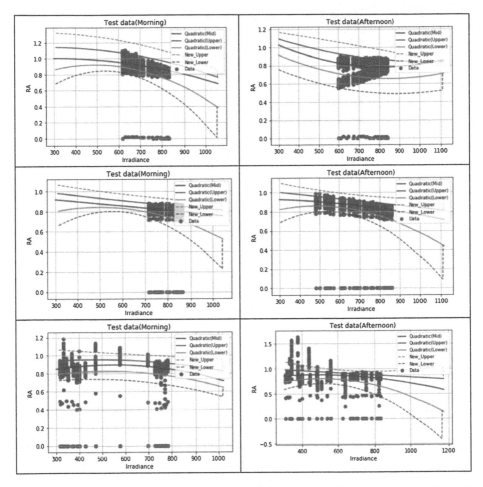

Fig. 6. RA distribution with respect to irradiance in the morning and afternoon, respectively, for Plant 1, 2, and 3.

Table 2. The numbers of the detected abnormal points and the points after merge

	No. of abnormal data points			No. of points after merge		
	Plant 1	Plant 2	Plant 3	Plant 1	Plant 2	Plant 3
KNN	54	0	167	6	0	10
NLR	131	140	438	2	3	30

The ground truth of the device status came from the field engineers which went to the plants to check and maintain, if necessary, the devices. Table 3 presents the diagnosis result and shows none of the methods reported false diagnosis. However, the NN method failed to report 13 faulty devices from the three plants in total. The reason

Table 3. The predicted results by the methods based on the k-nearest-neighbor technique (in the upper half) and based on the nonlinear regression technique (in the lower half)

		Predicted class					
		Plant 1		Plant 2		Plant 3	
		Healthy	Faulty	Healthy	Faulty	Healthy	Faulty
Real class	Healthy	5	0	0	0	7	0
	Faulty	0	1	0	0	0	3
Real class	Healthy	0	0	0	0	17	0
	Faulty	0	2	0	2	0	13

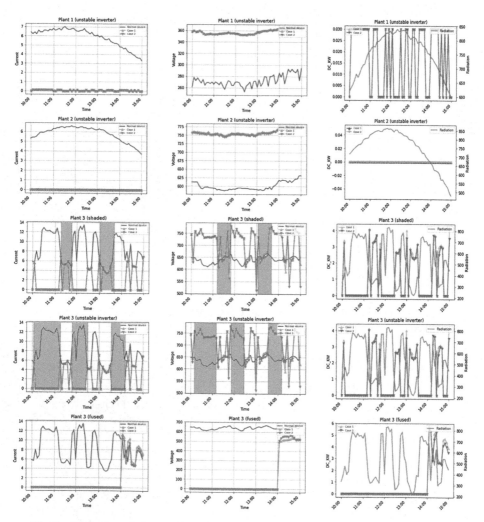

Fig. 7. Currents, voltages, and produced DC_KWs of the devices with various faults.

is that the NN is based on the historical data of the past seven days and if there are bad weather for more than seven days, the method cannot work as expected.

The first two rows in Fig. 7 present that an unstable inverter will have currents close to zero, voltages, higher than normal and unstable or zero DC powers. The last row shows that fused devices have current, voltage, and power all zero. Note that at 2 o'clock the faulty device was repaired.

5   Conclusion

In this paper, a detection method for faulty solar-power strings has been proposed. The RA range within which the values are considered normal is estimated by using nonlinear regression. To evaluate its performance, comparison is made with a method based on the KNN algorithm. The experimental results indicate that the proposed method can detect more faulty devices than the KNN approach, which can break under bad weather lasting for several days. Another advantage is that the proposed model is fast in detection since the model is constructed offline.

Acknowledgement. This work was partially supported by the grants from Ministry of Science and Technology, Reforecast Co., Ltd., and the Intelligent Recognition Industry Service Center.

References

1. Raza, M.Q., Nadarajah, M., Ekanayake, C.: On recent advances in PV output power forecast. Sol. Energy **136**, 125–144 (2016)
2. Europe SP: Global market outlook for solar power 2015–2019 Technical report Bruxelles: European Photovoltaic Industry Association (2015)
3. Oliver, M., Jackson, T.: The market for solar photovoltaics. Energy Policy **27**, 15 (1999)
4. Garoudja, E., Chouder, A., Kara, K., Silvestre, S.: An enhanced machine learning based approach for failures detection and diagnosis of PV systems. Energy Convers. Manage. **151**, 1246–1254 (2017)
5. Ding, H., et al.: Local outlier factor-based fault detection and evaluation of photovoltaic system. Sol. Energy **164**, 139–148 (2018)
6. Madeti, S.R., Singh, S.N.: Modeling of PV system based on experimental data for fault detection using kNN method. Sol. Energy **173**, 139–151 (2018)
7. Hsu, C.-C., Teng, C.-T., Cai, C.-J., Chang, A.: Real-time diagnosis of fault type for grid-connected photovoltaic plants. In: The 29th International Conference on Information Management, 3 June 2017, CSIM, Taichung (2018)
8. Khalid, A.M., Mitra, I., Warmuth, W., Schacht, V.: Performance ratio – crucial parameter for grid connected PV plants. Renew. Sustain. Energy Rev. **65**, 1139–1158 (2016)
9. Pillai, D.S., Rajasekar, N.: A comprehensive review on protection challenges and fault diagnosis in PV systems. Renew. Sustain. Energy Rev. **91**, 18–40 (2018)
10. Pillai, D.S., Rajasekar, N.: Metaheuristic algorithms for PV parameter identification: a comprehensive review with an application to threshold setting for fault detection in PV systems. Renew. Sustain. Energy Rev. **82**, 3503–3525 (2018)

Evaluation of Performance Improvement by Cleaning on Photovoltaic Systems

Chung-Chian Hsu[1(✉)], Shi-Mai Fang[1], Arthur Chang[1],
and Yu-Sheng Chen[2]

[1] Big Data Research Center, National Yunlin University
of Science and Technology, Yunlin, Taiwan
hsucc@yuntech.edu.tw
[2] Reforecast Co., Ltd., Taipei, Taiwan
anson@reforecast.com.tw

Abstract. To keep high-performance operations in photovoltaic system is an important task. However, solar panels are subject to pollution in the natural environment. Possible pollutions include dust in the air, feces in birds and dust from burning materials, etc., which can cause solar energy performance reduced. In this paper, the effects by manual cleaning and natural cleaning are investigated and the result is aimed to help manager to determine the timing of cleaning. The Array Ratio (RA) was used to evaluate the daily power generation performance and various conditions which can prevent from obtaining reliable RA values were addressed. Experiments were conducted to verify the proposed approach. The results showed that the first manual cleaning has a significant cleaning effect of 10.11% and the second manual cleaning effect only 2.03% since before the cleaning there were several heavy rains, resulting in natural cleaning of the plant.

Keywords: Data analysis · Photovoltaic system · PV module cleaning · Performance evaluation · Array Ratio

1 Introduction

Maintenance of solar panels is important which influences power production. One of the maintenance problems is to determine when to clean dirty solar panels caused by dust or other pollutions. Over cleaning can lead to wasted cost and not enough cleaning leads to reduced production. Especially in a tropical island-type climate in Taiwan, it rains frequently in some seasons, which results in cleaning effect of the dirty solar panels, referred to as natural cleaning in contrast to manual cleaning by maintenance personnel. It is necessary to investigate the cleaning issue of solar plants in Taiwan.

Pollution loss varies in different areas. In the cleanest United Kingdom, if there is no cleaning in a month, the sunshine intensity will decrease by 5% ~ 6% and In Sudan, the reduced intensity of sunshine will be 9 times that of the UK. In cooler and wet environments, the accumulated pollutants may include dust in the air, feces from birds and other animals, dust from burning materials, leaves or pollen [1].

C.-Y. Chang et al. (Eds.): ICS 2018, CCIS 1013, pp. 270–279, 2019.
https://doi.org/10.1007/978-981-13-9190-3_28

The solar panels with loss of output caused by the natural environment pollution needs to be maintained by cleaning. Relevant research suggests using system parameters with comparison between cleaned solar panels and contaminated solar panels to build cleaning models. To determine the frequency of solar panel cleaning, a related data model is used to dynamically updating the recommended cleaning frequency through clean and contaminated solar panels [2]. To determine the economic cost of cleaning, power production efficiencies in Perth, Australia and Nusa Tenggara Timur (NTT), Indonesia were evaluated [3]. The energy output of the module was normalized by the maximum energy output under standard test conditions (STC) and compared. The results showed that the average decline rate of maximum output per month was 4.5% and 8%, respectively. The study found that the NTT solar plant needs manual cleaning in October, and the Perth solar plant requires manual cleaning in August and October. To determine the recommended cleaning frequency for a year, researchers used Helioscope with simulation of solar plant and determined 10% and 15% soiling levels by the dust transparent instrument, which is closest to those of the local Algerian Sahara sites desert, and then does not clean the solar case for one year [4]. It is found in the study that cleaning twice a year is profitable.

Most of the research on the cleaning frequency like those mentioned above was conducted under controlled environment with carefully maintained solar panels. To the best of our knowledge, there is no investigation on operational solar-power plants which connected grid network. In an uncontrolled environment, additional issues need to be taken into consideration, including module failure, the angle of the sun photometer, the direction of the solar panels, etc.

In this paper, we propose an approach to measure power production improvement resulted from cleaning on operational solar-power plants. The result is valuable and can help to determine the proper time for panel cleaning. We considered the additional issues mentioned above and avoided the need for parameters which are expensive to obtain. In essence, we monitor power production of the plants under good weather. Low power production indicates cleaning shall be scheduled. The approach requires only power output, irradiance, and string capacity.

2 Method

The solar plant used in this study located in central Taiwan is operational and connected to the grid network. The total capacity of the plant is 484.12 kw.

Array Ratio (RA) [5] of photovoltaic system was used to observe power production changes caused by natural environment pollution, natural cleaning by rainfall and manual cleaning. The approach we propose is to monitor the change of RA along time, especially, the RA before and after manual cleaning as well as natural cleaning. However, the calculation of RA is not a trivial task. An inappropriate conduct could lead to results which are not interpretable. In the section, we propose the method which can help to acquire reliable RA values and thus the change of RA values along the time.

2.1   Array Ratio

RA was used to evaluate production performance of individual panel strings every five minutes. To calculate RA, the ratio between production efficiency PE and normalized irradiance IRR, as expressed in Eq. (1). PE is measured with the ratio between string output referred to as DCKW and module capacity. IRR is the ratio between the actual amount of irradiance, irradiance, and under the standard test condition (STC), namely, 1000 w.

$$RA = \frac{PE}{IRR} = \frac{DCKW/capacity}{irradiance/1000} \qquad (1)$$

RA in Eq. (1) for each string is calculated every five minutes. The daily value RA_{day} is computed by aggregating all the calculated RA values obtained in a day and from all the strings, as shown in Eq. (2) where N is the set of modules in the plant, n indicates a single module, T is the set of total time points involved in the calculation, and t indicates a single time point. In this study, T includes the time points in the afternoon from 12:00 to 15:00.

$$RA_{day} = \frac{1}{|T|} \sum_{t \in T} \frac{1}{|N|} \sum_{n \in N} RA_{t,n} \qquad (2)$$

2.2   Factors Affect RA Values

The idea behind our approach is that RA shall keep roughly stable under normal operation conditions. However, unexpected situations such as bad weather, cloud, failed devices, panel direction, etc. can result in abnormal values. We thus compute RA under certain conditions only to avoid anomaly. The conditions keeping valid RA include irradiance threshold, effective PE range and RA difference threshold. There are no theoretical rules for setting those parameters. Therefore, we resort to extensive experiments looking for appropriate thresholds.

First, a data point is taken into account only which irradiance is higher than the irradiance threshold. For the points passed the first condition, their PE is calculated. Second, the effective PE range is set to eliminate faulty devices, which yield low power. Third, since RA shall be stable under good weather, abrupt change of RA shall be excluded. RA_{slope} in Eq. (3) measures the RA change between two time points.

$$RA_{slope} = |RA_{t+1} - RA_t| \qquad (3)$$

2.3   Effect of Panel Cleaning

After cleaning, RA shall improve. The percentage of improvement is used to quantize the effect of solar panel cleaning, as expressed in Eq. (4) where the parameter RA_{clean} indicates the daily average RA after cleaning and the parameter RA_{dirty} represents the daily average RA before cleaning.

$$RA_{imp} = \frac{RA_{clean} - RA_{dirty}}{RA_{dirty}} \times 100\% \qquad (4)$$

3 Conditions for Valid RA Values

3.1 Different Angles of Modules and Pyrheliometer

In a solar plant, there may be panel strings that are either eastward or westward. Since the sun rises eastward and falls westward, the eastbound solar panels will produce more power in the morning then the westbound panels while the westbound panels will produce more power in the afternoon. Similarly, pyrheliometer can be installed horizontally or along with the angle of the panels.

Figure 1(a) shows RA value will be between 0.7 and 0.8 in the morning while between 0.8 and 1.1 in the afternoon. In addition, the pyrheliometer was installed along with the panels eastward. The RA value higher than 1.0 will not be a problem since the comparison of the RA values is made in the same power plant rather than different ones which may have a different angle of the pyrheliometer

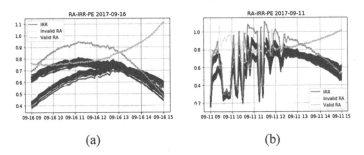

(a)   (b)

Fig. 1. IRR, PE and RA under (a) clean sky in all day and (b) shading in the morning. (Color figure online)

Figure 1(b) shows that the weather in the morning is unstable indicated by the unstable irradiance (depicted in the green line), and consequently yield the unstable, abnormal RA values (the yellow line) in the morning which are considered invalid RAs and excluded. Only the high, stable RAs in the afternoon are counted, which leads to a high average RA for the day. In this study, the daily average RA is calculated with valid RAs in between 12:00 ~ 15:00.

3.2 Threshold of Irradiance

Irradiance can be unstable due to unstable weather such as cloud. Consequently, RA values can be unstable as well. We need to exclude those data points which are collected under unstable irradiance.

Figure 2(a) shows that RA is unstable, usually becomes higher, in low irradiance. Figure 2(b) shows RA appears stable and will not be elevated under stable irradiance in good weather.

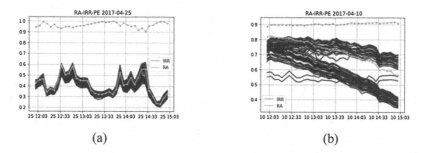

| (a) | (b) |

Fig. 2. RA with different irradiance levels: (a) low irradiance, (b) normal irradiance.

To acquire a proper threshold for the irradiance, we conducted experiments with various settings. Figure 3 shows at the irradiance threshold of 400 W/m2, there are days which have extreme high daily RAs. After inspection, those values are abnormal. The results with 500 W/m2 and 600 W/m2 are quite close. We use 500 W/m2 as the threshold for the subsequent experiments to avoid excluding too many points.

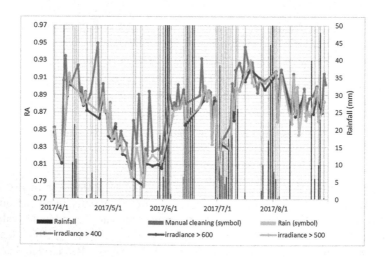

Fig. 3. Distribution of daily RAs with different irradiance thresholds.

Difference threshold of RA

Up to this point, the valid data points satisfy the following conditions: the time period for data points is 12:00 ~ 15:00, and the irradiance threshold is > 500 W/m2. In addition, the number of valid RAs shall be at least 20 and otherwise we ignore that day, i.e., do not calculate its daily average RA.

Still, some abnormal RAs can be observed as shown in Fig. 4(a). To tackle this problem, we further set a slope threshold referred to as RA_{slope}. As can be seen in Fig. 4(b) ∼ (d),

with smaller RA_{slope}, the number of valid RAs (indicated by the red dots) decreases. The results with $RA_{slope} \leqq 0.07$ and $RA_{slope} \leqq 0.05$ are about the same. In Fig. 4(d), it is clear that the threshold $RA_{slope} \leqq 0.03$ is to rigid, leading to the exclusion of too

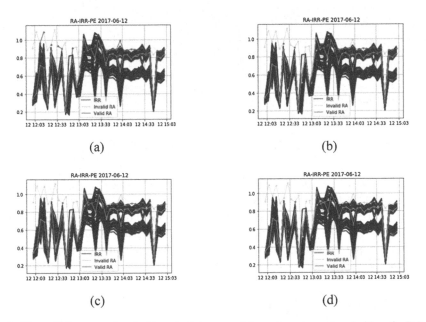

(a)

(b)

(c)

(d)

Fig. 4. The difference threshold of RA_{slope}: (a) not setup threshold of RA_{slope}, (b) $RA_{slope} \leqq 0.07$, (c) $RA_{slope} \leqq 0.05$, (d) $RA_{slope} \leqq 0.03$. (Color figure online)

many data points.

Figure 5 shows the RA results calculated with different RA_{slope} thresholds over a long period of time. As demonstrated, with RA_{slope} threshold 0.07 it seems there are still many abnormal points. With RA_{slope} threshold 0.05, it seems most of the daily RA values are reasonable. Nevertheless, more observations with additional experiments are needed. With RA_{slope} threshold 0.03, the line becomes smoother. However, only a few days are left and many valid days are excluded.

3.3   Effective Range of PE

It has been observed that the module fault occurred in a string will produce reduced power. In order to avoid including the fault module to the average calculation, production efficiency (PE) is aggregated for only a certain range of the individual PE values. Through the determination of the previous experiment, the condition increased the $RA_{slope} \leqq 0.05$ in this experiment. This experiment conditions includes:

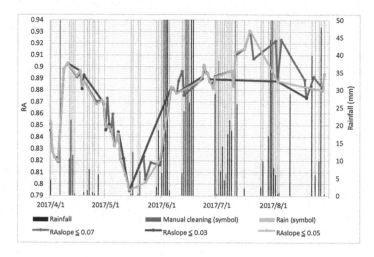

Fig. 5. The difference threshold of RA$_{slope}$.

experimental time 12:00 ~ 15:00, RA effective points $\geqq$ 20, threshold irradiance > 500 W/m2, threshold RA$_{slope}$ $\leqq$ 0.05.

Figure 6(a) presents the result without setting the threshold. It can be seen that there are several strings which have low PE values (indicated by the blue lines). Among those, two are quite evident, with the values less than 0.4. In Fig. 6(b) the effective range of the PE is set to the median $\pm$ 0.07. We can still observe low PEs. In contrast,

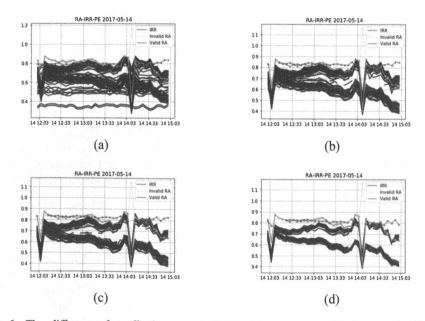

Fig. 6. The difference for effective range of PE: (a) not setup effective range, (b) PE median $\pm$ 0.07, (c) PE median $\pm$ 0.05, (d) PE median $\pm$ 0.03. (Color figure online)

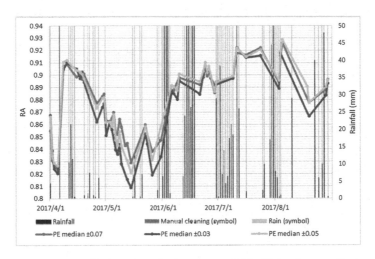

Fig. 7. The difference for effective range of PE. (Color figure online)

in Fig. 6(d) too many PEs are excluded and only a few strings remain. Therefore, it seems better to set the retention range of the PE by the median ± 0.5.

Figure 7 shows the RA results over a long time. No significant difference in the trend of the lines can be observed. However, we can see that a small range of PE values can result in low RA values. In particular, the green line representing the medium ± 0.03 is clearly low than the other two lines in several portions.

4 Experimental Results

The experiment is to observe the long-term change of RA from 2017/4/1 to 2017/8/31. The daily RA values were calculated for days under stable weather or at least having certain number of valid data points. The conditions for valid RA values are specified as the following: the time period is taken in between 12:00 and 15:00, the number of valid RA values shall be $\geqq 20$, the irradiance threshold > 500 W/m2, the threshold $RA_{slope} \leqq 0.05$, threshold PE range by PE median ±0.05.

Figure 8 shows the long-term RA change from 2017/4/1 to 2017/8/31 with manual cleaning on 2017/4/6 and 2017/7/11. We can see clearly that RA improves after manual cleaning. In early May, there was nearly no rains such that the RA decreased gradually. In early and mid-June, there were many heavy rains, which led to significant increases in RA. In late July, raining for several days also led to a slight increase in RA.

Table 1 shows the improvement after the two manual cleanings. The improvement after the first cleaning on 4/6 is significant, i.e., 10.11%. The improvement made by the second cleaning on 7/11 is marginal, i.e., 2.03%. The reason is because there were several heavy rains in June and July which have cleaned the panels and improved the RAs to near 0.9, leaving little room for improvement by manual cleaning. Having the analysis tool like shown in Table 1, the manager can decide when is the proper time to conduct manual cleaning of the solar-power plant.

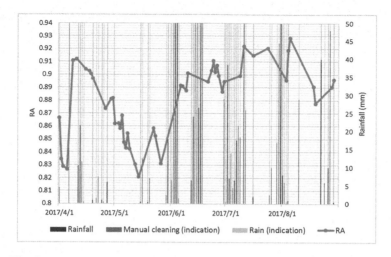

Fig. 8. Long-term observation of RA change, rainfall and manual cleaning.

Table 1. Efficiency improvement after cleaning on 4/6 and 7/11

Date	RA_{day}	RA_{imp}
2017/4/5 (dirty day)	0.824	
2017/4/8 (clean day)	0.907	
2017/4/6 (cleaning day)		10.11%
2017/7/9 (dirty day)	0.898	
2017/7/16 (clean day)	0.916	
2017/7/11 (cleaning day)		2.03%

5 Conclusion

In this study, we employed data analysis techniques to investigate the effect of solar-panel cleaning by analyzing collected data from a solar-power plant in central Taiwan. The cleaning effect is measured by the improvement on the daily RA value after the cleaning. Calculating the RA value is not a trivial task and needs to consider factors which prevent from obtaining reliable RAs. We discussed the factors and proposed methods to tackle the problems. Extensive experiments were conducted to verify the proposed methods. The results look promising. Consequently, the proposed approach can be used to help managers to determine when to clean solar-power plants such that a large improvement of power production after cleaning can be obtained.

Acknowledgement. This work was partially supported by the grants from Ministry of Science and Technology, Reforecast Co., Ltd., and the Intelligent Recognition Industry Service Center.

References

1. Ghazi, S., Sayigh, A., Ip, K.: Dust effect on flat surfaces – a review paper. Renew. Sustain. Energy Rev. **33**, 742–751 (2014)
2. Mei, H., Shen, Z., Zeng, C.: Study on cleaning frequency of grid-connected PV modules based on related data model. In: 2016 IEEE International Conference on Power and Renewable Energy (ICPRE), pp. 621–624. IEEE Press Shanghai (2016)
3. Tanesab, J., Parlevliet, D., Whale, J., Urmee, T.: Energy and economic losses caused by dust on residential photovoltaic (PV) systems deployed in different climate areas. Renew. Energy **120**, 401–412 (2018)
4. Fathi, M., Abderrezek, M., Grana, P.: Technical and economic assessment of cleaning protocol for photovoltaic power plants: case of Algerian Sahara sites. Sol. Energy **147**, 358–367 (2017)
5. Ayompe, L.M., Duffy, A., McCormack, S.J., Conlon, M.: Measured performance of a 1.72 kW rooftop grid connected photovoltaic system in Ireland. Energy Convers. Manag. **52**, 816–825 (2011)

egoStellar: Visual Analysis of Anomalous Communication Behaviors from Egocentric Perspective

Mei Han[1(✉)], Qing Wang[1(✉)], Lirui Wei[1(✉)], Yuwei Zhang[1(✉)], Yunbo Cao[2(✉)], and Jiansu Pu[1(✉)]

[1] Visual Analytics of Big Data Lab, UESTC, Chengdu, China
hanmei1993@126.com, vincent.w.qing@gmail.com,
413095866@qq.com, 494479914@qq.com,
jiansu.pu@uestc.edu.cn
[2] School of Information and Software Engineering, UESTC, Chengdu, China
uestc2008@126.com

Abstract. Detection and analysis of anomalous communication behaviors in cellar networks are extremely important in identifying potential advertising agency or fraud users. Visual analytics benefits domain experts in this problem for its intuitiveness and friendly interactive interface in presenting and exploring large volumes of data. In this paper, we propose a visual analytics system, egoStellar, to interactively explore the communication behaviors of mobile users from an ego network perspective. Ego network is composed of a centered individual and the relationships between the ego and his/her direct contacts (alters). Based on the graph model, egoStellar presents an overall statistical view to explore the distribution of mobile users for behavior inspection, a group view to classify the users and extract features for anomalous detection and comparison, and a ego-centric view to show the interactions between an ego and the alters in details. Our system can help analysts to interactively explore the communication patterns of mobile users from egocentric perspectives. Thus, this system makes it easier for the government or operators to visually inspect the massive communication behaviors in a intuitive way to detect and analyze anomalous users. Furthermore, our design can provide the researchers a good opportunity to observe the personal communication patterns to uncover new knowledge about human social interactions. Our proposed design can be applied to other fields where network structure exists. We evaluated egoStellar with real datasets containing the anomalous users with extremely large contacts in a short time period. The results show our system is effective in identifying anomalous communication behaviors, and its front-end interactive visualizations are intuitive and useful for analysts to discover insights in data.

Keywords: Mobile users · Ego-centric · Anomalous users · Visual analysis

© Springer Nature Singapore Pte Ltd. 2019
C.-Y. Chang et al. (Eds.): ICS 2018, CCIS 1013, pp. 280–290, 2019.
https://doi.org/10.1007/978-981-13-9190-3_29

1 Introduction

The booming of information and communication technology nurtures the big data era [1]. Among all these large volumes of data, communication data generated from celluar network recording how people interact with each other though mobile phones. The accumulation of such mobile communication records introduces new mechanisms for experts to study the human communication behaviors. And analyzing these behaviors not only helps finding the common communication patterns for mobile users, but more importantly facilitates the detection and analysis of customers with anomalous behaviors in communication networks who are potential advertising agencies or fraud users. Visual analytics benefits domain experts in this problem for its intuitiveness representation of context information and additional evidence via interactive interface for result analyzing and exploring. The Ego Networks (ENs) examine the ties connecting a target individual (ego) and his/her direct contacts (alters). Most of the extant research on communication networks are from the overall perspective regardless of the personal network features, and they were carried out based on either statistics or machine learning methods [5–7]. In this paper, we propose egoStellar to explore the communication behaviors of mobile users from an ego network perspective. Specifically, we extract the ECNs from the communication data, and portray the ECNs with six network metrics [11]. In order to explore anomalous behaviors via the visual inspection of ego-centric networks, we further design three views for interactive investigations: the first view is the statistical view, which uses the interactive scatter design to capture the holistic correlations and distributions of different ECN features for all egos. The second view is the group view, which uses pixel-based design to classify different ECNs into groups. Last but not least, we propose the third ego-centric view for uses, which shows the proportions of local and alien, unidirectional and bidirectional alters together with the interactions between the bidirectional alters by applying a new novel glyph-based design shaped from galaxy. In summary, our contributions in this paper are: (1) **System:** We build ECNs based on the communication data and introduce a novel visual analytics system for interactively exploring the mobile users' communication behaviors from ego network perspectives. (2) **Visualization:** We propose a new novel glyph design and layout algorithms shaped from galaxy to efficiently detect and analyze, and compare users with different communication patterns. Our design helps the experts to grasp the overall, the group-level, and the personal level of ECN status of the users thus facilitates the anonymous users detection and analysis. (3) **Evaluation:** We have evaluated egoStellar with real datasets containing the anomalous users with extremely large contacts in a short time period to demonstrated its effectiveness and usability. Through quantitative measurements of the design performance and qualitative interviews with domain experts, the results show our system is effective in identifying anomalous communication behaviors, and its front-end interactive visualizations are intuitive and useful for analysts to discover insights in data.

2 Related Work

The widespread of mobile communication and Online Social Network (OSN) accumulates the relevant data so that we are able to study the social networks at large scale [5, 6]. Onnela et al. [12] uncovered the existence of the weak tie effect. Eagle et al. [6] found it possible to infer 95% of friendships accurately based only on the mobile communication data. Saramäki et al. [13] showed that individuals have robust and distinctive social signatures persisting overtime. Wang et al. [11] studied the communication network from egocentric perspective, and find that the out-degree of a user plays a crucial role in affecting its ECN structure. As illustrated above, much attentions have been paid to uncovering the overall features of the ego communications networks. Ego network has also been a heated topic in the information visualization community recently. Shi et al. [14] proposed a new 1.5D visualization design to reduce the visual complexity of dynamic networks without sacrificing the topological and temporal context central to the focused ego. Liu et al. [15] raised a constrained graph layout algorithm "EgoNetCloud" on dynamic networks to prune, compress, and filter the networks in order to reveal the salient part of the network. Wu et al. [16] presented a visual analytics system named "egoSlider" for exploring and comparing dynamic citation networks from macroscope, mesoscope, and microscope levels. Cao et al. [17] proposed "TargetVue", which detected the anomalous users of online communication system via unsupervised learning. Liu et al. [18] introduced "egoComp", the storyflow-like links design, into the node-link graph in order to reveal the relations between two ego networks. Most of the research mainly focus on visualizing the statistical features of the peer to peer interactions within the OSNs or citation networks, but the research on detailed ego communication networks and communication patterns are still insufficient.

3 Data and Methods

He call detail records are collected by mobile operators for billing and network traffic monitoring. The basic information of such data sets contains the IDs of callers and callees, time stamps, call durations, base station numbers, charge information and so on. The dataset used in this study covers 7 million people of a Chinese provincial capital city for half a year spanning from Jan. to Jun. 2014. According to the operator the users choose, all of the users can be divided into two categories, namely, the local users (customers of the mobile operator who provide this data set) and the alien users (customers from the other operators). The mobile communication network can be modeled as a directed graph G(V; E) with the number of nodes and links being $|V| = N$ and $|E| = L$, respectively. Link weight is defined as wij for a directed link lij, which is the number of calls that user i has made to user j, and it represents the link strength between two users.

People usually make calls to maintain their social relationships [13]. The directions of communication divided the alters into two sets for an ego i: the in-contact set C_i^{in} and the out-contact set C_i^{out}. The size of C_i^{in} and C_i^{out} are in-degree k_i^{in} and out-degree k_i^{out}, respectively. k_i^{in} represents the ECN size ego i maintains, and k_i^{in} can reflect the influence of ego i in the network. In this paper, we mainly focus on k_i^{out}, because it represents the number of alters an ego intends to spend cognitive resources to maintain. We further define the node weight of an ego as $W_i^d = \sum_{j \in C_i^{out}} w_{ij}^d$ to indicate the total amount of energy an ego spend on maintaining his/her social relationships. In fact, the call durations are also important in communication behaviors and the link weight in "duration" perspective can be defined as $W_i = \sum_{j \in C_i^{out}} w_{ij}$, where w_{ij}^d is the call duration from i to j. To further investigate the properties of the ECNs, another three metrics are also introduced, namely, average node weight $\overline{w}$, attractiveness balance η, and tie balance θ. For ego i, the average node weight $\overline{w}_i$ is defined as:

$$\overline{w}_i = \frac{1}{k_i^{out}} \sum_{j \in C_i^{out}} w_{ij} \tag{1}$$

where w_{ij} is the weight of link l_{ij}, and k_i^{out} is the size of ECN. This metric indicates the average emotional closeness between an ego and the alters [13, 19]. Considering the communication directions, we introduce the attractiveness balance (AB) to measure such relationships between an ego and the network. It is defined in a straight forward way:

$$\eta_i = \frac{k_i^{in}}{k_i^{out}} \tag{2}$$

The attractiveness balance $\eta = 1$ means that the number of contacts a user calls is equal to the number of contacts who call him/her, suggesting the balance of the attractiveness. Large η implies strong attractiveness of an ego while small η refers to a weaker attractiveness. Apart from the attractiveness balance, communication directions also distinguishes bidirectional alters (who appear in both C_i^{in} and C_i^{out} from the uni-directional ones (who only appear in either C_i^{in} or C_i^{out}). Usually, the reciprocal relationships are stronger than the unidirectional relationships, thus they can be viewed as strong and weak ties [21]. Thus, we introduce another structural balance metric named tie balance (TB), which is defined as the Jaccard distance[22] between C_i^{in} and C_i^{out}. Mathematically, it reads:

$$\theta_i = \frac{|C_i^{in} \cap C_i^{out}|}{|C_i^{in} \cup C_i^{out}|} \tag{3}$$

$\theta = 1$ means all of ego i's direct contacts have bidirectional links with ego i, while $\theta = 0$ means ego i even has no reciprocal contacts. Of course, the above two kinds of ECNs are all extremely imbalance.

4 Visual Analytics System

4.1 System Overview

In this section, we introduce "egoStellar", whose design borrows the idea of galaxy. Like our solar system, an egocentric network is composed of a centered ego (like the sun), and all the other alters around him/her (like the other planets). The design goal of this visual analytics system is to give the analysts different levels of mobile users' calling behaviors: from the overall level of statistics, via group level statistics, to egocentric communication behaviors. To achieve this goal, we design 3 views for the corresponding level. Figure 2 illustrates the system architecture and the data processing pipeline of this visual analytics system. The system has two main parts as illustrated in Fig. 2(a), and they are "Computing End" and "Visual Representation End", which are connected via network. "Computing End" is a parallel computing cluster, which is composed of a Hadoop Distributed File System (HDFS), a customized Apache Spark parallel computing platform [24], and a "CompAgent". "CompAgent" receives computing tasks from the "Visual Representation", and cache the intermediate computing results for it. The "VisAgent" receives the data, and transmit the computing tasks to the "CompAgent". It can also transform data for visualization and send them to the "User Interface".

4.2 Visual Design

In this section, the three views are described conceccutively. Firstly, the Statistical View is present to show the distribution of users according to their egonetwork size, which is from the macroscopic perspective; Secondly, the users are divided into different groups according to the correlation between the ego network size and communication frequency, which is the mesoscopic perspective; Most importantly, the behaviors of the specific users are shown in the Egocentric View, which is the microscopic perspective.

Statistical View. Due to the scaling problem, it is not easy to observe the rare items in the traditional distribution chart, and log scale suffers from its unintuitiveness. Rare items are significant for detecting abnormal users in our case, thus we design the multi-scale distribution view, in which we show the distribution for the majority of the population, and use bubbles to represent the rare items. This Statistical View is more efficient and practical than directly visualizing such communication data for quickly grasping the data features. According to Wang's research [11], the size of ECN plays a crucial role in affecting other ECN properties, so we show the distribution of the egonetwork sizes in the first place as in Fig. 1(a).

Group View. With the help of statistical view, it is easy to figure out great quantity users' contacts are in 200 or less. In order to explore users' distribute of the relationship about contacts number and call frequency, we develop the Group View with a chessboard layout, also we classify clusters under the density of users' distribute.

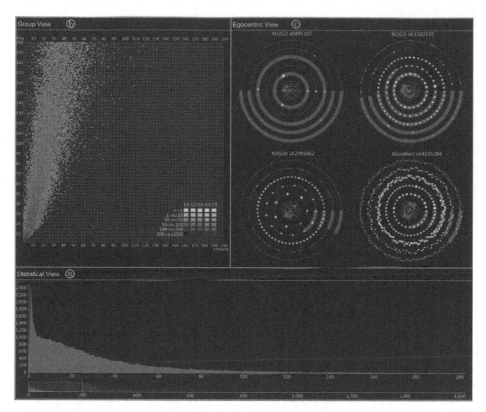

Fig. 1. (a) The visualization of users contacts and call frequency in 200 or less; (b) in this section, users communication structure in different clusters are represented as sky map to explore users features; (c) Monitoring users contacts in the entire telecommunications network.

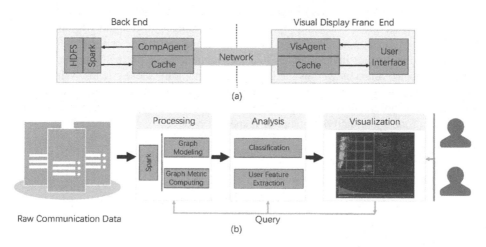

Fig. 2. The system architecture and data processing pipeline. (a) The system architecture; (b) The data processing pipeline.

With the classified clusters, we can figure out some specific user groups (one or several points in the view) we are interested in. In order to explore the distribute of users' coordinates, we map a series of sequence of colors to represent the number of users, refer to the bottom right corner in Fig. 1(b). The five clusters can be found in Fig. 1, as classified with the user density and the relationship of contacts and call frequency, and it can be seen that the "G1" has dark colors, also there are also many dark colors in the "G3", meanwhile, we interest in the "G2", some points have a few contacts with a quantity of frequency, with the "G4", covering the most points in right; we also interested in some points whose call frequency and contact ratio nearly equals 1. For further analysis, we display Egocentric View.

Egocentric View. With statistical view and group view, the analysts may interested in some specific users either for their representativeness or uniqueness. In fact, comprehending the social relationships and the communication strength of an ego can help to infer his/her personal social conditions. In order to fulfill these requirements and display the communication structure of users distinctly, this analytics system presents a microscopic user ego view with a sky map, which provides the following advantage: (1) Clearly display alien alters and local alters; (2) sky map layout have scalability to display the user with many contacts; (3) The layout display the character of the ego user clearly. In sky map, the alters which have a background is local user, the arc length of background represent the percent of the number of local alters, and the alter located in the near pathway means that the center user has more interconnection with the alter. and the inner ring displayed to compare the call frequency of center user with the alter, meanwhile, the outer ring compare the call duration of center user with the alter, and yellow displayed the called and purple represented the dialing. for the center, it takes a radar map to display the eight attributes of the central user which can be found in Fig. 3. Till now, the three views of the proposed visual analytics system have been fully presented in great details. The overall Statistical view provides the glimpse of all the users and their contacts distribute, and it helps the analysts promptly grasp the most users' property patterns. In order to get further information about the patterns located in the first view, the group view is proposed to compare egos within and without groups by applying glyph design. This view can help the analysts figure out interesting egos who need to be further investigated. Then the signature view presents the interactions between ego and alters as well as the interactions among the close friends. With all the above views, analysts are able to investigate the communication data from macroscopic, mesoscopic, and microscopic levels. This system can help the experts to know better about the social activity status of a specific user.

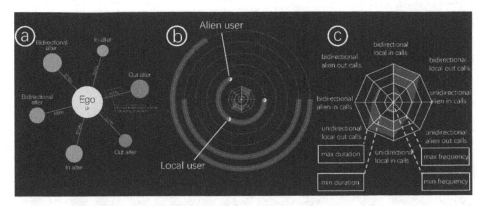

Fig. 3. Egocentric view: the source of data metric and the display of egocentric view. (a) the data metric of users; (b) This section put the design of the egocentric. (c) The detail information of ego center.

5 Case Study

In Fig. 1, the user "N1" from "G2" has few contacts but high calling frequency, and it interacts with its local alters at very high frequency. From the operator's perspective, it is a loyal user for its strong social relationships are all within this operator; There are lots of users in "G3", and "N2" is taken as an example, the user has intense communication with the bidirectional alters and lots of incoming calls from the other operators, thus it can be infered that it is a loyal user, meanwhile, it has the potential to attract the users from the other operators for it receives lots of calls from the other operators; For the users in "G4", like "N3", it has lots of contacts and has more interactions with local users, especially local bidirectional users (the center glyph), so this is an active and loyal user. All the above users have reasonable communication behaviors (both strong and weak social relationships are observed) and are normal users.

The last user "A1", in Fig. 1(c) has large number of contacts, however this user is outside of the scope of any existing group. In fact, this user calls lots of alien users, but doesn't have any strong relationships recorded, it looks more like an abnormal user, for example the telecom spammer. Figure 4 shows "A2" from "G1" and "A3" from "G5", according to definition, these are the users with very small and large ego networks, both of them are abnormal users. Among them, "A2" may have other mobile number in service at the same time, the egonetwork we obtained only contains part of its communication behaviors, and this is an alarm for the operator, and it calls for new business strategies to attract these users back. "A3" has 788 contacts (including many external contacts), the operator should try to maintain such heavy telecom user. From the above, we can see that this visual analytics system can help the operator to better understand the communication behaviors of both normal users and abnormal users, thus can help in making more personalized and profitable strategies.

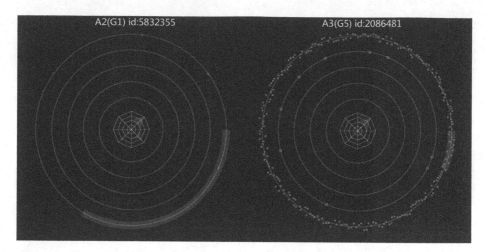

Fig. 4. In this section, we apply the visual analytics system in the task of abnormal user detection. The goal of this task is to find the abnormal users whose communication behaviors are very different and obtain the useful information to support the analysts of the mobile operator.

6 Discussion and Conclusion

The case study has demonstrated the efficacy of our visualization method in exploring large communication networks from egocentric perspective. The design of the statistical view can present the overall users' contacts distributions; the glyph based group view makes it easier to compare several users from the distribution of their contacts and call frequency at the same time; the stacked egocentric view can present the detail communication information of an ego. For example, this system can help to detect the service number and telecom-spammer.

Nevertheless, our method also suffers from several limitations. First of all, egocentric view can only show four egos at a time now. Secondly, the center of egocentric view high dimension information, and cannot display the ego's relationship network. The advantage is that such ratios can help the operator to estimate its market shares, and the disadvantage is the lost of the exact number of different kinds of alters.

As future works, the potential research direction is to present the ego-information of the ego and alters at the same time to improve mobility predictions.

Acknowledgments. This work was supported by the National Natural Science Foundation of China (Grant Nos. 61502083 and 61872066).

References

1. Manyika, J., et al.: Big data: the next frontier for innovation, competition, and productivity (2011). http://www.mckinsey.com/businessfunctions/business-technology/our-insights/big-data-the-nextfrontier-for-innovation. Accessed 10 Aug 2016

2. Barabási, A.L.: The origin of bursts and heavy tails in human dynamics. Nature **435**, 207–211 (2005)
3. Borgatti, S.P., Mehra, A.M., Brass, D.J., Labianca, J.: Network analysis in the social sciences. Science **323**, 892–895 (2009)
4. Roberts, S.G.B., Dunbar, R.I.M.: Communication in social networks: effects of kinship, network size, and emotional closeness. Pers. Relat. **18**, 439–452 (2011)
5. Onnela, J.P., et al.: Analysis of a large-scale weighted network of one-to-one human communication. New J. Phys. **9**, 179–206 (2007)
6. Eagle, N., Pentland, A.S., Lazer, D.: Inferring friendship network structure by using mobile phone data. Proc. Natl. Acad. Sci. U.S.A. **106**, 15274–15278 (2009)
7. Japkowicz, N., Stefanowski, J.: A machine learning perspective on big data analysis. In: Japkowicz, N., Stefanowski, J. (eds.) Big Data Analysis: New Algorithms for a New Society. SBD, vol. 16, pp. 1–31. Springer, Cham (2016). https://doi.org/10.1007/978-3-319-26989-4_1
8. Hey, T.: The fourth paradigm – data-intensive scientific discovery. In: Kurbanoğlu, S., Al, U., Erdoğan, P.L., Tonta, Y., Uçak, N. (eds.) IMCW 2012. CCIS, vol. 317, p. 1. Springer, Heidelberg (2012). https://doi.org/10.1007/978-3-642-33299-9_1
9. Keim, D., Andrienko, G., Fekete, J.-D., Görg, C., Kohlhammer, J., Melançon, G.: Visual analytics: definition, process, and challenges. In: Kerren, A., Stasko, J.T., Fekete, J.-D., North, C. (eds.) Information Visualization. LNCS, vol. 4950, pp. 154–175. Springer, Heidelberg (2008). https://doi.org/10.1007/978-3-540-70956-5_7
10. Mazza, R.: Introduction to Information Visualization. Springer, London (2009). https://doi.org/10.1007/978-1-84800-219-7
11. Wang, Q., Gao, J., Zhou, T., Hu, Z., Tian, H.: Critical size of ego communication networks. Europhys. Lett. **114**, 58004 (2016)
12. Onnela, J.P., et al.: Structure and tie strengths in mobile communication networks. Proc. Natl. Acad. Sci. U.S.A. **104**, 7332–7336 (2007)
13. Saramäki, J., Leicht, E.A., López, E., Roberts, S.G.B., Reed-Tsochas, F., Dunbar, R.I.M.: Persistence of social signatures in human communication. Proc. Natl. Acad. Sci. U.S.A. **111**, 942–947 (2014)
14. Shi, L., Wang, C., Wen, Z., Qu, H., Liao, Q.: 1.5D egocentric dynamic network visualization. IEEE Trans. Vis. Comput. Graphics **21**, 624–637 (2015)
15. Liu, Q., Hu, Y., Shi, L., Mu, X., Zhang, Y., Tang, J.: EgoNetCloud: event based egocentric dynamic network visualization. In: IEEE Conference on Visual Analytics Science and Technology, pp. 65–72 (2015)
16. Wu, Y., Pitipornvivat, N., Zhao, J., Yang, S., Huang, G., Qu, H.: EgoSlider: visual analysis of egocentric network evolution. IEEE Trans. Vis. Comput. Graphics **22**, 260–269 (2016)
17. Cao, N., Shi, C., Lin, S., Lu, J., Lin, Y., Lin, C.: TargetVue: visual analysis of anomalous user behaviors in online communication systems. IEEE Trans. Vis. Comput. Graph. **22**, 280–289 (2016)
18. Liu, D., Guo, F., Deng, B., Wu, Y., Qu, H.: EgoComp: a nodelink based technique for visual comparison of ego-network (2016). http://vacommunity.org/egas2015/papers/IEEEEGAS2015-DongyuLiu.pdf. Accessed 10 Aug 2016
19. Zhou, W.X., Sornette, D., Hill, R.A., Dunbar, R.I.M.: Discrete hierarchical organization of social group sizes. Proc. R. Soc. B **272**, 439–444 (2005)
20. Brzozowski, M.J., Romero, D.M.: Who should I follow? Recommending people in directed social networks. In: Fifth International AAAI Conference on Weblogs and Social Media, pp. 458–461 (2011)

21. Zhu, Y., Zhang, X., Sun, G., Tang, M., Zhou, T., Zhang, Z.: Influence of reciprocal links in social networks. PLoS One **9**, e103007 (2014)
22. Levandowsky, M., Winter, D.: Distance between sets. Nature **234**, 34–35 (1971)
23. Brown, J.J., Reingen, P.H.: Social ties and word-of-mouth referral behavior. J. Consum. Res. **14**, 350–362 (1987)
24. Zaharia, M., Chowdhury, M., Franklin, M.J., Shenker, S., Stoica, I.: Spark: cluster computing with working sets. HotCloud **10**, 95 (2010)

Visual Analysis for Online Communities Exploration Based on Social Data

Lirui Wei[1(✉)], Qinghua Hu[1(✉)], Mei Han[1(✉)], Yuwei Zhang[1(✉)],
Chao Fan[1(✉)], Yunbo Rao[2(✉)], and Jiansu Pu[1(✉)]

[1] VisBig Lab, School of Computer Science and Technology,
UESTC, Chengdu, Sichuan, China
lirui_wei@163.com
[2] School of Information and Software Engineering,
UESTC, Chengdu, Sichuan, China
uestc2008@126.com

Abstract. As the result of Social media data being unprecedentedly available, we are provided so many substantial opportunities to explore social circle from many perspectives. Many researches have deep understandings of the correlation between social relation online and that on real world. These researches make conclusions from perspectives of statistics only but they cannot explain specific reasons underlying those conclusions. Obviously we can separate an individual's social circle into several groups such as family group, classmate group and co-worker group etc. Aimed at labeling the friend groups online, in this paper, we implement a visual analytic system to exploring correlation between communities resulted from label propagation algorithm in online social friendship network of a centric user and each friend's offline POI distribution of such places where the centric user has also visited. To demonstrate the reasonability and utility, we give 3 cases in details based on social media data of the online friendship and offline movement information provided by Tencent (the largest social service platform in China).

Keywords: Friendship network · POI occurrence · Community detection · Visual analysis

1 Introduction

Online social network has replaced traditional social model and has become one of the main ways of social communication. The massive, heterogeneous and multidimensional social data poses great challenges for such researches.

Two types of those data are widely studied: online user friend relationship data and offline location check-in data of users. On the one hand, there is a lot of work to do based on these two types of social media data. On the other hand, the spatial and temporal characteristics of the location check-in data we obtain are too sparse and Irregular, so we have to combine the users' online friendship data and the check-in with location information in our visual analysis. We decide the social friend circle and all friends' check-in location data of a single user as the research object in our work. It is

© Springer Nature Singapore Pte Ltd. 2019
C.-Y. Chang et al. (Eds.): ICS 2018, CCIS 1013, pp. 291–301, 2019.
https://doi.org/10.1007/978-981-13-9190-3_30

easy to think of building a friendship network based on friendships among the friends of centric user. After the completion of our preliminary network diagram, we found that friends in the network of friends have different levels of social gathering. We use the label propagation algorithm [1] to divide the network of friends into several communities. Then we use the center friends' check-in location data with POI information of center user to explain different communities. For example, a community has a high locus similarity with the center user at home then we can conclude that the community is the central user's family member.

2 Related Work

According to the current situation of visual analysis of social media data, Y Wu and N Cao divides all visual analysis of social data into two categories in A Survey on Visual Analytics of Social Media Data [2]. The visual analysis of understanding user behavior in social networks is subdivided into two main directions: analyzing social network structure and exploring social network content.

2.1 Visual Analysis of Social Media Data

(1) Analyzing the Structure of Social Networks: The graph theory is the most commonly used and most intuitive way to study the network structure. However, when the scale of social networks has increased to a certain extent, the problem of overlapping is unacceptable and interaction has become more and more hysteretic. The solution to these problems in field of visual analysis is that the visual system interacts with the user to select the visual part of the network. For example, in the Vizster system proposed by Heer and Boyd, a force-directed graph is used to visualize social networks, and users are allowed to interactively select local network areas and highlight this part of the local network for relevant interaction and analysis [3]. In addition, van Ham and van Wijk also focused on force layout graph as visual component, but they proposed new layout algorithms to emphasize social communities [4]. Edge clustering technology [5] can effectively solve the problem of visual occlusion by modifying the connection path of edges in the network [6].

Different views in the visualization system can display different aspects of data. Click selection and other interactive operations can display a local network view with a certain semantic meaning [8]. There are ways to define the local network or obtain the analysis of the main areas of interest by means of feature extraction of the data. For example, an analyst can use Top-N [7] nodes based on different feature to select the most critical N nodes for correlation analysis. When higher-level semantic information related to a social network can be obtained, these valuable semantic information in the social network can help cluster the nodes in the social network to better understand the structure of the network [9]. Chi et al. proposed a unified social network clustering framework IOLAP based on multivariate factors, which can directly model 4D information for people, relationships, content and time [10]. More sophisticated algorithms like the topic probability model [11] can also be applied to create classified social networks.

(2) **Analyzing Social Network Content:** Due to the complexity of collective behavior, similar behaviors from different groups of people must be integrated prior to visualization. Understanding when and where and what information is transmitted on social networks is a very popular research topic. Lei et al. [14] proposed that image propagation depends on the relevance of its interpretation and user preferences. Niu et al. [12] analyzed a large number of video trajectories of spreading and revealed several interesting models of video transmission on social networks. Zhao et al. [13] studied the behavior of users' scoring behaviors on social network and proposed a matrix factorization model based on scorer-related scoring items, hobbies, scoring habits, and behavior propagation processes. The design of Google Ripples [15] is simple and effective. Whisper's [16] visual design is more complex and can analyze social data more efficiently. Compared to the previously mentioned analysis and visualization techniques that applid on group behavior, only a few visualization techniques are used to analyze the ego-centric social behavior. PeopleGarden [17] is one of the earliest studies of this type of such visual analysis. It visualizes the activities of the members of the online community as a glyph of the flower, and then different users are randomly placed into PeopleGarden. Although it visualizes the interaction between users, it does not mention when and how often these interactions occurred. Involving them, The visual design introduced next solves these problems. Cao et al. [18] proposed Episogram to use their designed icons to visualize user posts and replies on social networks. Based on this work, Cao et al. [19]. TargetVue also based on user-centered visual analysis of abnormal user behavior on Twitter. For each user, some defined behavior characteristics are extracted, and then an anomaly detection algorithm is used to detect the suspicious user group.

2.2 Label Propagation Algorithm

In our work, there is also a clear community structure in a user's social network built based on the center user's friendship. In order to extract the feature information of these communities from the network, we must divide the network and use the tag propagation algorithm to divide the communities of the friends network. There are many ways to divide the community of the network, but the results of most of the community division algorithms depend on preset parameters such as the number of associations or the size of the community, and the time complexity of these algorithms is exponential.

Unlike those community partitioning algorithms, the label propagation algorithm does not depend on any parameter settings and has linear time complexity. The most critical propagation condition for the label propagation algorithm is to assume that a certain node x has x_1, x_2, x_3,..., x_k adjacent nodes at a certain moment, and each neighbor node has been divided into a certain community. Every these k nodes must belong to one of G_{i1}, G_{i2},..., G_{im}, (m $\leq$ k) communities, and G_{iy} (iy belongs to i1, i2, ..., im) contains $N(x)_{iy}$ (iy belongs i1,i2,...,im) neighbor nodes of x, the community label of node x will change to the label of group of Maxim of $N(x)_{iy}$.

3 Task Abstraction

our research task need to collect feature from friendship data and location data and then design visual schema for features from these two aspect. Feature more, we need to implement a friendly, interactive, visual system based on the last two steps and finally explore valuable information by combine visual result of these two dataset through our system.

3.1 Friendship Network and Friend Groups

All friends of the centric user can develop friendship among them, which can be abstracted into a friendship network. First step of our task is to visualize such friendship network. However, it is unmeaning to visualize the friendship network only for the reason that no valuable information we can obtain by just analyzing this blank network, so we need to more feature to draw on this blank friendship network. That is group information. Intuitively, clustering friend groups appears in the blank friend network. It is reasonable in real world for various kinds of groups based on relation type among his or her friends consist of total friends of an individual. For example, an individual owns family member group while there are co-work group, classmate group, entertainment (e.g. party or eating or movie) group. Feather step of our task is to detect these friend groups completely based on friendship network structure. In the network filed, community detection is an important research branch for a long time and many algorithms are designed to solve this problem. Among them label propagation algorithm is an efficiently functional method which result is independent on input parameter and stable. According to this, on one hand our task is applying this algorithm to our friendship network to divide friends of an individual into different groups to meet the situation in real word and on the other hand our visual task requires us to encode these group features with visual elements in visualization way.

3.2 Movement Information and Occurrence

Considering that the sparse and not sequential location data is collected by user check-in activity so that we cannot apply traditional methods to analyze spatial-temporal data on this dataset. To make best use of it, we define occurrence of every friend as the location point, which the centric user and this friend both have visited. Our research task to visualize the location data requires occurrence feature extraction from the row sparse movement data but it is the only task we need to do. Such occurrences obtained with the unique POI tags so that the next processing step is to cluster all occurrences of every friend of the centric user by their POI tags. Finally, we need to work out visual design and implement of extracted POI feature.

3.3 Combination

Friendship data represents online social circle while location information represents offline sphere of social activity. The last general task of our research requires us to combine friend groups information from friendship data and POI distributions of occurrences to analyze the reason why such friend groups come into being in friendship network of the centric user by POIs tags distribution of members in every group.

4 System Overview

Our system (Fig. 1) is composed of friendship network view (Fig. 1(a)), POI temporal sequence view (Fig. 1(b)) and scatter plot (Fig. 1(c)) showing the distribution between number of common friends and movement similarity (CN-MS). By label propagation algorism, the friend network (Fig. 1(a)) of a centric user based on its friend links online are divided into friend groups in which arbitrary friend node owns links to nodes in its group no less than nodes out of its group. In addition, connection information both connecting the node itself with other groups and connecting group the node belonging to with other groups are encoded to every friend node in this network.

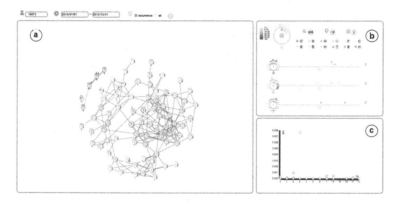

Fig. 1. System overview. (a) Groups in which arbitrary friend node owns links to nodes in its group no less than nodes out of its group. (b) Poi temporal sequence in which ticks represent 24 h in a day and the POI icons are arranged in descend order measured by its frequency to displays distribution of occurrences in 24 h of a node. (c) Scatter plot showing the distribution between number of common friends and movement similarity (CN-MS).

4.1 Analytic Pipeline

Our analytic system is a web-based application using full- stack web developing technique of JavaScript library (e.g. Mon- goose.js, node.js, express.js, d3.js) to assist users to explore realistic tags (e.g. classmates, co-workers, or family members) of friend groups in a centric user's friend network based on check-in records with POI information. We extract cluster features from friend network and occurrence features from check-in data. To efficiently display all information we obtained, we design friend node component and poi temporal sequence component to visualize details of group information and POI distribution of occurrences of a centric user. Rendering the views by data driven document JavaScript library (d3.js), all these view components make up to our system and user interaction is also an important part of our system (Fig. 2).

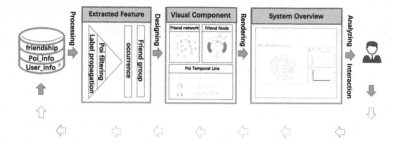

Fig. 2. System pipeline. The raw data is cleaning and stored into the Mongo DB for the use of feature extraction. Data processing aims to extract the occurrence feature and group feature. After feature extraction, we design three visual components to present feature information we extracted to finally render system view. we also implement Interaction as a key step in our pipeline loop.

5   Visualization Design

This visual analytic system is aimed to aid analysts in understanding the practical significance of the friends groups online. Directed by this goal, we design friend node component in (Fig. 3(1)) representing simple vertex in network and POI temporal sequence component (Fig. 3(2)) stretching distribution of occurrence of arbitrary friend node on 24-h temporal line.

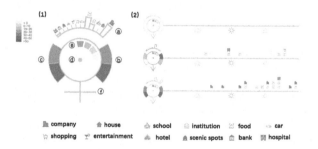

Fig. 3. Friends node and temporal sequence.

5.1   Friend Node

We visually code all information obtained by feature extraction in this friend node (Fig. 3(1)). For a node, a kind of color represents one friend group of centric user. On the left side of the big circle, this arc-shaped area (Fig. 3(c)) represents the connections between the groups owning this node and other groups. On the right side, this arc-shaped area (Fig. 3(b)) represents the connecting links between the friend node itself and other groups. For this node as the hub of its group it owns all connecting links its group has. On the top, arc with 12 ticks (Fig. 3(a)) displays POI distribution of occurrences between this friend node and the centric user. Observed from anti-clockwise direction, every tick respectively represents company, school, house, institution, food, car, shopping, entertainment, hotel, tourist attractions, bank, and hospital.

On the bottom (Fig. 3(f)), the gender symbol shows the gender of this friend. In the center, increasingly blue grids (Fig. 3(e)) like a dashboard shows friend age from less than 0 to over 50 years old with a gap of 10 years old. In the most center area, the size of small circle (Fig. 3(d)) represents that how many friends this friend node has.

5.2 POI Temporal Sequence

To explore the POI and temporal regularity of the POI distribution either in the same or different friend groups we have clustering, we design POI temporal sequence (Fig. 3 (2)) in which ticks represent 24 h in a day and the POI icons are arranged in descend order measured by its frequency to displays distribution of occurrences of a node in 24 h if the temporal data is good enough.

5.3 Interactions

Apart from direct interaction with the force-directed layout algorithm, there are other interactions in the friend network view. For example, selecting node in the friend network view will also be visualized in the POI timeline view. System users can arbitrarily select nodes in one friend group or in different groups to explore more information, as we will illustrate in case study part. Basically, system users can input the centric user ID and time period to generate all views. Likewise, they can select to display either all POI information of friends or only the occurrences with centric user.

6 Case Study

We implement a web-based system using JavaScript. To evaluate the effectiveness and availability of our system, we carry out three case studies based on data collected from Jul. 1, 2012 to Dec. 30, 2012 in a coastal city in China.

6.1 Case One

In this case (Fig. 4), first of all we can find out that there are two friends who have frequently visited the same places with the centric user. Then we check the friend network view finally to find out that two friend nodes having frequently visited the same place with the centric user are divided into the same group by applying label propagation algorithm. We can also find that it is a girl who almost has been to the same place at every hour in a day on the POI temporal sequence while the centric user is a boy. Our system successfully distinguishes high frequent occurrence group from other groups in the friends network view, in other word we can label corresponding group of high movement similarity with centric user after clustering its friends circle by combining online friendship data and offline check-in data with POIs.

Fig. 4. Case 1. Close friends having higher movement similarity offline are divided into the same group based on online friend network.

6.2   Case Two

In this case (Fig. 5) we can explore more valuable information combining visual result of our system and visual analysis. The orange group shares no connected edge with the blue group. Otherwise, the blue group in circle includes most friends who have higher movement similarity with the centric user. In other word, there are two completely separate groups in friends network in the condition that one group almost has no movement similarity with centric user while many members of the another group always visited the same bank with the centric user. For the no movement similarity group, the analysis result indicates either the members of it are online friends who never meet the centric user in the real word and keep a friendship in virtual cyber world only or they are remote friends in the situation that they used to interact with the centric user in the real word but somehow the centric user move to another place far away from them. There is one typical example for such a case that a young man grew up in his hometown until this man graduated from his senior school and then go to his college or go to work in another city so that his hometown friend group like the orange group both has no movement similarity with him and no connections with his new friend group like the blue group. In this case many members of the new friend group with high movement similarity with the centric user always visited the same bank during working time indicating this group is a workmate group for the centric user. We analyze the reason why isolate groups structure come into being in the friend network view because these groups either isolate or remote from the centric user both in the cyber and real world.

Fig. 5. Case 2. Friends whether having occurrence with centric user are divided into different groups and there is no connection between bank group and no occurrence group. (Color figure online)

6.3   Case Three

Not only can our visualizing system identify group with high movement similarity or it distinguishes remote groups from close group, but also can our system identify groups in network view into different categories of POI. In this case (Fig. 6) all friends of the centric user are divided into many groups with many colors. Especially, the orange group in circle visited the same school most while the green group in circle visited same company most with the centric user. For the blue group in circle, none of the nodes have visited the same place with the centric user. We can illustrate this visual result by the way that individual has different friend communities in real world such as family group, classmate groups, workmate groups and so on. Correspondingly in the network of virtual cyber world members in the same group has much stronger links more than members of other groups. It is reasonable that members of family group meet the centric user in the home most while members of classmate group meet centric user in the school most leading to different categories group with different POI labels. In this case there are school POI type and company POI type as observed both in friend nodes and POI temporal sequences.

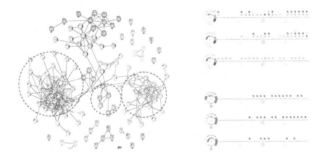

Fig. 6. Case 3. Not only online friend groups are distinguished by whether having occurrences with centric user, but also these groups have different kinds of POIs of occurrences with centric user. (e.g. In this case, there are school group and company group). (Color figure online)

7   Conclusion

The main direction of this paper is based on the popular visual analysis of social data in the current visualization field and the main data comes from the online social friend relationship data and offline check-in location data. Based on these two different data, we used visualization theory to perform association between them and view presentation. Eventually, the valuable information of these two kinds of data is mined and the signing location information was used to reasonably explain the communities in social network. The main contributions of our work are as follows:

(1) **Heterogeneous social data analysis:** We combine the association of these two kinds of data mentioned to perform feature extraction and conduct effective visual analysis of heterogeneous social data

(2) **Visual design:** Visualization design prototypes of various data are proposed to efficiently display information conveyed by such data.
(3) **Visualization system:** Using JavaScript full-stack development technology to complete the entire visual system.

Acknowledgments. This work was supported by the National Natural Science Foundation of China (Grant Nos. 61502083 and 61872066).

References

1. Raghavan, U.N., Albert, R., Kumara, S.: Near linear time algorithm to detect community structures in large-scale networks. Phys. Rev. E Stat. Nonlinear Soft Matter Phys. **76**(3 Pt 2), 036106 (2007)
2. Wu, Y., Cao, N., Gotz, D., Tan, Y.P., Keim, D.A.: A survey on visual analytics of social media data. IEEE Trans. Multimed. **18**(11), 2135–2148 (2016)
3. Heer, J., Boyd, D.: Vizster: visualizing online social networks. In: Proceedings of IEEE Symposium on Information Visualization, pp. 3239 (2005)
4. Holten, D.: Hierarchical edge bundles: Visualization of adjacency relations in hierarchical data. IEEE Trans. Vis. Comput. Graph. **12**(5), 741–748 (2006)
5. Cui, W., Zhou, H., Qu, H., Wong, P.C., Li, X.: Geometry-based edge clustering for graph visualization. IEEE Trans. Vis. Comput. Graph. **14**(6), 1277–1284 (2008)
6. van Ham, F., van Wijk, J.J.: Interactive visualization of small world graphs. In: Proceedings of IEEE Symposium on Information Visualization, pp. 199–206 (2004)
7. Perer, A., Guy, I., Uziel, E., Ronen, I., Jacovi, M.: Visual social network analytics for relationship discovery in the enterprise. In: Proceedings of IEEE Conference on Visual Analytics Science and Technology, pp. 71–79 (2011)
8. Perer, A., Shneiderman, B.: Balancing systematic and flexible exploration of social networks. IEEE Trans. Vis. Comput. Graph. **12**(5), 693–700 (2006)
9. Shneiderman, B., Aris, A.: Network visualization by semantic substrates. IEEE Trans. Vis. Comput. Graph. **12**(5), 733–740 (2006)
10. Chi, Y., Zhu, S., Hino, K., Gong, Y., Zhang, Y.: iOLAP: a framework for analyzing the internet, social networks, and other networked data. IEEE Trans. Multimed. **11**(3), 372–382 (2009)
11. Negoescu, R.-A., Gatica-Perez, D.: Modeling Flickr communities through probabilistic topic-based analysis. IEEE Trans. Multimed. **12**(5), 399–416 (2010)
12. Niu, G., Fan, X., Li, V.O., Long, Y., Xu, K.: Multi-source-driven asynchronous diffusion model for video-sharing in online social networks. IEEE Trans. Multimed. **16**(7), 2025–2037 (2014)
13. Zhao, G., Qian, X., Xie, X.: User-service rating prediction by exploring social users' rating behaviors. IEEE Trans. Multimed. **18**(3), 496–506 (2016)
14. Lei, C., Liu, D., Li, W.: Social diffusion analysis with common-interest model for image annotation. IEEE Trans. Multimed. **18**(4), 687–701 (2016)
15. Viégas, F., et al.: Google+ ripples: a native visualization of information flow. In: Proceedings of the International Conference on World Wide Web, pp. 1389–1398 (2013)
16. Cao, N., Lin, Y.-R., Sun, X., Lazer, D., Liu, S., Qu, H.: Whisper: tracing the spatiotemporal process of information diffusion in real time. IEEE Trans. Vis. Comput. Graph. **18**(12), 2649–2658 (2012)

17. Xiong, R., Donath, J.: PeopleGarden:creatingdataportraitsforusers. In: Proceedings of the ACM Symposium on User Interface Software and Technology, pp. 37–44 (1999)
18. Cao, N., Lin, Y.-R., Du, F., Wang, D.: Episogram: visual summarization of egocentric social interactions. Comput. Graph. Appl. **36**, 72–81 (2015)
19. Gilbert, E., Karahalios, K.: Using social visualization to motivate social production. IEEE Trans. Multimed. **11**(3), 413–421 (2009)

Forecasting Monthly Average of Taiwan Stock Exchange Index

Wei-Ting Sun[1], Hsin-Ta Chiao[2]([✉]), Yue-Shan Chang[3], and
Shyan-Ming Yuan[1]

[1] Department of Computer Science, National Chiao Tung University,
Hsinchu, Taiwan
weitin.sun@gmail.com, smyuan@cs.nctu.edu.tw
[2] Department of Computer Science, Tunghai University,
Taichung, Taiwan
josephchiao@thu.edu.tw
[3] Department of Computer Science and Information Engineering,
National Taipei University, New Taipei City, Taiwan
ysc@mail.ntpu.edu.tw

Abstract. Futures market has high leverage and the characteristics of over-performing returns. Hence, it always attracts lots of investors. However, three major kinds of institutional traders are more influential than individual investors in Taiwan. In this paper, a monthly predicting model for the weighted price index of the Taiwan Stock Exchange (TAIEX) was built based on correlation and regression analysis by using the following parameters: Dow Jones industrial index, NASDAQ index, M1A, M1B, M2 annual growth rate, US dollar exchange rate, economic monitoring indicator and global oil prices. Then, based on the prediction results, we define two trading strategies and apply them in trading MTX (mini Taiwan index futures). The evaluation result shows that both the two trading strategies have good returns.

Keywords: Correlation analysis · Regression analysis · Stock

1 Introduction

Taiwan stock futures (TX) were launched by the Taiwan Futures Exchange in 1998, and the trading target was the Taiwan weighted stock index. The mini Taiwan index futures (MTX) was launched in 2001, and the transaction target is the same as Taiwan stock futures [1, 2]. The difference between TX and MTX lies in the contract value and the required security deposit. In the past 10 years, the trading volume of both TX and MTX has been increasing year by year. In particular, the trading volume of MTX in 2016 was 8 times that of 2007, which represents the increasingly hot trading in the futures market. Stock futures provide investors with an investment approach other than stocks, which has high market liquidity, and transaction costs are much lower than stocks. Therefore, stock futures have the functions of hedging, price discovery and speculation. However, because the required minimum deposit is much lower than the contract value, stock futures are highly leveraged, high-risk investment tools.

© Springer Nature Singapore Pte Ltd. 2019
C.-Y. Chang et al. (Eds.): ICS 2018, CCIS 1013, pp. 302–309, 2019.
https://doi.org/10.1007/978-981-13-9190-3_31

Moreover, because the three major kinds of institutional traders have the advantages of capital size and better information sources, they usually outweigh many individual investors in profitability.

Since the trading targets of Taiwan stock futures and mini Taiwan index futures are all Taiwan weighted stock indices, the linkage between futures and stocks must be highly correlated. Therefore, the purposes of this paper are:

- To identify the factors that affected the weighted stock index of Taiwan in recent years.
- To predict the monthly average of the Taiwan weighted stock index by analyzing factors in historical data.
- To use the monthly average to judge the trend of the Taiwan stock market, and provide trading strategies on investing in mini Taiwan index futures.

We first refer to the literature on the stock market and futures market to find out the factors that may affect the stock price, such as: Dow Jones industrial index, NASDAQ index, monetary aggregates (M2, M1A, M1B), gold price, economic monitoring indicator, US dollar exchange rate, the balance of margin loan and stock loan, various international crude oil prices [3], etc. Then, we use correlation analysis and p-value approach to filter out factors that are more relevant to Taiwan weighted stock index. Then, we will find variables with better predictive power by using simple linear regression and here only one factor is considered as an independent variable at a time in simple linear regression. Finally, multiple linear regressions are used to combine multiple factors [4] and we will use the results of regression analysis to predict the monthly average of Taiwan weighted stock index. The reason for using the monthly average is to spread short-term risks, like the 9/11 attacks. If the forecast period is extended to the monthly interval, the impact of these short-term factors can be reduced.

Finally, we propose two trading strategies for mini Taiwan index futures. Through the tests based on historical data, we found that our prediction model can achieve the highest average accuracy by using the combination of the following three factors: the monthly average of Dow Jones industrial index, the monthly average of NASDQ index, and the M2 annual growth rate. Therefore, the prediction model in this paper mainly uses these three factors to do forecast. In the evaluation section, we will show the investment performances of these two proposed strategies and both of them have good investment returns.

2 Related Works

After analyzing the related literature, we did not found any related works for predicting the monthly average of the weighted stock index of Taiwan. Chuang in [5] mentioned that the public information of the three major kinds of institutional traders has considerable explanatory power on Taiwan index futures, and among which foreign investment institutes have the greatest influence. Since the futures market is still dominated by institutional traders, individual investors need to track the public information of the institutional traders to adjust the trading strategy to achieve higher profit. Hsieh [6] pointed out that the exchange rate has a certain degree of relationship and influence with the stock market, and analyzed the impact of exchange rate on Taiwan weighted stock price index, including the exchange rate changes between the New Taiwan dollar against the US dollar, the Chinese yuan, the Hong Kong dollar and the euro. Liu [7] explored the timing relationship among Taiwan weighted stock index, Taiwan stock index futures and Taiwan stock index options. It was observed that the futures price discovery ability was 30 min ahead of the option and 45 min ahead of the stock spot. Chang [8] studies the impact of the following three factors on the rise and fall of Taiwan stock index futures: the open interest of Taiwan stock index futures, the trading volume of Taiwan stock index futures and the net foreign investment of Taiwan stock index futures. Lu [9] attempted to use time series, regression analysis, and neural network to predict the next day closing index of Taiwan stock futures. Six variables were selected by stepwise regression analysis, including the 10-day moving average, the 10-day BIAS, the basis difference, the 9 days K, the open interest, and the Shanghai composite index. Wang [10] explored the linkages among the international oil price, change rate of currency exchange and the Taiwan stock price index, based on the historical data since January 2000 to September 2008. Wu [11] analyzed the market capital flow through the self-organizing map network and the reverse-transfer neural network in the Taiwan stock and futures market in order to identify potential behaviors of market capital flows as an investment aid for investors. Yang [12] made an empirical study on whether the daily close-to-close rate of return of the NASDAQ index has spillover effect on both investment reward and volatility of Taiwan stock market. According to the empirical results, NASDAQ has a statistically significant reward spillover effect for Taiwan stock index. The most significant impact is on the daily return of the Taiwan stock market. Hsieh [13] used a variety of time series methods to explore the linkage between Taiwan weighted stock price index, crude oil spot, crude oil futures, gold spot and gold futures. Using the nonparametric co-integration method, it is found that there is a long-term stable equilibrium relationship between the stock price index, crude oil and gold price. The analysis results show that the price of crude oil has the greatest influence. Therefore, when investing in the stock market, investors have to pay attention to the impact of oil price fluctuations. Sou [14] used an empirical research method to establish a trading strategy for Taiwan stock price index futures by additionally referencing the KD value of the day as well as the positive and negative price difference between Taiwan stock index futures.

3   TAIEX Index Prediction

In this paper, we have to collect the required historical data for prediction model creation and model performance evaluation. Table 1 shows the types, the sampling intervals and the data sources (web sites) of these historical data. The data are gathered either by a Java language crawler or manual downloading from the web sites listed in Table 1. For some types of data (whose Avg field is Y) in Table 1, we will calculate their respective monthly averages, and use their monthly averages in the subsequent data analysis process.

We calculate the correlation coefficient and p-value for each data type in Table 1 and the monthly average of the Taiwan weighted stock price index. Then we can

Table 1. Types, sampling intervals and data sources of historical data

Data type	Avg	Sampling interval	Data sources
Taiwan weighted stock index	Y	2010.01–2016.12	TWSE homepage [1]
The balance of margin loan	Y	2010.01–2016.12	TWSE homepage [1]
The balance of stock loan	Y	2010.01–2016.12	TWSE homepage [1]
Dow Jones industrial index	Y	2010.01–2016.12	Quandl homepage [15]
NASDAQ index	Y	2010.01–2016.12	Quandl homepage [15]
Gold price	Y	2010.01–2016.12	Quandl homepage [15]
M1A annual growth rate	N	2010.01–2016.12	TW central bank [16]
M1B annual growth rate	N	2010.01–2016.12	TW central bank [16]
M2 annual growth rate	N	2010.01–2016.12	TW central bank [16]
MTX index	N	2014.01–2016.12	TAIFEX homepage [2]
Economic monitoring indicator	N	2010.01–2016.12	TW NDC homepage [17]
US dollar exchange rate	Y	2010.01–2014.12	TPEFX homepage [18]
NYMEX crude oil	Y	2010.01–2014.12	Anue homepage [19]
WTI crude oil	Y	2010.01–2014.12	Anue homepage [19]
Brent crude oil	Y	2010.01–2014.12	Anue homepage [19]
RBOB gas	Y	2010.01–2014.12	Anue homepage [19]

observe that between 2010 and 2014, the following variables whose correlation coefficient with Taiwan weighted stock price index are more than 0.3: the Dow Jones industrial index, the NASDAQ index, the annual growth rate of M2, the economic monitoring indicator, and the NYMEX crude oil. From 2010 to 2014, the three variables of Dow Jones industrial index, NASDAQ index and M2 annual growth rate are all of moderately positive correlation, and even highly positive correlation can be achieved in a single year. In addition, similar results can also be observed by using the P-value approach. The following variables have a p-value of less than 0.05 (which means that the correlation is significant) with the Taiwan weighted stock price index: the Dow Jones industrial index, the NASDAQ index, the annual growth rate of M2, the economic monitoring indicator, the NYMEX crude oil, the balance of margin loan, and the gold price.

Therefore, we select to use each of the above-mentioned variables whose p-value is less than 0.05 as the independent variable to perform simple linear regression with the dependent variable, Taiwan weighted stock price index. Here we take the historical data of 60 months (from January 2010 to November 2014) as the training set for simple linear regression, and we will use the trained linear model to predict the Taiwan weighted stock price index for one month later (i.e., the monthly average of January 2015). Then, we will use the same simple linear regression training method based on the historical training data of the previous 60 month to predict the monthly average Taiwan weighted stock price index from February 2015 to December 2016. From the results of simple linear regression, it is found that the variables with better predictive ability are the Dow Jones industrial index, the NASDAQ index, the annual growth rate of M2, the gold price, and economic monitoring indicator.

We then can produce various variable combinations based on the variables selected by the procedure of simple linear regression. Using multiple linear regressions, a linear prediction model with multiple variables is generated for each of the above-mentioned variable combinations. For evaluating each prediction model, we use the historical data of the previous 22 months as the training set to predict the month average of Taiwan weighted stock price index from January 2015 to December 2016. However, since to choose a model is actually related to the profitability of trading and the prediction accuracy of the stock price trend, we will return to this issue after introducing our proposed trading strategies.

4 Trading Strategies

In this paper, we propose two trading strategies. In trading strategy 1, in the first MTX trading day of each month in the experimental interval, we enter into the arena. If the forecasted index is higher than the index of the last month, we buy one MTX LOT of the month. In contrast, if the forecasted index is lower than the index of the last month, we sell one LOT MTX. Here the contract value of one MTX LOT is the MTX index multiplied by 50 New Taiwan dollars. If the MTX index reaches the forecasted value before the clearance day, we will perform liquidation directly in advance. In contrast, if it does not, we will perform liquidation at the clearance day. In trading strategy 2, we also enter into the arena in the first trading day of each month in the experimental interval. If the forecasted index is higher than index of the last month, we buy one MTX LOT of that month. However, if the forecast index is lower than the index of the last month, we sell one LOT MTX. Here we always perform liquidation at the clearance day.

After we describe the proposed trading strategies, we can go back to discuss the issue of selecting which variables to form the best prediction model by using multiple linear regressions. We first use the method defined in the second trading strategy to generate the data of investment profit points and profit accuracy ratio, which shows how well the model can correctly predict the index in a coming month to go up or go down so that positive profit is generated or not. Each point in MTX is 50 New Taiwan dollars. Here we select the profit accuracy ratio as our main filtering factor. For predicting the index from 2015 to 2016, if we set the criteria that the average profit accuracy ratio within two years needs to be at least 58.3%, and the average annual profit accuracy ratio is not less than 50%, there are only nine variable combinations remain. Table 2 shows these variable combinations as well as the profit points and the profit accuracy ratio of each variable combination. We find that the combination of the monthly average of the Dow Jones industrial index, the monthly average of NASDAQ index, and the annual growth rate of M2 can achieve the highest average accuracy ratio and the second highest profitability. Therefore, we chose them as the independent variables of the prediction model based on multiple linear regressions in this paper.

Table 2. Accuracy and profit points of various variable combinations

Variable combinations	Year	Accuracy	Profit points
NASDAQ, M2	2015	66.7	764
	2016	66.7	1442
Dow Jones, NASDAQ, gold price	2015	58.3	376
	2016	58.3	1294
Dow Jones, NASDAQ, M2	2015	66.7	911
	2016	66.7	1350
NASDAQ, M2, economic indicator	2015	50	408
	2016	83.3	2166
Dow Jones, gold price, economic indicator	2015	66.7	912
	2016	66.7	1180
NASDAQ, M2, gold price, economic indicator	2015	50	408
	2016	83.3	2166
Dow Jones, NASDAQ, M2, economic indicator	2015	50	474
	2016	75	1510
Dow Jones, NASDAQ, gold price, economic indicator	2015	58.3	868
	2016	66.7	394
Dow Jones, NASDAQ, M2, gold price, economic indicator	2015	50	474
	2016	75	1510

5   Evaluation

Table 3 shows the investment profit in 2014 and 2015 of the prediction model that uses the Dow Jones industrial index, the NASDAQ index, and the annual growth rate of M2 as independent variables. The principal used in this experiment is 100,000 New Taiwan dollars, and the trading volume is one LOT. The administration fee of Taiwan Futures Exchange is 17.5 New Taiwan dollars and the Futures trading tax rate is 0.002%.

Table 3. The profit table of the two trading strategies

Strategies	Year	Monthly maximum profit (NTD)	Monthly maximum loss (NTD)	Annual profit (NTD)	Annual net profit (NTD)	Profit accuracy rate	Return rate
Strategy 1	2015	27350	20550	39350	38715	75	38.7
	2016	27900	16400	47150	46521	66.7	46.5
Strategy 2	2015	27350	21850	45550	44914	66.7	44.9
	2016	27900	16400	67500	66871	66.7	66.9

As shown in Table 3, both trading strategies have good investment performance. The reason why the profit accuracy rate of trading strategy 1 in 2015 is higher than that of trading strategy 2 is described in detailed below. For October 2015, the trading strategy 1 predicts that the index is going downward. Since the MTX index reaches the forecast point of 8162 on October 1, 2015, the trading strategy 1 will not wait until the clearance day and performs liquidation immediately. Hence, the profit is 18 points. On the contrary, since the trading strategy 2 needs to perform liquidation until the clearance day in October 2015, it lost 437 points.

In terms of net profit, since the operations of the trading strategy 1 make the decision of liquidation based on the forecasted points, the date for performing liquidation may be earlier than the clearance day. This may result in that the profit and loss are different from the trading strategy 2. The trading strategy 1 performs liquidation early in March, May, June, October and July 2016. Although the maximum loss in a single month is smaller than that of the trading strategy 2, the maximum profit in a single month is also smaller than that of the trading strategy 2. Therefore, the return rate of the trading strategy 2 is higher than that of the trading strategy 1.

6 Conclusions

In this paper, we used literature analysis to identify a variety of factors that might affect Taiwan stock market in the past. Then, by using correlation analysis and p-value approach analysis, we found out the most important factors related to Taiwan stock price index, including: US Dow Jones industrial index, US NASDAQ index and M2 annual growth rate. We also use these parameters to create a prediction model to forecast the monthly average index through multiple linear regressions. Finally, we propose two trading strategies based on the prediction model. The first strategy takes the day achieving the predicted index as the day to exit positions, and the second one takes the clearance day as the day to exit positions. The evaluation results showed that the first strategy has higher trend prediction accuracy, while the second strategy has a higher rate of return. Therefore, if an investor wants to pursue higher returns and can withstand higher investment risks, the second trading strategy is recommended. In contrast, conservative investors can choose the first trading strategy. Moreover, based on the historical data from 2014 to 2016, the simulation results showed that both of the two trading strategies yield good investment returns.

References

1. TWSE Homepage. http://www.twse.com.tw/en/
2. TAIFEX Homepage. http://www.taifex.com.tw/enl/eIndex
3. Billingsley, R., Chance, D.: The pricing and performance of stock index futures spreads. J. Futures Mark. **19**, 931–955 (1998)
4. Forslund, G., Åkesson, D.: Predicting share price by using multiple linear regression. Bachelor Thesis in Mathematical Statistics, Vehicle engineering, KTH (2013)
5. Chuang, J.: The Returns and the explanatory power of the data of the three major institutional traders on the future markets in Taiwan. Master Thesis, Institute of Finance, National Chiao Tung University (2017)

6. Hsieh, H.: A study of the effect of EUR, USD and Asia main currency exchange rates upon Taiwan weighted stock index. Master Thesis, Department of International Business, National Kaohsiung University of Applied Sciences (2015)
7. Liu, Y.: A study of lead/lag relationship among Taiwan stock index, futures, and options. Master Thesis, Department of Financial Engineering and Actuarial Mathematics, Soochow University (2015)
8. Chang, S.: The determinants of Taiwan stock index futures. Master Thesis, College of Management, Da-Yeh University (2014)
9. Lu, L.: A study for the forecasting of Taiwan stock exchange capitalization weighted stock index. Master Thesis, Department of Shipping and Transportation Management, National Taiwan Ocean University (2014)
10. Wang, J.: Association analysis of exchange rate, global oil prices and Taiwan stock index returns. Institute of Finance, Ling Tung University (2009)
11. Wu, Y.: Applying intelligent systems on Taiwan stock and futures market capital flows analysis. Master Thesis, Institute of Information Management, National Chiao Tung University (2009)
12. Yang, S.: Dynamic conditional correlation analysis of NASDAQ and Taiwan stock market. Master Thesis, Global MBA, National Chiao Tung University (2009)
13. Hsieh, C.: A research of the interactive relationship among the price of stock, gold and crude oil: Taiwan study. Master Thesis, Department of Economics, Feng Chia University (2006)
14. Sou, H.: A trading strategy of Taiwan stock weighted index futures. Master Thesis, EMBA, National Chiao Tung University (2006)
15. Quandl homepage. https://www.quandl.com
16. Homepage of Taiwan central bank. https://www.cbc.gov.tw/mp.asp?mp=2
17. Homepage of national development council of Taiwan. https://www.ndc.gov.tw/en/
18. Homepage of Taipei foreign exchange market development foundation. http://www.tpefx.com.tw/web/index/index.jsp
19. Anue homepage. https://www.cnyes.com/

Incorporating Prior Knowledge by Selective Context Features to Enhance Topic Coherence

Chuen-Min Huang[✉]

National Yunlin University of Science and Technology,
Douliou, Yunlin, Taiwan
jennyhuang921@gmail.com

Abstract. Latent variable model has been widely used to extract topics from document collections, but this unsupervised mode makes it difficult to interpret the topics covered by the constructed cluster due to no artificial tags. Considering the influence of preprocessing on subsequent data mining, this study extracts news feature words from CSCP word segmentation method and named entity identification (NER). For NER, names of people, places, organizations are extracted by syntax rules and verified by Wikipedia. In terms of CSCP, the probability of continuing characters, the distribution probabilities and numbers of links before and after the character are used to constantly merge the unit words, extract the important narrative words effectively, and then conduct Unigram, Compounds and Mixture word processing. The corpus of words obtained after word processing by CSCP and NER were used as LDA prior knowledge. Finally, the topic coherence of NER and CSCP is evaluated by UMass Topic Coherence Measurement. The experimental results show that Compounds are of specific meaning; Mixtures represents its diverse scope; Unigrams and NER are relatively short, while NER can accurately represent the important features of news content, the topic is more cohesive. In terms of efficiency, NER-LDA takes the longest, while it had the highest degree of topic coherence.

Keywords: Topic model · Topic coherence · Named entity recognition · CSCP · LDA

1 Introduction

Topic model research hopes to mine the underlying themes of the text. Ideally, the words included in each topic should be semantically related. Applying Latent Dirichlet Allocation (LDA) to mine hidden topics in text help to reduce data complexities to some extent, is a kind of extended Bayesian probability application [1]. However, subsequent studies have found that the topic generated by this model is not easy to be interpreted, and there is a significant gap between the model and people's cognition. Therefore, many improved models of X-LDA are derived [2]. In order to improve the interpretability of topics, discussions on knowledge-based topic models (KBTM) and Entity Topic Models (ETM) have also emerged, claiming to consider context compatibility and topic coherence. Among the KBTM and ETM studies, the most representative of KBTM is the DF-LDA model [3], which provides users to set the

© Springer Nature Singapore Pte Ltd. 2019
C.-Y. Chang et al. (Eds.): ICS 2018, CCIS 1013, pp. 310–318, 2019.
https://doi.org/10.1007/978-981-13-9190-3_32

must-links and cannot links, and assumes that these links are correct. These two links are recursive dependent transitive dependencies. If A, B/B, C are must links, then A and C must also link, making it A, B, C will belong to the same topic. Such transitive relationships, resulting in forced connections that causes many unrelated or irrelevant words to be linked together.

The bag-of-words assumption of topic model has gained recognition in terms of computational efficiency, whereas it is impractical in many language model applications where word order is essential. Hence, the question into whether unigram is sufficient to represent the context is worth further investigation. Wallach [4] proposed a bigram model by computing a bigram estimator and smoothed by the marginal frequency estimator to give the predictive probability. Results indicated the topics inferred using LDA contained more function words than the new model, and the new model exhibits better predictive accuracy than either a hierarchical Dirichlet bigram or a unigram topic model. Huang [5] compared Unigrams, Compounds, and Mixtures in terms of topic coherence and performance, the result shows that the Compounds and Mixtures illustrate more precise and accurate meaning and demonstrate computational efficiency than the Unigram based model.

Lexical chain (LC) is a sequence of words, which is in lexical cohesion relations with each other and they tend to indicate portions of the context that form semantic units; they could serve further as a basis for a segmentation and a summarization generation [6]. To extract key sentences as a surrogate of a text, we proposed a novice word segmentation method - Chinese Syntactic Chain Processing (CSCP) based on LC theory. The Unigrams, Compounds, and Mixtures generated from LC will become prior knowledge and be applied to process CSCP-LDA.

Traditional LDA does not consider named entities recognition. Newman et al. proposed entity topic model, called CorrLDA2, modeling word topic as a distribution over entity topics [7], while the experimental results showed unreasonable clustering of entities. Hu et al. [8] proposed an entity-centered topic model (ECTM) to summarize the correlation among entities, words and topics. The results demonstrated a lower perplexity and better in clustering of entities than traditional LDA and CorrLDA2, while they only experimented with small data sets. In [9], they analyzed the writing structure and observed each possible syntactic rule from the composition of most commonly used part of speech (POS) to its extended POS variation. Compared with other automatic rule construction and quasi-machine learning methods, they obtained a better performance particularly on the precision rate. Based on the above studies, this study adopted the method of [9] to extract name entities as prior knowledge to process NER-LDA.

The rest of the paper is organized as follows. In Sect. 2, we introduce applied techniques based on the framework of model and discuss the validation of the capabilities of our model with respect to iterations, topic coherence and performance; in the final section, we conclude the work and discuss possible directions for future research.

2 Applied Techniques

2.1 Use CSCP to Extract Descriptive Sentences

The fundamental idea of building CSCP is a bottom-up concatenating process based on the intensity and significance degree of distribution rate to extract meaningful descriptors from a string by processing the direct link and the inverted link in parallel. A directed graph is a set of nodes connected by edges, where the edges have a direction associated with them. The forward distribution rate is as in Eq. (1) and the reverse distribution rate is as in Eq. (2). D(i, j) represents the forward link from endpoint i to endpoint j; ~D(y,z) represents the reverse link from endpoint y to endpoint z. The threshold is 0.5. The process will be iterated until no concatenation can be found, and this iteration process will generate a series of short and long LCs from the string. Figure 1 shows two merged words "消防" and "猛男" were obtained. A detailed steps of diagram construction depicted in [10].

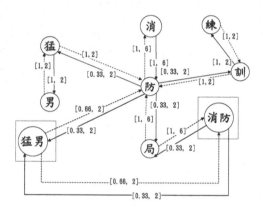

Fig. 1. Merge endpoints and create new link edges

Significant words are determined by Eq. (3). As for f_a, f_b and f_c are the frequencies of a, b, and c, respectively. When the Compounds frequency (f_c) "消防猛男" is equal to any of the wrapped sub-strings "消防" (f_a) and "猛男" (f_b), indicating that the substring has no specific meaning, it should be deleted. Then we calculate the word frequency of the feature words in the sentence. If the word frequency is higher, it indicates that the sentence is more likely to be the core of the news. Finally, we take the first quintile and concatenate into a news summary as Table 1.

This experiment uses Yahoo! Taiwan news from June to August 2014, including three categories of finance, politics and life. 6,000 pieces were selected from each of the three categories, and 2,000 pieces were randomly selected from the above three categories and mixed into the fourth mixed category. The CSCP method was used to extract 13,330 sentences from financial category, 12,228 sentences from life, 12,878 sentences from politics and 12,888 sentences from the three mixed categories. Unigram, Compounds, and Mixture word processing are performed separately to extract

Table 1. News summarization

News content	(1)信心回升美4月借貸攀升，美國消費者4月借貸攀升，信用卡債成長速度為逾12年來最快。 (2)美聯社報導，美國聯邦準備理事會昨天表示，4月信用借貸整體增加268億美元，3月增幅為195億美元。 (3)這對美國經濟是一大鼓勵，顯示消費者有信心透過借貸來增加消費。 (4)當中新貸學貸太高，增加180億美元，信用卡債即餐增加88億美元。 (5)上揚幅為12.3%，是自2001年11月以來最快增速，當時美國政府在911恐怖政擊後，呼籲民眾消費，成刺激經濟。 (6)美國4月借貸持續攀升，使總借貸增至史上新高的3.18兆美元。
CSCP word frequency	信心:2、增加:4、消費者:2、信用:3、美國:5、借貸:6…
Word frequency in summation	1. 信心(2)回升美 4月借貸(6)攀升，美國(5)消費者(2)4 月借貸(6)攀升，信用卡債成長速度為逾 12 年來最快:21 2. 這對美國(5)經濟是一大鼓勵，顯示消費者(2)有信心(3)透過借貸(6)來增加(4)消費:20

different types of feature words to observe the degree of topic cohesiveness. To extract Unigrams, we removed monosyllabic words from the datasets because the words with only one character are usually function words or do not carry enough lexical meaning, while we keep all the words to generate Compounds because Compounds may consist of monosyllabic words. Compounds generation is based on two concatenated words with verified morphological features including concatenated V+N, V+V, N+V, N+N, and A+N. Mixture word combines the Unigrams and Compounds processing results. If the Unigram word is included in the Compounds, the Eq. (3) is used as the basis for the word selection. The word processing result is shown as Fig. 2.

Category	Unigram	Uni-freq	Compound	Com-freq	Mixture	Mix-freq	NER	NER-freq
Finance	34,068	369,532	146,960	241,148	160,771	274,461	48,070	612,786
Life	43,863	343,372	158,039	221,575	176,452	261,507	48,858	523,416
Politics	43,093	351,047	143,961	229,052	158,460	261,390	37,431	572,844
Mixture	43,186	383,400	164,100	232,383	181,503	267,609	47,011	569,718

Fig. 2. Word processing result

$$D(i,j) = \text{Threshold V ForwardLink}(\text{Node}_i) > 1 \qquad (1)$$

$$\sim D(y,z) = \text{Threshold V BackwardLink}(Node_y) > 1 \qquad (2)$$

$$\begin{aligned} &\text{remove}(a), \text{ if } f_c = f_a \\ &\text{remove}(b), \text{ if } f_c = f_b \end{aligned} \qquad (3)$$

2.2 Use NER to Extract Descriptors

In recognizing person name, we applied 54 syntax rules to obtain candidate features, from which to further identify the monosyllabic or two-character combinations of surname and given name based on a name concatenation formula as Eq. (4), where P *(PER)* is the probability of name composition. *Freq Lc(i, i + 1)* represents the frequency of the combination of a single or two-character Nb with the subsequent first character, and *Freq Lc(i, i + 2)* represents the frequency of the combination with the subsequent two characters. When the word frequency of Lc(0, 2) is less than Lc(0, 1), P (PER) is less than 1, indicating that the last character should be combined as the name. On the contrary, it means that the last two characters should be combined as a person's name. If the Nb length is not 1 or 2, that means the Nb can be directly determined as a person's name. For practical considerations, our experiment only deals with the most frequent 2–4 characters of person names. Applying the combination of extended POS composition, we not only successfully extracted persons' jobs, job portfolio, but also identify more related features to enhance the accuracy of the name. To improve recognition accuracy of location and organization, we applied 11 syntax rules to obtain candidate features and referred to geographical directories of Infobox in Wikipedia for verification. A detailed steps of NER recognition and disambiguation depicted in [9].

$$P(PER) = \frac{Freq\ Lc(i, i+2)}{Freq\ Lc(i, i+1)} \ if \ \begin{cases} P(PER) < 1, PER \in Lc(i, i+1) \\ P(PER) \geq 1, PER \in Lc(i, i+2) \end{cases}, \ i = 0 \quad (4)$$

2.3   Evaluate Topic Coherence of LDA

In the given news set file $M = \{d_1, \ldots d_n\}$, the word set $W = \{w_1, \ldots w_n\}$ is generated from the aforementioned CSCP and NER processes, respectively. Each word w_i has a parameter z_k corresponding to the topic distribution, represented by $K(W - 1)$. Here K is the number of topics, and W is the number of words. All topics will be estimated and inferred using the Gibbs sampling program. The choice of parameters is based on the original optimal preset values of α and β, which are $\alpha = 0.1$ and $\beta = 0.01$, respectively. The execution steps are described below.

(1) For all d docs sample $\theta_d \sim \text{Dir}(\alpha)$
(2) For all i topics samples $\varphi_k \sim \text{Dir}(\beta)$
(3) For each of the valid N_{wd} from CSCP-Unigram, Compounds, Mixture word w_i in document d, and from NER word w_i in document d, respectively
   (a) Sample a topic $z_i \sim \text{Mult}(\theta_d)$
   (b) Sample a $w_i \sim \text{Mult}(\varphi_{zi})$.

Most studies create model through user participation, which is feasible for a small number of data sets. However, for huge amounts of data, it is obviously not practical to involve users in the extraction of prior knowledge. In addition, the calculation of word associations as well as the marking of documents will be costly. This method relies only on the co-occurrence relationship of words in the documents and does not require other external resources or manual labeling. To assess the quality of the model results to topics in this experiment, we adopted perplexity as evaluation criteria as Eq. (5): the lower the confused value, the better the results of semantic cohesion. The lowest perplexity value will be used to determine the number of LDA topics.

$$perplexity = exp\left\{ -\frac{\sum_{d=1}^{M} logP(w_d)}{\sum_{d=1}^{M} N_d} \right\} \tag{5}$$

Where $P(w_d)$ denotes the generative probability of the word type with respect to Unigrams, Compounds, Mixtures and NER, respectively in the document d, which M as the number of news. We ran the states of iterations from 1 to 1000 incremented by 100 per time for the three types of words. Results showed that the perplexity values of all types of words decrease sharply at the very beginning and soon converge at 100 and reach stable at the 200 iterations as Fig. 3. Be cautious, we used 300 iterations for the following LDA experiments. Figure 4 shows the change of the perplexity value in different topic numbers after running 300 iterations. From the figure, it can be found that the perplexity values of the Compounds-LDA and Mix-LDA models all drop sharply in the number of topics 10 to 20. For Unigram-LDA and NER-LDA, the perplexity values of the two are similar and the performance is relatively flat. We selected 90 as the number of topics since it reached a stable level for all kinds of LDA.

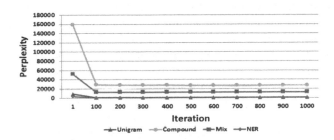

Fig. 3. Process of iterations

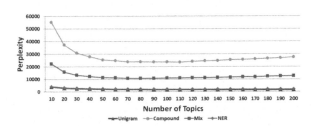

Fig. 4. Perplexity vs. number of topics

After the iteration processing, we conducted a performance analysis. All the simulations were performed on an Intel(R) Core (TM) i5-4460 (3.2 GHz) with 16G Memory. Figure 5 displays the performance in seconds corresponding to the number of topics for four models. It is known from the data that Compounds performs the best, Mixtures ranks the second, Unigrams stands the third, and NER take the longest time. The result suggests that performance may be proportional to the number of words, and it also indicates performance is inversely proportional to perplexity measurement.

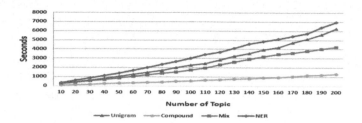

Fig. 5. Performance vs. number of topics

We adopted UMass Topic Coherence [2] as topic coherence measurement. In Eq. (6), where D(v) is the number of times the word v appears, and $D(v, v')$ is the number of times the words v and v' appear simultaneously in the same document. $V^{(t)} = \left(v_1^{(t)}, \ldots, v_M^{(t)} \right)$ means that there are M subject words in the subject t. In order not to make Log zero, we added 1 as a smoothing coefficient. Figure 6 shows the evaluation results of the UMass Topic Coherence. Even though NER-LDA didn't perform efficiently, the results demonstrated that NER-LDA is the most cohesive. It is speculated that the reason may be that people, things, time, and location are the focus of the news, furthermore, the extracted name entities have few meaningless words, making the topic more cohesive as a whole. Followed by Compounds, the worst are the Unigrams and Mixtures.

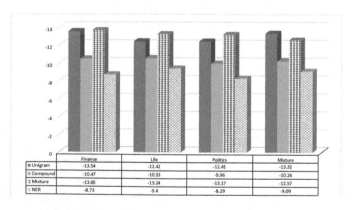

	Finance	Life	Politics	Mixture
Unigram	-13.54	-12.42	-12.41	-13.32
Compound	-10.47	-10.53	-9.96	-10.24
Mixture	-13.65	-13.24	-13.17	-12.57
NER	-8.73	-9.4	-8.29	-9.09

Fig. 6. UMass topic coherence evaluation results

$$C\left(t; V^{(t)}\right) = \sum_{m=2}^{M} \sum_{l=1}^{m-1} \log \frac{D\left(v_m^{(t)}, v_l^{(t)}\right) + 1}{D\left(v_l^{(t)}\right)} \qquad (6)$$

3   Conclusion

The basic concept of LDA topic model is to treat a document as a set of words without any prior knowledge, grammar or word order. However, subsequent studies have found that the topic generated by this model is not easy to be interpreted, and there is a significant gap between the model and people's cognition. In order to improve the interpretability of the topic, past research has led to modeling through user participation, which is feasible for a small number of data sets. Whereas, for the massive data, it is obviously not practical to let the user participate in the extraction of prior knowledge. This study proposes a CSCP word segmentation method to obtain important textual sentences and form summarizations, from which Unigram, Compounds, and Mixture words were extracted to enhance performance of subsequent LDA processing. Meanwhile, we also conducted NER-LDA topic model analysis for the named entities of the news. The corpus of words obtained after word processing by CSCP and NER were used as LDA prior knowledge. After the evaluation by UMass Topic Coherence, the experimental results show that NER can accurately represent the important features of news content, the topic is more cohesive than the others. Compounds are of specific meaning since it is based on two concatenated words with verified morphological features; Unigrams can express a wide range of meanings; Mixtures can present a more diverse representation, while both show less content cohesion. This study found that measurement of topical coherence by perplexity value is not the same as that of UMass Topic Coherence. Although both show NER performs the best, the results of Compounds are obviously different. It is recommended that future research continue to explore the reasons for the differences.

Acknowledgment. This research is supported by Ministry of Science and Technology, Taiwan, R.O.C. under grant number MOST 105-2221-E-224-053.

References

1. Blei, D.M., Ng, A.Y., Jordan, M.I.: Latent dirichlet allocation. J. Mach. Learn. Res. **3**, 993–1022 (2003)
2. Mimno, D., Wallach, H.M., Talley, E., Leenders, M., McCallum, A.: Optimizing semantic coherence in topic models. In: EMNLP, pp. 262–272 (2011)
3. Andrzejewski, D., Zhu, X., Craven, M.: Incorporating domain knowledge into topic modeling via Dirichlet Forest priors. In: ICML, pp. 25–32 (2009)
4. Wallach, H.M.: Topic modeling: beyond bag-of-words. In: Proceedings of the 23rd International Conference on Machine Learning, Pittsburgh, Pennsylvania, USA, pp. 977–984 (2006)
5. Huang, C.-M.: Investigating topic coherence and task performance for varied types of words in LDA, pp. 260–265 (2017)
6. Shanthi, V., Lalitha, S.: Lexical chaining process for text generations. In: International Conference on Process Automation, Control and Computing (PACC), pp. 1–6 (2011)
7. Newman, D., Chemudugunta, C., Smyth, P.: Statistical entity-topic models. In: Proceedings of the 12th ACM SIGKDD International Conference on Knowledge Discovery and Data Mining, Philadelphia, PA, USA, pp. 680–686 (2006)

8. Hu, L., Li, J., Li, Z., Shao, C., Li, Z.: Incorporating entities in news topic modeling. In: Zhou, G., Li, J., Zhao, D., Feng, Y. (eds.) NLPCC 2013. CCIS, vol. 400, pp. 139–150. Springer, Heidelberg (2013). https://doi.org/10.1007/978-3-642-41644-6_14
9. Huang, C.-M.: Using part-of-speech tagging based approach with Wikipedia to assist Chinese named entity recognition and disambiguation (in Chinese). J. Libr. Inform. Sci. Res. **11**(2), 139–179 (2017)
10. Huang, C.-M.: Applying lexical chain theory to extract context descriptors as web image annotation. Commun. ICISA: Int. J. **15**(2), 22–39 (2014)

Parallel, Peer-to-Peer, Distributed and Cloud Computing

Accelerated Parallel Based Distance Calculations for Live-Cell Time-Lapse Images

Hui-Jun Cheng[1], Chun-Yuan Lin[1,2,3,4(✉)], and Chun-Chien Mao[2]

[1] AI Innovation Research Center,
Chang Gung University, Taoyuan 33302, Taiwan
d0000l4642@cgu.edu.tw, cyulin@mail.cgu.edu.tw
[2] Department of Computer Science and Information Engineering,
Chang Gung University, Taoyuan 33302, Taiwan
m0429001@cgu.edu.tw
[3] Division of Rheumatology, Allergy and Immunology,
Chang Gung Memorial Hospital, Taoyuan 33305, Taiwan
[4] Brain Research Center, National Tsing Hua University,
Hsinchu 30013, Taiwan

Abstract. Live-cell time-lapse images with particles generated by experiments are useful for observing results, even for proposing novel hypotheses. By identifying particles and cells as objects from these images and then calculating measures from them, such as the distances, they can be quantized for the relationship of particles and cells. However, this work is very time-consuming when calculating the distances among a large number of images. Hence, a very important issue will be presented here in order to accelerate the calculations. In this paper, we will propose parallel algorithms for calculating particle-cell distances, abbreviate to a PCD problem. Two parallel PCD algorithms, called $PPCD_{OMP}$ and $PPCD_{CUDA}$, will be developed by using OpenMP and CUDA. After the experimental tests, the $PPCD_{OMP}$ with 16 CPU threads achieves 11.7 times by comparing with the PCD algorithm in a single thread; however, the $PPCD_{CUDA}$ with 256 GPU threads per thread block only achieves 3.2 times. Therefore, the $PPCD_{OMP}$ algorithm is suitable for analyzing live-cell time-lapse images with particles based on the shared memory environments.

Keywords: Live-cell time-lapse images · Particle-cell distance · GPU · OpenMP · CUDA

1 Introduction

Live-cell time-lapse images with particles by biological experiments are useful for observing results, even for proposing novel hypotheses. For example, calcium phosphate-based mineralo-organic particles can form spontaneously and ubiquitously in biological fluids [1–5]. Despite the fact they are actually non-living objects in circulation in human blood and other body fluid, they are involved not only in physiological calcification processes such as bone and teeth formation but also in pathological conditions that include atherosclerosis, chronic kidney disease, and ectopic calcification [6–9]. Due to their morphological nature and association with protein factors, these mineral complexes can interact with certain host cells, leading to cellular

© Springer Nature Singapore Pte Ltd. 2019
C.-Y. Chang et al. (Eds.): ICS 2018, CCIS 1013, pp. 321–329, 2019.
https://doi.org/10.1007/978-981-13-9190-3_33

internalization and subsequent activation of pro-inflammatory responses [3, 4]. On the other hand, the exact nature of host cell recruitment by these complexes as well as subsequent particle-cell interactions remains to be elucidated in order to further understand the downstream consequences.

For particle-cell interactions, by identifying particles and cells as objects from these images and then calculating measures from them, such as the distances, they can be quantized for the relationship of particles and cells. In order to accomplish the purpose, a particle-cell relation mining method, abbreviate to *PCRM*, has been proposed [10], for live-cell time-lapse images. The *PCRM* is novel method to identify and track each particle and cell in these images and then calculates the measures, not only for tracking single particle and/or cell in the past works, listed in the review article [11]. In the *PCRM* method, there are four phases: *object identification*, *objects tracking*, *measures calculation*, and *relation mining*. In the *object identification* phase, for each live-cell time-lapse image, the boundary of each particle and cell was detected at first, and the splitting or merging problem for an object then was solved; it means that each particle or cell was identified in each live-cell image. After that, in the second phase: *objects tracking*, for a time series of live-cell images, each particle or cell was tracked from the first live-cell image to the last one; it means that for a certain particle, the location(s) in each image was known. As mentioned in above, there are several measures [11, 12] used for the particle-cell relationship. Hence, in the third phase: *measures calculation*, the distances, a commonly-used factor, between any two of particle and cell in each live-cell image were calculated as the inputs for the next (fourth) phase. For the final phase: *relation mining*, the input measures in all live-cell images were further analyzed and then concluded that they are matched the observations of experiments or not. The details of *PCRM* method for live-cell time-lapse images can be found in the literature [10]. However, the work in the third phase (*measures calculation*) is very time-consuming when calculating the distances among a large number of images. Hence, a very important issue will be presented here in order to accelerate the calculations.

It is a feasible direction to apply parallel technologies and multi-core devices into the above issue. The feasibility of using massive computational devices to enhance the performance of many programs has received the considerable attention in recent years, especially for many-core devices, such as FPGAs [13] and Cell/Bes [14]. In recent years, the Intel Xeon E5-v5 and E5-v6 servers were released and they contained up to 20 or more Xeon CPUs, even for more than 40 threads by using the hyper-threading technique. It made the shared memory programming, such as OpenMP [15], may be suitable for the high performance computing field due to the low cost and high scalability. Current high-end graphics processing units, abbreviated to GPUs [16], which contain up to thousands of cores per-chip, are widely used in the high performance computing community. As a massively multi-threaded processor, GPU expects the thousands of concurrent threads to fully utilize its computing power. The ease of access GPUs by using the compute unified device architecture, abbreviated to CUDA [17], has made the supercomputing available widely.

In this paper, we will propose efficient parallel algorithms for calculating particle-cell distances, abbreviate to a PCD problem. Two parallel PCD algorithms, called PPCD$_{OMP}$ and PPCD$_{CUDA}$, will be developed by using OpenMP and CUDA. The majority idea in these two algorithms is how to assign the jobs into multi-core CPUs or multi-core GPUs. For the PPCD$_{OMP}$, the job of calculating distances among all particles and all cells in a live-cell image is assigned to a CPU; for the PPCD$_{CUDA}$, the job of calculating distances among all particles and all cells in a live-cell image is assigned to a thread block of a GPU card, and then a distance calculation among a particle and a cell is assigned to a thread in a thread block. The total of 61 live-cell images are recorded by the NIS-Elements (Nikon) as the text images in the experiments for these two algorithms. After the experimental tests, the PPCD$_{OMP}$ with 16 CPU threads achieves 11.7 times by comparing with the sequential PCD algorithm in a single CPU thread; the PPCD$_{CUDA}$ with 256 GPU threads per thread block only achieves 3.2 times. These results are proved that the proposed parallel algorithm PPCD$_{OMP}$ under the share memory environment is suitable for applying in the *PCRM* method in order to analyze the particle-cell interactions with a large number of live-cell images (time series) during the experiments.

2   Method

In this paper, there are 61 live-cell images are generated from the biological experiment and then recorded by the NIS-Elements (Nikon). In order to avoid unnecessary repetitive descriptions, the details of live-cell images generations can be found in the literature [10].

As mentioned above, the goal of the third phase (*measures calculation*) in the *PCRM* method is to calculate the shortest particle-cell distance for each particle in each live-cell image. In order to explain the calculations of shortest particle-cell distances, first three phases of *PCRM* method were described briefly in the following:

(i)   *object identification phase*

Assume that there are t live-cell time-lapse images, where $t = \{0, 1, 2, ..., f\}$. The symbol P^t and C^t are used to present the t-th particle image and cell image, respectively. By using image mask and dilate techniques, each particle and cell was detected in each particle and cell image, respectively. In an image P^t, assume that there are i particles, where $i = \{0, 1, 2, ..., n^t\}$ and the symbol P_i^t is used to present the i-th particle; similarly, assume that there are j cells, where $j = \{0, 1, 2, ..., m^t\}$, and the symbol C_j^t is used to present the j-th cell in an image C^t. Assume that there are a pixels in the boundary of a particle P_i^t, where $a = \{0, 1, 2, ..., u_i^t\}$, and these pixels can be used to present a particle P_i^t. The symbol $P_{a,i}^t$ can be used to present the a-th pixel in a particle P_i^t and a pixel $P_{a,i}^t$ has the x and y coordinates: $X_{a,i}^{P,t}$ and $Y_{a,i}^{P,t}$. Similarly, assume that there are b pixels in the boundary of a cell C_j^t, where $b = \{0, 1, 2, ..., v_j^t\}$, and these pixels can be used to present a cell C_j^t. The symbol $C_{b,j}^t$ can be used to present the b-th pixel and a pixel $C_{b,j}^t$ has the x and y coordinates: $X_{b,j}^{C,t}$ and $Y_{b,j}^{C,t}$. For all particle (or cell) images, a series of two-dimensional arrays are used to store the x and y coordinates of all pixels in the boundary of each particle (or cell).

(ii)   *objects tracking phase*

In this phase, each particle P_i in every particle image P^t will be tracked. In practice, the number of particles in each particle image may be not the same since several particles may be touched with each other during the procedure of moving. Therefore, the splitting or merging problems should be solved in this phase. For a particle P_i^t in t-th particle image, a certain particle in $(t+1)$-th particle image with the shortest distance can be found at first by calculating their x and y coordinates (or overlapping). Therefore, for each particle P_i^t in a particle image P^t, its x and y coordinates of all of pixels should be extracted in order to do the calculations mentioned in the first phase. After that, these two particles in two consecutive images (t-th and $(t+1)$-th) can be seen as the same particle, defined as P_i. When all particles in all of pair of consecutive images are processed according the above way. Finally, the moving pathway of each particle P_i can be tracked in live-cell time-lapse images. Although the above way is focused on the practice tracking, it is also suitable for the cell tracking.

(iii) *measures calculation phase*

Various measures can be calculated in this phase, such as shortest particle-cell distances. Before calculating the distance measure, for each cell C_j^t in a cell image C^t, its x and y coordinates of all of pixels also should be extracted. After that, for a particle P_i^t in a particle image P^t, a shortest distance by comparing with all of cells in a cell image C^t can be obtained. This shortest distance is defined as a shortest particle-cell distance D for P_i^t as follows.

$$D(P_i^t) = Min\left(\sqrt{\left(X_{a,i}^{P,t} - X_{b,j}^{C,t}\right)^2 + \left(Y_{a,i}^{P,t} - X_{b,j}^{C,t}\right)^2} \right)$$

As mentioned in the *object identification* phase, we also can use a one-dimensional array to store $D(P_i^t)$ for a particle P_i^t in a particle image P^t. For all particle images, a two-dimensional array is used. Since the number of particles in each particle image may be not the same (as mentioned in the objects tracking phase), the length of columns in this two-dimensional array is various. This two-dimensional array only is a temporary data in this phase.

Assume that there are f live-cell images, each image has n particles and m cells. In a live-cell image, a particle has m particle-cell distances between it and one of cells. The shortest particle-cell distance of a particle in a live-cell image is obtained from m particle-cell distances. As mentioned in the *object identification* phase, for live-cell images, a particle or a cell can be seen as a set of pixels (u pixels for particle, v pixels for cell) with x and y coordinates. Therefore, a particle-cell distance between a particle and a cell is to calculate the Euclidean distances from any two of pixels, one in particle and another in cell, at first, and then find the shortest Euclidean distances. For a particle in a live-cell image, the time complexity is O(muv) to find the shortest Euclidean distances; the time complexity is O($nmuv$) for all particles in a live-cell image; the time complexity is O($fnmuv$) for all particles in all live-cell image. Hence, it is time-consuming work to calculate all of shortest particle-cell distances in all live-cell images.

When designing a *PPCD* algorithm, there are several ways to assign the jobs mentioned above to multi-core devices (CPU/GPU). For the algorithm PPCD$_{OMP}$, the way adopt is to assign live-cell images to multi-core CPUs sequentially. Therefore, the shortest particle-cell distances for all particles in a live-cell image is calculated in a CPU. The pseudocode of the PPCD$_{OMP}$ is listed below.

Pseudo code of PPCD$_{OMP}$

```
#define ALL_IMG 61

void getSHORTESTDIS(item* v, item* c, result* mindis)
{
    int img = 0, vi = 0, vj = 0, cj = 0, vx = 0, vy = 0,
        cx = 0, cy = 0, x = 0;
    double dis = 0;
    int threadid = 16;

#pragma omp parallel num_threads(threadid) private(img,
x, vi, vj, cj, init_ci, fin_ci, vx, vy, cx, cy, dis)

    image = omp_get_thread_num();

    for(x = 0; x < ALL_IMG; x += threadid){
      if(img +x < ALL_IMG){
        init_ci = c-> o_i[img+x];
        fin_ci = c-> o_n[img+x] + init_ci - 1;
      for(vi = v-> o_i[img+x]; vi < v-> o_i[img+x] + v->
          o_n[img+x]; vi++)

          if(mindis-> overlap_mark[vi] == 0){
            mindis-> min_dis[vi] = 1000;

            for(vj = v-> p_i[vi]; vj < v-> p_i[vi] + v->
                p_n[vi]; vj++)
              vx = v-> x_coord[vj];
              vy = v-> y_coord[vj];

              for(cj = c-> p_i[init_ci]; cj < c->
                  p_i[fin_ci] + c-> p_n[fin_ci]; cj++)
                cx = c-> x_coord[cj];
                cy = c-> y_coord[cj];
                dis = sqrt((vx-cx) * (vx-cx) +
                            (vy-cy) * (vy-cy));
                if(dis < mindis-> min_dis[vi])
                  mindis-> min_dis[vi] = dis;
}
```

For the algorithm PPCD$_{CUDA}$, the way adopt is to assign live-cell images to thread blocks in a GPU card sequentially. The job in a thread block still is to calculate the shortest particle-cell distances for all particles in a live-cell image. However, there are many threads in a thread block. Each calculation of Euclidean distance is assigned to a thread. The pseudocode of the PPCD$_{CUDA}$ is listed below.

Pseudo code of PPCD$_{CUDA}$

```
#define GPU_IMG 61

__global__ void kernel_getSHORTESTDIS (
      const int * __restrict__ dv_oi,
      const int * __restrict__ dv_on,
      const int * __restrict__ dv_pi,
      const int * __restrict__ dv_pn,
      const int * __restrict__ dv_x,
      const int * __restrict__ dv_y,
      const int * __restrict__ dc_oi,
      const int * __restrict__ dc_on,
      const int * __restrict__ dc_pi,
      const int * __restrict__ dc_pn,
      const int * __restrict__ dc_x,
      const int * __restrict__ dc_y,
      double *dr_mindis,
      const int * __restrict__ dr_overlap)
{

int vi = 0, vj = 0, cj = 0, cx = 0, cy = 0, init_ci = 0,
fin_ci = 0;
__shared__ int vx;
__shared__ int vy;
__shared__ double dis[threadsnum];
double buff; int image = blockIdx.x;

if(image < GPU_IMG)
   init_ci = dc_oi[image];
   fin_ci = dc_on[image] + init_ci - 1;

   for(vi = dv_oi[image]; vi < (dv_oi[image]+
      dv_on[image]); vi++)
      if(dr_overlap[vi] == 0)

      for(vj = dv_pi[vi]; vj < (dv_pi[vi] + dv_pn[vi]);
         vj++)
         vx = dv_x[vj];
         vy = dv_y[vj];

         for(cj = dc_pi[init_ci]; cj < (dc_pi[fin_ci] +
            dc_pn[fin_ci]); cj += threadsnum)

            cx= dc_x[cj+threadIdx.x];
            cy = dc_y[cj+threadIdx.x];
            dis[threadIdx.x]=sqrt((double)(vx-cx) * (vx-
                                    cx) + (vy-cy) * (vy-
cy));

            for(int i = 0; i < THREADS; i++)

               if(buff > dis[i])
                  buff = dis[i];

               if(buff < dr_mindis[vi])
               dr_mindis[vi] = buff;
}
```

3   Experimental Results

In this work, the $PPCD_{OMP}$ and $PPCD_{CUDA}$ algorithms were implemented by C +OpenMP and C+CUDA, respectively, on Intel E5-2650 v2 machine and a GPU card. The Intel Xeon E5-2650 v2 machine has 16 Xeon CPUs, each is 2.0 GHz, and 128 GB RAM. The GPU card is NVIDIA Tesla K20m with 2496 cuda cores, each is 706 MHz, and 5G RAM. The 61 live-cell images were used to evaluate these two algorithms. The $PPCD_{OMP}$ algorithm was tested by 1, 2, 4, 8, and 16 threads on Intel E5-2650 v2 machine, respectively; the $PPCD_{CUDA}$ algorithm was tested on NVIDIA Tesla K20m with 61 thread blocks, each block has 64, 128, 256 and 512 threads, respectively.

Table 1 shows the computation time by the $PPCD_{OMP}$ algorithm on Intel E5-2650 v2 machine with various numbers of live-cell images. From Table 1, we can see that the computation time decreases when the number of threads increases. The maximal speedup ratio by comparing with 1 CPU thread is 11.66 by 16 threads. Table 2 shows the computation time by the $PPCD_{CUDA}$ algorithm on NVIDIA Tesla K20m with various numbers of live-cell images. From Table 2, the computation time is not able to always decrease when the number of threads increases. The maximal speedup ratio by comparing with 1 CPU thread is only 3.23 by 256 threads. By comparing Table 1 with Table 2, the capability of $PPCD_{CUDA}$ by a NVIDIA Tesla K20m card is similar to the capability of $PPCD_{OMP}$ by Intel E5-2650 v2 machine with 4 threads.

Table 1. The computation time by the $PPCD_{OMP}$ algorithm.

$PPCD_{OMP}$	16 images	32 images	60 images	61 images
1 thread	6.88	13.29	23.8	24.2
2 threads	3.5	6.84	12.2	12.27
4 threads	1.84	3.54	6.24	6.38
8 threads	1.1	2.04	3.81	3.82
16 threads	0.59	1.81	2.13	2.08

(unit: second)

Table 2. The computation time by the $PPCD_{CUDA}$ algorithm.

$PPCD_{CUDA}$	16 images	32 images	60 images	61 images
64 threads	7.99	8.73	9.73	9.67
128 threads	7.02	7.22	8.12	8.15
256 threads	6.28	6.66	7.51	7.49
512 threads	6.01	6.33	10.38	10.29

(unit: second)

328 H.-J. Cheng et al.

4 Conclusion

Live-cell time-lapse images can be used to observe the particle and cell activities and then understand the interactions between particle(s) and cell(s). However, the computations of measures of particle and cell relations are time-consuming. Hence, in this paper, two algorithms, PPCD$_{OMP}$ and PPCD$_{CUDA}$, were proposed to accelerate the speed of analyzing the relation of particles and cells. By the experimental tests, the PPCD$_{OMP}$ algorithm achieved good enough speedup ratios when analyzing 61 live-cell images. Therefore, the PPCD$_{OMP}$ algorithm is suitable for analyzing particle and cell images in the shared memory environments.

Acknowledgments. Part of this work was supported by the Ministry of Science and Technology under the grant MOST 107-2221-E-182-063-MY2. This work also was supported by the Higher Education Sprout Project funded by the Ministry of Science and Technology and Ministry of Education in Taiwan. The authors would like to thank the anonymous reviewers and experts discussed with us in the past.

References

1. Martel, J., Young, J.D.: Purported nanobacteria in human blood as calcium carbonate nanoparticles. Proc. Natl. Acad. Sci. U.S.A. **105**(14), 5549–5554 (2008). https://doi.org/10.1073/pnas.0711744105
2. Young, J.D., Martel, J., Young, L., Wu, C.Y., Young, A., Young, D.: Putative nanobacteria represent physiological remnants and culture by-products of normal calcium homeostasis. PLoS ONE **4**(2), e4417 (2009). https://doi.org/10.1371/journal.pone.0004417
3. Peng, H.H., Martel, J., Lee, Y.H., Ojcius, D.M., Young, J.D.: Serum-derived nanoparticles: de novo generation and growth in vitro, and internalization by mammalian cells in culture. Nanomedicine **6**(4), 643–658 (2011). https://doi.org/10.2217/nnm.11.24
4. Peng, H.H., et al.: Physicochemical and biological properties of biomimetic mineralo-protein nanoparticles formed spontaneously in biological fluids. Small **9**(13), 2297–2307 (2013). https://doi.org/10.1002/smll.201202270
5. Martel, J., Peng, H.H., Young, D., Wu, C.Y., Young, J.D.: Of nanobacteria, nanoparticles, biofilms and their role in health and disease: facts, fancy and future. Nanomedicine **9**(4), 483–499 (2014). https://doi.org/10.2217/nnm.13.221
6. Hohling, H.J., Arnold, S., Plate, U., Stratmann, U., Wiesmann, H.P.: Analysis of a general principle of crystal nucleation, formation in the different hard tissues. Adv. Dent. Res. **11**(4), 462–466 (1997). https://doi.org/10.1177/08959374970110041301
7. Hamano, T., et al.: Fetuin-mineral complex reflects extraosseous calcification stress in CKD. J. Am. Soc. Nephrol. **21**(11), 1998–2007 (2010). https://doi.org/10.1681/ASN.2009090944
8. Schlieper, G., et al.: Ultrastructural analysis of vascular calcifications in uremia. J. Am. Soc. Nephrol. **21**(4), 689–696 (2010). https://doi.org/10.1681/asn.2009080829
9. Jahnen-Dechent, W., Heiss, A., Schafer, C., Ketteler, M.: Fetuin-a regulation of calcified matrix metabolism. Circ. Res. **108**(12), 1494–1509 (2011). https://doi.org/10.1161/CIRCRESAHA.110.234260

10. Cheng, H.J., Wei, J.D., Peng, H.H., Liu, Y.J.: Particle-cell detecting and tracking in live-cell time-lapse images. In: 14th International Symposium on Pervasive Systems, Algorithms and Networks & 11th International Conference on Frontier of Computer Science and Technology & Third International Symposium of Creative Computing (ISPAN-FCST-ISCC), pp. 352–356 (2017). https://doi.org/10.1109/ispan-fcst-iscc.2017.58

11. Meijering, E., Dzyubahyk, O., Smal, I.: Methods for cell and particle tracking. Methods Enzymol. **504**, 183–200 (2012). https://doi.org/10.1016/B978-0-12-391857-4.00009-4

12. Jaqaman, K., Loerke, D., Mettlen, M., Kuwata, H., Grinstein, S., Schmid, S.L., Danuser, G.: Robust single-particle tracking in live-cell time-lapse sequences. Nat. Methods **5**(8), 695–702 (2008). https://doi.org/10.1038/nmeth.1237

13. Oliver, T., Schmidt, B., Maskell, D.L.: Reconfigurable architectures for bio-sequence database scanning on FPGAs. IEEE Trans. Circuits Syst. II-Express Briefs **52**, 851–855 (2005). https://doi.org/10.1109/TCSII.2005.853340

14. Szalkowski, A., Ledergerber, C., Krahenbuhl, P., Dessimoz, C.: SWPS3 – fast multi-threaded vectorized Smith-Waterman for IBM Cell/B.E. and x86/SSE2. BMC Res. Notes **1**, 107 (2008). https://doi.org/10.1186/1756-0500-1-107

15. Cramer, T., Schmidl, D., Klemm, M., Mey, D.A.: OpenMP programming on Intel R Xeon Phi TM coprocessors: an early performance comparison. In: Many-Core Applications Research Community Symposium, pp. 38–44 (2012)

16. Liu, W., Schmidt, B., Voss, G., Schroder, A., Muller-Wittig, W.: Bio-sequence database scanning on a GPU. In: 20th IEEE International Parallel & Distributed Processing Symposium (2006). https://doi.org/10.1109/ipdps.2006.1639531

17. Nickolls, J., Buck, I., Garland, M., Skadron, K.: Scalable parallel programming with CUDA. ACM Queue **6**, 40–53 (2008). https://doi.org/10.1145/1365490.1365500

Order Analysis for Translating NESL Programs into Efficient GPU Code

Ming-Yi Yan$^{(\boxtimes)}$, Ming-Hsiang Huang$^{(\boxtimes)}$, and Wuu Yang$^{(\boxtimes)}$

National Chiao Tung University, Hsinchu, Taiwan, R.O.C.
martin81325c@gmail.com, mnnuahg@gmail.com, wuuyang28@gmail.com

Abstract. The language NESL aims to facilitate GPU programming. In order to utilize the computation power of GPUs, NESL programs must be translated into efficient low-level code for execution. We propose a new translation technique. In NESL, *apply-to-each* is the main construct to extract parallel computation capability of GPUs. The result of apply-to-each is a sequence of elements. In traditional translation, the order of the elements in a sequence is *always* preserved. However, sometimes, the order need not be preserved and hence a faster method (which may not preserve the order of elements) for calculating the sequence may be employed. We propose the *order analysis* to determine if the order of elements in a sequence needs to be preserved. Order analysis is based on the *taint analysis*. In our experiments, we obtained 8.76x speedup on average.

Keywords: GPU · NESL · Order analysis · Parallel computation · Taint analysis

1   Introduction

NESL [1] is a first-order functional language designed to support nested data parallelism, which is important for implementing algorithms with irregular nested loops and for divide-and-conquer algorithms. General-purpose graphics processing units (GPUs) provide a large number of parallel threads; threads in the same warp execute the same instructions at the same time. To utilize the abundant parallel capability in GPUs, there are several works [2,3] focusing on translating NESL programs for the GPU models, such as CUDA. *Partial flattening* [4,5] is a technique that translates C programs together with annotations on parallel loops to CUDA programs. It supports irregular nested parallelism on GPUs. We have constructed a translator, *NESL2C*, that translates NESL programs into C programs with annotations for partial flattening.

Data parallelism in NESL is exploited through the *apply-to-each* construct, {*body* : *rbinds* | *sieve*}. In this construct, the sieve part is optional. For example,

---

This work is supported, in part, by Ministry of Science and Technology, Taiwan, R.O.C., under contract MOST 105-2221-E-009-078-MY3.

C.-Y. Chang et al. (Eds.): ICS 2018, CCIS 1013, pp. 330–337, 2019.
https://doi.org/10.1007/978-981-13-9190-3_34

in the expression $\{x + 1 : x \ in \ [1, -2, 3] \mid x > 0\}$, the increment operation is performed on every element in the sequence $[1, -2, 3]$ that satisfies the predicate $(x > 0)$. Hence, the result is the sequence $[2, 4]$. In this paper, an apply-to-each construct with a sieve part is called a *filtered sequence*.

In traditional translation of a filtered sequence, the order of the elements in a filtered sequence must always be preserved. However, the elements may be arbitrarily rearranged without affecting the final result in some cases. For example, when we calculate the sum of the elements in a filtered sequence, the order of elements is insignificant. In this case, it is possible to use a faster method in the translated code.

In this paper, we propose the *order analysis*, which conservatively determines if the order of elements in a filtered sequence is insignificant. According to order analysis, NESL2C adopts one of two translation approaches: If the element order in a filtered sequence needs to be preserved, NESL2C makes use of the *parallel prefix-sum* method [7] in the translation. Otherwise, the faster *warp-aggregated atomics* [8] method is used. Warp-aggregated atomics dramatically decrease the number of atomic instructions and hence improve the performance. However, this approach does not preserve the element order. Our experiment shows that the new NESL2C translator indeed generates faster code when the element order is insignificant.

2   Order Analysis

Order analysis aims to decide whether different orders of elements in a filtered sequence affect the output of a program. For each filtered sequence *seq* in a NESL program, we want to decide if the output of the function that *seq* belongs to is influenced by the order of the elements in *seq*. For this purpose, we may consider the filtered sequence as the tainted *source*. Then the order analysis can be conducted with the taint-analysis technique [6].

2.1   Type Tree

A NESL program consists of expressions. Each expression has a type. The type of an expression is represented by a *type tree*, which is a tree of type nodes. A type node denotes either a primitive type (*int*, *float*, *char*, or *bool*) or a type constructor (*sequence* or *tuple*). A sequence is a list of elements having the same type. Hence a sequence constructor has one child node which is the type of the elements in the sequence. A tuple is a pair of elements. The pair of elements may have different types. Hence, a tuple constructor has two child nodes. Figure 1 shows three examples of type trees. A type tree may be written as a type expression. For example, the type expressions for the three type trees in Fig. 1 are $[int]$, $([int], [int])$, $[[int]]$, respectively, where "[ ]" denotes the sequence constructor and "( )" denotes the tuple constructor.

During the order analysis, each sequence type node of a type tree has an *order status*, which may be either T or F, where T means the order of the elements in this sequence may be changed while F has the opposite meaning. The order status of a sequence type node is written as a subscript of the type expression. In Fig. 1, a gray rectangle represents a sequence with a T order status and a white rectangle represents a sequence with an F order status. In addition, an expression is considered as an *tainted expression* if it contains at least one sequence with a T order status.

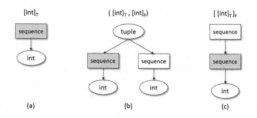

Fig. 1. Three type trees and their order status.

Consider the expression $[1, 2, 3]$. Assume its type tree is shown in Fig. 1 (a). Since the order status of the sequence type node is T, the actual sequence could be any one of $[2, 1, 3]$, $[3, 1, 2]$ or $[3, 2, 1]$, *etc.*

2.2 Kinds of Influence

In NESL2C, a NESL program is represented as an AST (abstract syntax tree). Order analysis performs a depth-first visit to find a filtered sequence, say v. Then we will mark v as tainted (by marking its order status as T) and locate the *parent expression* of v. Then the taint rules (stated in Sect. 2.4) are applied to determine the influence of v on the parent expression. After the influence of v on the function it belongs to is analyzed, erase the order status of every node in AST and the visit proceeds to find the next filtered sequence. The above analysis is repeated for every filtered sequence in the AST.

Let v be a node in the AST. The *parent expression* of v is the expression denoted by the lowest ancestor node of v in the AST that represents an expression. Note that nodes for *rbind, in, assign,* and *bind* do not represent expressions. All other nodes in an AST represent expressions.

Assume A is a filtered sequence with the T order status (so A is tainted). Assume B is the parent expression of A. There are three kinds of influences A may have on B, which are *ValueAffected, OrderAffected* and *NothingAffected.*

1. ValueAffected: If there is any sub-expression in B whose value may change due to the assumption that A is tainted, the influence would be ValueAffected. Note that if the value of the sub-expression is a sequence and only the order of the elements changes while the collection of the elements remain the same, we do not consider it as ValueAffected. For example, let A be the expression 'a', whose value is the sequence $[1, 2, 3]$. Assume A is tainted. Let B be the

parent expression $a[0]$. Then the value of B could be 1, 2, or 3. In this case, the influence of A on B is ValueAffected.

2. OrderAffected: If there is any sequence node within B in which the order of the elements would be affected due to the assumption that A is tainted, the influence would be OrderAffected. Note that other value of the sub-expressions have to remain the same. For example, in the expression "$A{+}{+}[1, 2, 3]$" ($++$ means string concatenation), if A is tainted (that is, the element order of A is changed), then the element order in the parent expression "$A{+}{+}[1, 2, 3]$" may also be changed.

3. NothingAffected: If the value of the expression B will not change even if A is tainted, the influence of A on B is NothingAffected. For example, assume the value of expression A is $[1, 2, 3, 4, 5, 6]$ and B be the parent expression $\#A$ (i.e., the length of A). The value of B is always 6 even if A is tainted.

Depending on the influence, we have different treatments. First, if the influence of the filtered sequence A on its parent expression B is OrderAffected, we need to further analyze the influence of A on B's parent expression and so on. Second, if the influence of A on B is ValueAffected, it means we have to use the method that preserve the order of the elements in A, otherwise the value of B may be different. Third, if the influence of A on B is NothingAffected, it means we do not have to preserve the element order in A. Hence we can use any faster method to compute A. Besides, when the parent expression is the whole function body and we still got OrderAffected, the final influence type will be OrderAffected and we have to preserve the order since the output of the function is affected. In the end, we will get an influence type for each filtered sequence.

2.3 Affected Range

We may build a lattice to compare the seriousness of various influences. Among the three kinds of influences, ValueAffected is the most serious while NothingAffected is the least because in case of ValueAffected, the NESL2C cannot adopt faster methods to implement filtered sequences and in case of NothingAffected NESL2C is free to choose any faster implementation methods. We use *affected range* to distinguish the seriousness in case of the OrderAffected influence.

Given two type trees α and β, they are *comparable* if they are identical type trees though the order status of certain nodes may differ. We say the affected range of α is *less than or equal to* that of β, denoted by $AffectedRange_\alpha \leq AffectedRange_\beta$, if the set of all the sequence nodes with the T order status in α is a subset of that of β. Figure 2 shows such an example, in which the sequence nodes with the T order status are colored gray.

The standard subset relation $\leq$ forms a lattice. This subset lattice is augmented with the ValueAffected node, which is greater than all other subsets. The NothingAffected node is combined with empty subset as a single node. It is smaller than all other nodes. The final augmented lattice for the type trees in Fig. 2 is shown in Fig. 3.

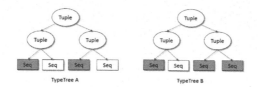

Fig. 2. $AffectedRange_A \leq AffectedRange_B$.

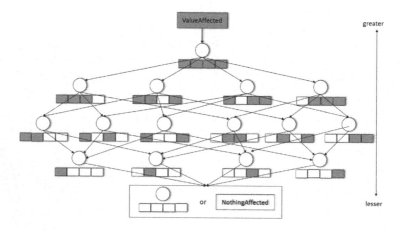

Fig. 3. The lattice of the affected range.

2.4   Taint Policy

The taint policy is a set of rules for propagating the taints among nodes in the AST. We use the following notations in our taint rules.

- We use English letters (e.g., A, B, E) to denote expressions.
- We use Greek letters (e.g., α, β, γ) to denote type trees and affected ranges. The two English letters V and N are used to represent the two affected ranges ValueAffected and NothingAffected, respectively.
- $E : <\alpha>$ means the affected range of E is less than or equals to the affected range α. For example, $E : <[int]_T>$.
- $\alpha \cup \beta$ means the join of the two affected ranges α and β. The sequence nodes with the T order status in $\alpha \cup \beta$ is the union of those in α and β. All other sequence nodes in $\alpha \cup \beta$ have the F order status. For the two special affected ranges V and N, $\alpha \cup V$ will be V while $\alpha \cup N$ will be α.
- $\#E$ denotes the number of elements in set (or sequence) E.
- $x \sim R(0, n)$: x is an arbitrary but unknown number between 0 and n.
- $F(E)_k$ means calling function F with argument E. The subscript k means the depth of the recursion is at most k.

Each rule is of the form:

$$\frac{current\ expression : <affected\ range>; preconditions}{parent\ expression : <affected\ range>}$$

Rules are read from top to bottom, left to right. Given an expression with its affected range and assuming the preconditions are satisfied, we can derive the affected range of the parent expression. For each kind of parent expression, we have one or more rules. Due to the paper limit, we show and discuss only important rules. The rest of the rules are stated in [9].

- Rule 1 introduces a taint to every filtered sequence.
- For rule 8, the parent expression is an apply-to-each construct with more than one binding in *rbinds*. For now we have the affected ranges of E_1 to E_n. Since a binding may affect later bindings, the affected range of this construct is considered ValueAffected if at least one of $u_1, \ldots, u_n$ is T. For example, $\{x + y : x \ in \ [1, 2, 3]; \ y \ in \ [4, 5, 6]\}$. If the order status of $[1, 2, 3]$ is T (the element order may change), the value of the construct may be different. In contrast, if all u_i's are F, we can further analyze the affected range of the *body* and the *sieve* parts with the rules, which are denoted as γ_1 and γ_2, respectively. Since all u_i's are F, the order status of the whole construct is also F. Hence, the affected range of the construct will be $[\gamma_1 \cup \gamma_2]_F$.
- For rule 10, the parent expression is an if-else construct and the value of the expression is not a sequence. (NOTE: if it is a sequence, we use other rules.) For now we have the affected range of *then* (E_1) and *else* (E_2) parts, which are α_1 and α_2, respectively. Since they would both affect the affected range of the parent expression, the affected range would be the join of α_1 and α_2, which is $\alpha_1 \cup \alpha_2$.

$$\overline{\{body : rbinds \mid sieve\} : <[\alpha]_T>} \tag{1}$$

$$\frac{E_1 : <\alpha_1>; E_2 : <\alpha_2>; \ldots; E_n : <\alpha_n>; \forall 1 \le i \le n, \alpha_i \ne V}{[E_1, E_2, \ldots, E_n] : <[\alpha_1 \cup \alpha_2 \cup \ldots \cup \alpha_n]_F>} \tag{2}$$

$$\frac{E_1 : <\alpha_1>; E_2 : <\alpha_2>; \alpha_1 \ne V; \alpha_2 \ne V}{(E_1, E_2) : <(\alpha_1, \alpha_2)>} \tag{3}$$

$$\frac{E : <[\alpha]_->; \alpha \ne V; I \sim R(0, \#E - 1)}{E[I] : <\alpha>} \tag{4}$$

$$\frac{E : <[\alpha]_u>; \alpha \ne V; \neg(I \sim R(0, \#E - 1))}{E[I] : <(u = T?V : \alpha)>} \tag{5}$$

$$\frac{E_1 : <\alpha_1>; E_2 : <\alpha_2>; \alpha_1 \ne V; \alpha_2 \ne V}{E_1 + +E_2 : <\alpha_1 \cup \alpha_2>} \tag{6}$$

$$\frac{E : <[\alpha]_->; \alpha \ne V}{\#E : <N>} \tag{7}$$

$$\frac{\begin{array}{l} E_1 : <[\alpha_1]_{u_1}>, E_2 : <[\alpha_2]_{u_2}>, \ldots, E_n : <[\alpha_n]_{u_n}>; \\ \forall 1 \le i \le n, \alpha_i \ne V; n \ge 2; \\ X_1 : <\alpha_1>, \ldots, X_n : <\alpha_n> \vdash body(X_1, \ldots, X_n) : <\gamma_1>; \gamma_1 \ne V; \\ X_1 : <\alpha_1>, \ldots, X_n : <\alpha_n> \vdash sieve(X_1, \ldots, X_n) : <\gamma_2>; \gamma_2 \ne V; \end{array}}{\begin{array}{c} \{body(X_1, \ldots, X_n) : X_1 \ in \ E_1, \ldots, X_n \ in \ E_n \mid sieve(X_1, \ldots, X_n)\} : \\ <(\exists i \ni u_i = T)? \ V : [\gamma_1 \cup \gamma_2]_F> \end{array}} \tag{8}$$

$$E : <\alpha>, \alpha \neq V;$$
$$\frac{X : <\alpha> \vdash body(X) : <\beta>}{(let \ X = E \ in \ body(X) : <\beta>} \quad (9)$$

$$\frac{E_1 : <\alpha_1>, E_2 : <\alpha_2>, \alpha_1 \neq V, \alpha_2 \neq V; \alpha_1 \neq [\beta]_u, \alpha_2 \neq [\beta]_u, \forall \beta}{(if \ Cond \ then \ E_1 \ else \ E_2) : <\alpha_1 \cup \alpha_2>} \quad (10)$$

$$\frac{E : <[\alpha]_->; \alpha \neq V}{sum(E) : <N>} \quad (11)$$

$$E : <\alpha>;$$
$$E : <\alpha> \vdash F_1(E) : <\beta>;$$
$$\forall i < k, A : <\alpha>, \ assume \ F_i(A) : <\beta>;$$
$$E : <\alpha> \vdash P : <\alpha>, \forall P \in argument \ of \ recursive \ call \ F(P);$$
$$\frac{E : <\alpha>, \forall R \in recursive \ call \ of \ F, R(P) : <\beta> \vdash F(E) : <\beta>}{F_k(E) : <\beta>} \quad (12)$$

3 Experimental Evaluation

Our computing platform is an Intel Core i7-7700 3.6 GHz CPU with 16 GB memory running 64-bit Ubuntu version 16.04. The experiments are run on a NVIDIA GTX770 graphic card with 4 GB memory and the version of CUDA SDK is 7.5.

Figure 4 shows the speedup of the warp-aggregated atomics method compared to the parallel prefix-sum method. There are six benchmarks that can be implemented with both the warp-aggregated atomics and the parallel prefix sum. For *Quick Select* and *Median Finding*, since the main computations are the creation of filtered sequences, we can get dramatic improvement, which is about 19.03x and 17.51x speedup, respectively. For other benchmarks, the main computations include many operations, such as user-defined functions, built-in functions or built-in operators, in addition to creating filtered sequences. Despite this, these benchmarks can still benefit from the faster method and get more than 2x speedup. The average speedup is 8.76x.

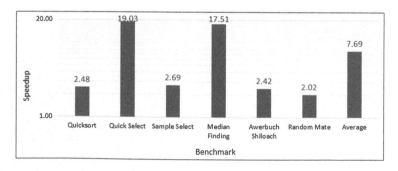

Fig. 4. Speedup of the warp-aggregated atomics method compared to the parallel prefix-sum method.

4   Conclusion

When building a NESL filtered sequence with CUDA code, we have to make use of the methods like parallel prefix-sum if the order of the elements is significant. However, when the order of the elements is insignificant, we can make use of faster methods, such as warp-aggregated atomics, that do not preserve the order of the elements to build the filtered sequence. According to our experiment, the average speedup is 8.76x when the element order is insignificant. We propose the order analysis to conservatively determine if the element order is insignificant.

References

1. Blelloch, G.E., Hardwick, J.C., Chatterjee, S., Sipelstein, J., Zagha, M.: Implementation of a portable nested data-parallel language. J. Parallel Distrib. Comput. 102–111 (1994)
2. Bergstrom, L., Reppy, J.: Nested data-parallelism on the GPU. In: Proceedings of 17th ACM SIGPLAN International Conference on Functional Programming, pp. 247–258 (2012)
3. Zhang, Y., Mueller, F.: CuNesl: compiling nested data-parallel languages for SIMT architectures. In: Proceedings of 41st International Conference on Parallel Processing (ICPP), pp. 340–349 (2012)
4. Huang, M.-H., Yang, W.: Partial flattening: a compilation technique for irregular nested parallelism on GPGPUs. In: Proceedings of 45th International Conference on Parallel Processing (ICPP) (2016)
5. Huang, M.-H.: PFACC: an OpenACC-like programming model for irregular nested parallelism. Ph.D. thesis, National Chiao Tung University (2018)
6. Schwartz, E.J., Avgerinos, T., Brumley, D.: All you ever wanted to know about dynamic taint analysis and forward symbolic execution (but might have been afraid to ask). In: Proceedings of IEEE Symposium on Security and Privacy, pp. 317–331 (2010)
7. Harris, M., Sengupta, S., Owens, J.D.: Parallel prefix sum (scan) with CUDA. GPU Gems **3**(39), 851–876 (2007)
8. Adinets, A.: CUDA Pro Tip: optimized filtering with warp-aggregated atomics. CUDA Pro Tip (2014)
9. Yan, M.-Y.: Order analysis for translating NESL programs into efficient GPU Code. Master's thesis, National Chiao Tung University (2018)

Auto-scaling in Kubernetes-Based Fog Computing Platform

Wei-Sheng Zheng and Li-Hsing Yen[✉][iD]

Department of Computer Science, National Chiao Tung University, Hsinchu, Taiwan
`kweisamx0322@gmail.com, lhyen@nctu.edu.tw`

Abstract. Cloud computing benefits emerging Inter of Things (IoT) applications by providing virtualized computing platform in the cloud. However, increasing demands of low-latency services motivates the placement of computing platform on the edge of network, a new computing paradigm named fog computing. This study assumes container as virtualized computing platform and uses Kubernetes to manage and control geographically distributed containers. We consider the design and implementation of an auto-scaling scheme in this environment, which dynamically adjusts the number of application instances to strike a balance between resource usage and application performance. The key components of the implementation include a scheme to monitor load status of physical hosts, an algorithm that determines the appropriate number of application instances, and an interface to Kubernetes to perform the adjustment. Experiments have been conducted to investigate the performance of the proposed scheme. The results confirm the effectiveness of the proposed scheme in reducing application response time.

Keywords: Container · Fog computing · Kubernetes · Scalability

1 Introduction

Internet of thing (IoT) technology supports the connectivity of smart devices to the Internet. A typical IoT application architecture is a fleet of wireless sensors or autonomous vehicles connected to a central cloud in the Internet, where an IoT application server running to collect data from or send instructions to these devices. This architecture suffers from excessive latency between the server and devices and also imposes high traffic load on the backhaul network. Therefore, when latency is a key parameter to the IoT application or when numerous IoT devices are involved, it is needed to place IoT servers in the vicinity of IoT devices. This calls for fog computing.

Fog computing deploys cloud service on the edge of the Internet, i.e., to the proximity of cloud users. For Infrastructure as a Service (IaaS), cloud service is embodied by virtual machines (VMs) or containers. Container is a light-weight virtualization technology that uses cgroups and Linux namespaces to isolate execution environment of applications. Compared with VMs, containers consumes

© Springer Nature Singapore Pte Ltd. 2019
C.-Y. Chang et al. (Eds.): ICS 2018, CCIS 1013, pp. 338–345, 2019.
https://doi.org/10.1007/978-981-13-9190-3_35

less resource, has a lower loading/starting time, and is easier to manage and control. For this reason, there have been some approaches using container technology to build IoT platform [3,5].

Docker is a popular container management software that manages containers hosted by a single machine. Ismail et al. [8] used Docker to deploy an edge computing platform. Bellavista and Zanni [2] proposed fog-oriented framework with Docker container for IoT applications. Their experiments demonstrate the feasibility and scalability of fog-based IoT platform.

However, Docker is not suitable for managing a cluster of containers spanning a bunch of machines. Kubernetes [9] (*k8s* for short) manages a cluster of containers that span multiple physical hosts. It cooperates with container management software such as Docker and Rocket [11] to control and manage physically scattered containers. Tsai et al. [12] built a fog platform with Raspberry Pi and Kubernetes, on which TensorFlow was deployed and tested.

Auto-scaling is a mechanism that monitors the load status of all application instances and accordingly adjusts the number of instances. Without this, some applications may not fully utilize precious resource allocated to them while other heavily-loaded applications may need resource more than allocated to alleviate and distribute the load. Kubernetes has a native function for container auto-scaling. But it considers only CPU utilization and thus only applies to computation-intensive applications. In fact, whether an application is lightly or heavily loaded should be specific to the application.

Our work took Kubernetes as an orchestrator that instantiates, manages, and terminates containers in multiple-host environments for fog applications, where each host acts as a fog node. On this platform, we developed a dynamic auto-scaling scheme that strikes a balance between resource consumption and application load. Our scheme collects load status from fog nodes, computes an appropriate number of application instances with respect to the load, and cooperates with Kubernetes to adjust the number of application instances. We conducted experiments to compare the performance of the proposed design with the native scheme. The results indicate that the proposed solution significantly reduces application response time.

The rest of this paper is organized as follows: Sect. 2 reviews related literature and background. Section 3 details the proposed approach for the fog computing. Section 4 presents our experimental results and Sect. 5 concludes this work.

2   Background and Related Work

Although fog computing differs from cloud computing in many ways, fog computing is not to replace cloud computing because fog platform may not have enough computation resource for some applications. Therefore, we may integrate fog computing and cloud computing to create a more comprehensive solution [10].

Yu et al. [13] proposed a framework for fog-enabled data processing in IoT systems to support low-latency service requested by real-time data applications. Their framework preprocesses sensory data uploaded from sensors at the fog computing platform before further forwarding them to the cloud. This approach effectively reduce the amount of data to be forwarded.

Hu et al. [7] considered running face identification and resolution scheme, which is computation-intensive, on fog platform. The fog-based resolution scheme efficiently performs the designated task. Hao et al. [6] identified some research challenges and problems with fog computing.

As a high-scalability system for OpenStack, ref [1] used a master node that controls the number of VMs running a certain application. The master node also severs as a single entry point for all requests for the application. All requests coming to the master node are queued and then dispatched by the master node to a VM. They also designed automatic scaling-up and scaling-down algorithm, which makes the platform stable and load balance. The problem of this approach is that the master node then becomes a performance bottleneck. We needs a mechanism that separates auto-scaling controller from traffic entry points.

Chang et al. [4] proposed an approach to monitoring Kubernetes container platform. The approach includes a monitoring mechanism that provides detailed information like utilization ratio of system resource and QoS metrics of application. The information enables an sophisticated resource provisioning strategy that performs dynamic resource dispatch. However, the system model used only one machine and did not explain the setting of their parameters.

3   A New Dynamic Fog Computing Architecture

We propose a fog computing platform based on a collection of physically distributed containers that is orchestrated by Kubernetes. In this platform, an application instance runs in a single container. More than one application instances may be instantiated on several physical hosts. This is to distribute the load of the application and also extend the service coverage of the application. However, as IoT devices may roam or dynamically participate in and out, the distribution of application instances may not match the distribution of requests coming from devices. As a result, loads on application instances may not be even. The main purpose of our design is to dynamically probe the load status of each application instance, based on which the most appropriate number of application instances that matches the current load and request status can be calculated. With this information, our design then communicates with Kubernetes for the adjustment of application instances, hopefully resulting in a better instance distribution that matches the current request needs from devices.

3.1   System Architecture

Pod and *Service* are two features of Kubernetes that are essential to the comprehension of our work. Pod is a package of one or containers that share common network namespace, storage, and some policies for restart and healthy check. Pod is the basic control and management unit of Kubernetes and each Pod has its own life cycle. In our work, we always run a single application instance in one Pod. Therefore, n Pods should be created if we should run n application instances.

Service helps dispatch requests to target Pods. Multiple Pods may be identified by outside users using a single IP address. When a packet destined to some IP address is received by the system, any Pod that is configured with the destination IP address can serve the request with equal probability. Kubernetes dispatch packets to all candidate Pods in a round-robin manner, which helps system evenly distribute requests to all serving Pods.

Kubernetes is a client-server architecture that consists of *Master* and *Nodes*. Master controls the whole kubernetes cluster, stores information and opens API for other users or nodes. Nodes is under the control and management of Master.

Master has four components: *Etcd, Controller Manager Server, Scheduler,* and *APIServer*. Etcd is a distributed key-value store that keeps data across all machines in a reliable way. Controller Manager Server handles any situation of the cluster to ensure stability of Kubernetes. Scheduler decides by which node a newly created Pod is to be hosted. It keeps track of node status, like CPU and memory usage, to select a suitable node for hosting the Pod. Finally, APIServer exports all function using RESTful API for information gathering and operation request.

Kubernetes Node consists of two components: *Kubelet* and *Kube-proxy*. Kubelet running on every node collects node information, including data, volume, image, status for containers, then connects to APIServer for information synchronization with Master. Kubelet also executes instructions from Master. Kube-proxy handles network routing for the accomplishment of service. It also supports basic load balance (round-robin request dispatch).

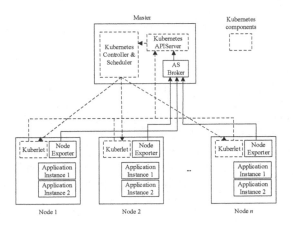

Fig. 1. System architecture

Kubernetes has a native mechanism for auto-scaling (needs installing heapster) that considers only CPU usage. Users could specify the maximal number of application instances, but the actual number of application instances activated is under the control of Kubernetes. We addressed this issue by developing *Auto Scaling Broker* (AS Broker) to dynamically adjust the number of Pods by users.

Figure 1 shows the whole architecture in including Kubernetes and AS Broker.

3.2 Design of AS Broker

We did not modify the round-robin packet dispatch policy of Kube-proxy, though this policy does not consider the current loads of nodes. We also left Scheduler untouched, so Pod placement is also handled by Kubernetes. However, we developed AS Broker to bypass load status reported by Kubelet to Master as we aim at a customized auto-scaling scheme.

AS Broker is a service running in a Pod on Master. It communicates through APIServer with Controller and Scheduler of Kubernetes to obtain a list of nodes where application instances are currently running. It then collects node information from all nodes. It the number of application instances should be adjusted, it then sends a request through APIServer for Pod number adjustment.

There are three major tasks of AS Broker: getting machine information from nodes, estimating an appropriate number of application instances, and requesting Master to exercise the result. For the first task, we run an open-source software *Node Exporter* in a Pod on each node to get information like CPU and memory usage from the physical machine on which it is running. To enable outside access of the information locally kept by Node Exporter, we opens a port on each Pod running Node Exporter so that AS Broker can send a HTTP GET to get node information there. The information consists of raw data of the node status, based on which we can get CPU usage ratio as defined in (1).

$$CPU_{usage} = (usertime + systemtime + nicetime)/\Delta, \tag{1}$$

where *usertime* and *systemtime* are the CPU time spent on user and kernel modes, respectively, *nicetime* is the CPU time spent on adjusting the program scheduler or setting priority for programs, and Δ is the time interval of probe.

In a large-scale system, deploying exactly one Pod running Node Exporter on each node manually may not be viable. We use function *DaemonSet* of Kubernetes to automate this task.

AS Broker probes node information every Δ seconds, and runs Algorithm 1 every T_s seconds to determine the best number of application instances n. If n is different from the current number, AS Broker then asks Kubernetes Controller through APIServer to keep n instances.

The following notations are for Algorithm 1. Let S be the set of all nodes that host the target application instances. For every node $i \in S$, let u_i^c be the CUP utilization ratio and u_i^m be the memory usage. Define T_c and T_m be the thresholds of CPU utilization and memory usage to trigger an adjustment. Parameter α is a factor that indicates the weighting between CUP utilization and memory usage. It should be high (close to 1) for computation-intensive applications. Parameter

β is an adjustment factor that keeps the value of n not exceeding the maximal number of Pods allowed for the applications.

Algorithm 1. best-instance-number(S, $\{u_i^c\}$, $\{u_i^m\}$)

Parameter
α: weighting factor between U_c and U_m
β: adjustment factor
   Output
n: number of Pods (application instances)

1: **if** $\exists i \in S, u_i^c > T_c$ or $u_i^m > T_m$ **then**
2:    $U_c = \sum_{i \in S} u_i^c / |S|$ $\triangleright$ Avg. CPU utilization
3:    $U_m = \sum_{i \in S} u_i^m / |S|$ $\triangleright$ Avg. memory usage
4:    $n = (\alpha * U_c + (1 - \alpha) * U_m) / \beta$
5: **else**
6:    $n = 1$
7: **end if**
8:

---

4 Experimental Results

Our fog platform consisted of four PCs. Each PC has a 3.2 GHz i5-6500 CPU and 8 GB RAM. The operating system is Ubuntu 16.04LTS. Kubernetes version is 1.6.1. Among them, three PCs were Nodes and the other was Master. AS Broker ran on the Master.

We used another PC to generate and send requests to the fog platform. We used *stress* program to generate CPU and memory load to emulate the processing of requests. Every request took 15-second execution time and 50-MB memory space. The inter-arrival time of requests was an exponential distribution with mean $1/\lambda$, rendering request arrivals a Poisson process with mean arrival rate λ. All requests were sent toward to an application and directed by Kubelet to a Node where an application instance was running. We varied the value of scaling interval T_s to investigate the impact of T_s on performance. Because instantiating a container took three seconds, the value of T_s was ranged from 10 to 60 seconds. Figure 2 shows the experiment environment.

We varied the value of λ and ran a 600-s trial with $T_s = 20$ for each setting of λ. Figure 3 shows cumulative probabilities of the number of Pods for different λ. We can see that with $\lambda = 1$, 47% of the time there were only six or fewer application instances (Pods). When λ was set to 2, the percentage dropped to 30%. It was 10% with $\lambda = 4$. When λ was 5, there were 8 or 9 application instances running 80% of the time.

We also tested application response time with and without AS Broker. Figure 4 shows the result with $\alpha = 0.8$, $T_s = 30$, and $\lambda = 1$. Clearly, though response time dynamically changes, the result with AS Broker is better than that without almost at every time point. This result demonstrates the effectiveness of the proposed scheme.

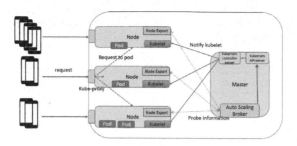

Fig. 2. Experiment environment

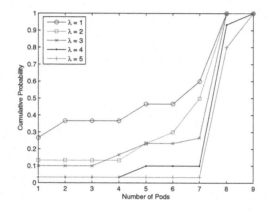

Fig. 3. Number of pods (application instances) with different λ

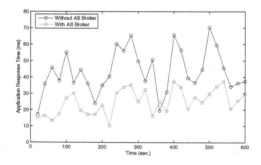

Fig. 4. Application response time with and without AS Broker ($\alpha = 0.8$, $T_s = 30$, $\lambda = 1$)

5   Conclusions

We has proposed an auto-scaling scheme for Kubernetes-based fog computing platform. It uses an open-source software Node Exporter running in a Pod on each node to get machine information. AS Broker collects machine information to determine the most appropriate number of application instances. It then asks

Kubernetes to keep the desired number of Pods. Experimental results confirm the effectiveness of the proposed scheme in reducing application response time.

References

1. de la Bastida, D., Lin, F.J.: OpenStack-based highly scalable IoT/M2M platforms. In: IEEE International Conference on Internet of Things, Exeter, UK, June 2017
2. Bellavista, P., Zanni, A.: Feasibility of fog computing deployment based on Docker containerization over RaspberryPi. In: Proceedings of the 18th International Conference on Distributed Computing and Networking, January 2017
3. Brogi, A., Mencagli, G., Neri, D., Soldani, J., Torquati, M.: Container-based support for autonomic data stream processing through the fog. In: Heras, D.B., Bougé, L. (eds.) Euro-Par 2017. LNCS, vol. 10659, pp. 17–28. Springer, Cham (2018). https://doi.org/10.1007/978-3-319-75178-8_2
4. Chang, C.C., Yang, S.R., Yeh, E.H., Lin, P., Jeng, J.Y.: A kubernetes-based monitoring platform for dynamic cloud resource provisioning. In: IEEE Global Communications Conference, December 2017
5. Dupont, C., Giaffreda, R., Capra, L.: Edge computing in IoT context: horizontal and vertical Linux container migration. In: Global Internet of Things Summit, June 2017
6. Hao, Z., Novak, E., Yi, S.: Challenges and software architecture for fog computing. IEEE Internet Comput. **21**(2), 44–53 (2017)
7. Hu, P., Ning, H., Qiu, T., Zhang, Y., Luo, X.: Fog computing based face identification and resolution scheme in internet of things. IEEE Trans. Ind. Inform. **13**(4), 1910–1920 (2017)
8. Ismail, B.I., Goortani, E.M., Karim, M.B.A.: Evaluation of Docker as edge computing platform. In: 2015 IEEE Conference on Open Systems, Bandar Melaka, Malaysia, August 2015
9. kubernetes: production-grade container orchestration. https://kubernetes.io/
10. Mebrek, A., Merghem-Boulahia, L., Esseghir, M.: Efficient green solution for a balanced energy consumption and delay in the IoT-fog-cloud computing. In: 16th International Symposium on Network Computing and Applications, Cambridge, MA, USA, October 2017
11. Rocket: a security-minded, standards-based container engine. https://coreos.com/rkt
12. Tsai, P.H., Hong, H.J., Cheng, A.C.: Distributed analytics in fog computing platforms using TensorFlow and Kubernetes. In: 19th Asia-Pacific Network Operations and Management Symposium, Seoul, South Korea, September 2017
13. Yu, T., Wang, X., Shami, A.: A novel fog computing enabled temporal data reduction scheme in IoT systems. In: IEEE Global Communications Conference, December 2017

Information Technology Innovation, Industrial Application and Internet of Things

A General Internet of Thing System with Person Emotion Detection Function

Wen-Pinn Fang$^{(\boxtimes)}$, Wen-Chi Huang, and Yu-Chien Chang

Department of Information Communication,
Yuan Ze University, Taoyuan City, Taiwan
wpfang@saturn.yzu.edu.tw

Abstract. This paper proposes an internet of things system which can generates the map of people emotion around the campus. The system can identify someone's emotion who stays in a school. Based on image retrieving, face detection and emotion recognition method, the emotion information can be gotten, store in the database and user can query the instance of emotion around the campus by the system. The query function is combined into an exist system which the authors proposed previously. The application of the system includes provide the professor to observe the students' statement and adjust the teaching mode, activity result evaluation. Some system demonstration is also shown in the paper.

Keywords: Emotional statistics · Expression analysis · Internet of Things

1 Introduction

Nowadays, it is convenient for us to get the image from the cameras. There are already many applications, such as smartphone, monitor and so on. It is common for not only teenagers but also elders to take a selfie with their phone and upload to social media to share their life. That is, it is easy to get images and analyze them. After analyzing images, it can use the technology of Internet of Thing (IoT) to upload the data to the Internet platform. In this paper, an IoT system which can generate the map of people emotion around the campus has been proposed.

Emotion Information is an important information in many field, such as shopping mall management, performance evaluation, student reaction information …and so on feedback. For instance, a department manager choices right method to increase the performance of promotion by their customer's emotion distribution data. Based on these feedbacks, these occupations can clearly know their customers' reaction. According to the information showing on the map, these occupations can adjust their plan. In order to analyze emotion from images and upload the information to the IoT platform, there are three steps: First of all, capturing the photo from the camera and detecting the human face. Second, build a database of human facial emotion and build the emotion chart. Last, upload the result to the platform and show on the correspondence map. With this map, it is possible to get the information of the emotions on this map at a glance. In this paper, it experiments in the campus. Count people's emotion in the campus and uploading to the cloud. Finally, the emotion statistic can be shown on the map.

© Springer Nature Singapore Pte Ltd. 2019
C.-Y. Chang et al. (Eds.): ICS 2018, CCIS 1013, pp. 349–357, 2019.
https://doi.org/10.1007/978-981-13-9190-3_36

The rest of this paper is organized as follows: the related work and introduce the technology is shown in Sect. 2; the method is proposed in Sect. 3; Experimental results are shown in Sect. 4. Finally, the discussion is represented in Sect. 5.

2   Related Work

2.1   Emotion Detect

Facial Expression is directly way to express sentiment, it is common to identify emotion by detecting facial expression. There are some common ways to detect facial expression. One is capturing facial features, through those positions to determine expression [1]. The other one is Facial Action Coding System (FACS) which is one of the most widely system for the analysis of facial expression [2]. There are also some exist products that can detect emotion, such as Google, Microsoft and so on. These products can make it easy to plug sensors into the network, but it is not often combine with complex devices to network. In this paper, it proposes to combine the high-level information.

2.2   Internet of Things (IoT)

Internet of Things (IoT) is the network that realize the things interconnection through the communication or Internet. The basic idea of IoT is able to interact with other things through unique addressing schemes, such as RFID or wireless sensor [3]. To connect devices and network, the company of IBM and Eurotech introduce a message protocol-Message Queue Telemetry Transport (MQTT). MQTT is a connectivity protocol of machine-to-machine (M2M) and Internet of Things (IoT). It is able to provide routing for small, cheap, low power and low memory devices in vulnerable and low bandwidth networks [4].

3   System Architecture

This paper proposes to generate a map of people emotion in campus. To realize the emotion map, it is divided to two parts. One is detecting emotion, the other is the Internet platform of internet of thing (See Fig. 1). To approach this system, there are two methods, one is Cloud Computing (See Fig. 2(a)), the other is Edge Computing (See Fig. 2(b)). In Fig. 3, it proposes the way to determine the method, referring to the image size, Ram usage or network transmission quality. According to the different requirement, it can decide the different method to make it efficient.

In this paper, it detects human face by some camera. Therefore, it gets the images from the video streaming. After getting the image, separating from the background to recognize the human face, and capturing the features on the face. According to the position of the features and expression database, mating the emotion result. In this

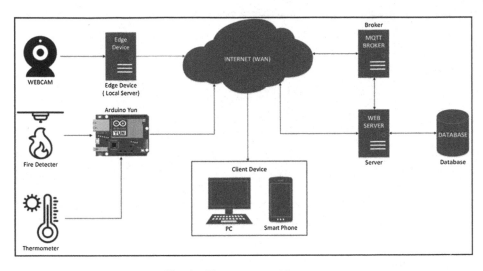

Fig. 1. The system architecture

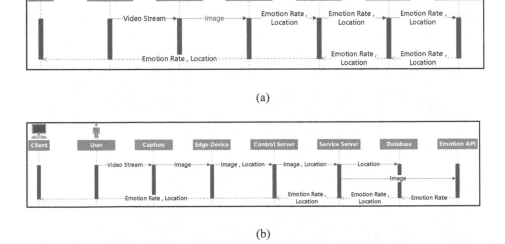

(a)

(b)

Fig. 2. System architecture (a) cloud computing solution, (b) edge Computing solution

paper, it designs an emotion chart which contains the scores and the corresponding emotions. With this chart, adding up the nearby score. Then, uploading the score to the IoT system. In this paper, it also proposes a platform to record these data and show on the map.

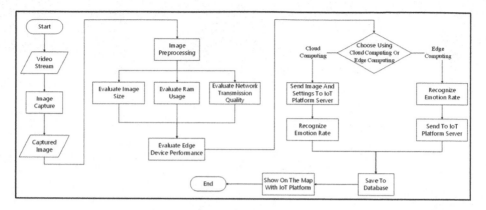

Fig. 3. The program flow

4 Experiment

There are some experiment results about this system. In Fig. 4, it processed the image to detect the human and capture the features on the face. After capturing the features, it can measure the feature position to estimate the emotion. According to the emotion database, mark the result on the image shown in Fig. 5, adding up the score of the emotion chart which the authors proposed previously, and average it to percent. The result of this image is 88%. Then, the IoT platform update the information and in

Fig. 4. An example of detecting human face and capturing the features

Fig. 5. An example of emotion detecting result

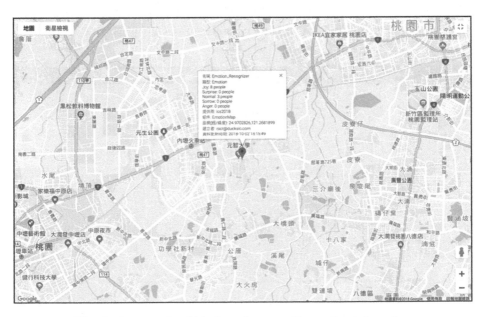

Fig. 6. An example which show the map with emotion information

Fig. 6, the information is shown on the map. In Fig. 7, it lists the Statistics chart of this experiment. In Fig. 8, this IoT platform combine with the traditional sensors and emotion detection, the value of the emotion detection is stand for the proportion of the joy in the picture. This is system was also experiment in class, the professor did the roll call by taking a photo, using this system to analyze the students' statement (Fig. 9). The experiment picture of students' statement using online emotion recognition API in the proposed system.

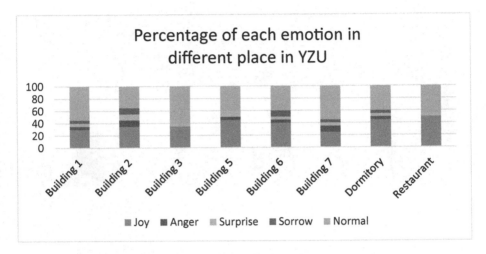

Fig. 7. The statistics of the experiment on the IoT platform

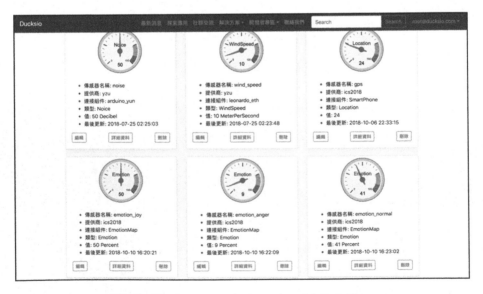

Fig. 8. The meter page in the proposed IoT platform

Fig. 9. The experiment picture of multi-face recognition

5   Discuss and Future Work

This paper proposes an internet of thing system which can generate the map of people emotion around the campus. The traditional IoT platform usually record about rainfall, humidity, temperature and so on. These data are recorded not frequently. In proposed system, it not only retrieves environment sensor, but also get emotion recognition result from video streaming with image based method. Because the character of video streaming, not every frame has he information of emotion or the recognition rate is not 100%. For the sake to reduce the cost of system, the bandwidth and the computational power are limited, there are two method to realize the system: Cloud Computing and Edge Computing to solve this problem. Cloud Computing is computing the data after uploading to the cloud. Edge Computing is transferring the information after computing the data. Using the method of Edge Computing can filter the image to decline the probability of unable to recognize. To make the system more efficiently, it can according to the camera level to decide the computing method. Though the microprocessor can transfer the data to the server, there are some limit, such as Arduino can transfer the data through the Internet, it cannot process too complex information. In

(a)

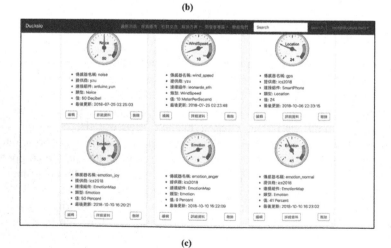

(b)

(c)

Fig. 10. The Comparison (a) one of the IoT platform in Taiwan (b) one of the IoT platform abroad (c) this system

Fig. 10 is the comparison of the exit internet of things platform. It is obviously that the platform that proposes in this paper plug the emotion sensor. In this paper, this system connects with Arduino and camera to realize the high-information Internet of Things platform, and it also can register sensor with mobile, as shown in Fig. 11. At present, no one has seen the combination of the emotion and the Internet of Things. In the future, it will combine with more high-level device to make a hybrid platform.

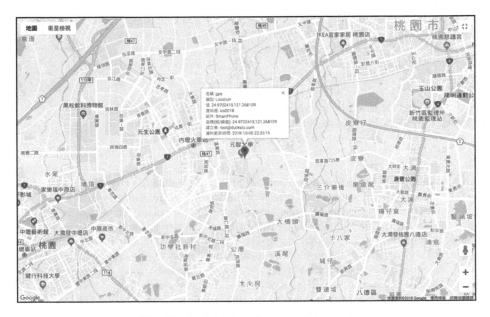

Fig. 11. Smartphone also can be a sensor

References

1. Fang, W.-P., Huang, W.-C.: Based on image emotional analysis of photos on social medias. Taiwan E-Learning Forum (2018)
2. Ekman, P., Friesen, W.V.: Facial Action Coding System: A Technique for the Measurement of Facial Movement. Consulting Psychologists Press, San Francisco (1978)
3. Atzori, L., Iera, A., Morabito, G.: The Internet of Things: a survey. Comput. Netw. **54**(15), 2787–2805 (2010)
4. Al-Fuqaha, A., Guizani, M., Mohammadi, M., Aledhari, M., Ayyash, M.: Internet of Things: a survey on enabling technologies, protocols and applications. IEEE Commun. Surv. AMP Tutor. **17**(4), 2347–2376 (2015)

A Biometric Entrance Guard Control System for Improving the Entrance Security of Intelligent Rental Housing

Jerry Chao-Lee Lin[1], Jim-Min Lin[1], and Vivien Yi-Chun Chen[2,3]($\boxtimes$)

[1] Department of Information Engineering and Computer Science,
Feng Chia University, Taichung, Taiwan
jerrypull@hotmail.com, jimmy@fcu.edu.tw
[2] Department of Architecture, Wuchang University of Technology,
Wuhan, China
vivichen11082017@gmail.com
[3] Department of Architecture, Fujian University of Technology,
No. 33 Xueyuan Road, Minhou County, Fuzhou, Fujian, China
61201817@fjut.edu.cn

Abstract. With the rapid development of the information and communication technology, the security requirement of the entrance guard control systems has significantly increased. In recent years, the rise and popularity of various portable smart devices, including traditional keys, inductive buckles, inductive magnetic disks, biometrics, and so on. It has been already ripe that the biometrics, especially the finger-print identification technology from intelligence mobile phones, intelligence watches, etc., has matured and become an important member of an entrance guard control system. This research is to enhance the entrance guard control management in the traditional rental housing industry with a new generation of intelligent ultrasonic bio-metric entrance guard control system. In addition to preventing loss of cards and copy of keys, the research can also have the feature of achieving remotely monitor of the rental situation of a rented house. Even if it is not in the local area, the security of the rental house can be immediately controlled by the system to achieve the optimization result of the unattended intelligent lease access control system. Finally, the of goal of this study is to provide a convenient and safe living environment for rental houses.

Keywords: Biometric · Entrance guard control system · Rental housing ·
3D screen ultrasonic fingerprint identification technology

1 Introduction

An Entrance Guard Control System refers to the software and hardware system that controls the entry and exit of specific personnel into a specific place. It is usually used in lots of space, like office gates, elevators, factories, warehouses, or MRT, laboratories, military offices, and even personal residences. The equipment is generally required to include four parts/devices: Automatic Identification System, Electronic Control

© Springer Nature Singapore Pte Ltd. 2019
C.-Y. Chang et al. (Eds.): ICS 2018, CCIS 1013, pp. 358–367, 2019.
https://doi.org/10.1007/978-981-13-9190-3_37

Lock, Power Supply, and Outgoing Device. Among them, the automatic identification system is to identify the user identity, and the electronic control lock is used to control the opening of the door. The power supply mainly maintains the normal operation of the entrance guard control system, and does not be affected by whether the supply of the main power system is out of order. The out-of-office device allows personnel to quickly open in the controlled area.

The most important aspect of the access control system is "security", which is to ensure the correctness and stability of the user's identity to prevent non-specific personnel from entering. In recent years, the rapid development of access control systems has not only added additional functions including time control, entry and exit, but also enhanced security and diverse identification methods, including various screening devices and biometrics. Traditional access control systems are developed by door locks, usually placed at important entrances and exits, and are a software and hardware integration system for controlling personnel access. Its safety and convenience are the most important performance indicators. "Security" refers to the reliability of the system to prevent illegal intrusions. "Convenience" refers to the means and time that legitimate users need to pass the system. The main technology is "identity." The traditional mechanical door lock only recognizes the key itself, but does not recognize the key holder. The structure of the key is easy to copy. Although it is easy to use, the security is obviously insufficient.

User identification is the core of the access control system. Strictly speaking, the earliest use of traditional keys does not really identify users. However, the size of the key is usually very small and sturdy, easy to carry, easy to use, and does not require any power when unlocked, therefore it is still the most versatile device. Because of the structure simplicity, the key is easy to copy and the key still needs to be carried by the user. Thus, it is indeed with the concerns of loss.

The new generation of door locks is electronically an important component of the access control system. Mainly by electronic sensors and related software programs to enhance their security, electronic sensors can be composed of simple buttons to extremely complex personal physiological sensing components, and the collected data are thus processed through the clamp signal of legal users. With the development of technology, the currently available electronic locks have been quite diverse, with their own advantages and disadvantages. The identification of its identity includes three types of portable identification devices, passwords and biometrics. Recently, biometric identification technology has developed rapidly, and its uniqueness and non-reproducibility are its advantages. The fingerprint recognition technology of the previous generation is susceptible to external factors such as dirt, oil stains, moisture and other external factors that affect the identification function.

Therefore, this study aims to integrate a new generation of screen 3D ultrasonic fingerprint recognition technology and face recognition technology to construct the concept of access control management subsystem. The identification of fingerprint recognition is the first verification level, and the second is the use of face recognition. Two levels of verification. At the same time, the user captures the fingerprint of the fingerprint reader and sends the facial image of the fingerprint recognizer to the facial recognition system and compares the facial database with the facial image captured by the camera. In this way, it is confirmed that the fingerprint reader and the face recognizer are the same person, and the function of the access control management is enhanced by the two-factor authentication of biometrics and face recognition. At the same time, for the application of lease control and rental housing management, a back-end integrated management system was designed. The completed system helps the homeowner control the entry and exit of tenants and visitors, thereby protecting tenant access and prevention. In this study, a dual-certified access control system with the 3D ultrasonic fingerprint recognition and face recognition on the new generation of screens will provide security, convenience, and dual protection for the system.

2 Fingerprint Identification System

Biometric identification is the core technology of user identification in all access control systems. Commonly used identification methods include fingerprint, face, iris, retina, palm vein, voiceprint, etc. Various techniques are as follows:

2.1 Fingerprint Identification System

The fingerprint identification system is a type of fingerprint authentication using a fingerprint. Due to the uniqueness and non-reproducibility of fingerprints, fingerprint locks become extremely secure locks. However, it also has some problems, such as the fingerprint screening rate cannot reach 98%, so some people cannot use, the reliability of the fingerprint lock circuit, and the fingerprint sensor may also be affected by the environmental humidity. In order to avail the benefits of higher user convenience, hygiene, and improved accuracy, contact less 3D fingerprint recognition techniques have recently been introduced [1]. Using the unique fingerprint information on the human finger to identify, the principle is that each person's fingerprint has a texture feature called minutiae, that is, the distribution pattern of the ridges and valleys in the fingerprint, such as the ridges end, splits, splits and joins, or just one point, these lines become the main flaws in fingerprint recognition.

The hand-fingerprint fingerprint identification device can be divided into three types, show in Table 1. One is optical and the other is capacitive. However, one of the main forces at present is to develop a new generation of 3D optical-like fingerprint identification technology, which is fingerprint recognition under 3D ultrasonic screen.

2.1.1 Optical Fingerprint Identification

Optical fingerprint recognition illuminates the fingerprint texture of the finger by self-illumination of the OLED screen, and allows the sensing elements under the hidden screen to be identified, thereby achieving an identification comparison effect. The fingerprint pressing position is composed of optical components such as acrylic or glass. The advantage is that the price is low and durable, and the disadvantage is that the volume is large.

Table 1. Differences in three fingerprint identifications

	Capacity	Optical	Ultrasonic
Technical principle			
Advantage	cheap price, long life, wide applicability	thin and light <1mm, easy to package	high security, thin and light <1mm
Disadvantage	big size, large thickness, low security, medium stain resistance	high price, low antistatic, low stain resistance	high price, high recognition rate, high stain resistance
Application product	trunk, NB, remote control, safe, other appliances	mobile phone, NB, tablet	mobile phone, NB, tablet

Source: take https://www.qualcomm.com/

2.1.2   Capacitive Fingerprint Identification

Capacitive fingerprint identification is to miniaturize and integrate a high-density capacitive sensor into a wafer. When the fingerprint is pressed against the surface of the wafer, the internal miniature capacitive sensor forms a different amount of charge according to the aggregation of the peaks and valleys of the fingerprint. The image of the fingerprint. The advantages are thin and small, and the disadvantages are erosion of the surface of the wafer and electrostatic protection, high cost and poor durability.

2.1.3   The Fingerprint Recognition Under the Ultrasonic 3D Screen

The fingerprint recognition under the ultrasonic 3D screen is that the screen does not need to be turned on at the highest brightness when the fingerprint is recognized, and the fingerprint form of the finger is constructed by using ultrasonic waves to form a 3D graphic, which is compared with the information existing on the terminal. Its advantage is that the density of the skin is the same as the density of the air through ultrasound, and it has a good performance for some waterproof, oil-proof and penetrating properties. Compared with optical fingerprinting and capacitive fingerprint recognition, the ultrasonic signal has better penetrability, which can reduce fingerprint dirt, grease and sweat interference while achieving fingerprint recognition, and will not be unlocked under water. It has an impact and is more widely applicable.

2.1.4   Face ID Recognition System

The Face ID recognition system is a non-contact and high-speed identification system [2–4]. Traditional face recognition systems mostly use 2d images. The techniques using 2D images are subdivided into three categories [5]: real view-based matching, pose transformation in image space, and pose transformation in feature space. Real view-based matching: Consists of representing the individuals in the gallery with different rotations and look for the individual to be identified in this gallery, once his pose has been determined. In [6], a method with a gallery of 15 images per individual which covers pose variability with ±40° in yaw and ±20° in tilt has been proposed. Identification process is typically a template matching algorithm with templates around the eyes, nose, and mouth, where the only difference is that it matches a probe face image with gallery face images in similar poses. These methods are easy from an algorithmic point of view but are difficult to exploit practically since they need images of faces in several orientations [7]. Therefore, when using the face 3D model identification system for identity authentication, the infrared floodlight turns on and scans the user's face. The infrared camera detects the user's line of sight. When the user's attention is on the lens, the structured light is emitted. The device will use a pattern of more than 30,000 infrared dots to project into the face area, and the infrared camera will take a picture as a structured light receiver. The distance obtained by the proximity sensor using Time Of Flight technology is calculated to obtain the head. 3D model.

The identity verification mode principle of the face id recognition system can be divided into two: one-to-one: In one-to-one authentication, the user first enters the user name or code, and the system removes the user from the database. The image is then taken by the camera to capture the user's face image and determine whether it is the same or not. The second category is one-to-many: in the case of one-to-many identity search verification, the user does not need to enter the user name, and the system compares the facial image captured by the camera with all users in the database. So the face is a password, there is no need to remember the password, and there are no concerns about theft or loss.

Face ID recognition technology has seven major advantages: (1) non-contact: the collection of face images is different from fingerprints, palm prints need to touch the palm-grain special collection equipment, and the collection of palm prints does not have any wear on the equipment, nor Hygiene, easy to cause the objection of the collector, and the face image acquisition device is the camera, no need to touch. (2) Non-intrusive: The photo can be taken automatically by the camera, no manpower, just in front of the camera. (3) Friendly: A human face is a biological feature that is exposed after a person is born, so its privacy is not as strong as palm prints and irises, so the collection of faces is not as unacceptable as the palm print collection. (4) Intuitive: We judge who is a person. It is the most intuitive way to look at this person's face. It does not mean that palm prints, irises, etc. require relevant experts to judge. (5) Fast: The face collection from the camera surveillance area is very fast, because its non-intervention and non-contact, the face acquisition time is greatly shortened. (6) Convenient: Face-collecting front-end equipment - the camera can be seen everywhere, it is not a special device, so it is easy to operate. (7) Good scalability: The acquisition terminal can completely adopt the camera equipment of the existing video surveillance system. The scalability of the back-end application determines that face recognition can be applied in many fields such as access control, blacklist monitoring, and face photo search.

3 Rental Housing Management Simulation System

In this section, we focus on the application of fingerprint identification and face recognition technology to construct the entrance guard control management subsystem. The two functions of biometrics are used to enhance the function of access control management. At the same time, we design the back-end integrated management system for the application of access control personnel. The completed system can control the entry and exit of personnel and thus serve as the basis for the safety of the tenant. as shown in Fig. 1.

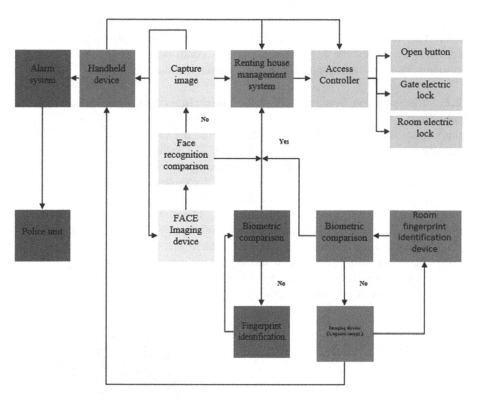

Fig. 1. Schematic diagram of rental housing management simulation system

3.1 Building a Two-Factory Rental Housing Entrance Guard Control System Management Application Platform

This study proposes to establish a dual-certified rental entrance guard control system management application platform. The overall architecture can be divided into two parts, namely, the identification system end and the server management end. The identification system uses ultrasonic fingerprint identification, with ultrasonic fingerprint identification module and network camera built in above the module. The first layer of authentication uses ultrasonic fingerprint screening. It is proposed to use short-range fixed-type ultrasonic recognition module. The system preset fingerprint recognition module is about 45 cm away from the circle; the second layer is for face capture and comparison. It is planned to use the network camera built in the fingerprint identification module to capture the face and perform real-time people. Face recognition. The system sets the instant face capture when the entry and exit personnel enters the photographic screen and the face size exceeds 150 × 150 pixels (Pixel) in the photographic screen. The tested face needs to be about 40–50 cm away from the camera to be effective. Capture function.

3.2 Certification and Operation Process

The dual authentication process of this system. The first level is fingerprint identification. The fingerprint identification module first obtains the tenant information. This information provides the face recognition and confirmation of the next level. The following describes the design of the ramp authentication system.

3.2.1 "Snapdragon Sense ID" 3D Ultrasonic Fingerprint Identification Technology

Snapdragon Sense ID technology is different from the common capacitive touch fingerprinting technology currently on the market. The technical principle referenced in this paper is Qualcomm (QUALCOMM) Snapdragon Sense ID, as shown in Fig. 2. Figure 3, mainly through Ultrasonic technology for fingerprint scanning, the technical principle is to use high-frequency sound waves to directly penetrate the outer layer of the skin, detect finger 3D details and unique fingerprint features including fingerprint ridges and sweat pores, and establish fingerprint authentication information that is difficult to imitate. Sound waves can traverse entities. Obstacle, can be used on glass, aluminum, stainless steel, sapphire and plastic materials, and will not affect the scanning results due to the interference of dirt, sweat or detergent on the hand, and avoid using the same place for detection. This means that any position on the screen can be identified.

Fig. 2. Principle of ultrasonic recognition
Source: take https://www.qualcomm.com/

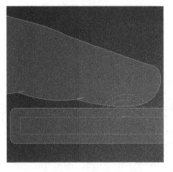

Fig. 3. Ultrasonic identification diagram

3.2.2 Face Recognition

The face recognition authentication is divided into a martial arts program. The first program is the part of the face that is captured. The image is identified by the features such as the facial features of the face. The face image must be obtained before the face recognition. The face detection and retrieval program uses the Source Code 人 of the face recognition provided by the OpenCV library to display the face position detection and capture program. The face detection and the captured face image are normalized. The second procedure is to compare the face database image with the face captured by the first program. The same member is sent to the backend server for subsequent processing, and vice versa, if the member does not match, it is impossible to pass.

(1) Face capture

In the face detection part, the instant image is obtained by the network camera set up on the identification system end, and the face detection is performed through the OpenCV function, and the OpenCV uses the Haar feature [8] as the distinguishing feature, as shown in Fig. 4. In addition, using the Cascade Adaboost splitter as a learning mechanism, the basic principle of the splitter is to use more than one hundred sample images, and use Haar-like features to perform the training of the splitter. The training samples can be divided into two types. The face of the splitter, which requires pictures of faces and non-faces, but the samples of non-faces need to be higher than the samples of faces, all samples must be normalized, and Haar-like features are obtained. A divider for detecting faces. Through the cvRectangle function in OpenCV, we can use cvRect to specify the size and position of the rectangle to be drawn on the specified image. These rectangles are the position of the face we detected, frame the face image and capture the face image. In order to obtain the identification result, the face image file is created, and different face images are stored for identification.

Through the Haar-like feature database to find features that match the face features, the program will first introduce this set of features, and the second program will use the set of well-recognized face features and instant images to judge the face features. In the live image, the face part may be traced and the face range is marked with a border. When the face size does not reach the detection size set by the system, the face size is not captured and the face range is marked. The face size is larger than the size we set, and the face size is captured and marked.

(2) Face recognition

The face sample is first collected. The image normalization is mainly based on the linear interpolation, the normalized image size of 40×40 pixels, and the grayscale image face brightness. Adjust to normalize the change of brightness, and then reduce the face image size to 10×10 pixels through the second wavelet transform. The purpose is to maintain the maximum information under the image, which can improve

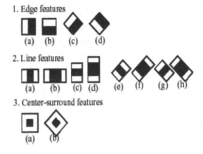

Fig. 4. Face recognition system process; Source: take https://www.opencv.org/

the speed of identification, and finally through linear discriminant analysis. The main purpose is to open the characteristic distance between members, and make the sample distance of each member denser. Each image in the database can be obtained through linear discriminant analysis.

3.3   Security Management System

In the rental management system, the overall rental management interface can have higher management results through the most practical planning and hierarchical functions. It is mainly divided into eight main functions, namely system management, renting, signing, housekeeping, maintenance, accounts receivable, leaseback and log-out system, as shown in Fig. 5.

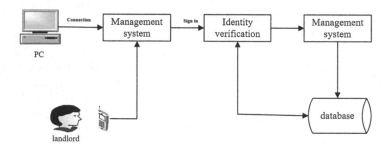

Fig. 5. System login diagram

4   Conclusions and Remarks

The contribution of this research in the dual biometrics authentication intelligent rental housing management system is built-in display by the ultrasonic fingerprint identification module, which is composed of a built-in network camera and a three-machine integrated machine. It has practical value for reliable safety improvement.

In the past, the traditional rental market was using RFID or a key. It was easy to have lost or invalid doubts. Its security was not very good, and the improvement of its security and convenience was the focus of this research.

The system proposed in this study intends to use the management of access control security and rental housing management as the main axis, according to the structure and environment of the house for the planning and design of software and hardware, in order to achieve the optimization of intelligent rental housing security management operations. The system integrates the 3D ultrasonic fingerprint recognition and face recognition technology to construct the access control management subsystem, and strengthens the access control management function by means of ultrasonic fingerprint identification and face recognition. The integrated management system is designed to facilitate the administrator and the landlord. The system used can help the manager or the landlord to control the entry and exit of the instant tenants and the visitor's situation, thereby improving the safety of the safety of the tenants. The intelligent rent management system with dual biometrics proposed in this article is reliable. The practical value of safety improvement.

Future research directions may continue to study in the face + finger vein + fingerprint. At present, this research is a simulation system, and the next research will try to make and implement the product.

References

1. Kumar, A., Kwong, C.: Towards contactless, low-cost and accurate 3D fingerprint identification. IEEE Trans. Pattern Anal. Mach. Intell. **37**(3), 681–696 (2015)
2. Crouzet, S.M., Thorpe, S.J.: Low-level cues and ultrafast-face detection. Front. Psychol. **2**, 342 (2011). https://doi.org/10.3389/fpsyg.2011.00342
3. Crouzet, S.M., Kirchner, H., Thorpe, S.J.: Fast saccades toward faces: face detection in just 100 ms. J. Vision **10**(4), 1–17 (2010)
4. Burton, A.M., Bindemann, M.: The role of view in human face detection. Vision Res. **49**(15), 2026–2036 (2009)
5. Zhang, X., Gao, Y.: Face recognition across pose: a review. Pattern Recogn. **42**(11), 2876–2896 (2009)
6. Beymer, D.: Face recognition under varying pose. In: Proceedings of the IEEE Conference on CVPR, Seattle, pp. 756–761 (1994)
7. Nadil, M., Feryel, A., Abdenour, S., Sahbi, L.H.: KCCA-based technique for profile face identification. EURASIP J. Image Video Process. **1**, 1–13 (2017)
8. Viola, P., Jones, M.: Rapid object detection using a boosted cascade of simple features. In: IEEE Computer Society Conference on Computer Vision and Pattern Recognition (CVPR), vol. 1, pp. 511–518 (2001)

Inception Network-Based Weather Image Classification with Pre-filtering Process

Li-Wei Kang[1,2,3]($\boxtimes$), Tian-Zheng Feng[2,3], and Ru-Hong Fu[2]

[1] Graduate School of Engineering Science and Technology,
National Yunlin University of Science and Technology,
Yunlin, Taiwan
lwkang@yuntech.edu.tw
[2] Department of Computer Science and Information Engineering,
National Yunlin University of Science and Technology, Yunlin, Taiwan
[3] Artificial Intelligence Recognition Industry Service Research Center,
National Yunlin University of Science and Technology, Yunlin, Taiwan

Abstract. Visual data (e.g., images/videos) captured from outdoor visual devices are usually degraded by turbid media, such as haze, rain, or snow. Hence, weather conditions would usually disrupt or degrade proper functioning of vision-based applications, such as transportation systems or advanced driver assistance systems, as well as several other outdoor surveillance-based systems. To cope with these problems, removal of weather effects (or the so-called deweathering) from visual data has been critical and received much attention. Therefore, it is important to provide a preprocessing step to automatically decide the current weather condition for input visual data, and then the corresponding proper deweathering operations (e.g., removals of rain or snow) will be properly triggered accordingly. This paper presents an inception network-based weather image classification framework relying on the GoogLeNet by considering the two common weather conditions (with similar characteristics), including rain and snow, in outdoor scenes. For an input image, our method automatically classifies it into one of the two categories or none of them (e.g., sunny or others). We also evaluate the possible impact on image classification performance derived from the image preprocessing via filtering. Extensive experiments conducted on open weather image datasets with/without preprocessing are conducted to evaluate the proposed method and the feasibility has been verified.

Keywords: Weather images · Preprocessing · Filtering · Classification · Recognition · Deep learning · Convolutional neural networks · Inception networks · GoogLeNet

This work was supported in part by Ministry of Science and Technology (MOST), Taiwan, under the Grant MOST 105-2628-E-224-001-MY3. This work was also financially supported by the "Artificial Intelligence Recognition Industry Service Research Center" from The Featured Areas Research Center Program within the framework of the Higher Education Sprout Project by the Ministry of Education (MOE) in Taiwan.

C.-Y. Chang et al. (Eds.): ICS 2018, CCIS 1013, pp. 368–375, 2019.
https://doi.org/10.1007/978-981-13-9190-3_38

1 Introduction

Different weather conditions, such as haze, rain, or snow would cause unpleasing visual effects in visual data (e.g., images/videos) [1]. Such effects may significantly degrade the performances of several outdoor vision systems, such as outdoor surveillance-based object detection, tracking, and recognition, scene analysis and classification, as well as vision-assisted transportation systems and advanced driver assistance systems (ADAS) applications [2]. To cope with the problems, removal of weather effects (or the so-called deweathering) from images/videos has been recently important and received much attention [3–5] (e.g., dehazing, *i.e.*, removal of haze [6–10], deraining, *i.e.*, removal of rain [11–24], and desnowing, *i.e.*, removal of snow [11, 24, 25]). To promptly apply the proper deweathering operation for an input image captured by outdoor visual devices, it is important to first correctly decide the weather condition in the image. Hence, weather image classification is essential for vision-based outdoor applications [26–41]. Based on our explorations of the state-of-the-art approaches, a key technique in the literature consists of the three main steps. The first step is to extract the regions of interests (ROIs) from a weather image (e.g., extraction of the sky region). Then, the second stage is usually to extract some features or descriptors to represent each ROI, followed by the third step applying some classifier to achieve classification of the weather condition for this image. Such approaches may work well for images with clear and easily extracted ROIs. However, for an image without specific or easily-extracted ROI region(s) for describing the weather condition of the image, such approaches may not work well.

To achieve better weather classification performance, deep learning techniques [42–44] have been successfully applied to the applications of weather image classification recently [33, 36, 37, 39–41]. For example, a deep learning-based weather image classification framework based on AlexNet [42] was presented in [33] to classify an input weather image into one of the two classes including sunny and cloudy. Furthermore, a two-class (sunny or cloudy) weather image classification framework based on collaborative learning was presented in [36], where the data-driven convolutional neural network (CNN) feature and well-selected weather-specific features are combined. In addition, a CNN-based multi-task framework was developed in [39] which aims to concurrently tackle weather category classification task and weather-cues segmentation task. In this paper, by considering currently most popular deweathering operations, including deraining [11–24] and desnowing [11, 24, 25], we present a preprocessing framework for weather image classification by considering the three classes of rainy, snowy, and the one (e.g., sunny) for none of the two aforementioned classes. That is, our goal is to automatically online decide the weather condition for an input image captured by any outdoor sensors equipped with deweathering functionalities, and properly trigger the corresponding deweathering operation.

Inspired by the great success achieved by deep learning in numerous perceptual tasks [42–44], we propose to apply the inception network-based deep learning to perform weather image classification relying on GoogLeNet [43]. The main idea of the inception network [43] is based on finding out how an optimal local sparse structure in a CNN can be approximated and covered by readily available dense components. The key is to simultaneously deploy multiple convolution operations with multiple filters and pooling layers in parallel within the same layer. As a result, both of the depth and width of the network are increased while keeping the computational budget constant. On the other hand, before feeding an image into the deep network, we also study the possible impact on classification performance by applying pre-filtering operation [45] to the image for possibly facilitate to extract weather cues.

Fig. 1. Examples of training images (used in the proposed deep model) of (**a**) rain [22, 23]; (**b**) snow [25]; and (**c**) sunny [34, 35].

2 Proposed Inception Network-Based Weather Image Classification Framework

2.1 Problem Formulation and Preprocessing

The main goal of this paper is to learn a classifier to classify each input image to one of the three classes, including rainy, snowy, and other (or none of above). Inspired by the preprocessing of image filtering applied in several image denoising applications, such as image deraining [12–24] and image deblocking [46–49], we propose to first apply the low-pass filtering to an input image I to obtain the low-frequency part of I, denoted by I_{LF}. Then, we calculate the high-frequency part of I as $I_{HF} = I - I_{LF}$. That is, it is expected that some weather cues, such as rain streaks or snow streaks, would be included in the high-frequency part of the image, while the other image basic components are included in the low-frequency part. Based on the suggestion of [46–49], the BM3D (block-matching and 3D filtering) algorithm [45] is selected as the low-pass filter in our method is, which is based on an enhanced sparse representation in transform domain, achieved by grouping similar 2D image fragments (blocks) into 3D data arrays. In our framework, all of the training and testing images are preprocessed via the above-mentioned filtering process to obtain their corresponding high-frequency images while the low-frequency parts are ignored. By collecting a set of N preprocessed training images $\{x^{(i)}\}$ with corresponding labels $\{y^{(i)}\}$, $i = 1, 2, \ldots, N$, our goal is to learn a classifier by optimizing the cross-entropy loss function defined as:

$$\mathcal{L}(\omega) = \sum_{i=1}^{N} \sum_{c=1}^{C} -\mathbf{I}\{y^{(i)} = c\} \log P\left(y^{(i)} = c | x^{(i)}; \omega\right) + \lambda \|\omega\|_2, \qquad (1)$$

where C denotes the number of classes considered ($C = 3$ is used in this paper), I is an indicator function, $y^{(i)} = c$ denotes that the i-th training image belongs to the c-th class, $P(y^{(i)} = c|x^{(i)}; \omega)$ is the predicted probability of the class c given the image $x^{(i)}$, and ω is the weighting parameter set to be learned, and λ is a regularization parameter.

2.2   Network Learning

To realize our inception network-based weather image classification framework, we apply GoogLeNet [43] to be the core of our method. The concept of the inception network mainly comes from the "network in network" presented in [50], which increases the representational power of neural networks with deeper nets needed for image classification purpose. In our method, we directly apply GoogLeNet with modification of output size set to be 3 (the original size of 1,000 was set for the ILSVRC2014 classification contest of 1,000 image classes). Different from the weather classification task presented in 33 with fine-tuning AlexNet 42 to achieve two-class weather classification, this paper proposes to fine-tune GoogLeNet to achieve three-class weather classification.

To train our inception network, we selected the images for training from the Rainy Image Dataset provided by [22, 23], and the Snow100K dataset provided by [25]. In addition, for the other class (not in both of rain and snow classes), we used the related images from the Multi-class Weather Image (MWI) Dataset provided by [34, 35]. Examples of training images are shown in Fig. 1. To optimize the cross-entropy loss function defined in Eq. (1). The proposed model was trained by the back-propagation algorithm with batch SGD (stochastic gradient descend) [51], such that the softmax loss is minimized.

3   Experimental Results

To evaluate the performance of the proposed weather image classification framework, we used the built-in pre-trained GoogLeNet deep architecture within the Caffe software of version 0.15.13 [52] on a PC equipped with Intel® Core™ Core i5-4590 processor, 12 GB memory, and NVIDIA GeForce GTX 1060 GPU. In addition, to establish our training and testing datasets, we randomly extracted 75% of the images from our collected images (from Rainy Image Dataset, [22, 23], Snow100 K dataset [25], and MWI Dataset [34, 35]) for training our deep model, and the rest 25% images were used for testing. The process was performed several times to obtain the final classification accuracy. During the training process, the learning rate is set to 0.01, and our network is trained with a batch-size of 128 in 100 epochs. The weather image classification accuracies of different epochs with and without applying the pre-filtering process obtained by the proposed method were shown in Fig. 2. It can be observed from Fig. 2 that the accuracies with pre-filtering process used are better than those without applying the pre-filtering process before the 30th epoch. That is, the pre-filtering process based on BM3D [45] might be useful for extracting some weather cues for the types of weather conditions revealing high-frequency property, such as rain streaks and snow streaks. Therefore, better classification accuracies would be achieved in earlier epochs with the assistant of the preprocessing. However, with the number of epochs increased, the deep network would learn better features for classification with higher accuracies, and the advantage of the pre-filtering operation would be non-obvious.

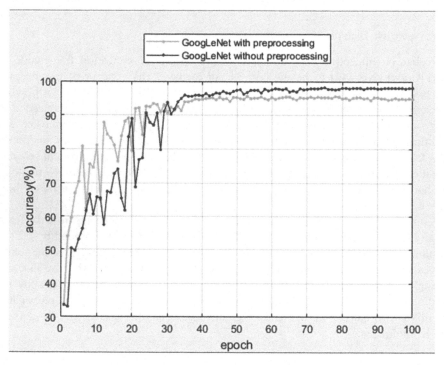

Fig. 2. The weather image classification accuracies of different epochs with and without applying the pre-filtering process obtained by the proposed method.

4   Conclusions

In this paper, we have proposed an inception network-based weather image classification framework with pre-filtering process for classifying each input image into one of the three classes, including rainy, snowy, and other. By applying the GoogLeNet deep CNN model to achieve efficient weather image classification with pre-filtering operation, we found that the pre-filtering process would be useful for extracting some weather cues for the types of weather conditions revealing high-frequency property (e.g., rain streaks and snow streaks), resulting in better accuracies in earlier training epochs. Such preprocessing technique is compatible to several recent state-of-the-art methods for removing weather effects (e.g., [12–24]). This property might be useful for designing a complete system for weather effect detection and removal, which is worthy to be investigated further.

References

1. Nayar, S.K., Narasimhan, S.G.: Vision in bad weather. In: IEEE International Conference on Computer Vision, pp. 820–827 (1999)
2. Shehata, M.S., et al.: Video-based automatic incident detection for smart roads: the outdoor environmental challenges regarding false alarms. IEEE Trans. Intell. Transp. Syst. 9, 349–360 (2008)
3. Narasimhan, S.G., Nayar, S.K.: Interactive deweathering of an image using physical models. In: IEEE Workshop on Color and Photometric Methods in Computer Vision (2003)
4. Kumari, A., Sahoo, S.K.: Real time image and video deweathering: the future prospects and possibilities. Optik-Int. J. Light Electron Opt. 127, 829–839 (2016)
5. Li, Y., You, S., Brown, M.S., Tan, R.T.: Haze visibility enhancement: a survey and quantitative benchmarking. Comput. Vis. Image Underst. 165, 1–16 (2017)
6. He, K., Sun, J., Tang, X.: Single image haze removal using dark channel prior. IEEE Trans. Pattern Anal. Mach. Intell. 33, 2341–2353 (2011)
7. Yeh, C.H., Kang, L.W., Lin, C.Y., Lin, C.Y.: Efficient image/video dehazing through fog density analysis based on pixel-based dark channel prior. In: IEEE International Conference on Information Security and Intelligent Control (2012)
8. Yeh, C.H., Kang, L.W., Lee, M.S., Lin, C.Y.: Haze effect removal from image via haze density estimation in optical model. Opt. Express 21, 27127–27141 (2013)
9. Cai, B., Xu, X., Jia, K., Qing, C., Tao, D.: DehazeNet: an end-to-end system for single image haze removal. IEEE Trans. Image Process. 25, 5187–5198 (2016)
10. Yeh, C.H., Huang, C.H., Kang, L.W., Lin, M.H.: Single image dehazing via deep learning-based image restoration. In: APSIPA Annual Summit and Conference (2018)
11. Barnum, P.C., Narasimhan, S., Kanade, T.: Analysis of rain and snow in frequency space. Int. J. Comput. Vis. 86, 256–274 (2010)
12. Fu, Y.H., Kang, L.W., Lin, C.W., Hsu, C.T.: Single-frame-based rain removal via image decomposition. In: IEEE International Conference on Acoustics, Speech, and Signal Processing (2011)
13. Kang, L.W., Lin, C.W., Fu, Y.H.: Automatic single-image-based rain streaks removal via image decomposition. IEEE Trans. Image Process. 21, 1742–1755 (2012)
14. Kang, L.W., Lin, C.W., Lin, C.T., Lin, Y.C.: Self-learning-based rain streak removal for image/video. In: IEEE International Symposium on Circuits and Systems (2012)
15. Huang, D.A., Kang, L.W., Yang, M.C., Lin, C.W., Wang, Y.C.F.: Context-aware single image rain removal. In: IEEE International Conference on Multimedia and Expo (2012)
16. Chen, D.Y., Chen, C.C., Kang, L.W.: Visual depth guided image rain streaks removal via sparse coding. In: IEEE International Symposium on Intelligent Signal Processing and Communication Systems (2012)
17. Huang, D.A., Kang, L.W., Wang, Y.C.F., Lin, C.W.: Self-learning based image decomposition with applications to single image denoising. IEEE Trans. Multimedia 16, 83–93 (2014)
18. Liu, P.H., Lin, C.Y., Yeh, C.H., Kang, L.W., Lo, K.S.H., Hwang, T.H.: Rain removal using single image based on non-negative matrix factorization. In: International Computer Symposium. Frontiers in Artificial Intelligence and Applications. IOS Press (2014)
19. Chen, D.Y., Chen, C.C., Kang, L.W.: Visual depth guided color image rain streaks removal using sparse coding. IEEE Trans. Circuits Syst. Video Technol. 24, 1430–1455 (2014)
20. Kang, L.W., Yeh, C.H., Chen, D.Y., Lin, C.T.: Self-learning-based signal decomposition for multimedia applications: a review and comparative study. In: APSIPA Annual Summit and Conference (2014)

21. Kang, L.W., Yu, C.M., Lin, C.Y., Yeh, C.H.: Image and video restoration and enhancement via sparse representation. In: Biometrics: Concepts, Methodologies, Tools, and Applications, pp. 501–528. IGI Global (2017)
22. Fu, X., Huang, J., Zeng, D., Huang, Y., Ding, X., Paisley, J.: Removing rain from single images via a deep detail network. In: IEEE Conference on Computer Vision and Pattern Recognition (2017)
23. Fu, X., Huang, J., Ding, X., Liao, Y., Paisley, J.: Clearing the skies: a deep network architecture for single-image rain removal. IEEE Trans. Image Process. **26**, 2944–2956 (2017)
24. Wang, Y., Liu, S., Chen, C., Zeng, B.: A hierarchical approach for rain or snow removing in a single color image. IEEE Trans. Image Process. **26**, 3936–3950 (2017)
25. Liu, Y.F., Jaw, D.W., Huang, S.C., Hwang, J.N.: DesnowNet: context-aware deep network for snow removal. IEEE Trans. Image Process. **27**, 3064–3073 (2018)
26. Kurihata, H., et al.: Rainy weather recognition from in-vehicle camera images for driver assistance. In: IEEE Intelligent Vehicles Symposium, pp. 205–210 (2005)
27. Roser, M., Moosmann, F.: Classification of weather situations on single color images. In: IEEE Intelligent Vehicles Symposium, pp. 798–803 (2008)
28. Yan, X., Luo, Y., Zheng, X.: Weather recognition based on images captured by vision system in vehicle. In: International Symposium on Neural Networks, pp. 390–398 (2009)
29. Shen, L., Tan, P.: Photometric stereo and weather estimation using Internet images. In: IEEE Conference on Computer Vision and Pattern Recognition, pp. 1850–1857 (2009)
30. Bossu, J., Hautiere, N., Tarel, J.: Rain or snow detection in image sequences through use of a histogram of orientation of streaks. Int. J. Comput. Vision **93**, 348–367 (2011)
31. Chen, Z., Yang, F., Lindner, A., Barrenetxea, G., Vetterli, M.: How is the weather: automatic inference from images. In: IEEE International Conference on Image Processing, pp. 1853–1856 (2012)
32. Lu, C., Lin, D., Jia, J., Tang, C.K.: Two-class weather classification. In: IEEE Conference on Computer Vision and Pattern Recognition, pp. 3718–3725 (2014)
33. Elhoseiny, M., Huang, S., Elgammal, A.M.: Weather classification with deep convolutional neural networks. In: IEEE International Conference on Image Processing, pp. 3349–3353 (2015)
34. Zhang, Z., Ma, H.: Multi-class weather classification on single images. In: IEEE International Conference on Image Processing, pp. 4396–4400 (2015)
35. Zhang, Z., Ma, H., Fu, H., Zhang, C.: Scene-free multi-class weather classification on single images. Neurocomputing **207**, 365–373 (2016)
36. Lu, C., Lin, D., Jia, J., Tang, C.K.: Two-class weather classification. IEEE Trans. Pattern Anal. Mach. Intell. **39**, 2510–2524 (2017)
37. Lin, D., Lu, C., Huang, H., Jia, J.: RSCM: region selection and concurrency model for multi-class weather recognition. IEEE Trans. Image Process. **26**, 4154–4167 (2017)
38. Chu, W.T., Zheng, X.Y., Ding, D.S.: Camera as weather sensor: estimating weather information from single images. J. Vis. Commun. Image Represent. **46**, 233–249 (2017)
39. Li, X., Wang, Z., Lu, X.: A multi-task framework for weather recognition. In: ACM Multimedia, pp. 1318–1326 (2017)
40. Guerra, J.C.V., Khanam, Z., Ehsan, S., Stolkin, R., McDonald-Maier, K.: Weather classification: a new multi-class dataset, data augmentation approach and comprehensive evaluations of convolutional neural networks. arXiv:1808.00588 (2018)
41. Kang, L.W., Chou, K.L., Fu, R.F.: Deep learning-based weather image recognition. In: IEEE International Symposium on Computer, Consumer and Control (2018)
42. Krizhevsky, A., Sutskever, I., Hinton, G.E.: ImageNet classification with deep convolutional neural networks, p. 25. Adv. Neural Inf. Process, Syst (2012)

43. Szegedy, C., et al.: Going deeper with convolutions. In: IEEE Conference on Computer Vision and Pattern Recognition (2015)
44. LeCun, Y., Bengio, Y., Hinton, G.E.: Deep learning. Nature **521**, 436–444 (2015)
45. Dabov, K., Foi, A., Katkovnik, V., Egiazarian, K.: Image denoising by sparse 3D transform-domain collaborative filtering. IEEE Trans. Image Process. **16**, 2080–2095 (2007)
46. Chiou, Y.W., Yeh, C.H., Kang, L.W., Lin, C.W., Fan-Jiang, S.J.: Efficient image/video deblocking via sparse representation. In: IEEE Visual Communication and Image Processing Conference (2012)
47. Kang, L.W., Chuang, B.C., Hsu, C.C., Lin, C.W., Yeh, C.H.: Self-learning-based single Image super-resolution of a highly compressed image. In: IEEE International Workshop on Multimedia Signal Processing (2013)
48. Yeh, C.H., Kang, L.W., Chiou, Y.W., Lin, C.W., Fan Jiang, S.J.: Self-learning-based post-processing for image/video deblocking via sparse representation. J. Vis. Commun. Image Represent. **25**, 891–903 (2014)
49. Kang, L.W., Hsu, C.C., Zhuang, B., Lin, C.W., Yeh, C.H.: Learning-based joint super-resolution and deblocking for a highly compressed image. IEEE Trans. Multimedia **17**, 921–934 (2015)
50. Lin, M., Chen, Q., Yan, S.: Network in network. CoRR abs/1312.4400 (2013)
51. LeCun, Y., et al.: Backpropagation applied to handwritten zip code recognition. Neural Comput. **1**, 541–551 (1989)
52. Jia, Y., et al.: Caffe: convolutional architecture for fast feature embedding. In: ACM Multimedia, pp. 675–678 (2014)

Defect Mapping of Lumber Surface by Image Processing for Automatic Glue Fitting

Hsien-Huang Wu[1](✉), Chung-Yuan Hung[1], Bo-jyun Zeng[1], and Ya-Yung Huang[2]

[1] Department of Electrical Engineering,
National Yunlin University of Science and Technology, Douliu, Taiwan
wuhp@yuntech.edu.tw
[2] Graduate School of Engineering Science and Technology,
National Yunlin University of Science and Technology, Douliu, Taiwan

Abstract. While automated optical inspection (AOI) is an effective means to evaluate the quality of wood product, there are very few other applications of AOI in the domestic wood factories. For example, defects of holes or cavities on the surface of wood product currently are still found and filled with glue by human labor. In this paper, we propose using the laser triangulation method of 3D machine vision, to detect defects (holes or cavities) for a large area of lumber surface, and the information collected can be used in the automatic filling machine for further filling process. This method proved to be unaffected by wood surface texture, and can identify the cavity defect with a size larger than 1 mm under the speed of 3.6 m/min for wood with 1.5 m wide.

Keywords: Automated Optical Inspection (AOI) · Triangulation method · Lumber surface · Defect detection

1 Introduction

In the production process of the wood flooring, the staff of quality control needs to check if the surface is flat or not. If there is a hole or crack, the staff fills glue in the defect before follow-up process. Currently, the action of detection and filling glue is mostly executed manually.

In recent years, with the rise of industrial automation, regardless of the technological or traditional industries, manual production has been replaced by automated production. The products of mass production must be inspected for quality management. Manual inspection consumes a lot of human resources, and the inspectors may have different standards for the defects and feel fatigue after a period of time. These factors easily lead the defective products to go downstream. It's a situation that the manufacturers and customers are not happy to see. Nowadays, due to the fact that Automated Optical Inspection (AOI) is booming, the replacement of manual inspection with computer vision can not only improve the quality of products and maintain stability, but also can effectively reduce the waste of raw materials and human labor errors.

In 1998, DT Pham and RJ Alcock conducted a literature collation on the classification and defect detection of wood-based products based on computer vision [1]. It is

© Springer Nature Singapore Pte Ltd. 2019
C.-Y. Chang et al. (Eds.): ICS 2018, CCIS 1013, pp. 376–384, 2019.
https://doi.org/10.1007/978-981-13-9190-3_39

suggested that Automated Visual Inspection (AVI) can detect only the wood surface, and is easy to be affected by shadows, stains, textures, and misjudgment. It also emphasized the importance of lighting in the detection system.

In 2015, Hashim et al. reviewed the automatic visual inspection of wood surfaces [2], and listed related studies using different types of sensors and combination of sensors, as shown in Tables 1 and 2. The multi-sensor approach has a better performance reported in many literatures, but the single sensor is more often used. This is because single optical sensor has the advantage of lower cost, and the ability to be quickly implemented for defect detection on wood surface [3].

Table 1. Related studies on visual sensors for inspection of wood surface defects

Vision sensors	References
Laser scanner	[4]
Optical camera	[5–7]
Optical distance	[8]

Table 2. Related studies on multi sensors for inspection of wood surface defects

Sensor fusion	References
Laser scanner Video camera	[9, 10]
Optical camera Color camera X-ray scanner	[11]

The area camera combined with bright-field front light illumination is used by a lot of related research [5–7, 12, 13]. Results of these research show good performance in the grading, sorting, and cutting of lumber; however, if the found defect is a sound knot on wood, we do not know if it exists a real depression on the wood surface. One approach to avoid this problem for imaging the lumber surface is based on the triangulation using a laser scanner [4], where a line laser light source with grayscale camera are the most widely used [9, 10, 14, 15]. This method has been widely used in the steelmaking industry on-line flatness measurement [16], weld quality inspection [17], and automatic tire inspection [18]. In 1999, Conners et al. patented the wood surface detection system [19] and in 2008, Taylor et al. patented the method of surface detection of wood [20]. In both patents, we can see the application of the laser triangulation method.

Most of the previous research is conducted for surface defect detection on a single and slender lumber. In this paper, we focus on a large area of wood surface for assessing the feasibility of the triangulation method.

2 Method

2.1 Laser Triangulation Method

Laser triangulation method is composed of three elements of camera, laser light source, and the target object. In the laser triangulation system, the laser light projected onto the surface of the object can be observed from the perspective of the camera. The observed stripe cannot get the true height value of the object. However, the angle between the projector and the camera combined with careful calibration can accurately deduce the height of each pixel based on the contour information on the object surface. The basic geometric model can be represented by an active triangulation system, as shown in the following Fig. 1:

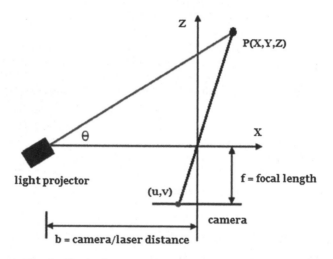

Fig. 1. The basic geometry of active optical triangulation

A light projector is placed at a distance b from the camera projection center which is called baseline. The projector emits an optical plane perpendicular to the XZ plane and is at an angle θ to the baseline. If there is an object in the visible range of the camera and the light plane emitted by the projector intersects the surface of the object, then the intersection point P, and the curve formed by P projection to the image plane is called stripe. Because the points on the stripes are present in the light plane emitted by the projector, it establishes a one-to-one relationship between the image and the three-dimensional coordinate system [21], and the relationship can be formulated as

$$\begin{bmatrix} X \\ Y \\ Z \end{bmatrix} = \frac{b}{f \cot \theta - x} \begin{bmatrix} x \\ y \\ f \end{bmatrix}$$

By measuring a number of objects of known heights, and recording the stripe of the image and its corresponding object height, a LUT (look-up table) can be built.

2.2   Building Look-Up Table

First, we adjust the laser projector so that projection on the platform, which is used to move the target object, can create a stripe parallel to the image plane of the x-axis. Then we place several calibration elements on the platform and record the different height of the location respectively. The following is the calibration results for the application which has the largest height of 45.15 mm. For each real height we have a corresponding position deviation from the stripe in the image, and they were recorded as (height, deviation) pairs. If there exists a linear relationship between the height and deviation, then we can use a simple interpolation method to obtain the height of each point given a deviation value.

In order to verify this linear relation, we calculate the height difference ΔH between two adjacent object points and divided by its corresponding deviation difference Δh in image, and represent it as σ (depth per pixel):

$$\sigma = \Delta H / \Delta h$$

We found that each σ is not the same, as shown in the Table 3. Therefore, if σ is used directly in the interpolation method to predict the height, there will exist a great error.

Table 3. Depth per pixel

Real height (H)	Deviation in the image (h)	Depth/pixel (σ)
45.15	335	
35.15	395	0.167
25.10	451	0.179
15.07	505	0.186
5.07	557	0.192
0	583	0.203

After observing the change of σ values, we use the curve fitting based on the least squares method to replace the commonly used linear interpolation method [22]. The relationship formula is represented as follows:

$$y = ax^2 + bx + c$$

The (h, H) pairs are used as (x, y) and substituted into the formula. Through the implementation of the Cramer's rule, we can find the parameters a, b, and c. Given these three parameters, the deviation h observed in the stripe can be used as x(h) to find the height of the surface of the object y(H). For verification, the more accurate results using quadratic curve fitting are listed in Table 4, where the errors of estimation are all less than 0.1 mm.

Table 4. Using quadratic curve fitting to forecast the height of the object

Real height	Forecast height	Error
45.15	45.178	0.028
35.15	35.074	0.075
25.10	25.143	0.043
15.07	15.107	0.039
5.07	5.018	0.052
0	0.019	0.019

Although the fitting error is small, we cannot guarantee that we can get the same deviation in the image each time for the same height of object. Because it may be affected to the surface smoothness, scratches, reflective and other factors. Therefore, we will claim the current system has an accuracy of ±0.5 mm.

2.3 Flow of Image Processing

While controlling the rotation of the motor to move the measured object, the motor sends a pulse signal at each fixed distance (for example, from an encoder) so the position of each projected stripe can be accurately recorded. The signal triggers the camera to grab the image and each image is executed by the same image processing flow as shown in Fig. 2. We can get the object surface contour depth information for each stripe. After the entire surface of the object are scanned, the collected depth information stored in the memory can be stitched to form a 2.5D image for the scanned surface.

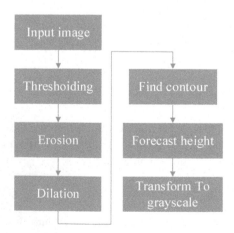

Fig. 2. Image processing flow

3   Results

The proposed lumber surface defect detection system is built on a desktop computer as an experimental platform. The computer has an Intel i7-6700 CPU with 16 GB memory, and Windows 7 Professional 64 bit operating system. The software development environment is Microsoft Visual Studio 2015 and using C# as the development language. The image processing library used is EmguCV.

An industrial grayscale camera of resolution 1280 × 1024 with a cctv lens having focal length of 16 mm was used. As for the laser, we chose a 650 nm red light laser module. Motionnet remote motion control architecture was used to control the SMMC Ezi-SERVO DC closed loop stepping servo motor for moving the target object. Motion module from the slave module sends the trigger signal to control the timing of the camera.

Figure 3(a) shows a small lumber surface acquired by a digital camera. Figure 3(b) is its corresponding 2.5D image that is generated line-by-line and then stitched together after scanning the area by the proposed method. Figure 3(c) is the result after binarizing the 2.5D to show the cavity on the lumber surface.

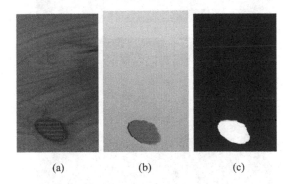

(a)   (b)   (c)

Fig. 3. Various image format of the lumber surface: (a) 2D image, (b) 2.5D image (3) cavity image

To acquire the 2.5D information for a wide area of wood surface, more than one camera is needed to cover the required FOV (field of view). In the following experiment, we use two identical cameras with a FOV of197 mm and placed them side-by-side. Through the stitching in the x-direction, we can detect the lumber surface about 394 mm wide. The accuracy about 0.15 mm per pixel (197 mm/1280～0.15 mm). Figure 4(b) is the 2.5D result of the lumber surface shown in Fig. 4(a). Since the large area of the wood is made of several strips of lumber, the groove between the boards is not defect and should be removed and the final results are shown in Fig. 4(c).

In the result image, the accuracy of the x-axis is the width of the FOV divided by the resolution (that is 0.15 mm); the accuracy of the y-axis is determined by the distance between two trigger signals. At present, the defect detection is conducted by moving the lumber 1 mm for each triggered image acquisition. The grayscale value of

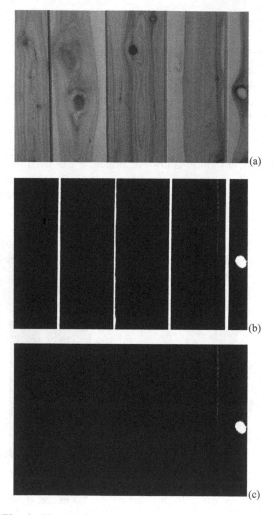

Fig. 4. The result image of using two identical camera

the coordinate (x, y) in the result image is the depth information. According to the rules of x and y axis above, we can find the depth and locate the defects position in Fig. 4(c).

4   Conclusion

At present, the proposed system uses two cameras to inspect the surface of the lumber board and the speed of inspection is about 95 mm per second with very stable acquisition and processing. The system can correctly find the holes or cavities on the surface of the wood, and was not at all affected by wood surface texture. In the future, we hope the system can combine with the gumming machine to automatically fill the cavities on the lumber surface. It then can reduce the cost of a large number of human resources and effectively reduce the waste of raw materials and errors caused by human labor. This eventually will lead the lumber production line gradually towards the goals of industrial automation.

References

1. Pham, D.T., Alcock, R.J.: Automated grading and defect detection: a review. Forest Prod. J. **48**, 34–42 (1998)
2. Hashim, U.R., Hashim, S.Z., Muda, A.K.: Automated vision inspection of timber surface defect: a review. Jurnal Teknologi **77**, 127–135 (2015)
3. Estévez, P.A., Perez, C.A., Goles, E.: Genetic input selection to a neural classifier for defect classification of radiata pine boards. Forest Prod. J. **53**, 87 (2003)
4. Hu, C., Tanaka, C., Ohtani, T.: Locating and identifying splits and holes on sugi by the laser displacement sensor. J. Wood Sci. **49**, 492–498 (2003)
5. Estevez, P., Fernandez, M., Alcock, R., Packianather, M.: Selection of features for the classification of wood board defect. In: Ninth International Conference on Artificial Neural Networks, pp. 347–352 (1999)
6. Niskanen, M., Silvén, O., Kauppinen, H.: Experiments with SOM based inspection of wood. In: International Conference on Quality Control by Artificial Vision (QCAV2001), pp. 311–316 (2001)
7. Hu, C., Tanaka, C., Ohtani, T.: Locating and identifying sound knots and dead knots on sugi by the rule-based color vision system. J. Wood Sci. **50**, 115–122 (2004)
8. Francini, F., Longobardi, G., Sansoni, P., Euzzor, S., Ciamberlini, C.: Identification of timber deformations. J. Opt. A: Pure Appl. Opt. **4**, 406–412 (2002)
9. Lee, S.-M., Abbott, A.L., Schmoldt, D.L.: Surface shape analysis of rough lumber for wane detection. Comput. Electron. Agric. **41**, 121–137 (2003)
10. Lee, S.-M., Araman, P.A., Abbott, A.L., Winn, M.: Automated grading, upgrading, and cuttings prediction of surfaced dry hardwood lumber. In: Proceedings of 6th International Symposium on Image and Signal Processing and Analysis, pp. 371–376 (2009)
11. Kline, D.E., Surak, C., Araman, P.A.: Automated hardwood lumber grading utilizing a multiple sensor machine vision technology. Comput. Electron. Agric. **41**, 139–155 (2003)
12. Hittawe, M.M., Muddamsetty, S.M., Sidibé, D., Mériaudeau, F.: Multiple features extraction for timber defects detection and classification using SVM. In: IEEE International Conference on Image Processing (ICIP), pp. 427–431 (2015)
13. Cavalin, P., Oliveira, L., Koerich, A., Britto, A.: Wood defect detection using grayscale images and an optimized feature set. In: 32nd Annual Conference on Industrial Electronics, IECON 2006, pp. 3408–3412 (2006)
14. Astrand, E., Astrom, A.: A single chip multi-function sensor system for wood inspection. In: 12th IAPR International Conference on Pattern Recognition, pp. 300–304 (1994)
15. 林建忠:雷射測距技術與研究現況. Photonics Industry & Technology Development Association (PIDA) (1999)
16. Molleda, J., Usamentiaga, R., García, D.F.: On-line flatness measurement in the steelmaking industry. Sensors **13**, 10245–10272 (2013)
17. Huang, W., Kovacevic, R.: A laser-based vision system for weld quality inspection. Sensors **11**, 506–521 (2011)
18. Frosio, I., Borghese, N.A., Tirelli, P., Venturino, G., Rotondo, G.: Flexible and low cost laser scanner for automatic tyre inspection. In: IEEE Instrumentation and Measurement Technology Conference (I2MTC), pp. 1–5 (2011)

19. Conners, R.W., Kline, D. E., Araman, P.A., Xiangyu Xiao, R., Drayer, T.H.: Defect detection system for lumber. United States Patent (1999)
20. Taylor, T.J., Seattle, W.: Methods for detecting compression wood in lumber. United States Patent (2008)
21. Trucco, E., Verri, A.: Introductory Techniques for 3-D Computer Vision, pp. 44–47. Prentice-Hall, Inc. (1998)
22. Alex@UEA: Least Squares Regression for Quadratic Curve Fitting. In: CodeProject (2011)

Software Testing Levels in Internet of Things (IoT) Architecture

Teik-Boon Tan^(⊠) 🆔 and Wai-Khuen Cheng^(⊠) 🆔

Universiti Tunku Abdul Rahman, Kampar, Malaysia
{tantb, chengwk}@utar.edu.my

Abstract. Testing the Internet of Things (IoT) solution is complex as it involves a diversification of implementation of smart objects that adopt a diverse and complex communication protocols. It is doubtful whether tests done in IoT solution have been adequately sufficient and scalable. This paper proposed a mapping of the IoT architecture to the conventional software test levels. The test levels shall provide a better view for tester to conduct tests based on different focus of the level.

Keywords: Internet of Things · Testing · Test levels · Challenges of IoT tests

1 Introduction

The applications of Internet of Things (IoT) with the Big Data trend is seen to be the trend for the next few years as more and smart objects are entering into the market with the expectation of 25 to 50 billions connected devices by the year 2025 [1]. One can say that IoT shall be providing huge potential for growth in development of applications from various fields. It could be for smart cities, smart farming, health tracking and management. Generally, IoT comprises of growing number of heterogeneous smart objects that are interconnected for data exchange using different protocols over the Internet [2]. The primary concept is to connect every "Things" to the Internet which can be implemented infrastructure of sensors that are deployed in buildings, external areas and carry within a body. The scales IoT implementation can be either very small or big scales. The diversification of IoT platform (implemented everywhere and different scales) has given rise on how testers are able to test sufficiently in such environment. At presence, testers tend to focus only on the local devices or the edges as the main test objects which can be regarded as insufficient to cover the communication of devices in large scale IoT solutions [3]. This paper outlines how the traditional software test levels can be adopted to provide views to test level in the IoT architecture. The representation shall be useful for tester to focus on the relevant aspect of the IoT implementations.

© Springer Nature Singapore Pte Ltd. 2019
C.-Y. Chang et al. (Eds.): ICS 2018, CCIS 1013, pp. 385–390, 2019.
https://doi.org/10.1007/978-981-13-9190-3_40

2   Background

Arguably IoT seems to be similar to the normal software in terms of functionality especially when functionality tests have to be conducted. IoT implementation however poses a problem of isolation of tests as there is a need to combine different hardware, software and network diversification. Network of IoT platform can include different protocols for data transmission and data exchange [4]. Testing is challenging in a large scale IoT implementation there shall be high amount of collaborative devices with requirements of complexed coordination due to the size [5]. Hence, there is need for proper levels of view of IoT platform in testing.

3   IoT Architecture

In this section, the general architecture of IoT is discussed. The architecture is a generic IoT architecture that have three main components namely Devices, Gateways and Communications and Application component [6]. Devices consist of the hardware that operates at variety of environment that can include indoor, outdoor, underwater and wearables. Most of these devices are tightly coupled to the platform implementation [7].

At middle layer shall be the gateways where the gateways shall be centre point of communication amongst the devices. The two common approaches of IoT communication shall be Constrained Application Protocol (CoAP) [8] and Message Queue Telemetry Transport (MQTT) [9]. The exchange of data shall involve communication between the sensors, sensors to gateways and gateways to gateways.

Application layer is actually concerning how to provide useful and accurate service to the ultimate users of the IoT system. The main focus shall be the data. The data shall be refined and further processed in accordance to the needs of the application. Data can be transferred to a Cloud Platform for further data analytic [10].

4   Software Test Levels

Software testing contains both verification (all specified requirements have been fulfilled) and validation processes (all the outcomes or test objects is complete). The processes is used in software testing for detecting bugs, for ensuring quality of products fulfilled and ensuring the application is for fit for its purpose [11].

Conventionally, the broad tests of software can be categorized into functional and non-functional tests. Software tests are further categorized to test levels to have better definition of software tests boundaries and test purposes. The tests levels are unit test, integration test, system test and acceptance test (see Fig. 1).

Unit is the component identifiable or testable parts of the program. It is the starting part of tests to be conducted in software testing involving codes. It is a technical test of the components therefore it is conducted by the developer of the unit. Unit testing is test to be done in isolation of other units. Isolation is achievable using the skeletal implementation of other related component using stubs and drivers.

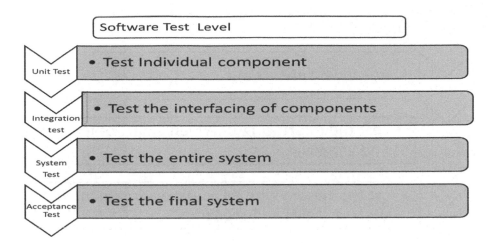

Fig. 1. Test levels of software.

Integration test is to test the interfacing part of the units or components of the software. The units are joint or integrated part by part to test whether the integration contains any defects or not. The tester needs to decide on how these components are integrated. The approaches can be big-bang integration, bottom-up and top-down.

System test is to test the system as a whole in the similar environment of the actual system. The software is tested in accordance to the needs of software requirement specifications and software design specification. Tests shall be conducted at the development side from development perspective to ensure the software fulfils requirements defined. Standard tests are on the usage of the system in actual environment. Business processes and use cases shall be used as the basis for tests. Some non-functional requirements can be tested in this level.

Acceptance test is the validation process as to decide whether the software can be accepted by the user or client. Acceptance testing is primarily to establish confidence in the product and evaluate whether the software is fit to be used. It is from the perspective of the users. The tests therefore involved different angle of the software. It can be on contractual, legal, user acceptance, testing the software in multiple configurations and operational [12].

5 Test Levels for IoT Architecture and Challenges

IoT architecture as a matter fact can have similar software test levels.

With reference to the Fig. 2, IoT architecture can be broken into level similar to the software test levels. The same levels are applied but with different test items and test techniques to be employed as IoT is a type of solution involved multiple smart objects with diverse communication requirements and protocols.

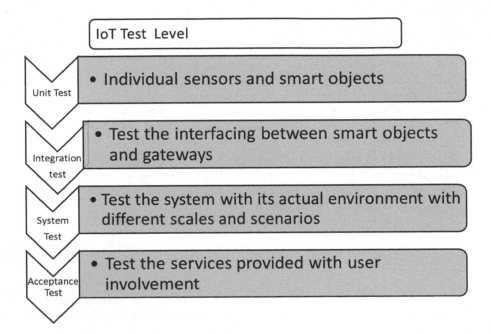

Fig. 2. Test levels of IoT.

5.1 Unit Test Level

At the component level, the identifiable units of IoT platform are actually the smart objects, sensors and gateways. In following the standard practice of Unit testing, each object in the IoT architecture is tested individually to ensure there are no defects or faults occurrence when tested. Units that are related to the unit under test needs to be replaced with skeletal units (with stubs or drivers) just provide feedbacks on data. Testers need to test whether sensors and smart objects are able to make measurement and able to exchange data. In addition, gateways are to be tested for data collections and aggregation.

Unit testing in IoT poses a challenge to tester as these units are constrained devices [7, 13] or they have limited resources. These devices are basically constrained low powered feature (sensors need to operate a few years), at times limited connectivity availability, low storage and hardware dependent.

5.2 Integration Test Level

In integration test tester needs to start joining or integrate component of things and gateway to test the interfaces induce any fault when integrated. The IoT platform consists of various networks devices and communication protocols [14]. The integration technique can be similar to the software integration test technique like top down or bottom up. Integration tests ought to cover failure in communication from the sensors, interfacing different types of sensors, capability of gateway to handle communication from multiple sensors and capability of gateways to handle different types of communication protocols (MQTT, CoAP, etc.).

Integration test poses challenges of combination of devices and network structure in testing. Tester needs to either simulate the environment for integration to be done or provide actual environment (test bed) for testing [14].

5.3 System Test Level

System test level means that the IoT solution to be tested as a whole system. It is tests to be executed before the actual deployment at the actual site. The system needs to be very similar or the same as the real implementation. The test is to be done by tester from the perspective of developer.

Due to the nature of heterogeneous nature of IoT and the complexity it is appropriate to test or simulate the IoT application before deployment. However, tests conducted are small scales and tend to be localized with only partial integration of devices and gateways [5], Preparing environment that can be used in modelling and testing IoT applications is hard due especially in the large scale IoT scenarios. Tester can only rely on good simulation tools and techniques for scalability.

Tester can rely on IoT simulation tools for preparing the tests before deployment. However not all simulators are suitable to model all supported architecture and components like sensors and gateways. Testbeds environment provided is expensive, hard to use and hard to maintain where there is change of setting [15].

5.4 Acceptance Test Level

Acceptance Test is on whether the service provided by system is acceptable to ultimate users. One of the test that is suitable for IoT platform is user acceptance test. User shall determine the IoT solution is able to provide useful and fitting service to them.

There are large quantities of data in IoT platform as multiple sensors are deployed to get measurement of things at the deployed sites. Acceptance test in IoT shall be to test the data intensive functionalities of the system. Acceptance testing therefore shall cover data profile development from aggregation of data, analysis of data and application to domains.

The challenge of acceptance test is on quality of service of data transmission and important metrics to be used for analytics [16]. Tester needs to ensure quality of connections and measurements as sensor nodes can be dispersed and ever changing in behavior.

6 Conclusion

The key of good testing is always test in isolation. Isolation is able to help tester to trace and identify which device, component, interface or sub-part causes failures in the system. The software test level from unit test, integration test, system test to acceptance test, separate the focus of part of the software that needs to be tested. Test level approach can be applicable to IoT architecture as well. Testers however need to be aware what shall be tested in each level of the IoT test level. In the unit test level the focus is on individual functionality of the sensors, smart objects and gateways. Secondly in the integration test level the primary concern is to test integration the IoT devices part by part and it is more a localize test of sub-components. The communication and exchanges of data are the main tests to be conducted. Thirdly, the system test is on the testing the entire IoT solution. Unlike the integration test, the system test requirement requires a more complex test that could involve large scale testing. Simulation tools can be adopted to simulate the environment. The fourth level is the acceptance test in which a user centric approach shall be adopted. The ultimate aim is to ensure the user is able to use and apply the data collected to a particular domain. The proposed test level is to allow tester to determine what to be tested in IoT and there are still challenges to be solved.

References

1. Evans, D.: The Internet of Things - how the next evolution of the internet is changing everything, CISCO white paper (2011)
2. Rosenkranz, P., Wählisch, M., Baccelli, E., Ortmann, L.: A distributed test system architecture for open-source IoT software. In: Proceedings of the 2015 Workshop on IoT Challenges in Mobile and Industrial Systems - IoT-Sys 2015 (2015)
3. Hagar, J.D.: Software test architectures and advanced support environments for IoT. In: IEEE International Conference on Software Testing, Verification and Validation Workshops (ICSTW), Vasteras, pp. 252–256 (2018)
4. Gardašević, G., et al.: The IoT architectural framework, design issues and application domains. Wirel. Pers. Commun. **92**, 127–148 (2017)
5. Kim, H., et al.: IoT-TaaS: towards a prospective IoT testing framework. IEEE Access **6**, 15480–15493 (2018)
6. Ojie, E., Pereira, E.: Exploring dependability issues in IoT applications. In: Proceedings of the Second International Conference on Internet of Things, Data and Cloud Computing (2017)
7. Marinissen, E.J., et al.: IoT: source of test challenges. In: 21th IEEE European Test Symposium (ETS), Amsterdam, pp. 1–10 (2016)
8. Constrained Application Protocol. http://coap.technology
9. Message Queue Transport. http://mqtt.org/
10. Kanstrén, T., Mäkelä, J., Karhula, P.: Architectures and experiences in testing IoT communications. In: IEEE International Conference on Software Testing, Verification and Validation Workshops (ICSTW), Vasteras, pp. 98–103 (2018)
11. Myers, G.: The Art of Software Testing, 2nd edn. (2004)
12. Bourque, P., Fairley, R.E.: Guide to the Software Engineering - Body of Knowledge (2014)
13. Bormann, A.K.C., Ersue, M.: Terminology for constrained node networks. Internet Engineering Task Force (IETF), Informational 2070-1721 (2014)
14. D'Angelo, G., Ferretti, S., Ghini, V.: Simulation of the Internet of Things. In: International Conference on High Performance Computing & Simulation (HPCS), Innsbruck, pp. 1–8 (2016)
15. Rosenkranz, P., Wählisch, M., Baccelli, E., Ortmann, L.: A distributed test system architecture for open-source IoT software. In: Proceedings of the 2015 Workshop on IoT Challenges in Mobile and Industrial Systems, pp. 43–48 (2015)
16. Kanstrén, T.: Experiences in testing and analysing data intensive systems. In: IEEE International Conference on Software Quality, Reliability and Security Companion (QRS-C), Prague, pp. 589–590 (2017)

The Modeling of Path Planning for Fire Evacuation

Ching-Lung Chang$^{(\boxtimes)}$ and Yi-Lin Tsai

Department of CSIE, National Yunlin University of Science and Technology,
Douliu, Taiwan
chang@yuntech.edu.tw

Abstract. Based on the sensing network to implement the fire emergency escape path planning. Unlike other planning methods, this paper uses grid technology to consider factors such as the impact of crowd density on travel time, smoke diffusion, and the upper limit of space/aisle accommodation. At the time of the fire, the evacuation path planning problem at each location is transformed into the optimization. In the model, a balanced evacuation was considered to achieve the goal of evacuation of the crowd. In the paper, the simulated annealing algorithm was used to solve the optimization model and the experimental results were verified.

Keywords: Emergency evacuation · Optimal modeling · Simulated annealing · Load balancing

1 Introduction

According to statistics, about 90% of modern people are in the indoor environment. Buildings are now moving toward complications and tall buildings, so once an emergency is encountered. Such as earthquakes, fires, etc., this kind of environment is easy to cause evacuation, it is easy to squeeze in the same area or lose its way, causing heavy casualties. From the information provided by the Fire Department Global Information Network of the Ministry of the Interior, we can know the damage, financial and martyrdom causes caused by fire.

The use of sensing networks for fire escape route planning has always been an important issue. The paper [1] uses sensing network technology and uses Ad Hoc transmission to transmit environmental information back to the control center. The system architecture is shown in Fig. 1. Considering multiple security exit environments, the sensing nodes are divided into environment sensing nodes and exit sensing nodes, and the environment sensing nodes detect the fire points. The message is sent back to the control center as an Ad Hoc network. The control center decides the area affected by the control center, and the export to each sensing node establishes the shortest path tree. Then using the developed algorithm, adjust the shortest path tree where the sensing node is located. Consider balanced evacuation to get the shortest crowd evacuation time goal.

Paper [2] considers floor issues and congestion issues. Floor problems are solved by adding stairs between floors, as shown in Fig. 2. This article is based on per-person

© Springer Nature Singapore Pte Ltd. 2019
C.-Y. Chang et al. (Eds.): ICS 2018, CCIS 1013, pp. 391–398, 2019.
https://doi.org/10.1007/978-981-13-9190-3_41

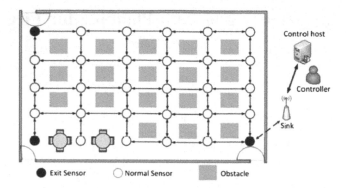

Fig. 1. Indoor emergency evacuation guidance system architecture Indoor.

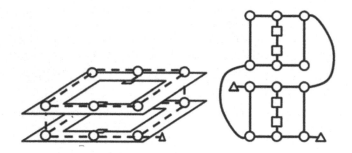

Fig. 2. Solve floor problems.

path planning, using the Dijkstra algorithm to plan the path. When congestion occurs, look at the time they spend on the second escape route, and let the second escape route take the second escape route if it is shorter. If the encounters are the same, one randomly chooses to take the second escape route. This is done in order to achieve the complete evacuation, so as to achieve the goal of the minimum time for evacuation.

The paper [3] uses a region as a unit to do path planning, considers the capacity of an outlet and a node, and makes a risk assessment of the path. Because the shortest path is not always the same as the route with the least risk, the factors considered are elevators, floors, and local observations. The higher the risk, the greater the weight, and the weight is an asymmetric function. So this paper is to find the minimum weight and load balancing as the goal.

2   Path Planning Modeling

The purpose of this paper's fire evacuation route planning is to complete the evacuation of the personnel in the shortest possible time and to avoid prolonged evacuation time leading to more casualties. The avoidance of congestion in escape is one of the most effective methods, so we consider the evacuation of each area and the number of walkways that can be accommodated, the time needed to move, the location of the exit, the impact of crowd density on the movement rate of the crowd, and the location of the fire at the opposite floor and the spread of smoke to get the minimum time for evacuation.

Different from other papers to find evacuation routes by algorithm, this dissertation changes the evacuation route problem into a linear programming model. Establish models to consider the factors mentioned in the above Syria, such as the location of personnel, capacity constraints, population density and other factors. The minimum time to get all personnel evacuated to a safe location of purpose. We consider the impact of population density on population movement rate. We consider the impact of population density on the rate of population movement.

2.1 Optimization Modeling

Translate the problem of evacuation path planning into network traffic problems in order to obtain the best or nearly optimal solution. The main purpose is to find out the evacuation time and minimize it.

Given Parameters:

Graph G = (N, L): N is {1, 2, ..., n} which collects all of nodes in the network. L is the link set which represents to the walkways, stairs within in the building. The link (i, j) has the parameters of link length lij and link capacity cij.

S: The set of nodes where people are when an emergency occurs, also known as a set of source nodes. The symbol si is the number of users at nodes i when the fire occur, where i ☐ S.

☐ i: The smoke diffuse time from the fire occur location to the node i. If ☐ i = 0 mean the location i is the fire occur point.

f((i, j), p): The moving time of p people pass through link (i, j), where link (i, j) ☐ L.

E: Stands for the virtual exit. The capacity of node E (i.e. cE) is infinity. The moving time from the exit node to the E is zero.

T = {0, 1, ..., K}: Convert the continuous time to discrete time. Where time 0 mean the fire occurs time and time K mean the maximum time of evacuation.

M: is a large value.

Decision Variables

x_{ij}^d: $x_{ij}^d = 1$, if link (i, j) is an escape path of source node d; $x_{ij}^d = 0$, otherwise.

$\bar{\delta}_i^t$: the number of people who escaped at node i at time t, where $i \in N$, $t \in T$.

$^d\delta_i^t$: the number of people who escaped from source node d at node i at time t, where $i \in$ N, $t \in T$, $d \in S$.

$^dr_i^t$: if $^dr_i^t = 1$ means the people who escaped from source node d will arrives at node i at time t, where $i \in N$, $t \in T$, $d \in S$.

Objective function: min Φ

subject to

$$\sum_{\{j:(i,j)\in L\}} x_{ij}^d - \sum_{\{j:(j,i)\in L\}} x_{ji}^d = \begin{cases} 1, & if\ i = d \\ -1, & if\ i = E \\ 0, & otherwise \end{cases} , \text{where } d \in S, i \in N \quad (1)$$

$$\sum_{t \in T} {}^d r_j^t \times t = x_{ij}^d \left(\sum_{t \in T} {}^d r_i^t \times \left(t + f\left((i,j), \bar{\delta}_i^t \right) \right) \right), i \in N, d \in S, (i,j) \in L \quad (2)$$

$$\sum_{t \in T} {}^d r_i^t \le 1, i \in N, d \in S \quad (3)$$

$$^d \delta_i^t = {}^d r_i^t \times \bar{\delta}_d^0, i \in N, t \in T, d \in S \quad (4)$$

$$\bar{\delta}_i^t = \sum_{d \in S} {}^d \delta_i^t, i \in N, t \in T \quad (5)$$

$$\sum_{(i,j) \in L} \sum_{d \in S} {}^d r_i^t \times x_{ij}^d \le 1, i \in N, t \in T \quad (6)$$

$$\bar{\delta}_i^t \le \sum_{d \in S} x_{ij}^d \times {}^d r_i^t \times u_{ij}, t \in T, i \in N, (i,j) \in L \quad (7)$$

$$\bar{\delta}_i^t \le c_i, i \in N, t \in T \quad (8)$$

$$^d r_i^t \times t \le \Phi, d \in S, i \in N, t \in T \quad (9)$$

Among them, the constrain (1) is that the source node finds a way to reach the exit node; the restriction formula (2) is to calculate the number of people who reach the node j in the d escape path; The constrain (3), (4), and (5) are used to calculate the value of the $^d \delta_i^t$ and value $\bar{\delta}_i^t$. In our formulation, people in the same source node must be evacuated at the same route. This requirement is provided by constrain (6). Equations (7) and (8) are capacity constrain. Equation (9) is used to calculate the longest time spent in fire evacuation.

2.2   Simulated Annealing

In order to solve our linear programming model, we use simulated annealing algorithm to solve this model. Simulated Annealing (SA) is one of the methods used to solve the optimization problem to find the best solution or approximate solution. Mainly based on the principle of statistical thermodynamics, simulating the phenomenon that the object can achieve the lowest temperature state during annealing, a global optimization method has been developed. The operation of SA is shown below.

1. Set initial parameters. The starting temperature of this paper is 1000°, the end temperature is 10°, the cooling rate is 0.95, and the number of overlapping bands is 1000.
2. Use the Dijkstra algorithm to generate the initial solution. After determining the initial solution, check whether the capacity of the node or the link is exceeded and whether the smoke has passed through the dense smoke area. If it does not match, adjust the path so that it meets the feasible solution.
3. Zero the number of iterations.

4. Generate new neighborhood solutions centered on the current solution.
5. Use Metropolis acceptance rules to decide whether to accept the neighborhood solution as the current solution.
6. Then increase the number of overlaps and then determine if the number of cools has been reached. If it does, cool it. If not, go back to the fourth step.
7. After cooling down, it is necessary to judge whether the end temperature has been reached. If the current solution is reached, it is the final solution; if not, it will return to the third step.

3 Simulation Results

3.1 Simulation Environment

In order to understand the application of the proposed method to buildings with different indoor structures, we simulated two topologies (a) and (b) in Fig. 3 to observe possible results. The circle in the figure is a node, the line between the circle and the circle is a link, the triangle is a virtual node, and the nodes of the same color are the same floor, wherein the green is the first layer, the blue is the second layer, and the red is the third layer. The number of people, capacity, length, etc. of each topology are listed in Table 1.

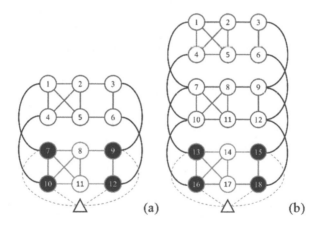

Fig. 3. Simulation topologies. (Color figure online)

3.2 Simulation Results

In the same topographical environment, the proposed method and the reference [4] has three comparisons: cumulative number of escapes, crowd in the area, and the relationship between the number of people above the fire floor and time.

In the case of the average population distribution, Figs. 4 and 5 show the cumulative number of people who have escaped buildings per second. It can be seen from

Table 1. Parameters used in each topology

	Topology (a)	Topology (b)
Number of nodes	12	18
Total people	18	25
Number of source nodes	5	7
Number of floors	2	3
Capacity of area	5–10	5–10
Capacity of walkway	5–10	5–10
Length of walkway	1–5	1–5

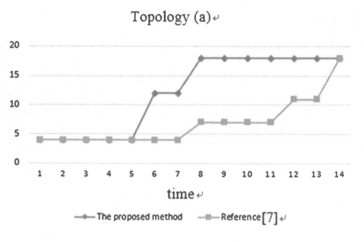

Fig. 4. The cumulative number of escapes in Topology (a)

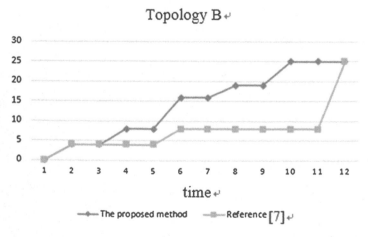

Fig. 5. The cumulative number of escapes in Topology (b)

these figures that the proposed method has the least escape time. Comparing with the reference [4], evacuation time of the proposed method is about 43% faster in topology (a), evacuation time of the proposed method is about 17% faster in topology (b).

The degree of congestion is the number of people in the area divided by the maximum capacity of the area. At each time point, the most crowded area in the time zone is taken. In the case of the average population distribution, Figs. 6 and 7 show the degree of congestion. Because we consider the impact of population density on the rate of movement of the crowd, the degree of congestion in the proposed method is better than reference [4].

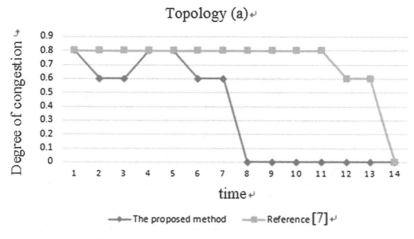

Fig. 6. Degree of congestion in Topology (a)

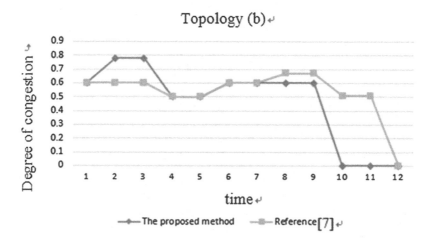

Fig. 7. Degree of congestion in Topology (b)

4 Checklist of Items to Be Sent to Your Conference Contact

This work applies technology of Wireless Sensor Network to propose an optimization-based model for the fire emergency evacuation problem and designs the heuristic approach to solve this problem. The proposed optimization-based model considers more factors including population density, smoke spread, the capacity of each area, the capacity of the walkways or staircases, the time required to move people in each area and walkway, the location where the fires occurred, the number of people in the area, the location of the exits, the area of the fire, escape direction, and the effect of population density on population movement rate. Thanks to more considerations, we get better results.

References

1. Radianti, J., Granmo, O.-C., Bouhmala, N., Sarshar, P., Yazidi, A., Gonzalez, J.: Crowd models for emergency evacuation: a review targeting human-centered sensing. In: Proceedings of the 46th Annual Hawaii International Conference on System Sciences (HICSS 2013), pp. 156–165. IEEE, Wailea, Hawaii, January 2013
2. Tabirca, T., Brown, K.N., Sreenan, C.J.: A dynamic model for fire emergency evacuation based on wireless sensor networks. In: Proceedings of International Symposium on Parallel Distributed Computing, pp. 29–36, June 2009
3. Hadzic, T., Brown, K.N., Sreenan, C.J.: Real-time pedestrian evacuation planning during emergency. In: Proceedings of IEEE International Conference on Tools Artificial Intelligence, pp. 597–604 (2011)
4. Escolar, S., Villa, D., Villanueva, F., Cantarero, R., Lopez, J.: An adaptive emergency protocol for people evacuation in high-rise buildings. In: IEEE Symposium on Computers And Communication (ISCC). https://doi.org/10.1109/iscc.2016.754376

Smart Automated Rubber Mixer System Implemented by Internet of Things for Tire Manufacturing

Yu-Chen Jhu and Chien-Chou Lin(⊠)

National Yunlin University of Science and Technology, Yunlin, Taiwan, R.O.C.
linchien@yuntech.edu.tw

Abstract. In this paper, a PC/PLC integrated mixer system is proposed and implemented. The proposed system uses a PLC (Programmable Logic Controller) to control the mixing stage and two PCs for monitoring the whole process and dispatching the daily manufacturing order. One of PCs works as a database server that provides a web interface to the manufacturing manager. In the central control room, the manufacturing manager dispatches the manufacturing order, including formulas and the number of batches. These commands are sent to another PC, an industrial PC, which can communicate with the PLC. Some parameters are also sent to PLC via this IPC, e.g., the times of each step. The IPC gathers the system information and checks that all materials are met the criterion. The IPC also shows the real-time manufacturing information on the screen to inform the operators. With the integration of the advantages of PC's networking capabilities, data storage capacity and PLC's real-time control, the proposed system provides a new generation of industrial 4.0 automated production system which is more stable and can improve the quality of production.

Keywords: Automation · Internet of Thing · Sensors · Website remoting · PLC · Rubber mixer · Tire manufacturing

1 Introduction

Nowadays, tires manufacturing is based on a common-used processes and machinery in many tire factories over the world. There are many procedures with several materials in the whole tire manufacturing. The most important material is rubber because more than 80% material of a tire is rubber [1]. The quality of a tire is depended on rubbers. Different types of tires are made by different rubbers. Tire rubber is a mixture composed of natural/synthetic rubber, carbon fiber, sulfur mixing. During tire rubber preparing procedure, all the materials, including natural/synthetic rubber, carbon fiber, sulfur…etc., are mixed by the rubber mixer [2, 3]. In order to obtain the rubber with a stable quality, the filler and raw rubber have to be mixed fully in the mixer. In this paper, we focus on this important procedure of the whole tire manufacturing, tire rubber mixing, to improve the software and the workflow of the conventional rubber mixer and collect the sensor data during the mixing process.

© Springer Nature Singapore Pte Ltd. 2019
C.-Y. Chang et al. (Eds.): ICS 2018, CCIS 1013, pp. 399–405, 2019.
https://doi.org/10.1007/978-981-13-9190-3_42

Recently, Internet of Things (IoT) is new technology widely used in manufacturing [4]. However, for over 50-years-old tire companies, IoT technology is absent from the conventional rubber mixers. In general, the conventional rubber mixers were controlled by the PLC and all materials were prepared by the operators. The automatic mixing procedure was programmed in the PLC and the operator pressed the start button after material preparing ready. At the same time, the operators were asked to measure and to record the weights of materials accorder the daily production schedule.

The conventional complete operations are described as follows. First, the supervisor dispatches the daily production schedule in the central control room including formulas and the number of batches. The operator inputs the production data by using the human-machine interface (HMI) and then starts to prepare for the materials. When the materials are prepared ready, the operator starts the rubber mixer system.

Usually, the rubber mixing process concludes following steps [5, 6]: (i) Master motor starting up and starting operation. (ii) Drop door closed, Ram up. (iii) Starting automatic mixing steps. (iv) Hopper door opened; Compound input; Hopper door closed; Weight down. (v) Ram up; Hopper door opened; Chemical powders input; Ram down. (vi) Time's up; Oil used; Ram up; Oil input; Ram down; Time's up. (vii) Mixing completed; Ram up; Ram down; Dump door opened; Ram down; Hopper door closed. (viii) Mixing completed; Wait for a predetermined time period; Ram up; Drop door closed; Hopper door opened. (ix) Bake to step (ii), and start a new cycle.

In order to implement an IoT-based rubber mixer, five issues have to be addressed. Firstly, the server in central control room doesn't have the real-time status of the mixer control system. The supervisor cannot know the current mixing situation in central control room. The second issue is about the accuracy of the used material. In conventional rubber system, material weighing and the weighing results are judged by the operators, while, with this way, it is easy to influence the amount of the used material. The third problem is about the method of production recording. In the past, production record was processed by operators' handwriting. Although this method has been operating for several years, it still has some problems and mistakes that caused by human carelessness. The fourth problem is about the system flexibility. The control system of the convenient rubber mixer is used by the PLC, so the flexibly of PLC is limited. Therefore, the supervisors cannot modify manufacturing parameters easily. The last problem is sensor data collection. Because the PLC cannot store data, those data during mixing, including mixing temperature, energy consumption…etc. will be discarded after a process cycle. It is hard to archive smart manufacturing.

This paper proposes an integrated system, which is composed of a PC and PLC to improve the automation ability and adjustability of the conventional rubber mixer. The advantage of the former is multi-tasking, good networking and huge data storage and the advantage of the latter are good at real-time control and robust for industrial applications. The rest of this paper is organized as follows. In Sect. 2, we propose an Integrated PC/PLC Rubber Mixer System. Section 3 shows and discusses the experimental results. Section 4 draws the conclusion of this paper.

2   The Proposed Integrated PC/PLC Rubber Mixer System

In Fig. 1, the proposed system consists of three PC systems and one PLC system. The PCs include a master PC in the central control room, a database server in headquarter, and an IPC in the working space. The proposed system has five key functions. Firstly, the server in the central control room will issue the daily production schedule to the PC of the mixer system, which includes the number of batches and the formulas. The PC sets the production parameters into the PLC. During the manufacture process, the PC-based mixer system updates its working information into the server. The second key function is that the system measures the weights of the used raw materials, which guarantees a high accuracy of the used material. The electronic scales measure the materials including raw rubber and chemical drugs, and the system is ready to next step until the materials are between acceptable tolerances of specifications. This approach can reduce the errors caused by personnel. In the third function, the daily measurement record of the used material is synchronized into the database of headquarter. These data are easy to report as variant formats for analysis. The fourth function is the system flexibility. The parameters of the mixing process can be modified by PC easily. Therefore, this function provides the manager to modify some of the parameters for testing and developing new products. The last function is that the whole mixing process is monitored, and the data is also recorded. While the PLC has no extra storage, the PC's storage can collect the whole data during mixing process, e.g., temperature change, energy consumption…etc. These data are very important for the applications of Industrial 4.0.

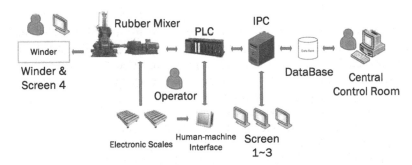

Fig. 1. The hardware configuration of the proposed system.

2.1   Hardware Configuration

The hardware configuration of the proposed system is shown in Fig. 1. The server PC provides a web interface for the supervisor to set the production schedule, formula, and dashboard format. The database server is a storage for store the setting information and production data during mixing process.

The IPC is a controller for the proposed system. The main functions of the IPC are (i) downloading the daily production schedule from the database, (ii) displaying the raw rubber weight, chemical weight, the batches of mixing, and mixing temperature on the four screens, respectively, (iii) collecting the data of the mixing process, (iv) storing the collected data into the database and (v) dispatching the parameters to PLC, including weight criteria and time of steps.

In the proposed system, there are four monitors to display the information of mixing process. One is for the measuring the weight of rubbers as shown in Fig. 2(a). Another is for the measuring weight of prepared chemical powders as shown in Fig. 2(b). The winder status is displayed on another one as shown in Fig. 2(c).

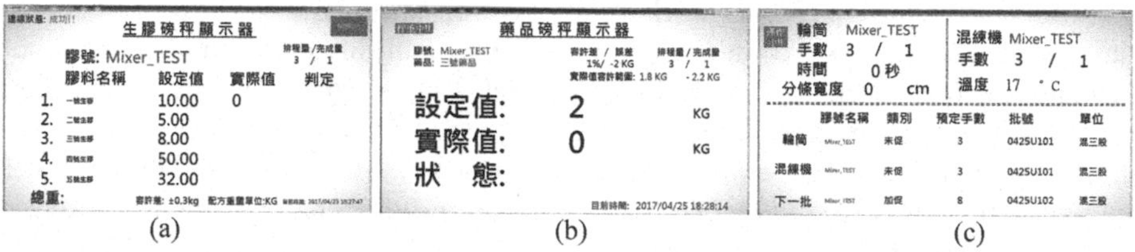

Fig. 2. (a) Raw rubber scale monitor. (b) Chemical powders scale monitor. (c) Winder monitor.

The materials are measured by two electric scales mounted on the conveyer. The weight criteria are used to check the weights from two electric scales, which are for raw rubber and specified chemical powders. In order to collect the temperature, a temperature sensor is installed on the mixer machine. The sensor data is obtained by the PLC and then the IPC is querying the data in the PLC.

2.2   Software Architecture

The software of the proposed system is implemented by several modules, including user management module, raw material setting module, formulas setting module, production schedule module, information display, temperature record monitor module and production report. The functions of the user management module are adding or deleting users and setting the permissions of users.

The raw material setting module provides adding or deleting the oil types, chemical powders and raw rubbers. Rubber mixtures have the specific formulas and tire company kept them confidential [7]. The proposed system provides the supervisor to edit the amount of materials used in a specific formula.

The production schedule module provides supervisors to edit the schedule of manufacturing, including types of rubbers, amount of each batch and numbers of batch of daily. This module also shows the status of manufacturing in real-time. The real-time information of the mixer including schedule, number of batches are shown in another monitor in Fig. 3. Manufacturing reports with variant formats are also provided.

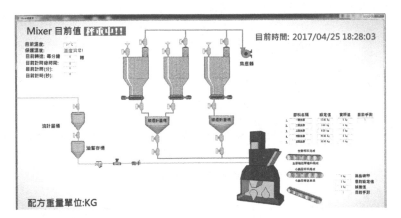

Fig. 3. The real-time information of the mixer including schedule, numbers of batches.

3   Experimental Results

3.1   The Proposed Operating Procedures

In order to improve the manufacturing performance, a new process of manufacturing is proposed. Firstly, the supervisor sets the daily production schedule in the central control room. The schedule will be synchronized to the IPC and then the information will be dispatched to PLC. The dispatched data included the weights of individual materials and the time of each mixing steps. While an operator checks weights of all material in the conventional system, the measured weight is compared with the pre-determined weight by the proposed system. Only within an acceptable tolerance, the mixing process is ready. The measured weights of all material and the data of the mixing process are also collected by IPC and then are stored into the database. When all the material preparing is ready, operator puts the materials into the mixer and turns on the mixer to start the automated mixing steps. After finishing a batch of material mixing, the finished mixing rubber drains out and goes into the winder to reduce its temperature.

3.2   Data Acquisition and Analysis

Rubber quality and work safety are affected by mixing temperature. A temperature measurement example of several mixing processes in one day is shown in Fig. 4. Basically, it is easy to see that there are three sections in the figure. Three sections are the temperature varying during morning shift, lunch time and later shift. Before the mixing process, the rubber mixer has to be warm-up to 95° to guarantee the initial temperature of every mixing processes is higher than 90°. It is obviously that the temperatures of the first trials are lower than others.

In Fig. 5, several temperature curves of each batches are shown. Because of the difference(s) of the initial temperature, these curves are divided into two groups. The upper half shows the temperature change of mixing in normal times, and the range is from 110° to 125°. The other half contains two temperature curves: the first batch's temperature changes in morning shift and in later shift.

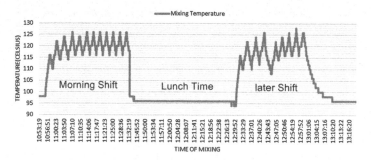

Fig. 4. Temperature during mixing procedures.

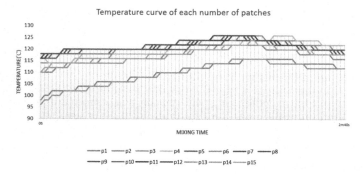

Fig. 5. Temperature curve of each number of batches.

4   Conclusion

Unlike the conventional rubber mixer (a pure PLC system) has five main issues for Industry 4.0 applications, the proposed system gathers many manufacturing data and reduces the errors, which are caused by human carelessness. The collected data are recorded into the database, including mixing temperature, material weighing results, and mixing time etc. The system also provides that supervisor and QC/QA people can manage for the process flow easily by checking the production report. In recent years, big data analysis is an important research topic, especially manufacturing data for Industry 4.0. In this research, a scheme for long-term collecting manufacturing data is implemented. In future works, new formulas or new procedures of tire manufacturing based on big data analysis will be proposed to improve the performance of products and to reduce the cost of material.

References

1. Amari, T., Themelis, N.J., Wernick, I.K.: Resource recovery from used rubber tires. Resour. Policy **25**(3), 179–188 (1999)
2. Rowhani, A., Rainey, T.J.: Scrap tyre management pathways and their use as a fuel—a review. Energies MDPI Open Access J. **9**(11), 1–26 (2016)
3. Lutsey, N.P., Regnier, J., Burke, A., Melaina, M.W., Bremson, J., Keteltas, M.: Assessment of tire technologies and practices for potential waste and energy use reductions. Institute of Transportation Studies, Working Paper Series, Institute of Transportation Studies, UC Davis (2006)
4. Lee, K., Kim, D., Choi, H.R., Park, B., Cho, M., Kang, D.: Application of IoT to inventory management in the tire industry. Information **19**(11), 5001–5005 (2016)
5. Sharma, A.R.: A review on rubber compound mixing in banbury mixer at tire industries. Int. J. Eng. Res. Rev. **2**(4), 106–109 (2014)
6. George, N.: Rubber Mixing. US Patent 2,067,458 (1937)
7. Grossman, R.F.: Mixing procedures for specific compounds. In: Grossman, R.F. (ed.) The Mixing of Rubber, pp. 125–162. Springer, Dordrecht (1997). https://doi.org/10.1007/978-94-011-5824-4_8

Indoor Navigation Based on a Gait Recognition and Counting Scheme

Tin Chang[1], Tzu-Hsuan Chung[1], En-Wei Lin[1], Jun-Jie Lai[1],
Xin-Hong Lai[1], Wen-Fong Wang[1(✉)], Chuan-Yu Chang[1],
and Ching-Yu Yang[2]

[1] Department of Computer Science and Information Engineering,
National Yunlin University of Science and Technology, Douliu, Taiwan
{EM10617005, B10417029, B10417002, B10417048, B10417061,
wwf, chuanyu}@yuntech.edu.tw
[2] Department of Computer Science and Information Engineering,
National Penghu University of Science and Technology, Magong, Taiwan
chingyu@npu.edu.tw

Abstract. GPS satellite positioning is currently a system used by people for navigation. As urban buildings become larger and their internal usages more diverse, the internal structure of the buildings turns into complex. Indoor positioning with GPS is often blocked by buildings, so that GPS is unable to accurately locate a user's position inside buildings. Currently, dead reckoning techniques can improve this issue in indoor positioning. However, the techniques need the deployment of many sensing devices in indoor environment, and the estimated distance would still result in serious errors. In this situation, it leads to the high cost of labor, materials, and equipment. In this study, we develop a gait recognition and counting scheme based on a self-made sensor to collect spatial data and user walks. The scheme can accurately calculate the number of walking steps, and then calculate the distance by effectively reducing the distance error.

Keywords: Indoors navigation · Gait · Accelerometer

1 Introduction

With the evolution of positioning technology, the quality of positioning and navigation systems are greatly improved. In outdoor positioning, GPS and Wi-Fi are mainly used. The system accuracy can be less than 10 m. As users are in tourism or search for landmark locations, it's a great application in a wide range of services. However, this accuracy is not enough to satisfy the needs of indoor positioning applications. For example, the positioning error by GPS in indoor spaces is often quite large, and it is also difficult to correctly locate a user's position. Therefore, the accuracy of indoor navigation and positioning is particularly concerned. In early days, Wi-Fi has always been considered as the most suitable technology for indoor positioning, but the shortcomings are also obvious. For instance, the accuracy is not good, the installation is not easy, and the power consumption is too high.

© Springer Nature Singapore Pte Ltd. 2019
C.-Y. Chang et al. (Eds.): ICS 2018, CCIS 1013, pp. 406–414, 2019.
https://doi.org/10.1007/978-981-13-9190-3_43

In recent years, various schemes have been proposed. In a factory, infrared rays and lasers are used as positioning guides for equipment automation. Since the protocols for communication of various devices are all in diverse wireless communications, the positioning data cannot be exchanged, so that it cannot be widely used. In this study, a self-made sensor and gait recognition model are proposed to accurately compute the number of user's walking steps, which in turn assists in the positioning function of the sensor device.

Indoor positioning technology and gait analysis become more interesting in recent years. Traditional schemes for indoor positioning have various types of infrastructure, including infrared, narrow-band radio, ultrasound, ultra-wideband (UWB), wireless information (Wi-Fi) signal strength, radio frequency identification (RFID), inertial measurement unit (IMU), vision, etc. [1–3]. Due to the high cost of equipment, the deployment of positioning service cannot be popular. Recently, the progression of microelectronics causes the integration of many sensors, including accelerometers, magnetometers, and gyroscopes, more possible. These schemes not only have lower prices, but also are easy to carry. In recent years, extensive research on pedestrian dead reckoning (PDR) and navigational calculations is done, and there are also many PDR systems that use pedometers or accelerometers to detect gait [4–7]. Since there is no complete gait analytical model for counting steps in user's walking, the error rate of distance estimation is rather high indoors [8–10]. In this paper, a specific gait recognition and counting scheme is proposed to improve this issue.

This paper is organized as follows. Section 2 describes the research materials in the study. The method of indoor navigation proposed in this study is sketched in Sect. 3. The experimental results are discussed in Sect. 4. Finally, a conclusion is given in Sect. 5.

2 Materials

2.1 Experimental Instruments

In this study, a sensor module has an accelerometer, a gyroscope, and a magnetometer. For the accelerometer, it calculates the degree of displacement in the 3-dimensional directions through piezoelectric effects and has three dimension coordinates (X, Y, Z) to determine the acceleration values of external motions. The X, Y, and Z acceleration values related to human walking are generated by the accelerometer as the user walks. They can be calculated and drawn a sinusoidal wave similar to a sine wave. When a sensor device driver receives a waveform generated by the vibrations of the X, Y, and Z acceleration values, it will determine whether it is a step through the acceleration values.

For the gyroscope, it is not used in this research work since the magnetometer provides the orientation information. To accurately determine the azimuth of a user's walking direction, the magnetometer can determine the magnetic field strength by measuring the change of the resistance from the user's movement. In this application, the main purpose of using the magnetometer is to be as a compass for helping the establishment of a 2 dimensional coordinate system, which can provide users with a reference orientation when navigating indoors.

2.2 Gait Description

A complete gait is mainly divided into a standing phase (stance) and a swinging phase (swing) as shown in Fig. 1. The stance phase accounts for about 60% of the entire gait cycle time, and the swing phase 40% of the cycle time. In Fig. 1, there are seven gait events, i.e., toe off, feet adjacent, tibia vertical, initial contact, opposite toe off, heel rise, and opposite initial contact. The events subdivide the two phases into seven gait stages. For the stance phase, it includes the stages of loading response, mid-stance, and terminal stance; for the swing phase, it includes the stages of pre-swing, initial swing, mid-swing, and terminal swing [11, 12].

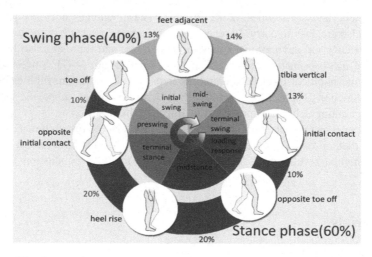

Fig. 1. A gait cycle with two phases, seven events, and seven stages

In Fig. 2, a signal waveform based on the root values of the sum of squares from every (X, Y, Z) acceleration of gait movements is presented. In the figure, each acquired gait data in 3-dimensional acceleration values is synthesized as a root value of the sum of squares from every (X, Y, Z) acceleration. In this way, the wearing directional deviation of a sensor module can be suppressed.

Since the collected physiological signals from the sensor modules are generated from electronic components and instruments, many noises such as electrical, swaying, muscle tail, and other noises are mixed together. To remove these noises, a signal spectrum analysis must be done before the followed signal processing. To discover the major spectrum of gait signals, fast Fourier transform is applied to analyze the frequency spectrum distribution of the acquired gait signals such as shown in Fig. 2. The spectrum analyzed results of the gait signals can be found in Fig. 3. It is obvious that all the major signals can be detected below 15 Hz.

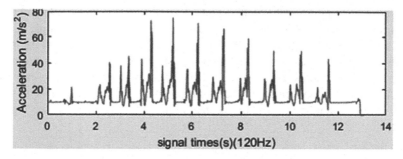

Fig. 2. The signal waveform with the root values of the sum of squares from every (X, Y, Z) acceleration of gait movements

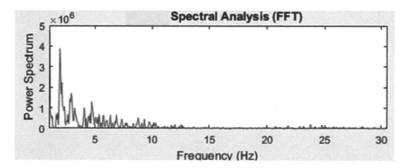

Fig. 3. The frequency spectrum distribution of acquired gait signals after fast Fourier transform

3 Methods

3.1 Gait Description

In order to collect the gait signals, a gait signal recording system is developed as shown in Fig. 4. In the figure, self-made sensor modules are installed inside of the insoles of a pair of shoes, and then the gait signals are acquired and communicated to a mobile phone APP for the initial signal processing of gait information.

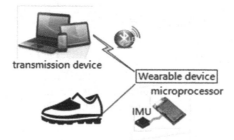

Fig. 4. A gait signal recording system

As shown in Fig. 4(a), the gait signals are acquired by the acceleration sensor modules, which are placed in the insoles of shoes. The signals have multiple peaks and troughs with different magnitudes, all of which are involved in the walking process. The resulting gait characteristics, including the step frequency, the number of steps, etc., can be determined as shown in Fig. 4(b). From the periodicity of each step, the above gait characteristics can be applied to the segmentation of gait cycles to get step counts for the calculation of moving distance in the indoor navigation (see Fig. 4(b)), (Fig. 5).

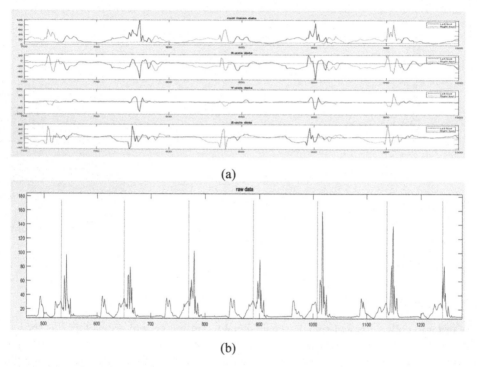

(a)

(b)

Fig. 5. (a) The gait acceleration signals acquired by the sensors; (b) The signals in the form of the root of sum of the square after the signal's segmentation

3.2   Indoor Positioning Computation

Step Length Estimation
Roughly speaking, the average human step length is about height (h) minus 100 cm. However, if a user's gait is arbitrary and irregular, then the average step length should be estimated a little greater than the above estimated value. Therefore, we adopt the

following formula (1) to estimate the average step length (d) in the specific azimuth of one user's walking direction:

$$d = h * 0.5 \tag{1}$$

Dimension Coordinate Conversion

Suppose that one specific entrance of a big building is designated to be as the original point for the indoor navigation service of that building. Then, based on the first movement from the original point, any temporary stop can be marked with a location record by applying a mutual conversion scheme between a 2-dimension coordinate system and a polar coordinate system. That is, convert a detected polar coordinate into a 2-dimension X and Y coordinate, where the polar coordinate distance is equal to a step number timed by step length and again timed by the trigonometric value of an azimuth, after a directional movement by walking. The following formula (2), (3) is the X, Y conversion coordinate formula, where n stands for the number of steps, d the average step length, and θ the specific azimuth of one user's walking direction.

$$X = n * d * cos\theta \tag{2}$$

$$Y = n * d * sin\theta \tag{3}$$

The number of walking steps and the walking direction of a user are obtained through sensing one specific walking behavior, and the obtained data are used to compute the coordinate values of the X and Y axes in a pseudo 2-dimension plane.

In addition, we developed a pseudo map creation subsystem, which is automatically activated on every second to synthesize the proper spatial map corresponding to the indoor walking environment. Accordingly, a user needs only to press the button in the indoor navigation APP program executing on the touch panel of a smart phone for adding a new coordinate, and then a new locational coordinate for the current position or a special location mark (such as exit, stairs, classroom, etc.) will be inserted into the map database for later usage.

Dimension Coordinate Conversion

Before the action of indoor navigation, the interface of the indoor navigation will first post a message to request a calibration action to the magnetometer of the smart phone to reduce orientation errors. At the same time, the user's information is recorded, including the user's step length and initial position XY coordinates. The next step is to ask the user to choose to arrive at the destination. Then the coordinates of the destination and the coordinates of the initial position are transformed by two-dimensional coordinate transformation. After calculating the average steps and the estimated distance of the user's walking, the magnetometer is activated to relocate the walking direction, and then an optimal walking path algorithm is devised to plan the forward path and navigate the user to his/her destination.

4 Experimental Results

In this study, the smart phone used is ASUS Zenfone 3 (Z012DA) with Andoird 8.0 operating system, and its processor is Qualcomm Snapdragon 625, eight cores, 2 GHz. To test the performance of the indoor navigation APP, two sets of testing scenarios were proposed and set up, namely "straight-line walking and then L-shaped cornering" and "S-curved continuous cornering".

In the test of the straight-line walking and then L-shaped cornering test, we found that the APP can effectively distinguish between cornering and straight-line walking. In

Table 1. Experimental results of the "straight-line walking and then L-shaped cornering" test.

Number	Test data	Result	Accuracy
1	50	49	98%
2	50	50	100%
3	50	50	100%
4	50	49	100%
5	50	50	98%
6	50	50	100%
7	50	50	100%
8	50	50	100%
9	50	50	100%
10	50	49	98%

Table 1, it can be found that nearly 100% accuracy can be obtained after a field trial testing. In this test, only a slight error had occurred to cause the miscounting of walking steps in the gait signal analysis due to the acquired gait signal's defects. Evidently, the experimental results shown in Table 1 support the effectiveness of the distance estimation in the indoor navigation.

In Table 2, the experimental results of the S-curved continuous cornering test are dropped, and it can be found the miscounting error does not exceed 2 steps. Actually, it does not affect the distance estimation used in the indoor navigation. One possible reason for miscounting the walking steps is probably due to the measurement of the specific azimuth of one user's walking direction. Although this test reveals a slight high error rate in estimating distance during S-curved continuous cornering, the navigation results are still acceptable.

Table 2. Experimental results of the "S-curved continuous cornering" test

Number	Test data	Result	Accuracy
1	50	49	98%
2	50	48	96%
3	50	48	96%
4	50	50	100%
5	50	49	98%
6	50	48	96%
7	50	49	98%
8	50	50	100%
9	50	50	100%
10	50	49	98%

5   Conclusion

In this study, a gait-based indoor navigation scheme for walking inside modern huge and complex buildings was proposed. This scheme integrates the techniques of gait signal analysis and 2-dimension spatial coordinate conversion to position users' locations for navigation. To test the performance of this system, two testing scenarios were devised, and from the analyzed gait signals for the distance estimation in navigation, our scheme can provide accurate results for indoor navigation. In comparison with previous works, our method has the benefits of low cost for installation and easy for deployment.

Acknowledgements. This work was financially supported by the "Intelligent Recognition Industry Service Center" from The Featured Areas Research Center Program within the framework of the Higher Education Sprout Project by the Ministry of Education (MOE) in Taiwan. Simultaneously, the authors are also grateful to the MOST, Taiwan, for supporting this study under the contracts MOST 107-2637-E-224-004.

References

1. Hightower, J., Borriello, G.: Location systems for ubiquitous computing. Computer **34**(8), 57–66 (2001)
2. Liu, H., Darabi, H., Banerjee, P., Liu, J.: Survey of wireless indoor positioning techniques and systems. IEEE Trans. Syst. Man Cybern. C Appl. Rev. **37**(6), 1067–1080 (2007)
3. Challamel, R., Tome, P., Harmer, D., Beauregard, S.: Performance assessment of indoor location technologies. In: Proceedings of the IEEE/ION Position, Location Navigation Symposium, pp. 624–632 (2008)
4. Ladetto, Q., Gabaglio, V., Merminod, B., Terrier, P., Schutz, Y.: Human walking analysis assisted by DGPS, pp. 1–4. GNSS, Edinburgh (2000)
5. Ladetto, Q.: On foot navigation: continuous step calibration using both complementary recursive prediction and adaptive Kalman filtering. In: Proceedings of the ION GPS, pp. 1735–1740 (2000)

6. Ladetto, Q., Merminod, B.: An alternative approach to vision techniques: Pedestrian navigation system based on digital magnetic compass and gyroscope integration. In: Proceedings of the 6th World Multiconference on Systemics, Cybernetics (2002)
7. Mezentsev, O., Collin, J., Lachapelle, G.: Pedestrian dead reckoning—a solution to navigation in GPS signal degraded areas? Geomatica **59**(2), 175–182 (2005)
8. Fang, L.: Design of a wireless assisted pedestrian dead reckoning system—the NavMote experience. IEEE Trans. Instrum. Meas. **54**(6), 2342–2358 (2005)
9. Judd, T.: A personal dead reckoning module. In: Proceedings of the ION GPS, vol. 97, pp. 47–51 (1997)
10. Jirawimut, R., Ptasinski, P., Garaj, V., Cecelja, F., Balachandran, W.: A method for dead reckoning parameter correction in pedestrian navigation system. IEEE Trans. Instrum. Meas. **52**(1), 209–215 (2003)
11. Neumann, D.: Kinesiology of the Musculoskeletal System: Foundations for Rehabilitation, 2nd edn. Elsevier, Health Sciences, Amsterdam (2013). ISBN 0323266320
12. Magee, D.: Orthopedic Physical Assessment, 6th edn. Elsevier, Health Sciences, Amsterdam (2014). ISBN 1455709751

Exploration on the Design of Sport Prescription and the Behavior of College Students

Li Yu-Chiang[2([⊠])], Jun-Yi Lin[1], and Wen-Fong Wang[1]

[1] Department of Computer Science and Information Engineering,
National Yunlin University of Science and Technology,
123 University Rd. Sec. 3, Douliou, Yunlin 64002, Taiwan
[2] Graduate School of Technological and Vocational Education,
National Yunlin University of Science and Technology,
123 University Rd. Sec. 3, Douliou, Yunlin 64002, Taiwan
jiangly@yuntech.edu.tw

Abstract. The results of this study show the college students' personal test records, which the average index of college students' cardiorespiratory strength (3 min) is 29.32, the average index of muscle fitness (1 min sit-ups) 37.71, the average score of softness sitting (frontal bend) 26.53, the average index of body mass index 37.71, and the average index of explosive force (established long jump) 174.63. The goals of exercise is to strengthen muscle fitness, heart and lung, endurance, and weight control. The type/project is ranked first in selecting medium-intensity activities, followed by high-impact activities such as jogging, and finally low-impact activities. Set the exercise target frequency for the selected sports to take the first place in 3 days a week. The exercise intensity is mostly due to the fact that people have diabetes mellitus and are a little tired (or load), but most of them are painful. The duration of exercise is 1 point per 5 min, the average index is 8.81, and most of them are 8 to 10 points each time. Therefore, the most frequent duration of each exercise is 40 to 50 min.

Keywords: Muscle fitness · Body mass index

1 Introduction

The main purpose of this study is to investigate the design of exercise prescription and the behavior of college students. From the news of the World Health Organization (WHO), every suicide event represents 10 to 20 self-inflicted attempts; and those who have previously committed self-deprecating behavior are more likely to rehabilitate than the average person. Among the young people aged 15 to 24, they rank second in the top ten causes of death. The causes of suicide include the disintegration of family values, the death of loved ones, social ambiguity and interpersonal dredging, emotional frustration, affirmation of personal achievement, financial distress, legal entanglement, drug abuse, serious physical illness, mental illness, etc.

The university's general curriculum design really needs to cover these different needs-oriented to help college students improve their ability to resist stress. The only

C.-Y. Chang et al. (Eds.): ICS 2018, CCIS 1013, pp. 415–422, 2019.
https://doi.org/10.1007/978-981-13-9190-3_44

way to reduce stress is exercise. This course is a general-purpose course offered at the university. The students are very enthusiastic, a total of 67 students. The purpose is to understand the sports behavior of college students and explore the sports habits and sports behaviors of college students through the intervention of the curriculum. Through the understanding and reflection of the course, I design my own tailor-made sports prescriptions for myself and my family, so as to promote the health of individuals and family members. The curriculum development design is better for sports prescriptions, in response to the advent of aged society, and will be applied in the future. Developed to the community elders' smart mobile device exercise prescription APP to jointly promote the health of all people.

2   Research Materials

The purposes of this study are to understand the concept of consciousness of college students' sports behavior. Next, understand the current situation of college students' sports behavior. Thirdly, understand the changes in sports behavior of college students before and after the intervention. Finally, understand the design of college sports prescriptions and the application of the future.

2.1   Terminology

- College student: The university student referred to in this study refers to a bachelor's degree student who is enrolled in the day school of a higher education institution established under the University Law and awarded a bachelor's degree or higher.
- Exercise prescription: Exercise Prescription refers to a sports science program that plans to improve physical fitness and health promotion.
- Willingness to exercise: Exercise Concern is the motivation for individuals to participate in various types of sports activities, and "competitiveness" is the best motivation for increasing exercise.
- Sports benefit: The exercise benefit is the different benefits of participating in various types of sports to the health of the body and mind.
- Muscle fitness: The importance of improving muscle fitness Maintaining good muscle strength and muscular endurance is very helpful in promoting health, preventing injury and improving work efficiency. When muscle strength and endurance decline, muscles themselves are often unable to perform daily activities and stress. Work load, prone to muscle fatigue and pain.
- Body mass index: The World Health Organization recommends measuring the degree of obesity by the Body Mass Index (BMI), which is calculated by dividing the body weight (kg) by the square of the height (meter). The National Health Service recommends that adult BMI in China should be maintained between 18.5 (kg/m^2) and 24 (kg/m^2). Too thin, too heavy or too fat can hinder health. Studies have shown that overweight or obesity (BMI $\geq$ 24) is a major risk factor for chronic diseases such as diabetes, cardiovascular disease, and malignant tumors; and too thin health problems can lead to malnutrition, osteoporosis, sudden death and other health problems.

2.2   Literature Discussion

With reference to the literatures, through data collection and exercise prescription design, data collation, analysis, induction, analysis, etc., to establish the theoretical basis of research, and according to the literature, a questionnaire tool to explore whether there is a significant difference in the performance of college students' healthy exercise behaviors was developed.

In 2002, the WHO proposed an active aging policy framework, advocated from the three aspects of "health, participation and security", not only to take into account the physical, psychological, social and other aspects of health, but also to improve the quality of life of the population. At present, the health care service industry is also the main force of the smart mobile device App for the mobile health market.

Regular exercise has many benefits for the health of the body, including increasing cardiac contractility, maximum ventilation, vascular elasticity and function, blood fat, heme concentration, aerobic enzymes, muscle glycogen content, myoglobin, stress relief, anxiety and depression reduction, self-confidence and vitality, mood, attention and cognitive ability, and working and learning efficiency [2]. Modern people face potential pressure every day, which can lead to mental stress and various stress symptoms. The environment for early human survival is bad. The pressure is mainly from the acquisition and fighting of food. The reaction under stress is physical activity. It is "fight or flight". The pressure of modern people comes from psychology. When stress causes heart rate to accelerate, blood pressure rises, blood vessels shrink, blood flow slows, blood vessels are easily blocked, and if you do not get through exercise. Solution, over time, may cause digestive diseases such as cardiovascular diseases and stress ulcer, decreased immune function, weakened body, fatigue, and poor work performance. However, proper exercise can strengthen competitiveness, stabilize emotions, and improve depression. Help sleep, improve physical and mental health.

3   Research Materials

According to the purpose of this study, we collect and conduct general counseling courses, collect relevant literature and indicators, and develop questionnaires on college sports behaviors to understand the health concept awareness of Taiwanese college students' sports behavior and the ability to design sports prescriptions. The purpose of this chapter is to develop the scale and research process, the scale and the design of the exercise prescription design, including research design, research tools, research participants and research procedures and data analysis.

3.1   Research Architecture

In the general education curriculum, design sports prescription and education checklist, the intervention process is divided into three stages (see Fig. 1). The first stage of pre-exercise health and safety filtering and questionnaires: including personal health history and physical activity questionnaires, such as gender, height, weight, blood pressure, medical history, health status, psychological and emotional status, medication situation, exercise experience, bone and joint problems, working status, health status, family inheritance, and others.

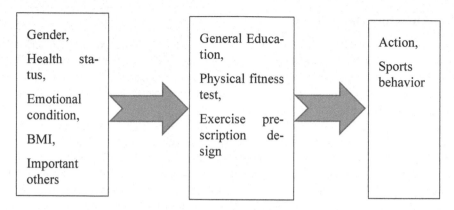

Fig. 1. Stages of a fitness assessment

The second stage of fitness assessment:

1. Fill in the fitness test consent form.
2. Ask students to read the exercise prescription physical fitness test sequence, test Environment and conditions [2].
3. The physical fitness testing project is based on the physical fitness testing program of the Ministry of Education's Sports Department (see Table 1).

Table 1. Students and national health fitness testing: physical fitness testing and testing items.

Project	Student health fitness test	National health fitness test
Cardiorespiratory endurance	800 or 1600 m run away test or 3 min boarding test	3 min boarding test
Muscle fitness	1 min sit-up	1 min sit-up
Softness	Sitting posture	Sitting posture
Body composition	Body mass index	Body mass index, Waist to hip ratio
Instant force	Standing long jump	none

Personal fitness test records Physical fitness test items include gait analysis records, EKG/HR (heart rhythm) records, 800 or 1600 m running (cardiopulmonary endurance), 3 min (cardiopulmonary endurance), 1 min supine Sit up (muscle fitness), sitting forward bend (softness), body composition (BMI, waist circumference, hip circumference), standing long jump (explosive force).

The preparation of the third stage exercise prescription content:

1. Confirm the purpose of exercise: reduce weight, strengthen cardiorespiratory strength, and muscle fitness
2. Choose the main mode of exercise that is favorite and convenient: high impact activity, medium intensity life dynamics, and low impact activities.
3. Setting sports training goals for selected sports: exercise frequency, intensity, and holding continued time.

The implementation of the fourth stage exercise prescription:

1. The initial stage (for 4–6 weeks): fill out the basic record of prescription exercise every week, the main invited sports include warm-up exercises, major sports, relaxation exercises and total time.
2. Improvement stage (for 4–8 weeks): During the promotion period, a record form is required every week. In order to track the effects of exercise, when the fitness is greatly improved, the exercise continues to increase by 10% every 2 weeks; increase the main exercise to 30 min after the dynamic strength to establish a cardio resistance basis; exercise intensity increases by 5% per week. The exercise intensity is 40 to 85% of the retained heart rate.
3. Maintenance period (after 6 months): During the promotion period, a record is required every week. Apply a recording table to track the effects of exercise. As participants' fitness has reached satisfactory level, there is no intention to increase the load; maintain the same amount of training to maintain the body can. Exercise should be diverse, enjoy fun, avoid boring and withdraw; training goals. It should be reassessed to make it practical.

4   Research Results

The purpose of this study is to understand whether there is a change in the student's athletic behavior after the intervention of the University's general education course and the sports science curriculum. This course consists of 67 students. This questionnaire is used to inform students to fill in a networking health-informatics database through an online teaching system. Road questionnaire, take a free answer, and recover 35 copies of the effective questionnaire. The students in the curriculum of the revision course are mostly students of the engineering school, the proportion is 94.28%, the design college 2.4%, and the management college 2.8%. The gender ratio is 77.14% for boys and 22.86% for girls, and the frequency of student movement is Week exercise 2 times, the highest rate of 15.3%; exercise duration from 30 min to 1 h up to 12.34%; the most commonly engaged sports for running 37.14%, followed by walking (31.42%) and playing basketball (28/.57%), The motivation for exercise is reduce stress up to 23%, followed by hobbies (19%) and health promotion (16%); the benefits of exercise are promoted to the most health, followed by stress reduction and weight control; the reasons for obstructing regular exercise. The main reason is that there is no time (work or class is too busy), followed by bad weather and laziness and no perseverance; whether important people will affect exercise habits of 67.60%, and those who do not affect 32.40%; who will affect your exercise habits. The most peers are friends, followed by family members and physicians; in the general education unit, the sports prescription unit is the most popular among the students, followed by the yoga unit; the students are encouraged to increase their health and sports related knowledge by up to 38.20%, followed by a student appointment or recommendation ratio of 35.26%. It improves the quality and efficiency of sports 14.71%; the innovation proposal for the curriculum to increase the proportion of extracurricular leisure enterprises to visit the curriculum unit is up to 26.45%. Secondly, expect to increase the Pilates course unit and boxing aerobic course unit. The most popular theme of the prescription is the weight control exercise prescription design, followed by the exercise prescription design for hypertension and heart disease; whether the curriculum design through the general education exercise prescription will increase the individual's concern to exercise as high as 96.97%. In the general education course of the university, the proportion of general education courses related to health needs to be as high as 55.83%.

The results of this study showed that the college students' personal test record showed that the average index of college students' cardiorespiratory strength (3 min), which were shown in Table 2, is 29.32; the average index of muscle fitness (1 min sit-ups), which were shown in Table 3, is 37.71; the average score of softness sitting (frontal bend), which were shown in Table 4, is 26.53; the average index of body mass index is 37.71; the average index of explosive force (established long jump) is 174.63; the target of exercise is to strengthen muscle fitness, and the second goal is to strengthen heart and lung. Endurance, and finally weight control; in choosing the main sports side that is like and convenient. The type/project is ranked first in selecting medium-intensity activities, followed by high-impact activities such as jogging, and finally low-impact activities.

Table 2. One sample test for cardiopulmonary ability.

t	df	Sig. (2-tailed)	Mean difference	95% Confidence interval of the difference	
				Lower	Upper
30.38	45	0.0	29.325	27.38	31.27

Set the exercise target frequency for the selected sports to take the first place in 3 days a week. The exercise intensity is mostly due to the fact that the body has sweaty people and the body is a little tired (or load), but most of them are painful. The duration of exercise is 1 point every 5 min, the average index is 8.81, and most of them are 8 to 10 points each time. Therefore, the most frequent duration of each exercise is 40 to 50 min.

Table 3. One sample test for muscle fitness.

t	df	Sig. (2-tailed)	Mean difference	95% Confidence interval of the difference	
				Lower	Upper
24.00	45	0.0	37.713	34.55	40.88

Table 4. One sample test for softness.

t	df	Sig. (2-tailed)	Mean difference	95% Confidence interval of the difference	
				Lower	Upper
8.227	45	0.0	26.53	20.04	33.03

5   Conclusions and Recommendations

Most of the college students have little interpersonal interaction. Some college students are addicted to the virtual world of the Internet. They are extremely inexperienced in education. The tolerance for frustration is also decreasing. The number of depression cases is increasing. The number of counseling staff is insufficient, the counselors are exhausted, and student counseling cases increase. Therefore, there are frequent suicides on campus. In order to promote the physical and mental health of college students, reduce depression and improve their ability to resist stress, exercise is the best way. Through the comprehensive curriculum fitness test and exercise prescription design, students reflect on the importance of exercise after the intervention. Benefits, and then develop exercise habits, and affect family, friends, etc., develop good sports behaviors, and establish healthy behavior patterns. Such a general education course is quite meaningful and worthy of promotion.

Acknowledgments.   The major project goal of this work is a trial for providing the students of the Engineering school to cast themselves into a field of promoting health conditions of elders in the proximal communities around campus for a university social responsibility. The financial support of this work is from the Higher Education Sprout Project of National Yunlin University of Science & Technology.

References

1. Cai, S., Lin, Y., Cai, Y.: Analysis of the willingness to use mobile health app by method destination chain model. Master thesis, Yuanpei Medical Science and Technology University, Chiayi, Taiwan, ROC (2015)
2. Fang, C.-L.: Exercise Prescriptions. Far Du Publishing Co., Ltd., Taipei, ROC (2017)
3. Sun, C., Chen, Y.: Study on College students' attitudes towards leisure sports—taking Mingdao university students as an example. Leisure Holisic Wellness (2), 10–12 (2009)

4. Ye, W., Zhang, Z., Zhang, J., Huang, W.: Research on the motivation of college students. Leisure Holisic Wellness (7), 91–99 (2012)
5. Hou, T., Yang, M.: A Study on the motivation and satisfaction of college students' participation in fitness exercises—taking Mingdao university as an example. Leisure Holisic Wellness (13), 24–41 (2016)

Algorithms and Computation Theory

A Diagonal-Based Algorithm
for the Constrained Longest Common
Subsequence Problem

Siang-Huai Hung[1], Chang-Biau Yang[1($\boxtimes$)], and Kuo-Si Huang[2]

[1] National Sun Yat-sen University, Kaohsiung, Taiwan
cbyang@cse.nsysu.edu.tw
[2] National Kaohsiung University of Science and Technology, Kaohsiung, Taiwan

Abstract. Given two sequences A and B of lengths m and n, respectively, and another constrained sequence C with length r, the *constrained longest common subsequence* (CLCS) problem is to find the *longest common subsequence* (LCS) of A and B with the constraint that C is contained as a subsequence in the answer. Based on the diagonal concept for finding the LCS length, proposed by Nakatsu *et al.*, this paper proposes an algorithm for obtaining the CLCS length efficiently in $\mathrm{O}(rL(m-L))$ time and $\mathrm{O}(mr)$ space, where L denotes the CLCS length. According to the experimental result, the proposed algorithm outperforms the previously CLCS algorithms.

Keywords: Longest common subsequence · Constrained LCS ·
Diagonal-based strategy

1 Introduction

The goal of the *longest common subsequence* (LCS) problem is to calculate the identity or similarity of two sequences. It can be applied to several fields, such as bioinformatics, file plagiarism, and voice recognition [7].

A *subsequence* is gotten by deleting zero or more symbols from the original sequence or string. Given two sequences (or strings) $A = a_1a_2a_3 \cdots a_m$ and $B = b_1b_2b_3 \cdots b_n$, $|A| = m \leq n = |B|$, the LCS problem is to find the common subsequence of A and B whose length is the longest. A lot of algorithms have been proposed for solving the LCS problem [6,8]. Several variations of the LCS problem have also been proposed, such as the *constrained longest common subsequence* (CLCS) problem [3,5,11] and the *merged longest common subsequence* (MLCS) problem [12].

Given two sequences $A = a_1a_2a_3 \cdots a_m$, $B = b_1b_2b_3 \cdots b_n$, $|A| = m \leq n = |B|$, and a constrained sequence $C = c_1c_2c_3 \cdots c_r$, $|C| = r$, the *constrained longest*

This research work was partially supported by the Ministry of Science and Technology of Taiwan under contract MOST 104-2221-E-110-018-MY3.

C.-Y. Chang et al. (Eds.): ICS 2018, CCIS 1013, pp. 425–432, 2019.
https://doi.org/10.1007/978-981-13-9190-3_45

common subsequence (CLCS) problem, proposed by Tsai [11], is to find the LCS of A and B such that C is contained as a subsequence in the answer. Tsai [11] presented a *dynamic programming* (DP) algorithm with $O(m^2 n^2 r)$ time and space. Peng also presented a DP algorithm with $O(mnr)$ time and space [9]. Chin *et al.* proved that the CLCS problem is equivalent to a special case of the *constrained multiple sequence alignment* (CMSA) problem and presented a DP algorithm with $O(mnr)$ time and space [3].

Arslan and Eğecioğlu [2] improved the algorithm complexity of Tsai from $O(m^2 n^2 r)$ to $O(mnr)$ by modifying the recurrence formula. Deorowicz [4] rewrote the DP formula of Chin *et al.* and applied the approach proposed by Hunt and Szymanski [6], then proposed an algorithm in $O(r(mL' + R) + n)$ time, where $L' = |LCS(A, B)|$ and R is the total number of match pairs between A and B. Deorowicz's algorithm is more efficient when the alphabet size is large.

In 2010, Peng *et al.* [10] proposed an algorithm in $O(mnr)$ time and $O(nr)$ space for the weighted CPSA (WCPSA) problem. In the WCPSA problem, some constraints can be ignored by adopting proper constraint weights. In 2012, Ann *et al.* [1] proposed an efficient algorithm for the run-length encoded (RLE) sequences, which are often used to represent the secondary structure of proteins, in $O(mnR_C + mNr + Mnr)$ time, where M, N and R_C are the numbers of runs of A, B and C, respectively. In their algorithm, the *range minimum querying* (RMQ) technique is invoked. Ho *et al.* [5] observed that the values of most corresponding CLCS lattice cells are identical in two consecutive layers when the alphabet size is small. They proposed an algorithm to avoid redundant computation by clarifying whether the lattice cells need to be calculated or not.

The organization of this paper is as follows. Section 2 introduces some preliminaries of the CLCS problem. In Sect. 3, we will propose a new algorithm, based on the diagonal scheme, for solving the CLCS problem. The diagonal scheme is inspired by the LCS algorithm proposed by Nakatsu *et al.* [8]. In Sect. 4, we show the experimental results of our algorithm and compare its efficiency to some previously published algorithms. Finally, the conclusion is given in Sect. 5.

2   Preliminaries

A sequence (string) $S = s_1 s_2 s_3 \cdots s_{|S|}$ is composed of characters over a finite alphabet Σ. The sequence notations are described as follows.

- s_i: the ith character of sequence S.
- $|S|$: the length of sequence S.
- $i..j$: the range from indexes i to j.
- $S_{i..j}$: the substring of sequence S from indexes i to j. We set that $S_{i..j} = \emptyset$ if $j < i$.

2.1   The Longest Common Subsequence Problem

A *subsequence* is gotten by deleting zero or more character from the original sequence. Given two sequences $A = a_1 a_2 a_3 \cdots a_m$ and $B = b_1 b_2 b_3 \cdots b_n$, where

$m \leq n$, the LCS problem is to find the longest common subsequence of A and B. In 1974, Wagner and Fischer [13] proposed an algorithm with $O(mn)$ time and space to solve the LCS problem by the *dynamic programming* (DP) approach.

Nakatsu *et al.* [8] proposed an algorithm to solve the LCS problem in $O(n(m - L'))$ time, where $L' = |LCS(A, B)|$. Evidently, if L' is close to m, the time complexity tends to be linear. That is, the algorithm is very efficient when the two sequences are very similar. For the prefix $A_{1..i}$ of A, let $j = d_{i,s}$ denote the smallest index j of B such that $|LCS(A_{1..i}, B_{1..j})| = s$. Nakatsu *et al.* [8] used $d_{i,s}$ to solve the LCS problem as follows.

$$d_{i,s} = \begin{cases} \infty & \text{if } i = 0, \\ \min\{j, d_{i-1,s}\} & \text{if there exists a smallest index} j \text{ such that} \\ & a_i = b_j \text{ and } j > d_{i-1,s-1} \text{ for } s \geq 2, \\ d_{i-1,s} & \text{if there is no such } j. \end{cases} \tag{1}$$

2.2   The Constrained Longest Common Subsequence Problem

Given two sequences A, B, and a constrained sequence $C = c_1 c_2 c_3 \cdots c_r$, the *constrained longest common subsequence* (CLCS) problem is to find the LCS of A and B such that C is also a subsequence in this LCS. Let the solution of the *constrained longest common subsequence* (CLCS) problem be denoted as $CLCS(A, B, C)$. For example, suppose that $A = \text{ccdbbcbdcd}$, $B = \text{dccbbcdbcb}$, and $C = \text{db}$. We have $LCS(A, B) = \text{ccbbcbc}$ and $|LCS(A, B)| = 7$. When C is considered, $CLCS(A, B, C) = \text{dbbcdc}$ and $|CLCS(A, B, C)| = 6$. It is clear that $|LCS(A, B)| \geq |CLCS(A, B, C)|$.

3   The Diagonal-Based Algorithm

The proposed CLCS algorithm is inspired by the LCS algorithm of Nakatsu *et al.* [8]. The time and space complexities of our algorithm are $O(rL(m - L))$ and $O(mr)$, respectively, where $L = |CLCS(A, B, C)|$, $|A| = m$, $|B| = n$, $m \leq n$, and $|C| = r$. Accordingly, it performs well for the short CLCS since L is small, or for similar sequences since L is close to m.

Definition 1. *Let $D_{i,l}$, $i, l \geq 1$, denote a set of 3-tuple elements $\langle i', j, h \rangle$, $i' \leq i$ such that the constrained common subsequence of length l can be obtained, where $a_{i'} = b_j$, i' and j are the match indexes of A and B, the suffix $C_{r-h+1..r}$ (with length h) has not been included yet in the solution.*

By Definition 1, a 3-tuple element $\langle i', j, h \rangle \in D_{i,l}$ means the prefix $C_{1..k}$ has been included in the solution, $h = r - k$, that is, $|CLCS(A_{1..i'}, B_{1..j}, C_{1..r-h})| \geq l$. With the same feasible solution length, we prefer smaller values of j and h, because it requires a shorter prefix of B and includes more constraints in C. Accordingly, we define the *domination* concept as follows.

Definition 2. *For any two 3-tuple elements $\langle i_1, j_1, h_1 \rangle$ and $\langle i_2, j_2, h_2 \rangle$, where $\langle i_1, j_1, h_1 \rangle \neq \langle i_2, j_2, h_2 \rangle$, we say that $\langle i_1, j_1, h_1 \rangle$ dominates $\langle i_2, j_2, h_2 \rangle$ if $(j_1 \leq j_2$ and $h_1 \leq h_2)$ or $(i_1 < i_2$ and $j_1 = j_2$ and $h_1 = h_2)$.*

We use one array $limitB$ and one matrix $NextMatch_B$ [12] to improve the efficiency for finding $|CLCS(A, B, C)|$. $limitB[k]$ records the largest index j such that $c_k = b_j$ and and there is no feasible solution for $c_k = b_{j'}$, $j' > j$. On the boundaries, we set $limitB[0] = 0$. For example, suppose that $B = $ dccbbcdbcb, $limitB = \{0, 7, 10\}$ for $C = $ db, and $limitB = \{0, 7, 8, 9\}$ for $C = $ dbc. $limitB[k]$ can be built by Eq. 2.

$$limitB[k] = \begin{cases} 0 & \text{if } k = 0, \\ \max\{j|c_k = b_j\} & \text{if } k = r, \\ \max\{j|c_k = b_j, j < limitB[k+1]\} & \text{if } 1 \le k \le r - 1. \end{cases} \qquad (2)$$

For each $\langle i', j', h' \rangle \in D_{i-1,l-1}$, we extend it to $\langle i, j, h \rangle \in D_{i,l}$ if it can get a longer CLCS candidate. We denote this operation as $\text{EXTENSION}(\langle i', j', h' \rangle) = \langle i, j, h \rangle$. Some properties are described as follows.

(1) Naturally, $i \ge i' + 1$. If $i > m$, then $D_{i,l} = \emptyset$.
(2) $j = NextMatch_B[a_i][j']$. If $j > n$, then $\langle i, j, h \rangle$ is not valid and it cannot be appended into $D_{i,l}$.
(3) If $a_i = b_j = c_{r-h'+1}$, we update $h = h' - 1$; otherwise, $h = h'$.
(4) $\langle i, j, h \rangle$ is valid if $j \le limitB[r - h + 1]$. Otherwise, it is not valid and it cannot be appended into $D_{i,l}$.

After gathering $D_{i,l}$ from the extension of $D_{i-1,l-1}$, we combine $D_{i-1,l}$ and current $D_{i,l}$ together, and then perform the domination operation on this composite set to obtain a new $D_{i,l}$, where every pair of 3-tuple elements are not dominated by each other. This procedure is denoted as $D_{i,l} = \text{DOMINATION}(\text{EXTENSION}(D_{i-1,l-1}) \cup D_{i-1,l})$. Note that $D_{i,0} = \{\langle 0, 0, r \rangle\}$ for initialization. Table 1 shows an example of $D_{i,l}$ for this procedure.

Lemma 1. *If there exists* $\langle i', j, h \rangle \in D_{i,l}$, $1 \le i' \le i$ *and* $l \ge 1$, *we get* $|CLCS(A_{1..i'}, B_{1..j}, C_{1..r-h})| \ge l$, *where* $D_{i,l} = \text{DOMINATION}(\text{EXTENSION}(D_{i-1,l-1}) \cup D_{i-1,l})$ *and* $D_{0,0} = D_{i,0} = \{\langle 0, 0, r \rangle\}$.

Proof. By the properties of EXTENSION, each $\langle i', j, h \rangle \in D_{i,l}$ should be valid. If $\text{EXTENSION}(D_{i-1,l-1} = \langle i'', j', h' \rangle) = \langle i', j, h \rangle$, $i' \ge i'' + 1$, j is the next match index and $j > j'$, then the length of a feasible solution in $D_{i,l}$ is the length in $D_{i-1,l-1}$ plus one. So $|CLCS(A_{1..i'}, B_{1..j}, C_{1..r-h})| \ge l$. ∎

Theorem 1. *If* $\langle i', j, 0 \rangle \in D_{i,l}$ *and there is no other* $\langle i'', j'', 0 \rangle \in D_{i,l}$, $i, l \ge 1$, $i' \ne i''$ *and* $j \ne j''$, $|CLCS(A_{1..i'}, B_{1..j}, C)| = l$, *where* $D_{i,l} = \text{DOMINATION}(\text{EXTENSION}(D_{i-1,l-1}) \cup D_{i-1,l})$ *and* $D_{0,0} = D_{i,0} = \{\langle 0, 0, r \rangle\}$.

Proof. By Lemma 1, $|CLCS(A_{1..i'}, B_{1..j}, C)| \ge l$. By Definition 1, we know $h = 0$ means the constrained sequence C has been included in the feasible solution. Definition 2 ensures $\langle i', j, 0 \rangle$ is better than $\langle i'', j'', 0 \rangle$. We conclude $|CLCS(A_{1..i'}, B_{1..j}, C)| = l$. ∎

Algorithm 1. Computing the length of CLCS.

Input: Sequences $A = a_1a_2a_3 \ldots a_m$, $B = b_1b_2b_3 \ldots b_n$ and $C = c_1c_2c_3 \ldots c_r$
Output: Length of $CLCS(A, B, C)$

1: Construct the arrays of $limitB$ and $NextMatch_B$
2: $L \leftarrow 0$ $\triangleright L = |CLCS(A, B, C)|$
3: **if** any $limitB[k] = 0$, $1 \leq k \leq r$ **then return** 0
4: **for** $t = 1 \rightarrow m$ **do** $\triangleright$ round t
5:      $D_{t-1,0} \leftarrow \{\langle 0, 0, r \rangle\}$, $l \leftarrow 1$
6:      **for** $i = t \rightarrow m$ **do**
7:          **for each** $\langle i', j', h' \rangle \in D_{i-1,l-1}$ **do**
8:              $j \leftarrow NextMatch_B[a_i][j']$
9:              $k \leftarrow r - h' + 1$
10:             **if** $j \leq n$ and $h' = 0$ **then**
11:                 Insert $\langle i, j, 0 \rangle$ into $D_{i,l}$
12:             **else if** $j \leq limitB[k]$ **then**
13:                 Insert $\langle i, j, h' - 1 \rangle$ into $D_{i,l}$ if $a_i = c_k$
14:                 Insert $\langle i, j, h' \rangle$ into $D_{i,l}$ if $a_i \neq c_k$
15:          $D_{i,l} \leftarrow \text{DOMINATION}(D_{i,l} \cup D_{i-1,l})$
16:          **if** $D_{i,l} = \emptyset$ **then**
17:             **break**
18:          Find the largest L such that $\langle i'', j'', 0 \rangle \in D_{i,L}$
19:          $l \leftarrow l + 1$
20:      **if** $((m - t) \leq L)$ **then**
21:          **return** L
22: **for** $l = L \rightarrow 0$ **do**
23:      **if** $\langle i'', j'', 0 \rangle \in D_{i,l}$ **then return** l
24: **return** 0

Function 1. Domination.

1: **function** DOMINATION(set D)
2:      Initialize: $list[0..r] \leftarrow \emptyset$
3:      **for each** $\langle i, j, h \rangle \in D$ **do** $\triangleright list[h]$ stores one $\langle i, j, h \rangle$
4:          **if** $list[h] = \emptyset$ **then**
5:             Insert $\langle i, j, h \rangle$ into $list[h]$
6:          **else if** $\langle i, j, h \rangle$ dominates $\langle i', j', h \rangle \in list[h]$ **then**
7:             Remove $\langle i', j', h \rangle$ from $list[h]$ and insert $\langle i, j, h \rangle$ into $list[h]$
8:      Set $D \leftarrow \emptyset$
9:      $p \leftarrow 0$, $q \leftarrow 1$
10:      **while** $p \leq r$ and $q \leq r$ **do** $\triangleright list[p]$ compares with $list[q]$
11:          **if** $\langle i, j, p \rangle \in list[p]$ dominates $\langle i', j', q \rangle \in list[q]$ **then**
12:             Remove $\langle i', j', q \rangle$ from $list[q]$
13:             $q \leftarrow q + 1$
14:          **else**
15:             $p \leftarrow q$, $q \leftarrow q + 1$
16:      Insert each $\langle i, j, h \rangle \in list[h]$ into D
17:      **return** D

Table 1. An example for the construction of $D_{i,l}$ with $A = $ ccdbbcbdcd, $B = $ dccbbcdbcb and $C = $ db, where a strikethrough symbol means that the 3-tuple element is dominated and thus removed.

Round t	Length(l)							
	0	1	2	3	4	5	6	7
1	$D_{0,0}$ $\langle 0,0,2 \rangle$	$D_{1,1}$ $\langle 1,2,2 \rangle$	$D_{2,2}$ $\langle 2,3,2 \rangle$	$D_{3,3}$ $\langle 3,7,1 \rangle$	$D_{4,4}$ $\langle 4,8,0 \rangle$	$D_{5,5}$ $\langle 5,10,0 \rangle$		
2	$D_{1,0}$ $\langle 0,0,2 \rangle$	$D_{2,1}$ $\langle 1,2,2 \rangle$ ~~$\langle 2,2,2 \rangle$~~	$D_{3,2}$ $\langle 3,7,1 \rangle$ $\langle 2,3,2 \rangle$	$D_{4,3}$ $\langle 4,8,0 \rangle$ $\langle 3,7,1 \rangle$ $\langle 4,4,2 \rangle$ $\langle 5,5,2 \rangle$	$D_{5,4}$ $\langle 4,8,0 \rangle$ ~~$\langle 5,8,0 \rangle$~~ ~~$\langle 5,10,0 \rangle$~~	$D_{6,5}$ $\langle 6,9,0 \rangle$ ~~$\langle 5,10,0 \rangle$~~ $\langle 6,6,2 \rangle$	$D_{7,6}$ $\langle 7,10,0 \rangle$	
3	$D_{2,0}$ $\langle 0,0,2 \rangle$	$D_{3,1}$ $\langle 3,1,1 \rangle$ ~~$\langle 1,2,2 \rangle$~~	$D_{4,2}$ $\langle 4,4,0 \rangle$ ~~$\langle 3,7,1 \rangle$~~ $\langle 2,3,2 \rangle$	$D_{5,3}$ ~~$\langle 4,8,0 \rangle$~~ $\langle 5,5,0 \rangle$ ~~$\langle 3,7,1 \rangle$~~ $\langle 4,4,2 \rangle$ ~~$\langle 5,4,2 \rangle$~~	$D_{6,4}$ ~~$\langle 4,8,0 \rangle$~~ $\langle 6,6,0 \rangle$ $\langle 5,5,2 \rangle$ ~~$\langle 6,6,2 \rangle$~~	$D_{7,5}$ ~~$\langle 6,9,0 \rangle$~~ $\langle 7,8,0 \rangle$ $\langle 6,6,2 \rangle$	$D_{8,6}$ $\langle 7,10,0 \rangle$ $\langle 8,7,1 \rangle$	$D_{9,7}$ $\langle 9,9,1 \rangle$
4	$D_{3,0}$ $\langle 0,0,2 \rangle$	$D_{4,1}$ $\langle 3,1,1 \rangle$ ~~$\langle 4,4,2 \rangle$~~	$D_{5,2}$ $\langle 4,4,0 \rangle$ ~~$\langle 5,4,0 \rangle$~~ $\langle 2,3,2 \rangle$	$D_{6,3}$ $\langle 5,5,0 \rangle$ ~~$\langle 6,6,0 \rangle$~~ $\langle 4,4,2 \rangle$ ~~$\langle 6,6,2 \rangle$~~	$D_{7,4}$ $\langle 6,6,0 \rangle$ ~~$\langle 7,8,0 \rangle$~~ $\langle 5,5,2 \rangle$ ~~$\langle 7,5,2 \rangle$~~	$D_{8,5}$ ~~$\langle 7,8,0 \rangle$~~ $\langle 8,7,0 \rangle$ $\langle 6,6,2 \rangle$ ~~$\langle 8,7,1 \rangle$~~	$D_{9,6}$ ~~$\langle 7,10,0 \rangle$~~ $\langle 9,9,0 \rangle$ $\langle 8,7,1 \rangle$	$D_{10,7}$ $\langle 9,9,1 \rangle$

Theorem 2. *Algorithm 1 solves the CLCS problem in $O(rL(m - L))$ time and $O(mr)$ space.*

Proof. The algorithm terminates when it finds $|CLCS(A, B, C)| = L$. The number of rounds (t) is no more than $m - L$. The inner loop is executed at most L times. $|D_{i,l}| \leq r$, because of the domination property. It means that operation EXTENSION is performed at most r times in each cell. Hence, the time complexity of Algorithm 1 is $O(rL(m - L))$. Since $|D_{i,l}| \leq r$, the space required in each cell is $O(r)$. The space in different rounds can be reused. Thus, the space complexity of the algorithm is $O(Lr) = O(mr)$.

4   Experimental Results

This section presents the experimental results of the proposed algorithm compared with the algorithms of Chin *et al.* [3], Arslan and Eğecioğlu [2], Deorowicz [4], and Ho *et al.* [5]. The experimental environment is a computer running 64-bit Windows 7 OS with 3.30 GHz CPU (Intel Core i5-4590) and 8 GB RAM. These algorithms are implemented in C++ by Code::Blocks 13.12 with the GNU compiler collection GCC 4.8.1. In the experiment, the *similarity* of two sequences A and B is defined in Eq. 3.

$$similarity(A, B) = \frac{LCS(A, B)}{\min\{|A|, |B|\}}. \tag{3}$$

The program is executed 100 times for each parameter combination: $|C|$ $\in \{2, 4\}$, $|\Sigma| = 256$, and $|A| = |B| = 1000$. Figure 1 shows that our algorithm has better performance than other algorithms obviously. Furthermore, our algorithm needs fewer execution time when the similarities more than 70% or less than 20%. With higher similarity, the number of match pairs between A and B increases, hence our algorithm will find the feasible solution faster. On the other hand, with lower similarity, the number of match pairs between A and B decreases, our algorithm needs to compute fewer match pairs, it reduces the computation time.

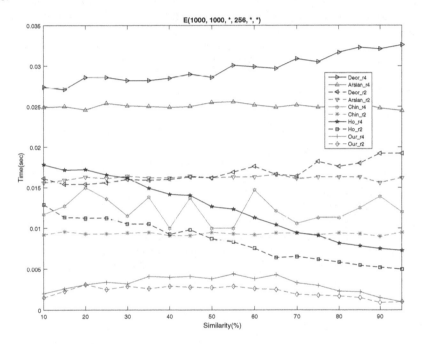

Fig. 1. The execution time (in seconds) for various similarities from 10% to 95% with $|A| = 1000$, $|B| = 1000$, $|C| \in \{2, 4\}$, and $|\Sigma| = 256$. `Chin_r4` represents the algorithm of Chin *et al.* with $|C| = 4$ and `Our_r2` represents our algorithm with $|C| = 2$.

5   Conclusion

This paper proposes a diagonal-based algorithm for solving the constrained longest common subsequence (CLCS) problem in $O(rL(m - L))$ time and in $O(mr)$ space, where m, r, and L denote the lengths of input sequences A, C, and CLCS length, respectively. As the experimental results show, our algorithm requires less execution time while the number of match pairs of A and B is small or their similarity is higher than 70%. The proposed algorithm uses $O(mr)$ space

432   S.-H. Hung et al.

to store the 3-tuple elements for finding $|CLCS(A, B, C)|$. In the future, it is worthy of discussing the properties of the 3-tuple elements between neighboring cells for reducing redundant calculation.

References

1. Ann, H.Y., Yang, C.B., Tseng, C.T., Hor, C.Y.: Fast algorithms for computing the constrained LCS of run-length encoded strings. Theor. Comput. Sci. **432**, 1–9 (2012)
2. Arslan, A.N., Eğecioğlu, Ö.: Algorithms for the constrained longest common subsequence problems. Int. J. Found. Comput. Sci. **16**(06), 1099–1109 (2005)
3. Chin, F.Y.L., Santis, A.D., Ferrara, A.L., Ho, N.L., Kim, S.K.: A simple algorithm for the constrained sequence problems. Inform. Process. Lett. **90**(4), 175–179 (2004)
4. Deorowicz, S.: Fast algorithm for the constrained longest common subsequence problem. Theor. Appl. Inform. **19**(2), 91–102 (2007)
5. Ho, W.C., Huang, K.S., Yang, C.B.: A fast algorithm for the constrained longest common subsequence problem with small alphabet. In: Proceedings of the 34th Workshop on Combinatorial Mathematics and Computation Theory, Taichung, Taiwan, pp. 13–25 (2017)
6. Hunt, J.W., Szymanski, T.G.: A fast algorithm for computing longest common subsequences. Commun. ACM **20**(5), 350–353 (1977)
7. Kruskal, J.B.: An overview of sequence comparison: time warps, string edits, and macromolecules. SIAM Rev. **25**(2), 201–237 (1983)
8. Nakatsu, N., Kambayashi, Y., Yajima, S.: A longest common subsequence algorithm suitable for similar text strings. Acta Inform. **18**, 171–179 (1982)
9. Peng, C.L.: An approach for solving the constrained longest common subsequence problem. Master's Thesis, Department of Computer Science and Engineering, National Sun Yat-Sen University, Kaohsiung, Taiwan (2003)
10. Peng, Y.H., Yang, C.B., Huang, K.S., Tseng, K.T.: An algorithm and applications to sequence alignment with weighted constraints. Int. J. Found. Comput. Sci. **21**, 51–59 (2010)
11. Tsai, Y.T.: The constrained longest common subsequence problem. Inform. Process. Lett. **88**, 173–176 (2003)
12. Tseng, K.T., Chan, D.S., Yang, C.B., Lo, S.F.: Efficient merged longest common subsequence algorithms for similar sequences. Theor. Comput. Sci. **708**, 75–90 (2018)
13. Wagner, R., Fischer, M.: The string-to-string correction problem. J. ACM **21**(1), 168–173 (1974)

Designing an Algorithm to Improve the Diameters of Completely Independent Spanning Trees in Crossed Cubes

Kung-Jui Pai[(✉)] [iD]

Department of Industrial Engineering and Management,
Ming Chi University of Technology, New Taipei City, Taiwan, ROC
poter@mail.mcut.edu.tw

Abstract. Let T_1, T_2 be spanning trees in a graph G. If for any two vertices u, v of G, the paths from u to v in T_1, T_2 are vertex-disjoint except end vertices u and v, then T_1, T_2 are called two completely independent spanning trees (CISTs for short) in Pai and Chang [12] proposed an approach to recursively construct two CISTs in several hypercube-variant networks, including crossed cubes. For every kind of n-dimensional variant cube, the diameters of two CISTs for their construction are $2n - 1$. In this paper, we give a new algorithm to construct two CISTs T_1 and T_2 in n-dimensional crossed cubes, and show that $\operatorname{diam}(T_1) = \operatorname{diam}(T_2) = 2n - 2$ if $n \in \{4, 5\}$; and $\operatorname{diam}(T_1) = \operatorname{diam}(T_2) = 2n - 3$ if $n \geq 6$ where $\operatorname{diam}(G)$ is the diameter of graph G.

Keywords: Interconnection networks ·
Completely independent spanning trees · Crossed cubes · Diameter

1 Introduction

Let G be a simple undirected graph with vertex set $V(G)$ and edge set $E(G)$. For two vertices $u, v \in V(G)$, an (u, v)-path is a path connecting u and v. Two (u, v)-paths P_1 and P_2 are called *openly disjoint* if they are vertex-disjoint apart from their end vertices. Let T_1, T_2 be *spanning trees* of G. If for any two vertices u, v of G, the paths from u to v in T_1, T_2 are pairwise openly disjoint, then T_1, T_2 are called two *completely independent spanning trees* (abbreviated as CISTs) in G. Since the topology of the network can be modeled as a graph that vertices are treated as nodes and edges represent links between the nodes. The CIST problem can be applied to the fault-tolerant broadcasting problem in networks.

In 2001, the CIST problem was first introduced by Hasunuma [6, 7], and the decision problem as to whether there exist two CISTs in a general graph G has been shown NP-hard [7]. Thus, related investigations tended to study k CISTs on certain families of graphs [3, 6, 7, 9, 11–13], for $k \geq 2$. For example, there exist two CISTs on 4-connected maximal planar graphs [7], several hypercube-variant networks [12], and the Cartesian product of two 2-connected graphs [9]. Some studies provide degree-based conditions that are sufficient for graphs admitting CISTs [1, 2, 5, 8, 10].

© Springer Nature Singapore Pte Ltd. 2019
C.-Y. Chang et al. (Eds.): ICS 2018, CCIS 1013, pp. 433–439, 2019.
https://doi.org/10.1007/978-981-13-9190-3_46

The *diameter* of a graph G, denoted by $\text{diam}(G)$, is the greatest distance between any two vertices in G. It represents the lower bound on required time in the worst case for performing some fundamental operations in the corresponding network, such as routing, broadcasting, data aggregation, and so on. In 2016, Pai and Chang [12] proposed an approach to recursively construct two CISTs, including crossed cubes, in several hypercube-variant networks. For each n-dimensional variant cube, the diameters of two CISTs for their construction are $2n - 1$. Recently, we have improve the diameters of CISTs in locally twisted cubes [13]. Unfortunately, the previous technique cannot be applied to reduce the diameters of CISTs in n-dimensional crossed cubes. In this paper, we provide an algorithm for constructing two CISTs T_1 and T_2 in crossed cubes, and show that $\text{diam}(T_1) = \text{diam}(T_2) = 2n - 2$ if $n \in \{4,5\}$; and $\text{diam}(T_1) = \text{diam}(T_2) = 2n - 3$ if $n \geq 6$.

2 Preliminaries

In this paper, we shall adopt the following notation. Vertices in crossed cubes are encoded by using binary strings. For the sake of brevity, sometimes the labels will change to their decimal. A binary string B of length n is denoted by $b_{n-1}b_{n-2}...b_1b_0$, where $b_i \in \{0, 1\}$ for $0 \leq i \leq n - 1$. For a labeled graph G and a binary string B, we use G^x to denote the graph obtained from G by prefixing the binary string of every vertex with x. Two binary strings $B = b_1b_0$ and $A = a_1a_0$ are pair-related, denoted $B \sim A$, if and only if $(B, A) \in \{(00, 00), (10, 10), (01, 11), (11, 01)\}$. The n-dimensional crossed cube CQ_n is the labeled graph with the following recursive fashion [4]:

(1) CQ_1 is the complete graph on two vertices with labels 0 and 1.
(2) For $n \geq 2$, CQ_n is composed of two subcubes CQ_{n-1}^0 and CQ_{n-1}^1 such that two vertices $B = 0b_{n-2}...b_1b_0 \in V(CQ_{n-1}^0)$ and $A = 1a_{n-2}...a_1a_0 \in V(CQ_{n-1}^1)$ are joined by an edge if and only if (i) $b_{n-2} = a_{n-2}$ if n is even, and (ii) $b_{2i+1}b_{2i} \sim a_{2i+1}a_{2i}$ for $0 \leq i < \lfloor (n - 1)/2 \rfloor$, where B and A are called the $(n - 1)$-neighbors to each other, and denote as $N_{n-1}(B) = A$ or $N_{n-1}(A) = B$.

Figure 1 depicts CQ_4. In order to show the correctness of our construction, we rely on the following properties.

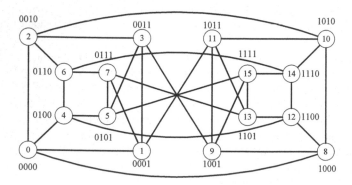

Fig. 1. A crossed cube CQ_4.

Theorem 1 [6]. *Let $k \geq 2$ be an integer. $T_1, T_2, \ldots, T_k$ are CISTs in a graph G if and only if they are edge-disjoint spanning trees of G and for any $u \in V(G)$, there is at most one T_i such that u is not a leaf (i.e., u is an internal vertex of T_i).*

Theorem 2 [1]. *A connected graph G has two CISTs if and only if there is a partition of $V(G)$ into V_1 and V_2, which is call a CIST-partition, such that*

(1) *for $i \in \{1, 2\}$, the subgraph of G induced by V_i, denoted by $G[V_i]$, is connected;*
(2) *the bipartite graph $B(V_1, V_2, G)$ with vertex set $V(G)$ and edge set $\{(x, y) \in E(G): x \in V_1, y \in V_2\}$ has no tree component, that is, every connected component H of B (V_1, V_2, G) satisfies $|E(H)| \geq |V(H)|$.*

Theorem 3 [12]. *A Let G_n be the n-dimensional variant hypercube (including crossed cube) for $n \geq 4$ and suppose that T_1 and T_2 are two CISTs of G_n. For $i \in \{1, 2\}$, let T'_i be a spanning tree of G_{n+1} constructed from T_i^0 and T_i^1 by adding an edge $(u_i, v_i) \in E (G_{n+1})$ to connect two internal vertices $u_i \in V(T_i^0)$ and $v_i \in V(T_i^1)$, which are called the port vertices of T_i^0 and T_i^1, respectively. Then, T'_1 and T'_2 are two CISTs of G_{n+1}.*

3   Main Results

We first consider CQ_4 as shown in Fig. 1 and construct two spanning trees of CQ_4 with diameter 6 as shown in Fig. 2. It is easy to check that both T_1 and T_2 are edge-disjoint, and every vertex of CQ_4 is an internal vertex either in T_1 or T_2. By Theorem 1, the two spanning trees are CISTs of CQ_4. Then, we have the following lemma.

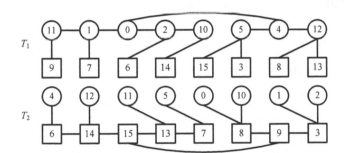

Fig. 2. Two CISTs of CQ_4. Circular vertices are internal vertices in T_1 and square vertices are internal vertices in T_2.

Lemma 4. *There exist two CISTs with diameter 6 in CQ_4.*

Then, we consider the recursive construction of two CISTs in high-dimensional crossed cubes by Theorem 3. It notes that the center of a tree is defined as the set of vertices which minimize the maximum distance from other vertices. In Fig. 2, T_1 and T_2 are two CISTs of CQ_4, and they have center vertices 0 and 15, respectively. We choose vertex 0 at T_1^0 in CQ_4^0 and vertex 16 ($= 0 + 2^4 = N_4(0)$) at T_1^1 in CQ_4^1 as the port vertices. After adding an edge $(0, 16)$ to connect T_1^0 and T_1^1, we have T'_1 with diameter 7 in CQ_5. By the pair-related property of crossed cubes, 4-neighbor of vertex 15 is vertex 21 (= $5 + 2^4$). According to Theorem 3, construct T_2' by adding an edge (15, 21) to connect T_2^0 and T_2^1 is erroneous because vertex 5 is a leaf in T_2. We need to find a center v in T_i^0 and a center u in T_i^1 such that $u = N_n(v)$, i.e. $u = v + 2^n$, for $i \in \{1, 2\}$. Considering the pair-related property of crossed cubes, only four vertices 0(000), 2 (0010), 8(1000) and 10(1010) in CQ_4 meet the above condition. The idea of designing algorithms has emerged. The subject of the algorithm is to find two CISTs T_1 with the center 0, T_2 with the center 10, and diameters of both T_1, T_2 are all limited.

Algorithm A: Finding 2 CISTs in CQ_n while $n \geq 5$
Input: A graph G and p // p : vertices number of G
Output: s[0, ..., $p-1$]   // s[i] = 1 (or 2) : vertex i is in V_1 (or V_2)
step 1. s[0] ← 1; s[1] ← 1; s[2] ← 1; s[8] ← 1;
step 2. h[0] ← 0; h[1] ← 1; h[2] ← 1; h[8] ← 1;   // h[i] : the level of vertex i
step 3. s[10] ← 2; s[11] ← 2; s[14] ← 2; s[26] ← 2;
step 4. h[10] ← 0; h[11] ← 1; h[14] ← 1; h[26] ← 1;
step 5. **if** expandT(1, 4) = TRUE **then**
step 6.   **if** expandT(2, 4) = TRUE **then**
step 7.   construct the bipartite graph $B(V_1, V_2, G)$ according s[0, ..., $p-1$] and G;
step 8.   **for** each component H in $B(V_1, V_2, G)$
step 9.   **if** $|E(H)| \geq |V(H)|$ **then**
step 10.   output s[0, ..., $p-1$];   // s[...] is a CIST-partition by Theorem 2
step 11.   **end if**
step 12.   **end for**
step 13.   **end if**
step 14. **end if**

Procedure expandT(t, c)   // t = 1 (or 2) for T_1 (or T_2), c : number of vertices in T_t
step 1. **if** $c < p / 2$ **then**
step 2.   **for** $v \leftarrow 0$ **to** $p - 1$ **do**   // select a vertex v
step 3.   **if** s[v] = 0 **then**   // vertex v is not in V_1 or V_2
step 4.   **for** $u \leftarrow 0$ **to** $p - 1$ **do**   // find vertex u in T_t
step 5.   **if** s[u] = t **and** v is adjacent to u **and** h[u] ≤ 2 **then**
step 6.   s[v] ← t;
step 7.   h[v] ← h[u] + 1;
step 8.   expandT(t, $c + 1$)
step 9.   **end if**
step 10.   **end for**
step 11.   **end if**
step 12.   **end for**
step 13.   **Return** FALSE;
step 14. **else**
step 15.   **Return** TRUE;
step 16. **end if**

According to Theorem 2, we need to partition $V(CQ_n)$ into V_1 and V_2. In fact, all vertices in V_1 are internal vertices in the CIST T_1, and all vertices in V_2 are internal vertices in the CIST T_2. The procedure expandT(t, c) is recursive function that expands one vertex in T_t at a time while $t \in \{1, 2\}$ and c is number of vertices in T_t. h$[0...p - 1]$ record the level of each vertex while p is number of vertices in G. A vertex u can be added to T_t if the level of its neighbor less than or equal to 2. This requirement is for good diameters of CIST. After the end of the recursion, we have a subtree of T_1 with $p/2$ vertices. Taking T_1 in Fig. 3 as an example, each circular vertex is added at a time. Vertex 29 can be added in T_1 since the level of vertex 7 is equal to 2. After the recursive function expandT(1, 4) ends, we have a subtree of T_1 which is induced by circular vertices.

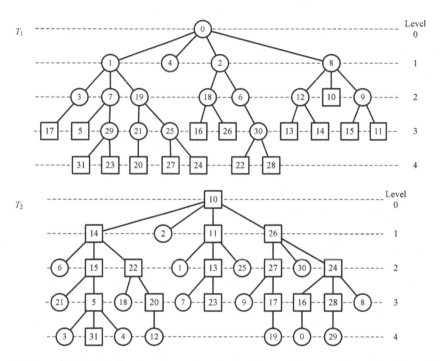

Fig. 3. Two CISTs of CQ_5. Circular vertices and square vertices are belonged to V_1 and V_2, respectively.

Algorithm A is designed for finding two CISTs in CQ_n while $n \geq 5$, vertices 0, 1, 2, 8 are added into V_1 and vertices 10, 11, 14, 26 are added into V_2 in steps 1 to 4. It is used to speed up operation time and reducing the height of the tree. In steps 5 and 6, Algorithm A call expandT(1, 4) and expandT(2, 4) to find CISTs T_1 and T_2 with only $|V|/2$ internal vertices, respectively. Then, we have s$[0, ..., p - 1]$, since s$[u] = t$ for vertex u is belong to T_t. In steps 7 to 10, the bipartite graph $B(V_1, V_2, G)$ can be constructed according s$[0, ..., p - 1]$ and G. By using Depth-first search in the textbook, all components in $B(V_1, V_2, G)$ can be found. Next, if $|E(H)| \geq |V(H)|$ for each component H, then s$[0, \ldots, p - 1]$ represent the CIST-partition according Theorem 2.

By computing results, we have two CISTs in CQ_5, as shown in Fig. 3, with the following lemma.

Lemma 5. *There exist two CISTs with diameter* 8 *in* CQ_5.

According to Theorem 3, we can choose the pairs $\{0, 2^n\}$ and $\{10, 10 + 2^n\}$ as port vertices for building two CISTs of CQ_{n+1} by using induction on n. Let T_1' and T_2' be the two constructed CISTs of CQ_{n+1}. According to the construction, if follows that

$$\mathrm{diam}\left(T_i'\right) = 2\frac{\mathrm{diam}(T_i)}{2} + 1, \text{for } i\{1, 2\} \tag{1}$$

We obtain the following theorem by combining Lemma 4, 5 and solving the Eq. (1) under the base case $\mathrm{diam}(T_i) = 8$ when $n = 5$ and $i \in \{1, 2\}$.

Theorem 6. *For* $n \geq 4$, *the crossed cubes* CQ_n *admits two CISTs* T_1 *and* T_2 *with diameter described below. For* $i \in \{1, 2\}$,

$$diam(T_i) = \begin{cases} 2n - 2 & \text{if } n \in \{4, 5\} \\ 2n - 3 & \text{if } n \geq 6 \end{cases} \tag{2}$$

4   Concluding Remarks

As aforementioned, we have designed an algorithm to find two CISTs T_1 with the center 0 and T_2 with the center 10 in CQ_5, and the diameter of both T_1, T_2 is 8. Choosing the pairs $\{0, 2^n\}$ and $\{10, 10 + 2^n\}$ as port vertices for building two CISTs of CQ_{n+1}, the diameters of CISTs in CQ_n have been improved for $n \geq 5$. However, it still remains an open question whether the diameters of CISTs in hypercubes, parity cubes, and Möbius cubes can be improved.

Acknowledgments.   This research was partially supported by MOST grants 107-2221-E-131-011 from the Ministry of Science and Technology, Taiwan.

References

1. Araki, T.: Dirac's condition for completely independent spanning trees. J. Graph Theory **77**, 171–179 (2014)
2. Chang, H.Y., Wang, H.L., Yang, J.S., Chang, J.M.: A note on the degree condition of completely independent spanning trees. IEICE Trans. Fundam. **E98-A**, 2191–2193 (2015)
3. Darties, B., Gastineau, N., Togni, O.: Completely independent spanning trees in some regular graphs. Discrete Appl. Math. **217**, 163–174 (2017)

4. Efe, K.: The crossed cube architecture for parallel computation. IEEE Trans. Parallel Distrib. Syst. **3**, 513–524 (1992)
5. Fan, G., Hong, Y., Liu, Q.: Ore's condition for completely independent spanning trees. Discrete Appl. Math. **177**, 95–100 (2014)
6. Hasunuma, T.: Completely independent spanning trees in the underlying graph of a line digraph. Discrete Math. **234**, 149–157 (2001)
7. Hasunuma, T.: Completely independent spanning trees in maximal planar graphs. In: Goos, G., Hartmanis, J., van Leeuwen, J., Kučera, L. (eds.) WG 2002. LNCS, vol. 2573, pp. 235–245. Springer, Heidelberg (2002). https://doi.org/10.1007/3-540-36379-3_21
8. Hasunuma, T.: Minimum degree conditions and optimal graphs for completely independent spanning trees. In: Lipták, Z., Smyth, W.F. (eds.) IWOCA 2015. LNCS, vol. 9538, pp. 260–273. Springer, Cham (2016). https://doi.org/10.1007/978-3-319-29516-9_22
9. Hasunuma, T., Morisaka, C.: Completely independent spanning trees in torus networks. Networks **60**, 59–69 (2012)
10. Hong, X., Liu, Q.: Degree condition for completely independent spanning trees. Inform. Process. Lett. **116**, 644–648 (2016)
11. Matsushita, M., Otachi, Y., Araki, T.: Completely independent spanning trees in (partial) k-trees. Discuss. Math. Graph Theory **35**, 427–437 (2015)
12. Pai, K.J., Chang, J.M.: Constructing two completely independent spanning trees in hypercube-variant networks. Theor. Comput. Sci. **652**, 28–37 (2016)
13. Pai, K.J., Chang, J.M.: Improving the diameters of completely independent spanning trees in locally twisted cubes. Inform. Process. Lett. **141**, 22–24 (2019)

A Measure and Conquer Algorithm for the Minimum User Spatial-Aware Interest Group Query Problem

Chih-Yang Huang[1]([⊠]) [iD], Po-Chuan Chien[2] [iD], and Yen Hung Chen[1]

[1] Department of Computer Science, University of Taipei, Taipei, Taiwan (R.O.C.)
user@hcy.idv.tw, yhchen@utaipei.edu.tw
[2] Research Center for Information Technology Innovation, Academia Sinica,
Taipei, Taiwan (R.O.C.)
dibery@citi.sinica.edu.tw

Abstract. Location-based social networks are important issues in the recent decade. In modern social networks, websites such as Twitter, Facebook, and Plurk, attempt to get the accurate address positions from their users, and try to reduce the gap between virtuality and reality. This paper mainly aims at both the interests of Internet users and their real positions. This issue is called the spatial-aware interest group query problem (SIGQP). Given a user set U with n users, a keywords set W with m words, and a spatial objects set S with s items, each of which contains one or multiple keywords. If a user checks in a certain spatial object, it means the user could be interested in that part of keywords, which is countable to clarify the interests of the user. The SIGQP then tries to find a k-user set U_k, $k \le n$, such that the union of keywords of these k users will equal to W, and additionally, the diameter (longest Euclidean distance of two arbitrary users in U_k) should be as small as possible. The SIGQP has been proved as NP-Complete, and two heuristic algorithms have been proposed. Extended from SIGQP, the main problem of this paper prioritizes in finding the smallest k for U_k to cover all the keywords, with the users' distance as the secondary criterion, called as "minimum user spatial-aware interest group query problem" (MUSIGQP). This paper further designs an exact algorithm on a measure-&-conquer-based method to precisely solve this problem, and a performance analysis is given.

Keywords: Spatial-aware interest group query problem ·
NP-Complete · Exact algorithms · Computing problem ·
Group queries · Location-based service

1 Introduction

Mobile phone positioning and social network have been seen as significant and innovative issues in the recent decade [26]. The goal of group queries in location-based social networks is to find a group of users where members are close to each other and have same interests [19,32].

© Springer Nature Singapore Pte Ltd. 2019
C.-Y. Chang et al. (Eds.): ICS 2018, CCIS 1013, pp. 440–448, 2019.
https://doi.org/10.1007/978-981-13-9190-3_47

Li et al., proposed the spatial-aware interest group query problem (SIGQP) in order to combine the issues of positioning and group queries in location-based social networks [8, 18]. Given n user sets in $U = \{u_1, u_2, ..., u_n\}$, s spatial objects in $S = \{p_1, p_2, ..., p_s\}$ and m keywords in $W = \{w_1, w_2, ..., w_m\}$, with each spatial object consisting of one or more keywords, it is feasible to count the value of interests of a user if it checks in some spatial objects. The normalized interest value of user u over keyword w is indicated as $I(u, w)$, which is illustrated in Eq. 1, where $count(u, p)$ is the total time of the user u checking in the spatial object p, and the collection of i spatial objects that user u has been is denoted as $S_u = \{p_1', p_2', ..., p_i'\}$.

$$I(u, w) = \frac{count(u, w)}{\sum\limits_{p \in S_u} count(u, p)} \qquad (1)$$

We then furthermore consider a more general case where a user is interested in multiple keywords, collected as a set W'. The interest score $I(u, W')$ over that keyword group is evaluated as the aggregation of the interest values of all keywords in W' (i.e., $\sum_{w \in W'} I(u, w)$). A spatial-aware interest group (SIG) query is defined to find a user set U_k with k users, $k \leq n$, to cover all m keywords. Furthermore, an adjustment α is introduced so that we can adjust the weight between the interest and the distance of the users, and the maximization objective function (where the maximization target is the $Rank$ of the selected U_k) is defined in Eq. 2 [18].

$$Rank_\alpha(U_k) = \alpha \times \min\{I(u, W) | u \in U_k\} + (1 - \alpha)(D(U) - D(U_k)) \qquad (2)$$

$D(U)$ and $D(U_k)$ are the diameters of the user sets U and U_k, which is the farthest Euclidean distance between any two users in that set, and can be calculated by $\max_{i,j \in U_k} \sqrt{(x_i - x_j)^2 + (y_i - y_j)^2}$.

When $\alpha = 1$, the distance of users would be irrelevant, and using the fewest group of users to cover all the keywords will be the main issue. We call this problem as a minimum user spatial-aware interest group query problem (MUSIGQP), and highlight on the keywords coverage over the users' distance. In this case, the minimum set cover (MSC) method, an exact algorithm, can be applied, and we can derive an exact answer toward MUSIGQP. Because MSC uses least number of sets to cover all keywords, the result of MUSIGQP will consist of as least groups as possible. However, this would totally ignore the factor of the distances, so in later sections, we will show how to deal with the distances between users by integrating the concept of distance into the MSC algorithm.

Our contribution is as follows: To our knowledge, there is no MUSIGQP research for the design of non-trivial brute force exact algorithms, and as an enhancement to existent approximation solutions, we provide a precise solution of the problem. In real world applications, every check-in place could be seen as a spatial object p in MUSIGQP, and there are some features or keywords for those places. For example, Starbucks is representative of the words "food", "coffee", or "drink", while Vie Show Cinemas is the symbol of the words "movie" and "popcorn". Also, every word could be seen as a keyword in MUSIGQP. If a user checks in a Starbucks coffee shop, it means the user would be interested in words (keywords) like "coffee" or "drink". Our algorithms on MUSIGQP consider not only the keywords but also the users' distances. It makes the users have the common interests and stay in the near spots. Broadcasting the advertisements and marketing are possible applications for MUSIGQP.

2 Related Work

With the development of location-aware devices, ubiquitous Internet, and the techniques of social computing, access to the position as well as social information of a user are more available. A lot of researches [16,17,19,32] are aiming at finding a group of users who are close and interested in the common issues, based on group queries in location-based social networks. For example, the issue of expert collaboration queries is to find a group of experts who know all the skills, and their distances are not far.

If we consider spatial query processing, R-tree and R* tree are available. In the recent 30 years, there are a lot of queries we can use, such as k-nearest-neighbor queries [11,14,15,24,27], range queries [23,29], and closest-pair queries [4,10,28]. There are also some researches [3,5,20,25,31,33] combining spatial query processing and keywords. In addition, some researches propose group and team query on social network [2,9,16,17,19,32]. Li [18] and the others identify $Rank_\alpha(U_k)$ and SIGQP [1,21,30] and develop two heuristic algorithms, based on the technique of IR-tree [3]. They reduce the set cover problem into a SIGQP [8] and prove it as NP-Complete. However, SIGQP is similar to maximum coverage problem [12,22]. It can be solved by $(1 - 1/e)$-approximation algorithm [12] ($e \approx 2.718$) through Greedy skills. Its lower bound of approximation rate is $(1 - 1/e) + o(1) \approx 0.632$ [6,12].

3 Problem Formulation and Solution Approach

In a SIGQP, we consider a situation where a user set $U = \{u_1, u_2, \ldots, u_{|U|}\}$, a spacial object set $S = \{p_1, p_2, \ldots, p_{|S|}\}$, and a keyword set $W = \{w_1, w_2, \ldots, w_{|W|}\}$ exist, and satisfy $\forall u \in U, \exists p \in S \land p \in u$ and $\forall p \in S, \exists w \in W \land w \in p$, from which we can infer that an element $u \in U$ is factually a set of keywords $w \in W$, and that every user in the user set will be inherently associated with a group of keywords using the transitive law.

Since the goal of a MUSIGQP is to select a user set $U' \subseteq U$ such that all keywords in W are covered, we can, without loss of generality, eliminate the spatial object group S from the problem and construct the direct relationship between a user and a keyword. Because our goal is still to select a U' such that the union of keywords from all users in U' will be equal to W, we can restate the MUSIGQP as a minimum set cover (MSC) problem, by regarding W as the universe set, and U as the collection of sets. user_set is denoted as a group of users and each of user has its position as well as part of keywords.

In the following subsections, we will be concentrated on the exact solution approach of minimum set cover problems.

3.1 Measure and Conquer Exact Algorithm for MSC

Fomin, Grandoni, and Kratsch proposed an algorithm to exactly solve the MSC problem by finding the minimum number of sets required to cover all the keywords [7]. However, such number does not help when we wish to find out which sets are chosen. Therefore, we modify this algorithm, which is illustrated in Fig. 1, so that the algorithm returns the actually selected sets.

The input of the algorithm msc is a user set M, where each user obtains some keywords, and its output is still a user set. First, if M is empty, a null set will be returned, and when the keywords of user u_1 is the subset of another user u_2, we can still derive the correct answer by removing user u_1 from M as if it is not existent in the beginning because choosing u_2 always produces no worse result than choosing u_1. In addition, if user u_3 has some unique keywords (that is, those keywords are not existent in other users), we must select u_3 in the final answer. When every user in M has only two keywords, a graph matching method can be applied, and finally, it returns the smaller user set between the recursion of whether or not selecting an arbitrary user u_4 from M in the final result.

Removing a user u from input set M, denoted as $M \backslash \{u\}$ in the algorithm, is achieved by totally ignoring that user, and has no impact on other users in the set, while on the other hand, selecting a user u in the final result, denoted as $del(u, M)$, will additionally eliminate all keywords of u from other users in M. Reasoning of the above method is similar to that in [7], and the algorithm 2_msc(S) is a kind of graph matching [13].

```
1  user_set msc(user_set M) {
2      if (|M| = 0)
3          return ∅; // base case (empty set)
4      if (∃ u₁, u₂ ∈ M and u₁ ⊆ u₂)
5          return msc(M\{u₁});
6      if (∃ u₃ ∈ M s.t. only u₃ has a certain keyword w ∈ W)
7          return u₃ ∪ msc(del(u₃, M));
8      if (∀ u ∈ M s.t. |u| = 2)
9          return 2_msc(M)  // 2_msc(M) is a kind of graph matching
10     choose an arbitrary user u₄ ∈ M
11     return min{msc(M\{u₄}), u₄ ∪ msc(del(u₄, M))};
12 }
```

Fig. 1. Algorithm msc for the minimum set cover problem on MUSIGQP.

3.2 Measure and Conquer Exact Algorithm for MSC with Consideration of Distance

When there are multiple combinations of groups that can satisfy the criteria that every keyword is selected, we would show an inclination to choose the group whose diameter, calculated by the max distance between user (i,j) in the group, is smaller. The standard method described in the above subsection does not, however, take the Euclidean distance between users into consideration; consequently, such a method may not be able to derive the desired solution.

To handle such situations, we will need to take the distance between users into account. The modified version, denoted as exact_MUSIGQP later in this paper, is illustrated in Fig. 2

```
1   user_set exact_MUSIGQP(user_set M) {
2       if(|M| = 0)
3           return ∅ // base case
4       if(∃u₁,u₂ ∈ M and u₁ ⊆ u₂)
5           return msc(M\{u₁})
6       if(∃u₃ ∈ M s.t. only u₃ has a certain keyword w ∈ W)
7           return u₃∪msc(del(u₃,M))
8       if(∀u ∈ M s.t.|u| = 2)
9           return 2_msc(M) // 2_msc(M) is a kind of graph matching
10      choose an arbitrary user u₄ ∈ M
11      return min_dist{msc(M\{u₄}), u₄∪msc(del(u₄,M))}
12  }
```

Fig. 2. Algorithm exact_MUSIGQP with consideration of distance on MUSIGQP.

In the last line, we change the min to min_dist, which will evaluate the set size first, and when the size of the two sets are equal, the group who has a smaller diameter will be returned. The algorithm of min_dist is presented in Fig. 3, description of the diameter function is given in Fig. 4.

```
1   user_set min_dist(user_set grpA, user_set grpB) {
2       if |grpA| < |grpB|
3           return grpA
4       else if |grpA| > |grpB|
5           return grpB
6       else if diameter(grpA) < diameter(grpB) // size equal
7           return grpA
8       return grpB // the last possibility
9   }
```

Fig. 3. Choose the set with a smaller size and a smaller diameter

Regarding the correct solution set as Opt, we can say that a user set u may or may not be in Opt. If $u \in Opt$, then the solution is then further found by selecting u and remove all keywords in u from other existent users; otherwise, the solution is found by eliminating u from the user set. In this way, we are capable of traversing all possible combination of groups, and because in each

```
1  diameter(user_set grp) {
2      d = 0 // the diameter
3      for each element pair (A, B) in grp
4          if Euclidean_distance(A, B) > d
5              d = Euclidean_distance(A, B)
6      return d
7  }
```

Fig. 4. Measure the diameter of a group

step of the recursion, we choose the one with a smaller diameter, in the global scope, we can achieve the optimal solution.

In the next section, we will mainly utilize this method to solve MUSIGQP and the symbols used in our problem definition is organized in Table 1.

4   Performance Evaluation

The algorithm is implemented in Java. The models of the CPU and RAM are Intel Core i7 2.2 GHz and 16 GB 1600 MHz DDR3, respectively.

Our algorithm is tested on a situation where k users, $k \in [10, 170]$, $k/2$ keywords (interests), and all k users will stand in the position where $0 \leq x \leq k$, $0 \leq y \leq k$ in the Euclidean space. Each user has a random group of keywords and a random position. The experimental result is plotted in Fig. 5, with every k users conducted 100 times and take the average. Owing to the fact that the time complexity of this algorithm is in exponential time, the running time in presented in logarithm of base 2.

It is inferred that the transformation of MUSIGQP into MSC algorithm is feasible. The time complexity of the designed algorithm would be $O(2^{0.465n})$ upper bound. On the other hand, $\Omega(2^{0.396n})$ and $\Omega(2^{0.142n})$ would be the possible lower bounds. This theorem is on the ground of A Measure & Conquer Approach

Table 1. Symbols shown in this paper

Symbol	Description
U	A user set with n users, which is $\{u_1, u_2, u_3, \ldots, u_n\}$
W	A keyword set with m words, which is $\{w_1, w_2, w_3, \ldots, w_m\}$
S	A spatial object set with p items, which is $\{p_1, p_2, p_3, \ldots, p_s\}$
S_u	The collection of all i spatial objects that user u has been, which is $\{p'_1, p'_2, p'_3, \ldots, p'_i\}$
$D(U)$	The farthest Euclidean distance between two arbitrary users in the user set U
$I(u, w)$	Interest score of user u over the keyword (set) w
α	Weight adjustment coefficient between the distance and the weight

for the Analysis of Exact Algorithms described in [7]. Thus, we could decrease the time complexity of MUSIGQP and transform MUSIGQP into MSC.

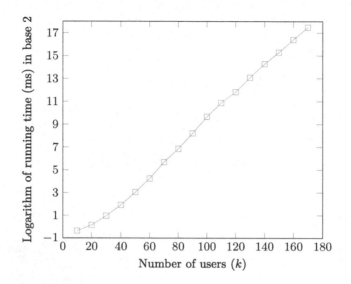

Fig. 5. Running time versus the value of k users in exact algorithm.

5   Conclusion

In this paper, we investigated the spatial-aware interest group query problem and provide two algorithms to solve MUSIGQP, with their performance being analyzed.

These algorithms are based on the MSC algorithm proposed in [7]. We transform MUSIGQP into MSC. The first exact algorithm doesn't take the Euclidean space into consideration, while the second one does. Both of them take $O(2^{0.465n})$ upper bounds, which is lower than $O(2^n)$, the time complexity of a brute force method.

All in all, we provide the exact_MUSIGQP algorithm and try to decrease the time complexity.

Acknowledgment. This research was supported by the Ministry of Science and Technology in Taiwan under the grants MOST 107-2813-C-845-025-E.

References

1. Chen, L., Cong, G., Jensen, C.S., Wu, D.: Spatial keyword query processing: an experimental evaluation. In: Proceedings of the VLDB Endowment, vol. 6, pp. 217–228. VLDB Endowment (2013)
2. Chen, S.J., Lin, L.: Modeling team member characteristics for the formation of a multifunctional team in concurrent engineering. IEEE Trans. Eng. Manag. **51**(2), 111–124 (2004)
3. Cong, G., Jensen, C.S., Wu, D.: Efficient retrieval of the top-k most relevant spatial web objects. Proc. VLDB Endow. **2**(1), 337–348 (2009)
4. Corral, A., Manolopoulos, Y., Theodoridis, Y., Vassilakopoulos, M.: Closest pair queries in spatial databases. In: ACM SIGMOD Record, vol. 29, pp. 189–200. ACM (2000)
5. De Felipe, I., Hristidis, V., Rishe, N.: Keyword search on spatial databases. In: IEEE 24th International Conference on Data Engineering, ICDE 2008, pp. 656–665. IEEE (2008)
6. Feige, U.: A threshold of ln n for approximating set cover. J. ACM (JACM) **45**(4), 634–652 (1998)
7. Fomin, F.V., Grandoni, F., Kratsch, D.: A measure & conquer approach for the analysis of exact algorithms. J. ACM (JACM) **56**(5), 25 (2009)
8. Garey, M.R., Johnson, D.S.: Computers and y: A Guide to the Theory of NP-Completeness (Series of Books in the Mathematical Sciences). Computers and Intractability, vol. 340 (1979)
9. Garg, N., Konjevod, G., Ravi, R.: A polylogarithmic approximation algorithm for the group steiner tree problem. J. Algorithms **37**(1), 66–84 (2000)
10. Hjaltason, G.R., Samet, H.: Incremental distance join algorithms for spatial databases. In: ACM SIGMOD Record, vol. 27, pp. 237–248. ACM (1998)
11. Hjaltason, G.R., Samet, H.: Distance browsing in spatial databases. ACM Trans. Database Syst. (TODS) **24**(2), 265–318 (1999)
12. Hochbaum, D.S.: Approximating covering and packing problems: set cover, vertex cover, independent set, and related problems. Approx. Algorithms NP-Hard Probl. 94–143 (1997)
13. Karpiński, M., Karpinski, M., Rytter, W.: Fast Parallel Algorithms for Graph Matching Problems, vol. 9. Oxford University Press, Oxford (1998)
14. Katayama, N., Satoh, S.: The SR-tree: an index structure for high-dimensional nearest neighbor queries. In: ACM Sigmod Record, vol. 26, no. 2, pp. 369–380 (1997)
15. Kolahdouzan, M., Shahabi, C.: Voronoi-based k nearest neighbor search for spatial network databases. In: Proceedings of the Thirtieth International Conference on Very Large Data Bases, vol. 30, pp. 840–851. VLDB Endowment (2004)
16. Lappas, T., Liu, K., Terzi, E.: Finding a team of experts in social networks. In: Proceedings of the 15th ACM SIGKDD International Conference on Knowledge Discovery and Data Mining, pp. 467–476. ACM (2009)
17. Li, C.T., Shan, M.K.: Team formation for generalized tasks in expertise social networks. In: 2010 IEEE Second International Conference on Social Computing (SocialCom), pp. 9–16. IEEE (2010)
18. Li, Y., Wu, D., Xu, J., Choi, B., Su, W.: Spatial-aware interest group queries in location-based social networks. Data Knowl. Eng. **92**, 20–38 (2014)

19. Liu, W., Sun, W., Chen, C., Huang, Y., Jing, Y., Chen, K.: Circle of friend query in geo-social networks. In: Lee, S., Peng, Z., Zhou, X., Moon, Y.-S., Unland, R., Yoo, J. (eds.) DASFAA 2012. LNCS, vol. 7239, pp. 126–137. Springer, Heidelberg (2012). https://doi.org/10.1007/978-3-642-29035-0_9
20. Long, C., Wong, R.C.W., Wang, K., Fu, A.W.C.: Collective spatial keyword queries: a distance owner-driven approach. In: Proceedings of the 2013 ACM SIGMOD International Conference on Management of Data, pp. 689–700. ACM (2013)
21. Martins, B., Silva, M.J., Andrade, L.: Indexing and ranking in Geo-IR systems. In: Proceedings of the 2005 Workshop on Geographic Information Retrieval, pp. 31–34. ACM (2005)
22. Nemhauser, G.L., Wolsey, L.A., Fisher, M.L.: An analysis of approximations for maximizing submodular set functions-I. Math. Program. 14(1), 265–294 (1978)
23. Pagel, B.U., Six, H.W., Toben, H., Widmayer, P.: Towards an analysis of range query performance in spatial data structures. In: Proceedings of the Twelfth ACM SIGACT-SIGMOD-SIGART Symposium on Principles of Database Systems, pp. 214–221. ACM (1993)
24. Papadias, D., Shen, Q., Tao, Y., Mouratidis, K.: Group nearest neighbor queries. In: Proceedings of the 20th International Conference on Data Engineering, pp. 301–312. IEEE (2004)
25. Rocha-Junior, J.B., Gkorgkas, O., Jonassen, S., Nørvåg, K.: Efficient processing of top-k spatial keyword queries. In: Pfoser, D., et al. (eds.) SSTD 2011. LNCS, vol. 6849, pp. 205–222. Springer, Heidelberg (2011). https://doi.org/10.1007/978-3-642-22922-0_13
26. Ross, P.E.: Top 11 technologies of the decade. IEEE Spectrum 48(1), 27–63 (2011)
27. Roussopoulos, N., Kelley, S., Vincent, F.: Nearest neighbor queries. In: ACM Sigmod Record, vol. 24, pp. 71–79. ACM (1995)
28. Shin, H., Moon, B., Lee, S.: Adaptive multi-stage distance join processing. In: ACM SIGMOD Record, vol. 29, pp. 343–354. ACM (2000)
29. Tao, Y., Xiao, X., Cheng, R.: Range search on multidimensional uncertain data. ACM Trans. Database Syst. (TODS) 32(3), 15 (2007)
30. Wu, D., Cong, G., Jensen, C.S.: A framework for efficient spatial web object retrieval. VLDB J. 21(6), 797–822 (2012)
31. Wu, D., Yiu, M.L., Jensen, C.S., Cong, G.: Efficient continuously moving top-k spatial keyword query processing. In: 2011 IEEE 27th International Conference on Data Engineering (ICDE), pp. 541–552. IEEE (2011)
32. Yang, D.N., Shen, C.Y., Lee, W.C., Chen, M.S.: On socio-spatial group query for location-based social networks. In: Proceedings of the 18th ACM SIGKDD International Conference on Knowledge Discovery and Data Mining, pp. 949–957. ACM (2012)
33. Zhou, Y., Xie, X., Wang, C., Gong, Y., Ma, W.Y.: Hybrid index structures for location-based web search. In: Proceedings of the 14th ACM International Conference on Information and Knowledge Management, pp. 155–162. ACM (2005)

A Minimum-First Algorithm for Dynamic Time Warping on Time Series

Bo-Xian Chen[1], Kuo-Tsung Tseng[2], and Chang-Biau Yang[1(✉)]

[1] National Sun Yat-sen University, Kaohsiung, Taiwan
cbyang@cse.nsysu.edu.tw
[2] National Kaohsiung University of Science and Technology, Kaohsiung, Taiwan

Abstract. In the *time series classification* (TSC) problem, the calculation of the distance of two time series is the kernel issue. One of the famous methods for the distance calculation is the *dynamic time warping* (DTW) with $O(n^2)$ time complexity, based on the dynamic programming. It takes very long time when the data size is large. In order to overcome the time consuming problem, the *dynamic time warping with window* (DTWW) combines the warping window into DTW calculation. This method reduces the computation time by restricting the number of possible solutions, so the answer of DTWW may not be the optimal solution. In this paper, we propose the minimum-first DTW method (MDTW) that expands the possible solutions in the minimum first order. Our method not only reduces the required computation time, but also gets the optimal answer.

Keywords: Time series classification · Dynamic time warping · Dynamic programming · Minimum first order

1 Introduction

The *time series classification* (TSC) problem [9,12,13] is to determine which category the given time series belongs to. The TSC problem can usually be applied in several fields, such as word recognition [2], gesture recognition [6], robotics [4], finance, and biometrics [14].

There are several measurement skills for solving the TSC problem, such as the distance methods [11,18], and the shapelet methods [7,17]. Taking the distance method for instance, the idea of *Euclidean distance* (ED) is direct and simple [5]. However, it cannot solve the time distortion problem. the *dynamic time warping* (DTW) [3] overcomes the time distortion problem and reports the optimal solution. It is a pity that the time complexity of DTW is $O(n^2)$. When the lengths of input time series are large, the distance calculation with DTW needs much time.

This research work was partially supported by the Ministry of Science and Technology of Taiwan under contract MOST 107-2221-E-110-033.

To improve the computation efficiency of DTW, many *dynamic time warping with window* (DTWW) methods [8,15,16] have been presented in the past years. The main concept of these methods is to avoid some terrible alignments and then to reduce the unnecessary computations. All these DTWW methods utilize predefined windows and they face the same issue that the result may not be optimal since some computations are omitted. We then present the minimum-first DTW method (MDTW) with an adaptive window which calculates the minimum first and stops if and only if the optimal result is obtained.

The rest of this paper is organized as follows. Section 2 presents some well-known DTWW methods. We present our MDTW method in Sect. 3. Section 4 shows the experimental results that state the efficiency of our method. Finally, Sect. 5 concludes the paper and provides some advices for future works.

2   Dynamic Time Warping with Window

DTW is time-consuming since it requires $O(n^2)$ time to find the answer. Therefore, the concept of *dynamic time warping with window* (DTWW) was proposed by Itakura [8] in 1975, and Sakoe and Chiba [16] in 1978. Both of their methods belong to the global constraint. The goal of constraints is to let the warping path be closer to the diagonal and avoid the undesired path. In the method of Sakoe and Chiba, assume that the warping windows size is r. Then the path is only permitted within the width r, i.e. $|i - j| < r$. The warping path of Itakura's algorithm is bounded by two slopes S and $\frac{1}{S}$. Sakoe and Chiba used a diagonal with a fixed width.

The well-known global constraints, proposed by Sakoe with Chiba, Itakura, and Ratanamahatana with Keogh are shown in Fig. 1. It is worth to notice that white cells are not calculated for time-saving, so the answer may not be optimal. The spirit of our MDTW method is like DTWW methods. What is in common among MDTW and DTWW is to reduce calculated cells, but DTWW

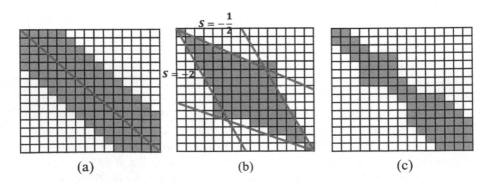

Fig. 1. Three warping windows of DTWW. (a) Sakoe-Chiba band [16], bounded by $|i - j| < r = 5$. (b) Itakura parallelogram [8], bounded by slopes $S = -2$ and $S = -\frac{1}{2}$. (c) Ratanamahatana-Keogh band [15].

restricts the range of calculated cells with predefined windows, while MDTW changes the calculating order of cells. More specifically, MDTW calculate cells by the minimum-first order and stops if the optimal answer is obtained. Thus, the remaining cells can be ignored for time-saving.

3 Our Method

In this Section, we propose our MDTW method which is a method with an adaptive window that avoids the disadvantage of DTWW. MDTW combines the concept of dynamic time warping with an adaptive window and gets the globally optimal answer much faster.

3.1 An Example for Illustrating Our Method

We first give an example to demonstrate our concept in Fig. 2. Given two time series $A = \{2, 9, 8, 8, 5, 4, 2, 1, 5\}$ and $B = \{3, 7, 4, 1, 3, 2, 1, 7\}$, we first initialize a two-dimensional matrix M to calculate the DTW distance between A and B. The top-left (yellow) cell is calculated as the starting point, as shown in Fig. 2a.

In the beginning, we expand three adjacent cells from cell $M[1, 1]$, then we insert these expanded cells, $\langle value, row\ index, column\ index \rangle$ denoted as $\langle MV, i, j \rangle$, into a priority queue Q. Thus, we have $Q = \{\langle 3, 2, 2 \rangle, \langle 6, 1, 2 \rangle, \langle 7, 2, 1 \rangle\}$, shown as the blue cells in Fig. 2b. Next, we pop out the minimal cell from Q. In Fig. 2b, the minimal cell $\langle MV, i, j \rangle$ in Q is $\langle 3, 2, 2 \rangle$ (the blue circled cell). So, $M[2, 2]$ (blue circled) is the next cell to be expanded, and its current cumulative distance is 3.

In Fig. 2c, expanded from $M[2, 2] = 3$, so get three cells $M[3, 2] = 4$, $M[2, 3] = 8$ and $M[3, 3] = 7$. After inserting these cells into Q, and we get $Q = \{\langle 4, 3, 2 \rangle, \langle 6, 1, 2 \rangle, \langle 7, 2, 1 \rangle\ \langle 7, 3, 3 \rangle\ \langle 8, 2, 3 \rangle\}$. This time, the minimal cell in Q is $\langle 4, 3, 2 \rangle$ ($M[3, 2] = 4$). Repeat the procedure until the bottom-right cell is expanded. In Fig. 2b to h, the orange cells are the current minima, which are expanded to blue cells. The circled cells are the next minima and Fig. 2i shows the final result.

1NN-DTW (one nearest neighbor DTW) is one of well-known methods used in the TSC problem [4, 10]. The straightforward method for 1NN-DTW is to search the database of time series one by one, and to obtain the time series having the minimum DTW distance with the query series. In the above example, the value of $M[9, 8]$ is a new threshold for searching time series. If the current minimal value exceeds the threshold, we can stop the calculation of the current time series, even we do not reach the most bottom-right cell. If the distance is less than the current threshold, the threshold is updated.

3.2 The Irreplaceable Property

This section introduces the irreplaceable property of DTW. Based on this property, the value of each expanded cell cannot be updated any more.

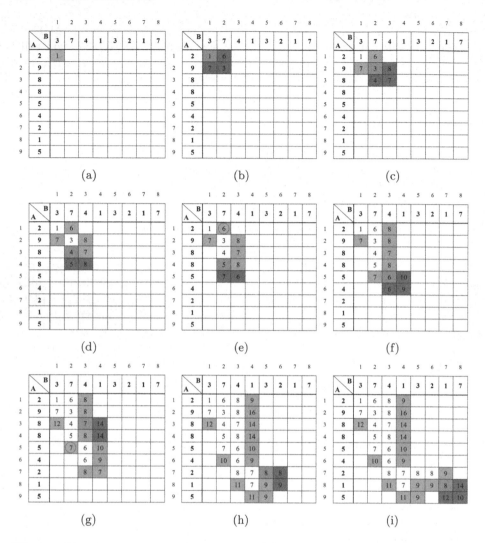

Fig. 2. The expansion steps of our MDTW with two time series $A = \{2, 9, 8, 8, 5, 4, 2, 1, 5\}$ and $B = \{3, 7, 4, 1, 3, 2, 1, 7\}$. (Color figure online)

Theorem 1. *If the lattice M for calculating the DTW distance is expanded with the minimum first order, then the expanded cells already have their cumulative distances, and their values cannot be replaced afterwards.*

Proof. The DP formula for calculating DTW distance with M for $A = \{a_1, a_2, \cdots, a_m\}$, $B = \{b_1, b_2, \cdots, b_n\}$ is given as follows.

$$M_{i,j} = \begin{cases} 0 & \text{if } i = 0 \text{ and } j = 0, \\ \infty & \begin{array}{l} \text{if } i = 0 \text{ or } j = 0, \\ \text{and } i \neq j, \end{array} \\ dis(a_i, b_j) + \min \begin{cases} M_{i-1,j} \\ M_{i,j-1} & \text{if } 1 \leq i \leq m \text{ and } 1 \leq j \leq n. \\ M_{i-1,j-1} \end{cases} \end{cases} \quad (1)$$

It is clear that the value of $M_{i,j}$ comes from the minimum of $M_{i-1,j}$, $M_{i,j-1}$ and $M_{i-1,j-1}$. Suppose that $M_{i,j}$ is expanded from $M_{i-1,j-1}$. In this situation, $M_{i-1,j-1}$ the minimum of $M_{i-1,j}$, $M_{i,j-1}$ and $M_{i-1,j-1}$, and $M_{i-1,j-1}$ is extracted from the queue before the other two. Accordingly, when $M_{i-1,j}$ or $M_{i,j-1}$ is extracted from the queue, $dis(a_i, b_j) + M_{i-1,j}$ or $dis(a_i, b_j) + M_{i,j-1}$ cannot be the answer of $M_{i,j}$. In other words, the value of $M_{i,j}$ cannot be replaced afterwards.

If $M_{i,j}$ is expanded from $M_{i,j-1}$ or $M_{i-1,j}$, it can be proved similarly.

3.3 The Minimum First Order

The pseudo code of our MDTW algorithm is shown in Algorithm 1. The threshold T is set to infinity initially, and it is updated along with the time series one by one. So, T may become lower and lower or unchanged. If we find the most similar time series, we can reduce much more calculation in later searches. Based on Theorem 1, we do not need to initialize the two-dimensional matrix, and we need only to record the expanded cells instead. We expand the cells until we get the bottom-right cell or the minimal value in queue Q exceeds T.

Algorithm 1. Minimum first DTW (MDTW)

Input: two time series A, B and threshold T
Output: *distance of* A *and* B   ▷ if $MV > T$, then return null
1: $i, j = 1$
2: $MV = |a_i - b_j|$ ▷ current minimal value
3: $Q = \{\langle MV, i, j \rangle\}$ ▷ insert unexpanded cells into queue
4: **while** $T > MV$ **do**
5:     **if** $(i + 1, j)$ is not in Q and does not exceed boundary **then**
6:         Insert $\langle |a_{i+1} - b_j| + MV, i + 1, j \rangle$ into Q
7:     **end if**
8:     **if** $(i, j + 1)$ is not in Q and does not exceed boundary **then**
9:         Insert $\langle |a_i - b_{j+1}| + MV, i, j + 1 \rangle$ into Q
10:    **end if**
11:    **if** $(i + 1, j + 1)$ is not in Q and does not exceed boundary **then**
12:        Insert $\langle |a_{i+1} - b_{j+1}| + MV, i + 1, j + 1 \rangle$ into Q
13:    **end if**
14:    **if** (m, n) in Q **then**
15:        **return** MV of cell (m, n)
16:    **end if**
17:    $\langle MV, i, j \rangle \leftarrow \min(Q)$ ▷ minimal value of MV in Q
18: **end while**

---

4   Experimental Results

The computer environment of our experiments is Intel(R) Core(TM) i7-4790 CPU @ 3.6 GHz and memory 8 GB RAM. The experimental datasets come from UEA & UCR time series repository [1]. There are totally 85 classes in the repository, where each of them has its own distinct training set size, testing set size, time series length and different number of classes. Since they are open datasets, we omit the detailed description of the datasets.

To improve 1NN-DTW, the concept of threshold T can also be applied. When the DTW distance of the query series and one target series is calculated, once the distance exceeds T, we can stop the distance calculation. Here, this improvement is denoted as TDTW.

Figure 3 shows ratios of the computational time and expanded cells of TDTW and MDTW compared with the original DTW method with the threshold and our method MDTW. It is obvious that lines of MDTW are almost lower than the lines of TDTW. In other words, MDTW gets optimal answer with less computational time and fewer expanded cells. The ratio of expanded cells for MDTW are between 0.01 (the best case - Wafer) and 0.85 (the worst case - ShapeletSim), and most of them are nearly between 0.1 to 0.3. This shows that MDTW expands fewer cells to get the optimal answer. The average ratio of the computational time for MDTW is less than 0.3.

It is worth to be discussed in future that our MDTW method beats TDTW in 83 datasets, but takes more time than the original DTW and TDTW in datasets Phoneme and ShapeletSim. Though we expand fewer cells in both cases, the computational times are longer than the original DTW method. We shall investigate the features of these two datasets, so that we may improve our MDTW method.

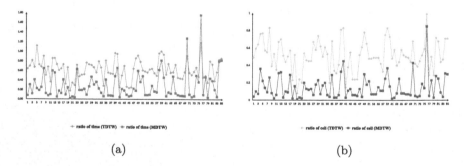

(a)   (b)

Fig. 3. The ratios of computational time and expanded cells of TDTW and MDTW (a) Ratios of execution time. (b) Ratios of expanded cells.

5   Conclusion

In this paper, we propose the minimum-first DTW method (MDTW) for calculating the DTW distance of two time series. MDTW expands the lattice cells with the minimum-first order, The computation is like DTW with an adaptive window. MDTW finds the optimal answer and reduces the computational time. As the experiment results show, most cases (83/85) in the experimental datasets require less computational time than the original DTW, and the ratios of expanded cell that we have to calculate are between 0.1 and 0.3.

Our method performs very well on similar but distorted data, because the warping path is almost along the diagonal direction. However, the performance of our method in the dataset which falls and rises extremely is bad, because the DTW distance is large and many cells have to be expanded.

Our method saves much more time for the TSC problem. In the future, dynamic adjustment of increment in every turn may be studied, and we may try to discover more relationships between cells or the method of pruning unnecessary cells. Moreover, we may design a measure method to evaluate whether our method can perform well or not in advance.

References

1. Bagnall, A., Lines, J., Bostrom, A., Large, J., Keogh, E.: The great time series classification bake off: a review and experimental evaluation of recent algorithmic advances. Data Min. Knowl. Discov. **31**(3), 606–660 (2016)
2. Bailly, A., Malinowski, S., Tavenard, R., Chapel, L., Guyet, T.: Dense bag-of-temporal-SIFT-words for time series classification. In: Douzal-Chouakria, A., Vilar, J.A., Marteau, P.-F. (eds.) AALTD 2015. LNCS (LNAI), vol. 9785, pp. 17–30. Springer, Cham (2016). https://doi.org/10.1007/978-3-319-44412-3_2
3. Bellman, R., Kalaba, R.: On adaptive control processes. IRE Trans. Autom. Control **4**(2), 1–9 (1959)
4. Buza, K., Nanopoulos, A., Schmidt-Thieme, L.: Time-series classification based on individualised error prediction. In: 2010 IEEE 13th International Conference on Computational Science and Engineering (CSE), pp. 48–54. IEEE (2010)
5. Ding, H., Trajcevski, G., Scheuermann, P., Wang, X., Keogh, E.: Querying and mining of time series data: experimental comparison of representations and distance measures. Proc. Very Large Data Bases Endow. **1**(2), 1542–1552 (2008)
6. Hamilton, J.D.: Time Series Analysis, vol. 2. Princeton University Press, Princeton (1994)
7. Hills, J., Lines, J., Baranauskas, E., Mapp, J., Bagnall, A.: Classification of time series by shapelet transformation. Data Min. Knowl. Discov. **28**(4), 851–881 (2014)
8. Itakura, F.: Minimum prediction residual principle applied to speech recognition. IEEE Trans. Acoust. Speech Signal Process. **23**(1), 67–72 (1975)
9. Jain, B.J., Spiegel, S.: Time series classification in dissimilarity spaces. In: Proceedings of 1st International Workshop on Advanced Analytics and Learning on Temporal Data, Porto, Portugal (2015)
10. Jeong, Y.S., Jeong, M.K., Omitaomu, O.A.: Weighted dynamic time warping for time series classification. Pattern Recogn. **44**(9), 2231–2240 (2011)
11. Lines, J., Bagnall, A.: Time series classification with ensembles of elastic distance measures. Data Min. Knowl. Discov. **29**(3), 565–592 (2015)
12. Luczak, M.: Univariate and multivariate time series classification with parametric integral dynamic time warping. J. Intell. Fuzzy Syst. **33**(4), 2403–2413 (2017)

13. Morel, M., Achard, C., Kulpa, R., Dubuisson, S.: Time-series averaging using constrained dynamic time warping with tolerance. Pattern Recogn. **74**, 77–89 (2018)
14. Parthasaradhi, S.T., Derakhshani, R., Hornak, L.A., Schuckers, S.A.: Time-series detection of perspiration as a liveness test in fingerprint devices. IEEE Trans. Syst. Man Cybern. Part C (Appl. Rev.) **35**(3), 335–343 (2005)
15. Ratanamahatana, C.A., Keogh, E.: Making time-series classification more accurate using learned constraints. In: Proceedings of the 4th SIAM International Conference on Data Mining, pp. 11–22. SIAM, Florida (2004)
16. Sakoe, H., Chiba, S.: Dynamic programming algorithm optimization for spoken word recognition. IEEE Trans. Acoust. Speech Signal Process. **26**(1), 43–49 (1978)
17. Shah, M., Grabocka, J., Schilling, N., Wistuba, M., Schmidt-Thieme, L.: Learning DTW-shapelets for time-series classification. In: Proceedings of the 3rd IKDD Conference on Data Science (CODS), p. 3. ACM, New York, March 2016
18. Stefan, A., Athitsos, V., Das, G.: The move-split-merge metric for time series. IEEE Trans. Knowl. Data Eng. **25**(6), 1425–1438 (2013)

A Note on Metric 1-median Selection

Ching-Lueh Chang$^{(\boxtimes)}$ (iD)

Department of Computer Science and Engineering, Yuan Ze University,
Taoyuan, Taiwan
clchang@saturn.yzu.edu.tw

Abstract. METRIC 1-MEDIAN asks for $\operatorname{argmin}_{p=1}^{n} \sum_{q=1}^{n} d(p,q)$, breaking ties arbitrarily, given a metric space $(\{1, 2, \ldots, n\}, d)$. Let A be any deterministic algorithm for METRIC 1-MEDIAN making each point in $\{1, 2, \ldots, n\}$ involve in only $O(1)$ queries to d. We show A to not be $o(\log n)$-approximate.

Keywords: 1-median · Closeness centrality · Metric space

1 Introduction

For each positive integer n, $[n] \equiv \{1, 2, \ldots, n\}$. Given a metric space $([n], d)$, METRIC 1-MEDIAN asks for

$$\operatorname*{argmin}_{p \in [n]} \sum_{q \in [n]} d(p, q),$$

breaking ties arbitrarily. An algorithm for METRIC 1-MEDIAN may query for $d(p, q)$ for any $p, q \in [n]$. Indyk [3,4] designs a Monte Carlo $O(n/\epsilon^2)$-time $(1+\epsilon)$-approximation algorithm for METRIC 1-MEDIAN, where $\epsilon > 0$.

Chang [1, Corollary 10] gives a deterministic, $O(\exp(O(1/\epsilon)) \cdot n)$-query, $(\epsilon \log n)$-approximation and nonadaptive algorithm for METRIC 1-MEDIAN, where $\epsilon > 0$ is any constant. For infinitely many n, his algorithm makes $O(1)$ queries concerning each point in $[n]$. We show that such a property forbids his algorithm to be $o(\log n)$-apppproximate. As in previous lower bounds for METRIC 1-MEDIAN, our proof uses the adversarial method (see [2] and the references therein).

Chang [2] shows that METRIC 1-MEDIAN has no deterministic $o(n^{1+1/(h-1)})$-query $(2h \cdot (1-\epsilon))$-approximation algorithms for any constant $\epsilon > 0$ and any integer-valued $h = h(n) \geq 2$ satisfying $h = o(n^{1/(h-1)})$. His result does not imply ours in any obvious way.

Supported in part by the Ministry of Science and Technology of Taiwan under grant 107-2221-E-155-006-MY2.

2   Main Result

For all metric spaces $([n], d)$ and algorithms A for METRIC 1-MEDIAN, define

$$Q_A^d \equiv \left\{ (p, q) \in [n]^2 \mid A^d \text{ queries for } d\,(p, q) \right\}$$

to be the set of queries of A with oracle access to d, where (p, q) is interpreted as an unordered pair. So the maximum number of queries concerning a point is

$$\deg_A^d \equiv \max_{p \in [n]} \left| \{ q \in [n] \mid (p, q) \in Q_A^d \} \right|.$$

Theorem 1. *Let A be a deterministic algorithm for* METRIC 1-MEDIAN *satisfying $\deg_A^d = O(1)$ for all metric spaces $([n], d)$. Then A is not $o(\log n)$-approximate.*

Proof. Assume without loss of generality that A does not query for $d(p, p)$ for any $p \in [n]$. We will construct d as A queries. In particular, d is fully determined after A outputs.

Answer each query of A by 1. So $d(p, q) = 1$ if A ever queries for $d(p, q)$, where $(p, q) \in [n]^2$. Consider the undirected graph $G = ([n], Q)$, where Q denotes the set of all queries (as unordered pairs in $[n]^2$) of A. By padding dummy queries, assume $\text{diam}(G) = O(\log n)$ without loss of generality (e.g., pick an $O(1)$-regular expander $G' = ([n], E')$ and assume $E' \subseteq Q$ by padding). All queries of A, having been answered by 1, are clearly consistent with d_G. Denote the output of A by p^*. As $\deg_A^d = O(1)$ for all metric spaces $([n], d)$, G has a maximum degree of $O(1)$. So there exists a small constant $\epsilon > 0$ such that p^* has distance in G greater than $\epsilon \log n$ to at least $n - \sqrt{n}$ points. That is,

$$U \equiv \{ q \in [n] \mid d_G\,(p^*, q) > \epsilon \log n \}$$

satisfies $|U| \geq n - \sqrt{n}$. Define an undirected graph $H = ([n], Q \cup (U \times U))$ by adding to G an edge between each pair of points in U. Because $d_G(p^*, q) > \epsilon \log n$ for all $q \in U$ and $|U| \geq n - \sqrt{n}$,

$$\sum_{q \in U} d_H\,(p^*, q) \geq |U| \cdot \epsilon \log n = \Omega\,(n \log n). \tag{1}$$

For each $u \in U$,

$$\begin{aligned}
\sum_{q \in [n]} d_H\,(u, q) &= \sum_{q \in U} d_H\,(u, q) + \sum_{q \in [n] \setminus U} d_H\,(u, q) \\
&\leq |U| + \sum_{q \in [n] \setminus U} d_H\,(u, q) \\
&\leq |U| + O(\log n) \cdot (n - |U|) \\
&\leq n + o\,(n),
\end{aligned} \tag{2}$$

where the first, second and third inequalities follow from $H = ([n], Q \cup (U \times U))$, $\text{diam}(H) \leq \text{diam}(G) = O(\log n)$ and $|U| \geq n - \sqrt{n}$, respectively.

As $H = ([n], Q \cup (U \times U))$, $d_H(p, q) = 1$ for all $(p, q) \in Q$. Consequently, A^{d_H} outputs p^* (recall that A outputs p^* if every query is answered by 1). So Eqs. (1)–(2) forbid the output of A^{d_H} to be $o(\log n)$-approximate. In particular, A^{d_H} outputs a point with average d_H-distance to other points $\Omega(\log n)$ times the minimum possible.

Theorem 1 forbids Chang's [1, Corollary 10] deterministic $O(n)$-query algorithm to be $o(\log n)$-approximate. But in general, it is open whether METRIC 1-MEDIAN has a deterministic $O(n)$-query $o(\log n)$-approximation algorithm.

References

1. Chang, C.-L.: Metric 1-median selection with fewer queries. Technical Report arXiv: 1612.08654 (2016)
2. Chang, C.-L.: Metric 1-median selection: query complexity vs. approximation ratio. ACM Trans. Comput. Theory **9**(4), Article 20 (2018)
3. Indyk, P.: Sublinear time algorithms for metric space problems. In: Vitter, J., Larmore, L, Leighton, F. (eds.) The 31st Annual ACM Symposium on Theory of Computing 1999, pp. 428–434. ACM, New York (1999). https://doi.org/10.1145/301250.301366
4. Indyk, P.: High-dimensional computational geometry. Ph.D. thesis, Stanford University (2000)

Accelerating Secret Sharing on GPU

Shyong Jian Shyu$^{1(\boxtimes)}$ ⓘ and Ying Zhen Tsai^2

^{1} Department of Computer Science and Information Engineering,
Ming Chuan University, Taoyuan 33348, Taiwan
sjshyu@mail.mcu.edu.tw
^{2} Center for Artificial Intelligence in Medicine, Chang Gung Memorial Hospital,
Taoyuan 33305, Taiwan
alonestilllove@gmail.com

Abstract. A (k, n) threshold secret sharing scheme encrypts a secret s into n parts (called shares), which are distributed to n participants, such that any k participants can recover s using their shares, any group of less than k ones cannot. A robust threshold sharing scheme provides not only the perfect security, but also the tolerance of a possible loss of up to $n{-}k$ shares. When the size of s grows large (such as multimedia data), the efficiency of the encoding/decoding on s becomes a major problem. We designed efficient implementations for Kurihara et al.'s threshold secret sharing scheme on parallel GPU platforms in a personal computer. Experimental results show that the parallel GPU implementation could achieve an appealing speedup over the sequential CPU implementation when dealing with the sharing of multimedia data.

Keywords: Secret sharing · Threshold scheme · Parallel computing

1 Introduction

Secret sharing aims at protecting a secret among a group of participants in such a way that only those participants satisfying some predefined requirement could recover the secret, while others cannot. A typical example for the predefined requirement is the number of participants, called *threshold*. Consider a set of n participants and a threshold k. A (k, n) *threshold secret sharing scheme* (TSSS) encrypts a secret s into n parts (called *shadows*), which are distributed to the n participants, such that any k participants can recover s using their shadows, any group of less than k ones cannot. A robust threshold sharing scheme provides not only the perfect security, but also the tolerance of a possible loss of up to $n{-}k$ shadows.

Shamir [1] developed a (k, n)-TSSS relying on polynomial interpolation in 1979. The scheme is with perfect security and based on operations in *Galois field*. Kurihara et al. proposed another (k, n)-TSSS, which is also with perfect security and based on

This research was supported in part by the Ministry of Science and Technology, Taiwan, under Grants MOST 103-2221-E-130-002-MY3 and 107-2221-E-130-016.

XOR (eXclusive-OR) operations, in 2008 [2]. In their experiments, the latter scheme is 5 (45) times faster than the former in the encoding (decoding) process for sharing a 4.5 MB data in $(k, n) = (3, 11)$ in a personal computer.

Our interest in this paper is to accelerate Kurihara et al.'s scheme by GPGPU (general-purpose computing on graphics processing units; GPU for short) [3]. The rest of this paper is organized as follows. Section 2 introduces the Kurihara et al.'s scheme. Our parallel algorithms designed for their scheme and suitable for running on GPU are presented in Sect. 3. Experimental results are compared and discussed in Sect. 4. Section 5 gives the concluding remarks.

2 Kurihara et al.'s Scheme

2.1 Original Idea

Consider prime n_p, secret s, k and n where $s \in \{0, 1\}^{d(np-1)}$ for $n_p \geq n$ and $d > 0$. The encoding algorithm in Kurihara et al.'s scheme is formally described as follows. Note that secret s is decomposed into $s_1, s_2, \ldots, s_{np-1}$ with d bits each and $s_0 = 0^d$.

Encoding: *Encode*
Input: k, n, prime n_p ($\geq n$), d (>0) and secret $s \in \{0, 1\}^{d(n_p-1)}$
Output: $(w_0, w_1, \ldots, w_{n-1})$

---

1. $s_0 = 0^d$, $s = s_1 \| s_2 \| \ldots \| s_{n_p-1}$
2.   for (each i, $0 \leq i \leq k-2$)
     {   for (each j, $0 \leq j \leq n_p-1$)
             $r_j^i = \text{random}(\{0, 1\}^d)$
     }
3.   for (each i, $0 \leq i \leq n-1$)
     {   for (each j, $0 \leq j \leq n_p-2$)
         $w_{(i,j)} = (\bigoplus_{h=0}^{k-2} r_{h \times i+j}^i) \oplus s_{j-i}$

         $w_i = w_{(i, 0)} \| w_{(i, 1)} \| \ldots \| w_{(i, n_p-2)}$
     }
4.   return $(w_0, w_1, \ldots, w_{n-1})$

When any group of k participants collects their shadows, they could recover the secret s by the decoding algorithm described in the following.

S. J. Shyu and Y. Z. Tsai

Decoding: *Decode*
Input: k shadows $w_{t_0}, w_{t_1}, \ldots, w_{t_{k-1}}$
Output: secret s

---

1.   for (each i, $0 \leq i \leq k-1$)
$$w_{t_i} = w_{(t_i, 0)} \parallel w_{(t_i, 1)} \parallel \ldots \parallel w_{(t_i, n_p-2)}$$
2. $\mathbf{w} = (w_{(t_0, 0)}, w_{(t_0, 1)}, \ldots, w_{(t_0, n_p-2)}, w_{(t_1, 0)}, w_{(t_1, 1)}, \ldots, w_{(t_1, n_p-2)},$
$$\ldots, w_{(t_{k-1}, 0)}, w_{(t_{k-1}, 1)}, \ldots, w_{(t_{k-1}, n_p-2)})^T$$
3. $\mathbf{M} = MAT(t_0, t_1, \ldots, t_{k-1})$
4. $(s_1, s_2, \ldots, s_{n_p-1})^T = \mathbf{M} \cdot \mathbf{w}$
5. $s = s_1 \parallel s_2 \parallel \ldots \parallel s_{n_p-1}$
6.   return s

Note that shadow w_{t_i} is decomposed into n_p-1 parts with d bits each for $0 \leq i$ $k-1$ (step 1). Then, $\mathbf{w}$ is a $k(n_p-1)$ binary vector consisting of the $k(n_p-1)$ decomposed parts (step 2). The function MAT would produce the recovering matrix $\mathbf{M}$ (step 3). The n_p-1 parts of the secret s can be obtained by applying $\mathbf{M} \cdot \mathbf{w}$ (step 4). Then, secret s is recovered (step 5). MAT is operated as follows where *FG* and *BG* denote forward and backward substitutions in Gaussian elimination.

MAT
Input: $t_0, t_1, t_2, \ldots, t_{k-1}$
Output: $\mathbf{M}$

---

1.   for (each i, $0 \leq i \leq k-1$)
       {   for (each j, $0 \leq j \leq n_p-2$)
             $\mathbf{v}_{(t_i, j)} = VEC(t_i, j)$
       }
2. $\mathbf{G} = (\mathbf{v}_{(t_0, 0)}, \mathbf{v}_{(t_0, 1)}, \ldots, \mathbf{v}_{(t_0, n_p-2)}, \ldots, \mathbf{v}_{(t_1, 0)}, \mathbf{v}_{(t_1, 1)}, \ldots, \mathbf{v}_{(t_1, n_p-2)},$
$$\ldots, \mathbf{v}_{(t_{k-1}, 0)}, \mathbf{v}_{(t_{k-1}, 1)}, \ldots, \mathbf{v}_{(t_{k-1}, n_p-2)})^T$$
3. $\begin{bmatrix} \mathbf{G}_2 & \mathbf{G}_1 & \mathbf{J}_1 \\ \varnothing & \mathbf{G}_0 & \mathbf{J}_0 \end{bmatrix} \leftarrow FG([\mathbf{G} \ \mathbf{I}_{k(n_p-1)}]) = [\check{\mathbf{G}} \ \mathbf{J}]$
4. $[\mathbf{I}_{n_p-1} \ \mathbf{M}] = BG([\mathbf{G}_0 \ \mathbf{J}_0])$
5.   return $\mathbf{M}$

2.2   Dealing with a Large Binary Data

To deal with a binary data D with size N bytes, we simply decompose the data into $\lambda = N/(l(n_p - 1))$ segments where $l = 1, 2, 4$ or 8 bytes, corresponding to $d = 8, 16, 32, 64$ bits, respectively, in the *Encode* and *Decode* algorithms. Then, each segment j is encoded by the *Encode* algorithm into n parts, say $y_{1j}, y_{2j}, \ldots, y_{nj}$, under the given (k, n) structure. The concatenated result $Y_i = y_{i1} \cup y_{i2} \cup \ldots \cup y_{i\lambda}$ from the λ segments constitutes shadow i for participant i for $1 \leq i \leq n$.

Any k participants with k shadows, say $Y_{t_1}, Y_{t_2}, \ldots, Y_{t_k}$, are able to recover D. They decompose Y_{t_i} into $\lambda = N/(l(n_p-1))$ segments, namely $y_{t_i 1}, y_{t_i 2}, \ldots, y_{t_i \lambda}$, for $1 \leq i \leq k$. Applying the *Decode* algorithm onto $y_{t_1 j}, y_{t_2 j}, \ldots, y_{t_k j}$, they obtain the decoded result d_j for $1 \leq j \leq \lambda$. The original secret is thus $D = d_1 \cup d_2 \cup \ldots \cup d_\lambda$.

3   Parallel Implementations

To utilize the multiple cores in GPU, we divide the data into fine grains so that each grain can be processed by the *thread*, which is the elementary processing unit in a core. For binary data D with N bytes in a computer with word size l bytes, we assume that the number of the threads that could operate simultaneously on GPU is *maxT*. Our parallel encoding algorithm is formally presented as follows.

Parallel Encoding: *PE*
Input: k, n, secret D, n_p, N, l, *maxT*
Output: n shadows $Y_1, Y_2, \ldots, Y_n$

$PE(k, n, D, n_p, N, l, maxT)$
1. $q = N/(n_p-1)$, $\lambda = \lceil q/l \rceil$, $\eta = \lceil \lambda/maxT \rceil$
2.   Allocate memory of Y_j for $1 \leq j \leq n$ in CPU and GPU
3.   for (each region e_j of D, $1 \leq j \leq \eta$)
     {   __paralleldo<<*maxT*>>__
         $\{y^r_{1j}, y^r_{2j}, \ldots, y^r_{nj}\} = Encode(k, n, e^r_j, n_p)$
         // e^r_j: segment r in region j, $1 \leq r \leq maxT$
         __parallelend<<*maxT*>>__
         copy $\{y_{1j}, y_{2j}, \ldots, y_{nj}\}$ back to CPU where
         $y_{ij} = y^1_{ij} \cup y^2_{ij} \cup \ldots \cup y^{maxT}_{ij}$ for $1 \leq i \leq n$
     }
4.   for (each participant i, $1 \leq i \leq n$)
         $Y_i = y_{i1} \cup y_{i2} \cup \ldots \cup y_{i\eta}$
5.   return $(Y_1, Y_2, \ldots, Y_n)$

Note that e^r_j denotes segment r in region e_j for $1 \leq r \leq maxT$ and $1 \leq j \leq \eta$. The secret D with N bytes is decomposed into λ segments with $l(n_p-1)$ bytes each and further η regions with *maxT* segments each. Conceptually, the program codes between __paralleldo<<*maxT*>>__ and __parallelend<<*maxT*>>__ are executed in parallel (with *maxT* threads) on GPU.

The function $Encode(k, n, e^r_j, n_p)$ in step 3 of *PE* encodes segment r in region e_j of D in parallel where each thread runs the aforementioned *Encode* algorithm to encode e^r_j into n shares: $y^r_{1j}, y^r_{2j}, \ldots, y^r_{nj}$. All *maxT* threads encodes the *maxT* segments simultaneously in a region. The encoded results $y_{1j}, y_{2j}, \ldots, y_{nj}$ of region e_j for $1 \leq j \leq \eta$ on GPU would be copied back to CPU $y_{ij} = y^1_{ij} \cup y^2_{ij} \cup \ldots \cup y^{maxT}_{ij}$ for $1 \leq i \leq n$. The n shadows are formed at step 4 ($Y_i = y_{i1} \cup y_{i2} \cup \ldots \cup y_{i\eta}$ for $1 \leq i \leq n$).

The parallel decoding algorithm is as follows.

Parallel Decoding: *PD*
Input: k, n_p, $\mathcal{T} = \{Y_{t_1}, Y_{t_2}, \ldots, Y_{t_k}\}$, $\mathcal{P} = \{t_1, t_2, \ldots, t_k\}$

Output: secret D

$PD(k, n_p, \mathcal{T}, \mathcal{P}, N, l, maxT)$

1. $q = N/(n_p-1)$, $\lambda = \lceil q/l \rceil$, $\eta = \lceil \lambda/maxT \rceil$
2. $\mathbf{M} = MAT(t_1, t_2, \ldots, t_k)$
3. Allocate memory of D in CPU and GPU
4. for (each region e_j containing $y_{t_1 j}, y_{t_2 j}, \ldots, y_{t_k j}$, $1 \le j \le \eta$)
    { __paralleldo<<$maxT$>>__
        $d_j^r = DecodeM(k, n_p, \mathcal{T}, \mathbf{M}, e_j^r)$
    __parallelend<<$maxT$>>__
        copy $\mathcal{D}_j = d_j^1 \cup d_j^2 \cup \ldots \cup d_j^{maxT}$ back to CPU
    }
5. return $D = \mathcal{D}_1 \cup \mathcal{D}_2 \cup \ldots \cup \mathcal{D}_\eta$

The function $DecodeM(k, n_p, \mathcal{T}, \mathbf{M}, e_j^r)$ in step 4 decodes d_j^r according to $y_{t_1 j}^r, y_{t_2 j}^r, \ldots, y_{t_k j}^r$ in segment r of region e_j by applying the *Decode* algorithm yet without step 3 (which computes $\mathbf{M}$). In fact, $\mathbf{M}$ is computed once at step 2 of *PD* and used $\eta \cdot maxT$ times in step 4 for all η regions. The decoded result $\mathcal{D}_j$ ($= d_j^1 \cup d_j^2 \cup \ldots \cup d_j^{maxT}$) corresponding to region e_j would be copied back to CPU for $1 \le i \le \eta$. Then, the original secret D ($= \mathcal{D}_1 \cup \mathcal{D}_2 \cup \ldots \cup \mathcal{D}_\eta$) could be attained in CPU.

4   Experimental Results

The sequential platform was a personal computer running Windows 7 with i7-4790 (3.6 GHz) CPU and 8 GB memory. The sequential programs were coded in C++ Builder. With the same personal computer, our parallel platform was a GeForce GTX760 video card, which consists of 1152 cores and 2 GB memory. The parallel programs were coded in Visual Studio 2015 with CUDA 8.0.

The size of the binary test data was 15.9 MB. Table 1 explores the execution times of our sequential implementations based on the *Encode* and *Decode* algorithms under different d's and (k, n)'s where n_p was set to be the same as n.

It is easily seen from Table 1 that the performance of $d = 64$ is the best among the four alternatives for a given setting of (k, n). This is reasonable that a larger segment due to a larger d reduces the number of segments (i.e. λ, which is actually the number of calls to the *Encode* (*Decode*) function) and consequently shortens the execution time.

Let *PE* and *PD* denote the parallel execution times of our parallel encoding and decoding algorithms, respectively. Table 2 summarizes the results of *PE* and *PD* by different d's.

Likewise, the performance of $d = 64$ is the better than those of the other three.

Table 1. Comparison of sequential implementations using different d's.

(k, n)	Encode				Decode			
d	8	16	32	64	8	16	32	64
(2, 5)	1.22	0.77	0.52	0.39	0.47	0.22	0.11	0.06
(2, 11)	2.23	1.26	0.73	0.55	0.89	0.44	0.22	0.12
(2, 23)	4.31	2.26	1.25	0.81	1.98	0.91	0.47	0.25
(2, 31)	5.65	2.93	1.61	1.05	2.57	1.28	0.66	0.34
(2, 43)	7.82	4.04	2.17	1.15	3.65	1.84	0.94	0.50
(4, 5)	2.51	1.68	1.22	1.03	0.87	0.44	0.22	0.11
(4, 11)	4.32	2.51	1.53	1.17	1.73	0.86	0.44	0.23
(4, 23)	8.05	4.35	2.45	1.72	3.49	1.78	0.87	0.47
(4, 31)	10.47	5.59	3.09	2.09	4.96	2.45	1.25	0.67
(4, 43)	14.40	7.53	4.09	2.67	7.13	3.57	1.78	0.94
(6, 11)	6.32	3.65	2.34	1.84	2.48	1.23	0.61	0.34
(6, 23)	11.69	6.35	3.62	2.64	6.30	3.28	1.61	0.84
(6, 31)	15.18	8.11	4.52	3.14	11.51	5.85	2.92	1.47
(6, 43)	20.86	10.91	5.94	4.09	18.44	9.52	4.81	2.43
(8, 11)	8.44	4.90	3.15	2.51	3.43	1.70	0.86	0.47
(8, 23)	15.26	8.32	4.79	3.48	11.70	6.15	3.11	1.56
(8, 31)	19.83	10.61	5.98	4.17	18.49	9.44	4.67	2.43
(8, 43)	27.10	14.32	7.85	5.27	30.31	15.30	7.89	3.93

We choose the best results from Tables 1 and 2 (i.e., those of $d = 64$) and compute the speedup ratios (i.e., Encode/PE and Decode/PD) in Table 3.

It is not hard to realize that when k is fixed, the performances of Encode and PE grow as n increases. On the other hand, for a fixed n, the their execution times also go larger as k increases. These are lucid because a larger n (k) induces more computations for a fixed k (n). In our experiments with respect to various (k, n)'s, the speedup ratios are 2–6. For a particular instance, say $(k, n) = (8, 11)$, PE takes 0.41 s, which is about 6.14 times faster than Encode that spends 2.51 s.

Let us focus on the speedup ratios for encoding. Concerning a fixed n, they increase as k grows, since the computations in step 2 of Encode increases with k (while those in step 3 are fixed for given n and n_p). Yet, for a fixed k, they reduce as n grows. We may say that the time needed in the computations in step 3, which grow as n and n_p, dominate the gain from the parallel execution on GPU.

Regarding Decode and PD, their performances grow as k increases for a fixed n. For a fixed k, they also grow slightly as n increases. Consider $(k, n) = (8, 43)$. PD (0.44 s) is about 8.89 times faster than Decode (3.93 s).

In terms of speedup ratios, they are about 1.7–8.8. In addition, they increase as n for a fixed k; besides, as k for a fixed n. It means that our parallel decoding algorithm tends to achieve a better speedup (over the sequential implementation) as k (or n) increases on GPU.

Table 2. Comparison of parallel implementations using different d's.

(k, n)	PE				DE			
d	8	16	32	64	8	16	32	64
(2, 5)	0.27	0.16	0.19	0.21	0.06	0.05	0.06	0.04
(2, 11)	0.44	0.28	0.24	0.26	0.12	0.06	0.06	0.04
(2, 23)	0.57	0.46	0.38	0.32	0.21	0.11	0.12	0.05
(2, 31)	1.36	0.85	0.68	0.65	0.30	0.16	0.10	0.06
(2, 43)	2.21	1.27	1.11	0.96	0.51	0.28	0.16	0.09
(4, 5)	0.43	0.19	0.18	0.21	0.14	0.08	0.10	0.07
(4, 11)	0.53	0.30	0.24	0.28	0.17	0.11	0.07	0.07
(4, 23)	0.98	0.62	0.50	0.51	0.46	0.26	0.16	0.11
(4, 31)	1.44	0.88	0.72	0.66	0.91	0.47	0.28	0.16
(4, 43)	2.35	1.32	1.11	0.97	1.33	0.69	0.39	0.22
(6, 11)	0.78	0.40	0.28	0.30	0.28	0.16	0.13	0.10
(6, 23)	1.16	0.72	0.57	0.53	0.94	0.48	0.30	0.17
(6, 31)	1.66	0.94	0.80	0.74	1.41	0.74	0.40	0.25
(6, 43)	2.62	1.41	1.11	1.05	1.97	1.01	0.56	0.33
(8, 11)	0.87	0.49	0.36	0.41	0.35	0.22	0.17	0.13
(8, 23)	1.47	0.81	0.64	0.62	1.19	0.62	0.39	0.22
(8, 31)	1.89	1.13	0.88	0.78	1.86	0.96	0.56	0.32
(8, 43)	2.86	1.60	1.20	1.06	2.56	1.35	0.75	0.44

Table 3. Comparison of sequential and parallel implementations.

(k, n)	Encoding			Decoding		
	Encode	PE	Encode/PE	Decode	PD	Decode/PD
(2, 5)	0.39	0.21	1.90	0.06	0.04	1.75
(2, 11)	0.55	0.26	2.08	0.12	0.04	3.26
(2, 23)	0.81	0.50	1.62	0.25	0.05	5.56
(2, 31)	1.05	0.65	1.60	0.34	0.06	5.36
(2, 43)	1.15	0.96	1.19	0.50	0.09	5.31
(4, 5)	1.03	0.21	4.90	0.11	0.07	1.68
(4, 11)	1.17	0.28	4.25	0.23	0.07	3.39
(4, 23)	1.72	0.51	3.38	0.47	0.11	4.11
(4, 31)	2.09	0.66	3.18	0.67	0.16	4.16
(4, 43)	2.67	0.97	2.75	0.94	0.22	4.22
(6, 11)	1.84	0.30	6.14	0.34	0.10	3.44
(6, 23)	2.64	0.53	4.98	0.84	0.17	4.87
(6, 31)	3.14	0.74	4.23	1.47	0.25	5.94
(6, 43)	4.09	1.05	3.91	2.43	0.33	7.33
(8, 11)	2.51	0.41	6.14	0.47	0.13	3.52
(8, 23)	3.48	0.62	5.66	1.56	0.22	7.09
(8, 31)	4.17	0.78	5.31	2.43	0.32	7.70
(8, 43)	5.27	1.06	4.99	3.93	0.44	8.89

5 Concluding Remarks

We designed, implemented and tested efficient parallel algorithms on GPU for Kurihara et al.'s threshold secret sharing scheme in this paper. The experimental results demonstrate that the parallel GPU implementation could achieve an appealing speedup over the sequential CPU implementation when dealing with the sharing of multimedia data. The improvement on the decoding time is particularly appealing especially when k or n becomes large. These merits encourage the practical applications of sharing media data directly in cloud services, or distributed database.

In this stage, our parallel implementation of the decoding algorithm is more robust than that of the encoding one. In the near future, we shall try to improve the performance of our parallel encoding algorithm. Surely, more experiments involving larger media data, more efficient GPU platform (with more GPU cores), sophisticated GPU programming, and so on will be conducted to explore how these factors affect the performances of our parallel algorithms.

References

1. Shamir, A.: How to share a secret. Commun. ACM **22**(11), 612–613 (1979)
2. Kurihara, J., Kiyomoto, S., Fukushima, K., Tanaka, T.: On a fast (k, n)-threshold secret sharing scheme. IEICE Trans. Fundam. **E91-A**(9), 2365–2378 (2008)
3. Nvidia: Cuda GPUs. https://developer.nvidia.com/cuda-gpus

An $O(f)$ Bi-approximation for Weighted Capacitated Covering with Hard Capacity

Hai-Lun Tu[1]([✉]), Mong-Jen Kao[2], and D. T. Lee[3]

[1] Department of Computer Science and Information Engineering,
National Taiwan University, Taipei, Taiwan
d95019@csie.ntu.edu.tw
[2] Department of Computer Science and Information Engineering,
National Chung Cheng University, Chiayi City, Taiwan
mjkao@cs.ccu.edu.tw
[3] Institute of Information Science, Academia Sinica, Taipei, Taiwan
dtlee@ieee.org

Abstract. We consider capacitated vertex cover with hard capacity (HCVC) on f-hypergraphs. In this problem, we are given a hypergraph $G = (V, E)$ with a maximum edge size f. Each (hyper)edge is associated with a demand and each vertex is associated with a weight (cost), a capacity, and an available multiplicity. The objective is to find a minimum-weight vertex multiset, or cover, such that the demands of the edges can be met by the capacities of the vertices and the multiplicity of each vertex does not exceed its available multiplicity.

In this paper we present an $O(f)$ bi-approximation for partial HCVC. As the demand served is at least the ratio of $(1-\epsilon)$, we have an $O(1/\epsilon)f$-approximation algorithm. This gives a parametric trade-off between the total demand to be covered and the cost of the resulting demand assignment.

Keywords: Capacitated covering with hard capacity · Partial cover · Bi-approximation

1 Introduction

In this paper, we consider capacitated vertex cover with hard capacity (HCVC) on f-hypergraphs. In HCVC, we are given a hypergraph $G = (V, E)$ with a maximum edge size f. Each (hyper)edge is associated with a demand and each vertex is associated with a weight (cost), a capacity, and an available multiplicity. The objective is to find a minimum-weight vertex multiset, or cover, such that the demands of the edges can be met by the capacities of the vertices and the multiplicity of each vertex does not exceed its available multiplicity. A demand assignment is *feasible* if the demand of each edge is fully-assigned to (fully-served by) its incident vertices and the multiplicity of each vertex does not exceed its available multiplicity. In other words, HCVC asks for a feasible demand assignment function h such that the total cost $w(h)$ is minimized.

C.-Y. Chang et al. (Eds.): ICS 2018, CCIS 1013, pp. 468–475, 2019.
https://doi.org/10.1007/978-981-13-9190-3_51

Background and the Related Work. The capacitated vertex cover generalizes vertex cover in that a demand-to-service assignment model is evolved from the original 0/1 covering model. For classical vertex cover, it is known that an f-approximation can be obtained by LP rounding and duality [1,6]. Khot and Regev [9] showed that, assuming the unique games conjecture, approximating this problem to a ratio better than $(f - \epsilon)$ is NP-hard for any $\epsilon > 0$ and $f \geq 2$.

For hard capacities, Chuzhoy and Naor [3] considered capacitated covering with hard capacities (HCVC) and unit demand. For unweighted HCVC, they gave a 3-approximation using randomized rounding with a specific patching procedure. They showed that the weighted version of HCVC is at least as hard as the set cover problem. Due to this reason, subsequent work on HCVC has focused on the unweighted version. For weighted capacitated set cover with unit demand, they presented a $(\ln \delta + 1)$-approximation, where δ is the maximum size of the sets. This approach further extends to a $(\ln \max_S f(S) + 1)$-approximation for submodular set cover, which was proved by Wolsey [12]. [2,4,10] improved the approximation result subsequently. Recently, Kao [7] presented an f-approximation for any $f \geq 2$ and closed the gap of approximation for this problem.

For partial HCVC for f-hypergraphs, Cheung et al. [2] presented a $(2f + 2)$ $(1 + \epsilon)$-approximation. Shiau et al. [11] improved it to a tight f-approximation.

In this paper we present an $O(f)$ bi-approximation for partial HCVC. This gives a parametric trade-off between the total demand to be covered and the cost of the resulting demand assignment.

2 Definition

In this problem, we are given a hypergraph $G = (V, E \subseteq 2^V)$ where each $e \in E$ is associated with a demand $d_e \in \mathbb{R}^{\geq 0}$ and each $v \in V$ is associated with a weight (or cost) $w_v \in \mathbb{R}^{\geq 0}$, a capacity $c_v \in \mathbb{R}^{\geq 0}$, and an available multiplicity $m_v \in \mathbb{Z}^{\geq 0}$. The demand of an edge is the amount of service it requires. The capacity of a vertex v is the amount of service each multiplicity of that vertex can provide to $e \in E[v]$.

The objective is to find a vertex multiset, or, cover, represented by a demand assignment function $h \colon E \times V \to \mathbb{R}^{\geq 0}$, such that the following two constraints are met:

1. $\sum_{v \in e} h_{e,v} \geq d_e$ for all $e \in E$,
2. $x_v^{(h)} \leq m_v$ for all $v \in V$, where $x_v^{(h)} := \left\lceil \sum_{e \colon e \in E, v \in e} h_{e,v}/c_v \right\rceil$,

and $w(h) = \sum_{v \in V} w_v \cdot x_v^{(h)}$ is minimized. A demand assignment function h is said to be *feasible* if the two constraints above are met.

Partial Cover. We relax the covered demand to assure that at least β-fraction of total demand is covered. Let $\Pi = (V, E, d_e, w_v, c_v, m_v)$ be an instance for

HCVC. For any $0 \leq \beta \leq 1$, a demand assignment h is said to be β-feasible if

$$\sum_{e \in E} \min \left\{ d_e, \sum_{v \in e} h_{e,v} \right\} \geq \beta \cdot \sum_{e \in E} d_e, \text{ and } x_v^{(h)} \leq m_v \text{ for all } v \in V.$$

Let $\mathcal{F}_1$ denote the set of 1-feasible demand assignments. We say that a demand assignment h forms a (β,γ)-partial-cover if h is β-feasible and $w(h) \leq \gamma \cdot \min_{h' \in \mathcal{F}_1} w(h')$.

3   The Algorithm and Result

In this section, we present our algorithm and result about partial HCVC. We used primal-dual with local charging scheme to solve the problem. And we have $1 - \epsilon, O(1/\epsilon)f)$-partial-cover for partial cover, which means the served demand is at least the ratio of $1 - \epsilon$ and we have an $O(1/\epsilon)f$-approximation algorithm.

3.1   LP Relaxation and the Dual LP

Let $\Pi = (V, E, d_e, w_v, c_v, m_v)$ be an input instance of HCVC. The natural LP relaxation of HCVC for an instance Π is given below in LP (1). There are two sets of variables, $h_{e,v}$ and x_v, which correspond to the demand assignment function and the multiplicities of the vertices, respectively.

$$
\begin{aligned}
\text{Minimize} \quad & \sum_{v \in V} w_v \cdot x_v && (1)\\
& \sum_{v \in e} h_{e,v} \geq d_e, && \forall e \in E\\
& c_v \cdot x_v - \sum_{e \in E[v]} h_{e,v} \geq 0, && \forall v \in V\\
& x_v \leq m_v, && \forall v \in V\\
& d_e \cdot x_v - h_{e,v} \geq 0, && \forall e \in E, \ v \in e\\
& x_v, h_{e,v} \geq 0, && \forall e \in E, \ v \in e
\end{aligned}
$$

The first inequality states that the demand of each edge has to be fully-served. The second inequality connects the multiplicity function and the demand assignment function. The third inequality constraints the multiplicity of each vertex. The fourth inequality, which states that the multiplicity of a vertex cannot be zero if some demand is assigned to that vertex, is introduced to bound the integrality gap of the relaxation.

The dual linear program of the relaxation of (1) is given in (2). There are four sets of variables y_e, z_v, $g_{e,v}$, and η_v, which can be interpreted as a packing program as follows. We want to raise the values of y_e for all $e \in E$. However, the value of each y_e is constrained by z_v and $g_{e,v}$ that are further constrained by w_v for each $v \in e$.

$$\text{Maximize} \quad \sum_{e \in E} d_e \cdot y_e - \sum_{v \in V} m_v \cdot \eta_v$$

$$(2)$$

$$c_v \cdot z_v + \sum_{e \in E[v]} d_e \cdot g_{e,v} - \eta_v \leq w_v, \forall v \in V$$

$$y_e \leq z_v + g_{e,v}, \qquad\qquad \forall v \in V, \; e \in E[v]$$

$$y_e, z_v, g_{e,v}, \eta_v \geq 0, \qquad\qquad \forall v \in V, \; e \in E[v]$$

The fourth set of variables, η_v, complicates the structure of the packing program in that it allows us to pack even more values into y_e in the cost of a deduction in the objective value. This provides a certain degree of flexibility, and handling this flexibility would be one of the major challenges for this problem.

3.2 A Primal-Dual Schema for HCVC

In this section, we present our extended primal-dual algorithm for HCVC. The algorithm that we present extends the framework developed for the soft capacity model [5,8]. In the prior framework, the demand is assigned immediately when a vertex from its incident edges gets saturated. In our algorithm, we keep some of decisions pending until we have sufficient capacity for the demands. We store the dual values in both $g_{e,v}$ and z_v, depending on the amount of unassigned demand that v possesses in its incident edges. This ensures that, the cost of each multiplicity is charged only to the demands that it serves.

To obtain a solid bound for this approach, however, we need to ensure that the vertices whose multiplicity limits are attained receive sufficient amount of demands to charge to. This motivates our flow-based procedure Self-Containment for dealing with the pending decisions. During this procedure, a natural demand assignment is also formed.

The Algorithm. We present our extended primal-dual algorithm DUAL-HCVC below. This algorithm takes as input an instance $\Pi = (V, E, d, w, c, m)$ of HCVC and outputs a feasible primal demand assignment h together with a feasible dual solution $\Psi = (y_v, z_v, g_{e,v}, \eta_v)$ for Π.

The algorithm starts with an initially zero dual solution and eventually reaches a locally optimal solution. During the process, the values of the dual variables in Ψ are raised gradually and some inequalities will meet with equality. We say that a vertex v is *saturated* if the inequality $c_v \cdot z_v + \sum_{e \in E[v]} d_e \cdot g_{e,v} - \eta_v \leq w_v$ is met with equality.

Let $E^\phi := \{e : e \in E, d_e > 0\}$ be the set of edges with non-zero demand and $V^\phi := \{v : v \in V, m_v \cdot c_v > 0\}$ be the set of vertices with non-zero capacity. For each $v \in V$, we use $d^\phi(v) = \sum_{e \in E[v] \cap E^\phi} d_e$ to denote the total amount of demand in $E[v] \cap E^\phi$. For intuition, E^ϕ contains the set of edges whose demands are not yet processed nor assigned, and V^ϕ corresponds to the set of vertices that have not yet saturated.

In addition, we maintain a set S, initialized to be empty, to denote the set of vertices that have saturated and that have at least one incident edge in E^ϕ. Intuitively, S corresponds to vertices with pending assignments.

The algorithm works as follows. Initially all dual variables in Ψ and the demand assignment h are set to be zero. We raise the value of the dual variable y_e for each $e \in E^\phi$ simultaneously at the same rate. To maintain the dual feasibility, as we increase y_e, either z_v or $g_{e,v}$ has to be raised for each $v \in e$. If $d^\phi(v) \leq c_v$, then we raise $g_{e,v}$. Otherwise, we raise z_v. In addition, for all $v \in e \cap S$, we *raise* η_v to the extent that keeps v saturated.

When a vertex $u \in V^\phi$ becomes saturated, it is removed from V^ϕ. Then we invoke a recursive procedure Self-Containment$(S \cup \{u\}, u)$, which is a flow-based procedure, to compute a pair (S', h'), where

- S' is a maximal subset of $S \cup \{u\}$ whose capacity, if chosen, can fully-serve the demands in $E[S'] \cap E^\phi$, and
- h' is the corresponding demand assignment function (from $E[S'] \cap E^\phi$ to S').

If $S' = \emptyset$, then we leave the assignment decision pending and add u to S. Otherwise, S' is removed from S and $E[S']$ is removed from E^ϕ. In addition, we add the assignment h' to final assignment h to be output. This process repeats until $E^\phi = \emptyset$. Then the algorithm outputs h and Ψ and terminates.

We also note that, the particular vertex to saturate in each iteration is the one with the smallest value of $w^\phi(v)/\min\{c_v, d^\phi(v)\}$, where $w^\phi(v) := w_v - (c_v \cdot z_v + \sum_{e \in E[v]} d_e \cdot g_{e,v} - \eta_v)$ denotes the current slack of the inequality associated with $v \in V^\phi$.

Properties of DUAL-HCVC. In the following, we briefly describe basic properties of our algorithm. Since the algorithm keeps the constraints feasible when increasing the dual variables, we know that Ψ is feasible for the dual LP for Π. We first show that h is a feasible demand assignment for Π as well. Then we derive properties which will be used when establishing the bi-approximation factor in the next section.

Feasibility of the Demand Assignment h. We begin with procedure Self-Containment. Let $(S', \tilde{h}')$ be the pair returned by Self-Containment$(S \cup \{u\}, u)$. The following lemma shows that S' is indeed maximal.

Lemma 1. *If there exists a $B \subseteq S \cup \{u\}$ such that B can fully-serve the demand in $E[B] \cap E^\phi$, then $B \subseteq S'$.*

The following lemma states the feasibility of this primal-dual process.

Lemma 2. E^ϕ *becomes empty in polynomial time. Furthermore, the assignments computed by* Self-Containment *during the process form a feasible demand assignment.*

The Cost Incurred by h. We consider the cost incurred by the partial assignments computed by Self-Containment. Let V_S denote the set of vertices that have been included in the set S. For any vertex v that has saturated, we use (S'_v, h'_v) to denote the particular pair returned by Self-Containment such that $v \in S'_v$. Note that, this pair (S'_v, h'_v) is uniquely defined for each v that has saturated. Therefore, we know that $h_{e,v} = (h'_v)_{e,v}$ holds for any $e \in E[v]$.

In the rest of this section, we will simply use $h_{e,v}$ when it refers to $(h'_v)_{e,v}$ for simplicity of notation. Recall that $D_{h'_v}(v)$ denotes the amount of demand that v receives in h'_v. We have the following proposition for the dual solution $\Psi = (y_e, z_v, g_{e,v}, \eta_v)$, which follows directly from the way in which the dual variables are raised.

Proposition 1. *For any $v \in V$ such that $d^\phi(v) > c_v$ when saturated, the following holds:*

- $z_v = y_e$ *for all $e \in E[v]$ with $h_{e,v} > 0$.*
- $\eta_v > 0$ *only when $v \in V_S$.*

The following lemma gives the properties for vertices in V_S.

Lemma 3. *For any $v \in V_S$, we have*

1. $D_{h'_v}(v) = m_v \cdot c_v$.
2. $w_v \cdot m_v = D_{h'_v}(v) \cdot y_e - m_v \cdot \eta_v$ *for all $e \in E[v]$ such that $h_{e,v} > 0$.*

The following auxiliary lemma, which is carried over from the previous primal-dual framework, shows that, for any vertex v with $d^\phi(v) \leq c_v$ when saturated, we can locate at most c_v units of demands from $E[v]$ such that their dual value pays for w_v. This statement holds intuitively since v is saturated.

Lemma 4. *For any $v \in V$ with $d^\phi(v) \leq c_v$ when saturated, we can compute a function $\ell_v \colon E[v] \to \mathbb{R}^{\geq 0}$ such that the following holds:*

(a) $0 \leq h_{e,v} \leq \ell_v(e) \leq d_e$, for all $e \in E[v]$.
(b) $\sum_{e \in E[v]} \ell_v(e) \leq c_v$.
(c) $\sum_{e \in E[v]} \ell_v(e) \cdot y_e = w_v$.

Intuitively, Proposition 1 and Lemma 3 provide a solid upper-bound for vertices whose capacity is fairly used. However, we remark that, this approach does not yield a solid guarantee for vertices whose capacity is barely used, i.e., $D_{h'_v}(v) \ll c_v$. The reason is that the demand that is served (charged) by vertices that have been included in S, i.e., those discussed in Lemma 3, cannot be charged again since their dual values are inflated during the primal-dual process.

3.3 $(1 - \epsilon, O(1/\epsilon)f)$-partial-cover for Partial Cover

In this section we modify algorithm DUAL-HCVC to Partial-HCVC(α), where $\alpha \geq 2$ is the target parameter to be decided later. The algorithm builds on the primal-dual scheme given in §3.2. It keeps track of the y_e values during its execution. Whenever there are demands to assign, it makes sure that the demands are able to pay for the cost. To obtain the feasibility guarantee, a procedure DemandRecycle is used to collect the demands that were left unassigned in previous iterations. The following information is maintained in the algorithm:

1. $\hat{y}$: the current y-value of the edges in E^ϕ.
2. $E^\times$: the set of edges whose demand is processed and left unassigned.
3. d_e^r and y_e for each $e \in E^\times$: the amount of demand that is processed and left unassigned for edge e and its y-value, respectively.

In each iteration, the algorithm updates the value of $\hat{y}$ by adding to it the amount of y-value that was raised for edges in E^ϕ. Let u be the vertex which becomes saturated in the current iteration, and (S', h') be the pair returned by procedure Self-Containment$(S \cup \{u\}, u)$. If $S' = \emptyset$, then we add u to S and iterate as described before. Otherwise, we use a procedure DemandRecycle$(u, h', E^\times, y, d^r)$, described in the next paragraph, to collect demands from $E[u] \cap E^\times$.

Let h'' be the assignment function returned by DemandRecycle$(u, h', E^\times, y, d^r)$. The algorithm checks if the y-values of the demands collected in h' and h'' are sufficient to pay for the cost of the vertex u. In particular, if

$$\hat{y} \cdot \sum_{e \in E[u] \cap E^\phi} h'_{e,u} + \sum_{e \in E[u] \cap E^\times} h''_{e,u} \cdot y_e \geq \frac{1}{\alpha} w_u,$$

then it performs the assignments suggested by h' and h''. Otherwise, the demand that is assigned to u in h' is added to $E^\times$ and left unassigned. In this case, the algorithm also records the corresponding y-values and the amount of residue demands. This process is repeated until all the demand is processed and E^ϕ becomes empty.

The Procedure DemandRecycle$(u, h', E^\times, y, d^r)$ works as follows. Let $\langle h'_v, v \rangle$ denote the amount of demand v receives in h'. If $\langle h'_u, u \rangle \geq c_u$, then it returns a null assignment. Otherwise, it scans the edges in $E[u] \cap E^\times$ in non-increasing order according to their y-values and collects the residue demands until either u gets c_u amount of demands in total or nothing is left to be collected.

In the following, we show that, for any $s \geq 1$, $\hat{h}$ forms an $(s/(s+1), sf)$-partial-cover with a properly chosen α.

Since we collect the demands from $E^\times$ in non-ascending order according to their y-values in the procedure DemandRecycle, we know that, if the demands collected by the procedure could not pay for the cost, sufficient amount of demand from the vicinity has already been served. This gives the following lemma regarding the $(\frac{\alpha-1}{f+\alpha-2})$-feasibility of $\hat{h}$.

Lemma 5. $\hat{h}$ is $(\frac{\alpha-1}{f+\alpha-2})$-feasible provided that $\alpha \geq 2$.

Let OPT(G) denote the cost of the optimal demand assignment for G. The following lemma bounds the cost incurred by $\hat{h}$.

Lemma 6. *For $\alpha \geq 2$, we have $w(\hat{h}) \leq \alpha \cdot \mathrm{OPT}(G)$.*

By Lemmas 5–6, and the fact that

$$\frac{sf - 1}{(s+1)f - 2} \geq \frac{sf}{(s+1)f}$$

for any $s \geq 1$ and $f \geq 2$, we have the following theorem.

Theorem 1. *For any $s \geq 1$, algorithm Partial-HCVC(sf) computes an $\left(\frac{s}{s+1}, sf\right)$-partial-cover for HCVC on f-hypergraphs in polynomial time.*

References

1. Bar-Yehuda, R., Even, S.: A linear-time approximation algorithm for the weighted vertex cover problem. J. Algorithms **2**(2), 198–203 (1981)
2. Cheung, W.-C., Goemans, M.X., Wong, S.C.-W.: Improved algorithms for vertex cover with hard capacities on multigraphs and hypergraphs. In: Proceedings of the Twenty-Fifth Annual ACM-SIAM Symposium on Discrete Algorithms, SODA 2014, pp. 1714–1726 (2014)
3. Chuzhoy, J., Naor, J.S.: Covering problems with hard capacities. SIAM J. Comput. **36**(2), 498–515 (2006)
4. Gandhi, R., Halperin, E., Khuller, S., Kortsarz, G., Srinivasan, A.: An improved approximation algorithm for vertex cover with hard capacities. In: Baeten, J.C.M., Lenstra, J.K., Parrow, J., Woeginger, G.J. (eds.) ICALP 2003. LNCS, vol. 2719, pp. 164–175. Springer, Heidelberg (2003). https://doi.org/10.1007/3-540-45061-0_15
5. Guha, S., Hassin, R., Khuller, S., Or, E.: Capacitated vertex covering. J. Algorithms **48**(1), 257–270 (2003)
6. Hochbaum, D.S.: Approximation algorithms for the set covering and vertex cover problems. SIAM J. Comput. **11**(3), 555–556 (1982)
7. Kao, M.-J.: Iterative partial rounding for vertex cover with hard capacities. In: Proceedings of the Thirty-First Annual ACM-SIAM Symposium on Discrete Algorithms, SODA 2017 (2017)
8. Kao, M.-J., Liao, C.-S., Lee, D.T.: Capacitated domination problem. Algorithmica **60**(2), 274–300 (2011)
9. Khot, S., Regev, O.: Vertex cover might be hard to approximate to within 2-epsilon. J. Comput. Syst. Sci. **74**(3), 335–349 (2008)
10. Saha, B., Khuller, S.: Set cover revisited: hypergraph cover with hard capacities. In: Czumaj, A., Mehlhorn, K., Pitts, A., Wattenhofer, R. (eds.) ICALP 2012. LNCS, vol. 7391, pp. 762–773. Springer, Heidelberg (2012). https://doi.org/10.1007/978-3-642-31594-7_64
11. Shiau, J.-Y., Kao, M.-J., Lin, C.-C., Lee, D.T.: Tight approximation for partial vertex cover with hard capacities. In: 28th International Symposium on Algorithms and Computation, ISAAC 2017, 9–12 December 2017, Phuket, Thailand, pp. 64:1–64:13 (2017)
12. Wolsey, L.A.: An analysis of the greedy algorithm for the submodular set covering problem. Combinatorica **2**(4), 385–393 (1982)

A Lyapunov Stability Based Adaptive Learning Rate of Recursive Sinusoidal Function Neural Network for Identification of Elders Fall Signal

Chao-Ting Chu[1]($\boxtimes$) and Chian-Cheng Ho[2]

[1] Internet of Things Laboratory,
Chunghwa Telecom Laboratories, New Taipei City, Taiwan
chaot@cht.com.tw
[2] Department of Electrical Engineering, National Yunlin University
of Science and Technology, Douliu, Taiwan

Abstract. This paper presents an adaptive learning rate of recursive sinusoidal function neural network (ALR-RSFNN) with Lyapunov stability for identification elders fall signal. The older human signal analysis has been a research topic in health care fields that algorithms are implemented in wearable device real time to detect fall situation. However, the code size of the microcontroller in wearable device is limited, and the neural network learning rate choice is important which influencs neural network convergence performance. The recursive sinusoidal function neural network uses sine wave modulation input function to reduce train times in traditional Gaussian function vertex and width. Moreover, we utilize adaptive learning rate to guarantee network stability. In the experimental results, the ALR-RSFNN identify human fall signal accurately and reliably. In addition, we use wearable device combined BLE (Bluetooth low energy) to feedback output response real time.

Keywords: Sine wave · Neural network · Health care · Adaptive learning rate

1 Introduction

Recently, researchers have shown an increasing interest in fitness fields [1, 2] which advance is easily portable to combine different algorithms analysis and user body signal. The research of fitness fields has been combined health care application [3–5] to analyse body signal. Bertozzi et al. [3] proposed health-care interventions with games for user which the games show low-cost and high-impact approach to help user detection body signal. Carvalko et al. [4] presented crowdsourcing biological specimen identification; the consumer technology applied to health-care access have satisfactory output response. Khazaei et al. [5] design a health informatics for neonatal intensive care units; the experimental results discussed an analytical modeling perspective in health informatics. It is becoming increasingly difficult to ignore the user falls signal [6–8] alarm that helps older user to avoid danger situation. In [6], a development and evaluation of a prior-to-impact fall event detection algorithm have been published by

© Springer Nature Singapore Pte Ltd. 2019
C.-Y. Chang et al. (Eds.): ICS 2018, CCIS 1013, pp. 476–484, 2019.
https://doi.org/10.1007/978-981-13-9190-3_52

Liu et al. [6]. There are shown prior-to-impact algorithm detection fall event real time and feedback to backstage processed. Lee et al. [7] discussed a inertial sensing-based pre-impact detection of falls involving near-fall scenarios, in which the proposed algorithms detection of falls involving near-fall scenarios have satisfactory performance. Yu et al. [8] presented an online one class support vector machine-based person-specific fall detection system for monitoring an elderly individual in a room environment. The experimental results shows person-specific fall detection system estimation fall signal real time.

A considerable amount of literature about neural network has been published. These studies used neural network [9–12] for classification fields. Martin et al. [9] proposed a detection and classification of single and combined power quality disturbances using neural networks that are shown neural networks applied power quality disturbances to detection and classification. In [10], Deshpande et al. are shown the research about fully connected cascade artificial neural network architecture for attention deficit hyperactivity disorder classification from functional magnetic resonance imaging data, in which the functional magnetic resonance complex imaging data used neural network classification have contentment output performance. Mohammed et al. [11] presented an enhanced fuzzy min–max neural network for pattern classification. The fuzzy min–max neural network classify different pattern in experimental results. More recently, literature has published that offers satisfactory classify performance about different type neural network for Hermite function [12–14]. In [12], a Hermite functional link neural network for solving the van der pol–duffing oscillator equation have been proposed by Mall et al., in which the Hermite functional link neural network have multivariate input layer to improve complex van der pol–duffing oscillator equation. Lin et al. [13] shows tracking control of thrust active magnetic bearing system via Hermite polynomial-based recurrent neural network. The neural network with Hermite polynomial estimated nonlinear magnetic bearing system uncertainty real time. Ma et al. [14] developed a constructive feedforward neural networks using Hermite polynomial activation functions that experimental results have satisfactory output response.

This paper proposes a ALR-RSFNN identification and analysis for elders fall situation in wearable devices. The features of ALR-RSFNN identification use different frequency modulation function in input layer to map extensive complex input signal, and we utilize adaptive learning rate to guarantee network stability. Moreover, we implement acceleration sensor with BLE (Bluetooth low energy) feedback body signal in wearable device. In the experimental result, it shows the rotation memory neural network algorithms have estimated fall detection signal and have higher satisfactory output response than traditional performance index.

2 Wearable Device System Architecture

Figure 1 is the sensor board setting situation. We set sensor board in user pockets, and the acceleration sensor signal transmits by Bluetooth low energy. Figure 2 is the sensor board function diagram. Firstly, the sensor board uses coin battery to support system power. Secondly, acceleration sensors collect body's three-axis signal and use ALR-RSFNN algorithms to identify user fall situation. Finally, we use BLE function to transmit three-axis signal to remote PC which shows experimental results and notice.

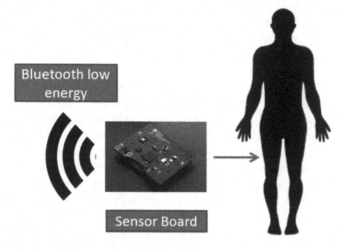

Fig. 1. Wearable device setting situation

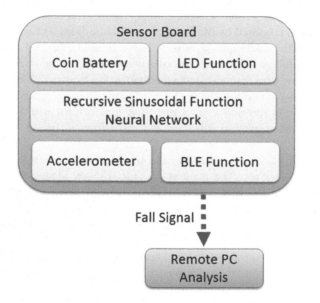

Fig. 2. Wearable device function diagram

3   Identification of ALR-RSHNN

The ALR-RSFNN is shown in Fig. 3. The ALR-RSFNN used recursive neurons weight record previous and current signal, and frequency modulation function input layer to identify fall signal. We used sport signal input to ALR-RSFNN. The user sport signal used 3-axis accelerations. Define coordinate system x, y, z are located axis, and the accelerations with the geodetic coordinate system are a_x, a_y, a_z. Therefore, we define performance index of resultant acceleration norm as

$$\varsigma = \sqrt{a_x^2 + a_y^2 + a_z^2} \tag{1}$$

The ALR-RSHNN input layer used Gaussian function which equation shows as

$$H_j(\varsigma) = \sin(j \cdot \varsigma \cdot \beta) + \alpha + r_j H_j(t-1, \varsigma) \tag{2}$$

where j is the node, $\alpha, \beta > 0$, t is the sample time.
Hence, we obtain output of ALR-RSHNN as

$$\psi = \sum_{i=1}^{j} H_i w_i \tag{3}$$

where w_i is the output weight.
The energy convergence function define as

$$E = \frac{1}{2} e^2 \tag{4}$$

where $e = x_d - \psi$, x_d is the target identify results.
Hence,

$$\Delta w_j(t) = -\eta_1 \frac{\partial E}{\partial w_j} = \eta_1 e \frac{\partial \psi}{\partial w_j} = \eta_1 e \frac{\partial \left(\sum_{i=1}^{j} H_i w_i \right)}{\partial w_j} = \eta_1 e H_j \tag{5}$$

$$\begin{aligned}
\Delta r_j(t) &= -\eta_2 \frac{\partial E}{\partial r_j} = -\eta_4 \frac{\partial \frac{1}{2} (x_d - \psi)^2}{\partial r_j} \\
&= \eta_2 e w_j \frac{1}{2} \left(\frac{\partial H_j}{\partial r_j} + \frac{\partial H_j(t-1)}{\partial r_j} \frac{\partial H_j(t)}{\partial H_j(t-1)} \right) \\
&= \eta_2 e w_j \frac{1}{2} \left(H_j(\varsigma, t-1) + H_j(\varsigma, t-2) r_j \right)
\end{aligned} \tag{6}$$

where $\eta_1, \eta_2 > 0$.
For the adaptive learning rate that let Lyapounv function choose

$$V_s = \frac{1}{2}e^2(k) \tag{7}$$

where k is the simple time. From (7), we know

$$\Delta V_s = V_s(k) - V_s(k-1) = \Delta e(k)\left(e(k) + \frac{1}{2}\Delta e(k)\right) \tag{8}$$

where $\Delta e(k) = e(k) - e(k-1)$.

Define the error variation as

$$\Delta e(k) = \left[\frac{\partial e(k)}{\partial W_s}\right]^T \Delta W_s \tag{9}$$

where $W_s = \left[[W_f]^T \ [W_r]^T\right]^T_{1\times 2},$ $W_f = [w_1, \ldots, w_j]_{1\times j},$ $W_r = [r_1, \ldots, r_j]_{1\times j}.$

Consolidate total learning rate matrix as

$$\eta_s = \begin{bmatrix} \eta_1 & 0 \\ 0 & \eta_2 \end{bmatrix}_{2\times 2} \tag{10}$$

ALR-RSFNN learning rate parameter variation can be written as

$$\Delta W_s = -\eta_s \frac{\partial V_s(k)}{\partial W_s} = -e(k)\begin{bmatrix} \eta_1 & 0 \\ 0 & \eta_2 \end{bmatrix}\left[\left[\frac{\partial e(k)}{\partial W_f}\right]^T \left[\frac{\partial e(k)}{\partial W_r}\right]^T\right]^T \tag{11}$$

Substituting (11) into (8), we have

$$\Delta e(k) = \left[\frac{\partial e(k)}{\partial W_s}\right]^T \Delta W_s = -e(k)\left(\eta_1\left\|\frac{\partial e(k)}{\partial W_f}\right\|^2 + \eta_2\left\|\frac{\partial e(k)}{\partial W_r}\right\|^2\right) \tag{12}$$

Define as

$$R = \eta_1\left\|\frac{\partial e(k)}{\partial W_f}\right\|^2 + \eta_2\left\|\frac{\partial e(k)}{\partial W_r}\right\|^2 \tag{13}$$

Substituting (13) into (11), we get

$$\Delta V_s = \Delta e(k)\left(e(k) + \frac{1}{2}\Delta e(k)\right) = -\frac{1}{2}e^2(k)(2R - R^2) \tag{14}$$

Limit $0 < R < 2$, so that

$$0 < \eta_m < \frac{2}{\left\|\frac{\partial e(k)}{\partial W_f}\right\|^2 + \left\|\frac{\partial e(k)}{\partial W_r}\right\|^2} \tag{15}$$

where $\eta_m = \max_{i=1 \to 2} \eta_i$.

Finally, the learning rate define as (15), in which we can guarantee the Lyapunov function $V_s \geq 0$ and $\Delta V_s \leq 0$ to ensure ALR-RSFNN convergence.

For the experimental results, we choose performance index as

$$\chi = \frac{1}{((x_d - \mu)^r + 1)} \tag{16}$$

where x_d is the target result, r is the choose square.

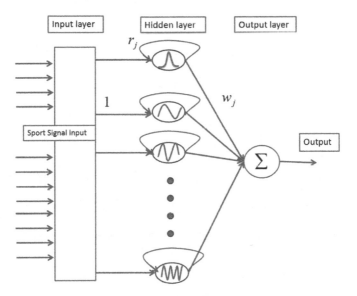

Fig. 3. ALR-RSFNN structure

4 Experimental Results

The remote PC shows person fall signal experimental results. Figure 4 shows the ALR-RSFNN train error state which shows error convergence in 500 times. Figures 5, 6, 7 and 8 show the Volunteer 1 to Volunteer 3 sport signal for different resultant acceleration and identify results. The have been obtained fall single in four Volunteer which have satisfactory response.

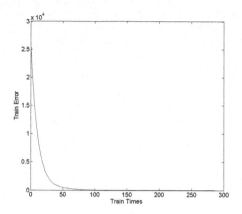

Fig. 4. ALR-RSFNN train error convergence situation.

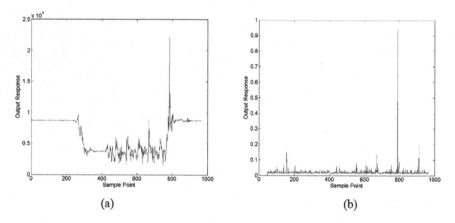

(a)   (b)

Fig. 5. Volunteer 1 sport signal (a) resultant acceleration, (b) ALR-RSFNN identify situation.

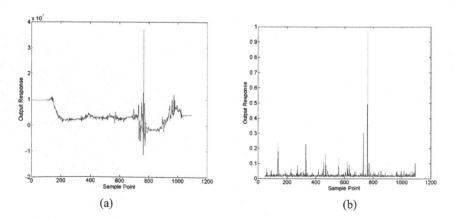

(a)   (b)

Fig. 6. Volunteer 2 sport signal (a) resultant acceleration, (b) ALR-RSFNN identify situation.

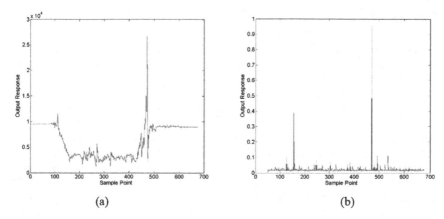

(a)   (b)

Fig. 7. Volunteer 3 sport signal (a) resultant acceleration, (b) ALR-RSFNN model identify situation.

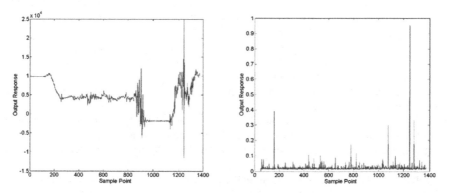

Fig. 8. Volunteer 4 sport signal (a) resultant acceleration, (b) ALR-RSFNN model identify situation.

5 Conclusion

The fall detection is an important research topic in health care fields which assists with older adult home safety. This paper successful uses ALR-RSFNN algorithms and implements in wearable device that has higher performance detection fall signal and feedback remote PC. The experimental results show ALR-RSFNN algorithms have better identification of fall signal event than traditional resultant acceleration in all-volunteer situation.

Acknowledgment. This work was supported in part by the "Intelligent Recognition Industry Service Center" of Higher Education Sprout Project, Ministry of Education, Taiwan.

References

1. Yuan, B., Li, B., Weise, T., Yao, X.: A new memetic algorithm with fitness approximation for the defect-tolerant logic mapping in crossbar-based nanoarchitectures. IEEE Trans. Parallel Distrib. Syst. **18**(6), 846–859 (2014)
2. Chu, C.T., Chiang, H.K., Hung, J.J.: Dynamic heart rate monitors algorithm for reflection green light wearable device. In: International Conference on Intelligent Informatics and Biomedical Sciences, vol. 62, no. 8, pp. 438–445 (2015)
3. Bertozzi, E., et al.: Health-care interventions with games: a low-cost, high-impact approach. IEEE Consum. Electron. Mag. **4**(3), 80–82 (2015)
4. Carvalko, J.R., Morris, C.: Crowdsourcing biological specimen identification: consumer technology applied to health-care access. IEEE Consum. Electron. Mag. **4**(1), 90–93 (2015)
5. Khazaei, H., Bressan, N.M., McGregor, C., Pugh, J.E.: Health informatics for neonatal intensive care units: an analytical modeling perspective. IEEE Trans. Biomed. Circ. Syst. **3** (1), 3000109 (2015)
6. Liu, J., Lockhart, T.E.: Development and evaluation of a prior-to-impact fall event detection algorithm. IEEE Trans. Biomed. Eng. **61**(7), 2135–2140 (2014)
7. Lee, J.K., Robinovitch, S.N., Park, E.J.: Inertial sensing-based pre-impact detection of falls involving near-fall scenarios. IEEE Trans. Neural Syst. Rehabil. Eng. **63**(2), 258–266 (2016)
8. Yu, M., Yu, Y., Rhuma, A., Naqvi, S.M.R., Wang, L., Chambers, J.A.: An online one class support vector machine-based person-specific fall detection system for monitoring an elderly individual in a room environment. IEEE J. Biomed. Health Inform. **17**(6), 1002–1014 (2013)
9. Martin, V.R., Rene, R.T., Alfredo, J.Q.R.R., Arturo, G.P.: Detection and classification of single and combined power quality disturbances using neural networks. IEEE Trans. Ind. Electron. **61**(5), 2473–2482 (2014)
10. Deshpande, G., Wang, P., Rangaprakash, D., Wilamowski, B.: Fully connected cascade artificial neural network architecture for attention deficit hyperactivity disorder classification from functional magnetic resonance imaging data. IEEE Trans. Cybern. **45**(12), 2668–2679 (2015)
11. Mohammed, M.F.W., Lim, C.P.: An enhanced fuzzy min–max neural network for pattern classification. IEEE Trans. Neural Netw. Learn. Syst. **26**(3), 417–429 (2015)
12. Mall, S., Chakraverty, S.: Hermite functional link neural network for solving the van der pol–duffing oscillator equation. IEEE Trans. Control Syst. Technol. **28**(8), 1574–1598 (2016)
13. Lin, F.J., Chen, S.Y., Huang, M.S.: Tracking control of thrust active magnetic bearing system via hermite polynomial-based recurrent neural network. IET Electr. Power Appl. **4**(9), 701–714 (2010)
14. Ma, L., Khorasani, K.: Constructive feedforward neural networks using Hermite polynomial activation functions. IEEE Trans. Neural Networks **16**(4), 821–833 (2015)

Multi-recursive Wavelet Neural Network for Proximity Capacitive Gesture Recognition Analysis and Implementation

Chao-Ting Chu[1($\boxtimes$)] and Chian-Cheng Ho[2]

[1] Internet of Things Laboratory, Chunghwa Telecom Laboratories,
New Taipei City, Taiwan
chaot@cht.com.tw
[2] Department of Electrical Engineering, National Yunlin University
of Science and Technology, Douliu, Taiwan

Abstract. This paper presents a multi-recursive wavelet neural network (MRWNN) with proximity capacitive gesture recognition. Recently, the capacitive sensor technologies have been developed for proximity methods that sensing electronic varies around sensor detection point, but the user gesture signals are time-variant. The MRWNN have multi layers recursive weight to record last signal variation, and we utilize microcontroller with MRWNN to identify algorithms and implement proximity capacitive gesture recognition. Moreover, we show MRWNN weight convergence analysis of the MRWNN signal identifier. In the experimental results, we show MRWNN can recognize patterns of different gesture signal accurately and reliably. In addition, we use wearable device combined with BLE (Bluetooth Low Energy) feedback output response immediately.

Keywords: Microcontroller · Proximity capacitive · Gesture recognition · Wavelet

1 Introduction

Recently, researchers have shown increasing interest in IOT fields [1, 2] which detect different sensor situation and feedback users. The health care with sensor control system has been developed which make some researchers [3–5] to propose researches in different applications. Semnani et al. [3] proposed a semi-flocking algorithm for motion control of mobile sensors in large-scale surveillance systems that the proposed semi-flocking algorithm monitor motion situation immediately. Usman et al. [4] presented a mobile agent-based cross-layer anomaly detection in smart home sensor networks using fuzzy logic, in which fuzzy logic used expert knowledge methods anomaly detection smart home sensor networks. Kafi et al. [5] shows a congestion control protocols in wireless sensor networks, in which the researches discussed wireless sensor technical future trends. It is becoming increasingly difficult to ignore the user biological signal [6–8] analysis that fall detection alarm to help older users to avoid danger situation. Inertial sensing-based pre-impact detection of falls involving near-fall scenarios has been proposed by Lee et al. [6] which predicted human falls alert

© Springer Nature Singapore Pte Ltd. 2019
C.-Y. Chang et al. (Eds.): ICS 2018, CCIS 1013, pp. 485–494, 2019.
https://doi.org/10.1007/978-981-13-9190-3_53

before near-fall scenarios. In [7], a development and evaluation of a prior-to-impact fall event detection algorithm has been published by Liu et al. There are shown prior-to-impact algorithm detection fall event real time and feedback to backstage processed. Yu et al. [8] presented an online one class support vector machine-based person-specific fall detection system for monitoring an elderly individual in a room environment. The experimental results show person-specific fall detection system estimation fall signal real time.

A considerable amount of literature has been published on neural network. These studies used neural network [9–12] applied to classification fields. In [9], Deshpande et al. showed the research about fully connected cascade artificial neural network architecture for attention deficit hyperactivity disorder classification from functional magnetic resonance imaging data, in which the functional magnetic resonance complex imaging data used neural network classification has contentment output performance. In [10], a Hermite functional link neural network for solving the van der pol–duffing oscillator equation have been proposed by Mall et al., in which the Hermite functional link neural network have multivariate input layer to improve complex van der pol–duffing oscillator equation. Ma et al. [11] developed a constructive feedforward neural networks using Hermite polynomial activation functions that experimental results have satisfactory output response. A recent study by wavelet and neural network involve in control and identify [12–14] fields. Devi et al. [12] shows diagnosis and classification of stator winding insulation faults on a three-phase induction motor using wavelet and MNN, in which wavelet neural network classify stator winding insulation faults have satisfactory response in experimental results. Duan et al. [13] proposed EMG-Based identification of hand motion commands using wavelet neural network combined with discrete wavelet transform. The wavelet neural network detected hand sway of EMG signal and identified user motion state. For the control fields, a squirrel-cage induction generator system using wavelet petri fuzzy neural network control for wind power applications have been presented by Tan et al. [14] that shows proposed algorithms control induction generator system track command speed precisely.

The smart home securities have been a research topic in internet of things fields that securities algorithms build in real-time processor to recognize user identification. This paper proposes proximity capacitive gesture recognition with MRWNN. The features of MRWNN have multi layers recursive weight to record last signal vary, and the wavelet activation function classify user input signal. The Sect. 4 shows the MRWNN weight convergence prove to identify user gesture situation. Finally, we implement proximity capacitive sensor with BLE (Bluetooth low energy) module feedback user hand signal. In the experimental results shows the MRWNN algorithms identify different gesture signal that have satisfactory output response.

2 Wearable Device System Architecture

Figure 1 is the capacitive sensor board. We use capacitive proximity mode sensing methods to obtain user gesture capacitive variation, and the microcontroller uses MRWNN train and learn user gesture. Finally, the Bluetooth module transmits identification results and user gesture capacitive variation to remote PC.

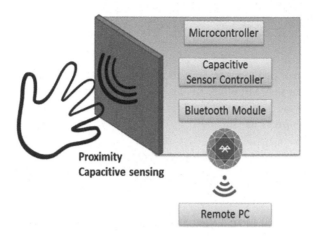

Fig. 1. Capacitive sensor board

Figure 2 is the capacitive sensor board function diagram. Firstly, the sensor pad obtains capacitive varying signal. Secondly, capacitive sensor controller collects user gesture signal and uses identify system to identify user gesture. Finally, we use Bluetooth module to transmit identification signal to remote PC which shows experimental results and notice.

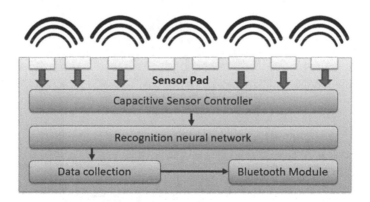

Fig. 2. Capacitive sensor board function diagram

3 Identification of MRWNN

The MRWNN construct is shown in Fig. 3 which uses multi-recursive weight to identify user gesture signal. We use capacitance signal input to MRWNN and train identification eigenvalues. The user capacitance signal used electric field situation in sensor pad. Define gesture vector equation as

$$\tau(t) = \sum_{i=1}^{n} G_i(t) \tag{1}$$

where n is the sensor pad number. G_i is the capacitance sensing signal from sensor pad. t is the sample times. A MRWNN has an input layer, a membership layer, a rule layer and an output layer. The input signal of MRWNN is user gesture signal, in which equation can be express as

$$u_i(N) = \tau(N) + O_i^{(1)}(N-1) \tag{2}$$

$$O_i^{(1)}(N) = u_i^{(1)}(N) \tag{3}$$

where u_i is the input of input layer. O_i^1 is the output of input layer. N is the $N-th$ iteration.

The membership layer can be express as

$$h(x) = -x \exp\left(-\frac{x^2}{2}\right) \tag{4}$$

$$u_{ij}^{(2)} = \frac{O_i^{(1)} - n_{ij}}{\gamma_{ij}} \tag{5}$$

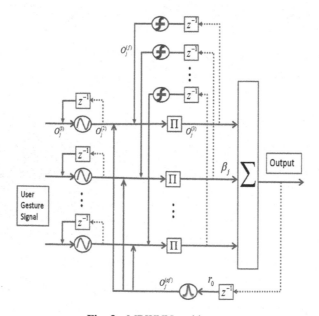

Fig. 3. MRWNN architecture

$$O_{ij}^{(2)} = h\left(u_{ij}^{(2)}\right) \tag{6}$$

Where $j = 1, 2, \ldots,$ n. n_{ij} and γ_{ij} is the translation and dilation, respectively. u_i^2 is the input of membership layer. O_j^2 is the output of membership layer. The superscript (2) represents membership layer. The subscript j is the neurons numbers of the membership layer.

The recursive rule layer can be express as

$$u_j^f(N) = O_j^{(3)}(N-1) \tag{7}$$

$$O_j^f(N) = f\left(u_j^f(N)\right) \tag{8}$$

$$f(x) = \frac{1}{1 + \exp(-x)} \tag{9}$$

where exp is exponential function. u_i^f is the input of recursive rule layers. O_i^f is the output of recursive rule layers. Superscript f represents recursive rule layer. Superscript (3) represents the rule layer.

The rule layer can be express as

$$u_j^{(3)} = O^{of} \cdot O_j^f \cdot O_{1j}^{(2)} \cdot O_{2j}^{(2)} \tag{10}$$

$$O_j^{(3)} = u_j^{(3)} \tag{11}$$

where $u_j^{(3)}$ is the input of rule layer. $O_j^{(3)}$ is the output of rule layer.

The recursive of output layer can be express as

$$u^{of}(N) = r_o \cdot y(N-1) \tag{12}$$

$$O^{of}(N) = \exp\left(-\left(u^{of}(N)\right)^2\right) \tag{13}$$

where r_o is a not adjust recursive weight of output layer. u^{of} is the recursive input of output layer. O^{of} is the recursive output of output layer. Superscript of is the output layer.

Finally, the output layer is

$$u^{(4)} = \sum_{j=1}^{5} \beta_j \cdot O_j^{(3)} \tag{14}$$

$$U = y(N) = O^{(4)} = u^{(4)} \tag{15}$$

where β_j is the weight between rule layer and output layer. $u^{(4)}$ is the input of output layers. U is the output of output layers. Superscript (4) represents the output layer.

4   Training Algorithm of the MRWNN Identification System

The MRWNN system is trained using the back-propagation learning algorithm, where a gradient vector is calculated recursively. The energy function is defined as

$$E = \frac{1}{2}e^2 \tag{16}$$

where $e = x_d - U$, x_d is the target identify results.

The error of the output layer is defined as Eq. (17).

$$\delta^{(4)} = -\frac{\partial E}{\partial y(N)} = -\frac{\partial E}{\partial e} \cdot \frac{\partial e}{\partial y(N)} \approx e \tag{17}$$

The weights between output and wavelet layers are updated as Eqs. (18)–(19).

$$\Delta\beta_j = -\frac{\partial E}{\partial \beta_j} = -\frac{\partial E}{\partial y(N)} \cdot \frac{\partial y(N)}{\partial u^{(4)}} \cdot \frac{\partial u^{(4)}}{\partial \beta_j} = \eta_\beta \delta^{(4)} O_j^{(3)} \tag{18}$$

$$\beta_j(N+1) = \beta_j(N) + \Delta\beta_j \tag{19}$$

where η_β is the learning rate of output layer.

Let the rule layer and membership layer error as

$$\delta_j^{(3)} = -\frac{\partial E}{\partial O_j^{(3)}} = -\frac{\partial E}{\partial y(N)} \cdot \frac{\partial y(N)}{\partial u^{(4)}} \cdot \frac{\partial u^{(4)}}{\partial O_j^{(3)}} = \delta^{(4)}\beta_j(N) \tag{20}$$

$$\delta_{1j}^{(2)} = -\frac{\partial E}{\partial O_{1j}^{(2)}} = -\frac{\partial E}{\partial y(N)} \cdot \frac{\partial y(N)}{\partial u^{(4)}} \cdot \frac{\partial u^{(4)}}{\partial O_j^{(3)}} \cdot \frac{\partial O_j^{(3)}}{\partial u_j^{(3)}} \cdot \frac{\partial u_j^{(3)}}{\partial O_{1j}^{(2)}} = \delta_j^{(3)} O^{of} O_j^f O_{2j}^{(2)} \tag{21}$$

$$\delta_{2j}^{(2)} = -\frac{\partial E}{\partial O_{2j}^{(2)}} = -\frac{\partial E}{\partial y(N)} \cdot \frac{\partial y(N)}{\partial u^{(4)}} \cdot \frac{\partial u^{(4)}}{\partial O_j^{(3)}} \cdot \frac{\partial O_j^{(3)}}{\partial u_j^{(3)}} \cdot \frac{\partial u_j^{(3)}}{\partial O_{2j}^{(2)}} = \delta_j^{(3)} O^{of} O_j^f O_{1j}^{(2)} \tag{22}$$

Therefore, the updated data of translation and dilation, we get

$$\Delta n_{ij} = -\eta_n \frac{\partial E}{\partial n_{ij}}$$

$$= -\eta_n \frac{\partial E}{\partial y(N)} \cdot \frac{\partial y(N)}{\partial u^{(4)}} \cdot \frac{\partial u^{(4)}}{\partial O_j^{(3)}} \cdot \frac{\partial O_j^{(3)}}{\partial u_j^{(3)}} \cdot \frac{\partial u_j^{(3)}}{\partial O_{ij}^{(2)}} \cdot \frac{\partial O_{ij}^{(2)}}{\partial u_{ij}^{(2)}} \cdot \frac{\partial u_{ij}^{(2)}}{\partial n_{ij}} \qquad (23)$$

$$= \eta_n \frac{\delta_{ij}^{(2)}}{\gamma_{ij}} \left[1 - \left(u_{ij}^{(2)} \right)^2 \right] \exp \left[-\frac{\left(u_{ij}^{(2)} \right)^2}{2} \right]$$

$$\Delta \gamma_{ij} = -\eta_\gamma \frac{\partial E}{\partial \gamma_{ij}}$$

$$= -\eta_\gamma \frac{\partial E}{\partial y(N)} \cdot \frac{\partial y(N)}{\partial u^{(4)}} \cdot \frac{\partial u^{(4)}}{\partial O_j^{(3)}} \cdot \frac{\partial O_j^{(3)}}{\partial u_j^{(3)}} \cdot \frac{\partial u_j^{(3)}}{\partial O_{ij}^{(2)}} \cdot \frac{\partial O_{ij}^{(2)}}{\partial u_{ij}^{(2)}} \cdot \frac{\partial u_{ij}^{(2)}}{\partial \gamma_{ij}} \qquad (24)$$

$$= \eta_\gamma \frac{\delta_{ij}^{(2)} u_{ij}^{(2)}}{\gamma_{ij}} \left[1 - \left(u_{ij}^{(2)} \right)^2 \right] \exp \left[-\frac{\left(u_{ij}^{(2)} \right)^2}{2} \right]$$

where η_m is the learning rates for the translation of wavelet function. η_σ is the learning rates for the dilation of wavelet function.

Hence,

$$n_{ij}(N+1) = n_{ij}(N) + \Delta n_{ij} \qquad (25)$$

$$\gamma_{ij}(N+1) = \gamma_{ij}(N) + \Delta \gamma_{ij} \qquad (26)$$

For the experimental results, we choose performance index as

$$\Psi = \frac{\sigma}{((x_d - \xi)^p + 1)} \qquad (27)$$

where x_d is the target result, p is the choose square, σ is the constant.

5   Experimental Results

The remote PC shows person gesture capacitive varies signal experimental results. Figure 4 shows the MRWNN identify system train error state and identify results which used error train about 400 times. In addition, the recognition results are show close to 1 that MRWNN identify results have clear recognition different user gesture in Fig. 5.

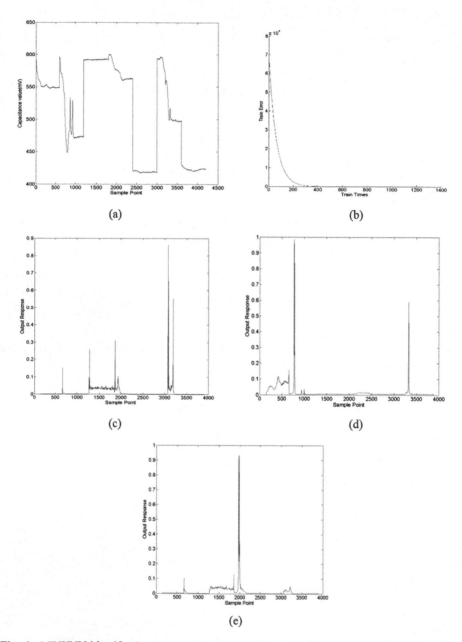

Fig. 4. MRWNN identify situation (a) capacitive sensing data, (b) train error, (c) identify results of user first gesture, (d) identify results of user second gesture, (e) identify results of user third gesture.

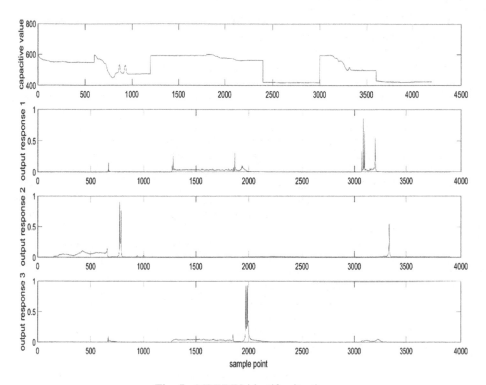

Fig. 5. MRWNN identify situation

6 Conclusion

The user gesture detection is an important research topic in smart home application that different gesture combined security identification and intelligent interaction in home life. This paper successful used MRWNN algorithms implemented in microcontroller that has high performance detection user gesture and feedback remote PC. The experimental results show MRWNN algorithms analysis different user gesture and clear to identify the true user gesture.

Acknowledgment. This work was supported in part by the "Intelligent Recognition Industry Service Center" of Higher Education Sprout Project, Ministry of Education, Taiwan.

References

1. Lin, X., Adhikary, A., Wang, Y.P.E.: Random access preamble design and detection for 3GPP narrowband IoT systems. IEEE Wirel. Commun. Lett. **5**(6), 640–643 (2016)
2. Chu, C.T., Chiang, H.K., Hung, J.J.: Dynamic heart rate monitors algorithm for reflection green light wearable device. In: International Conference on Intelligent Informatics and Biomedical Sciences, vol. 62, no. 8, pp. 438–445 (2015)

3. Ha, U., Lee, Y., Kim, H.T., Roh, J., Kim, B.C., Yoo, H.J.: A Wearable EEG-HEG-HRV multimodal system with simultaneous monitoring of tES for mental health management. IEEE Trans. Biomed. Circuits Syst. **9**(6), 758–766 (2015)
4. Brugarolas, R., et al.: Wearable heart rate sensor systems for wireless canine health monitoring. IEEE Sens. J. **16**(10), 3454–3464 (2016)
5. Wiens, A.D., Etemadi, M., Roy, S., Klein, L., Inan, O.T.: Toward continuous, noninvasive assessment of ventricular function and hemodynamics: wearable ballistocardiography. IEEE J. Biomed. Health Inform. **22**(1), 1435–1442 (2015)
6. Semnani, S.H., Basir, O.A.: Semi-flocking algorithm for motion control of mobile sensors in large-scale surveillance systems. IEEE Trans. Cybern. **45**(1), 129–137 (2015)
7. Fazio, M., Puliafito, A.: Cloud4sens: a cloud-based architecture for sensor controlling and monitoring. IEEE Commun. Mag. **41**(47), 4–8 (2015)
8. Kafi, M.A., Djenouri, D., Othman, J.B., Badache, N.: Congestion control protocols in wireless sensor networks: a survey, and future trends. IEEE Commun. Surv. Tutor. **16**(3), 1369–1390 (2014)
9. Giles, C.L., Miller, C.B., Chen, D., Chen, H.H., Sun, G.Z., Lee, Y.C.: Learning and extracting finite state automata with second-order recurrent neural networks. Neural Comput. **4**(3), 518–527 (1992)
10. Kim, Y., Moon, T.: Human detection and activity classification based on micro-doppler signatures using deep convolutional neural networks. IEEE Trans. Ind. Electron. **13**(1), 8–12 (2016)
11. Bu, N., Okamoto, M., Tsuji, T.: A hybrid motion classification approach for EMG-based human–robot interfaces using bayesian and neural networks. IEEE Trans. Rob. **25**(3), 502–511 (2009)
12. Gupta, H.P., Chudgar, H.S., Mukherjee, S., Dutta, T.: A continuous hand gestures recognition technique for human-machine interaction using accelerometer and gyroscope sensors. IEEE Sens. J. **16**(16), 6425–6432 (2016)
13. Chang, J.Y.: Nonparametric feature matching based conditional random fields for gesture recognition from multi-modal video. IEEE Trans. Pattern Anal. Mach. Intell. **38**(8), 1612–1625 (2016)
14. Lefter, I., Burghouts, G.J., Rothkrantz, L.J.M.: Recognizing stress using semantics and modulation of speech and gestures. IEEE Trans. Affect. Comput. **38**(8), 162–175 (2017)

Paired-Domination Problem on Distance Hereditary Graphs

Ching-Chi Lin[1(✉)], Keng-Chu Ku[2], Gen-Huey Chen[2], and Chan-Hung Hsu[2]

[1] Department of Computer Science and Engineering,
National Taiwan Ocean University, Keelung, Taiwan
`lincc@mail.ntou.edu.tw`
[2] Department of Computer Science and Information Engineering,
National Taiwan University, Taipei, Taiwan
`{r04922075,ghchen,b04902130}@ntu.edu.tw`

Abstract. A paired-dominating set of a graph G is a dominating set S of G such that the subgraph of G induced by S has a perfect matching. In [*Paired domination in graphs*, Networks, 32:199–206, 1998], Haynes and Slater introduced the concept of paired-domination and showed that the problem of determining minimum paired-dominating sets is NP-complete on general graphs. Ever since then many algorithmic results are studied on some important classes of graphs. In this paper, we extend the results by providing an $O(n^2)$-time algorithm on distance-hereditary graphs.

Keywords: Paired-domination · Perfect matching · Distance-hereditary graphs · NP-complete

1 Introduction

For a graph $G = (V, E)$, a vertex subset $S \subseteq V(G)$ is said to be a *dominating set* of G if every vertex not in S is adjacent to at least a vertex in S. The domination problem involves finding a minimum dominating set of a graph G, which has been received great attention and intensively studied by researchers [10]. Since the domination problem is NP-complete on general graphs [21], many attempts have been made in designing approximation algorithms [2], proving NP-completeness and providing polynomial-time algorithms on special classes of graphs [4,7,17,19]. Furthermore, many variations of the domination problem has been investigated due to different requirements of different applications. The most commonly studied variants of domination are paired, independent, connected, and total dominating sets.

A dominating set S is called a *paired, independent, connected,* and *total* dominating set of G if the subgraph of G induced by S has a perfect matching, has no edges, is connected, and has no isolated vertices, respectively. It is proved that

This work is partially supported by the Ministry of Science and Technology under the Grants No. MOST 106-2221-E-019-014-, and MOST 107-2221-E-019-016-.

© Springer Nature Singapore Pte Ltd. 2019
C.-Y. Chang et al. (Eds.): ICS 2018, CCIS 1013, pp. 495–502, 2019.
https://doi.org/10.1007/978-981-13-9190-3_54

the problems of finding minimum paired, independent, connected, or total dominating sets are all NP-complete. However, they become polynomial-time solvable on certain special classes of graphs. Some selected recent results of above variants of domination problems on special classes of graphs are summarized in Table 1, in which we use "NPC" and "P" respectively to denote "NP-complete" and "polynomial-time solvable". The classes include bipartite, chordal, split, strongly chordal, interval, circular-arc, circle, permutation, distance-hereditary, and tree graphs.

Table 1. Results on variants of domination problem on special classes of graphs.

Graph class	Domination	Paired	Independent	Connected	Total
Bipartite	NPC [4]	NPC [14]	NPC [17]	NPC [29]	NPC [29]
Chordal	NPC [7]	NPC [14]	P [18]	NPC [27]	NPC [28]
Split	NPC [4, 17]	NPC [14]	P [18]	NPC [27]	NPC [27]
Strongly chordal	P [19]	P [13]	P [18]	P [31]	P [9]
Interval	P [7]	P [14]	P [18]	P [31]	P [5]
Circular-arc	P [10]	P [15]	P [10]	P [10]	P [10]
Circle	NPC [25]	unknown	unknown	NPC [25]	NPC [25]
Permutation	P [20]	P [26]	P [20]	P [8]	P [8]
Distance-hereditary	P [12]	P[a]	P [11]	P [32]	P [12]
Tree	P [16]	P [30]	P [6]	P [1]	P [28]

[a]The main result of this paper.

In this paper we focus our attention only on the paired-domination problem. The idea of a paired-dominating set arose from the area monitoring problem, which requests that each guard is assigned another adjacent guard as a backup. Haynes and Slater [23] introduced the concept of paired-domination problem and showed that the problem of determining minimum paired-dominating sets is NP-complete on general graphs. Ever since then many algorithmic results are studied on some important classes of graphs [13–15, 26, 30] as shown in Table 1. One can refer to [24] for more recent results regarding this problem. In particular, Qiao et al. [30] proposed an $O(n)$-time algorithm on trees for this problem. However, it is still unknown whether the problem can be solved in polynomial time for circle graphs. The purpose of this paper is to extend the above results by providing an $O(n^2)$-time algorithm for distance-hereditary graphs.

The remainder of this paper is organized as follows. Section 2 describes an $O(n^2)$-time algorithm for finding a minimum paired-dominating set of G. In Sect. 3, we propose a detailed implementation of the algorithm. Finally, we give concluding remarks and suggest some direction for future work in Sect. 4.

2   Algorithm for Distance-Hereditary Graphs

Given a distance-hereditary graph G, this section establishes an $O(n^2)$-time algorithm for finding a minimum paired-dominating set of G by making use of dynamic programming. First, some preliminaries are briefly introduced. Let $G = (V, E)$ be a graph with vertex set $V(G)$ and edge set $E(G)$. Moreover, we let $n = |V(G)|$ and $m = |E(G)|$. A edge subset $M \subseteq E(G)$ is said to be a *matching* if no two edges in M share a common vertex in G. In addition, if M contains all vertices of G, then M is a *perfect matching*. A vertex subset $S \subseteq V(G)$ is said to be a *dominating set* of G if every vertex not in S is adjacent to a vertex in S. For a vertex subset $S \subseteq V(G)$, the subgraph induced by S, denoted by $G[S]$, is the graph whose vertex set is S and whose edge set is $\{xy \in E(G) \mid x, y \in S\}$.

A *paired-dominating* set of a graph G is a dominating set S of G such that the subgraph of G induced by S has a perfect matching. The *neighborhood* of a vertex v, denoted by $N_G(v)$, is the set of all vertices adjacent to v in G. The *closed neighborhood* $N_G[v] = \{v\} \cup N_G(v)$. Two vertices u and v are called *true twins* if $N[u] = N[v]$. Similarly, u and v are called *false twins* if $N(u) = N(v)$. A vertex v is called a *pendant vertex* attached to vertex u if $deg(v) = 1$ and u is the only neighbor of v. For any ordering $(v_1, v_2, \ldots, v_n)$ of $V(G)$, let G_i denote the subgraph of G induced by $\{v_1, v_2, \ldots, v_i\}$. An ordering $(v_1, v_2, \ldots, v_n)$ of $V(G)$ is called a *one-vertex-extension ordering* of G if v_i is a pendant vertex or is a twin of some vertex v_j in G_i for $1 \leq i \leq n$.

A graph G is called a *distance-hereditary graph*, if each pair of vertices has the same distance in every connected induced subgraph containing them. Bandelt and Mulder [3] showed that a graph is distance-hereditary if and only if it has a one-vertex-extension ordering. Moreover, they presented an $O(n + m)$-time algorithm for finding a one-vertex-extension ordering of a distance-hereditary graph of n vertices and m edges.

Lemma 1 ([3,22]). *A graph is distance-hereditary if and only if it has a one-vertex-extension ordering. Moreover, given a distance-hereditary graph G, a one-vertex-extension of G can be generated in $O(n + m)$ time.*

2.1   Decomposition Trees

On the other hand, Chang *et al.* [11] consider the distance-hereditary graphs from a viewpoint of edge connections between two special vertex sets, which are called *twin sets*. A graph G with a single vertex v is regarded as a distance-hereditary graph with twin set $TS(G) = \{v\}$. Given two distance-hereditary graphs G_l and G_r, with twin sets $TS(G_l)$ and $TS(G_r)$, respectively, a new distance-hereditary graph G can be formed by one of the following three operations: *true twin operation*, *false twin operation* and *attachment operation*.

- True twin operation (denoted by $G = G_l \otimes G_r$)

$$V(G) = V(G_l) \cup V(G_r).$$
$$E(G) = E(G_l) \cup E(G_r) \cup \{uv \mid u \in TS(G_l) \text{ and } v \in TS(G_r)\}.$$
$$TS(G) = TS(G_l) \cup TS(G_r).$$

– False twin operation (denoted by $G = G_l \odot G_r$)

$$V(G) = V(G_l) \cup V(G_r).$$
$$E(G) = E(G_l) \cup E(G_r).$$
$$TS(G) = TS(G_l) \cup TS(G_r).$$

– Attachment operation (denoted by $G = G_l \oplus G_r$)

$$V(G) = V(G_l) \cup V(G_r).$$
$$E(G) = E(G_l) \cup E(G_r) \cup \{uv \mid u \in TS(G_l) \text{ and } v \in TS(G_r)\}.$$
$$TS(G) = TS(G_l).$$

Suppose a distance-hereditary graph G is constructed by a sequence of operations described above. Then, the sequence of operations can be represented abstractly by a full binary tree T, which is called *decomposition tree*. The leaves in T are precisely the vertices of G. We annotate each internal vertex in T by $\otimes$, $\odot$, or $\oplus$ to represent a true twin operation, false twin operation, or attachment operation, respectively. In a decomposition tree, each leaf indicates a distance-hereditary graph $G[\{v_i\}]$ with twin set $TS(G[\{v_i\}]) = v_i$ for $1 \le i \le n$. Each rooted subtree is corresponding to a distance-hereditary graph with vertices and operations specified in the subtree. Each internal node indicates an operation to perform on the two distance-hereditary graphs corresponding to the left subtree and right subtree, respectively.

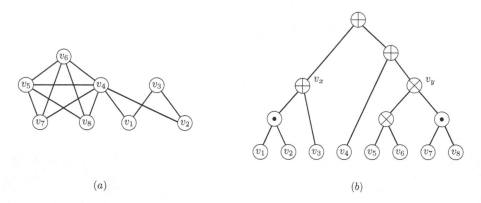

(a)   (b)

Fig. 1. (a) A distance-hereditary graph G. (b) The corresponding decomposition tree T for the distance-hereditary graph G in (a).

Figure 1 shows an illustrative example, in which Fig. 1(b) depicts the corresponding decomposition tree T for the distance-hereditary graph G in Fig. 1(a). Notice that v_x is an internal vertex of T annotated by $\oplus$, and $G[\{v_1, v_2\}]$ and $G[\{v_3\}]$ are the two distance-hereditary graphs, with twin sets $\{v_1, v_2\}$ and $\{v_3\}$, respectively corresponding to the left subtree and right subtree of internal vertex

v_x. Then, by the definition of attachment operation $\oplus$, the distance-hereditary graph corresponding to the subtree rooted at v_x is $G[\{v_1, v_2, v_3\}]$ with twin set $\{v_1, v_2\}$. Meanwhile, the distance-hereditary graph corresponding to the subtree rooted at v_y is $G[\{v_5, v_6, v_7, v_8\}]$ with twin set $\{v_5, v_6, v_7, v_8\}$. Chang [11] et al. showed that a graph G is distance-hereditary if and only if it has a decomposition tree. Moreover, given a distance-hereditary graph G, they presented an $O(n + m)$-time algorithm for constructing a decomposition tree T of G.

Lemma 2 ([11]). *Given a distance-hereditary graph G, a decomposition tree T of G can be generated in $O(n + m)$ time.*

2.2   The Algorithm

Our algorithm adopts dynamic programming strategy for finding a minimum paired-dominating set of G. For a vertex $v \in T$, let $L(v)$ denote the set of leaf vertices of the subtree rooted at v. The algorithm first constructs a decomposition tree T of G rooted at κ. Then, the algorithm iteratively determines paired-dominating sets of $G[L(v)]$ for each $v \in T$ in a bottom-up manner. Clearly, a paired-dominating set of G will be computed at the end of the loop as we have $G[L(\kappa)] = G$. Before describing the approach in detail, four types of paired-dominating sets $D_1(G), D_2(G), D_3(G)$ and $D_4(G)$ of G are introduced below for the purpose of describing the recursive formulas used in developing algorithms.

$D_1(G) = \{D \mid D$ is a minimum dominating set of G, $D \cap TS(G) = \emptyset$, and $G[D]$ has a perfect matching$\}$.

$D_2(G) = \{D \mid D$ is a minimum dominating set of G, $D \cap TS(G) \neq \emptyset$, and $G[D]$ has a perfect matching$\}$.

$D_3(G) = \{D \mid D$ is a minimum dominating set of $G - TS(G)$, $D \cap TS(G) = \emptyset$, and $G[D]$ has a perfect matching$\}$.

$D_4(G) = \{D \mid D$ is a minimum dominating set of $G - TS(G)$, $D \cap TS(G) \neq \emptyset$, $G[D - X]$ has a perfect matching for some vertex set $X \subseteq D \cap TS(G)\}$.

For each paired-dominating set $D \in D_4(G)$, let $\alpha(D)$ and $\beta(D)$ denote the minimum and the maximum cardinality of X, respectively. Furthermore, let $\gamma_k(G)$ denote the cardinality of any paired-dominating set $D \in D_k(G)$ of G for $1 \leq k \leq 4$. Clearly, either $\gamma_1(G)$ or $\gamma_2(G)$ is the cardinality of a minimum paired-dominating set of G. In the remain of this paper, we focus on the determination numbers $\gamma_1(G)$ and $\gamma_2(G)$. One can construct a minimum paired-dominating set by recording choices that led to the optimal value.

In order to obtain $\gamma_1(G)$ and $\gamma_2(G)$, we use dynamic programming method to iteratively compute $\gamma_k(G[L(v)])$ for $1 \leq k \leq 4$ in a bottom-up manner. One internal vertex of T is considered in each iteration of the loop. For simplicity, we define $\hat{\gamma}_k(v) = \gamma_k(G[L(v)])$. The algorithm first constructs a decomposition tree T of G. Initially, it assigns $\hat{\gamma}_1(\ell) = \infty$, $\hat{\gamma}_2(\ell) = \infty$, $\hat{\gamma}_3(\ell) = 0$, and $\hat{\gamma}_4(\ell) = 1$ for each leaf $\ell \in T$. The algorithm then iteratively processes the internal vertices in T. In each iteration of the repeat loop, we find a vertex v of T whose left child

v_l and right child v_r are marked as "DONE", which implies that the dominating numbers $\hat{\gamma}_k(v_l)$ and $\hat{\gamma}_k(v_r)$ with $1 \leq k \leq 4$ have been determined. Given the dominating numbers $\hat{\gamma}_k(v_l)$ and $\hat{\gamma}_k(v_r)$, we will propose $O(|L(v_l)| \cdot |L(v_r)|)$-time dynamic programming procedures to compute $\hat{\gamma}_k(v)$ in Sects. 3, Since κ is the root of T, either $\hat{\gamma}_1(\kappa)$ or $\hat{\gamma}_2(\kappa)$ is a minimum paired-dominating set of G. The algorithm is detailed below.

Algorithm 1. Minimum paired-dominating sets in distance-hereditary graphs.

Input: A distance-hereditary graph G.
Output: The cardinality of a minimum paired-dominating set of G.
1: construct a decomposition tree T of G;
2: **for** each leaf $\ell \in T$ **do**
3:     let $\hat{\gamma}_1(\ell) \leftarrow \infty$ and $\hat{\gamma}_2(\ell) \leftarrow \infty$;
4:     let $\hat{\gamma}_3(\ell) \leftarrow 0$ and $\hat{\gamma}_4(\ell) \leftarrow 1$;
5:     mark ℓ as DONE;
6: **end for**
7: **repeat**
8:     find a vertex v of T whose left child v_l and right child v_r are marked as DONE;
9:     compute $\hat{\gamma}_k(v)$ by using $\hat{\gamma}_k(v_l)$ and $\hat{\gamma}_k(v_r)$ determined in the previous iterations with $1 \leq k \leq 4$;
10:     mark v as DONE;
11:     release the space used by v_l and v_r;
12: **until** all nodes of T are marked as DONE
13: let κ be the root of T;
14: **return** $\min\{\hat{\gamma}_1(\kappa), \hat{\gamma}_2(\kappa)\}$.

Below we consider the complexity analysis. Since the dynamic programming procedures can be completed in $O(|L(v_l)| \cdot |L(v_r)|)$ time, the recurrence for the running time of the repeat loop at Steps (7)–(12) is then

$$T(|L(v)|) = T(|L(v_l)|) + T(|L(v_r)|) + O(|L(v_l)| \cdot |L(v_r)|).$$

Using the substitution method, we show that the running time of Steps (7)–(12) is $O(n^2)$. Suppose that $T(|L(v)|) \leq c \cdot |L(v)|^2$ for some constant c. Then, substituting this guess into the recurrence, we obtain

$$\begin{aligned}
T(|L(v)|) &\leq c \cdot |L(v_l)|^2 + c \cdot |L(v_r)|^2 + c \cdot |L(v_l)| \cdot |L(v_r)| \\
&\leq c \cdot (|L(v_l)|^2 + |L(v_r)|^2 + 2 \cdot |L(v_l)| \cdot |L(v_r)|) \\
&= c \cdot (|L(v_l)| + |L(v_r)|)^2 \\
&= c \cdot |L(v)|^2.
\end{aligned}$$

Thus, it takes $O(n^2)$ time to complete the repeat loop at Steps (7)–(12). Since the other steps can be completed in $O(n)$ time, the worst-case running time of Algorithm 1 is $O(n^2)$. Clearly, the proposed procedures in Sect. 3 will ensure the correctness of the algorithm, the main result of this paper is stated as the following theorem.

Theorem 1. *Given a distance-hereditary graph G, a paired-dominating set of G can be determined in $O(n^2)$ time.*

3   Implementation of the Algorithm

We omit all the details due to the page limit.

4   Conclusion and Future Work

In this paper, we have presented an algorithm for finding a paired-dominating set on distance-hereditary graphs. The algorithm uses dynamic programming to iteratively determine $D_1(G), D_2(G), D_3(G)$, and $D_4(G)$ in a bottom-up manner. When the graph is given in an adjacency list representation, our algorithm runs in $O(n^2)$ time. Below we present some open problems related to the paired-domination problem. It is known that circle graphs is a proper superfamily of distance-hereditary graphs. Therefore, it is interesting to study the time complexity of paired-domination problem in circle graphs. In [13], Chen *et al.* proposed an approximation algorithm with ratio $\ln(2\Delta(G)) + 1$ for general graphs and showed that the problem is APX-complete, i.e., has no PTAS. Thus, it would be useful if we could develop an approximation algorithm for general graphs with constant ratio. Meanwhile, it would be desirable to show that the problem remains NP-complete in planar graphs and design an approximation algorithm.

References

1. Arnborg, S., Proskurowski, A.: Linear time algorithms for NP-hard problems restricted to partial k-trees. Discrete Appl. Math. **23**, 11–24 (1989)
2. Ausiello, G., Marchetti-Spaccamela, A., Crescenzi, P., Gambosi, G., Protasi, M., Kann, V.: Complexity and Approximation. Springer, Berlin (1999). https://doi.org/10.1007/978-3-642-58412-1
3. Bandelt, H.J., Mulder, H.M.: Distance-hereditary graphs. J. Comb. Theory Series B **41**, 182–208 (1986)
4. Bertossi, A.A.: Dominating sets for split and bipartite graphs. Inf. Process. Lett. **19**, 37–40 (1984)
5. Bertossi, A.A.: Total domination in interval graphs. Inf. Process. Lett. **23**, 131–134 (1986)
6. Beyer, T., Proskurowski, A., Hedetniemi, S., Mitchell, S.: Independent domination in trees. In: The Proceedings of SEICCGTC 1977, pp. 321–328 (1977)
7. Booth, K.S., Johnson, J.H.: Dominating sets in chordal graphs. SIAM J. Comput. **11**, 191–199 (1982)
8. Brandstädt, A., Kratsch, D.: On the restriction of some NP-complete graph problems to permutation graphs. In: Budach, L. (ed.) FCT 1985. LNCS, vol. 199, pp. 53–62. Springer, Heidelberg (1985). https://doi.org/10.1007/BFb0028791
9. Chang, G.: Labeling algorithms for domination problems in sun-free chordal graphs. Discrete Appl. Math. **22**, 21–34 (1988)

10. Chang, M.S.: Efficient algorithms for the domination problems on interval and circular-arc graphs. SIAM J. Comput. **27**, 1671–1694 (1998)
11. Chang, M.-S., Hsieh, S., Chen, G.-H.: Dynamic programming on distance-hereditary graphs. In: Leong, H.W., Imai, H., Jain, S. (eds.) ISAAC 1997. LNCS, vol. 1350, pp. 344–353. Springer, Heidelberg (1997). https://doi.org/10.1007/3-540-63890-3_37
12. Chang, M.S., Wu, S.C., Chang, G.J., Yeh, H.G.: Domination in distance-hereditary graphs. Discrete Appl. Math. **116**, 103–113 (2002)
13. Chen, L., Lu, C.H., Zeng, Z.B.: A linear-time algorithm for paired-domination problem in strongly chordal graphs. Inf. Process. Lett. **110**, 20–23 (2009)
14. Chen, L., Lu, C.H., Zeng, Z.B.: Labeling algorithms for paired-domination problems in block and interval graphs. J. Comb. Optim. **19**, 457–470 (2010)
15. Cheng, T.C.E., Kang, L., Ng, C.T.: Paired domination on interval and circular-arc graphs. Discrete Appl. Math. **155**, 2077–2086 (2007)
16. Cockayne, E.: A linear algorithm for the domination number of a tree. Inf. Process. Lett. **4**, 41–44 (1975)
17. Corneil, D.G., Perl, Y.: Clustering and domination in perfect graphs. Discrete Appl. Math. **9**, 27–39 (1984)
18. Farber, M.: Independent domination in chordal graphs. Oper. Res. Lett. **1**, 134–138 (1982)
19. Farber, M.: Domination, independent domination, and duality in strongly chordal graphs. Discrete Appl. Math. **7**, 115–130 (1984)
20. Farber, M.: Domination in permutation graphs. J. Algorithms **6**, 309–321 (1985)
21. Garey, M.R., Johnson, D.S.: Computers and Intractability: A Guide to the Theory of NP-Completeness. Freeman, New York (1979)
22. Hammer, P.L., Maffray, F.: Completely separable graphs. Discrete Appl. Math. **27**, 85–99 (1990)
23. Haynes, T.W., Slater, P.J.: Paired domination in graphs. Networks **32**, 199–206 (1998)
24. Henning, M.A., McCoy, J., Southey, J.: Graphs with maximum size and given paired-domination number. Discrete Appl. Math. **170**, 72–82 (2014)
25. Keil, J.M.: The complexity of domination problems in circle graphs. Discrete Appl. Math. **42**, 51–63 (1993)
26. Lappas, E., Nikolopoulos, S.D., Palios, L.: An $O(n)$-time algorithm for the paired domination problem on permutation graphs. Eur. J. Comb. **34**, 593–608 (2013)
27. Laskar, R., Pfaff, J.: Domination and irredundance in split graphs. Technical Report 430, Clemson University (1983)
28. Laskar, R., Pfaff, J., Hedetniemi, S.M., Hedetniemi, S.T.: On the algorithmic complexity of total domination. SIAM J. Algebraic Discrete Methods **5**, 420–425 (1984)
29. Pfaff, J., Laskar, R., Hedetniemi, S.T.: NP-completeness of total and connected domination and irredundance for bipartite graphs. Technical Report 428, Clemson University (1983)
30. Qiao, H., Kang, L., Cardei, M., Du, D.Z.: Paired domination of trees. J. Global Optim. **25**, 43–54 (2003)
31. White, K., Farber, M., Pulleyblank, W.: Steiner trees, connected domination and strongly chordal graphs. Networks **15**, 109–124 (1985)
32. Yeh, H.G., Chang, G.J.: Weighted connected domination and Steiner trees in distance-hereditary graphs. Discrete Appl. Math. **87**, 245–253 (1998)

Rainbow Coloring of Bubble Sort Graphs

Yung-Ling Lai$^{(\boxtimes)}$ and Jian-Wen He

National Chiayi University, Chiayi 60004, Taiwan
yllai@mail.ncyu.edu.tw

Abstract. There are many kinds of edge colorings. This paper deals with a special edge coloring named rainbow coloring. Different from other edge colorings, the rainbow coloring requires every pair of vertices has a rainbow path between them. A rainbow path is a path P in graph G such that every edge on P has different color. A rainbow connected graph G is a graph such that there is a rainbow path between every pair of vertices. The rainbow connection number, denoted $rc(G)$, is the smallest number of colors to meet the conditions that the graph G is rainbow connected. The bubble sort graph, denoted as B_n, is a type of Cayley graph. This paper established the rainbow connection number of bubble sort graph.

Keywords: Edge coloring · Rainbow connection · Bubble sort graph

1 Introduction

There are many kinds of vertex coloring have been used in many types of graphs. This paper researched the bubble sort graph by using an edge coloring method which name is rainbow coloring. The difference between rainbow coloring and others is the former may be the same color on adjacent edges. A rainbow path is a path P in graph G without the same color to each pair of edges. If an edge-colored graph G has rainbow path between any two vertices which is rainbow connected. The rainbow connection number is the smallest number of colors to meet the conditions that the graph G is rainbow connected, denoted as $rc(G)$ [5]. A rainbow coloring of a connected graph G is an edge coloring $f : E(G) \rightarrow \{1, 2, \ldots, k\}$ such that there is a rainbow path between every pair of distinct vertices. The rainbow connection problem was proposed in 2008 by Chartrand, Johns, McKeon, and Zhang [8]. It is known that if G is a nontrivial connected graph of size m whose diameter denoted by $diam(G)$, then

$$diam(G) \leq rc(G) \leq m. \tag{1}$$

The precise rainbow connection number of several graph classes is known including complete multipartite graphs [3, 7], fan and sun graphs [18], wheel and Petersen graph [8], thorn graph [14], hypergraph [4], triangular pyramids [19], versatile pyramid network [20], random graph [10], random bipartite graphs [9], interval graphs [17], cartesian product [13], origami and pizza graphs [15], flower graph [11], stellar graphs [16] etc. For certain rainbow connection number, we know that $rc(G) = 1$ if and only if G is complete graphs [3], and $rc(G) = n - 1$ if and only if G is tree [3]. Some bounds are known for the rainbow connection number of graphs. For every

© Springer Nature Singapore Pte Ltd. 2019
C.-Y. Chang et al. (Eds.): ICS 2018, CCIS 1013, pp. 503–506, 2019.
https://doi.org/10.1007/978-981-13-9190-3_55

bridgeless graph G with radius r, $rc(G) \leq r(r+2)$ [2] while for bridgeless chordal graph G with radius r, $rc(G) \leq 3r$ [6]. Rainbow connection can be applied to message transmission between agencies. Messages need to be protected in the process of inter-agency transmission, and the transmitted message between the two agencies may need other agencies as intermediaries. We need a lot of passwords and firewalls to block intruders in such a way that there is at least one secured path between each pair of agencies, so the information transmitted along this path has no duplication of passwords. Let each agency be a vertex and the password between each pair of agencies is the color on that edge. Then the least number of passwords or firewalls required to complete the task is the rainbow connection number of that graph [12].

The bubble sort graph has $n!$ vertices and $n!(n-1)/2$ edges while its diameter is $n(n-1)/2$ [1]. Bubble sort graphs are attracting attention because by their simple, symmetric, and recursive structure. For a n-dimensional bubble sort graph B_n, each vertex $u = u_1, u_2, \ldots, u_n$ of B_n is a $n!$ permutation of integers $1, 2, \ldots, n$ which is adjacent to $u_1, u_2, \ldots, u_{t-1}, u_{t+1}, u_t, \ldots, u_n$ for $1 \leq t \leq n-1$. Similar to bubble sort, comparing adjacent element, only connect with two vertices that the element changes the same after swapping adjacent numbers. For example, the element of B_3 that the "123" only connect with "132" and "213". Figure 1 is an illustration of bubble sort graphs B_1, B_2, B_3. In this paper, we provide an algorithm to determine the exact value of $rc(B_n)$.

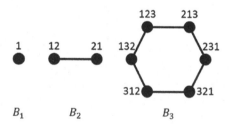

Fig. 1. An illustration of bubble sort graphs B_1, B_2, B_3.

2   Main Results

Proposition 1 (*from* [8]) *If G is a nontrivial connected graph of size m whose diameter denoted by $diam(G)$, then $diam(G) \leq rc(G) \leq m$.*

Proposition 2 (*from* [1]) $diam(B_n) = n(n-1)/2$.

Theorem 1 *Let B_n for $n \geq 2$, then $rc(B_n) = n(n-1)/2$.*
Proof: Define an edge coloring $f : E(G) \rightarrow \{1, 2, \ldots, n(n-1)/2\}$ as follows. For edge $e = (u, v)$ such that $u = (u_1, u_2, \ldots, u_n)$ and $v = (u_1, u_2, \ldots, u_{t-1}, u_{t+1}, u_t, \ldots, u_n)$ for $1 \leq t \leq n-1$, if $u_t = i$ and $u_{t+1} = j$ and $1 \leq i < j \leq n$, then

$$f(e) = (2n - i)(i - 1)/2 + (j - i) \tag{2}$$

Since $1 \leq i < j \leq n$, $\max\{f(e) | e \in E(B_n)\} = n(n-1)/2$. Since the edge is colored according to the exchange digits, those edge with different pair of digits exchanged will receive different color. By this coloring, for any pair of two vertices, the shortest path is a rainbow between them. Hence, $rc(B_n) \leq n(n-1)/2$. Figure 2 illustrated B_4 with all vertices labeled and Fig. 3 shows the 6-rainbow coloring on B_4. By Proposition 2, we know that $diam(B_n) = n(n-1)/2$, and by Proposition 1 $rc(G) \geq diam(G)$, therefore $rc(B_n) \geq n(n-1)/2$. That is, $rc(B_n) = n(n-1)/2$. ∎

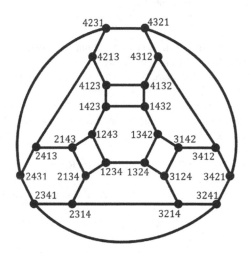

Fig. 2. An illustration of bubble sort graphs B_4.

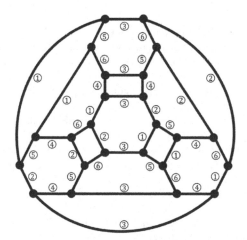

Fig. 3. A 6-rainbow coloring of B_4.

3   Conclusion

The bubble sort graph B_n has the property that the number of diameter growth is stable. When the n of the B_n increases, it is very easy to figure out how to color. The rainbow connection number of the bubble sort graph has been provided in this paper. There are also a lot of graph's rainbow coloring numbers waiting for us to fine out.

References

1. Akers, S.B., Krishnamurthy, B.: A group-theoretic model for symmetric interconnection networks. IEEE Trans. Comput. **38**(4), 555–566 (1989)
2. Basavaraju, M., Chandran, L.S., Rajendraprasad, D., Ramaswamy, A.: Rainbow connection number and radius. Graphs Comb. **30**(2), 275–285 (2014)
3. Caro, Y., Lev, A., Roditty, Y., Tuza, Z., Yuster, R.: On rainbow connection. Electron. J. Comb. **15**, R57 (2008)
4. Carpentier, R.P., Liu, H., Silva, M., Sousa, T.: Rainbow connection for some families of hypergraphs. Discrete Math. **327**, 40–50 (2014)
5. Chakraborty, S., Fischer, E., Matsliah, A., Yuster, R.: Hardness and algorithms for rainbow connection. J. Comb. Optim. **21**(3), 330–347 (2011)
6. Chandran, L.S., Das, A., Rajendraprasad, D., Varma, N.M.: Rainbow connection number and connected dominating sets. Electron. Notes Discrete Math. **38**, 239–244 (2011)
7. Chartrand, G., Johns, G.L., McKeon, K.A., Zhang, P.: The rainbow connectivity of a graph. Networks **54**(2), 75–81 (2009)
8. Chartrand, G., Johns, G.L., McKeon, K.A., Zhang, P.: Rainbow connection in graphs. Math. Bohemica **133**(1), 85–98 (2008)
9. Chen, X., Li, X., Lian, H.: Rainbow k-connectivity of Random Bipartite Graphs. arXiv:1212.6115v1 [math.CO] (2008)
10. Heckel, A., Riordan, O.: On the Threshold for Rainbow Connection Number r in Random Graphs. arXiv:1307.7747v1 [math.CO] (2013)
11. Kumala, I.S., Salman, A.N.M.: The rainbow connection number of a flower (Cm, Kn) graph and flower (C3, Fn) graph. Procedia Comput. Sci. **74**, 168–172 (2015)
12. Lai, Y.L., He, J.W.: Rainbow coloring of corona graphs. In: National Computer Symposium, pp. 224–226 (2017)
13. Liang, Y.J.: Rainbow Connection Numbers of Cartesian Product of Graphs. Master Thesis of National Dong Hwa University of Applied Mathematics, Hualien (2012)
14. Liu, Y., Wang, Z.: Rainbow connection number of the thorn graph. Appl. Math. Sci. **8**(128), 6373–6377 (2014)
15. Nabila, S., Salman, A.N.M.: The rainbow connection number of origami graphs and pizza graphs. Procedia Comput. Sci. **74**, 162–167 (2015)
16. Shulhany, M.A., Salman, A.N.M.: The (strong) rainbow connection number of stellar graphs. AIP Conf. Proc. **1708**(1), 060007 (2016)
17. Sudhakaraiah, A., Sreenivasulu, A., Deepika, E.G., Latha, V.R.: To find the equality of the rainbow connection number towards the diameter using interval graphs. Int. Refereed J. Eng. Sci. **2**(4), 15–21 (2013)
18. Sy, S., Medika, G.H., Yulianti, L.: The rainbow connection of fan and sun. Appl. Math. Sci. **7**(64), 3155–3159 (2013)
19. Wang, F.H., Sung, G.S.: Rainbow connection number in triangular pyramids. In: The 29th Workshop on Combinatorial Mathematics and Computation Theory, pp. 73–76 (2012)
20. Wang, F.H., Wu, Z.J.: On Finding a Rainbow Connection in a Versatile Pyramid Network. Master Thesis of Business Administration, Department of Information Management College of Business Chinese Culture University, Taipei (2012)

The Multi-service Location Problems

Hung-I Yu[1]($\boxtimes$)(iD), Mong-Jen Kao[2](iD), and D. T. Lee[1](iD)

[1] Institute of Information Science, Academia Sinica, Nankang, Taipei 115, Taiwan
{herbert,dtlee}@iis.sinica.edu.tw
[2] Institute of Computer Science and Information Engineering,
National Chung-Cheng University, Chiayi 621, Taiwan
mjkao@cs.ccu.edu.tw

Abstract. In this paper, we aim to provide a general study on the framework of *Multi-Service Location Problems* from a broader perspective and provide systematic methodologies for this category of problems to obtain approximate solutions. In this category of problems, we are to decide the location of a fixed number of facilities providing different types of services, so as to optimize certain distance measures of interest regarding how well the clients are served.

Specifically, we are to provide p types of services by locating $k \geq p$ facilities. Each client has a demanding list for the p types of services, and evaluates its service quality by its *service distance*, defined as its total transportation cost to those facilities offering the demanded services. Under this framework, we address two kinds of distance measures, the maximum service distance and the average service distance of all clients, and define the *p-service k-center* problem and the *p-service k-median* problem, according to the minimax and the minisum criteria, respectively. We develop a general approach for multi-service location problems, and propose a $(2p)$-approximation and a 4-approximation to the two problems, respectively.

Keywords: Multi-service location $\cdot$ k-center $\cdot$ k-median

1 Introduction

Locating facilities optimally for customer service provision has been a long-standing central issue in transportation and communication networks. In this category of problems, the typical scenario is to place one or multiple facilities wisely to form clusters so as to optimize certain intra-cluster distance measures of interest, e.g., *radius*, *average distance*, etc. This abstract description, for instances, was referred to as the classical *k-center problem* and *k-median problem*.

In the setting of these traditional location problems, it is assumed that all facilities provide a single type of service, and each client can be served by any one

Research supported by Ministry of Science and Technology of Taiwan under Grants No. MOST 106-2221-E-001-006-MY3.

C.-Y. Chang et al. (Eds.): ICS 2018, CCIS 1013, pp. 507–515, 2019.
https://doi.org/10.1007/978-981-13-9190-3_56

of them. However, in practical scenarios it is often the case that the customers have non-identical wish-lists for different types of services that are provided only by facilities of certain kinds. Take the freight traffic of logistics centers as an example. The company wants to open a number of logistics centers for providing transportation of various kinds of goods. The fact that goods come in different shapes and serve for different purposes makes the decision for the placement of logistic centers more challenging than one may have thought. For example, heavy industrial packages may require special storage condition and delivery mechanism and are mainly sent to industrial areas, while large amount of small personal parcels tend to be treated in a simpler fashion and sent to residential sections. Under such circumstances, the placement of these logistics centers has to be made in consideration of the interrelationship of their locations and potential customers in the vicinity.

Inspired by such scenarios, Yu et al. [15,16] introduced the *p-Service Center Problem*. In this problem, we are to place one service center (facility) for each of the p types of services we have. Each client, say, v, has a demanding list for each of the p services, represented by a vector w_v in $\mathbb{R}^p$. How well this client is served by these centers is then measured by its *service distance*, defined to be the sum of distances between v and the p service centers, weighted by its demand w_v. In other words, the service distance of v is the inner product $w_v \cdot \ell_v$, where ℓ_v is the vector in $\mathbb{R}^p$ representing the distances between v and the service centers. The objective of this problem is to place the centers carefully, so as to minimize the maximum service distance of the clients.

In [15,16], Yu et al. studied this problem under graph metrics. On general graphs, they showed that this problem is NP-hard and, for any given constant c, presented a p/c-approximation algorithm with running time exponential in c. Polynomial-time algorithms are developed when p is restricted to 2 and the input graph is a tree. In a follow-up work, Anzai et al. [2] showed that the p-service center problem is NP-hard even for split graphs with unit edge lengths. Recently, Ito et al. [7] showed that this problem is strongly NP-hard even for cycles. For tree graphs, they presented a weakly polynomial-time algorithm for general p, broadening the existing result of [15,16].

In this paper, we propose the framework of *multi-service location problems*, as the expansion and generalization of the p-service center problem. In this category of problems, we are given a distance metric $M = (V, d)$ defined over a ground set V of vertices and a demand vector function $w \colon V \to \mathbb{R}^p_{\geq 0}$. The objective is to decide the best locations of $k \geq p$ facilities providing p types of services, denoted $\mathcal{F} = (F_1, F_2, \ldots, F_p)$ with $\sum_{1 \leq i \leq p} |F_i| = k$, where $F_i \subseteq V$ represents the facilities providing the ith type of service for all $1 \leq i \leq p$, so as to optimize certain distance measures of interest.

Under this framework, we address two types of distance measures: (1) *maximum service distance*, $\max_{v \in V} w_v \cdot \ell_v$, which measures the maximum service distance of the clients. (2) *average service distance*, $\sum_{v \in V} w_v \cdot \ell_v$, which measures the sum of the service distances of the clients. Optimizing the two measures thereby defines the *p-service k-center* problem and the *p-service k-median* problem, respectively.

We aim to provide an algorithmic study on the framework of multi-service location problems, and develop a general approach that leads to good approximate solutions for different distance measures of interest.

Related Work. The classical k-center problem is known to be NP-hard [9], even in the Euclidean plane [12]. Moreover, for general distance metric, approximating this problem to a factor better than 2 is known to be NP-hard [6]. For Euclidean distance metric, the lower bound is 1.822 [5]. On the other hand, the k-center problem admits 2-approximation algorithms for general distance metrics [13].

Similarly, the classical k-median problem is NP-hard on general graphs [10] and in the Euclidean plane [12]. Also, it is NP-hard to approximate within factor $1 + 2/e$ for general metrics [8]. A number of different approximation algorithms have been developed for this problem. For the k-median and the weighted k-median problems under general metrics, the current best results are a $(2.675+\epsilon)$-approximation algorithm, proposed by Byrka et al. [3], and a 4-approximation algorithm, proposed by Charikar and Guha [4], respectively. When the underlying metric is Euclidean, Ahmadian et al. [1] gave an approximation algorithm of factor $2.633 + \epsilon$. Moreover, by applying randomized techniques, a series of work have been devoted to the Euclidean k-median problem, providing several randomized polynomial-time approximate schemes. See [11] for reference.

Our Results and Contribution. Our main contribution in this paper is a general approach on the design of approximation algorithms for the category of multi-service location problems. This approach is a dynamic-programming-like method, applied on the number of facilities allocated to each type of service. Although we have no access to the allocation number in an optimal solution, the optimal substructure of this problem allows us to preserve the quality of the approximate solutions for each individual type of service and employ a dynamic programming technique to approximate the best allocation. For the p-service k-median problem, the approach gives the following.

Theorem 1. *Given an α-approximation algorithm of the classical k-median problem, there is an α-approximation algorithm for the p-service k-median problem.*

Theorem 2. *Given an α-approximation algorithm of the classical k-center problem, there is an (αp)-approximation algorithm for the p-service k-center problem.*

Note that this approach works not only for median-type of problems but also for center-type of problems. It is because its algorithmic concept considers only the allocation number and is irrelevant to the underlying distance measure and the demand functions of the clients. Thus, the above theorems apply to any distance metric, if proper k-center or k-median algorithms exist under the specified metric. (Due to page limit, the proofs are omitted.)

In particular, by applying the approximation algorithms developed for the k-median problem [4] and the k-center problem [13] as oracle subroutines, we obtain two main results: a 4-approximation for the p-service k-median problem and a $(2p)$-approximation for the p-service k-center problem.

The rest of this paper is organized as follows. In Sect. 2, we give the formal definitions of the p-service k-center problem and the p-service k-median problem. We discuss the general approach and its applications in Sect. 3. Finally, we conclude with future directions in Sect. 4.

2   Preliminary

We say that $M = (V, d)$ forms a metric space if $d \colon V \times V \to \mathbb{R}_{\geq 0}$ is a metric (distance function) defined over the ground set V of vertices. For any element $v \in V$ and any subset $F \subseteq V$, we will extend the definition of the distance function d and use $d(v, F) := \min_{u \in F} d(v, u)$ to denote the distance between v and its closest vertex in F. For ease of description, let $d(v, F) = \infty$ if $F = \emptyset$.

For any subset $F \subseteq V$, we will use $|F|$ to denote the cardinality of F. For an ordered sequence of subsets of V, say, $\mathcal{F} = (F_1, F_2, \ldots, F_p)$, we will extend the notation and use $|\mathcal{F}| := \sum_{1 \leq i \leq p} |F_i|$ to denote the total cardinality of the subsets in this sequence.

In the framework of p-*Service k-Location Problem*, we will be considering a metric space $M = (V, d)$ and a demand function $w \colon V \to \mathbb{R}_{\geq 0}^p$ defined over V. Intuitively, the coordinates of the vector w_v represent the demand of the vertex v towards the p types of services, respectively.

Given an instance $\Pi = (M = (V, d), w)$ of the p-service k-location problem, the general objective is to compute an ordered sequence $\mathcal{F} = (F_1, F_2, \ldots, F_p)$ of p subsets of V, for which we call a p-*service tuple*, with $|\mathcal{F}| \leq k$ such that certain distance measure of interest is optimized.

In the following we make concrete definitions for distance measures and the specific problems we consider in this paper. We begin with the p-service distance, which measures how well an element $v \in V$ is served by a given set of facilities. For a p-service tuple $\mathcal{F} = (F_1, F_2, \ldots, F_p)$, we use the vector $\ell_{v, \mathcal{F}} := (d(v, F_1), d(v, F_2), \ldots, d(v, F_p)) \in \mathbb{R}^p$ to denote the distance between an element $v \in V$ and its closest service facility in F_i for each $1 \leq i \leq p$, respectively. The p-service distance of an element $v \in V$ is then defined to be $D(v, \mathcal{F}) := w_v \cdot \ell_{v, \mathcal{F}}$, the inner product of w_v and $\ell_{v, \mathcal{F}}$.

We consider two types of distance measures that evaluate how well the facilities are located for serving the clients in V. For a p-service tuple $\mathcal{F} = (F_1, F_2, \ldots, F_p)$, the p-*service radius* of $\mathcal{F}$ is defined as $\mathrm{Rad}(\mathcal{F}) := \max_{v \in V} D(v, \mathcal{F})$, and the p-*service average-distance* of $\mathcal{F}$ is defined as $\mathrm{Avg}(\mathcal{F}) := \sum_{v \in V} D(v, \mathcal{F})$. In the p-service k-center problem, the objective is to compute a p-service tuple $\mathcal{F}$ with $|\mathcal{F}| \leq k$ such that $\mathrm{Rad}(\mathcal{F})$ is minimized. Similarly, in the p-service k-median problem, our objective is to compute a p-service tuple $\mathcal{F}$ with $|\mathcal{F}| \leq k$ so as to minimize $\mathrm{Avg}(\mathcal{F})$.

Further Notations and Definitions. In this paper, for an instance $\Pi = (M, w)$ of the p-service k-location problem, our algorithm will be considering the projections of the demand vector function $w\colon V \to \mathbb{R}^p_{\geq 0}$ into lower-dimensional spaces. For any vector $w_v \in \mathbb{R}^p$ and any $1 \leq i \leq p$, we will use $w_v^{(i)}$ to denote the ith-coordinate of w_v. We implicitly extend this definition to vector functions as well. For any vector function $w\colon V \to \mathbb{R}^p$, we will use $w^{(i)}\colon V \to \mathbb{R}$ to denote the function formed by $w_v^{(i)}$ for all v.

For any $1 \leq i \leq p$ and any $i \leq j \leq k$, we will use the *i-service j-location projection* of the original instance Π to denote an instance of the i-service j-location problem, defined in the same metric space of Π with only the first i coordinates of w considered as the new demand function. Specifically, it is the instance (M, w_i), where $w_i \in \mathbb{R}^i$ is the vector function formed by the first i coordinates of w.

3   Our Main Approach

In this section, we present a general method applicable to both the two proposed problems. In this method, the algorithm tries to approximate the correct number of facilities allocated to each type of service in an optimal solution. During this process, existing approximation algorithms for single-service location problems are used as oracle subroutines.

3.1   The General Idea

Consider a specific p-service k-location problem and let Π be an instance of this problem. Suppose that $\mathcal{F}^* = (F_1^*, F_2^*, \ldots, F_p^*)$ is an optimal p-service tuple of Π. For any $1 \leq i \leq p$, by regarding the ith type of service individually, we can obtain an instance $\Pi^{(i)} = (M, w^{(i)})$ of the 1-service $|F_i^*|$-location problem and a corresponding feasible solution F_i^*. Let F_i be an optimal placement of the instance $\Pi^{(i)}$. It follows naturally that

$$\text{Measure}^{(i)}(F_i) \;\leq\; \text{Measure}^{(i)}(F_i^*), \qquad (1)$$

where $\text{Measure}^{(i)}$ is the 1-service distance function under consideration.

Intuitively, when we are given the allocation of facilities $|F_1^*|, |F_2^*|, \ldots, |F_p^*|$ in advance, a reasonably good approximate solution for the p-service k-location problem can be obtained by combining the solution we find for each $\Pi^{(i)}$.

However, as we have no access to the true value of $|F_i^*|$ for each i, we employ a dynamic-programming approach to approximate the desired allocation as follows. For any $1 \leq i \leq p$ and any $i \leq j \leq k$, let $\text{OPT}(i,j)$ denote the optimal i-service tuple of the i-service j-location projection of the instance Π. We compute an approximation $\tilde{\text{OPT}}(i,j)$ of $\text{OPT}(i,j)$ by the following recursion:

$$\tilde{\text{OPT}}(i,j) = \text{the best combination of } \left(\tilde{\text{OPT}}(i-1, j-q), F_{i,q} \right), 1 \leq q \leq j - i + 1,$$

where $F_{i,q}$ is an approximate solution to the instance $\Pi^{(i)}$ of the 1-service q-location problem. (For simplicity, let $\tilde{\mathrm{OPT}}(0, j)$ be an empty tuple for any j.) Provided that $F_{i,q}$ can be computed efficiently for each i and q, by Inequality (1), we know that $\tilde{\mathrm{OPT}}(i, j)$ will be a good approximation of $\mathrm{OPT}(i, j)$.

3.2 Applications

In the following we will elaborate this idea in more detail, with applications to the p-service k-median problem and the p-service k-center problem.

Minimizing the Average Service Distance. Consider the case that a p-service tuple $\mathcal{F}$ is evaluated by its p-service average-distance $\mathrm{Avg}(\mathcal{F})$. We can view each instance $\Pi^{(i)}$ as an instance of the 1-service q-location problem, for any $1 \leq q \leq k$, and define the distance measure for any $F \subseteq V$ as its 1-service average-distance in $\Pi^{(i)}$, $\mathrm{Measure}^{(i)}(F) := \sum_{v \in V} \left\{ w_v^{(i)} \cdot d(v, F) \right\}$.

Suppose that, for any $1 \leq i \leq p$ and any $1 \leq q \leq k$, we can obtain an α-approximation solution $F_{i,q}$ to the 1-service q-location instance $\Pi^{(i)}$ for some α. From the recursion stated above, for fixed i and j with $1 \leq i \leq p$ and $i \leq j \leq k$, we compute the approximation solution $\tilde{\mathrm{OPT}}(i, j)$ by constructing i-service tuples $\left(\tilde{\mathrm{OPT}}(i - 1, j - q), F_{i,q} \right)$ for $1 \leq q \leq j - i + 1$, and finding the index q^* whose corresponding tuple has the minimum i-service average-distance. In this way we have the following.

Lemma 3. *When the distance measure is p-service average-distance, for $1 \leq i \leq p$ and $i \leq j \leq k$, $\tilde{\mathrm{OPT}}(i, j)$ is a factor-α approximate solution of the i-service j-location projection of Π.*

By Lemma 3, if there exists a polynomial-time α-approximation algorithm for the 1-service k-location problem, we can find an α-approximation solution to any p-service k-location instance in polynomial time, since the recursive construction of $\tilde{\mathrm{OPT}}(p, k)$ calls the approximation algorithm at most pk times.

Theorem 4. *When the distance measure is p-service average-distance, there exists an α-approximation algorithm for the p-service k-location problem, provided that an α-approximation algorithm for the 1-service k-location problem is given.*

Below, we discuss several applications of this theorem to the p-service k-median problem in different distance metrics, while taking into consideration whether $p < k$ or $p = k$.

For the p-service k-median problem, to apply Theorem 4 we have to choose appropriate weighted k-median algorithms with respect to the distance metrics. In general metric spaces, we are considering the metric k-median problem. Most of the recent results for this problem do not deal with vertex weights and can not be applied here. So far, the best result considering weighted case is a 4-approximation algorithm proposed by Charikar and Guha [4]. By applying it to Theorem 4, we have the following.

Corollary 5. *There exists a polynomial-time 4-approximation algorithm for the p-service k-median problem in metric spaces.*

For graph metrics, since the weighted k-median problem in general graphs is known to have optimal vertex solutions [10], the above result also applies, given the all-pair shortest distance. Similarly, for the problem in Euclidean metrics, we still apply this result, since existing results for the Euclidean k-median problem and polynomial-time approximation schemes do not admit vertex weights.

On the other hand, for tree metrics, the weighted k-median problem is known to be polynomially solvable on trees. Here, we choose the dynamic programming algorithm of Tamir [14] with running time $O(kn^2)$, and obtain the following.

Corollary 6. *The p-service k-median problem on trees is polynomial-time solvable.*

When $p = k$, the problem becomes the p-service median problem briefly mentioned in [16]. By observing the recursion, we can see that only $F_{i,1}$ has to be computed for each $\Pi^{(i)}$. As a (1-service) 1-median instance, an optimal solution to each $\Pi^{(i)}$ can be obtained in polynomial time by classical 1-median algorithms. Thus, we have the following.

Corollary 7. *The p-service median problem is polynomial-time solvable in any distance metric.*

Minimizing the Maximum Service Distance. When the distance measure is the p-service radius, by viewing $\Pi^{(i)}$ as an instance of the 1-service q-location problem for some q, the distance measure of any subset F in $\Pi^{(i)}$ is the 1-service radius $\mathrm{Measure}^{(i)}(F) := \max_{v \in V} \left\{ w_v^{(i)} \cdot d(v, F) \right\}$.

Suppose again that, for any i and q, we can obtain an α-approximation solution $F_{i,q}$ to $\Pi^{(i)}$. By similar arguments, we can obtain the following.

Theorem 8. *When the distance measure is p-service radius, there exists an $(\alpha \cdot p)$-approximation algorithm for the p-service k-location problem, provided that an α-approximation algorithm for the 1-service k-location problem is given.*

It is easy to apply Theorem 8 to the p-service k-center problem. As mentioned before, the 1-service k-center problem is equivalent to the weighted k-center problem, for which Plesník [13] has a 2-approximation algorithm.

Corollary 9. *There exists a polynomial-time (2p)-approximation algorithm for the p-service k-center problem in metric graphs.*

4   Conclusion

We proposed the framework of the multi-service location problems, under which two representative problems in this category are considered. For this framework of problems, a general methodology is discussed to yield approximate solutions for these problems, provided that ground approximation oracle exists for the corresponding 1-service location problem.

We conclude with an open direction to explore for the multi-service location problem. While we obtained the best possible results for the median-type of problems, it is not clear if the same goal can be achieved for the center-type of problems. To be precise, can we break through the approximation guarantees of $O(p)$ for the p-service center problem and the p-service k-center problem?

References

1. Ahmadian, S., Norouzi-Fard, A., Svensson, O., Ward, J.: Better guarantees for k-means and Euclidean k-median by primal-dual algorithms. In: 2017 IEEE 58th Annual Symposium on Foundations of Computer Science (FOCS), pp. 61–72 (2017)
2. Anzai, T., Ito, T., Suziki, A., Zhou, X.: The multi-service center decision problem is NP-complete for split graphs. In: Proceedings of the 6th World Congress on Engineering and Technology, CET 2016 (2016)
3. Byrka, J., Pensyl, T., Rybicki, B., Srinivasan, A., Trinh, K.: An improved approximation for k-median and positive correlation in budgeted optimization. ACM Trans. Algorithms **13**(2), 23:1–23:31 (2017)
4. Charikar, M., Guha, S.: Improved combinatorial algorithms for the facility location and k-median problems. In: 40th Annual Symposium on Foundations of Computer Science, pp. 378–388 (1999)
5. Feder, T., Greene, D.: Optimal algorithms for approximate clustering. In: Proceedings of the Twentieth Annual ACM Symposium on Theory of Computing, STOC 1988, pp. 434–444. ACM, New York (1988)
6. Hochbaum, D.S., Shmoys, D.B.: A best possible heuristic for the k-center problem. Math. Oper. Res. **10**(2), 180–184 (1985)
7. Ito, T., Kakimura, N., Kobayashi, Y.: Complexity of the multi-service center problem. In: Okamoto, Y., Tokuyama, T. (eds.) 28th International Symposium on Algorithms and Computation (ISAAC 2017). Leibniz International Proceedings in Informatics (LIPIcs), vol. 92, pp. 48:1–48:12. Schloss Dagstuhl-Leibniz-Zentrum fuer Informatik, Dagstuhl (2017)
8. Jain, K., Mahdian, M., Saberi, A.: A new greedy approach for facility location problems. In: Proceedings of the Thiry-fourth Annual ACM Symposium on Theory of Computing, STOC 2002, pp. 731–740. ACM, New York (2002)
9. Kariv, O., Hakimi, S.L.: An algorithmic approach to network location problems. I: The p-centers. SIAM J. Appl. Math. **37**(3), 513–538 (1979)
10. Kariv, O., Hakimi, S.L.: An algorithmic approach to network location problems. II: The p-medians. SIAM J. Appl. Math. **37**(3), 539–560 (1979)
11. Kumar, A., Sabharwal, Y., Sen, S.: Linear-time approximation schemes for clustering problems in any dimensions. J. ACM **57**(2), 5:1–5:32 (2010)
12. Megiddo, N., Supowit, K.J.: On the complexity of some common geometric location problems. SIAM J. Comput. **13**(1), 182–196 (1984)
13. Plesník, J.: A heuristic for the p-center problems in graphs. Discrete Appl. Math. **17**(3), 263–268 (1987)
14. Tamir, A.: An $O(pn^2)$ algorithm for the p-median and related problems on tree graphs. Oper. Res. Lett. **19**(2), 59–64 (1996)

15. Yu, H.-I., Li, C.-C.: The multi-service center problem. In: Chao, K.-M., Hsu, T., Lee, D.-T. (eds.) ISAAC 2012. LNCS, vol. 7676, pp. 578–587. Springer, Heidelberg (2012). https://doi.org/10.1007/978-3-642-35261-4_60
16. Yu, H.I., Li, C.C., Lee, D.: The multi-service center problem. Theor. Comput. Sci. **705**, 58–74 (2018)

Total k-Domatic Partition and Weak Elimination Ordering

Chuan-Min Lee[✉]

Department of Computer and Communication Engineering, Ming Chuan University,
5 De Ming Rd., Guishan District, Taoyuan City 333, Taiwan
joneslee@mail.mcu.edu.tw

Abstract. The total k-domatic partition problem is to partition the vertices of a graph into k pairwise disjoint total dominating sets. In this paper, we prove that the 4-domatic partition problem is NP-complete for planar graphs of bounded maximum degree. We use this NP-completeness result to show that the *total* 4-domatic partition problem is also NP-complete for planar graphs of bounded maximum degree. We also show that the total k-domatic partition problem is linear-time solvable for any bipartite distance-hereditary graph by showing how to compute a weak elimination ordering of the graph in linear time. The linear-time algorithm for computing a weak elimination ordering of a bipartite distance-hereditary graph can lead to improvement on the complexity of several graph problems or alternative solutions to the problems such as signed total domination, minus total domination, k-tuple total domination, and total $\{k\}$-domination problems.

Keywords: Total domatic partition · Total domination ·
Weak elimination ordering · Distance-hereditary graph

1 Introduction

Let $G = (V, E)$ be a finite, simple, undirected graph with vertex set V and edge set E. It is understood that $|V| = n$ and $|E| = m$ if nothing else is stated. We also use $V(G)$ and $E(G)$ to denote vertex set and edge set of G, respectively. The *neighborhood* of v in G, denoted by $N_G(v)$, is the set of all neighbors of v. The *closed neighborhood* of v in G, denoted by $N_G[v]$, is the union of the sets $N_G(v)$ and $\{v\}$. The *degree* of a vertex v in G, denoted by $deg_G(v)$, is the number of neighbors of v.

A vertex u of a graph $G = (V, E)$ *dominates* a vertex v if $u \in N_G[v]$. A vertex u of G *totally dominates* a vertex v if $u \in N_G(v)$. A subset $D \subseteq V$ dominates a vertex v if $|D \cap N_G[v]| \geq 1$. A subset $D \subseteq V$ totally dominates a vertex v if $|D \cap N_G(v)| \geq 1$. A *dominating set* of G is a subset D of V such that D dominates every vertex v in V. A *total dominating set* of G is a subset D of V such that D totally dominates every vertex v in V.

© Springer Nature Singapore Pte Ltd. 2019
C.-Y. Chang et al. (Eds.): ICS 2018, CCIS 1013, pp. 516–523, 2019.
https://doi.org/10.1007/978-981-13-9190-3_57

A collection P of subsets $S_1, S_2, \ldots, S_\ell$ of a set S forms a *partition* of S if $S = \bigcup_{i=1}^{\ell} S_i$, and $S_i \cap S_j = \emptyset$ for any pair of sets S_i and S_j in P. A partition $P = \{V_1, V_2, \ldots, V_\ell\}$ of V is a *domatic partition* of a graph $G = (V, E)$ if V_i is a dominating set of G for $i = 1, 2, \ldots, \ell$. A partition $P = \{V_1, V_2, \ldots, V_\ell\}$ of V is a *total domatic partition* of G if V_i is a total dominating set of G for $i = 1, 2, \ldots, \ell$. The *domatic partition problem* is to find a domatic partition of G of maximum size. The *total domatic partition problem* is to find a total domatic partition of G of maximum size. The *domatic number* of G, denoted by $d(G)$, is the size of a maximum domatic partition of G. The *total domatic number* of G, denoted by $d_t(G)$, is the size of a maximum total domatic partition of G.

Let k be a positive integer. A k-*domatic partition* of G is a domatic partition P of G such that $|P| = k$. A *total* k-*domatic partition* of G is a total domatic partition P of G such that $|P| = k$. The k-domatic partition problem is to find a k-domatic partition of G. The total k-domatic partition problem is to find a total k-domatic partition of G.

Total domatic partitions are also known as *coupon colorings*. It has recently received attention from the combinatorial and algorithmic communities [4,5,13]. From the algorithmic point of view, the total 2-domatic partition problem on bipartite graphs is NP-complete [7]. The total 3-domatic partition problem is NP-complete, even when restricted to the 2-section graph of the order-interval hypergraph of a finite poset, regular graphs, bipartite graphs, and planar graphs [1,8,9].

For any fixed integer $k \geq 2$, the total k-domatic partition problem on split graphs is NP-complete [8,9]. The total domatic partition is polynomial-time solvable for threshold graphs [8] and cographs [5]. In [9], Lee et al. showed that the total k-domatic partition problem is polynomial-time solvable for graphs with balanced adjacency matrices [9]. Furthermore, they showed that the total k-domatic partition problem is linear-time solvable for any chordal bipartite graph G if a Γ-free form of the adjacency matrix of G is given. Lee [10] showed that the total k-domatic partition problem is NP-complete for doubly chordal graphs and cobipartite graphs, and showed that the problem is linear-time solvable for chordal bipartite graphs, bipartite permutation graphs, convex bipartite graphs.

In this paper, we prove that the 4-domatic partition problem is NP-complete for planar graphs of maximum degree 9. We use this NP-completeness result to show that the total 4-domatic partition problem is also NP-complete for planar graphs of maximum degree 10. We also show that the total k-domatic partition problem is linear-time solvable for any bipartite distance-hereditary graph by showing how to compute a weak elimination ordering of the graph in linear time.

2   NP-Completeness Results

Before presenting the NP-completeness results, we restate the k-domatic partition problem and the total k-domatic partition problem as decision problems.

(1) **The k-domatic partition problem:**
    Instance: A graph $G = (V, E)$ and a positive integer k.
    Question: Does G have a k-domatic partition?
(2) **The total k-domatic partition problem:**
    Instance: A graph $G = (V, E)$ and a positive k.
    Question: Does G have a total k-domatic partition?

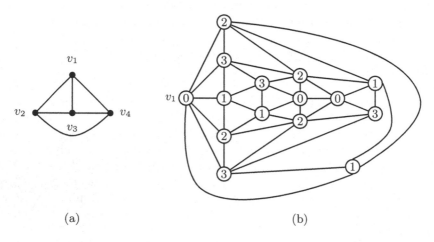

(a)   (b)

Fig. 1. (a) A planar graph of 4 vertices. (b) A planar graph of 15 vertices.

Theorem 1 (Goddard and Henning [6]). *For any planar graph G, $1 \leq d_t(G) \leq 4$. Moreover, these bounds are tight.*

Theorem 2.   *The 4-domatic partition problem is NP-complete for planar graphs of maximum degree 9.*

Proof. By Theorem 1, there exists a planar graph G with $d(G) = 4$. The 4-domatic partition problem for planar graphs of maximum degree 9 is clearly in NP. The 3-domatic partition problem is NP-complete for planar bipartite graphs of maximum degree 8 [11]. In the following, we show the NP-completeness of the 4-domatic partition problem for planar graphs of maximum degree 9 by a polynomial-time reduction from the 3-domatic partition problem for planar bipartite graphs of maximum degree 8.

Let $G = (V, E)$ be a planar bipartite graph of maximum degree 8. For each vertex $v \in V$, we construct a planar graph G_v of 4 vertices, as shown in Fig. 1(a) and connect v to the vertex v_1 of G_v. Let H be the resulting graph. Clearly, H is a planar graph of maximum degree 9 and the construction of H can be done in polynomial time.

Suppose that G has a 3-domatic partition $P = \{V_1, V_2, V_3\}$. Let $\hat{V}_0 = \emptyset$ and let $\hat{V}_i = V_i$ for $i = 1, 2, 3$. For each $v \in V$, we assign v_1 to $\hat{V}_0$, and v_i to $\hat{V}_{i-1}$ for $i = 2, 3, 4$. Clearly, $\hat{V}_0$, $\hat{V}_1$, $\hat{V}_2$, and $\hat{V}_3$ are dominating sets of H.

Conversely, we consider that H has a 4-domatic partition $\hat{P} = \{\hat{V}_0, \hat{V}_1, \hat{V}_2, \hat{V}_3\}$. Let v be a vertex in V and let $N_0[v] = N_G[v] \cap \hat{V}_0$. The subgraph G_v consists of 4 vertices and v is adjacent to only the vertex v_1 in G_v. Since $\hat{P}$ is a 4-domatic partition, the vertices v_1, v_2, v_3, v_4 of G_v are in different dominating sets of $\hat{P}$. We consider the following two cases.

Case 1: $v_1 \in \hat{V}_0$. Clearly, $\hat{V}_\ell \cap V$ dominates v for $1 \le \ell \le 3$. Let $V_0' = \hat{V}_0 \setminus N_0[v]$, $V_1' = \hat{V}_1 \cup N_0[v]$, and $V_i' = \hat{V}_i$ for $i \in \{2, 3\}$. Clearly, $V_\ell' \cap V$ dominates v for $1 \le \ell \le 3$.

Case 2: $v_1 \notin \hat{V}_0$. Let $\hat{V}_i \in \hat{P} \setminus \hat{V}_0$ contains the vertex v_1. Then, $N_0[v] \ne \emptyset$. For each $\hat{V}_j \in (\hat{P} \setminus \{\hat{V}_0, \hat{V}_i\})$, the set $\hat{V}_j \cap V$ dominates v since $\hat{V}_j$ is a dominating set of H and does not contain v_1. Let $V_i' = (\hat{V}_i \setminus \{v_1\}) \cup N_0[v]$, $V_0' = (\hat{V}_0 \setminus N_0[v]) \cup \{v_1\}$, and $V_j' = \hat{V}_j$ for each $\hat{V}_j \in (\hat{P} \setminus \{\hat{V}_0, \hat{V}_i\})$. Clearly, $V_\ell' \cap V$ dominates v for $1 \le \ell \le 3$.

Following the discussion above, we can obtain V_0', V_1', V_2', V_3' from $\hat{V}_0, \hat{V}_1, \hat{V}_2, \hat{V}_3$ such that $V_0' \cap V = \emptyset$ and $V_\ell' \cap V$ dominates each $v \in V$ for $1 \le \ell \le 3$. Then, G has a 3-domatic partition if and only if H has a 4-domatic partition. Hence, the 4-domatic partition problem is NP-complete for planar graphs of maximum degree 9.

Theorem 3. *The total 4-domatic partition problem is NP-complete for planar graphs of maximum degree 10.*

Proof. The total 4-domatic partition problem for planar graphs of maximum degree 10 is clearly in NP. Theorem 2 shows that the 4-domatic partition problem on planar graphs of maximum degree 9 is NP-complete. In the following, we show the NP-completeness of the total 4-domatic partition problem for planar graphs of maximum degree 10 by a polynomial-time reduction from the 4-domatic partition problem for planar graphs of maximum degree 9.

Let $G = (V, E)$ be a planar graph of maximum degree 9. For each vertex $v \in V$, we construct a planar graph G_v of 15 vertices, as shown in Fig. 1(b)[1], and connect v to v_1 of G_v.

Let H be the resulting graph. Clearly, H is a planar graph of maximum degree 10 and the construction of H can be done in polynomial time.

Following the arguments similar to those for proving Theorem 2, we can prove that G has a 4-domatic partition if and only if H has a total 4-domatic partition.

3   Bipartite Distance-Hereditary Graphs

A graph $G = (V, E)$ is called *distance-hereditary* if every pair of vertices are equidistant in every connected induced subgraph containing them. Distance-hereditary can be defined recursively by the following theorem.

---

[1] The graph is modified from [6].

520   C.-M. Lee

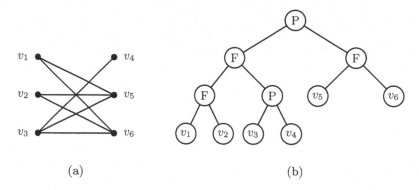

Fig. 2. (a) A bipartite distance-hereditary graph G. (b) A PF-tree of G.

Theorem 4 (Chang et al. [3])

1. *A graph consisting of only one vertex is distance-hereditary, and the twin set is the vertex itself.*
2. *If G_1 and G_2 are disjoint distance-hereditary graphs with twin sets $TS(G_1)$ and $TS(G_2)$, respectively, then the graph $G_1 \cup G_2$ is a distance-hereditary graph and the twin set of G is $TS(G_1) \cup TS(G_2)$. G is said to be obtained from G_1 and G_2 by a false twin operation.*
3. *If G_1 and G_2 are disjoint distance-hereditary graphs with twin sets $TS(G_1)$ and $TS(G_2)$, respectively, then the graph obtained by connecting every vertex of $TS(G_1)$ to all vertices of $TS(G_2)$ is a distance-hereditary graph and the twin set of G is $TS(G_1) \cup TS(G_2)$. G is said to be obtained from G_1 and G_2 by a true twin operation.*
4. *If G_1 and G_2 are disjoint distance-hereditary graphs with twin sets $TS(G_1)$ and $TS(G_2)$, respectively, then the graph obtained by connecting every vertex of $TS(G_1)$ to all vertices of $TS(G_2)$ is a distance-hereditary graph and the twin set of G is $TS(G_1)$. G is said to be obtained from G_1 and G_2 by a pendant vertex operation.*

Following Theorem 4, a binary ordered decomposition tree can be obtained in linear-time [3]. In this decomposition tree, each leaf is a single vertex graph, and each internal node represents one of the three operations: pendant vertex operation (labeled by P), true twin operation (labeled by T), and false twin operation (labeled by F.) This ordered decomposition tree is called a *PTF-tree*. It has $2n - 1$ tree nodes.

A graph is called a *bipartite distance-hereditary* graph if it is both *bipartite* and *distance-hereditary*. Bipartite distance-hereditary graphs form a subclass of distance-hereditary graphs. A bipartite distance-hereditary graph can be defined recursively by just two types of operations: false twin operation and pendant vertex operation. Therefore, its binary ordered decomposition tree is called a *PF-tree*. For a bipartite distance-hereditary graph G, we use $TS(G)$ to denote its twin set and use $PF(G)$ to denote its PF-tree. Clearly, a PF-tree can be constructed in linear time. Figure 2 shows an example of a PF-tree.

A vertex v of a bipartite graph $G = (V, E)$ is *weak simplicial* if (1) $N_G(v)$ is an independent, and (2) for each $x, y \in N_G(v)$, either $N_G(x) \subseteq N_G(y)$ or $N_G(y) \subseteq N_G(x)$. Let $(v_1, v_2, \dots, v_n)$ be an ordering of V and let G_i be the subgraph of G induced by $\{v_i, v_{i+1}, \dots, v_n\}$. An ordering $(v_1, v_2, \dots, v_n)$ of V is a *weak elimination ordering* of G if each vertex v_i is a weak simplicial vertex in G_i and for each $v_j, v_k \in N_{G_i}(v_i)$ with $j < k$, $N_{G_i}(v_j) \subseteq N_{G_i}(v_k)$.

Bipartite distance-hereditary graphs form a subclass of chordal bipartite graphs [2]. In the following, we give **Algorithm MakeSets** to compute a weak elimination ordering of any given bipartite distance-hereditary graph in $O(n)$ time.

Algorithm MakeSets:

Input: A PF-tree, $PF(G)$, of a connected bipartite distance-hereditary graph $G = (V, E)$ where $|V| > 1$ and the root r of $PF(G)$ is labeled by P.

Output: An ordered list $\mathcal{L}$ of sets that partition V.

1: Sort the nodes of $PF(G)$ in the postorder of the tree traversal;
2: Let $\mathcal{L}$ be an empty list of sets;
3: **for** $i = 1$ to $2n - 1$ **do**
4:     (Assume that i_1 and i_2 are the left and right children of node i, respectively
5:     if node i is a non-leaf node;)
6:     **if** node i is a leaf node which corresponds to vertex v **then**
7:         $TS(G_i) = \{v\}$;
8:     **end if**
9:     **if** node i is labeled by F **then**
10:        $TS(G_i) = TS(G_{i_1}) \cup TS(G_{i_2})$;
11:    **end if**
12:    **if** node i is labeled by P **then**
13:        assume that $TS(G_i) = TS(G_{i_1})$;
14:        let $S = TS(G_{i_2})$;
15:        append S to $\mathcal{L}$;
16:        **if** node i is the root of $PF(G)$ **then**
17:            append $TS(G_i)$ to $\mathcal{L}$;
18:        **end if**
19:    **end if**
20: **end for**

To illustrate, let G be the bipartite distance-hereditary graph with $V(G) = \{v_1, v_2, \dots, v_6\}$ and let $PF(G)$ be its PF-tree as shown in Fig. 2. The postorder of $PF(G)$ is $v_1, v_2, \text{F}, v_3, v_4, \text{P}, \text{F}, v_5, v_6, \text{F}, \text{P}$. Then, **Algorithm MakeSets** outputs the list of sets $\mathcal{L} = \{v_4\}, \{v_5, v_6\}, \{v_1, v_2, v_3\}$. We visit each set in order and arbitrarily output the vertices within each set and then we can obtain a new ordering, $v_4, v_5, v_6, v_1, v_2, v_3$. To simplify the discussion, we use $\langle L \rangle$ to denote an arbitrary ordering obtained from $\mathcal{L}$ in this fashion. Lemmas 1 and 2 can be easily verified.

Lemma 1. **Algorithm MakeSets** *runs in $O(n)$ time.*

Lemma 2. *If* **Algorithm MakeSets** *outputs* $\mathcal{L} = S_1, S_2, \ldots, S_r$ *for a bipartite distance-hereditary graph* $G = (V, E)$, *then* S_i *is an independent set of* G *for* $1 \le i \le r$.

Lemma 3. *If* **Algorithm MakeSets** *outputs* $\mathcal{L} = S_1, S_2, \ldots, S_r$ *for a bipartite distance-hereditary graph* $G = (V, E)$, *then* $\langle L \rangle = u_1, u_2, \ldots, u_n$ *is a weak elimination ordering.*

Proof. Let $1 \le i \le n$ and let G_i be the subgraph of G induced by $\{u_i, u_{i+1}, \ldots, u_n\}$. Consider three vertices u_i, u_j, and u_k with $i < j < k$ and u_i is adjacent to u_j and u_k. By Lemma 2, u_i, u_j, u_k are not in the same set of $\mathcal{L}$. Let $u_i \in S_a$ and $u_j \in S_b$. Clearly, $a < b$. Assume that the algorithm appends S_a to $\mathcal{L}$ as it visits the node ℓ. Then, node ℓ is labeled by P. By the algorithm, $S_a = TS(G_{\ell_2})$ and $TS(G_\ell) = TS(G_{\ell_1}) \subseteq S_b$. Therefore, $u_j, u_k \in TS(G_\ell)$. By Theorem 4, every vertex of S_a is adjacent to both vertices u_j and u_k. Suppose that there exists a vertex $u_p \notin S_a$ such that $u_p \in S_t$ is adjacent to u_j or u_k. We consider the following two cases.

Case 1: The algorithm appends S_t to $\mathcal{L}$ before it appends S_b to $\mathcal{L}$. Then, $p < j < k$. Therefore, every vertex of S_t is adjacent to both vertices u_j and u_k as we discussed above.

Case 2: The algorithm appends S_b to $\mathcal{L}$ before it appends S_t to $\mathcal{L}$. Then, $j < k < p$. Therefore, u_j and u_k are both adjacent to u_p.

Following the discussion above, we know that $N_{G_i}[v_j] \subseteq N_{G_i}[v_k]$ for $1 \le i \le n$. Hence, the ordering $\langle L \rangle = u_1, u_2, \ldots, u_n$ is a weak elimination ordering.

Theorem 5 (Lee [10]). *Given a chordal bipartite graph* $G = (A, B, E)$ *with a weak elimination ordering and a positive integer* $k \le \delta(G)$, *the vertices in* $A \cup B$ *can be partitioned into* k *total dominating sets* $D_1, D_2, \ldots, D_k$ *in* $O(n+m)$ *time.*

Theorem 6. *The total* k-*domatic partition problem can be solved in* $O(n + m)$ *time for distance-hereditary graphs.*

Proof. It follows from Lemmas 1 and 3 and Theorem 5.

Theorem 7 (Pradhan [12]). *For any chordal bipartite graph* $G = (A, B, E)$ *with a weak elimination ordering, the R-total domination problem can be solved in* $O(n + m)$ *time.*

Corollary 1. *The signed total domination, minus total domination,* k-*tuple total domination, and total* $\{k\}$-*domination problems are linear-time solvable for bipartite distance-hereditary graphs.*

Proof. The signed total domination, minus total domination, k-tuple total domination, and total $\{k\}$-domination problems are special cases of the R-total domination problem. By Lemmas 1 and 3 and Theorem 7, the corollary holds.

Acknowledgment. The work is supported by an internal research project of Ming Chuan University (2018/11/1–2019/3/31) and partially supported by Research Grant: MOST-106-2221-E-130-006 in Taiwan. The author is grateful to the anonymous referees for their valuable comments and suggestions to improve the presentation of this paper.

References

1. Bouchemakh, I., Ouatiki, S.: On the domatic and the total domatic numbers of the 2-section graph of the order-interval hypergraph of a finite poset. Discrete Math. **309**, 3674–3679 (2009)
2. Brandstädt, A., Le, V.B., Spinrad, J.P.: Graph Classes: A Survey. SIAM Monographs on Discrete Mathematics and Applications. SIAM, Philadelphia (1999)
3. Chang, M.-S., Hsieh, S., Chen, G.-H.: Dynamic programming on distance-hereditary graphs. In: Leong, H.W., Imai, H., Jain, S. (eds.) ISAAC 1997. LNCS, vol. 1350, pp. 344–353. Springer, Heidelberg (1997). https://doi.org/10.1007/3-540-63890-3_37
4. Chen, B., Kim, J.H., Tait, M., Verstraete, J.: On coupon colorings of graphs. Discrete Appl. Math. **193**, 94–101 (2015)
5. Chen, H., Jin, Z.: Coupon coloring of cographs. Appl. Math. Comput. **308**, 90–95 (2017)
6. Goddard, W., Henning, M.A.: Thoroughly distributed colorings. arXiv preprint arXiv:1609.09684 (2016)
7. Heggernes, P., Telle, J.A.: Partitioning graphs into generalized dominating sets. Nordic J. Comput. **5**, 128–142 (1998)
8. Koivisto, M., Laakkonen, P., Lauri, J.: NP-completeness results for partitioning a graph into total dominating sets. In: Cao, Y., Chen, J. (eds.) COCOON 2017. LNCS, vol. 10392, pp. 333–345. Springer, Cham (2017). https://doi.org/10.1007/978-3-319-62389-4_28
9. Lee, C.M., Wu, S.L., Chen, H.L., Chang, C.W., Lee, T.: A note on the complexity of the total domatic partition problem in graphs. J. Comb. Math. Comb. Comput. **108** (2017)
10. Lee, C.M.: Total k-domatic problem on some classes of graphs. Utilitas Mathematica, **109** (2018)
11. Poon, S.-H., Yen, W.C.-K., Ung, C.-T.: Domatic partition on several classes of graphs. In: Lin, G. (ed.) COCOA 2012. LNCS, vol. 7402, pp. 245–256. Springer, Heidelberg (2012). https://doi.org/10.1007/978-3-642-31770-5_22
12. Pradhan, D.: Complexity of certain functional variants of total domination in chordal bipartite graphs. Discrete Math. Algorithms Appl. **4** (2012)
13. Shi, Y., Wei, M., Yue, J., Zhao, Y.: Coupon coloring of some special graphs. J. Comb. Optim. **33**, 156–164 (2017)

An Approximation Algorithm for Star p-Hub Routing Cost Problem

Sun-Yuan Hsieh$^{(\boxtimes)}$, Li-Hsuan Chen, and Wei Lu

Department of Computer Science and Information Engineering,
National Cheng Kung University, Tainan 701, Taiwan
{hsiehsy, p76041166}@mail.ncku.edu.tw,
clhl00p@cs.ccu.edu.tw

Abstract. Given a metric graph $G = (V, E, w)$, a center $c \in V$, and an integer p, we discuss the Star p-Hub Routing Cost Problem in this paper. We want obtain a depth-2 tree which has a root and root is adjacent to p vertices called hubs. We call that this tree is a star p-hub tree and let the sum of distance in tree between all pairs of vertices be minimum. We prove the Star p-Hub Routing Cost Problem is NP-hard by reducing the Exact Cover by 3-Sets Problem to it. The Exact Cover by 3-Sets Problem is a variation of set cover problem and known NP-hard problem. After proving the Star p-Hub Routing Cost Problem is NP-hard, we present a 4-approximation algorithm running in polynomial time $O(n^2)$ for the Star p-Hub Routing Cost Problem.

Keywords: Graph theory · Algorithm · NP-hard · Approximation · Hub location · Star · Routing cost

1 Introduction

Among the available forms of interconnecting network, the intense exchange of entities among different areas impels the desire for more efficient architecture. Instead of directly routing flows from their origin node to the destination, a hub-and-spoke network is the architecture which can arise to better routing performance of nodes exchange flows. Hub-and-spoke network design consists of locating hubs from a set of candidate nodes, deciding which hub arcs will be installed and granted scale economies, and allocating non-hub nodes to hubs such that a given objective is optimized (O'Kelly and Miller 1994) [13]. The objective of this is the total cost to construct the connected network which usually composed of fixed setup costs for hubs and hub arcs, and of transportation costs. Hub location problems constitute an important class of problems in logistics which numerous applications in passenger/cargo transportation, postal services, telecommunications, etc. According to the definition of hub location problems, hubs are special facilities of the network responsible for switching, aggregating, transshipment and sorting. In many-to-many distributed systems, these hubs routing the flows either to their final destinations or to other hubs. Instead of serving each pair of service directly, hubs concentrate flows to take advantage of economies of scales. Hub facilities are inter-connected by hub arcs forming a hub level network, since the demand flows are routed in bulks through this sub-network, high-capacity

© Springer Nature Singapore Pte Ltd. 2019
C.-Y. Chang et al. (Eds.): ICS 2018, CCIS 1013, pp. 524–531, 2019.
https://doi.org/10.1007/978-981-13-9190-3_58

carriers can be used on those hub arcs so that lower unitary transportation cost can be attained. A complete network between the installed hubs equipped with efficient means of transport that allow a flow- independent discount factor to be applied to the inter-hub transportation costs.

Hub location problem is used in many situations in reality, including telecommunication system, traffic system, or medical system, etc. The target is different in different situation. Hub location problem has many different target functions. The k-hub median problem minimizes the total cost of output and the k-hub center problem minimize the diameter of output which had been proved that it is NP-hard and presented 4/3-inapproximity and a 5/3-approximation algorithm by Chen et al. [3].

In this paper, we discuss the Star p-Hub Routing Cost Problem(SpHRP) that output is a 2-level rooted tree and routing cost is minimum. We prove the problem SpHRP is NP-hard by reducing a NP-hard problem to SpHRP and present a approximation algorithm for SpHRP.

The rest of the paper is organized as follows. In the Sect. 2, we formally define the problem SpHRP. In the Sect. 3, we prove that SpHRP is NP-hard. In the Sect. 4, we present a approximation algorithm for SpHRP. We conclude the paper in Sect. 5.

2 Preliminaries

Let u, v be two vertices. $d_G(u, v)$ denotes distance between u, v in graph G and $d_T(u, v)$ denotes distance between u, v in tree T. Define $C(T) = \sum_{u,v \in V} d_T(u, v)$ called the routing cost of tree T and $c_s = \text{argmin}_{u \in V} \sum_{u,v \in V} d_T(u, v)$ called the center of minimum star. The input of the problem SpHRP is a metric, undirected, and complete graph, a vertex c and a parameter p. We want to obtain a tree that root is c, p vertices called hubs are adjacent to c and each of remaining vertices called terminal is adjacent to a hub. Our target is that minimizing routing cost. Routing cost is sum of distance between all pairs of vertices.

Star p-Hub Routing Cost Problem

Input: A undirected metric graph $G = (V, E, w)$, a vertex $c \in V$, and positive integer p.

Output: A depth-2 spanning tree T^* rooted by c called the central hub such that c has exactly p children (called hubs) and the routing cost of T^*, $C(T^*)$, is minimized.

To prove SpHRP is NP-hard, we need to reduce a NP-hard problem to SpHRP. Exact Cover by 3-Sets Problem (X3C) is a variation of set cover problem and a well known NP-hard problem [9]. Original set cover problem is that give a universal set and many subset of universal set and let union of the least subsets be universal set. In the problem X3C, the amount of member of universal set is multiple of three, every subsets are 3-sets, and each member of universal set appears in the union of chosen subsets once.

3   NP-Hardness

In this section, we prove that the problem SpHRP is a NP-hard problem with the problem X3C, which is one of NP-hard problem.

Exact Cover by 3-Sets Problem

Input: Given a set U, with $|U| = n = 3q$ (so, the size of U is a multiple of 3), and a collection S of 3-element subsets of U.
Output: Is there a subset S' of S where every element of U occurs in exactly one member of S'?

Theorem 1. *If the* Star p-Hub Routing Cost Problem *can be solved in polynomial time, then* Exact Cover by 3-Sets Problem *is polynomial time solvable.*

Proof. Let $(\mathcal{U}, \mathcal{S})$ be an input instance of Exact Cover by 3-Sets Problem. $\mathcal{U}$ is universal set and $\mathcal{S}$ is a collection of 3-element subset of $\mathcal{U}$. We construct a metric graph $G = (V \cup S \cup L \cup \{c\}, E, w)$ of the Star p-Hub Routing Cost Problem according to $(\mathcal{U}, \mathcal{S})$. First, we define the vertex set of G. c is a specified center. V corresponds to $\mathcal{U}$. For each subset $S_i \in \mathcal{S}$, we create a vertex s_i which belongs to S, and a vertex set L_i which contains b vertices and belongs to L.

It is obviously that any three vertices u, v, r in G satisfy $w(u, v) + w(v, r) \geq w(u, r)$. Thus G is a metric graph and we reduce input of X3C to input of SpHRP. Let T^* be an optimal solution of the Star p-Hub Routing Cost Problem with input graph G. We can construct T^* on condition that all vertex s in S is hub, all vertex l_i in L is terminal and is adjacent to s_i in S which creates l_i, all v_i in U is terminal and is adjacent to s_i which covers v_i, and v in U must be adjacent to the same vertex in S with the others two vertices in U. The routing cost in T^* is $C(T^*)$, where $C(T^*) = (4m^2 - 2m)b^2 + (6m^2 + 24mq - 2m - 12q)b + (2m^2 + 18mq + 36q^2 - 24q)$.

In the following, we will prove T^* is an optimal solution of the Star p-Hub Routing Cost Problem with input graph G. First, we prove that all vertex s in S is hub.

Claim 3.1. *In the T^*, all vertices in S are hubs and adjacent to c.*

Proof. Let T_1 be solution of SpHRP and T_1^* be optimal solution in T_1. We support that a vertex s belonging S is not a hub or adjacent to c in T_1. If the lower bound of the routing cost of T_1 is bigger than the routing cost of T^*, T_1 can't be T^*. When we calculating the lower bound of the routing cost of T_1, we just need to calculate cost between L instead of V because the lower bound won't increase when amount of vertices which are calculated are decrease.

We can sum up all minimum distance between each pair of vertices when calculating the lower bound of routing cost of T_1 by observing the above equation. A vertex l in L just has five possible location in solution. The first location is hub, and the other four possible location are terminals and distance to the hub is 1, 2, 3, 4, respectively. In the following, we will discuss sum of minimum distance from l to the other vertices when l in each possible location.

The first possible location is that l is a hub and adjacent to c. Up to m members in L can be put in this location.

(The remaining detailed proofs are omitted due to page limit.)

With Claim 3.1, we will prove the second condition of T^*.

Claim 3.2. *In the T^*, all vertices in L are adjacent to the vertex in S which creates it.*

Proof. Let T_2 be solution of SpHRP and T_2^* be optimal solution in T_2. We support that a vertex l in L is not adjacent to s in S which creates l in T_2. The vertex set V is consist of S, U, L', $\{l\}$, and $\{c\}$. Among them, L' is L excluding l.

$$\sum_{x,y \in A \cup B} d(x,y) = \sum_{x,y \in A} d(x,y) + 2 \times \sum_{x \in A, y \in B} d(x,y) + \sum_{x,y \in B} d(x,y)$$

Using the above equation, we simplify the calculation of the routing cost of T_2.

$$
\begin{aligned}
C(T_2) &= \sum_{x,y \in V} d_{T_2}(x,y) \\
&= \sum_{x \in L'} \sum_{y \in L'} d_{T_2}(x,y) + 2 \sum_{x \in L'} \sum_{y \in S \cup \{c\}} d_{T_2}(x,y) + \sum_{x \in S \cup \{c\}} \sum_{y \in S \cup \{c\}} d_{T_2}(x,y) \\
&\quad + 2 \sum_{y \in L' \cup S \cup \{c\}} d_{T_2}(l,y) + 2 \sum_{x \in U} \sum_{y \in L'} d_{T_2}(x,y) + 2 \sum_{x \in U} \sum_{y \in S \cup \{c\}} d_{T_2}(x,y) \\
&\quad + 2 \sum_{x \in U} d_{T_2}(x,l) + \sum_{x \in U} \sum_{y \in U} d_{T_2}(x,y)
\end{aligned}
$$

First, we calculate the lower bound of routing cost of T_2 between vertices in L'. (Claims 3.2.1 to 3.2.7 are omitted due to page limit.)

In the third part, we will prove the third condition of T^* with Claim 3.1 and Claim 3.2.

Claim 3.3. *In the T^*, all vertices in U are adjacent to the vertex in S which covers it.*

Proof. Let T_3 be solution of SpHRP and T_3^* be optimal solution in T_3. We support that a vertex v in U is not adjacent to s in S which covers v in T_3. The vertex set V is consist of S, U', L, $\{v\}$, and $\{c\}$. Among them, U' is U excluding v. Using the Eq. 1, we simplify the calculation of the routing cost of T_3.

$$
\begin{aligned}
C(T_3) &= \sum_{x,y \in V} d_{T_3}(x,y) \\
&= \sum_{x \in L} \sum_{y \in L} d_{T_3}(x,y) + 2 \sum_{x \in L} \sum_{y \in S \cup \{c\}} d_{T_3}(x,y) + \sum_{x \in S \cup \{c\}} \sum_{y \in S \cup \{c\}} d_{T_3}(x,y) \\
&\quad + 2 \sum_{y \in L \cup S \cup \{c\}} d_{T_3}(v,y) + 2 \sum_{x \in U'} d_{T_3}(x,v) \\
&\quad + 2 \sum_{x \in U'} \sum_{y \in L \cup S \cup \{c\}} d_{T_3}(x,y) + \sum_{x \in U'} \sum_{y \in U'} d_{T_3}(x,y)
\end{aligned}
$$

First, we calculate the lower bound of routing cost of T_3 between vertices in L. (Claims 3.3.1 to 3.3.6 with their proofs are omitted due to page limit.)

In the last part, we will prove the fourth condition of T^* with Claim 3.1, Claim 3.2, and Claim 3.3.

Claim 3.4. *In the* T^*, v_i *in* U *must be adjacent to the same vertex in* S *with the others two vertices in* U.

Proof. Let T_4 be solution of SpHRP and T_4^* be optimal solution in T_4. We support that a vertex v in U is not adjacent to the same vertex in S with the others two vertices in U in T_4. The vertex set V is consist of S, U', L, $\{v\}$, and $\{c\}$. Among them, U' is U excluding v. Using the Eq. 1, we simplify the calculation of the routing cost of T_4 of T_4.

$$
\begin{aligned}
C(T_4) &= \sum_{x,y \in V} d_{T_4}(x,y) \\
&= \sum_{x \in L} \sum_{y \in L} d_{T_4}(x,y) + 2 \sum_{x \in L} \sum_{y \in S \cup \{c\}} d_{T_4}(x,y) + \sum_{x \in S \cup \{c\}} \sum_{y \in S \cup \{c\}} d_{T_4}(x,y) \\
&\quad + 2 \sum_{x \in U} \sum_{y \in L \cup S \cup \{c\}} d_{T_4}(x,y) + \sum_{x \in U'} \sum_{y \in U} d_{T_4}(x,y) + \sum_{y \in U} d_{T_4}(v,y)
\end{aligned}
$$

Next, we calculate the lower bound of routing cost of T_4 between vertices in U and vertices in $L \cup S \cup \{c\}$.

Claim 3.4.1. $\sum_{x \in U} \sum_{y \in L \cup S \cup \{c\}} d_{T_4}(x,y) \geq (12mq - 6q)b + 9mq$.

Next, we will calculate the lower bound of routing cost of T_4 between vertices in U' and vertices in U.

Claim 3.4.2. $\sum_{x \in U'} \sum_{y \in U} d_{T_4}(x,y) \geq 36q^2 - 36q + 8$.

At last, we will calculate the lower bound of routing cost of T_4 between v which is not adjacent to the same vertex in S with the others two vertices in U and vertices in U.

Claim 3.4.3. $\sum_{y \in U} d_{T_4}(v,y) \geq 12q - 6$.

According above four parts, we can construct T^* on condition that all vertices in S are hubs, all vertices in L are terminals and adjacent to the vertex in S which creates it, all vertices in U are terminal and adjacent to the vertex in S which covers it, and each vertex v in U must be adjacent to the same vertex in S with the others two vertices in U.

When we know the structure of output of SpHRP, we can get output of X3C from output of SpHRP. Each hub in S which is adjacent to three vertices in U covers adjacent vertices in U. Obviously, all vertices in U are adjacent to a vertex in S. It means that all elements in U are covered and the hubs, vertices in S, which are adjacent to three vertices in U are the output of X3C. We prove that we can obtain the input of SpHRP from the input of X3C in polynomial time and obtain the output of X3C from the output of SpHRP in polynomial time. If we can solve SpHRP in polynomial time, we can solve X3C in polynomial time by obtaining the input of SpHRP from the input of X3C, solving SpHRP and obtaining the output of X3C from the output of SpHRP in polynomial time.

4 Approximation Algorithm

Next we will present a 4-approximation algorithm for the Star p-Hub Routing Cost Problem. Let c_s be the center of minimum star in G, $c_s = \text{argmin}_{v \in V} \sum_{u \in V} (u, v)$, and c_n be the nearest vertex of vertex c_s, $c_n = \text{argmin}_{v \in V} d_G(c_s, v)$. Let H^* be hubs in optimal solution T^* and $h_1^*, h_2^*, \ldots, h_p^*$ present each hub in H^*. H be hubs in our algorithm solution T and $h_1, h_2, \ldots, h_p$ present each hub in H.

We can get the following lemma.

Lemma 1. $C(T^*) \geq C(G)$.

Proof. Because input graph G is a metric graph, complete graph and satisfied triangle inequality, the minimum distance between two vertices is weight of edge between two vertices in G.

$$d_{T^*}(u, v) \geq d_G(u, v)$$

$$C(T^*) = \sum_{u \in V} \sum_{v \in V} d_{T^*}(u, v) \geq \sum_{u \in V} \sum_{v \in V} d_G(u, v) = C(G)$$

The routing cost of optimal solution T^* is bigger or equal than the routing cost of input graph G.

Lemma 2. $C(T^*) \geq n \sum_{v \in V} d_G(c_s, v)$.

Proof. $s_c = \text{arg min}_{v \in V} \sum_{u \in V} (u, v)$

$$C(T^*) \geq C(G) = \sum_{u \in V} \sum_{v \in V} d(u, v) = n \sum_{v \in V} d_G(c_s, v)$$

(The proofs of Lemmas 3 and 4 are omitted due to page limit.)

Lemma 3. $C(T^*) \geq n(n-1)d_G(c_s, c_n)$.

Lemma 4. $C(T^*) \geq 2(n-1) \sum_{i=2}^{p} d_G(h_i, c)$.

Algorithm APX

Step 1: Find c_s, center of minimum star. $c_s = \text{argmin}_{u \in V} \sum_{v \in V} (u, v)$.
Step 2: Find c_n, the nearest vertex of vertex c_s. $c_n = \text{argmin}_{v \in V} d_G(c_s, v)$.
Step 3: If vertex c_s is different from vertex c, let vertex c_s be h_1. Otherwise, let vertex c_n be h_1.
Step 4: Connect vertex c and vertex h_1.
Step 5: Pick $p-1$ vertices $\{h_2, h_3, \ldots, h_p\}$ closest to c from $V \backslash \{c, h_1\}$ and connect them to vertex c. Let $N_T(c) = \{h_1, h_2, h_3, \ldots, h_p\}$.
Step 6: Connect all vertices in $V \backslash \{c, h_1, h_2, \ldots, h_p\}$ to h_1 in T.
Step 7: Return the tree T.

Theorem 2. There is a 4-approximation algorithm for the Star p-Hub Routing Cost Problem running in time $O(n^2)$ where n is the number of vertices in the input graph.

Proof. There are two kinds of the output of algorithm. One is T_s that h_1 is vertex c_s, the other is T_n that h_1 is vertex c_n. We will prove that both routing cost of T_s and T_n are less or equal than four times of routing cost of optimal solution.

(The proofs of Lemmas 5 and 6 are omitted due to page limit.)

Lemma 5. $C(T_s) \leq 4C(T^*)$.

Lemma 6. $C(T_n) \leq 4C(T^*)$.

By Lemmas 5 and 6, we prove the routing cost of algorithm solution is less or equal than four times of the routing cost of optimal solution. Next, we will prove that the algorithm run in time $O(n^2)$. Obviously, finding center of the minimum induced star run in time $O(n^2)$, finding the nearest vertex of center of the minimum induced star run in time $O(n)$, picking $p - 1$ vertices closet to c run in time $O(n)$, and connecting two vertices run in time $O(1)$. The proposed algorithm is a 4-approximation algorithm running in time $O(n^2)$.

5 Conclusion

In this paper, we formally define the Star p-Hub Routing Cost Problem. Then, we prove the Star p-Hub Routing Cost Problem is NP-hard, by reducing a known NP-hard problem, the Exact cover by 3-sets problem, to our problem. In the last, we present a 4-approximation algorithm using minimum star to find hub to solve the Star p-Hub Routing Cost Problem. For the future work, it is interesting to see whether there exists an α-approximation algorithm and $\alpha < 4$ or to prove that for any $\varepsilon > 0$, it is NP-hard to approximate the Star p-Hub Routing Cost Problem to a ratio $4 - \varepsilon$.

References

1. Campos, R., Ricardo, M.: A fast algorithm for computing minimum routing cost spanning trees. Comput. Netw. **52**(17), 3229–3247 (2008)
2. Chen, L.H., Cheng, D.W., Hsieh, S.Y., Hung, L.J., Lee, C.W., Wu, B.Y.: Approximation algorithms for single allocation k-hub center problem. In: Proceedings of the 33rd Workshop on Combinatorial Mathematics and Computation Theory (CMCT 2016), pp. 13–18 (2016)
3. Chen, L.-H., Cheng, D.-W., Hsieh, S.-Y., Hung, L.-J., Lee, C.-W., Wu, B.-Y.: Approximation algorithms for the star k-hub center problem in metric graphs. In: Dinh, T.N., Thai, M.T. (eds.) COCOON 2016. LNCS, vol. 9797, pp. 222–234. Springer, Cham (2016). https://doi.org/10.1007/978-3-319-42634-1_18
4. Chen, L.-H., Hsieh, S.-Y., Hung, L.-J., Klasing, R., Lee, C.-W., Wu, B.Y.: On the complexity of the star p-hub center problem with parameterized triangle inequality. In: Fotakis, D., Pagourtzis, A., Paschos, V.T. (eds.) CIAC 2017. LNCS, vol. 10236, pp. 152–163. Springer, Cham (2017). https://doi.org/10.1007/978-3-319-57586-5_14

5. Chen, L.-H., Hsieh, S.-Y., Hung, L.-J., Klasing, R.: The Approximability of the p-hub center problem with parameterized triangle inequality. In: Cao, Y., Chen, J. (eds.) COCOON 2017. LNCS, vol. 10392, pp. 112–123. Springer, Cham (2017). https://doi.org/10.1007/978-3-319-62389-4_10

6. Wu, Y., et al.: Approximability and inapproximability of the star p-hub center problem with parameterized triangle inequality. J. Comput. Syst. Sci. **92**, 92–112 (2018)

7. Dionne, R., Florian, M.: Exact and approximate algorithms for optimal network design. Networks **9**(1), 37–59 (1979)

8. Fischetti, M., Lancia, G., Serafini, P.: Exact algorithms for minimum routing cost trees. Networks **39**(3), 161–173 (2002)

9. Garey, M.R., Johnson, D.S.: Computers and Intractability: A guide to the theory of NP-completeness. W. H. Freeman and Company, San Francisco (1979)

10. Hu, T.C.: Optimum communication spanning trees. SIAM J. Comput. **3**(3), 188–195 (1974)

11. Hochuli, A., Holzer, S., Wattenhofer, R.: Distributed approximation of minimum routing cost trees. In: Halldórsson, M.M. (ed.) SIROCCO 2014. LNCS, vol. 8576, pp. 121–136. Springer, Cham (2014). https://doi.org/10.1007/978-3-319-09620-9_11

12. Lin, W.C., Wu, B.Y.: A 2-approximation algorithm for the clustered minimum routing cost tree problem. In: Intelligent Systems and Applications: Proceedings of the International Computer Symposium (ICS) Held at Taichung, Taiwan, 12–14 December 2014, vol. 274, p. 3. IOS Press, April 2015

13. O'Kelly, M.E., Miller, H.J.: The hub network design problem: a review and synthesis. J. Transp. Geograph. **2**(1), 31–40 (1994)

14. Reddy, K.R.U.K.: A survey of the all-pairs shortest paths problem and its variants in graphs. Acta Universitatis Sapientiae, Informatica **8**(1), 16–40 (2016)

15. Wu, B.Y., Chao, K.M., Tang, C.Y.: Approximation algorithms for some optimum communication spanning tree problems. Discrete Appl. Math. **102**(3), 245–266 (2000)

16. Wu, B.Y., Lancia, G., Bafna, V., Chao, K.M., Ravi, R., Tang, C.Y.: A polynomial-time approximation scheme for minimum routing cost spanning trees. SIAM J. Comput. **29**(3), 761–778 (2000)

17. Yaman, H., Elloumi, S.: Star p-hub center problem and star p-hub median problem with bounded path lengths. Comput. Oper. Res. **39**(11), 2725–2732 (2012)

Tube Inner Circumference State Classification Optimization by Using Artificial Neural Networks, Random Forest and Support Vector Machines Algorithms

Wei-Ting Li, Chung-Wen Hung, and Ching-Ju Chen[✉]

National Yunlin University of Science and Technology, Douliou, Taiwan
chen.chingju@gmail.com

Abstract. Using Artificial Neural Networks, Random Forest and Support Vector Machines algorithms to optimize Tube inner circumference state classification and accomplish the process of Incoming Quality Control (IQC) is proposed in this paper. However, the traditional classification system is usually set the threshold by the developer in the early stages. The method is time-consuming and tedious to develop the module. In modern, machine learning technology can overcome the shortcomings of tradition classification system. However, machine learning exists a lot of algorithms, such as Artificial Neural Network (ANN), Random Forest (RF), Support Vector Machine (SVM), and so on. And, the different algorithms may cause the different characteristics and efficiencies, so it's necessary to compare the different algorithms at application. This paper will use a method, called grid search to find the best parameter, and compare these algorithms which has the best characteristic, efficiency and the parameter. Finally, it is found from the experimental results that the method of this paper is workable for actual dataset.

Keywords: Machine learning · ANN · RF ·
SVM and tube inner circumference

1 Introduction

In the past, the accuracy and development time of the traditional classification system is worse than machine learning. As the technology advances, the operational performance of the hardware was already satisfied machine learning with the complicated algorithms now. However, machine learning includes a lot of algorithms, the chopsticks tube data [1] will be used to compare accuracy and speed for ANN, RF, and SVM which are optimized. The contour perimeter, circle radius of circle fitting, two radii of ellipse fitting, maximum inscribed circle, and minimum inscribed circle are used by the developer to classify as "Normal", "Large", "Small", "Deformed" chopstick tube and "Empty" [1]. The accuracy of the result is about 91%. You must put more effort and time to try if you want to improve the accuracy. This paper will use the same training data and the test data to compare accuracy and calculating the speed for ANN, RF, and SVM which are optimized model, and how to find these parameters. In the results, the

© Springer Nature Singapore Pte Ltd. 2019
C.-Y. Chang et al. (Eds.): ICS 2018, CCIS 1013, pp. 532–540, 2019.
https://doi.org/10.1007/978-981-13-9190-3_59

accuracy of the test set is higher than the traditional method after the paper uses a grid search [2] to find the optimization parameters of these algorithms. Nevertheless, SVM is the most time-consuming in this paper, then ANN is the slowest at module calculating speed, and RF is the easiest to observe the structure of the algorithm.

2 Methodologies

2.1 Artificial Neural Network, ANN

This structure simulates the characteristics of nervous [3], and the nerves are connected to each other. Figure 1 shows the basic structure of ANN, which includes the input layer, hidden layers and the output layer, and the number of neurons and layer is mainly according to application design. If the module can't satisfy the complicated application, then increase the number of neurons or hidden layer, but the time of training will relatively increase. In the modern, graphics processing unit (GPU) can be used to accelerate parallel computing the complicated module.

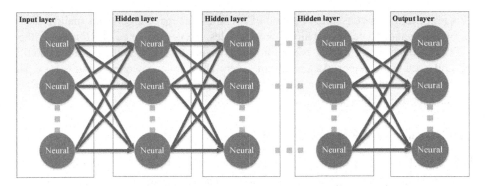

Fig. 1. Artificial Neural Network system architecture

Furthermore, ANN will use the active function [3], this paper used the sigmoid function. However, the value of each layer needs to pass the sigmoid function, and complete the prediction. This paper used cross-entropy [4] and backpropagation [5] to calculate cost and correct weight during training. The structure of ANN is simple, but we cannot understand the meaning for weight.

2.2 Decision Tree, DT

This algorithm is a tree structure on the application for classification or regression. In the process of the training module, it's mainly used to find the maximum information gain (IG) (1) of every parent node. D_p and D_j are the datasets of the parent node and the child node. The parameter f is the feature to perform the split. N_p is all of the samples at the parent node, N_n is the number of samples in the child node. The parameter I is our impurity measure. Then the parameter I will change with different Algorithm.

The algorithm included Iterative Dichotomiser 3 (ID3), C4.5, C5.0 [6], classification and regression trees (CART). The CART is used in the paper, and this algorithm is a binary method that likes the algorithm of ID3. The impurity measure of CART use Entropy (2) with ID3, parameter p is the proportion of c sample in nodes, but the algorithm of CART changes the impurity measure method to Gini index (3) method in building DT.

$$IG(D_p, f) = I(D_p) - \sum_{j=1}^{m} \frac{N_j}{N_p} I(D_j) \tag{1}$$

$$I_H(t) = -\sum_{i=1}^{c} [p(i|t) log_2 p(i|t)] \tag{2}$$

$$I_G(t) = 1 - \sum_{i=1}^{c} p(i|t)^2 \tag{3}$$

2.3   Random Forest, RF

This algorithm is the ensemble method of DT, the concept of algorithms mainly uses a lot of DT method to achieve majority voting rules, the performance of RF is better than a DT. The method of Bagging is used in random sampling to train the module, also this method used in this paper. As a result, the every DT can keep accurate results for a part of samples, and improve the problem of overfitting. You do not need to prune the RF if you use the RF method.

2.4   Support Vector Machine, SVM

The SVM [8, 9] is mainly to find the hyperplane (4) that can be divided into two categories such as Fig. 2. The $\vec{x}$ is the feature vector of input, $\vec{\omega}$ is the weight vector, b is the bias of hyperplane, pink line is the hyperplane that classify different sample into red dots and blue forks, red dots and blue forks are support vectors (SV); moreover, the hyperplane has to possess maximum distance (5) between hyperplane and SV.

$$h(\vec{x}) = \vec{\omega}^T \vec{x} + b \tag{4}$$

$$\vec{r} = \frac{h(\vec{x})}{\left\| \vec{\omega} \right\|} \tag{5}$$

If the application can't use linear SVM to classify, we can use the kernel function to increase the dimensions. The kernel function included radial basis function kernel (RBF), polynomial kernel, sigmoid kernel, inter kernel and so on. For example, Fig. 3 uses the polynomial kernel to increase two-degrees to three-degrees. The hyperplane can be found in high dimensions by this method, and the best kernel and the related parameters will be found by grid search in this paper.

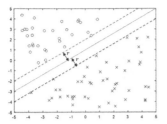 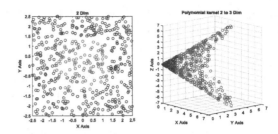

Fig. 2. Schematic that SVM classify the sample (Color figure online)

Fig. 3. Use the polynomial kernel to improve the dimensions

3 Experimental Result

In this section, this paper will use tube inner circumference state [1] as a sample to find the optimized algorithm which ANN, RF, and SVM, and improve the traditional method. The tube inner circumference state and feature [1] are displayed in Fig. 4. The white line is the contour of chopstick tube after image analysis, the green line is drawn by circle fitting, a rad line is drawn by ellipse fitting, a light blue line is the maximum inscribed circle, and the purple line is the minimum circumscribed circle. Furthermore, the ellipse can get the two feature is a radius. However, the result predicted by [1] are Normal, Large, Small, Deformed chopstick tube and Empty. The above information will be used in this experiment, and the data set will be divided into four to one which are training data and testing data in this experiment. Finally, the Tensorflow and OpenCV will be implemented and compared on NVIDIA TX2 platform in this paper.

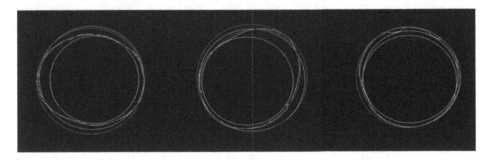

Fig. 4. Schematic diagram of chopsticks after image analysis (Color figure online)

3.1 Artificial Neural Network, ANN

The number of hidden units and hidden layers will be adjusted to optimize the ANN module. The range of hidden units is between 6 and 18, and the range of hidden layers is between 1 and 6. The weight of ANN is random in the beginning, so this training result is the average value of 5 times such as [10]. Furthermore, the parameters in machine learning are learning rate $\eta = 0.01$ and epochs are 7000. Table 1 indicates the test data accuracy of ANN with different parameters. Hidden units and hidden layers use the optimal solution about 16 units and 3 layers, the maximum accuracy of test data is 0.96857 shown in Table 1. With 12 units and 4 layers are also the optimal solution of hidden units and hidden layers, but the module with 4 hidden layers will spend more calculating time than 3. The module with 16 units and 3 layers be chosen in this paper.

Table 1. The accuracy of test data with the various number of parameter

Net\layer	1	2	3	4	5	6
6	0.56000	0.72000	0.89714	0.84857	0.90000	0.73714
7	0.62571	0.78571	0.84571	0.85429	0.88857	0.87429
8	0.57714	0.81714	0.89429	0.92571	0.88000	0.93714
9	0.61714	0.82286	0.93714	0.94857	0.86286	0.90286
10	0.62286	0.84000	0.94000	0.94571	0.94286	0.86857
11	0.60286	0.87429	0.92857	0.96286	0.95714	0.95429
12	0.68000	0.85714	0.94857	**0.96857**	0.95143	0.96286
13	0.65143	0.88571	0.96000	0.96572	0.96000	0.96000
14	0.63429	0.88286	0.94857	0.96286	0.96572	0.96000
15	0.63429	0.89429	0.94286	0.95429	0.96000	0.95429
16	0.68571	0.89429	**0.96857**	0.95429	0.93714	0.96572
17	0.68286	0.89429	0.94857	0.96000	0.95143	0.94857
18	0.68571	0.89714	0.94571	0.94571	0.95429	0.95429

This paper will train the module up to 17000 epochs used the module with 16 hidden units and 3 hidden layers, and the result is shown in Fig. 5. And then, the blue line is the loss from root-mean-square error, the red solid line is a curve of training accuracy, and the red dotted line is a curve of testing accuracy. The training set accuracy and the test set accuracy also arrive 0.985612 and 1. The result can prove the module is not overfitting, and the module is best for this experiment.

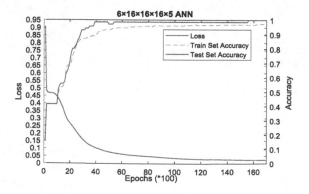

Fig. 5. Schematic diagram of chopsticks after image analysis

3.2 Random Forest, RF

RT mainly adjusted the number of DT and the maximum branch for every DT, this paper will adjust the maximum branch between 20 and 200, and the number of DT between 10 and 100. However, RF is easy to overfit during training and shown in Fig. 6. The red solid line is testing accuracy, the red dotted line is training accuracy, and the blue line is a branch of average. As a result, the testing set accuracy gradually decreases after each training, and this paper used early stopping [9] to improve the problem. Furthermore, RF used the random training set to build DT as the same as bagging algorithm, so this practice will use the average value from 10 times data.

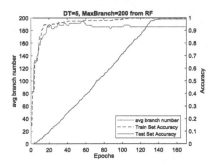

Fig. 6. The curve of DT training

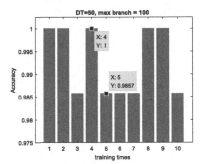

Fig. 7. Test accuracy of 50 DT and 100 branch

The result is shown in Table 2, the row and column are the numbers of DT and maximum branch. The range of table is large, so only show the quantity of DT between 20 to 80. There are 3 accuracies with optimal parameter close to 0.99286. The first, the number of DT and maximum branch are 70 and 160, the second are 30 and 180, and the third are 50 and 100. The module with parameters are 50 and 100 is more simple than others, so this module will be selected to reduce the complexity of this paper.

Table 2. Testing set recode from RT training.

MB\DT	20	30	40	50	60	70	80
20	0.97143	0.96286	0.96857	0.96429	0.95571	0.96429	0.97571
40	0.97571	0.98714	0.98857	0.98429	0.98142	0.98429	0.97857
60	0.98571	0.99000	0.98570	0.98000	0.98571	0.99000	0.98857
80	0.98429	0.98571	0.98429	0.98714	0.98429	0.99000	0.98571
100	0.99000	0.98571	0.98571	**0.99286**	0.98714	0.98571	0.98571
120	0.98571	0.99143	0.99143	0.98571	0.98714	0.98571	0.98429
140	0.99000	0.98571	0.98857	0.98429	0.99000	0.98857	0.98429
160	0.99000	0.98857	0.98714	0.98714	0.99000	**0.99286**	0.98571
180	0.98571	**0.99286**	0.98714	0.99000	0.98571	0.98571	0.98714
200	0.98571	0.99000	0.98571	0.98429	0.98571	0.98714	0.98571

Figure 7. displays the testing accuracy at each time of training, and the parameter of the module is 30 DT and 180 maximum branches. The x-axis is a quantity of training times. The y-axis is testing accuracy. As a result, the best module can easily arrive at in 100% for the testing accuracy in this experimental.

3.3 Support Vector Machine, SVM

The SVM mainly adjusted the kernel function and the parameters of function for the application, this paper will fix the cost penalization and iterations to look for the optimal module. Furthermore, this paper will try these kernel function: linear kernel, RBF, polynomial kernel, sigmoid kernel and inter kernel, to find the optimal parameters.

The training set accuracy and the test accuracy of a linear kernel and inter kernel showed in Table 3, a linear kernel is a normal linear SVM, inter kernel can reference the function (6), these two kernels don't have parameters to adjust.

$$K\left(\vec{x}, \vec{x}'\right) = min(\vec{x}, \vec{x}')\tag{6}$$

Table 3. Linear and inter kernel result

Information\kernel	Linear	Inter
Train set accuracy	0.838129	1.0
Test set accuracy	0.814286	0.985714

Polynomial kernel had to adjust two parameters (7), R and d are constant and the degree of a kernel function, setting the degree to 2, because of the high degree is very easy to overfit. In Table 4, this paper looks up for R between 0 to 1, but the data is too large, so only show the data between 0.545 to 0.55, and the optimal R is 0.548 for the test accuracy that is the highest value.

$$K\left(\vec{x}, \vec{x}'\right) = (\vec{x}'^{T}\vec{x} + R)^{d}\tag{7}$$

Table 4. Polynomial kernel result

R	0.545	0.546	0.547	0.548	0.549	0.55
Train set accuracy	0.87050	0.94245	0.93525	**0.95684**	0.91727	0.96043
Test set accuracy	0.87143	0.97143	0.98571	**1**	0.94286	0.97143

The kernel of RBF (8) can infinitely increase dimensions for a sample, γ is constant that influenced Euclidean Distance for the sample, and only γ between 0.903 and 0.908 be shown in Table 5 in this paper because the data range is too large. However, the optimal γ is 0.906 for the test accuracy that is the highest value.

$$K\left(\vec{x}, \vec{x}'\right) = e^{-\gamma\left|\left|\vec{x}-\vec{x}'\right|\right|^2} \tag{8}$$

Table 5. RBF kernel result

Gamma	0.903	0.904	0.905	0.906	0.907	0.908
Train set accuracy	0.98561	0.98561	0.98201	**0.98201**	0.98561	0.98561
Test set accuracy	0.97143	0.97143	0.98571	**1.0**	0.97143	0.97143

In finally, sigmoid kernel (8) has to adjust the constant R, a part of the result shown in Table 6, a sigmoid kernel is more suitable for the regressive application, so the accuracy is lower than other kernels.

$$K\left(\vec{x}, \vec{x}'\right) = tanh(\vec{x}'^{T}\vec{x} + R) \tag{9}$$

Table 6. Sigmoid kernel result

R	1	2	3	4	5	6
Train set accuracy	0.24101	0.34532	0.37050	0.37770	0.39928	0.33094
Test set accuracy	0.21429	0.37143	0.37143	0.37143	0.41429	0.31429

In conclusion, the optimal module of SVM will choose RBF with $\gamma = 0.906$, and the test accuracy is up to 0.982014.

4 Conclusion

The accuracy of testing can increase to 100% when this structure is complicated, and the accuracy is better than a traditional system is 91%. However, the complexity is not necessarily proportional to testing accuracy. The complex model is usually overfitting for the training set. When training the module, ANN and RF are simple, but the prediction of ANN is time-consuming. However, the training of SVM is more time consuming than ANN and RF, because has to set the parameter of a different kernel, and this method will be easy to do the hyperparameters. In the task of prediction, the calculating speed of SVM faster than and easier other. As a result, SVM is more suitable than other in an application of tube detection. Furthermore, we can select module are ANN and RF, if we do not care speed of predict.

The ratio is 4:1 for training and testing data in this experiment. The noise of testing data is lower than training data, and testing accuracy can easily increase to 100% because the sample is few and noise is not uniform. In part of the evaluation, there are still many places needed to improve. Such as: evenly distributed the noise, and optimize value is hyperparameters. The above are all important topics that is worth to discuss.

Acknowledgments. This work is partially supported by the Ministry of Science and Technology, ROC, under contract No. MOST 106-2221-E-224-025, and 106-2218-E150-001.

This work was financially supported by the "Intelligent Recognition Industry Service Center" from The Featured Areas Research Center Program within the framework of the Higher Education Sprout Project by the Ministry of Education (MOE) in Taiwan.

References

1. Hung, C.-W., Jiang, J.-G., Wu, H.-H.P., Mao, W.-L.: An automated optical inspection system for a tube inner circumference state identification. In: ICAROB (2018)
2. Yuanyuan, S., Yongming, W., Lili, G., Zhongsong, M., Shan, J.: The comparison of optimizing SVM by GA and grid search. In: 2017 13th IEEE International Conference on Electronic Measurement & Instruments (ICEMI), pp. 354–360, Yangzhou (2017). https://doi.org/10.1109/icemi.2017.8265815
3. Ross, J.: Fuzzy Logic with Engineering Application, 3rd edn, pp. 179–183. Wiley-Blackwell (2010)
4. Cross entropy available. http://en.wikipedia.org/wiki/Cross_entropy
5. Yusong, P.O.: Generalization of the cross-entropy error function to improve the error backpropagation algorithm. In: Proceedings of International Conference on Neural Networks (ICNN'97), vol. 3, pp. 1856–1861, Houston, TX, USA (1997). https://doi.org/10.1109/icnn.1997.614181
6. Pang, S.L., Gong, J.Z.: C.50 classification algorithm and its application on individual credit score for banks. Syst. Eng. Theor. Pract. **39**(12), 94–104 (2009)
7. Ho, T.K.: The random subspace method for constructing decision forests. IEEE Trans. Pattern Anal. Mach. Intell. **20**(8), 832–844 (1998). https://doi.org/10.1109/34.709601
8. Lin, C.-F., Wang, S.-D.: Fuzzy support vector machines. In: Learning and Soft Computing: Support Vector Machines, Neural Networks, and Fuzzy Logic Models, MITP (2001)
9. Ishikawa, M., Moriyama, T.: Prediction of time series by a structural learning of neural networks. Fuzzy Sets Syst. **85**(2), 167–176 (1996)
10. Shao, Y., Taff, G.N., Walsh, S.J.: Comparison of early stopping criteria for neural-network-based subpixel classification. In: IEEE Geoscience and Remote Sensing Letters, January 2011, vol. 8, no. 1, pp. 113–117. https://doi.org/10.1109/lgrs.2010.2052782

Cryptography and Information Security

A Secure User Authenticated Scheme in Intelligent Manufacturing System

Ming-Te Chen(ID), Hao-Yu Liu$^{(\boxtimes)}$, Chien-Hung Lai$^{(\boxtimes)}$, Wen-Shiang Wang$^{(\boxtimes)}$, and Chao-Yang Huang$^{(\boxtimes)}$

Department of Computer Science and Information Technology,
National Chin-Yi University of Technology, Taichung, Taiwan
`mtchen@ncut.edu.tw`, `qaz0921151415@gmail.com`, `azw987658p@gmail.com`,
`kevin22413180@gmail.com`, `jack373620@gmail.com`

Abstract. In recently years, intelligent manufacturing system is getting grown up. There are many manufacturing vendors that investigate to develop their intelligent manufacturing systems in their product line. Our government also promotes some cities of mid Taiwan to become intelligent cities in the future. However, we discover that there are no such stand cryptography modules or security modules in these systems and there are a lot of papers that indicated security problems in intelligent manufacturing system. When a legimate user attempts to login an intelligent manufacturing system, an attacker may pretend as a legal server to perform mutual authentication with this user. On one hand, the server also faced the same problem. That is called the men-in-the-middle problem. On the other hand, an attacker may lunch software to capture some users' login passwords. If a user's login password does not to be protected by security mechanisms of the intelligent manufacturing system, the attacker may login this system with captured passwords successfully and fetch secret data in advance. Besides, there are no such provable user authentication schemes for the intelligent manufacturing system in random oracle model. Due to above problems, we proposed a secure user authentication scheme for intelligent manufacturing system. Not only this scheme does not store each user's password in its database table, but also each user can change his/her own password after logging in successfully. Finally, we also give formal security proof in the random oracle model of the full version of this paper.

Keywords: Intelligent manufacturing system · Cryptography · Authentication · Random oracle model

1 Introduction

In recently years, there are many new research topics arising including Artificial Intelligence, Factory 4.0, Intelligent Manufacturing, Big Data and IOT. Some of them are getting hot in research area such as Artificial Intelligence. It can be used in medical area, industrial area, or other related areas. Besides, our government

© Springer Nature Singapore Pte Ltd. 2019
C.-Y. Chang et al. (Eds.): ICS 2018, CCIS 1013, pp. 543–549, 2019.
https://doi.org/10.1007/978-981-13-9190-3_60

also promotes new policies such as to transform some cities to become intelligent cities in the mid of Taiwan due to lots of cities in the mid of Taiwan that are manufacturing vendors located here. In these cities, among of them also import intelligent manufacturing systems into their product line to product their new products. However, these systems do not contain a standard security module or suitable user authentication mechanism. If an attacker pretends to be a legimate user and attempts to login in this system with captured random numbers or hash values without time period checking or revocation mechanism of users. Then he/she may login this system successfully by above captured information with non-neglible probability.

By the way, there are no such authentication schemes for intelligent manufacturing systems with fully security proof and also do not offer the mutual authentication to them. In order to solve these problems, we proposed a secure user authentication scheme for intelligent manufacturing system. Not only it could construct an efficient authenticated mechanism, but also give the formal security proof in the random oracle model. In the future, we will implement this proposed scheme to be the security mechanism for intelligent manufacturing system and also give the formal security proof in the full version of this paper.

2   Related Works and Security Definition

2.1   Related Works

In this section, we also survey some papers [1,16–19] and proposed a secure user authenticated scheme in intelligent manufacturing system [1]. By the way, these papers [16–19] described some security issues in intelligent manufacturing system. However, they could not provide a legimate user to change his/her password after authenticating with the system and also give the formal security proof among them. Besides, if an attacker replays some captured random values to pretend as some legimate users to the server, the server may accept this request to login without checking time period of these transmitted random values. It means that this scheme [1] does not provide forward security. In order to solve above problems, we proposed our secure user authenticated scheme with formal security proof.

2.2   Security Definition

In this proposed scheme, we give some security definitions as follows.

Definition 1. *Ind-cpa Secure*
In our scheme, we assume that our symmetric encryption/decryption algorithm is $\mathcal{SE} = (E_{pk_T}, D_{sk_T})$, where $T \in \{i, j\}$ and $i, j \in \{U, V\}$ and q_m and q_e are the number of the messages and the encryption queries, respectively. The attacker $\mathcal{A}$ can ask the encryption query on its chosen message (M_0, M_1). We assume that the encryption oracle is $E_{pk_T}(\cdot, \theta)$ with the security parameter θ and it takes M_b as the input in the following, where $b \in \{0, 1\}$. If $b = 1$, then $C \longleftarrow$

$E_{pk_T}(M_b, \theta)$. *Otherwise,* $C \longleftarrow E_{pk_T}(M_{1-b}, \theta)$ *and returns* C. *We consider the following experiment.*

$$Exp_{A,S\mathcal{E}}^{Ind-cpa-b}(\theta)$$
$$T \in \{i, j\}, \{M_0, M_1\} \longleftarrow \mathcal{A}^{E_{pk_{i,j}}(\cdot, \theta)}$$
$$b \in \{0, 1\}, C \longleftarrow E_{pk_T}(M_b, \theta)$$
$$b' \longleftarrow \mathcal{A}^{E_{pk_T}(\cdot, \theta)}(C, M_0, M_1)$$
$$Return\ b'.$$

The advantage function of an adversary $\mathcal{A}_{S\mathcal{E}}^{ind-cpa}(\theta)$ *is defined as* $Adv_{S\mathcal{E},\mathcal{A}}^{Ind-cpa}(\theta) = |Pr[Exp_{S\mathcal{E},\mathcal{A}}^{Ind-cpa-1}(\theta) = 1] - Pr[Exp_{S\mathcal{E},\mathcal{A}}^{Ind-cpa-0}(\theta) = 1]| < \varepsilon'$.

Theorem 1. *Assume* $S\mathcal{E}$ *is an Ind-cpa secure encryption scheme and* H_1 *and* H_2 *satisfy the random oracle assumptions. Our proposed user efficient authentication(UEA for short) is a secure user authentication scheme. In other words, if* $S\mathcal{E}$ *is* (t', ε') *ind-cpa secure, then*

$$Adv_{UEA}(\theta, t) \leq (I^2 q_s (Adv_{S\mathcal{E}}^{Ind-cpa}(\theta, t') + 1)),$$

where t' *is the maximum total experiment time including an adversary execution time,* I *is an upper bound on the number of parties, and* q_s *is an upper bound on the number of instances initiated in the experiment.*

3 The Proposed Scheme

The following is our proposed scheme and it contains three stages including the registration stage, the login stage and the password change stage.

3.1 Preliminary

In this subsection, we give some definitions in our proposed scheme and they are described as follows.

- U: The user attemps to authenticate with the intelligent manufacturing system server.
- V: The server in a intelligent manufacturing system would receive the registration of user, login request and password change requests.
- H_1: The hash function that it maps $Z_n^* \rightarrow \{0,1\}^*$ with collision-resistance.
- H_2: The hash function that it maps $Z_n^* \rightarrow \{0,1\}^*$ with collision-resistance.
- pw_U: The password was chosen in the first time registration and login verification usage for the user U.
- E_{pk_i}: The public key encryption function for the party's public key pk of i, where $i \in \{U, V\}$.
- D_{sk_i}: The public key decryption function for the party's secret key sk of i, where $j \in \{U, V\}$.
- t_i: The time period was chosen by the party $i \in \{U, V\}$ in order to prevent replay attack.
- r_i: The random value was chosen uniformly from Z_n^* by the party $i \in \{U, V\}$.

3.2   The Registration Phase

In this phase, a user U starts to registrate with a server called as V.

- First, U forwards his/her identity ID_U, public key pk_U, and certificate $cert_U$ to the server V.
- Then, after V receives these tuples, it could check the valid time period of $cert_U$ and U's certificate with public key pk_U. After checking certificate successfully, he/she prepares two hash functions that one is the H_1 and the other is the H_2, where $H_1 : Z_n^* \rightarrow \{0,1\}^*$ and $H_2 : Z_n^* \rightarrow \{0,1\}^*$.
- It also selects a password pw_U for the user U and computes the hash value $H_1(pw_U)$.
- Then, it encrypts $H_1(pw_U)$, forwards the result $E_{pk_U}(H_1(pw_U), pw_U)$ to the user U and finishes this stage.
- When the user U received the encryption text, he/she could decrypt it and check the validation of pw_U.
- After transmitting the password to the user U, V drops the password pw_U and stores the hash value $H_1(pw_U)$ in its table.

3.3   The Login Phase

When starting this login phase, a user U attemps to login this system and he/she performs the following steps.

- First, he/she prepares this authentication tuple $(ID_U, r_U, t_U, H_1(ID_U||r_U|| t_U))$ to the server V.
- After receiving this tuple from U, V verifies the each element with hash value $H_1(ID_U||r_U||t_U)$, where r_U is a random from Z_n^* and t_U is the valid time period in this login phase.
- After checking successfully, V chooses a random $r_V \in Z_n^*$ and computes $R_V = H_2(r_U + 1||H_1(r_V))$ and $R_V' = E_{pk_U}(H_1(pw_U) \cdot r_V \cdot t_V^{-1})$ with time period t_V.
- Finally, it drops the random value r_V and forwards (R_V, R_V', t_V) to the user U.
- When U receives this tuple, he/she could decrypt this cyphertext and obtains his/her own password hash value $H_1(pw_U) \cdot r_V \cdot t_V^{-1}$ from R_V' and let $H_1(pw_U) \cdot r_V \cdot t_V^{-1}$ as R_V''. Finally, he/she obtains the r_V from $R_V'' \cdot H_1(pw_U)^{-1} \cdot t_V = r_V$.
- In the next step, he/she checks the challenge $H_1(r_V)$ with r_V and also makes sure the following equation is valid or not.

$$R_V \overset{?}{=} H_2(r_U + 1||H_1(r_V)) \tag{1}$$

- After verifying it successfully, the user U computes $R_V^* = E_{pkv}(H_2(r_V + 1||H_1(pw_U)) \cdot t_V^{-1})$ and forwards R_V^* to the server V.
- When V received this tuple, it decryptes R_V^* with private key and computes $H_2(r_V + 1||H_1(pw_U))$. If above values are valid, the server accepted this authentication successfully and finished this phase with the user U.

3.4 The Password Changing Phase

In this phase, the server could allow user to change his/her password in a secure channel after above login successfully.

- First, a user U selects a new hash password value $H_1(pw_U')$ with his/her new own password pw_U' and computes $P_U = H_2(H_1(pw_U)\|H_1(pw_U'))$. Then the user drops his/her new password pw_U' after above hash value has computed.
- Then, he/she forwards $(H_1(pw_U'), P_U)$ to the server V.
- V uses P_U to verify user's old password $H_1(pw_U)$ and stores new password $H_1(pw_U')$ in the password table after both verification successfully.

4 Security Analysis

In this section, we provide security analysis and functional analysis about our proposed scheme.

4.1 Password Collision-Resistance

In our proposed scheme, the server only stores the hash value of each user's password. If an attacker obtains this hash value, he/she must have the neglible probability to guess the real password value from this hash value. I.e., he/she has to create a hash value to against the collision-resistence of our hash function with non-neglible advantage probability. We will provide full security proof in our full version of paper.

4.2 Without Password Reservation

In this proposed scheme, a user could change his/her old password after he/she performs login phase successfully. By the way, the server side only stores the hash value of password and drops this selected password after login successfully. So if an attacker gets some hash values, then he/she is not able to guess the real passwords as mentioned above with non-neglible probability in random oracle model.

4.3 Mutual Authentication

In our proposed scheme, the user U can register with the server V. Then the server V can verify his/her identity with $H_1(pw_U)$ in the third step of login phase. On the other hand, the user U can verify identity of server V's R_V' with R_V and t_V by decrypting R_V'. During the login phase, both side have to decrypt the ciphertext by their secret keys. It means that only the corresponding party would decrypt the ciphertext by his/her own private key.

4.4 Replay Attack Resistance

In this proposed scheme, we adopted the random value and timestamp value as our authentication message. If an attacker that he/she could capture authentication tuples during protocol and attemps to replay message to the server V. Then, the server V will check this message with time period t_U that it was used before in some transaction by some user. Hence, the server will deny this authentication request if the t_U was used before and it would log this record as the replay attack.

5 Conclusions

In this proposed scheme, we offer a secure authentication scheme for users to authenticate with the intelligent manufacturing system. Not only our scheme could against the replay attack with timestamp parameters to prevent replay attacks, but also it provides the mutual authentication with both sides with security proof in full version of this paper. In the future, it will be our goal to implement this proposed scheme and also construct more applications for intelligent manufacturing systems.

References

1. Sohn, Y., Cho, M., On, G., Chae, K.: A secure user authentication method in networked intelligent manufacturing systems. In: Proceedings of International Conference on Cyberworlds (CW 2005), pp. 122–129 (2005)
2. Fan, C.I., Ho, P.H., Hsu, R.H.: Provably secure nested one-time secret mechanisms for fast mutual authentication and key exchange in mobile communications. IEEE/ACM Trans. Networking **18**(3), 996–1009 (2010)
3. Bellare, M., Rogaway, P.: Entity authentication and key distribution. In: Stinson, D.R. (ed.) CRYPTO 1993. LNCS, vol. 773, pp. 232–249. Springer, Heidelberg (1994). https://doi.org/10.1007/3-540-48329-2_21
4. Bellare, M., Canetti, R., Krawczyk, H.: A modular approach to the design and analysis of authentication and key-exchange protocols. In: Proceedings of the Thirtieth Annual ACM Symposium on Theory of Computing, pp. 419–428 (1998)
5. Fan, C.I., Chan, Y.C., Zhang, Z.K.: Robust remote authentication scheme with smart cards. Comput. Secur. **24**(8), 619–628 (2005)
6. Juang, W.S., Wu, J.L.: Two efficient two-factor authenticated key exchange protocols in public wireless LANs. Comput. Electr. Eng. **35**(1), 33–40 (2009)
7. Fan, C.I., Lin, Y.H.: Provably secure remote truly three-factor authentication schemes with privacy protection on biometrics. IEEE Trans. Inf. Forensics Secur. **4**(4), 933–945 (2009)
8. Al-Riyami, S.S., Paterson, K.G.: Certificateless public key cryptography. In: Laih, C.-S. (ed.) ASIACRYPT 2003. LNCS, vol. 2894, pp. 452–473. Springer, Heidelberg (2003). https://doi.org/10.1007/978-3-540-40061-5_29
9. Girault, M.: Self-certified public keys. In: Davies, D.W. (ed.) EUROCRYPT 1991. LNCS, vol. 547, pp. 490–497. Springer, Heidelberg (1991). https://doi.org/10.1007/3-540-46416-6_42

10. Hu, B.C., Wong, D.S., Zhang, Z., Deng, X.: Certificateless signature: a new security model and an improved generic construction. Des. Codes Crypt. **42**(2), 109–126 (2007)
11. Shamir, A.: Identity-based cryptosystems and signature schemes. In: Blakley, G.R., Chaum, D. (eds.) CRYPTO 1984. LNCS, vol. 196, pp. 47–53. Springer, Heidelberg (1985). https://doi.org/10.1007/3-540-39568-7_5
12. Boneh, D., Franklin, M.: Identity-based encryption from the weil pairing. In: Kilian, J. (ed.) CRYPTO 2001. LNCS, vol. 2139, pp. 213–229. Springer, Heidelberg (2001). https://doi.org/10.1007/3-540-44647-8_13
13. Juels, A., Kaliski, B.S.: PORs: proofs of retrievability for large files. In: Proceedings of CCS 2007, pp. 584–597 (2007)
14. Shacham, H., Waters, B.: Compact proofs of retrievability. In: Pieprzyk, J. (ed.) ASIACRYPT 2008. LNCS, vol. 5350, pp. 90–107. Springer, Heidelberg (2008). https://doi.org/10.1007/978-3-540-89255-7_7
15. Mell, P., Grance, T.: Effectively and securely using the cloud computing paradigm. In: NIST (2009)
16. Morariu, C., Morariu, O., Borangiu, T.: Security issues in service oriented manufacturing architectures with distributed intelligence. In: Borangiu, T., Trentesaux, D., Thomas, A., McFarlane, D. (eds.) Service Orientation in Holonic and Multi-Agent Manufacturing. SCI, vol. 640, pp. 243–263. Springer, Cham (2016). https://doi.org/10.1007/978-3-319-30337-6_23
17. Chhetri, S.R., Rashid, N., Faezi, S., Al. Faruque, M.A.: Security trends and advances in manufacturing systems in the era of industry 4.0. In: Proceedings of IEEE/ACM International Conference on Computer-Aided Design (ICCAD), pp. 1039–1046 (2017)
18. Zhang, H., Nian, P., Chen, Y.: Intelligent manufacturing: the core leads industrial change in the future. In: Proceedings of 4th International Conference on Industrial Economics System and Industrial Security Engineering (IEIS), pp. 1–5 (2017)
19. Liu, Z., Liu, J.: Reliability evaluation of intelligent manufacturing equipment. In: Proceedings of 11th International Conference on Natural Computation (ICNC), pp. 108–112 (2015)

On Delegatability of a Certificateless Strong Designated Verifier Signature Scheme

Han-Yu Lin$^{(\boxtimes)}$ (iD), Chia-Hung Wu, and Yan-Ru Jiang

Department of Computer Science and Engineering,
National Taiwan Ocean University, Keelung 202, Taiwan
hanyu@mail.ntou.edu.tw

Abstract. A strong designated verifier signature (SDVS) is a special variant of digital signatures, since it only allows a designated recipient to verify the signer's signature. The transcript simulation property of such signatures also prohibits a designated verifier from arbitrarily transferring his/her conviction to any third party. When implemented in certificateless cryptosystems, a certificateless SDVS is unnecessary to manage public key certificates and deal with the key-escrow problem of conventional identity-based systems. In 2014, Shim pointed out a crucial security property called non-delegatability for SDVS schemes. This property states that anyone should not be able to generate a valid SDVS without obtaining either the signer's or the verifier's private key. In other worlds, a non-delegatable SDVS scheme must ensure that any malicious adversary cannot forge a valid signature even if he/she has gotten the shared secret value between a signer and an intended verifier. In this paper, we first demonstrate that a previously proposed efficient certificateless SDVS scheme is vulnerable to the delegatability attack and then further propose an improved variant.

Keywords: Delegatability · Certificateless · Strong designated verifier · Cryptanalysis · Digital signature

1 Introduction

A traditional digital signature scheme allows a signer to produce a valid signature with his/her private key such that anyone can verify the resulted signature with the signer's corresponding public key. To further control the capability of verifying a signature, Chaum and Antwerpen [2] proposed the so-called undeniable signature. In such schemes, a verifier must cooperate with the original signer to validate a given signature. Without the agreement of original signers, no recipient can perform the verification process solely. However, if a repudiated signer is unwilling to assist the recipient, the signature verification process cannot be carried out.

The notion of designated verifier proof was first addressed by Jakobsson *et al.* [12]. The idea of designated verifier signature (DVS) is to enable anyone to solely verify a given signature, yet only an intended recipient will be convinced of its authenticity. This is owing to the unique property of signer ambiguity for DVS schemes, i.e., a designated recipient is able to create a computationally indistinguishable transcript for himself.

© Springer Nature Singapore Pte Ltd. 2019
C.-Y. Chang et al. (Eds.): ICS 2018, CCIS 1013, pp. 550–558, 2019.
https://doi.org/10.1007/978-981-13-9190-3_61

Saeednia *et al.* [16] further added the designated verifier's private key into the signature verification process and hence transformed DVS into strong DVS (SDVS). It is obvious that without the designated verifier's private key, no one can verify a given SDVS. Combined with identity-based cryptography, Susilo *et al.* [18] put forward an ID-based SDVS scheme. In an ID-based system [17], a system authority (SA) is responsible for computing each user's private key from his/her public identifier which is also viewed as the corresponding public key. The key-escrow problem is a major drawback of this system, because a malicious SA can impersonate any legitimate user without being detected.

Integrated with message recovery techniques, Lee and Chang [14] presented SDVS schemes which allow a designated verifier to recover the original message from its signature. This helps with the reduction of communication overheads. Nevertheless, some extra computation efforts are still incurred for extracting the original message. Considering the bilinear pairing groups from elliptic curves, Kang *et al.* [13] proposed a new SDVS scheme based on ID-based systems. According to their evaluation, they claimed that the proposed approach exhibits better efficiency in terms of computational complexity and signature lengths. Unfortunately, Hsu and Lin [9] later showed that Kang *et al.*'s work cannot resist the universal forgery attack which means that a malicious adversary who leans nothing about the signer's private key can successfully derive a forged SDVS satisfying the signature verification equality. Using the hardness of discrete logarithm problems (DLP) [5], Lin *et al.* [15] realized a provably secure SDVS mechanism in the random oracle model.

In 2003, Al-Riyami and Paterson [1] introduced certificateless public key cryptography in which each user owns a partial private key and a secret value. The former is issued by the SA whereas the latter is chosen by the user himself. It can be seen that the SA only controls the partial private key of each user. Based on different computational assumptions, Huang *et al.* [10] and the Du-Wen [6] separately addressed certificateless strong designated verifier signature (CL-SDVS) mechanisms. However, Fan *et al.* [7] later found out that the work [6] presented by Du and Wen is vulnerable to known active attacks. So far, lots of CL-SDVS schemes [3, 4, 8, 11, 19] have been proposed.

In 2014, Shim [20] came up with an important property called non-delegatability for SDVS schemes. This property states that anyone should not be able to generate a valid SDVS without obtaining either the signer's or the verifier's private key. In other worlds, a non-delegatable SDVS scheme must ensure that any malicious adversary cannot forge a valid signature even if he/she has gotten the shared secret value between a signer and an intended verifier. In this paper, we will show that a previously proposed efficient CL-SDVS scheme by Yang *et al.* [21] could not withstand the delegatability attack. Specifically, a type-II adversary who acts as a malicious SA obtaining a shared secret between a signer and a designated verifier is capable of forging a valid signature. Additionally, we will introduce a secure variant by amending Yang *et al.*'s algorithms.

The rest of this paper is organized as follows. We will describe some mathematical backgrounds and computational assumptions in Sect. 2. The construction of Yang *et al.*'s work is briefly reviewed in Sect. 3. Section 4 first demonstrates the security flaw of Yang *et al.*'s scheme and then introduces our improved variant. Finally, a conclusion with the significance of this paper is given in Sect. 5.

2 Preliminaries

We describe some related mathematical backgrounds and computational assumptions as follows:

Bilinear Pairing
Let the notations of $(G_1, +)$ and $(G_2, \times)$ separately be an additive and a multiplicative group of the same prime order q and e: $G_1 \times G_1 \rightarrow G_2$ a bilinear map having the following properties:

Bilinearity:

$$e(P_a + P_b, Q) = e(P_a, Q)e(P_b, Q);$$

$$e(P, Q_a + Q_b) = e(P, Q_a)e(P, Q_b);$$

Non-degeneracy:
If P is a generator of G_1, then $e(P, P)$ is a generator of G_2.
Computability:
Given $P_a, P_b \in G_1$, the value of $e(P_a, P_b)$ can be efficiently computed by a polynomial-time algorithm.

Bilinear Diffie-Hellman Problem; BDHP
Given $P, aP, bP, cP \in G_1$ for some unknown $a, b, c \in Z_q{}^*$, the BDHP is to compute $e(P, P)^{abc} \in G_2$.

Bilinear Diffie-Hellman (BDH) Assumption
For every probabilistic polynomial-time algorithm $\mathcal{A}$, every positive polynomial $D(\cdot)$ and all sufficiently large k, the algorithm $\mathcal{A}$ can solve the BDHP with an advantage of at most $1/D(k)$, i.e.,

$$\Pr[\mathcal{A}(P, aP, bP, cP) = e(P, P)^{abc}; a, b, c \leftarrow Z_q^*, (P, aP, bP, cP) \leftarrow G_1{}^4] \leqslant 1/D(k).$$

The probability is taken over the uniformly and independently chosen instance and over the random choices of $\mathcal{A}$.

Definition 1. *The (t, ε)-BDH assumption holds if there is no polynomial-time adversary that can solve the BDHP in time at most t and with an advantage ε.*

3 Review of Yang *et al.*'s Scheme [21]

We briefly review the construction of Yang *et al.*'s work in this section. Their CL-SDVS scheme can be divided into six phases described as follows:

Setup: Taking a security parameter k as input, the Key Generation Center (KGC) will generate a master private key $s \in Z_q^*$ along with some public parameters $\{G_1, G_2, q, P,$

P_0, e, H_1, H_2} where $P_0 = sP$ is KGC's public key and (H_1, H_2) are two collision-resistant hash functions defined below:

$$H_1 : \{0,1\}^* \rightarrow G_1,$$
$$H_2 : \{0,1\}^* \times G_1^3 \rightarrow Z_q^*.$$

Partial-Private-Key-Extract: Given public parameters and a user identity ID_i, the KGC first chooses $r_i \in Z_q^*$ and then computes

$$Q_i = H_1(ID_i), \tag{1}$$

$$d_i = sQ_i. \tag{2}$$

The value d_i is the partial private key of ID_i and will be sent back via a secure channel.

User-Key-Extract: Given public parameters and a user identity ID_i, this algorithm first chooses a random number $x_i \in Z_q^*$ and computes

$$P_i = x_iP. \tag{3}$$

The values of x_i and P_i are the secret value and public key for ID_i, respectively.

CLSDVS-Sign: Let ID_A and ID_B be a signer and a designated verifier, respectively. To generate a CL-SDVS on the message m, ID_A first chooses $r \in_R Z_q^*$ and computes

$$U = rP, \tag{4}$$

$$h = H_2(m, U, P_A, x_AP_B), \tag{5}$$

$$V = rP_0 + hd_A, \tag{6}$$

$$T = e(V, Q_B). \tag{7}$$

Then, the computed CL-SDVS on the message m intended for ID_B is (U, T).

CLSDVS-Verify: Upon receiving m and its CL-SDVS (U, T), ID_B will perform the CLSDVS-Verify algorithm. First, ID_B computes

$$h' = H_2(m, U, P_A, x_BP_A), \tag{8}$$

and then checks if the following equality holds or not.

$$T = e(U + h'Q_A, d_B). \tag{9}$$

We show the correctness of Eq. (9). From Eq. (7), we have

$$
\begin{aligned}
T &= e(V, Q_B) &&\text{(by Eq. (7))}\\
&= e(rP_0 + hd_A, Q_B) &&\text{(by Eq. (6))}\\
&= e(rsP + H_2(m, U, P_A, x_A P_B)d_A, Q_B) &&\text{(by Eq. (5))}\\
&= e(rsP + H_2(m, U, P_A, x_A P_B)sQ_A, Q_B) &&\text{(by Eq. (2))}\\
&= e(rP + H_2(m, U, P_A, x_A P_B)Q_A, sQ_B)\\
&= e(rP + H_2(m, U, P_A, x_B P_A)Q_A, d_B)\\
&= e(rP + h'Q_A, d_B) &&\text{(by Eq. (8))}\\
&= e(U + h'Q_A, d_B) &&\text{(by Eq. (4))}
\end{aligned}
$$

CLSDVS-Simulation: The designated verifier ID_B can perform this algorithm to generate a valid transcript for himself. Given public parameters, a signer's identity ID_A, the signer's public key P_A and a message m, ID_B first chooses $r' \in_R Z_q^*$ and computes

$$
U' = r'P, \tag{10}
$$

$$
h' = H_2(m, U', P_A, x_B P_A), \tag{11}
$$

$$
T' = e(U' + h'Q_A, d_B). \tag{12}
$$

Here, (U', T') is a valid transcript on the message m designated for ID_B.

4 Security Flaw and Improvement

In this section, we will first demonstrate that the construction of Yang *et al.*'s work is delegatable, i.e., a type-II adversary is able to forge a valid CL-SDVS using a shared secret between the signer and the designated verifier. Then we further propose a secure variant by amending Yang *et al.*'s scheme.

4.1 Security Flaw of Yang *et al.*'s Scheme

In a certificateless cryptographic mechanism, we have to consider type-I and type-II adversaries. The former is able to replace legitimate users' public keys whereas the latter acts as a malicious KGC and thus can obtain users' partial private keys. According to the definition of non-delegatability introduced by Shim [20], any adversary obtaining shared secrets still cannot forge a valid CL-SDVS. Nevertheless, in Yang *et al.*'s scheme, suppose that a type-II adversary $\mathcal{A}$ who controls the partial private key d_A and further gets the shared secret $x_A P_B$. Then he can forge a CL-SDVS on an arbitrarily chosen message m' by computing

$$
U' = r'P \text{ where } r' \in_R Z_q^*, \tag{13}
$$

$$
h' = H_2(m', U, P_A, x_A P_B), \tag{14}
$$

$$V' = r'P_0 + h'd_A, \tag{15}$$

$$T' = e(V', Q_B). \tag{16}$$

It is clear that the forged (U', T') would be a valid CL-SDVS on the message m' intended for ID_B. Therefore, we claim that Yang $et\ al.$'s scheme is vulnerable to delegatability attacks under type-II adversaries.

4.2 Improved Variant

In this subsection, we introduce a modified variant based on Yang $et\ al.$'s construction. Since the Setup, Partial-Private-Key-Extract and User-Key-Extract phases are unmodified, we only present the other improved phases as follows:

CLSDVS-Sign: Let ID_A and ID_B be a signer and a designated verifier, respectively. To generate a CL-SDVS on the message m, ID_A first chooses $r, w \in_R Z_q^*$ and computes

$$l = w - x_A \bmod q, \tag{17}$$

$$U = rP, \tag{18}$$

$$h = H_2(m, U, P_A, x_A P_B, w P_B), \tag{19}$$

$$V = rP_0 + hd_A, \tag{20}$$

$$T = e(V, Q_B). \tag{21}$$

Then, the computed CL-SDVS on the message m intended for ID_B is $(l,\ U,\ T)$.

CLSDVS-Verify: Upon receiving m and its CL-SDVS $(l,\ U,\ T)$, ID_B will perform the CLSDVS-Verify algorithm. First, ID_B computes

$$W = lP + P_A, \tag{22}$$

$$h' = H_2(m, U, P_A, x_B P_A, x_B W), \tag{23}$$

and then checks if the following equality holds or not.

$$T = e(U + h'Q_A, d_B). \tag{24}$$

We show the correctness of Eq. (24). From Eq. (21), we have

$$
\begin{aligned}
T &= e(V, Q_B) && \text{(by Eq.\,(21))} \\
&= e(rP_0 + hd_A, Q_B) && \text{(by Eq.\,(20))} \\
&= e(rsP + H_2(m, U, P_A, x_A P_B, w P_B)d_A, Q_B) && \text{(by Eq.\,(19))} \\
&= e(rsP + H_2(m, U, P_A, x_A P_B, w P_B)sQ_A, Q_B) && \text{(by Eq.\,(2))} \\
&= e(rP + H_2(m, U, P_A, x_A P_B, w P_B)Q_A, sQ_B) && \\
&= e(rP + H_2(m, U, P_A, x_A P_B, (l + x_A)P_B)Q_A, sQ_B) && \text{(by Eq.\,(17))}
\end{aligned}
$$

$$= e(rP + H_2(m, U, P_A, x_A P_B, x_B(lP + P_A))Q_A, sQ_B)$$
$$= e(rP + H_2(m, U, P_A, x_A P_B, x_B W)Q_A, sQ_B) \qquad \text{(by Eq. (22))}$$
$$= e(rP + H_2(m, U, P_A, x_B P_A, x_B W)Q_A, d_B)$$
$$= e(rP + h'Q_A, d_B) \qquad \text{(by Eq. (23))}$$
$$= e(U + h'Q_A, d_B) \qquad \text{(by Eq. (18))}$$

CLSDVS-Simulation: The designated verifier ID_B can perform this algorithm to generate a valid transcript for himself. Given public parameters, a signer's identity ID_A, the signer's public key P_A and a message m, ID_B first chooses $r', l' \in_R Z_q^*$ and computes

$$W' = l'P + P_A, \qquad (25)$$

$$U' = r'P, \qquad (26)$$

$$h' = H_2(m, U', P_A, x_B P_A, x_B W'), \qquad (27)$$

$$T' = e(U' + h'Q_A, d_B). \qquad (28)$$

Here, (l', U', T') is a valid transcript on the message m designated for ID_B.

4.3 Security Analysis

As our improved variant is directly modified from Yang et al.'s construction, we will omit complete security proofs here. Interested readers can refer their literature for more details. We only show that the proposed variant is non-delegatable against the type-II adversary as Theorem 1.

Theorem 1. *The improved CL-SDVS variant is non-delegatable against the type-II adversary.*

Proof: Assume that a type-II adversary $\mathcal{A}$ attempts to forge a valid CLSDVS in our improved variant after obtaining the shared secret $x_A P_B$. According to our CLSDVS-Sign algorithm, he can easily derive the parameters of (U, h, V, T) by utilizing Eqs. (18) to (21). However, a valid CL-SDVS of our scheme must contain another valid parameter l which is derived from the signer's secret value x_A. Without having the knowledge of this information, the adversary $\mathcal{A}$ cannot make it. Still, if the adversary $\mathcal{A}$ tries to derive the secret value x_A from obtained shared secret $x_A P_B$, he will also be frustrated by the intractable elliptic curve discrete logarithm problem (ECDLP). Consequently, we claim that our improved CL-SDVS construction satisfies the property of non-delegatability.

5 Conclusions

Cryptographic mechanisms implemented on certificateless public key systems have been received much attention for recent years. In this paper, we focused on the significance of non-delegatability property for CL-SDVS schemes and showed that a previous construction introduced by Yang *et al.* could not fulfill such security requirement under the type-II adversary. Furthermore, we also propose a secure variant by adding an extra parameter into the signature generation algorithm. Although the computational cost is slightly increased, we believe that it is a worthy tradeoff for strengthened security level and the increased computation efforts are affordable in practical implementation.

Acknowledgement. This work was supported in part by the Ministry of Science and Technology of Republic of China under the contract number MOST 107-2221-E-019-017.

References

1. Al-Riyami, S.S., Paterson, K.G.: Certificateless public key cryptography. In: Laih, C.-S. (ed.) ASIACRYPT 2003. LNCS, vol. 2894, pp. 452–473. Springer, Heidelberg (2003). https://doi.org/10.1007/978-3-540-40061-5_29

2. Chaum, D., van Antwerpen, H.: Undeniable signatures. In: Brassard, G. (ed.) CRYPTO 1989. LNCS, vol. 435, pp. 212–216. Springer, New York (1990). https://doi.org/10.1007/0-387-34805-0_20

3. Chen, Y., Zhao, Y., Xiong, H., Yue, F.: A certificateless strong designated verifier signature scheme with non-delegatability. Int. J. Netw. Secur. **19**(4), 573–582 (2017)

4. Choi, K.Y., Park, J.H., Lee, D.H.: A new provably secure certificateless short signature scheme. Comput. Math Appl. **61**(7), 1760–1768 (2011)

5. Diffie, W., Hellman, M.: New directions in cryptography. IEEE Trans. Inf. Theor. **IT-22**(6), 644–654 (1976)

6. Du, H., Wen, Q.: Efficient and provably-secure certificateless short signature scheme from bilinear pairings. Cryptology ePrint Archive, 2007/250 (2007). http://eprint.iacr.org/2007/250

7. Fan, C.I., Hsu, R.H., Ho, P.H.: Cryptanalysis on Du-Wen certificateless short signature scheme. In: Proceedings of the Fourth Joint Workshop on Information Security (JWIS 2009), pp. 1–7 (2009)

8. He, D., Chen, J.: An efficient certificateless designated verifier signature scheme. Int. Arab J. Inf. Technol. **10**(4), 389–396 (2013)

9. Hsu, C.L., Lin, H.Y.: Universal forgery attack on a strong designated verifier signature scheme. Int. Arab J. Inf. Technol. **11**(5), 425–428 (2014)

10. Huang, X., Susilo, W., Mu, Y., Zhang, F.: Certificateless designated verifier signature schemes. In: Proceedings of the IEEE 20th International Conference on Advanced Information Networking and Applications (AINA 2006), vol. 2, pp. 15–19 (2006)

11. Islam, S.K.H., Biswas, G.P.: Provably secure certificateless strong designated verifier signature scheme based on elliptic curve bilinear pairings. J. King Saud Univ. Comput. Info. Sci. **25**(1), 51–61 (2013)

12. Jakobsson, M., Sako, K., Impagliazzo, R.: Designated verifier proofs and their applications. In: Maurer, U. (ed.) EUROCRYPT 1996. LNCS, vol. 1070, pp. 143–154. Springer, Heidelberg (1996). https://doi.org/10.1007/3-540-68339-9_13

13. Kang, B., Boyd, C., Dawson, E.: A novel identity-based strong designated verifier signature scheme. J. Syst. Softw. **82**(2), 270–273 (2009)

14. Lee, J.S., Chang, J.H.: Strong designated verifier signature scheme with message recovery. In: The 9th International Conference on Advanced Communication Technology, vol. 1, pp. 801–803 (2007)

15. Lin, H.Y., Wu, T.S., Yeh, Y.S.: A DL based short strong designated verifier signature scheme with low computation. J. Inf. Sci. Eng. **27**(2), 451–463 (2011)
16. Saeednia, S., Kremer, S., Markowitch, O.: An efficient strong designated verifier signature scheme. In: Lim, J.-I., Lee, D.-H. (eds.) ICISC 2003. LNCS, vol. 2971, pp. 40–54. Springer, Heidelberg (2004). https://doi.org/10.1007/978-3-540-24691-6_4
17. Shamir, A.: Identity-based cryptosystems and signature schemes. In: Blakley, G.R., Chaum, D. (eds.) CRYPTO 1984. LNCS, vol. 196, pp. 47–53. Springer, Heidelberg (1985). https://doi.org/10.1007/3-540-39568-7_5
18. Susilo, W., Zhang, F., Mu, Y.: Identity-based strong designated verifier signature schemes. In: Wang, H., Pieprzyk, J., Varadharajan, V. (eds.) ACISP 2004. LNCS, vol. 3108, pp. 313–324. Springer, Heidelberg (2004). https://doi.org/10.1007/978-3-540-27800-9_27
19. Tian, M., Huang, L., Yang, W.: On the security of a certificateless short signature scheme. Cryptology ePrint Archive, 2011/418 (2011). http://eprint.iacr.org/2011/419
20. Shim, K.A.: On delegatability of designated verifier signature schemes. Inf. Sci. **281**(10), 365–372 (2014)
21. Yang, B., Hu, Z., Xiao, Z.: Efficient certificateless strong designated verifier signature scheme. In: Proceedings of International Conference on Computational Intelligence and Security (CIS 2009), vol. 1, pp. 432–436 (2009)

Dynamic Key Management Scheme in IoT

Po-Wen Chi[1]($\boxtimes$) and Ming-Hung Wang[2]

[1] Department of Computer Science and Information Engineering,
National Taiwan Normal University, Taipei, Taiwan, R.O.C.
`neokent@gapps.ntnu.edu.tw`
[2] Department of Information Engineering and Computer Science,
Feng Chia University, Taichung, Taiwan, R.O.C.
`mhwang@fcu.edu.tw`

Abstract. While IoT becomes more and more popular, security becomes an important issue when IoT deployment. Considering there are lot of mobile device, it is frequent for member joining and leaving. Therefore, traditional key agreement schemes are not suitable for dynamic IoT environments. In this paper, we propose a dynamic key management scheme to avoid key update overhead when membership changing.

Keywords: Internet of Things (IoT) · Group key management

1 Introduction

IoT (Internet of Things) has enabled a large number of connected devices to communicate with each other inside a private network, e.g., factory, farm, school, etc. These devices transit sensor records, machine status, and even sensitive data. Thus, security issues raised in communication between devices have become crucial and need to be addressed. Currently, many systems have leveraged the public key infrastructure to achieve a secure data transmission. However, in a private IoT, the computation power may be insufficient to support the key management of such a large number of individual machines with different keys. Moreover, there are more and more wearable devices and these devices move around with people. So we need a new key management scheme to support the dynamic member environment.

In this study, we propose to a dynamic key management scheme for IoT. We divide sensors into three groups. One group is for mobile sensors and other two groups are for static sensors. The difference between these two static sensors is their computational power. For example, when a traveler checks in a hotel, he may get a lightweight device which can access other hotel facilities. The device belongs to the first group. When the user enters a room, the device can access other room's field agents through a control unit. The control unit belongs to group 2 and field agents belong to group 3. In this paper, we move most heavy computational works to the static and powerful node to support other

© Springer Nature Singapore Pte Ltd. 2019
C.-Y. Chang et al. (Eds.): ICS 2018, CCIS 1013, pp. 559–566, 2019.
https://doi.org/10.1007/978-981-13-9190-3_62

power constrained nodes' membership changing. We show that this scheme can decrease key update requirements even under frequent group 1 node handover events.

2 Background and Related Work

In this section, we briefly introduce the background techniques used in our scheme and some related works in this topic.

2.1 Blom's Key Pre-distribution Scheme [3]

Blom proposed a key pre-distribution scheme that allows any two nodes to find a secret key between them. Given total n nodes, one node does not require to store $n-1$ keys for other nodes. Instead, the node only takes $O(\lambda)$ memory space where λ is much smaller than n. The trade-off is that Blom's scheme is not fully resilient against the node capture attack. If an attacker compromises more than λ modes, the attacker can crack the system can get the pairwise key between any two nodes. This is called λ-secure. Blom's key pre-distribution scheme includes three phases which are briefly introduced as follows.

1. **Environment Setup.** Given total node number n, the trusted authority, which will be called **key server** later, first creates a generating matrix G of size $(\lambda + 1) \times n$. λ is a security parameter described above. This matrix G is public information. Any $\lambda+1$ columns of G must be linearly independent. This can be done through a Vandermonde matrix[1]. The key server first selects a prime q where $q > n$ and then randomly picks a primitive element s of $GF(q)$ to generate the matrix.
2. **Key Space Setup.** The key server randomly generates a symmetric matrix D of size $(\lambda + 1) \times (\lambda + 1)$ over $GF(q)$. D is kept secret and is not disclosed to any nodes. The key server calculates $A = (D \cdot G)^T$. For a node i, the key server distributes i-th row of A to the node.
3. **Pairwise Key Agreement.** Suppose node i and node j want to come out a pairwise secret key. Since D is symmetric, we can show that $A \cdot G$ is also symmetric. The proof is as follows.

$$A \cdot G = (D \cdot G)^T \cdot G = G^T \cdot D^T \cdot G = G^T \cdot D \cdot G = G^T \cdot A^T = (A \cdot G)^T.$$

Node i calculates $k_{i,j}$, which indicates the element located on i-th row and j-th column of the matrix $A \cdot G$. Note that node i can derive $k_{i,j}$ with i-th row of A. Node j calculates $k_{j,i}$ of $A \cdot G$ similarly. Since $A \cdot G$ is a symmetric matrix, we can have $k_{i,j} = k_{j,i}$ and therefore $k_{i,j}$ can be used as the pairwise key.

---

[1] In Blom's work, it is not required to use a Vandermonde matrix. Here we use the Vandermonde matrix for convenience and the storage issue.

In 2005, Du et al. applied this idea with a random key distribution idea to build a sensor key management scheme [4]. In this paper, we base Blom's key pre-distribution work to build a dynamic key management scheme for IoT. Because of the dynamic characteristic in IoT, λ-security is not acceptable. So we enhance Blom's work to support more than λ changes in IoT.

2.2   Related Works

There are lots of works regarding secure and efficient key management in IoT and sensor networks. When considering the membership changing issue, most researchers use group key management to update keys efficiently. Logical Key Hierarchy (LKH) [5] is one of the most common group key management scheme. LKH uses a tree structure to represent users and their own keys. The update process takes $O(\log n)$ messages for n users. One way function tree is another efficient group key management scheme based on the tree architecture [2]. Park et al. proposed a group key management based on Chinese Remainder Theorem so that one encryption key can be used for multiple decryption keys [6]. Abdmeziem et al. separate devices into several groups to reduce key update overhead [1]. Veltri et al. decrease membership changing overhead through time partitioning techniques [7].

Unlike the above techniques, in this paper we drop the group key idea and use dynamic key generation concept for applying dynamic IoT environments. So in our scheme, the key update process is not necessary.

3   Proposed Scheme

In this section, we will introduce our scheme and show how it works when handling membership changes. First, we give an overview of the proposed scheme. Then we introduce the attack model. In Sect. 3.3, we show how the dynamic key agreement works. Finally, we use the dynamic key agreement approach to build a IoT key management system.

3.1   Overview

Our proposed scheme is a two-tier key management architecture with three different roles, **user**, **broker** and **device**. The user is an entity that will move around and handover between brokers. The broker is an entity that is located in a fixed-position and will not join or leave the system. The broker is in charge of forwarding data between users and devices. Here the broker is semi-trusted which implies the broker cannot read the content of packets that it relays. The device is an entity that is also on a fixed position and belongs to some broker. When a user wants to communicate with a device, the user needs to transfer data to the broker first and the broker then sends data to the device. Each device belongs to different functional group, like the temperature sensor, the humidity sensor, the door lock, the IP camera and so on. All entities have their own unique identity in their role groups. There is an additional entity called **Key Distribution Center (KDC)** which is in charge of key management. The overall system model is shown in Fig. 1.

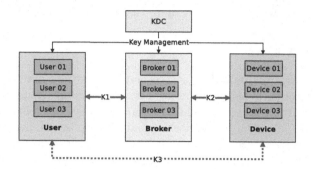

Fig. 1. System model.

In this model, there are three pairwise keys, K_1, K_2, K_3. They are used to protect the communication channels between the user and the broker, the broker and the device and the user and the device respectively. The dotted line in Fig. 1 implies the logical channel. When sending data to some device, the user will encrypt data through K_1 and K_3 and send the cipher to the broker. The broker then decrypts the cipher with K_1, re-encrypts with K_2 and forwards the new cipher to the device. The device finally derives data after decryption with K_2 and K_3.

Note that in this paper, the user also includes mobile devices, like wearable sensors.

3.2 Attacker Model

The attacker's goal is to get data access right without proper permission. For example, the attacker can be an outsider who is not allowed to get data but tries to decrypt data. Another example is that the attacker is a compromised device that attempts to get data which should be secret to it. In this case, undoubtedly, the compromised device can legally get data that it has right to access. So this case will not be considered as a successful attack.

3.3 Dynamic Pairwise Key Agreement Approach

In our system model, there will be three pairwise keys for three different channels. Here we just focus on the pairwise key agreement mechanism and the next subsection will show how this approach can be used to build a key management system in IoT. In this approach, we divide nodes into two groups and members belong to these two groups want to communicate with others. One group support dynamic membership while the other group is more static. There are five phases in this approach and are described below.

1. **Setup**(λ, m, n). Given two groups that have m and n members respectively. For simplicity, we call them group 1 and group 2. Let m is greater than n. KDC first creates a generating matrix G of size $(\lambda+1) \times (m'+n)$ where m' is much smaller than m. Any $\lambda+1$ columns of G must be linearly independent. KDC finds a transformation function ρ that maps from m to m'. We can use a hash function as the transformation function. KDC selects a prime q where $q > n$ and then randomly picks a primitive element s of $GF(q)$. The matrix will be:

$$G = \begin{bmatrix} 1 & 1 & 1 & \cdots & 1 \\ s & s^2 & s^3 & \cdots & s^{m+n} \\ s^2 & (s^2)^2 & (s^3)^2 & \cdots & (s^{m+n})^2 \\ & & \vdots & & \\ s^\lambda & (s^2)^\lambda & (s^3)^\lambda & \cdots & (s^{m+n})^\lambda \end{bmatrix}.$$

Each node only needs one element s to record G.

2. **Key Space Setup.** KDC randomly generates a symmetric matrix D of size $(\lambda + 1) \times (\lambda + 1)$ over $GF(q)$ with that all elements on the main diagonal are zeros. D is kept secret and is not disclosed to others. KDC also picks a pseudo random function σ. σ is secret to group 1 but is well known to group 2. KDC calculates $A = (D \cdot G)^T$. For node i in group 2, KDC distributes i-th row of A and σ to the node i. For a node j in group 1, KDC gets $(\rho(j)+n)$-th row of A as $\boldsymbol{v}$. Then KDC calculates $\boldsymbol{v}'$ as follows:

$$v'_k = v_k + \sigma(j,k) \cdot (s^{\rho(j)+n})^k, \forall k = 0, \ldots, \lambda.$$

KDC distributes $\boldsymbol{v}'$ to the node j. This implies every node j in group 1 has its own unique secret matrix D_j where the element on the main diagonal is $\sigma(j,k), \forall k = 0, \ldots, \lambda$. Other elements are same with those in D. For simplicity, we use A_j to indicate $(D_j \cdot G)^T$.

3. **Pairwise Key Agreement.** Suppose node j in group 1 and node i in group 2 want to come out a pairwise secret key. Since D_j is symmetric, we can show that $A_j \cdot G$ is also symmetric:

$$A_j \cdot G = (D_j \cdot G)^T \cdot G = G^T \cdot D_j^T \cdot G = G^T \cdot D_j \cdot G = G^T \cdot A_j^T = (A_j \cdot G)^T.$$

Node i calculates $k_{\rho(j)+n,i}$, which indicates the element located on $(\rho(j)+n)$-th row and i-th column of the matrix $A_j \cdot G$. As for node i in group 2, node i needs to calculate i-th row of A_j, $\boldsymbol{v}'$, from i-th row of A, $\boldsymbol{v}$, as follows:

$$v'_k = v_k + \sigma(j,k) \cdot (s^i)^k, \forall k = 0, \ldots, \lambda.$$

So node i can get $k_{i,\rho(j)+n}$ of the matrix $A_j \cdot G$. Because the matrix $A_j \cdot G$ is symmetric, $k_{i,\rho(j)+n} = k_{\rho(j)+n,i}$ and therefore node i and node j can share the same key.

4. **User Joining.** Here we focus on group 1 member joining. KDC assigns a new identity to the member and distributes the key space information for the new comer as described in the **Key Space Setup** phase. Note that existing deployed nodes do not need to do any changes.

5. **User Leaving**. Here we focus on group 1 member leaving. KDC simply broadcasts the node identity to the whole system. When the group 2 node receives the identity, it will simply add the identity to its revocation list. The group 2 member will reject the key agreement process with the group 1 member whose identity is on the revocation list.

In this pairwise key agreement approach, it is easily shown that computational cost required by the group 1 member is less than the group 2 member since the group 2 member needs additional $\lambda + 1$ pseudo random functions. The group 1 membership changing event costs almost nothing since the deployed environment does not require the key update process.

3.4 IoT Key Management Scheme

In our system model, there are three roles as shown in Fig. 1. In general, the user is dynamic while other two roles are static. That is, users join and leave frequently. As for the other two roles, they seldom changes once deployed. Besides, the broker is often more powerful than other two and the number of the user group is overwhelming.

K_1, K_2, K_3 are established from the approach described in Sect. 3.3. Note that there are three independent environments for three keys. According to the above characteristics, for K_1 and K_2, we make the broker in charge of the heavy computational work, which means the broker group is group 2 defined in the previous subsection. So the user and the device will not use too much computational power on pairwise key establishment. As for the K_3, since there are more users than devices, we prefer the device is group 2 and the user is group 1. To ease the device's computational burden, in our design, we make the broker to calculate $\sigma(j, k) \cdot (s^i)^k, \forall k = 0, \ldots, \lambda$ in the K_3 environment for the device. The broker attaches these elements to data when forwarding data to the device. That is, KDC puts σ of K_3 to the broker instead of the device. This can move some computational works to a more powerful entity. Note that the broker does not have any secret information D of K_3 and therefore it is impossible for the broker to derive the pairwise key K_3.

4   Evaluation

In this section, we discuss the computational overhead of our proposed scheme. We also discuss the probability of collusion attacks.

4.1   Computational Overhead

In this subsection, we will evaluate the computational costs required in our scheme. We implement our scheme on an Intel i7-7700 CPU including the user node, the group node and the device node. Though it is much more powerful than most IoT devices, here we just check the time difference. Since K_1, K_2, K_3 are from the same agreement scheme, here we just focus on K_1.

First, we check the pairwise key establishment part. Note that we do not care the environment setup phase and the key space setup phase run by KDC because KDC is much more powerful than other nodes and the setup process is infrequent. The evaluation result is shown in Fig. 2a. Group 1 is the user group and group 2 is the broker group. We can see that the group 1 node takes less computation time than the group 2 node. The reason is that group 2 node needs to recover the user's secret matrix from D. We use AES as our pseudo random function in our implementation. Note that the target group 1 number will not affect the computation time because it depends on $O(\lambda)$ instead of the mapping target group size.

Next, we compare the membership changing overhead in KDC between our method and LKH. The comparison result is presented in Fig. 2b. In the LKH scheme, when a node joins or leaves, existing nodes needs to update their keys related to the changing node. That is, given totally n nodes, KDC in LKH needs to encrypt $\log(n)$ times. As for our proposed scheme, KDC simply broadcasts the leaving node identity when a group 1 node leaves. For the node joining event, KDC distributes key agreement information to the newly coming node without informing existing nodes. That is, no encryption is required when membership changing. So the KDC computational cost in our scheme is almost zero.

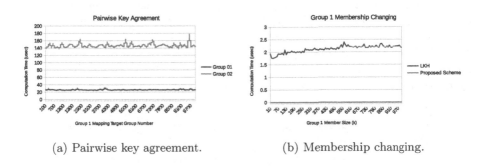

(a) Pairwise key agreement.   (b) Membership changing.

Fig. 2. Computational overhead.

4.2   Collusion Attack Analysis

In this subsection, we discuss how the collusion attack affect our key management system. There are three keys in our system and they are established through the same agreement approach. So here we just use K_1 as an example for analysis. Here are two groups here, the user group and the device group. Since any $\lambda + 1$ columns of the matrix G are linearly independent, an attacker must capture more than $\lambda + 1$ nodes with the same secret matrix D to recover D. However, since every node in the user group has its own secret, all colluded nodes cannot get secrets of other nodes.

Suppose one node in the broker group is compromised. That is, the secret pseudo random permutation function σ is released to an attacker. Because in our scheme, the user node identity is mapped to a smaller target group through a mapping function ρ, compromising one user node implies compromising all user nodes that map to the same target. Given the target group size m' and a security parameter λ. Suppose m' is much smaller than m, which is the user group size. The probability that all K_1 pairwise keys are broken with n compromised user nodes and one compromised broker node is

$$
P(n) = \begin{cases} 1 - \displaystyle\sum_{k=1}^{\lambda} \frac{1}{m'^n}(C_k^{m'} \cdot k^n), n > \lambda, \lambda < m' \\ \dfrac{1}{m'^n} \displaystyle\sum_{k=0}^{m'}(-1)^k \cdot C_k^{m'} \cdot (m'-k)^n, n > m', \lambda \geq m' \end{cases}.
$$

5 Conclusion and Future Work

In this paper, we propose an IoT pairwise key management scheme that supports partially dynamic membership which means this system supports only some kind of devices joining or leaving. The overhead of membership changing costs less than other existing techniques. Considering some practical scenarios, we believe that the proposed scheme is suitable for the IoT environment.

Our next step will focus on the membership changing handling of the other group. Though in our construction, the proposed approach can support up to λ nodes leaving, it cannot support node joining[2]. Besides, λ may not be enough in a dynamic environment. We will try to solve this problem to make the scheme more applicable.

References

1. Abdmeziem, M.R., Tandjaoui, D., Romdhani, I.: A decentralized batch-based group key management protocol for mobile internet of things (DBGK). In: 2015 IEEE International Conference on Computer and Information Technology; Ubiquitous Computing and Communications; Dependable, Autonomic and Secure Computing; Pervasive Intelligence and Computing, pp. 1109–1117, October 2015
2. Balenson, D., McGrew, D., Sherman, A.: Key management for large dynamic groups: One-way function trees and amortized initialization (1999)
3. Blom, R.: An optimal class of symmetric key generation systems. In: Beth, T., Cot, N., Ingemarsson, I. (eds.) EUROCRYPT 1984. LNCS, vol. 209, pp. 335–338. Springer, Heidelberg (1985). https://doi.org/10.1007/3-540-39757-4_22
4. Du, W., Deng, J., Han, Y.S., Varshney, P.K., Katz, J., Khalili, A.: A pairwise key predistribution scheme for wireless sensor networks. ACM Trans. Inf. Syst. Secur. 8(2), 228–258 (2005)
5. Harney, H.: Logical key hierarchy protocol. SMUG, March 1999
6. Park, M.H., Park, Y.H., Jeong, H.Y., Seo, S.W.: Key management for multiple multicast groups in wireless networks. IEEE Trans. Mobile Comput. 12(9), 1712–1723 (2013)
7. Veltri, L., Cirani, S., Busanelli, S., Ferrari, G.: A novel batch-based group key management protocol applied to the internet of things. Ad Hoc Netw. 11(8), 2724–2737 (2013)

---

[2] Of course, users can prepare a larger pool for new coming nodes.

Secure File Transfer Protocol for Named Data Networks Supporting Homomorphic Computations

Hsiang-Shian Fan$^{(\boxtimes)}$, Cheng-Hsing Yang$^{(\boxtimes)}$, and Chi-Yao Weng$^{(\boxtimes)}$

National Pingtung University, Pingtung, Taiwan
roi.ss.fan@gmail.com,
{chyang, cyweng}@mail.nptu.edu.tw

Abstract. Not only does Named Data Network (NDN) provide a higher performance than TCP/IP network, but also it can cope with the problem of limited IP addresses. Currently, some scholars have proposed a secure file transfer protocol, which is based on re-encryption for NDN, to ensure that files can be safely transferred between nodes or users. On the other hand, because of the popular craze of saving files on Cloud, the security of Cloud is in vogue. However, numerous of jobs must be done if the user wants to calculate encrypted files on Cloud. Furthermore, the process will make files exposed in danger for a long time. By using Homomorphic Encryption, we can perform operations of the encrypted files on Cloud, and the operations will be finished by Cloud. In this paper, we provide secure operations for a file transfer protocol based on homomorphic re-encryption for named data networks. Our scheme fuses the advantages of NDN, Homomorphic Encryption, and Re-Encryption. It is a low energy consumption system which offers transmission safety and handy calculation.

Keywords: Name data networks · Re-encryption · Homomorphic

1 Introduction

In recent years, with the flourishing growth of the Internet, humans' life style changes tremendously. Due to an increasing number of the Internet usage rate, people have become more and more.dependent on the Internet. Literally we cannot live without the Internet nowadays. However, people have to face several problems when sharing information online. Information security problem is the most important issue. If information security cannot be guaranteed, there will be no privacy between humans; in other words, it is a disaster.

Whether in a real world or an online world, resource decreasing is a serious issue that all humans must confront with. We not merely should make use of the remainder resources frugally but likewise search for new substitute resources. People widely used networks, which causes that TCP/IP may face various resource-consumed problems. Some behaviors will waste the network resources in the traditional network. One example is that some users access simultaneously the same content from video services, which leads to the server incurring extra costs. Another example is that a user will ask a

© Springer Nature Singapore Pte Ltd. 2019
C.-Y. Chang et al. (Eds.): ICS 2018, CCIS 1013, pp. 567–579, 2019.
https://doi.org/10.1007/978-981-13-9190-3_63

file from a trusted remote node rather than the nearby nodes, which will cause the network traffic to greatly increase. Therefore, a novel network architecture, which is called the named data network (NDN) [4, 5] and is based on data itself, was brought about to deal with the problems. It improves the performance of digital content distribution and resource utilization as compared with IP-address based networks. Some scholars have proposed an FTP-NDN system, which is a secure file transfer protocol for NDN based on re-encryption [7]. The system not only avoids the obsession of executing one-to-one encryptions between the demander and the owner, but also allows potential users to demand files without consuming too many resources.

Cloud storage is a non-neglectable memory space. People like to save data on Cloud nowadays. To ensure information security, most people will encrypt their files before uploading them. However, if a user wants to perform computations on encrypted files which had been uploaded to Cloud, it will be necessary to finish several works. The works are as follows. First, download the required files. Second, decrypt them and perform operations on them. Finally, encrypt the files and upload them to Cloud. The process not only performs too many redundant operations but also overstays the files in danger. Therefore, combining NDN [9] re-encryption system, and homomorphic encryption [11] and entrusting the calculations to Cloud, we can reduce the complexity of the process and improve safety of the files. In this paper, we design a homomorphic encryption scheme on the FTP-NDN system, which ensures information security by Boneh–Goh–Nissim Encryption mechanism (BGN). Our scheme can support homomorphic addition, subtraction, multiplication, division, on ciphertexts.

2 Related Works

2.1 Boneh–Goh–Nissim Encryption [6]

The BGN encryption scheme is one of the famous encryption schemes. The BGN scheme is known as the first encryption scheme to allow both homomorphic addition and homomorphic multiplication with a constant-size ciphertext. The process of the scheme has three steps, which are Key Generation, Encryption, and Decryption.

Key Generation
Given a security parameter $\lambda \in \mathbf{Z}^+$, generate a tuple (q_1, q_2, G) where q_1 and q_2 are two distinct large primes with λ bits. G is a cyclic group of order $q_1 q_2$, and e is a pairing map e: $G \times G \rightarrow G_1$. Let $N = q_1 q_2$. Pick up two random generators g and u from G and set $h = u^{q_2}$ with order q_1. Finally, $PK = \{N, G, G_1, e, g, h\}$ is the public key, and the private key $SK = q_1$.

Encryption
To encrypt a message m using the public key PK, pick a random number r from $\{1, 2, \ldots, N\}$ and compute:

$$C = g^m h^r \in G$$

Output C as the ciphertext.

Decryption

Decrypt ciphertext C by private key $SK = q_1$:

$$C^{q_1} = (g^m h^r)^{q_1} = (g^{q_1})^m$$

To recover the message m, it suffices to compute the discrete logarithm of C^{q_1} to the base g^{q_1}. Since $0 \le m \le T$, this takes expected time $O(\sqrt{T})$ using Pollard's lambda method.

Homomorphic Properties

The BGN scheme allows both additive and multiplicative homomorphisms with a constant-size ciphertext.

Additive Homomorphism

Given two ciphertexts $C_1 = g^{m_1} h^{r_1} \in G$ and $C_2 = g^{m_2} h^{r_2} \in G$ of messages $m_1, m_2 \in \{0, 1, \ldots, T\}$, pick a random number $r \in \{1, 2, \ldots N - 1\}$. Ciphertexts will achieve additive homomorphism by computing the product

$$C = C_1 C_2 h^r$$

$$= (g^{m_1} h^{r_1})(g^{m_2} h^{r_2}) h^r$$

$$- g^{m_1 + m_2} h^{r_1 + r_2 + r}$$

The plaintexts m_1 and m_2 have achieved additive homomorphism.

Multiplication Homomorphism

By using the bilinear map, we can multiply two encrypted messages together. Let

$$g_1 = e(g, g)$$

where g_1 is of order N, and let

$$h_1 = e(g, h)$$

where h_1 is of order q_1. There is a $\alpha \in \mathbf{Z}$, which contents

$$h = g^{\alpha q_2}$$

Suppose that there are two ciphertexts $C_1 = g^{m_1} h^{r_1} \in G$, $C_2 = g^{m_2} h^{r_2} \in G$. Pick a random number $r \in \mathbf{Z}_N$, and let

$$C = e(C_1, C_2)h_1^r \in G_1$$

The details are as follows:

$$C = e(C_1, C_2)h_1^r$$

$$= e(g^{m_1}h^{r_1}, g^{m_2}h^{r_2})h_1^r$$

$$= e(g^{m_1 + \alpha q_1 r_1}, g^{m_2 + \alpha q_2 r_2})h_1^r$$

$$= e(g, g)^{(m_1 + \alpha q_1 r_1)(m_2 + \alpha q_2 r_2)}h_1^r$$

$$= e(g, g)^{m_1 m_2 + \alpha q_2(m_1 r_2 + m_2 r_1 + \alpha q_2 r_1 r_2)}h_1^r$$

$$= e(g, g)^{m_1 m_2}h_1^{r + m_1 r_2 + m_2 r_1 + \alpha q_2 r_1 r_2}$$

Obviously, it has become a ciphertext of $m_1 m_2$, and in other words, it achieved multiplication homomorphism.

2.2 Named Data Network (NDN)

NDN [1] is a novel network architecture. It improves the performance of digital content distribution and resource utilization as compared with IP-address based networks. NDN is based on data rather than IP addresses. IP addresses are limited, in other words, it may be exhausted in the future. It won't be a problem if we use NDN [8, 10]. Numbers of scholars proposed new works that are interrelated with NDN. Figure 1 shows an example of the architecture of NDN.

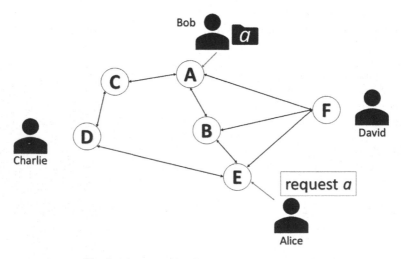

Fig. 1. An example of the architecture of NDN

In Fig. 1, each file has a unique name and contains the producer's signature. Users can upload files to nearby nodes and can request files from nearby nodes. Each node will keep files in its cache for a period time. For example, if Bob wants to upload a file to the system, he will send file a to one of his nearby nodes, which is node A. After that, Bob can be offline. Now, if Alice wants to request file a, she will send a request signal to her nearby node, which is node E. If node E has file a, it will send the file a to Alice immediately. However, if node E doesn't have file a, E will send a request signal to all of its adjacent nodes. The process will be repeatedly performed until E gets the file a. Eventually, Alice will get the file a from E. Similarly, Charlie and David could get the file from one of their nearby nodes.

2.3 File Transfer Protocol Based on Re-Encryption for Named Data Network Supporting Nondesignated Receivers (FTP-NDN)

It is a secure file transfer protocol [3] for NDN based on re-encryption. Figure 2 shows an example of the architecture of FTP-NDN.

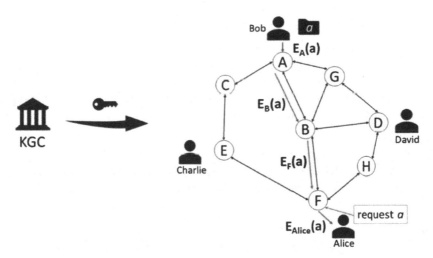

Fig. 2. An example of the architecture of FTP-NDN

In this system, there is a KGC, which is Key Generation Center. The center (KGC) will respond for key issuing. It issues private keys to every receiver. However, KGC only issues an re-encryption key to every node. Nodes will not get their private keys, so that nodes can only re-encrypt the file. They cannot decrypt it. For example, Bob uploads the file a to his adjacent node, which is node A. After encrypting file a by node A's public key, Bob can get offline. When Alice wants to request file a, she will send a request to her adjacent node, node F. Assuming that node F does not have file a, it will send a request to its adjacent nodes, and the request will be gradually broadcast in the system. Finally, node A got the request. After that node A will re-encrypt the ciphertext into a ciphertext of node B, and node B will re-encrypt the ciphertext into a ciphertext of node F. Finally, node F will re-encrypt the ciphertext to Alice, so Alice can decrypt file a by her private key.

3 Our Proposed Scheme

3.1 Mathematic Background

p: a large prime
$\mathbb{G}$: an additive group with order p
$\mathbb{G}_{\mathbb{T}}$: a multiplicative group with order p
P: a generator of $\mathbb{G}$
$e : \mathbb{G} \times \mathbb{G} \rightarrow \mathbb{G}_{\mathbb{T}}$

Define a Hash function: $H : \{0,1\}^{*} \rightarrow \mathbb{G}$

Bilinearity

$e(aP_1, bP_2) = e(P_1, P_2)^{ab}$ for any $P_1, P_2 \in \mathbb{G}$ and $a, b \in \mathbb{Z}_p^{*}$
$e(P_3 + P_4, P_2) = e(P_3, P_2) \cdot e(P_4, P_2)$ for any $P_2, P_3, P_4 \in \mathbb{G}$

Non-Degeneracy

$e(P_1, P_2) \neq 1_{\mathbb{G}_{\mathbb{T}}}$ whenever $P_1, P_2 \neq 1_{\mathbb{G}}$

To present the ciphertext by the form of BGN, we integrate the homomorphism property of BGN into the FTP-NDN system. Similar to the FTP-NDN system, there are five phases in our protocol, which are Setup, Registration, Uploading, Re-Encryption, and Decryption. They will be elaborated as follows.

Setup Phase

KGC (Key Generation Center) will randomly pick a number s as its master key and let sP be its public key. KGC will compute a re-encryption keys $RK_{i,j}$ for every node i with the adjacent node j, where the re-encryption key $RK_{i,j} = s\big(H(ID_j) - H(ID_i)\big)$.

Registration Phase

After KGC receives a user ID (ID_k) and user informations from user K, KGC will return user private key ($sH(ID_K)$) and node information to user K. At the same time, for every node F adjacent to user K, KGC will compute re-encryption key RK_{F,ID_K}, and send it to node F.

Uploading Phase

In order to upload a file m to an adjacent node A, the user will use the public key of node A to encrypt the file, which is $CT_{A,0}$. Before encrypting the file, user must pick a random number $r \in \mathbb{Z}_p^{*}$ for randomization. The details of $CT_{A,0}$ are as follows:

$$CT_{A,0} = \big(C_{2,0}, C_3\big)$$

where

$$C_{2,0} = e(P,P)^m * e(rH(ID_A), sP), \; C_3 = rP$$

The next two phases will be presented using ciphertext $CT_{A,0}$

Re-Encryption Phase

Node A can re-encrypt the file that received from the user to node B by using the re-encryption key $RK_{A,B} = s(H(ID_B) - H(ID_A))$. After node A re-encrypts the file to node B, ciphertext $CT_{A,0}$ will become ciphertext $CT_{B,1} = (C_{2,1}, C_3)$, which is a ciphertext of node B.

To re-encrypt the ciphertext, we only need to compute the first part of the ciphertext.

$$C_{2,1} = C_{2,0} \cdot e(RK_{A,B}, C_3)$$

$$= e(P,P)^m \cdot e(rH(ID_A), sP) \cdot e(s(H(ID_B) - H(ID_A)), rP)$$

$$= e(P,P)^m \cdot e(sH(ID_A), rP) \cdot e(sH(ID_B) - sH(ID_A), rP)$$

$$= e(P,P)^m \cdot e(sH(ID_A) + sH(ID_B) - sH(ID_A), rP)$$

$$= e(P,P)^m \cdot e(sH(ID_B), rP)$$

Decryption Phase

User Alice can decrypt ciphertext $CT_{Alice,j} = (C_{2,j}, C_3)$ by her private key $sk_{Alice} = sH(ID_{Alice})$. The operation is as follows:

$$\frac{C_{2,j}}{e(sk_{Alice}, C_3)}$$

$$= \frac{e(P,P)^m \cdot e(rH(ID_{Alice}), sP)}{e(sH(ID_{Alice}), rP)}$$

$$= \frac{e(P,P)^m \cdot e(rH(ID_{Alice}), sP)}{e(rH(ID_{Alice}), sP)}$$

$$= e(P,P)^m$$

Since $0 \le m \le T$, this takes expected time $O(\sqrt{T})$ to solve using Pollard's lambda method.

Additive Homomorphism

Given two ciphertexts $CT_{A,j,m_1} = (C_{2,j,m_1}, C_{3,m_1}) = (e(P,P)^{m_1} \cdot e(r_1 H(ID_A), sP), r_1 P)$ and $CT_{A,j,m_2} = (C_{2,j,m_2}, C_{3,m_2}) = (e(P,P)^{m_2} \cdot e(r_2 H(ID_A), sP), r_2 P)$, after finishing the operation below, we can ensure additively homomorphism.

$$C_{2,j,m_1} \cdot C_{2,j,m_2} = (e(P,P)^{m_1} \cdot e(r_1 H(ID_A), sP)) \cdot (e(P,P)^{m_2} \cdot e(r_2 H(ID_A), sP))$$

$$= e(P,P)^{m_1+m_2} \cdot e((r_1+r_2)H(ID_A), sP)$$

$$C_{3,m_1} + C_{3,m_2} = r_1 P + r_2 P = (r_1+r_2)P$$

Decryption Phase

User Alice can decrypt ciphertext $CT_{Alice,j,m_1+m_2} = \left(C_{2,j,m_1+m_2}, C_{3,m_1+m_2}\right)$ by her private key $sk_{Alice} = sH(ID_{Alice})$ as follows:

$$\frac{C_{2,j,m_1+m_2}}{e\left(sk_{Alice}, C_{3,m_1+m_2}\right)}$$

$$= \frac{e(P,P)^{m_1+m_2} \cdot e((r_1+r_2)H(ID_{Alice}), sP)}{e(sH(ID_{Alice}), (r_1+r_2)P)}$$

$$= \frac{e(P,P)^{m_1+m_2} \cdot e((r_1+r_2)H(ID_{Alice}), sP)}{e((r_1+r_2)H(ID_{Alice}), sP)}$$

$$= e(P,P)^{m_1+m_2}$$

Since $0 \le m_1 + m_2 \le 2T$, this takes expected time $O\left(\sqrt{2T}\right)$ to solve using Pollard's lambda method.

Subtractive Homomorphism

Given two ciphertexts $CT_{A,j,m_1} = \left(C_{2,j,m_1}, C_{3,m_1}\right)$ and $CT_{A,j,m_2} = \left(C_{2,j,m_2}, C_{3,m_2}\right)$.

In order to let the plaintext become $(m_1 - m_2)$, it is necessary to take (-1) power of the subtrahend and compute with the minuend. The definition of taking (-1) power of ciphertext is as follows:

$$\left(CT_{A,j,m_2}\right)^{-1} = \left(C_{2,j,m_2}^{-1}, -C_{3,m_2}\right)$$

After finishing the following operation, we can obtain subtractive homomorphism.

$$C_{2,j,m_1} * \left(C_{2,j,m_2}\right)^{-1} = e(P,P)^{m_1-m_2} \cdot e((r_1-r_2)H(ID_A), sP) = C_{2,j,m_1-m_2}$$

$$C_{3,m_1} - (C_{3,m_2}) = r_1 P + (-(r_2 P)) = (r_1 - r_2)P = C_{3,m_1-m_2}$$

Decryption Phase

User Alice can decrypt ciphertext $CT_{Alice,j,m_1-m_2} = \left(C_{2,j,m_1-m_2}, C_{3,m_1-m_2}\right)$ by her private key $sk_{Alice} = sH(ID_{Alice})$

$$\frac{C_{2,j,m_1-m_2}}{e\left(sk_{Alice}, C_{3,m_1-m_2}\right)}$$

$$= \frac{e(P,P)^{m_1-m_2} \cdot e((r_1 - r_2)H(ID_{Alice}), sP)}{e(sH(ID_{Alice}), (r_1 - r_2)P)}$$

$$= \frac{e(P,P)^{m_1-m_2} \cdot e((r_1 - r_2)H(ID_{Alice}), sP)}{e((r_1 - r_2)H(ID_{Alice}), sP)}$$

$$= e(P,P)^{m_1-m_2}$$

Since $0 \leq |m_1 + m_2| \leq 2T$, this takes expected time $O(\sqrt{2T})$ to solve using Pollard's lambda method. If the solving time exceeds the normal solving time a lot, it turns out that $(m_1 - m_2)$ is negative. We can get the target plaintext by taking (-1) power of the previous formula and solving it by Pollard's lambda method. The target plaintext will appear after adding a minus sign to the outcome of Pollard's lambda method.

Uploading Phase
In order to upload a file m to an adjacent node A, the user will use the public key of node A to encrypt the file. The result is $CT_{A,0}$. Before encrypting the file, user must pick a random number $r \in \mathbb{Z}_p^*$ for randomization. The details of $CT_{A,0}$ are as follows:

$$CT_{A,0} = (C_{2,0}, C_3)$$

where

$$C_{2,0} = m * e(rH(ID_A), sP), \quad C_3 = rP,$$

The next two phases will be presented using ciphertext $CT_{A,0}$.

Re-Encryption Phase
Node A can re-encrypt the file that received from the user to node B by using the re-encryption key $RK_{A,B} = s(H(ID_B) - H(ID_A))$. After node A re-encrypts the file to node B, ciphertext $CT_{A,0}$ will become ciphertext $CT_{B,1} = (C_{2,1}, C_3)$, which is a ciphertext of node B.

To re-encrypt the ciphertext, we only need to compute the first part of the ciphertext.

$$C_{2,1} = C_{2,0} \cdot e(RK_{A,B}, C_3)$$

$$= m \cdot e(rH(ID_A), sP) \cdot e(s(H(ID_B) - H(ID_A)), rP)$$

$$= m \cdot e(sH(ID_A), rP) \cdot e(sH(ID_B) - sH(ID_A), rP)$$

$$= m \cdot e(sH(ID_A) + sH(ID_B) - sH(ID_A), rP)$$

$$= m \cdot e(sH(ID_B), rP)$$

Decryption Phase

User Alice can decrypt ciphertext $CT_{Alice,j} = (C_{2,j}, C_3)$ by her private key $sk_{Alice} = sH(ID_{Alice})$. The operation is as follows:

$$\frac{C_{2,j}}{e(sk_{Alice}, C_3)}$$

$$= \frac{m \cdot e(rH(ID_{Alice}), sP)}{e(sH(ID_{Alice}), rP)}$$

$$= \frac{m \cdot e(rH(ID_{Alice}), sP)}{e(rH(ID_{Alice}), sP)}$$

$$= m$$

Multiplicative Homomorphism

Given two ciphertexts $CT_{A,j,m_1} = (C_{2,j,m_1}, C_{3,m_1}) = (m_1 \cdot e(r_1 H(ID_A), sP), r_1 P)$ and $CT_{A,j,m_2} = (C_{2,j,m_2}, C_{3,m_2}) = (m_2 \cdot e(r_2 H(ID_A), sP), r_2 P)$, after finishing the operation below, we can achieve multiplicative homomorphism.

The operation is as follows:

$$C_{2,j,m_1} \cdot C_{2,j,m_2} = (m_1 \cdot e(r_1 H(ID_A), sP)) \cdot (m_2 \cdot e(r_2 H(ID_A), sP))$$

$$= (m_1 \cdot m_2) \cdot e((r_1 + r_2)H(ID_A), sP)$$

$$C_{3,m_1} + C_{3,m_2} = r_1 P + r_2 P = (r_1 + r_2)P$$

Message m_1 and message m_2 can be multiplied owing to multiplicative homomorphism.

Decryption Phase

User Alice can decrypt ciphertext $CT_{Alice,j,m_1 \cdot m_2} = (C_{2,j,m_1 \cdot m_2}, C_{3,m_1 \cdot m_2})$ by her private key $sk_{Alice} = sH(ID_{Alice})$. The operation is as follows:

$$\frac{C_{2,j,m_1 \cdot m_2}}{e(sk_{Alice}, C_{3,m_1 m_2})}$$

$$= \frac{(m_1 \cdot m_2) \cdot e((r_1 + r_2)H(ID_{Alice}), sP)}{e(sH(ID_{Alice}), (r_1 + r_2)P)}$$

$$= \frac{(m_1 \cdot m_2) \cdot e((r_1 + r_2)H(ID_{Alice}), sP)}{e((r_1 + r_2)H(ID_{Alice}), sP)}$$

$$= (m_1 \cdot m_2)$$

Finally, the plaintext $(m_1 \cdot m_2) \bmod p)$ appears.

Divisible Homomorphism

Due to division is an inverse operation of multiplication, it is easy to achieve divisible homomorphism by take (-1) power of the divisor, and multiply it with the dividend. The details are as follows:

Given two ciphertexts $CT_{A,j,m_1} = (C_{2,j,m_1}, C_{3,m_1}) = (m_1 \cdot e(r_1 H(ID_A), sP), r_1 P)$ and $CT_{A,j,m_2} = (C_{2,j,m_2}, C_{3,m_2}) = (m_2 \cdot e(r_2 H(ID_A), sP), r_2 P)$. In order to make the plaintext become $\frac{m_1}{m_2} \bmod p$, taking (-1) power of divisor ciphertext CT_{A,j,m_2} then computing with dividend ciphertext CT_{A,j,m_1} is necessary. The definition of taking (-1) power of ciphertext is as follows:

$$\left(CT_{A,j,m_2}\right)^{-1} = \left(C_{2,j,m_2}^{-1}, C_{3,m_2}^{-1}\right)$$

where

$$\left(C_{2,j,m_2}\right)^{-1} = (m_2 \cdot e(r_2 H(ID_A), sP))^{-1}$$

$$\left(C_{3,m_2}\right)^{-1} = (r_2 P)^{-1} = -(r_2 P)$$

Then calculate $\left(CT_{A,j,m_2}\right)^{-1}$ and CT_{A,j,m_1}, that is to say, multiply the first part of the ciphertext. As for the second part of the ciphertext, we add them together.

$$C_{2,j,m_1} * \left(C_{2,j,m_2}\right)^{-1} = (m_1 \cdot e(r_1 H(ID_A), sP)) \cdot (m_2 \cdot e(r_2 H(ID_A), sP))^{-1}$$
$$= \frac{m_1}{m_2} \cdot e((r_1 - r_2) H(ID_A), sP)$$

$$C_{3,m_1} + \left(C_{3,m_2}\right)^{-1} = r_1 P + (-(r_2 P)) = (r_1 - r_2) P$$

The ciphertext of message m_1 and message m_2 have successfully transformed into the ciphertext of message $(\frac{m_1}{m_2} \bmod p)$. Hence, the ciphertext is provided with Divisible Homomorphism.

Decryption Phase

User Alice can decrypt ciphertext $CT_{Alice,j,\frac{m_1}{m_2}} = \left(C_{2,j,\frac{m_1}{m_2}}, C_{3,\frac{m_1}{m_2}}\right)$ by her private key $sk_{Alice} = sH(ID_{Alice})$. The operation is as follows:

$$\frac{C_{2,j,\frac{m_1}{m_2}}}{e\left(sk_{Alice}, C_{3,\frac{m_1}{m_2}}\right)}$$

$$= \frac{\frac{m_1}{m_2} \cdot e((r_1 - r_2) H(ID_{Alice}), sP)}{e(sH(ID_{Alice}), (r_1 - r_2)P)}$$

$$= \frac{\frac{m_1}{m_2} \cdot e((r_1 - r_2)H(ID_{Alice}), sP)}{e((r_1 - r_2)H(ID_{Alice}), sP)}$$

$$= \frac{m_1}{m_2}$$

Finally, the plaintext $\left(\frac{m_1}{m_2} \bmod p\right)$ appears.

4   Comparison

4.1   Encrypted Data Processing with Homomorphic Encryption [2]

Ding et al. have proposed additive homomorphism on a re-encryption scheme in 2017 [2]. They achieved additive homomorphism by representing the ciphertext as the form of Paillier Encryption Scheme [12, 13], which is the first scheme that attains homomorphism. Ding's work is also with a two-level decryption. It means that the message can be re-encrypted once. In other words, it is unidirectional and single-hop.

4.2   Comparisons with Our Proposed Scheme

There are plenty of nodes in an NDN system. All of them provide bidirectional transmission and multi-hop. Consequently, Ding's work cannot fit the NDN system. Although the FTP-NDN system fits the NDN system, it cannot achieve ciphertext additive homomorphism and ciphertext multiplicative homomorphism. Table 1 shows the comparisons among FTP-NDN [3], Ding's scheme [2], and our scheme.

Table 1. The comparisons among FTP-NDN, Ding's scheme, and our scheme.

	FTP-NDN [3]	Ding's [2]	Ours
Ciphertext additive homomorphism		✓	✓
Ciphertext multiplication homomorphism			✓
Bidirectional transmission	✓		✓
Ciphertext can be re-encrypted repeatedly	✓		✓

5   Conclusion

Nowadays, information security has become more and more important. People started to attach importance to the security of files. The resource sustainability is also a hot topic on the Internet. With the rise of the Internet usage rate, people have to economically use the resources on the Internet. An NDN file transfer protocol which offers homomorphic re-encryption not only staves the exhaustion of IP addresses in TCP/IP networks but also provides a safe space for message transmission and message operation. This system presents ciphertexts based on the BGN encryption scheme, and therefore, ciphertexts can achieve additive, subtractive, multiplicative, divisible homomorphisms, and OR, AND, NOT logic operation homomorphisms. Furthermore, the nodes will accomplish all calculations such that it is not necessary for the users to do any calculation. In conclusion, if this system has been widely used, it might bring a more convenient and more secure online word to humans.

Acknowledgement. This research was partially supported by the Ministry of Science and Technology of the Republic of China under the Grant MOST 106-2221-E-153-002, MOST 107-2221-E-153-001 and TWISC@NSYSU.

References

1. Claffy, K., Polterock, J., Afanasyev, A., Burke, J., Zhang, L.: The first named data networking community meeting (NDNcomm). In: Proceedings Workshop Named Data Networking, pp. 1–6 (2015)
2. Ding, W., Yan, Z., Deng, R.H.: Encrypted data processing with homomorphic re-encryption. Inf. Sci. **409–410**, 35–55 (2017)
3. Fan, C.-I., Chen, I.-T., Cheng, C.-K., Huang, J.-J., Chen, W.-T.: FTP- NDN: file transfer protocol based on re-encryption for named data network supporting non-designated receivers. IEEE Syst. J. **12**(1), 473–484 (2018)
4. Grassi, G., et al.: Vehicular inter-networking via named data. In: Proceedings of ACM 9th International ICST Conference Hot Mobile, pp. 116–125 (2013)
5. Hamdane, B., Msahli, M., Serhrouchni, A., Guemara, S.: Data-based access control in named data networking. In: Proceedings of International Conference on MDM Collaborative Computing: Networking, Applications and Worksharing, pp. 531–536 (2013)
6. Homomorphic Encryption - Springer, pp. 41–45 http://www.springer.com/cda/content/document/cda_downloaddocument/9783319122281-c1.pdf?SGWID=0-0-45-1487904-p177033600
7. Lu, R., Lin, X., Shao, J., Liang, K.: RCCA-secure multi-use bidirectional proxy re-encryption with master secret security. In: Chow, S.S.M., Liu, J.K., Hui, L.C.K., Yiu, S.M. (eds.) ProvSec 2014. LNCS, vol. 8782, pp. 194–205. Springer, Cham (2014). https://doi.org/10.1007/978-3-319-12475-9_14
8. Named data networking (2014). http://nameddata.net/publications/
9. Shang, W., Ding, Q., Marianantoni, A., Burke, J., Zhang, L.: Securing building management systems using named data networking. IEEE Netw. **28**(3), 50–56 (2014)
10. Zhang, L., et al.: Named data networking project. NDN Project Team, National Science Foundation (NSF), NDN Technical report, ndn-0001, USA (2010)
11. Somewhat Homomorphic Encryption. https://crypto.stanford.edu/~dwu4/talks/SecurityLunch0214.pdf
12. Paillier, P.: Public-key cryptosystems based on composite degree residuosity classes. In: Stern, J. (ed.) EUROCRYPT 1999. LNCS, vol. 1592, pp. 223–238. Springer, Heidelberg (1999). https://doi.org/10.1007/3-540-48910-X_16
13. Paillier, P., Pointcheval, D.: Efficient public-key cryptosystems provably secure against active adversaries. In: Lam, K.-Y., Okamoto, E., Xing, C. (eds.) ASIACRYPT 1999. LNCS, vol. 1716, pp. 165–179. Springer, Heidelberg (1999). https://doi.org/10.1007/978-3-540-48000-6_14

A Weighted Threshold Visual Cryptography

Tai-Yuan Tu, Tzung-Her Chen, Ji-min Yang,
and Chih-Hung Wang$^{(\boxtimes)}$

Department of Computer Science and Information Engineering,
National Chiayi University, Chiayi, Taiwan
{thchen, wangch}@mail.ncyu.edu.tw

Abstract. Over the past years, a visual secret sharing scheme gave each share the same ability to reconstruct the secret image. That means each participant had the same significance to reveal the secret. However, it is not realistic in real world for some applications. In this paper, the weighted (k, n)-threshold visual cryptography scheme is proposed, in which the secret image is encoded into some shares with different weights and the sum of weights for all shares has to be equal to n, according to the share-holders of different priority levels. In the decoding phase, when the shares with different weights are superimposed and the sum of weights of all stacking shares is equal to or larger than k, the secret is then visually recognizable. Otherwise, no information about secret image is revealed. The proposed scheme is the first weighted (k, n)-threshold visual cryptography method with no pixel expansion. It is suitable for applications in the real life.

Keywords: Cryptography · Visual cryptography ·
Weighted visual secret sharing · Probabilistic visual secret sharing

1 Introduction

Visual Cryptography (VC) is a secret sharing method for digital images without cryptographic computations for decryption. Blakly [1] and Shamir [14] (1979) first developed individually the concept of the secret sharing scheme. And then Naor and Shamir [13] (1995) extended the secret sharing idea into image research, and referred it as (k, n)-threshold VC. The (k, n)-threshold VC scheme is to encode a secret image composed of black and white pixels into n noise-like pieces (called shares or shadows), and then all n noise-like shares are distributed among n participants. While any set of at least k shares are stacked, the secret image can be visually revealed, whereas, any set of shares less than k cannot gain any information about the secret. Note that the secret image encrypted by VC can be decrypted by human visual system without complicated cryptographic mechanisms and computations.

Conventional VC potentially has two well-known disadvantages [2, 6, 10, 16–18]: (1) contrast distortion (2) pixel expansion. The contrast is the luminance difference between white and black pixels in the reconstructed image. The pixel expansion means the number of pixels in a share is used to encode a pixel of the original secret. Higher contrast can make the reconstructed image easier to be recognized by human visual

© Springer Nature Singapore Pte Ltd. 2019
C.-Y. Chang et al. (Eds.): ICS 2018, CCIS 1013, pp. 580–589, 2019.
https://doi.org/10.1007/978-981-13-9190-3_64

system. Smaller pixel expansion means less storage of shares. Conventional VSS schemes generally use two $n \times m$ basis Boolean matrices, B^0 and B^1, to encode the secret image into n share images. While decomposing the secret image into noise-like shares in VC-based VSS schemes, each pixel of the original secret image can be expanded into m black and white sub-pixels. That will result in more storage space of shares and much loss of contrast in the reconstructed image.

After Naor and Shamir, the discussions on the optimal pixel expansion and contrast for a VSS scheme can be found in [2, 6, 9, 11, 15, 17–20]. No matter the VC or the ProbVC (probabilistic VC [17–19]) is used, the average contrast in a stacked image will increase a constant amount while another share is stacked on in decoding phase. In other words, each share has the identical capability to restore the secret image; that means every participant is assigned the same privilege class. According to observation in the real world, however, participants might have different levels of duty; i.e., every participant in the secret image sharing scheme should be assigned to the different priority class. From the viewpoint of the management, we would consider each participant may have a unique priority, and design the corresponding share with different weight in response to his/her significance in the decoding phase.

Chen [4] proposed a weighted and progressive method based on pixel expansion, which causes the needs of more storage space and transmission time. Hou et al. [12] proposed a method called general model for priority-based progressive visual secret sharing (GPPVSS) in which every participant is assigned a unique privilege to recover the secret image. However, when the priority level increases, the highest privilege share decreases dramatically the capability to restore the secret image. In other words, the highest priority share provides fewer black spots and thus has little contrast improvement for the restored image.

Inspired by Yang's ProbVC [19], this paper proposes a weighted ProbVC scheme inherited the properties of ProbVC. In order to achieve the goal of assigning different weight to the share of each participant in different priority class, first each participant is assigned to a weight according to his/her duty in the organization. Next the basis matrix designed by Yang [19] is transformed into the weighted basis matrix in which the sum of the weights of all rows with different weight t is equal to n according to different priority class. After the weighted basis matrix construction satisfying different priority has been designed for encoding share with different priority t, and then each share with different weight t is created by the weighted basis matrix and dispatched to participant relying on his/her duty. While restoring the secret image, if the sum of weight of all stacking shares is greater than or equal to k, the secret image can be revealed. The proposed scheme is the first (k, n)-threshold ProbVC method with weight. It is suitable for applications in the real world.

2 The Proposed Scheme

This section is devoted to show the concept and the processes of how to construct the proposed weighted (k, n) non-expanded visual secret sharing scheme.

2.1 Preliminary

Prior to the description of the proposed method, some definitions are given.

Definition 1. A notation $\mu_{i,j}$ denotes the set of all $n \times 1$ column matrices with Hamming weight i of every column vector, and j denotes the matrices belonging to C_j where $j \in \{0, 1\}$.

For instance, $n = 4$, we have

$$\mu_{2,1} = \left\{ \begin{bmatrix} 1 \\ 1 \\ 0 \\ 0 \end{bmatrix}, \begin{bmatrix} 0 \\ 0 \\ 1 \\ 1 \end{bmatrix}, \begin{bmatrix} 1 \\ 0 \\ 1 \\ 0 \end{bmatrix}, \begin{bmatrix} 0 \\ 1 \\ 0 \\ 1 \end{bmatrix}, \begin{bmatrix} 1 \\ 0 \\ 0 \\ 1 \end{bmatrix}, \begin{bmatrix} 0 \\ 1 \\ 1 \\ 0 \end{bmatrix} \right\}.$$

Definition 2. OR-ed operation $L(V(k))$ is defined as follows. For $n \times 1$ Boolean matrix $M = [m_i]$, where $1 \leq i \leq n$, $L(V(k))$ represents the "OR"-ed operation of any k-tuple column vector V, i.e., $L(V(k)) = m_1 + m_2 + \ldots + m_k$.

Definition 3. Transfer operation $T(\cdot)$ is described as follows. Let $B = [b_{ij}]$ be an $n \times m$ Boolean matrix, where $1 \leq i \leq n$ and $1 \leq j \leq m$. $T(B)$ denotes the set of "m" $n \times 1$ column matrices

$$\left\{ \begin{bmatrix} b_{11} \\ b_{21} \\ \vdots \\ b_{n1} \end{bmatrix}, \begin{bmatrix} b_{12} \\ b_{22} \\ \vdots \\ b_{n2} \end{bmatrix}, \ldots, \begin{bmatrix} b_{1m} \\ b_{2m} \\ \vdots \\ b_{nm} \end{bmatrix} \right\}.$$

In the beginning, we first construct two white and black sets consisting of $n \times 1$ column matrices for a (n, n) ProbVSS scheme defined in Yang [19]. Let C_0 and C_1 be the white and black sets consisting of $n \times 1$ column matrices, respectively. Next according to the significance of the participant in the organization, it first classifies r priority levels and then assigns every participant a unique weighting value depending on the duty of each participant. Without losing the generality, it assumes that the priority level of participant i is assigned as t_i where $1 \leq t_i < n$, $t_1 + t_2 + \ldots + t_i = n$ for $i = 1 \ldots r$. According to the r priority levels, it uses OR-ed operation function $L(V(t_i))$ to construct the two priority sets C_0^p and C_1^p consisting of $r \times 1$ column matrices, respectively. For two sets C_0 and C_1 sets consisting of $n \times 1$ column matrices, let $M = [m_i]$ be a $n \times 1$ Boolean matrix. We choose t_1 rows among n rows and perform $L(V(t_1)) = m_1 + m_2 + \ldots + m_{t_1}$ for all $n \times 1$ matrices. Next we choose t_2 rows among remaining $(n - t_1)$ rows and perform $L(V(t_2)) = m_1 + m_2 + \ldots + m_{t_2}$ for all $(n - t_1) \times 1$ matrices. and so on. Finally perform $L(V(t_r)) = m_1 + m_2 + \ldots + m_{t_r}$ from remaining $(n - t_1 - t_2 - \ldots - t_{r-1})$ rows. After that, both priority sets C_0^p and C_1^p are shown as follows.

$$C_0^p = \left\{ \begin{bmatrix} L(V(t_1))_{11} \\ L(V(t_2))_{21} \\ \vdots \\ L(V(t_r))_{r1} \end{bmatrix}, \begin{bmatrix} L(V(t_1))_{11} \\ L(V(t_2))_{21} \\ \vdots \\ L(V(t_r))_{r1} \end{bmatrix}, \cdots \begin{bmatrix} L(V(t_1))_{11} \\ L(V(t_2))_{21} \\ \vdots \\ L(V(t_r))_{r1} \end{bmatrix} \right\}, C_1^p = \left\{ \begin{bmatrix} L(V(t_1))_{11} \\ L(V(t_2))_{21} \\ \vdots \\ L(V(t_r))_{r1} \end{bmatrix}, \begin{bmatrix} L(V(t_1))_{11} \\ L(V(t_2))_{21} \\ \vdots \\ L(V(t_r))_{r1} \end{bmatrix}, \cdots \begin{bmatrix} L(V(t_1))_{11} \\ L(V(t_2))_{21} \\ \vdots \\ L(V(t_r))_{r1} \end{bmatrix} \right\}$$

Definition 4. A weighted (k,n) non-expanded VSS scheme can be represented as two priority sets, white set C_0^p and black set C_1^p consisting of λ_0 and λ_1 $n \times 1$ matrices, respectively. When sharing a white (resp. black) pixel, the dealer first randomly chooses one $r \times 1$ column matrix in C_0^p(resp.C_1^p), and then randomly selects one row of this chosen column matrix to a relative share. The chosen matrix defines the color level of pixel in every one of the r shares. A weighted (k,n) threshold non-expanded VSS scheme is considered valid if following conditions are satisfied:

(1) For these λ_0 (resp. λ_1) column matrices in the set C_0^p(resp. C_1^p), the "OR"-ed value of any i-tuple column vector V is $L(V(i))$. And the sum of their weight is $(t_1 + t_2 + \ldots + t_i)$. These values of all matrices form a set S_0 (resp. S_1).

(2) While $(t_1 + t_2 + \ldots + t_i) \geq k$, The two sets S_0 and S_1 satisfy that $p_0 \geq p_{TH}$ and $p_1 \leq p_{TH} - \alpha$, where p_0 and p_1 are the appearance probabilities of the "0" (white color) in the set S_0 and S_1, respectively.

(3) For any subset $\{t_1, t_2, \ldots, t_q\}$ of $\{1, 2, \ldots, i\}$ with $t_q < k$ or $\sum_{i \in \{1, \ldots q\}} t_i < k$, the p_0

and p_1 are the same.

From above definition, the first two conditions are called condition contrast and the third condition is called condition security.

2.2   A Weighted (k,n)-Threshold VSS Scheme Without Pixel Expansion

Because (k,n) ProbVSS is based on conventional VSS introduced by Naor and Shamir [13], in which two $n \times m$ matrices B^0 and B^1 were defined for encoding white and black pixel of the original image, respectively. The parameter m denotes the shadow size.

Here we use function $T(\cdot)$ to transform two $n \times m$ matrices B^0 and B^1 into two sets $C_0 = T(B^0)$ and $C_1 = T(B^1)$ consisting of "m" $n \times 1$ column matrices, respectively.

We assign every participant a weighting value depending on the significance of each participant. Here we suppose that the priority level of participant i is assigned as t_i where $1 \leq t_i < k$ for $i = 1, \ldots, k$. Then according to the priority level, we use OR-ed operation function $L(V(t_i))$ to construct the two priority sets C_0^p and C_1^p consisting of "m" $r \times 1$ matrices, respectively. Finally, we use the two priority sets C_0^p and C_1^p to encode both white and black pixel of original image, respectively. Let $B^0 = \begin{bmatrix} b_{ij}^0 \end{bmatrix}$ and $B^1 = \begin{bmatrix} b_{ij}^1 \end{bmatrix}$ be two $n \times m$ Boolean matrices, where $1 \leq i \leq n$ and $1 \leq j \leq m$. $T(B^0)$ and $T(B^1)$ denote the sets of "m" $n \times 1$ column matrices respectively.

$$
C_0 = T(B^0) = \left\{ \overbrace{\begin{bmatrix} b_{11}^0 \\ b_{21}^0 \\ \vdots \\ b_{n1}^0 \end{bmatrix}, \begin{bmatrix} b_{12}^0 \\ b_{22}^0 \\ \vdots \\ b_{n2}^0 \end{bmatrix}, \cdots, \begin{bmatrix} b_{1m}^0 \\ b_{2m}^0 \\ \vdots \\ b_{nm}^0 \end{bmatrix}}^{m} \right\}, \quad C_1 = T(B^1) = \left\{ \overbrace{\begin{bmatrix} b_{11}^1 \\ b_{21}^1 \\ \vdots \\ b_{n1}^1 \end{bmatrix}, \begin{bmatrix} b_{12}^1 \\ b_{22}^1 \\ \vdots \\ b_{n2}^1 \end{bmatrix}, \cdots, \begin{bmatrix} b_{1m}^1 \\ b_{2m}^1 \\ \vdots \\ b_{nm}^1 \end{bmatrix}}^{m} \right\}
$$

The two priority sets C_0^p (from C_0) and C_1^p (from C_1) are shown as follows.

$$
C_0^p = \left\{ \overbrace{\begin{bmatrix} L(V(t_1))_{11} \\ L(V(t_2))_{21} \\ \vdots \\ L(V(t_r))_{r1} \end{bmatrix}, \begin{bmatrix} L(V(t_1))_{11} \\ L(V(t_2))_{21} \\ \vdots \\ L(V(t_r))_{r1} \end{bmatrix}, \cdots \begin{bmatrix} L(V(t_1))_{11} \\ L(V(t_2))_{21} \\ \vdots \\ L(V(t_r))_{r1} \end{bmatrix}}^{m} \right\}, \quad C_1^p = \left\{ \overbrace{\begin{bmatrix} L(V(t_1))_{11} \\ L(V(t_2))_{21} \\ \vdots \\ L(V(t_r))_{r1} \end{bmatrix}, \begin{bmatrix} L(V(t_1))_{11} \\ L(V(t_2))_{21} \\ \vdots \\ L(V(t_r))_{r1} \end{bmatrix}, \cdots \begin{bmatrix} L(V(t_1))_{11} \\ L(V(t_2))_{21} \\ \vdots \\ L(V(t_r))_{r1} \end{bmatrix}}^{m} \right\}
$$

Construction 1. Let B^0 and B^1 defined in the conventional (k,n) VSS scheme be the two $n \times m$ white and black matrices, respectively. The parameters of the share size is m, and the Hamming weight of "OR"-ed operation on any k of the n rows in white (resp. black) matrix is $(m-h)$ (resp. $m-l$) where $h > l$. A weighted (k,n) threshold VSS scheme has two priority white and black sets, C_0^p and C_1^p, consisting of "m" $r \times 1$ column matrices.

Theorem 1. The scheme from Construction 1 is a weighted (k,n) -threshold VSS scheme without pixel expansion. It can be constructed to have the parameter probability $p_{TH} = \frac{h}{m}$ and the contrast $\alpha = \frac{h-l}{m}$.

Proof. For a proof of the condition "security", according to the properties of B^0 and B^1 defined in the conventional (k,n) VSS scheme, any t (the sum of weights $< k$) rows of all the matrices obtained by permuting the columns of B^0 and B^1 contain the same matrices with the same frequencies. Moreover, two sets C_0^p and C_1^p are obtained by performing $L(V(t))$ of any t rows of the column matrices in two sets $C_0 = T(B^0)$ and $C_1 = T(B^1)$, respectively. Therefore, the same row in both C_0^p and C_1^p also contain the same matrices with same frequencies. Thus any one share or these t stacked shares cannot reveal anything about original image. The two priority sets are:

$$
C_0^p = \left\{ \overbrace{\begin{bmatrix} L(V(t_1))_{11}^1 \\ L(V(t_2))_{21}^1 \\ \vdots \\ L(V(t_r))_{r1}^1 \end{bmatrix}, \begin{bmatrix} L(V(t_1))_{11}^2 \\ L(V(t_2))_{21}^2 \\ \vdots \\ L(V(t_r))_{r1}^2 \end{bmatrix}, \cdots \begin{bmatrix} L(V(t_1))_{11}^m \\ L(V(t_2))_{21}^m \\ \vdots \\ L(V(t_r))_{r1}^m \end{bmatrix}}^{m} \right\}, \quad C_1^p = \left\{ \overbrace{\begin{bmatrix} L(V(t_1))_{11}^1 \\ L(V(t_2))_{21}^1 \\ \vdots \\ L(V(t_r))_{r1}^1 \end{bmatrix}, \begin{bmatrix} L(V(t_1))_{11}^2 \\ L(V(t_2))_{21}^2 \\ \vdots \\ L(V(t_r))_{r1}^2 \end{bmatrix}, \cdots \begin{bmatrix} L(V(t_1))_{11}^m \\ L(V(t_2))_{21}^m \\ \vdots \\ L(V(t_r))_{r1}^m \end{bmatrix}}^{m} \right\}
$$

If the sum of weights of any i rows is more than or equal to k, i.e., $(t_1 + t_2 + \ldots + t_i) \geq k$, then performing "OR"-ed operation on these i rows

$$\lambda = \left\{ L \begin{bmatrix} \begin{bmatrix} L(V(t_1))_{11}^1 \\ L(V(t_2))_{21}^1 \\ \vdots \\ L(V(t_{i-1}))_{i-11}^1 \\ L(V(t_i))_{i1}^1 \end{bmatrix} ,L \begin{bmatrix} L(V(t_1))_{11}^2 \\ L(V(t_2))_{21}^2 \\ \vdots \\ L(V(t_{i-1}))_{i-11}^2 \\ L(V(t_i))_{i1}^2 \end{bmatrix} ,\cdots,L \begin{bmatrix} L(V(t_1))_{11}^m \\ L(V(t_2))_{21}^m \\ \vdots \\ L(V(t_{i-1}))_{i-11}^m \\ L(V(t_i))_{i1}^m \end{bmatrix} \end{bmatrix} \right\} = \left\{ L \begin{bmatrix} b_{11}^1 \\ \vdots \\ b_{t_11}^1 \\ \vdots \\ b_{t_i1}^1 \end{bmatrix} ,L \begin{bmatrix} b_{11}^2 \\ \vdots \\ b_{t_11}^2 \\ \vdots \\ b_{t_i1}^2 \end{bmatrix} ,\cdots,L \begin{bmatrix} b_{11}^m \\ \vdots \\ b_{t_11}^m \\ \vdots \\ b_{t_i1}^m \end{bmatrix} \right\}$$

will get $S_0 = \{\overbrace{0,\ldots,0}^{h},\overbrace{1,\ldots,1}^{m-h}\}$ and $S_1 = \{\overbrace{0,\ldots,0}^{l},\overbrace{1,\ldots,1}^{m-l}\}$. The appearance probabilities of white color in S_0 and S_1 are $p_0 = \frac{h}{m}$ and $p_1 = \frac{l}{m}$, and thus the threshold probability is $p_{TH} = \frac{h}{m}$ and the contrast is $\alpha = \frac{h-l}{m}$.

3 Experimental Results

Here some related experiments of the proposed weighted visual secret sharing scheme are conducted in this section. We present the experimental results to demonstrate the performance of construction (k, n) VSS. The standard 512×512 black-white image is shown in Fig. 1(a). And another gray level image of size 512×512 pixels contains Lena. Since the halftone image is pretty suited for visual cryptography. So the gray-level image is transformed into a 512×512 halftone image as shown in Fig. 1(b). These two images are used as the secret images in the experiments.

(a)   (b)

Fig. 1. Two secret images.

The (3,5) VSS is taken as the example. The secret image is divided into two priority sets. They are $P_1 = \{t_1 = 2, t_2 = 2, t_3 = 1\}$ and $P_2 = \{t_1 = 2, t_2 = 1, t_3 = 1, t_4 = 1\}$, respectively. The three different priority shares of P_1 are shown in Fig. 2(a)–(c), respectively. The Fig. 2(d) to (e) are the superimposed results of any two out of the three shares. Figure 2(f) is the stacked result of all three shares.

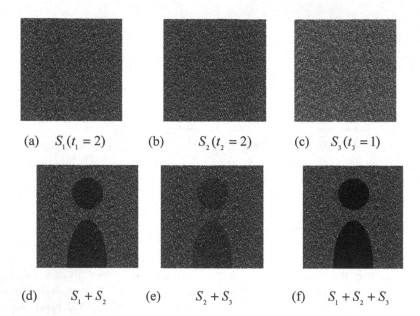

(a) $S_1(t_1 = 2)$ (b) $S_2(t_2 = 2)$ (c) $S_3(t_3 = 1)$

(d) $S_1 + S_2$ (e) $S_2 + S_3$ (f) $S_1 + S_2 + S_3$

Fig. 2. Experimental results 1: (a–c) three shares with different weight, (d–e) two shares stacked, and (f) all shares stacked.

The four different priority shares of P_2 are shown in Fig. 3(a)–(d), respectively. The Fig. 3(e) to (g) are the superimposed results of share1 (t_1) and share2 (t_2), share2 (t_2) and share3 (t_3) as well as share2 (t_2), share3 (t_3) and share4 (t_4). Finally, Fig. 3(h) is the stacked result of all four shares.

4 Discussions

After demonstrating the feasibility of the proposed scheme, comparisons with previous VSS methods are shown in Table 1. The benefits of the proposed scheme are: first, the size of each share equals to that of original secret image. Each share has no pixel expansion and it can save a lot of storage space. Second, each share has different weight according to the different significance of participant in the organization. That means each share has different ability to restore the secret image. Third, the progressive technique can make the secret image reveal with different level. That is, according to the participants' duty in the organization, each participant in the proposed scheme is assigned to different priority level in the real world.

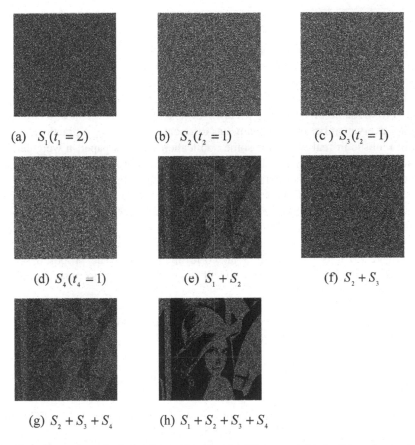

(a) $S_1(t_1 = 2)$ (b) $S_2(t_2 = 1)$ (c) $S_3(t_2 = 1)$

(d) $S_4(t_4 = 1)$ (e) $S_1 + S_2$ (f) $S_2 + S_3$

(g) $S_2 + S_3 + S_4$ (h) $S_1 + S_2 + S_3 + S_4$

Fig. 3. Experimental results 2: (a–d) four shares with different weight, (e–f) two shares stacked, (g) three shares stacked, and (h) all shares stacked.

Table 1. Comparison between related works and the proposed scheme

Schemes	Different priority	Visually progressive	No-Pixel expansion
Naor and Shamir [13]	No	No	No
Yang [19]	No	No	Yes
Cimato et al. [6]	No	No	Yes
Fang [7]	No	Yes	No
Chen and Lee [5]	No	Yes	Yes
Fang and Lin [8]	No	Yes	No
Chao and Lin [3]	No	Yes	Yes
Chen [4]	Yes	Yes	No
Hou et al. [12]	Yes	Yes	Yes
The proposed	Yes	Yes	Yes

5   Conclusions

Traditional (k, n)-threshold visual secret sharing (VSS) schemes encode a secret image into n sharing images, and the stacked image will reveal the secret while k or more shares are superimposed. Nevertheless, those methods did not give proper privileges according to the significance of participants and every participant in the scheme is assigned to the same privilege level. However, take the management of a company for example; every member of a company has different significance in practice. Therefore, it is not realistic in real world for some applications. In this paper, a weighted (k, n)-threshold non-expanded visual secret sharing scheme is proposed. The scheme shares the secret image among the participants with different weights. And the secret can be reconstructed if the sum of the weights of the participants is greater than or equal to the threshold k. Compared with other visual secret sharing schemes, the proposed scheme has the four characteristics: (a) every share has different privilege value (b) it is an "all-or-nothing" and a progressive scheme (c) the size of each share equals to the original secret image (d) it is suitable for real world applications. The proposed scheme is suitable for applications in the daily life. It has high potential to push the scheme to various applications.

Acknowledgements. This research was partially supported by Ministry of Science Technology, Taiwan, R.O.C., under contract no. MOST 105-2221-E-415 -012.

References

1. Blakley, G.: Safeguarding cryptographic keys. In: Proceedings AFIPS 1979 National Computer Conference, pp. 313–317, AFIPS Press, New York (1979)
2. Blundo, C., Santis, A.D., Stinson, D.R.: On the contrast in visual cryptography schemes. J. Crypt. **12**, 261–289 (1999)
3. Chao, K.Y., Lin, J.C.: User-friendly sharing of images: progressive approach based on modulus operation. J. Electronic Imaging **18**(3), 0330081–0330089 (2009)
4. Chen, S.K.: Weighted visual cryptography with non-expansible shares. J. Image Process. Commun. **5**(1), 1–6 (2013)
5. Chen, T.H., Lee, Y.S.: Yet another friendly progressive visual secret sharing scheme. In: Fifth International Conference on Intelligent Information Hiding and Multimedia Signal Processing (2009)
6. Cimato, S., Prisco, R.D., Santis, A.D.: Probabilistic visual cryptography schemes. Comput. J. **49**(1), 97–107 (2006)
7. Fang, W.P.: Friendly progressive visual secret sharing. Pattern Recogn. **41**, 1410–1414 (2008)
8. Fang, W.P., Lin, J.C.: Progressive viewing and sharing of sensitive image. Pattern Recogn. Image Anal. **15**(4), 632–636 (2006). https://doi.org/10.1134/S1054661806040080
9. Homiest, T., Krause, M., Simon, H.U.: Contrast optimal k out of n secret sharing schemes in visual cryptography. Theoret. Comput. Sci. **240**, 471–485 (2000)
10. Hou, Y.C.: Visual cryptography for color images. Pattern Recogn. **36**(7), 1619–1629 (2003)
11. Hou, Y.C., Chang, C.Y., Hsu, C.S.: Visual cryptography for color images without pixel expansion. In: Proceeding of CISST 2001, vol. I, pp. 239–245, Las Vegas (2001)

12. Hou, Y.C., Quan, Z.Y., Tsai, C.F.: General model for the priority-based progressive visual secret sharing. Journal of C.C.I.T, **42**(2), 33–48 (2013)
13. Naor, M., Shamir, A.: Visual cryptography. In: De Santis, A. (ed.) EUROCRYPT 1994. LNCS, vol. 950, pp. 1–12. Springer, Heidelberg (1995). https://doi.org/10.1007/BFb0053419
14. Shamir, A.: How to share a secret. Commun. ACM **22**(11), 612–613 (1979)
15. Thien, C.C., Lin, J.C.: Secret image sharing. Comput. Graph. **26**(5), 765–770 (2002)
16. Verheul, E.R., Van Tilborg, H.C.: Constructions and properties of k out of n visual secret sharing schemes. Design, Codes and Cryptography **11**(2), 179–196 (1997). https://doi.org/10.1023/A:1008280705142
17. Viet, D.Q., Kurosawa, K.: Almost ideal contrast visual cryptography with reversing. In: Okamoto, T. (ed.) CT-RSA 2004. LNCS, vol. 2964, pp. 353–365. Springer, Heidelberg (2004). https://doi.org/10.1007/978-3-540-24660-2_27
18. Wang, A., Zhang, L., Ma, N., Li, X.: Two secret sharing schemes based on boolean operations. Pattern Recogn. **40**, 2776–2785 (2007)
19. Yang, N.: New visual secret sharing schemes using probabilistic method. Pattern Recogn. Lett. **25**(4), 481–494 (2004)
20. Yang, C.N., Chen, T.S.: Aspect ratio invariant visual secret sharing schemes with minimum pixel expansion. Pattern Recogn. Lett. **26**, 193–206 (2005)

Enhancement of FTP-NDN Supporting Nondesignated Receivers

Arijit Karati, Chun-I Fan$^{(\boxtimes)}$, and Ruei-Hau Hsu

Department of Computer Science and Engineering,
National Sun Yat-sen University, Kaohsiung 80424, Taiwan
{arijit.karati,cifan,rhhsu}@mail.cse.nsysu.edu.tw

Abstract. Recently, Fan et al. proposed the File Transfer Protocol Based on Re-Encryption for Named Data Network (FTP-NDN) in order to reduce the cost that affects simultaneous access of same video services. The authors designed an elegant network architecture to deal with secure file transmission to the unknown potential customers. The technique is shown to be secured under Decisional Bilinear Diffie-Hellman (DBDH) assumption and computationally efficient than other existing techniques. Although, the protocol achieves data confidentiality, it does not provide node authentication during transmission in the NDN. In this paper, we propose an authentication scheme using the bilinear pairing. Performance evaluation shows that the proposed technique can be incorporated with considerable computation overhead.

Keywords: Confidentiality · Authenticity ·
Named Data Networking (NDN)

1 Introduction

In the modern digital era, Internet plays a vital role in making a data driven economy by integrating a number of objects into our daily lives. The Internet is the most common surface nowadays where people share their sensitive data among themselves. In the neoteric society, the data are not limited to textual form, rather it is now in the form of multimedia. Most of the users communicate with another by the help of IP address-based network although it is inefficient in content distribution. In this architecture, a user may face several problems, e.g., simultaneous access of a same file by several users, host authentication, etc. In this scenario, a recent communication architecture called Named Data Network (NDN) [8], built on hierarchical named data, solves the aforementioned problems. Evolution of this data-centric network architecture from the host-centric network architecture (IP) was primarily introduced by [6] in 2009. The motivation of NDN is to focus on the data (named as content) that a user wants

The work is supported by Information Security Research Center, National Sun Yat-sen University, Taiwan.

rather to provide a reference of a specific address (named as hosts) where the data is located. In the NDN architecture, a data owner generates a file that is to be shared over the network. Then, it sends the file by appending its signature in the network. On the other hand, anyone as a receiver can verify the owner's signature instead of authenticating hosts. The detailed process is further discussed in Fig. 1. However, security is the major concern in this architecture. Since it has several advantages over IP-address based communication, NDN is the prime focus to the researchers. In 2012, Etefia et al. [2] designed a NDN-based hierarchical network topology to support the military communications. The authors showed that the mobile communication can be merged with the NDN to acquire the other military goals. In the same year, Hamdane et al. [5] constructed a hierarchical identity based scheme for the NDN. Here, they appended a signature with the name of packet to enrich the security. After that, Grassi et al. [4] devised an efficient vehicular communication concept by introducing the NDN. In their construction, vehicles use the mobile networks to communicate with another vehicle. Recently, Fan et al. [3] designed a secure file sharing protocol, named as FTP-NDN, using bilinear pairings for the NDN. The authors showed that their protocol is also applicable for the nondesignated/unspecified users. Although, the work withstands many attacks, we notice that there is no node authentication during the public transmission of an encrypted file from the source to destination party. Hence, we improve the scheme to its next level by introducing the node authenticity feature. The proposed work is based on bilinear pairing and outputs satisfactory result.

Rest of the manuscript is structured as follows: Sect. 2 discusses some useful concepts to understand our work. Section 3 discusses Fan et al.'s designed FTP-NDN with its limitation(s). After that in Sects. 4 and 5, we discuss the proposed authentication technique for FTP-NDN and its performance analysis. Finally, Sect. 6 concludes the paper with some remarks.

2   Preliminaries

This section illustrates some backgrounds of the proposed authentication technique. Besides, Table 1 comprises a list of notations used in this article.

2.1   NDN Architecture

Named Data Networking (NDN) is a future Internet architecture invigorated by years of the technological research into the network usage. The concept of NDN is derived from the Content-Centric Networking (CCN) which was introduced by Van Jacobson in 2006. Figure 1 shows a typical file transfer protocol in the NDN. It is a network of several active nodes where a data consumer sends an interest packet to its nearest node in order to access a remote file, and the further communications are as follows:

Table 1. Notation table

Notation	Meaning
msk	KGC computed secure master key
$params$	KGC computed public parameters
ID_i	User/Node i's valid identity
sk_i, K_i	User i's secret key
$RK_{\{i,j\}}, K_i$	Node i's re-encryption key from Node i to j and secret key of Node i
p	Considerably large odd prime
G_1, G_2	Two same p-ordered cyclic groups, one additive and another multiplicative
P	Generator of group G_1
$k \in_R K$	k is chosen at random from set K
$\perp$	Unique symbol indicates *return nothing*
Z_p^*	$Z_p - \{0\}$

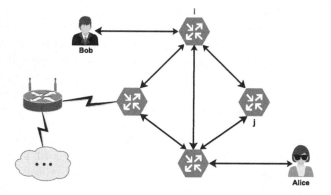

Fig. 1. Architectural overview of file transfer protocol in NDN

1. On receiving an interest packet, the nearest node finds whether it has file.
2. If it has file in its local cache, then
   - it answers the name and file as a data packet to the consumer.
3. Else, the node will request to its nearest nodes for file, and the process will continue until it touches the data source.
4. On receiving file, the node sends file to the requested consumer and keep a copy of file into its local cache temporarily for further same requests.

It may be noted that file can be provided by the nearest node to the consumer.

2.2   Identity-Based Encryption (IBE)

Novel concept of IBE was primarily introduced by Shamir [7] in 1984, however, the practical instantiation was drawn by Boneh [1] in 2001 using the bilinear pairings. The formal structure of IBE contains four following algorithms.

1. $(\mathsf{param}, \mathsf{msk}) \leftarrow \mathsf{Setup}(\mathsf{k})$: KGC runs the algorithm for security parameter k. It produces $params$, known to everyone and msk, known only to KGC.
2. $\mathsf{d_{ID}} \leftarrow \mathsf{Extract}(\mathsf{ID}, \mathsf{param}, \mathsf{msk})$: KGC runs the algorithm for input parameters $ID, param$, and msk. It produces user's private key d_{ID}.
3. $\mathsf{CT} \leftarrow \mathsf{Encrypt}(\mathsf{ID}, \mathsf{param}, \mathsf{m})$: A sender executes the algorithm for input parameters $ID, param$, and m. It outputs the ciphertext CT.
4. $\mathsf{m}/ \perp \leftarrow \mathsf{Decrypt}(\mathsf{d_{ID}}, \mathsf{param}, \mathsf{CT})$: A receiver executes the algorithm for input parameters $d_{ID}, param$, and CT. It outputs the plaintext m or $\perp$.

2.3 Bilinear Map

Assume, $(P, Q) \in_R (G_1)^2$ and $(x, y) \in_R (Z_p^*)^2$ are chosen at random. An efficiently-computable map $e : G \times G \rightarrow G_T$ is said to be an admissible bilinear pairing if it holds the following properties:

1. Bilinear: Always produces $e(xP, yQ) = e(P, Q)^{xy}$.
2. Non-degenerate: Satisfies $e(P, P) = 1$, where $1 \in G_T$ is the identity element.
3. Computable: One efficient algorithm is always exists to compute $e(P, Q)$.

2.4 Intractable Problem

This section discusses two polynomial time (t) hard problems which are used in this work. We define $(x, y, z, u) \in_R (Z_p^*)^4$ chosen at random.

Definition 1 (Computational Diffie-Hellman (CDH)). *For an algorithm $\mathcal{A}$, computation of $Z = xyP$ from given (P, xP, yP) is infeasible in time t. The advantage ϵ of $\mathcal{A}$ to breach CDH is mentioned as $\Pr\left[\mathcal{A}(xP, yP) = xyP\right] \geq \epsilon$*

Definition 2 (Decisional Bilinear Diffie-Hellman (DBDH)). *For $\mathcal{A}$, decision of $u = xyz$ from $(P, xP, yP, zP, e(P, P)^{xyz})$ and $(P, xP, yP, zP, e(P, P)^u)$ is infeasible in time t. The advantage ϵ of $\mathcal{A}$ to breach DBDH is mentioned as $\left|\Pr\left[\mathcal{A}(P, xP, yP, zP, e(P, P)^{xyz})\right] - \Pr\left[\mathcal{A}(P, xP, yP, zP, e(P, P)^u)\right]\right| \geq \epsilon$*

3 Overview of Fan et al.'s Protocol

In this section, we explain the construction and limitation of the file transfer protocol by Fan et al. [3].

3.1 Details of the FTP-NDN

The protocol comprises six following algorithms:

1. $\mathsf{param} \leftarrow \mathsf{Setup}(\mathsf{k})$: For a security parameter k, KGC computes public parameter $param$ by executing the following tasks.
   (a) considers a bilinear pairing $e : G \times G \rightarrow G_T$ and a generator $P \in_R G$.

(b) chooses a symmetric key cryptosystem that considers an encryption ($SymEnc$) and a decryption ($SymDec$) functions with a l-bit key.

(c) selects three cryptographic hash functions as $H : \{0,1\}^* \to G$; $H_1 : G_T \to \{0,1\}^l$, and $H_2 : \{0,1\}^* \times G_T \to Z_p^*$.

(d) sets $msk = (s)$ and compute $P_{pub} = sP$ as the public key for $s \in_R Z_p^*$.

(e) Publishes the public parameter as
$$param = \{G, G_T, p, P, e, SymEnc, SymDec, P_{pub}, H, H_1, H_2\}$$

2. $sk_i \leftarrow$ Extract(param, ID_i, s): On receiving sufficient input parameters, KGC outputs the user's public key $pk_i = H(ID_i)$ and private key $sk_i = sH(ID_i)$.

3. $RK_{i,j} \leftarrow$ ReKeyGen(param, ID_i, ID_j, s): On receiving sufficient inputs, KGC generates a key as $RK_{i,j} = s(H(ID_j) - H(ID_i))$ to re-encrypt a ciphertext received by an NDN node i for another NDN node (or a user) j.

4. $CT_{i,0} \leftarrow$ Enc(param, m, ID_i): On receiving a plaintext message $m \in \{0,1\}^*$ along with sufficient inputs, the encryption process is performed as follows:

(a) selects an element $K \in_R G_T$ and sets $r = H_2(m, K) \in Z_p^*$.

(b) sets the ciphertext $CT_{i,0} = (C_1, C_2, U_{i,0})$ where $C_1 = SymEnc_{H_1(K)}(m)$, $C_2 = rP$, $U_{i,0} = K \cdot e(rH(ID_i), P_{pub})$.

5. $CT_{j,k+1} \leftarrow$ ReEnc(param, $CT_{i,k}$, $RK_{i,j}$): On receiving $CT_{i,k} = (C_1, C_2, U_{i,k})$ with sufficient inputs, it calculates $U_{j,k+1} = U_{i,k} \cdot e(RK_{i,j}, C_2)$ and output the re-encrypted ciphertext as $CT_{j,k+1} = (C_1, C_2, U_{j,k+1})$. It can be noticed that $U_{j,k+1} = U_{i,k} \cdot e(RK_{i,j}, C_2) = K \cdot e(rH(ID_j), P_{pub})$.

6. $m/\perp \leftarrow$ Dec(param, $CT_{x,n}$, sk_x): On receiving sufficient inputs, the algorithm decrypts $m = SymDec_{H_1(K)}(C_1)$ where $K = U_{x,n} \cdot e(sk_x, C_2)^{-1}$. Finally it returns m if $C_2 \overset{?}{=} H_2(m, K)P$, otherwise, $\perp$.

3.2 Scope of Improvement in Fan et al.'s Protocol

Fan et al. showed that their protocol maintains confidentiality property under DBDH assumption, however, they didn't consider the authentication issue in between two adjacent nodes in the NDN. More specifically, an NDN node i forwards the ciphertext to its succeeding node $i+1$ without verifying the authenticity of ciphertext sent by its preceding node $i-1$. Therefore, an malicious node j can act like node $i-1$ and forward some unwanted ciphertext. In the next section we discuss an enhanced file transfer protocol based on [3] for the named data network.

4   Proposed Authentication for FTP-NDN

This section demonstrates the proposed authentication technique as a plugin for the Fan et al.'s FTP-NDN. The upgraded version of [3] with incorporated authentication constrains is discussed below.

1. param $\leftarrow$ Setup(k): For the security parameter k, KGC performs the same actions as discussed in Sect. 3.1 excepts the followings:

(a) chooses $(s, t) \in_R (Z_p^*)^2$ and sets $msk = (s, t)$.

(b) computes $P_{pub1} = sP$ and $P_{pub2} = tP_{pub1}$.

Finally, it publishes the public parameter as

$$param = \{G, G_T, p, P, e, SymEnc, SymDec, P_{pub1}, P_{pub2}, H, H_1, H_2\}$$

2. $sk_i \leftarrow$ Extract(param, ID_i, s): The algorithm acts as the same like in Sect. 3.1. In addition, it computes $K_i = tH(ID_i)$ in the NDN. Therefore the secret key of user i is $sk_i = (sH(ID_i), tH(ID_i))$.

3. $RK_{i,j} \leftarrow$ ReKeyGen(param, ID_i, ID_j, s): This algorithm executes same tasks defined in Sect. 3.1. In addition, it computes $K_i = tH(ID_i)$.

4. $CT_{i,0} \leftarrow$ Enc(param, m, ID_i): On receiving a plaintext message $m \in \{0,1\}^*$ along with sufficient inputs, the encryption performs as follows:

(a) selects an element $K \in_R G_T$ and sets $r = H_2(m, K) \in Z_p^*$.

(b) computes $C_1 = SymEnc_{H_1(K)}(m)$, $C_2 = rP$, $U_{i,0} = K \cdot e\,(rH(ID_i), P_{pub1})$, and $V_{i,0} = K \cdot e\,(K_{ID_{-1}}, hP_{pub1})$, where $h = H_1(K \cdot e\,(rH(ID_{i-1}), P_{pub1}))$. Finally, it sets ciphertext $CT_{i,0} = (C_1, C_2, U_{i,0}, V_{i,0})$.

5. $CT_{j,k+1} \leftarrow$ ReEnc(param, $CT_{i,k}$, $RK_{i,j}$): On receiving $CT_{i,k} = (C_1, C_2, U_{i,k}, C_{3,k})$ with sufficient inputs, it performs the followings:

(a) computes $X = U_{i,k} \cdot e(RK_{i,i-1}, C_2)$ and sets $h = H_1(X)$

(b) if $(V_{i,k} \neq e(H(ID_{i-1}), hP_{pub2}))$ then aborts the connection.

else,

   – sets $h' = H_1(U_{i,k})$ and computes $V_{j,k+1} = e(K_i, h'P_{pub1})$

   – calculates $U_{j,k+1} = U_{i,k} \cdot e(RK_{i,j}, C_2)$

   – outputs the re-encrypted text as $CT_{j,k+1} = (C_1, C_2, U_{j,k+1}, V_{j,k+1})$.

If it doesn't abort, then it is noticed that $V_{i,k} = e(H(ID_{i-1}), hP_{pub2})$ always hold as $e(H(ID_{i-1}), hP_{pub2}) = e(tH(ID_{i-1}), hP_{pub1}) = e(K_{i-1}, hP_{pub1})$ where $h = H_1(U_{i,k} \cdot e(RK_{i,i-1}, C_2)) = H_1(U_{i,k-1})$. Besides, we have $U_{j,k+1} = U_{i,k} \cdot e(RK_{i,j}, C_2) = K \cdot e(rH(ID_j), P_{pub})$.

6. $m/\perp \leftarrow$ Dec(param, $CT_{x,n}$, sk_x): On receiving sufficient inputs, the algorithm performs following:

(a) computes $Y = U_{x,n} \cdot e(RK_{x,x-1}, C_2)$ and sets $h = H_1(Y)$.

(b) if $(V_{x,n} \neq e(H(ID_{x-1}), hP_{pub2}))$, then returns $\perp$

else,

   – computes $K = U_{x,n} \cdot e(sk_x, C_2)^{-1}$.

   – decrypts $m = SymDec_{H_1(K)}(C_1)$.

   – if $C_2 \overset{?}{=} H_2(m, K)P$, returns m; otherwise returns $\perp$.

This completes the description of proposed authentication plugin mounted in Fan et al.'s FTP-NDN [3]. For better clarity, we further discuss it in Fig. 2. This picture considers five nodes (A, B, C, D, E), and two users $(Alice, Bob)$. In order to receive any remote file in the NDN, Alice requests to its nearby node C. On receiving the request, C checks whether it is present in its local memory or not. As we can see that the file does not exist, so, it asks its nearby nodes D, and then from D to A. The response comes in the reverse order, i.e., $Bob \rightarrow A \rightarrow D \rightarrow C \rightarrow Alice$ to achieve the file. Here, we mount our authentication technique suitably and the same is highlighted as blue.

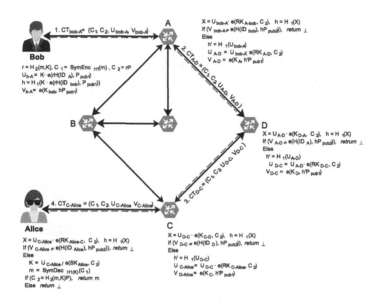

Fig. 2. The proposed authentication technique plugged in the Fan et al.'s FTP-NDN

5   Performance Measurement

This section discusses three essential aspects, such as, the computational, communication and storage costs. Here, we mention only the additional time required to active our technique in Fan et al.'s FTP-NDN [3]. Now, it illustrates each of the above mentioned aspects.

1. *Computational cost: Setup* algorithm executes one exponentiation along with the associated computation discussed in Fan et al. [3]. Similarly, each of *Extract* and *ReKeyGen* algorithms requires additionally one scalar multiplication operation. The *Enc* and *Dec* algorithms on the user sides require additionally two scalar point multiplications and two pairing computations to produce and verify a ciphertext respectively. The *Re-Enc* requires two scalar multiplication and three pairing computations.

2. *Communication cost:* The proposed technique requires one element along with the ciphertext size in Fan et al.'s [3] Protocol. Thus, additional computation cost due to authentication plugin is considered as $|G_T|$ which indicates the number of bits required to represent one element in G_T.

3. *Storage cost:* The proposed technique stores two additional keys, i.e., one during *Extract* and another during *ReKeyGen* algorithms. Therefore, the additional required memory is considered as $2|G_1|$.

Table 2 demonstrates the additional cost measured in different algorithms in Fan et al's FTP-NDN due to the integration of our authentication technique.

Table 2. Required additional cost measurement

	Encryption (User: Producer)	Decryption (User: Consumer)	Re-encryption (Node)	|Ciphertext|	Private Key (KGC)	Re-encryption Key (KGC)
Ours	$2T_s + 2T_p$	$2T_s + 2T_p$	$2T_s + 3T_p$	$\|G_T\|$	T_s	T_s

T_s: the cost of a scalar multiplication in an additive group; $|M|$: the length of M; T_p: the cost of a bilinear pairing;

6   Conclusion

Recently, Fan et al. designed an efficient File Transfer Protocol Based on Re-Encryption for Named Data Network (FTP-NDN). The protocol is useful where simultaneous secure transmission of same file/service are the constrain. The FTP-NDN is shown to be secured under Decisional Bilinear Diffie-Hellman (DBDH) assumption and computationally efficient than other existing techniques. However, The protocol doesn't support one main cryptographic aspect called authenticity property. In this work, we enhanced Fan et al.'s protocol by introducing an authentication techniques. Our technique is efficient and it can be mounted easily into the existing FTP-NDN. Besides, we measured performance of the proposed authentication technique and showed its efficiency.

References

1. Boneh, D., Franklin, M.: Identity-based encryption from the weil pairing. In: Kilian, J. (ed.) CRYPTO 2001. LNCS, vol. 2139, pp. 213–229. Springer, Heidelberg (2001). https://doi.org/10.1007/3-540-44647-8_13
2. Etefia, B., Gerla, M., Zhang, L.: Supporting military communications with named data networking: an emulation analysis. In: MILCOM, pp. 1–6 (2012)
3. Fan, C.I., Chen, I.T., Cheng, C.K., Huang, J.J., Chen, W.T.: FTP-NDN: file transfer protocol based on re-encryption for named data network supporting nondesignated receivers. IEEE Syst. J. **12**(1), 473–484 (2018)
4. Grassi, G., et al.: ACM hotmobile 2013 poster: vehicular inter-networking via named data. ACM SIGMOBILE Mobile Comput. Commun. Rev. **17**(3), 23–24 (2013)
5. Hamdane, B., Serrhrouchni, A., Fadlallah, A., El Fatmi, S.G.: Named-data security scheme for named data networking. In: 2012 Third International Conference on the Network of the Future (NOF), pp. 1–6. IEEE (2012)
6. Jacobson, V., Smetters, D.K., Thornton, J.D., Plass, M.F., Briggs, N.H., Braynard, R.L.: Networking named content. In: Proceedings of the 5th International Conference on Emerging Networking Experiments and Technologies, pp. 1–12. ACM (2009)

7. Shamir, A.: Identity-based cryptosystems and signature schemes. In: Blakley, G.R., Chaum, D. (eds.) CRYPTO 1984. LNCS, vol. 196, pp. 47–53. Springer, Heidelberg (1985). https://doi.org/10.1007/3-540-39568-7_5
8. Zhang, L., et al.: Named data networking (NDN) project. Relatório Técnico NDN-0001, Xerox Palo Alto Research Center-PARC 157, 158 (2010)

Flexible Hierarchical Key Assignment Scheme with Time-Based Assured Deletion for Cloud Storage

Ping-Kun Hsu[1], Mu-Ting Lin[1], and Iuon-Chang Lin[1,2(✉)]

[1] Department of Management Information Systems,
National Chung Hsing University, 250 Kuo-Kuang Road, Taichung 402, Taiwan
iclin@dragon.nchu.edu.tw
[2] Department of Photonics and Communication Engineering,
Asia University, Taichung, Taiwan

Abstract. Everyone now can store their files to the cloud, which makes life more convenience and don't worry about losing the storage device. However, the files store in the cloud is managed by someone may not trustable become a security concern. One of the solutions is encrypting the file and doing assured deletion on it. This paper proposed a time-based assured deletion in a flexible hierarchy structure. Clients will be distributed one derivation key depend on which class and when to over. Then client can use the derivation key to derivate the time-bound secret key to encrypt files. While the predetermined time passing, the secret key will be deleted and the file is unrecoverable. The proposed scheme provides the guarantee of files in the cloud, and also applies to the flexible hierarchy structure which may suitable in the organization.

Keywords: Time-bound · Assured deletion · Cloud storage · Hierarchy key assignment

1 Introduction

In recent years, cloud computing [13, 14] has become an attractive computing infrastructure. One of the attractive reasons is providing the unlimited storage space. For example, the Amazon Simple Storage Service [12] and Dropbox [11] are famous cloud storage providers. Individuals or organizations often require storing their data to avoid data loss, hardware or software failure and inevitable disasters. Instead of buying the storage media to backup these data, individuals or organizations can just outsource their data to the cloud storage provider, which provides storage resources to the data backup.

However, the security concerns of sensitive data become relevant as storing them to the third party. Users are unaware how the cloud service provider mange the information. In addition, it is no idea that whether the employee in the cloud storage provider has accessed or leakage the information. For example, the personal health records make patients can manage their health information in the cloud [15]. The information is highly sensitive. Intentionally or unintended leakage the records may threaten the patient's privacy or right and lead to unexpected consequences.

© Springer Nature Singapore Pte Ltd. 2019
C.-Y. Chang et al. (Eds.): ICS 2018, CCIS 1013, pp. 599–607, 2019.
https://doi.org/10.1007/978-981-13-9190-3_66

This paper proposed a time-based assured deletion for a flexible hierarchical key management scheme to provide the guarantees of the sensitive data in the cloud. The time-based assured deletion means the secret key has a life cycle, which will be deleted after the predetermined time passes. Then the file encrypted with the time-bound secret key can't recover anymore, it is called assured deletion. So even someone owns the file, without the time-bound secret key, he can't access. Besides, for the organization, this scheme also introduces a more flexible hierarchy to implement. The flexible hierarchy is like the Fig. 1, the user in class C_1 has the authority to access information in C_2 and C_4, but access C_3 is not allowed. The user in class C_2 can access C_3 and C_4, and the user in C_4 can also access C_2. It is not like traditional hierarchy that higher class can access the lower class. This flexible hierarchy is with anti-symmetric and transitive exceptions. The anti-symmetric policy means that C_i could access C_j and C_j can also access C_i, but C_i and C_j are two different classes. For example, the classes C_2 and C_4 are in this case as Fig. 1 show. The transitive exceptions means that C_i can access C_j and C_j can access C_k, but C_i cannot access C_k. For example, the classes C_1, C_2 and C_3 are in this case as Fig. 1 show. This hierarchy structure is more flexible and practical than traditional hierarchy structure in the real world.

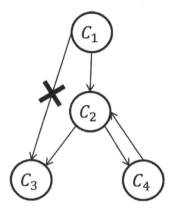

Fig. 1. An example of flexible hierarchy structure with anti-symmetric and transitive exceptions.

The organization of this paper is as follow. In the Sect. 2, related work briefly introduces the method of assured deletion and time-bound hierarchical key assignment. Section 3 introduces the proposed scheme applying on the time-based assured deletion to the flexible hierarchy structure in cloud. There has an example in the Sect. 4 to illustrate the proposed scheme. The security analysis of active and deleted files is provided in the Sect. 5. Finally, the conclusions is presented in the Sect. 6 of this paper.

2   Related Work

This section reviews other related works on assured deletion and time-bound hierarchical key assignment.

2.1 Assured Deletion

A file is requested to be deleted, but someone owns the copy of file and can discover it, making the file in danger. So assured deletion becomes an important guarantee of the file. There are two types of assured deletion. One is policy-based assured deletion [1]. This method means each file will associate with a file access policy. Each policy is with a control key, which is a public-private key pair. The control key is maintained by the key manager, it is a sever which responsible to cryptographic key management. Supposed there has a file associated with a policy, and this file will encrypt with a data key, which is symmetric-key encryption. This data key will further encrypt with the control key corresponding to the policy. When the policy is deleted, the corresponding control key will be revoked from the key manager. Therefore, when the policy with the file no longer exists, the data key and the encrypted file will not be recovered without the control key. It achieves the assured deletion. In the recent work of Tang et al., they extend the assured deletion to cloud backup system with version control [2] and further improved by Tezuka et al. [3]. The system provides the version control backup design to eliminate the storage of redundant data. It also allows the assured deletion that client can know which version or file in the cloud be assured deletion. While other versions or files that share the same data of the deleted one will remain unaffected. In some way, it is a good application to implement assured deletion to the file in the cloud.

The other type of assured deletion is time-based deletion. It is first introduces in [4]. Time-based deletion means the file can be securely deleted and inaccessible after a specific duration. The main idea in [4] is a file encrypted with a data key by the owner, and this data key will further encrypt with a control key by a key manager. The control key is time-limited, meaning it will be removed by the key manager when the predefined time is reached. Without the control key, the data key and the file remain encrypted. Even the cloud storage provider owns the copy of file, it still unrecoverable.

2.2 Time-Bound Hierarchical Key Assignment

To manage access in a hierarchy, the easiest way is the authorized users have the entire successor's security clearance class secret keys. In this way, the key management raised problem in the multilevel security. Akl and Taylor [5] first introduces the concept of super-key, and it also becomes the basis of lots of research [6–8, 10]. They use the top-down method. In their method, the trusted third party will assign each class a prime, secret key and public parameter. If $C_j < C_i$, the user in class C_i can derivate the secret key in C_j with his secret key and public parameters. However, this method needs large amount of storage to store the public parameters. Because the public parameter in class C_j is the product of the public prime of C_i. In 2003, Lin et al. proposed a new key assignment in a more flexible hierarchy [6]. The storage of public parameter is smaller than [5], because it is a single prime in each class.

In 2002, Tzeng [8] proposed a time-bound cryptographic key assignment. It is an extension of [5] with the concept of time. The scheme could apply on secure broadcasting and cryptographic key backup. In the scheme of Bertino et al. [9] proposed, they showed that Tzeng's scheme is applicable to secure broadcasting of XML documents. Besides, their scheme has based on the tamper-resistant to store the information; it greatly reduces the computation load and storage. In 2005, Yeh [10] also proposed a time-bound hierarchical key assignment, which is based on the RSA cryptographic system. Yeh's scheme is easy to understand and can apply to electronic article subscription system.

This paper is adopted by Lin et al.'s hierarchical key assignment and the tamper-resistant device in Bertino et al.'s scheme. In the Bertino et al.'s scheme, the device is tamper resistant and no one can recover the value or change the clock in it, so it also becomes the basis of this paper. The proposed scheme is aimed to apply time-based assured deletion to protect the file store in the cloud from someone who may discover it even had deleted.

3   The Time-Based Assured Deletion with Flexible Hierarchical Key Management Scheme

This section will introduce the key management with assured deletion in a hierarchy for a more flexible access control policy. In this scheme, the environment is based on the same start time, but the end time is depending on client. Besides, we adopt the tamper-resistant device which can prevent anyone to discover any information in it.

There have three roles in our scheme. One is Central Authority (CA). It is a third party that can be trusted. CA is responsible for generating parameters and issuing tamper-resistant device to clients. The tamper-resistant device includes a derivation key which can derive the secret key to encrypt or decrypt files for a time period. The secret key is based on a symmetric cryptosystem, like DES or AES. Another role is client. After receiving the device that CA gave, the client can do encryption or decryption of files, then save it in the cloud storage. Besides, if the client has authorized, it can access files in other classes. The other is cloud, the storage service provider. It is assumed that there have attackers in the cloud try to discover the file, whether it is deleted or not. The details of this scheme are described as follow:

3.1   Initiation

CA randomly chooses two large primes, p and q. Both of them must keep secret. Then, CA computes the product n, such that $n = p \times q$. CA also chooses another parameter a, which is relatively prime to n and the range is between 2 and $n - 1$.

For every class $\{C_1, C_2, \ldots, C_i\}$, CA chooses a set of distinct primes $\{e_1, e_2, \ldots, e_i\}$. Each e_i is relatively prime to $\phi(n)$, such as $\gcd(\phi(n), e_i) = 1$, and the range is $1 < e_i < \phi(n)$. For every time period, CA also chooses a set of distinct primes $\{g_1, g_2, \ldots, g_z\}$. Assumed the maximum time period is z, and it's an integer. For example, if the time period means one month, so $z = 12$ represents one year. Note that although the system is beginning at 1 and ending at z, it does not mean the system is constraint on this period of time. In addition, each g_z is relative prime to $\phi(n)$, and the range is $1 < g_z < \phi(n)$.

Next, CA will compute $\{d_1, d_2, \ldots, d_i\}$ and $\{h_1, h_2, \ldots, h_z\}$ for client class and time period respectively. Each d_i and h_z is multiplicative inverse of e_i and g_z. For example, $e_i d_i \equiv 1 \bmod \phi(n)$.

3.2   Key Assignment

In the key assignment phase, CA creates derivation key for every client in the classes $\{C_1, C_2, \ldots, C_i\}$. The derivation key is as follow:

$$DK_{i,z} = a^{\prod_{C_j \leq C_i} d_i \prod_{h_{StartTime} \leq h_{EndDate}} h_z} \bmod n \tag{1}$$

where *StartTime* means the start time of the system and *EndDate* means the time client wants to over, both of them assumed to be an integer. $C_j \leq C_i$ means the client in the class C_i has authority to access the files in C_j.

Then, CA issues the client a tamper-resistant device, which storing $DK_{i,z}$ and the parameters $\{n, e_j, \ldots, e_i, g_{StartTime}, \ldots, g_{EndDate}\}$. There has a secure clock embedded in this device to keep track of the correct and current time. Because the device is tamper resistant, no one can recover the parameter or change the time of secure clock.

3.3   Key Derivation

The client in class C_i can use the derivation key $DK_{i,z}$ and parameters in the tamper-resistant device to derivate the secret key to encrypt files in its class or access the other classes which has authority. The process of derivation of secret key to encrypt files in client's class is as follow:

$$
\begin{aligned}
SK_{i,t} &= (DK_{i,z})^{\prod_{C_k < C_i, k \neq i} e_k \prod_{g_t \leq g_{EndDate}} g_l} \bmod n \\
&= \left(a^{\prod_{C_j \leq C_i} d_i \prod_{h_{StartTime} \leq h_{EndDate}} h_z}\right)^{\prod_{C_k < C_i, k \neq i} e_k \prod_{g_t \leq g_{EndDate}} g_l} \bmod n \\
&= (a^{d_i})^{\prod_{h_{StartTime} < h_t} h_l} \bmod n,
\end{aligned}
\tag{2}
$$

where t means the deletion time of this file.

If the client in the class C_i wants to access files in the class C_j, the process of derivation of the secret key of class C_j is as follow:

$$SK_{j,t} = (DK_{i,z})^{\prod_{C_k < C_j, k \neq j} e_k \prod_{g_t \leq g_{EndDate}} g_l} \bmod n \tag{3}$$

After derivation, it doesn't have to store the secret key. The derivation key $DK_{i,z}$ can derivate it, if the client is in the right authority and timing.

The process of encryption and decryption of files in the Tang et al. scheme [1] needs to interact with key managers many times. If there are many clients in the system, the performance may be inefficient. Their scheme also needs a large amount of storage to store the private key created by every policies. In contrast, the interaction with CA in this scheme only at key assignment phase and when the time passes.

3.4   Assured Deletion

Client in this system can set the deletion time for files to do assure deletion, avoiding someone in the cloud could access even it had deleted. Some parameters in the tamper-resistant will be deleted by CA when time passes t For example, the client in C_i wants to access the file in C_j, so it has to derive the secret key $SK_{j,t}$. However, the parameters $\{g_{StartTime}, \cdots, g_{NowaDay-1}\}$ were deleted cause of the time passes. The process is as follow:

$$
\begin{aligned}
SK_{j,t} &= \left(DK_{i,z}\right)^{\prod_{C_k < C_j, k \neq j} e_k \prod_{g_{NowaDay} \leq g_{EndDate}} g_l} \bmod n \\
&= \left(a^{\prod_{C_j \leq C_i} d_i \prod_{h_{StartTime} \leq h_{EndDate}} h_z}\right)^{\prod_{C_k < C_j, k \neq j} e_k \prod_{g_{NowaDay} \leq g_{EndDate}} g_l} \bmod n \\
&= \left(a^{d_j}\right)^{\prod_{h_{StartTime} < h_{NowaDay}} h_l} \bmod n \\
&\neq \left(a^{d_j}\right)^{\prod_{h_{StartTime} < h_t} h_l} \bmod n,
\end{aligned}
\tag{4}
$$

where *NowaDay* means the time now. The secret key $SK_{j,t}$ cannot compute correctly, because the deleted parameters. So the file is said assuredly deleted. Noted that this assured deletion doesn't interaction with the cloud.

4   An Example

In the following example, the proposed scheme applies to the structure of an organization with cloud storage provider. The structure is in the Fig. 1. The clients in the class C_1 have highest authority, they can access and derivate the secret key in the class C_2 and C_4. However, they can't access the class C_3, it is restricted by the transitive exceptions. Clients in C_2 can access and derivate secret key in C_3 and C_4. Besides, the clients in C_4 can also access C_2, because the anti-symmetrical. At last, the clients in C_3 have the lowest authority, they can only access the files by C_3 as themselves.

Supposed the start time of the system is *StartTime* $= 1$ and the maximum time period $z = 12$. CA chooses the parameters $\{e_1, e_2, e_3, e_4\}$ and $\{g_1, g_2, \ldots, g_{12}\}$ for class and time period respectively, and calculate the modular n. There have two clients, one in C_1, and the other in C_2. Assumed the client in C_1 wants its *EndDate* be 6(supposed it be $U_{1,6}$), and the client in C_2 be 5($U_{2,5}$). CA then computes $DK_{1,6} = a^{d_1 d_2 d_4 h_1 h_2 h_3 h_4 h_5 h_6} \bmod n$ and $DK_{2,5} = a^{d_2 d_3 d_4 h_1 h_2 h_3 h_4 h_5} \bmod n$ for $U_{1,6}$ and $U_{2,5}$ respectively. Next, CA issues the tamper-resistant device $\{DK_{1,6}, e_1, e_2, e_4, g_1, g_2, \ldots, g_6, n\}$ and $\{DK_{2,5}, e_2, e_3, e_4, g_1, g_2, \ldots, g_5, n\}$ to them.

If the *NowaDay* is equal to the *StartTime*, $U_{2,5}$ wants to encrypt a file and set assured deletion time is 4. Then it can use the derivation key $DK_{2,5}$ to derive the secret key $SK_{2,4}$ by formula 2 as follow:

$$SK_{2,4} = (DK_{2,5})^{e_3 e_4 g_4 g_5} \bmod n$$
$$= (a^{d_2 d_3 d_4 h_1 h_2 h_3 h_4 h_5})^{e_3 e_4 g_4 g_5} \bmod n$$
$$= a^{d_2 h_1 h_2 h_3} \bmod n$$

Because $DK_{2,5}$ can calculate the secret key $SK_{2,4}$, $U_{2,5}$ doesn't have to store it. When $U_{1,6}$ wants to access the file encrypted with $SK_{2,4}$, it can also use its derivation key by formula 3 as follow:

$$SK_{2,4} = (DK_{1,6})^{e_1 e_4 g_4 g_5 g_6} \bmod n$$
$$= (a^{d_1 d_2 d_4 h_1 h_2 h_3 h_4 h_5 h_6})^{e_1 e_4 g_4 g_5 g_6} \bmod n$$
$$= a^{d_2 h_1 h_2 h_3} \bmod n$$

While time passing and the *NowaDay* become 6, the parameters $\{g_1, g_2, \ldots, g_5\}$ will be deleted in the tamper-resistant device. If $U_{1,6}$ wants to access the file with $SK_{2,4}$, it cannot decrypt this as follow:

$$SK_{2,4} = (DK_{1,6})^{e_1 e_4 g_6} \bmod n$$
$$= (a^{d_1 d_2 d_4 h_1 h_2 h_3 h_4 h_5 h_6})^{e_1 e_4 g_6} \bmod n$$
$$= a^{d_2 h_1 h_2 h_3 h_4 h_5} \bmod n$$
$$\neq a^{d_2 h_1 h_2 h_3} \bmod n$$

Without the parameters, the secret key cannot be derivate anymore. Note that the above computations are computing by the tamper-resistant. It can avoid the computation process being revealed. What the client has to do is entering the class and time it wants to encrypt or decrypt. Besides, the device is tamper resistant and had embedded a secure clock to control the correct time, no one could change the time of clock or values.

5   Security Analysis

This section discusses that the attacker cannot recover the file protected by the proposed scheme.

5.1   Active Files

An active files means it is accessible before the deletion time, but it may access by unauthorized users. In this scheme, if class C_i hasn't authority to access class C_j, its derivation key $DK_{i,z}$ will not include a hidden multiplicative inverse d_j. Therefore, the secret key $SK_{j,t}$ is unable to be derived by formula 4. However, if clients are authorized, the derivation key $DK_{i,z}$ will reveal about class C_j for clients to derive secret key $SK_{j,t}$ with other parameters.

This scheme also resists the common modulus attack. This kind of attack means the message is encrypted with two different exponent values both have the same modulus n and prime to each other. Then the message can be accessed without the private key d_i, this makes RSA cryptosystem insecure. Though all classes in this scheme use the same modulus n and different values of the exponents, it won't discover any data under the common modulus attack. Since no parameters are computed by power of e_i and g_i modular n and the secret key $SK_{i,t} = \left(a^{d_i}\right)^{\prod_{h_{StartTime} < h_t} h_l} \bmod n$ can compute by the tamper-resistant device, it's unnecessary to store. Besides, the parameters e_i and g_i are well protected by the tamper-resistant device, no one can change the value in it.

5.2 Deleted Files

A deleted file means being deleted and encrypted with the secret key $SK_{i,t}$ after the deletion time passing. Since the parameters $\{g_{StartTime}, \ldots, g_{NowaDay-1}\}$ which are smaller than $NowaDay$ will be deleted by the detection of secure clock in the tamper-resistant device. The secret key $SK_{i,t}$ without correct parameters, the result won't be correct as Sect. 3.4 shows.

6 Conclusions

The proposed time-based assured deletion with a flexible hierarchical key assignment scheme is solving the problem of storing sensitive information in the cloud storage, such as personal health records. By the concept of time, the secret key had given a life cycle. After the predetermined time, it will be deleted, making the file unrecoverable. Besides, the hierarchy structure in the scheme has security clearance and closer to the reality, increasing the security and flexible to the organization.

References

1. Tang, Y., Lee, P.C., Lui, C.S., Perlman, R.: Secure overlay cloud storage with access control and assured deletion. IEEE Tran. Dependable Secure Comput **9**(6), 903–916 (2012)
2. Rahumed, A., Chen, C.H., Tang, Y., Lee, P.C., Lui, C.S.: A secure cloud backup system with assured deletion and version control. In: International Conference on Parallel Processing Workshop, pp. 160–167 (2011)
3. Tezuka, S., Uda, R., Okada, K.: ADEC: assured deletion and verifiable version control for cloud storage. In: 26th IEEE International Conference on Advanced Information Networking and Applications, pp. 23–30 (2012)
4. Perlman, R.: File system design with assured delete. In: Proceedings Network and Distributed System Security Symposium (NDSS) (2007)
5. Akl, S.G., Taylor, P.D.: Cryptographic solution to a problem of access control in a hierarchy. ACM Trans. Comput. Syst. **1**(3), 239–248 (1983)
6. Lin, I.C., Hwang, M.S., Chang, C.C.: A new key assignment scheme for enforcing complicated access control policies in hierarchy. Future Gener. Comput. Syst. **19**(4), 457–462 (2003)

7. Wang, S.Y., Laih, C.S.: Merging: an efficient solution for a time-bound hierarchical key assignment scheme. IEEE Tran. Dependable Secure Comput. **3**(1), 91–100 (2006)
8. Tzeng, W.G.: A time-bound cryptographic key assignment scheme for access control in a hierarchy. IEEE Trans. Knowl. Data Eng. **14**(1), 182–188 (2002)
9. Bertino, E., Shang, N., Wagstaff, S.S.: An efficient time-bound hierarchical key management scheme for secure broadcasting. IEEE Trans. Dependable Secure Comput. **5**(2), 65–70 (2008)
10. Yeh, J.H.: An RSA-based time-bound hierarchical key assignment scheme for electronic article subscription. In: Proceedings of the 14th ACM International Conference on Information and Knowledge Management, pp. 285–286 (2005)
11. Dropbox. https://www.dropbox.com
12. Amazon Simple Storage Service (S3). http://aws.amazon.com/s3/
13. Armbrust, M., et al.: Above the clouds: a Berkeley view of cloud computing, Electrical Engineering and Computer Sciences, University of California at Berkeley, Technical report No. UCB/EECS-2009-28 (2009)
14. Dillon, T., Chen, W., Chang, E.: Cloud computing: issues and challenges. In: 24th IEEE International Conference on Advanced Information Networking and Applications, pp. 27–33 (2010)
15. Kaletsch, A., Sunyaev, A.: Privacy engineering: personal health records in cloud computing environments. In: International Conference on Information System (2011)

Malware Detection Method Based on CNN

Wen-Chung Kuo$^{(\boxtimes)}$ and Yu-Pin Lin

Department of Computer Science and Information Engineering,
National Yunlin University of Science and Technology, Yunlin, Taiwan, R.O.C.
simonkuo@yuntech.edu.tw, yupinlin0913@gmail.com

Abstract. With the widespread use of smartphones, many malware attacks such as user's private information is stolen or leaking have been proposed. Furthermore, the hacker can manipulate these smartphones to become a member of malicious attackers. Therefore, how to detect the malware application has become one of the most important issues. Until now, two detection methods (static analysis and dynamic analysis) were discussed. For the static analysis view, it observes the source code to determine whether it is a malware application. However, the source code will be processed (such as packing or confusion) before it is shared. Therefore, the static analysis method is not able to detect it because we cannot get the recover code correctly and completely. In order to overcome this disadvantage, a new detection method based on CNN (convolutional neural network) will be proposed in this paper. The major contribution of our proposed scheme is that we can decompress the APK (Android application package) file directly, to obtain the classes.dex file and then uses the training detection model to determine whether the input classes.dex is malicious code or not. Finally, according to the experiment results, our proposed scheme is available for all APKs with an accuracy rate is 94%.

Keywords: Static analysis · Dynamic analysis · Convolutional neural network · Android malware

1 Introduction

Until now, many mobile applications had been proposed with the widespread use of smartphones. According to Gartner's data [1], the smart phone is divided into two major operating systems, Android and iOS, the Android system has a high market share as shown in Table 1. In the Table 1, we can find that the market share of the Android operating system reaches 85.9%. In contrast, many malicious programs have also been proposed. According to Nokia's threat intelligence report in 2017 [2], the result is shown as Fig. 1. From Fig. 1, we can find that the ratio of malware operation systems are 68.5%, 27.96% and 3.54% for the Android system, Window/PC and others, respectively.

Therefore, the current discussion direction is how to detect the malware attacks based on Android system. Until now, the Android malware detection methods were divided into dynamic analysis and static analysis. For the static analysis, it observes the source code to determine whether it is a malware application. For dynamic analysis, it must install and execute the test application program. Consequence, we record its

C.-Y. Chang et al. (Eds.): ICS 2018, CCIS 1013, pp. 608–617, 2019.
https://doi.org/10.1007/978-981-13-9190-3_67

Table 1. Market share of mobile device operating system (unit: thousand units) [1]

Operating system	2017 units	2017 market share (%)	2016 units	2016 market share (%)
Android	1,320,118.1	85.9	1,268,562.7	84.8
iOS	214,924.4	14.0	216,064.0	14.4
Other OS	1,493.0	0.1	11,332.2	0.8
Total	1,536,535.5	100.0	1,495,959.0	100.0

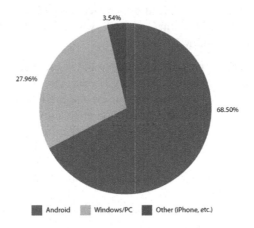

Fig. 1. Malware applications for each operating system [2]

runtime operations and then analyze whether it is a malware application. In general, dynamic analysis is more time consuming than static analysis because dynamic analysis requires the application to be installed and run for a period of time to record its operation. However, the source code will be processed (such as packing or confusion) before it is shared. Therefore, the static analysis method is not able to detect it because we cannot get the recover code correctly and completely. In order to improve this shortcoming, we will choose static analysis without decompiling the APK (Android application package) file, in other words, we decompress the APK file directly and get the classes.dex file for detection. Then we uses the training detection model to determine whether the input classes.dex is malicious code or not in this paper. According to the experiment results, our proposed scheme is available for all APKs with an accuracy rate is 94%.

The remainder of this paper is organized as follows: In Sect. 2, we review the related research methods. In Sect. 3, we proposes the CNN model-based detection method and then the experimental results are shown in Sect. 4. Finally, Sect. 5 presents the conclusions of our study.

2 Review the Related Methods

The installing process of an application for a smart phone can be divided into the following two steps. First, we can download the APK file from Google Play or the official website of the application. Then, we execute the APK file to install the application.

2.1 Introduce the APK File

The APK file is the abbreviation of Android application package, which is the Android installation package. The file format is ZIP, which usually includes classes.dex, AndroidManifest.xml, res and META-INF.

i. classes.dex file: Dalvik program executable file is generated by DEX compilation and dex is the abbreviation of Dalvik VM executes. In fact, the classes.dex file must be exist because the execution code required for the entire application operates. Therefore, hackers also embeds the malicious code into this file. In order to find the malicious code, we can detect this file directly.

ii. AndroidManifest.xml file: it can record the name, version and permissions of the application.

iii. META-INF folder: it stores the digital signature of the APK file to ensure the integrity of the APK file.

iv. res folder: This directory stores resource files such as image files and music files.

2.2 Convolutional Neural Networks (CNN) [3]

The convolutional neural network is a neural network structure which is used to process image classification problems. There are three major parts (convolution layers, pooling layers and fully connected layers) in the convolutional neural network shown as following:

i. Convolution layers: Linear filters are used to filter the input image and then these filters can extract the edge, color and shape information from the input image. Basically, each filter can operate on a sub-region of the input image and each sub-region will produce a single output value. According to these out values, each filter can generate a feature map.

ii. Pooling layers: In order to reduce the amount of subsequent calculations, It will reduce the image size of the feature image from the convolution layer. In general, it use the Max-pooling method which serves to maintain the maximum value in the block.

iii. Fully connected layers: Each neuron in this layer is connected to each neuron in the previous layer. As usually, in order to prevent the overfitting problem, the Dropout layer will follow the fully connected layer.

2.3   The Droiddetector Method [4]

2016, a malware detection method which combines the dynamic analysis and static analysis is proposed by Yuan *et al.* After decompressing the APK file, they decompile the AndroidManifest.xml and classes.dex file, respectively. Therefore, it can find out the sensitive permissions and API calls from the permission information by using static analysis. Furthermore, we also obtain its operation record when these APK file is executed on the sandbox. Finally, a feature set is generated from these information (sensitive permission, sensitive API call, operation record). Simultaneously, Yuan *et al.* select DBN (Deep Belief Networks) as a deep learning model. So, they use the feature set as input data to train the DBN model and then we can get the Android malicious application judgment model. When a new unknown APK file is obtained, the feature extraction is performed, the trained DBN model can determine whether the APK file is an Android malicious application or not. According to the simulation result [4], its accuracy is approached to 96% because they use a variety of features to detect. However, it also takes more time than static analysis alone.

2.4   Nix et al. [5] Proposed the Detection Method

In order to classify the Android malicious application, Nix *et al.* [5] proposed a pseudo-dynamic static analysis method in 2017. There are the following three steps to get the feature set. First, Nix *et al.* use the tool to decompile the APK file and get the smali code. Then, through the analyzer, they can find the API sequence, in other words, it is the API call flow for each group of systems. Finally, these API sequences are integrated into one API sequence feature set. Therefore, these API sequence feature set is taken as the input image to train their proposed the CNN model architecture to be the malware application family identification model. When a new malicious APK file wants to classify, we can decompile API and get the API sequence set. Then, we put this API sequence set to enter this trained CNN model to judge which belong to what the malicious application family is.

3   The Proposed Method

After our research discussion, we find that it is usually decompile the APK file to find useful information as a feature when the static analysis is used. However, there are many anti-compilation techniques (such as packing or confusion) are proposed to make decompile not necessarily successful. In order to improve this shortcoming, we will propose a method to decompress the APK file without decompile, so it will not be affected by the anti-compilation technology in this paper. Then, the data of the classes.dex file is converted into an image and we take it as the input image to train our proposed CNN model architecture to be the malware application identification model. When a new APK file wants to check, we use this trained CNN model to judge whether the malicious malware exits or not.In our scheme, the detection process are divided into three parts: extract the classes.dex file, create dataset, and detecting the APK file, as shown in Figs. 2, 3, and 4, respectively. The more detail methods will be introduced in the following sessions.

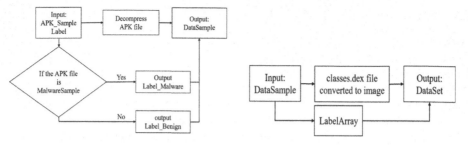

Fig. 2. Extract the classes.dex file

Fig. 3. Create dataset

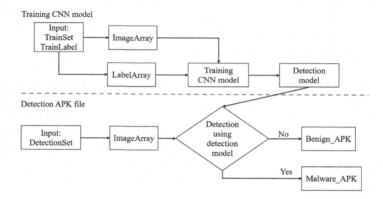

Fig. 4. Detection module

3.1 Extract the classes.dex File

All the input APK files are decompressed using the 7-ZIP tool. At the same time, according to the APK file from the benignsample set, the label is given to Label_-Benign, otherwise to Label_Malware. The operation steps are shown as Algorithm 1.

Algorithm 1. Extract the classes.dex file

Input : APK_Sample、Label
Output : DataSample
        for APK_Name in os.walk(APK_Sample) do:
            Decompress APK_Name extract all classes.dex file
            Store the classes.dex file in DataSample/APK_Name
            if (APK_Name from MalwareSample) do:
                Store the Label_Malware file in DataSample/APK_Name
            else :
                Store the Label_Benign file in DataSample/APK_Name

3.2   Create Dataset

All the labels are sequentially read into the LabelArray in the DataSample. According to the image size required by the CNN model, we decide the Image_size and then we give the same label to the classes.dex file from the same APK file. Furthermore, we want to calculate the compress_number, which represents the sum of the number of bytes needed to be averaged as the pixel value of the image when converting the classes.dex file into an image. For example: the classesArray length is 1000, the converted image is 10×10, then compress_number = $\lceil 1000/10 \times 10 \rceil$ = 10. This indicating that the values of the classesArray are grouped by 10 bytes, and the sum of each set of values is averaged as the pixel value of the image. After converting the bytes of the classesArray into the pixel values of the image, store them in the TrainSet and add the corresponding label of the classes.dex file to the TrainLabel. When all the classes.dex files have been converted, the TrainSet and the TrainLabel are the two data sets needed to train the CNN model, which are stored in the DataSet folder. The operation steps are shown as Algorithm.

Algorithm 2. Create dataset

Input : DataSample
Output : DataSet
Read all Label and add to LabelArray
Image_size ← 360*360
last_path ←"
Label_count ← -1
for FileName, dirPath in all classes.dex do:
    if last_path != dirPath do:
        Label_count += 1
    last_path ← dirPath
    classesArray ← read FileName byte
    compress_number ← [classesArray_size / Image_size]
    for i = 0 to Image_size do:
        for j = 0 to compress_number do:
            if ((i * compress_number + j) < classesArray_size):
                image[i] = image[i] + classesArray[i * compress_number + j]
            else:
                image[i] = image[i] + 0
        image[i] = image[i] / compress_number
    image add to TrainSet
    LabelArray[Label_count] add to TrainLabel
Store the TrainSet and TrainLabel in DataSet

3.3   Detecting APK File

The DetectionSet is a part of the sample from the DataSample, and the sample taken is not used during the training. The algorithm of the detection part, lines 1 to 13 are similar to the creation data set, where the second line of classes_CountArray is used to record that each APK file has several classes.dex files. Line 14 uses the trained CNN model to detect the DetectionSet, and the final result is output in the resultArray. Then, according to the classes_CountArray, the result array of the resultArray is used to determine the number of classes.dex files containing the malicious code. If the total_malware_count is greater than 0, the APK file is determined to be a malware application.

Algorithm 3. Detection APK file

Input : DetectionSet
Output : Detection APK file result(Benign/Malware)
    Image_size ← 360*360
    classes_CountArray ← Record how many classes.dex per APK file
    for all classes.dex do:
        classesArray ← Read classes.dex byte
        compress_number ← [classesArray_size / Image_size]
        for i = 0 to Image_size do:
            for j = 0 to compress_number do:
                if ((i * compress_number + j) < classesArray_size):
                    image[i] = image[i] + classesArray[i *
compress_number + j]
                else:
                    image[i] = image[i] + 0
                image[i] = image[i] / compress_number
        image add to DetectionSet
    resultArray = Model_CNN.predict(DetectionSet)
    number = -1
    for i = 0 to classes_CountArray_size do:
        total_malware_count = 0
        for j = 0 to classes_CountArray[i] do:
            number += 1
            total_malware_count = total_malware_count +
y_resultArray[number]
        if total_malware_count > 0:
            APK_result[i] = 1
        else :
        APK_result[i] = 0

4   Experimental

4.1   Experimental Environment

The equipment and environment tools are used shown as Table 2. Then, we use 1,166 APK samples which 523 benign samples are from Google Play [6] and 643 malware samples are from VirusShare [7] and National Center for High-performance Computing [8], respectively.

Table 2. Experimental environment

Item	Specification	Item	Specification
System version	Windows 10 64 bit	Anaconda3 [9]	5.1.0 64 bit
CPU	Intel (R) Core(TM) i7-8700K	Tensorflow [10]	1.8
Memory	40 GB	Keras [11]	2.1.6

4.2   Experimental Results

We will give two test results. Case 1. When the number of neurons was 500 and the image size was 360 × 360, the number of epochs will be tested, numbers were 30, 40, 50, 60 respectively. Case 2. The number of neurons will be tested, numbers were 500, 750 and 1000 respectively.

TP stands for correct judgment as malware sample, FP stands for false judgment as malware sample, TN stands for correct judgment as benign sample, FN stands for wrong judgment as benign sample. ACC (Accuracy) represents the correct proportion of all samples, TPR represents the proportion of correctly judged malware samples divided by all malware samples, TNR represents the proportion of correctly judged benign samples divided by all benign samples.

$$ACC = \frac{TP + TN}{TP + FP + TN + FN} \tag{1}$$

$$TPR = \frac{TP}{TP + FN} \tag{2}$$

$$TNP = \frac{TN}{TN + FP} \tag{3}$$

The accuracy of training the CNN model is judged by the results of classes.dex, and the symbol is represented as Train_ACC. The accuracy of detecting the APK file is the judgment result of the APK file, and the symbol is represented as Detection_ACC. In addition, TPR and TNR are only calculated when detecting the APK file portion.

Case 1. Number of Epochs Experiment
In this experiment, the number of neurons is set to 500, and the image size was 360 × 360. The number of epochs is 30, 40, 50, and 60, respectively. The experimental results of the epochs number, as shown in Table 3. We can observe that after the number of epochs to 30, Train_ACC does not increase much more. After the training, the Detection_ACC is the highest in 60 epochs, which is 3% more accurate than 30 epochs, but the time consumption is twice as long as 30 epochs, so we choose 30 epochs to carry out subsequent experiments.

Case 2. Number of Neurons Experiment
In this experiment, the epochs is set to 30, and the image size was 360 × 360, which was tested with 500, 750, and 1000 neurons, respectively. The results of the experimental results of the number of neurons are shown in Table 4. It was observed that the

Table 3. Number of epochs experiment

Epochs	Train_ACC (%)	Detection_ACC (%)	TPR (%)	TNR (%)
30	94	91	88	94
40	93	91	84	98
50	94	93	88	98
60	94	94	92	96

Table 4. Number of neurons experiment

Neurons	Train_ACC (%)	Detection_ACC (%)	TPR (%)	TNR (%)
500	94	91	88	94
750	94	92	90	94
1000	91	92	86	98

Train_ACC with a neuron number of 750 is the same as the Train_ACC with a neuron number of 500, but the neuron of 1000 does not give better results. At the end of the model training, the detection of 750 neurons is 1% more than that of 500 neurons. Finally, 750 neurons were selected for this paper.

5   Conclusion

In this paper, we propose the Android malicious application detection system based on CNN in order to solve the problem that the APK file cannot be properly decompiled when it is used the anti-compilation technology. In other words, we do not need to decompile the APK file and decompress it to obtain the classes.dex file directly. Then, by using the trained CNN detection model to determine whether the malicious code exist in the APK file or not. After the above simulation results, we can find that our proposed module is applicable to all APK files for initial Android malware detection.

Acknowledgement. This work was supported in part by the Ministry of Science and Technology of the Republic of China under Contract No. MOST 107-2218-E-110-014- and MOST 107-2218-E-492-003-.

References

1. https://www.gartner.com/newsroom/id/3859963
2. https://onestore.nokia.com/asset/201621/Nokia_2017_Threat_Intelligence_Report_EN.pdf
3. Kalash, M., Rochan, M., Mohammed, N., Bruce, N.D.B., Wang, Y., Iqbal, F.: Malware classification with deep convolutional neural networks. In: 9th IFIP International Conference on New Technologies, Mobility and Security (NTMS), pp. 1–5 (2018)
4. Yuan, Z., Lu, Y., Xue, Y.: Droiddetector: Android malware characterization and detection using deep learning. Tsinghua Sci. Technol. **21**(1), 114–123 (2016)

5. Nix, R., Zhang, J.: Classification of Android apps and malware using deep neural networks. In: International Joint Conference on Neural Networks (IJCNN), pp. 1871–1878 (2017)
6. Google Play. https://play.google.com/store/apps
7. VirusShare. https://virusshare.com/
8. https://www.nchc.org.tw/tw/
9. Anaconda. https://www.anaconda.com/what-is-anaconda/
10. Tensorflow. https://www.tensorflow.org/
11. Keras. https://keras.io/

Uncovering Internal Threats Based on Open-Source Intelligence

Meng-Han Tsai[1,2,3]($\boxtimes$), Ming-Hung Wang[4], Wei-Chieh Yang[1,2,3],
and Chin-Laung Lei[1]

[1] National Taiwan University, Taipei, Taiwan
{d02921015,d06921012,cllei}@ntu.edu.tw
[2] Institute for Information Industry, Taipei, Taiwan
[3] National Center for Cyber Security Technology, Taipei, Taiwan
[4] Feng Chia University, Taichung City, Taiwan
mhwang@fcu.edu.tw

Abstract. As the emerging threats of cybercriminals in recent years, how to efficiently and economically identify stealthy activities and attacks to avoid sensitive information leakage has been an important issue. However, due to business confidentiality and a lack of trust among information sharing, such valuable information is not exchanged transparently and not well utilized so far. In this study, we propose a hybrid method for internal threat identification. Our method leverages external open-source intelligence and applies it to internal network activities to uncover potential hacking campaigns among the network. We present the method consisting of collecting external intelligence, detecting internal infections, and identifying threats. We conduct our experiment under a tier-1 network in Taiwan. From the results, our method successfully identifies a number of famous hacking groups which are underneath threats in the large-scale network.

Keywords: Sinkhole server · Malicious domain names ·
Advanced persistent threat · Open source intelligence

1 Introduction

Emerging threats like cyber attacks have become more and more targeted, professional, and sophisticated on the Internet recently. Attackers intend to steal invaluable and sensitive information from the target network or organizations rather than to cause complete damage, for example, denial-of-service. However, as the expertise and stealthy characteristics of these experienced attackers, such as long-term reconnaissance, unknown vulnerabilities, and complicated attacking processes, detecting malicious activities and their related hacking groups remains a challenging issue until now.

Domain Name System (DNS) is a fundamental component of Internet infrastructures and plays an important role in both legit and illegal ways. In a wide

© Springer Nature Singapore Pte Ltd. 2019
C.-Y. Chang et al. (Eds.): ICS 2018, CCIS 1013, pp. 618–624, 2019.
https://doi.org/10.1007/978-981-13-9190-3_68

spectrum of malicious attacks such as drive-by downloads, phishing, Botnet communications, and advanced persistent threats (APT), DNS offers attackers agility and resilience to operate their malicious activities. Attackers utilize malicious domain names and DNS frequently to maintain the communications between the infected machines and their command and control (C&C) servers. Domain names provide flexibility of migrating malicious services and C&C servers for attackers. Moreover, they assist attackers to hide the true attack source behind proxy servers easily.

As DNS plays an important role in the broad spectrum of malicious services, many effective studies had been proposed to uncover internal infection and underneath threats using DNS traffic and information [2,4,9,10]. Among these studies, sinkhole is one of the successful measurement and remediation efforts to identify the infected machines. Generally speaking, DNS or IP sinkhole servers are managed in a specific manner by domain registries or security companies to monitor and defeat the malicious activities [3,7,8]. However, due to the cooperation confidentiality agreement between network owners and to avoid potential exposure to attackers, such schemes or information will not be disclosed to the public directly. Previous studies try to discover the potential sinkhole servers from a small subset of publicly known sinkholed IP addresses. However, utilizing the open-source intelligence (OSINT) and automating the results from Internet can also achieve the same goal without having essential prior knowledge.

In this study, we propose a method to identify internal infection and the underneath malicious activities by correlating internal DNS query records, HTTP request logs and external OSINT information including search engine results, online security services, and APT reports. We demonstrate successful identification of hacking campaigns and their related groups using our method over a tier-1 network in Taiwan. From the results, we hope to provide a hybrid and more economical detection method for enterprises or networks that are poorly managed in general due to the lack of resources and budgets.

2   Methodology

Our identification process is conducted through three major steps, including collecting sinkhole servers from OSINT, detecting internal infection through network activities and traffic, and identifying internal threats via trustworthy third parties. Figure 1 demonstrates the workflow of our method. We describe each stage in detail in the following paragraphs.

2.1   Collecting Sinkhole Servers

As a first step, we collect potential sinkhole server IPs or domain names using a number of online search engines. In addition to the well-known Google search

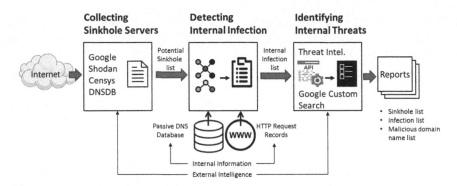

Fig. 1. The workflow of our proposed threat identification method

engine, many outstanding search engines, such as Shodan[1] and Censys[2], provide reconnaissance results and network service identification for researchers and security analysts. Furthermore, we also utilize DNSDB[3], a large passive DNS database (PDNS), to gather DNS name servers which may host sinkhole services or resolve the sinkholed domain names. The query methods on these major engines are described as follows:

- **Google:** we use Google hacking techniques to collect domain names of sinkhole servers with some keywords, such as *sinkhole*, *botnetsinkhole*, *sinkdns*, etc.
- **Shodan and Censys:** From our observation, many sinkhole web servers have a non-standard header contains X-Sinkhole or indicate themselves as sinkhole servers with Server: malware-sinkhole. These features help us to identify the potential sinkhole servers.
- **DNSDB:** We apply the same keywords while using Google search engines to DNSDB to find the sinkhole servers from the PDNS database.

Notice that in this part all the gathered domain names and their mapping IP addresses are considered and labeled as potential sinkhole servers since we do not have enough information about the ground truth. The list of potential sinkhole servers will be pruned in the second stage.

2.2 Detecting Internal Infection

To identify the potential infection inside a certain network, we first distinguish which internal machines have malicious activities, such as malicious domain names querying or HTTP requesting, to the potential sinkhole servers which we collected from the first stage. In this step, we construct the association of machines, domain names, and sinkhole servers to identify the potentially infected

---

[1] https://www.shodan.io/.

[2] https://censys.io/.

[3] https://www.dnsdb.info/.

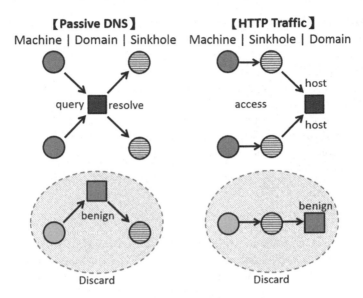

Fig. 2. Detecting internal infections and updating the sinkhole server list using Alexa database (Color figure online)

machines through a large scale passive DNS records [1,5,6] and HTTP request traffic collection. We build two tripartite graphs for each data collection: (1) from passive DNS records, we extract **which machine** (pink circle) is querying **what domain name** (red square) that is resolved to **which sinkhole server** (striped circle), and (2) from HTTP request traffic, we build a path from **which machine** (pink circle) is communicating with **which sinkhole server** (striped circle) using HTTP via **what domain name** (red square). The procedure is demonstrated in Fig. 2.

However, as our sinkhole server collection is based on keyword-based searching through major searching engines, some normal servers may be included once they match the keyword (e.g., sinkhole.com). To remove such mis-included servers from our list, we use the Alexa top 1 million sites[4] as a whitelist and perform an update of our list. The removal process is described in the bottom half of Figure 2. Once a connection exists between a sinkhole server in our list and any domain name in the whitelist (blue square), we discard the sinkhole server as well as the benign domain name from the list.

2.3   Identifying Internal Threats

The final step of the proposed method is the automated validation. We investigate discovered internal threats with two OSINT portal websites which are

---

[4] http://s3.amazonaws.com/alexa-static/top-1m.csv.zip.

ThreatMiner[5] and ThreatCrowd[6]. They both provide threat reports and correlation results of the indicator of compromise (IOC) for threat researchers to pivot
and make data enrichment. We send all discovered malicious domain names to
ThreatMiner and ThreatCrowd to check whether the domain names have been
mentioned in any APT reports or matched to any IOC. Besides ThreatMiner
and ThreatCrowd, we also leverage Google custom search engine which covers
many cyber threat intelligence (CTI) from different websites of security vendors
to conduct additional validations. Even though there is no complete list covering
all malicious domain names, in this step we strive to assure the identification is
accurate and extensive.

3   Evaluation

Our evaluation is conducted by identifying potential threats in real network
activities. To achieve this goal, we retrieve the DNS queries and HTTP requests
of a 9-month-long period. We correlate the aggregated sinkhole lists from the
external OSINT with the large-scale records of DNS queries and HTTP requests
inside a tier-1 network.

From the methodologies introduced in Sect. 2, we collected over 20 thousand IP addresses affiliated to 103 Autonomous System Numbers (via IP to
ASN mapping service provided by Team Cymru[7]). A total of 88 Internet service
providers/organizations/governments are in charge of these IP addresses. Table 1
presents the top 5 organizations in charge of the most sinkhole servers. From the
results, we find more than 99% of the sinkholes are belonging to Cogent Communications[8] and Team Cymru[9], while some companies share the remainder.

We use passive DNS method to collect DNS queries from February to October
2016 and record HTTP requests traffic from June to October 2016 as well. A
summary of DNS queries and HTTP requests collection is presented in Table 2.

Table 1. Top organizations of the sinkhole

Rank	Organization name	IP addresses of sinkhole servers
1	Cogent Communications	14,459
2	Team Cymru	5,960
3	Microsoft Corp	28
4	Lease Web	22
5	1and1	18

---

[5] https://www.threatminer.org/.
[6] https://www.threatcrowd.org/.
[7] https://www.team-cymru.com/IP-ASN-mapping.html.
[8] https://www.cogentco.com/.
[9] https://www.team-cymru.com/.

Table 2. Identification of malicious domain names and web accesses from the DNS queries and HTTP requests

Observation period	DNS: Feb. 2016–Oct. 2016
	HTTP: Jun. 2016–Oct. 2016
# DNS query	113,900,526,370
# HTTP request	54,299,643,745
# Malicious domain name	26,309
# Malicious web access	10,413

Table 3. Sample of identified groups and domain names

Group	Malicious domain name
PittyTiger	skypetm.com.tw; ey.avstore.com.tw; wmdshr.com
GhostNet	indexnews.org; lookbytheway.com; networkcia.com
APT10	avasters.com; yahooip.net
APT1	worthhummer.net
Lotus Blossom	wsi.dyndns.org
APT28	updatepc.org
Winnti Group	mini.reegame.net
Flea Group	windows.serveusers.com
Adwind RAT	jry123.ddns.net
DGA-based Botnet (Conficker)	nkunljuoznf.ws

Our results demonstrate that a total number of 26,309 malicious domain name queries and 10,413 malicious web accesses are identified. We validate the data collection inside the network through ThreatMiner, ThreatCrowd and Google custom search on major threat report sites. The results present that our method identifies more than 15 hacking groups which have ever involved with some APT and Botnet attacks. The sinkholed malicious domain names also indicate the existence of malwares and malicious activities in the network. A sample of our identification reports is shown in Table 3.

4   Conclusions and Future Work

As the emerging threats of cybercriminals, a number of professions and scholars are working on efficient methods for threat identification. In this paper, we propose a method to leverage a variety of external OSINT and internal network activities to provide an effective solution. Over 20 thousand IP address of sinkhole servers is collected through four platforms, including Google, Shodan,

Censys, and DNSDB. We validate our method through a 9-month-long network traces from a tier-1 network. From the results, our method successfully identifies a number of hacking groups as well as sinkholed malicious domain names which can be used for facilitating incident response or proceedings.

In this study, we demonstrate an approach to discover potentially infected machines and internal threats through a semi-automatic procedure. However, some issues remain to addressed in the future. First, we discover sinkhole servers using keyword-based search. The proposed method will include some servers not actually related to a "sinkhole server." Developing a reliable and extensive method for collecting sinkhole servers is required. Second, some steps in our current proposal are not fully automated. Decreasing manual intervention during the whole procedure is another task to be solved in the future.

References

1. Bilge, L., Sen, S., Balzarotti, D., Kirda, E., Kruegel, C.: Exposure: a passive DNS analysis service to detect and report malicious domains. ACM Trans. Inf. Syst. Secur. (TISSEC) **16**(4), 14:1–14:28 (2014)
2. Binde, B., McRee, R., O'Connor, T.J.: Assessing outbound traffic to uncover advanced persistent threat. SANS Institute Whitepaper, p. 16 (2011)
3. Kührer, M., Rossow, C., Holz, T.: Paint it black: evaluating the effectiveness of malware blacklists. In: Stavrou, A., Bos, H., Portokalidis, G. (eds.) RAID 2014. LNCS, vol. 8688, pp. 1–21. Springer, Cham (2014). https://doi.org/10.1007/978-3-319-11379-1_1
4. Ma, X., Zhang, J., Tao, J., Li, J., Tian, J., Guan, X.: DNSRadar: outsourcing malicious domain detection based on distributed cache-footprints. IEEE Trans. Inf. Forensics Secur. **9**(11), 1906–1921 (2014)
5. Perdisci, R., Corona, I., Giacinto, G.: Early detection of malicious flux networks via large-scale passive dns traffic analysis. IEEE Trans. Dependable Secure Comput. **9**(5), 714–726 (2012)
6. Rahbarinia, B., Perdisci, R., Antonakakis, M.: Segugio: efficient behavior-based tracking of malware-control domains in large ISP networks. In: The 45th Annual IEEE/IFIP International Conference on Dependable Systems and Networks (DSN), pp. 403–414. IEEE (2015)
7. Rahbarinia, B., Perdisci, R., Antonakakis, M., Dagon, D.: SinkMiner: Mining botnet sinkholes for fun and profit. In: The 6th USENIX Workshop on Large-Scale Exploits and Emergent Threats. USENIX (2013)
8. Ramachandran, A., Feamster, N.: Understanding the network-level behavior of spammers. In: ACM SIGCOMM Computer Communication Review, vol. 36, pp. 291–302. ACM (2006)
9. Wang, X., Zheng, K., Niu, X., Wu, B., Wu, C.: Detection of command and control in advanced persistent threat based on independent access. In: IEEE International Conference on Communications (ICC), pp. 1–6. IEEE (2016)
10. Zhao, G., Xu, K., Xu, L., Wu, B.: Detecting APT malware infections based on malicious dns and traffic analysis. IEEE Access **3**, 1132–1142 (2015)

Artificial Intelligence and Fuzzy Systems

A Comparison of Transfer Learning Techniques, Deep Convolutional Neural Network and Multilayer Neural Network Methods for the Diagnosis of Glaucomatous Optic Neuropathy

Mohammad Norouzifard[1](✉) ⓘ, Ali Nemati[2] ⓘ, Anmar Abdul-Rahman[3] ⓘ,
Hamid GholamHosseini[1] ⓘ, and Reinhard Klette[1] ⓘ

[1] School of Engineering, Computer and Mathematical Sciences,
Auckland University of Technology (AUT), Auckland, New Zealand
Mohammad.Norouzifard@aut.ac.nz
[2] School of Engineering and Technology, University of Washington, Tacoma, USA
[3] Department of Ophthalmology, Counties Manukau DHB, Auckland, New Zealand

Abstract. Early glaucoma diagnosis prevents permanent structural optic nerve damage and consequent irreversible vision impairment. Longitudinal studies have described both baseline structural and functional factors that predict the development of glaucomatous change in ocular hypertensive and glaucoma suspects. Although there is neither a gold standard for disease diagnosis nor progression, photographic assessment of the optic nerve head remains a mainstay in the diagnosis and management of glaucoma suspects and glaucoma patients. We describe a method aimed at both detecting pathologic changes, characteristic of glaucomatous optic neuropathy in optic disc images, and classification of images into categories glaucomatous/suspect or normal optic discs. Three different deep-learning algorithms used are transfer learning, deep convolutional neural network, and deep multilayer neural network that extract features automatically based on clinically relevant optic-disc features. Of the total of 455 cases extracted from the RIM-ONE public dataset (version 2), consisting of 348 training, 87 validation and 20 test cases, the proposed approach classified images with a training accuracy of 98.16%. We hypothesise that this approach can support the clinical decision algorithm in the diagnosis of glaucomatous optic neuropathy.

1 Introduction

Glaucoma is a chronic neurodegenerative disease characterised by loss of retinal ganglion cells, resulting in distinctive changes in the *optic nerve head* (ONH) and *retinal nerve fiber layer* (RNFL) [1]. It is the leading cause of global irreversible blindness [2]. According to Glaucoma New Zealand [3] statistics, approximately 91,000 New Zealanders who are aged 40 or older currently suffer from glaucoma while about 50% of them are unaware of having the disease.

ⓒ Springer Nature Singapore Pte Ltd. 2019
C.-Y. Chang et al. (Eds.): ICS 2018, CCIS 1013, pp. 627–635, 2019.
https://doi.org/10.1007/978-981-13-9190-3_69

The high intra- and interobserver variability in clinical examination [4] demands the use of ancillary techniques to assess the structure of the ONH and RNFL such as optic disc photography, confocal scanning laser ophthalmoscopy, scanning laser polarimetry, and optical coherence tomography. Similarly, selective perimetry techniques, including *short-wavelength automated perimetry* (SWAP) and *frequency-doubling technology* (FDT) perimetry, are being explored as replacements to *standard automated perimetry* (SAP) to provide earlier detection of visual field deficits [1].

Optic disc change supersedes visual field testing as a reference standard in both disease diagnosis and progression [1,5]. Structural change is detected earlier than visual field abnormalities in over half of patients progressing to an initial diagnosis of glaucoma [6]. Optic disc photography is the most commonly used technique to objectively document structural ONH damage due to its reproducibility and low cost [7]. In addition it has been used as an endpoint in randomized clinical trials: the *ocular hypertension treatment study* (OHTS), the *early manifest glaucoma trial* (EMGT), and the *European glaucoma prevention study* (EGPS) [1].

We present a decision support tool for differentiating normal optic nerves from those diagnosed with glaucoma/glaucoma suspects. The extracted parameters include cupping the area, vertical and horizontal cup to disc ratio. This research was conducted in order to detect slight changes in these parameters automatically using *digital fundus image* DFIs and dividing images into two different categories of glaucoma/glaucoma suspects and normal optic nerves. The *optic disc critical region* (ODCR) is the small region of the DFIs, and processing ODCRs takes less time in comparison with the processing of the DFIs; see Fig. 1.

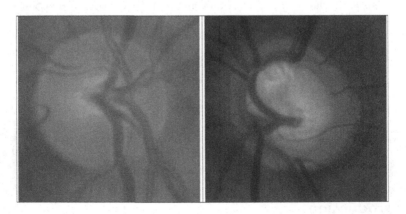

Fig. 1. Normal *(left)* and glaucoma *(right)* optic disc critical region on the RIM-ONE dataset [13]

We applied different deep learning algorithms such as transfer learning models, deep *convolutional neural network* (CNN), and deep *multilayer neural network* (MNN) to the ODCRs and extracted clinically relevant parameters automatically. The ODCR parts are available in DFIs in the RIM-ONE dataset as input to apply to the deep learning algorithms. Generally, deep CNN has developed for image segmentation and classification [8,9].

Transfer learning of machine learning techniques restores the weights and labelled data which are trained on the ImageNet dataset [10]. It can be applied to other tasks that are complicated such as glaucoma classification and robust optic disc segmentation [11]. Moreover, transfer learning models have been improved and developed to be applicable to small datasets. Recently, research studies indicated that many approaches that have been attempted to segment optic cup and optic disc have used unsupervised machine learning [12].

We employed a public retinal image database on optic nerve evaluation for two healthy and glaucoma categories that are exclusively focused on *optic nerve head* (ONH) segmentation. The second version (V2) of RIM-ONE dataset [13] is classified into two subsets: glaucoma and glaucoma suspects with a total of 200 images, and a normal subset including 255 images at different resolutions. The RIM-ONE dataset is publicly available and consists of healthy and glaucoma DFIs. It can also illustrate the accurate gold standard, the ONH, by professionals in this field. Three hospitals, Hospital Clínico San Carlos, Hospital Universitario Miguel Servet, and Hospital Universitario de Canarias, contributed to the development of this database.

The remainder of this article is structured as follows: In Sect. 2, methodology and details of MNN, CNN, transfer learning models and results of these deep learning algorithms are briefly explained; we evaluate six deep learning models and compare their accuracies. Section 3 concludes.

2   Methodology and Results

Deep learning demands extensive data for training. Optimised weights and image features are chosen during learning, and also for evaluation using accuracy metric. Then, the best model is selected. Finally, after training the selected model, the test dataset is used to check the quality of the trained model.

The research is aimed at classifying medical images; a high-quality deep learning model based on a limited number of low resolution (about 500×600) images from RIM-ONE V2 has been employed. Due to the small size of this image dataset, it is divided into three parts, approximately 75% for the training set, 20% for evaluation, and 5% for testing. In order to overcome the requirement of having a large number of images, we used transfer learning models which are applicable to the weights trained on a large number of images in ImageNet. For the evaluation of the proposed approach, it has been compared with three popular types of deep learning, called transfer learning, CNN and MNN. It was found that due to the lack of data, the aforementioned methods did not provide desirable results. By using transfer learning methods and adjusting the hyper-parameters, we were able to achieve improved results. Altogether, in this research we compare three methods for diagnosing glaucoma: CNN, MNN, and (four different) transfer learning methods which are represented as a block diagram in Fig. 2. This block diagram includes three supervised learning techniques and a deep learning approach. In the following, we explain briefly these three deep learning methods.

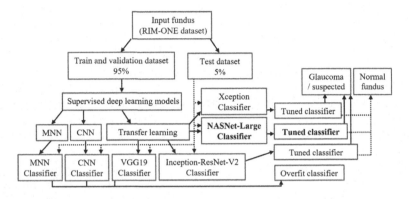

Fig. 2. Block diagram for glaucoma classification

Multilayer Neural Networks. The MNN has three fully-connected layers with, respectively, five, fifteen and five neurons in each layer. The ReLU activation function on the first three layers and the softmax activation function on the output layer were employed. All images are applied as an input vector to the first layer and then transferred to the hidden layers while each hidden layer is connected to preceding layers. The task of the activation function is to express an output which is given by some inputs.

Two training and validation scores have not converged into each other in one hundred epochs. Therefore, in this case, the MNN method is not applicable; it has an overfitting problem.

Convolutional Neural Networks. ConvNets [14,15] can learn weights and biased values from the processed images. The CNN had been employed to detect glaucoma by training seven convs' layers with an average accuracy of 92.68% [16] on the Drive database, which is a public dataset. In our work, a deep CNN was employed with six convolution-layer blocks. In the first block, two convolution-layers are available with sigmoid activation functions, and there are two convolution-layers with ReLU activation functions in the other five blocks. At the end of this ConvNet architecture, there are three fully connected layers with softmax activation function. It should be mentioned that the filter size is 3×3 and dropout is 5% in all blocks. Two training and validation scores have not converged into each other for the first one hundred epochs; thus the proposed method fails to meet the objectives because of overfitting.

Although the current CNN model works very well on big datasets, the transfer learning method can be deployed on the limited data set to get the best result.

Transfer Learning - VGG. The transfer learning (pre-trained) method is the state-of-the-art supervised machine learning technique. This model is developed and trained on a massive standard dataset (ImageNet) and then used for other tasks. Pre-trained algorithms are first trained on that dataset, and then weights and parameters are saved. Thus, it applies to deploy a pre-trained algorithm on glaucoma detection, but results are depending on setting the hyper-parameters so it is tricky to get trustworthy results. Pre-trained methods do not require segmentation of DFIs structures, so these algorithms can serve as a prior knowledge for measuring different glaucomatous symptoms associating with fundus segmentation. In this research, VGG19 [17] was deployed for glaucoma detection. This method has nineteen layers, and it has a default input size of 244 × 244 RGB images. As an output of VGG19 architecture, there are three fully connected layers, and all hidden layers have used ReLU activation function.

VGG19 is an appreciable architecture to evaluate a specific task, and it also works well on image classification for big image datasets. Scale jittering was used as one of data augmentation technique during training. The ReLU activation function was used after each convolution layer and trained with batch gradient descent. Two training and validation scores have not converged into each other in different epochs, up to fifty. Therefore, in this case, VGG19 is an overfit model and not applicable.

Transfer Learning - InceptionResNet. The Inception-ResNet [18] is applicable to glaucoma detection, and both validation and training loss scores converged into each other in ten epochs. The accuracy of test data with the Inception-ResNet method on the RIM-ONE dataset is 85%. In our study, we required most of the parameters to be trainable and only a small fraction was selected as a default. In order to optimize the training computational complexity, we used a cloud-based *graphics processing unit* (GPU).

Transfer Learning - Xception. Another pre-trained model to check the result of our application is Xception [19]. The Xception model is a linear stack of depthwise separable convolutional layers with residual connections [20]. A depthwise separable convolution is a kind of an Inception module [21] with a maximally large number of towers. This approach leads to the proposal of a novel deep CNN model inspired by Inception, where Inception modules have been replaced by depthwise separable convolutions. It slightly improved results compared to Inception V3 on ImageNet, and has the same number of parameters as Inception V3. Performance gains are not due to increased capacity but rather to a more efficient use of model parameters [19].

The default image input size is 299 × 299 in color format and training and validation input images feed into the model. In our study, convs layers were frozen, so available weights of Xception were transferred and from convs layers into fully connected layers. These fully connected layers were trained by input images. Accuracy and loss scores converged into each other. The best result is achieved on the 20th epoch: 90% of normal images and glaucoma cases are correctly identified.

Proposed Method Based on Transfer Learning - NASNet. In this study, another pre-trained model was used to recheck the result of our application. NASNet [22] is a pre-trained model that may be used for small databases. Our proposed model is explained in detail as follows: The feeding image size is 299×299. The proposed model is modified in the training phase by an augmentation. There are four fill-mode augmentations such as constant, nearest, reflect, and wrap. Due to the high performance, the best result was achieved using a proposed fill mode with "nearest" in augmentation. Furthermore, images have been horizontally filled. Other tuned factors are rotation range (equal to 40), width shift range (0.2), height shift range (0.2), shear range (0.2), zoom range (0.2), and channel shift range (10); the remaining factors are the same as NASNet defaults. The proposed model has 85,723,220 parameters, of those, 85,523,960 are trainable and the rest of them are non-trainable parameters. Our model has started by calling the NASNet-Large model with ImageNet weights. The model was flattened to build a long feature unit vector and use it by a fully connected layer to make a decision for the final classification with the softmax activation function; dropout is assumed to be 0.1. Freezing layers have been used, except in the fully connected layers. The proposed model uses the Adam optimizer and a lower learning rate of $1e-5$ since our model is fine-tuning to achieve our goal which is a better performance and accuracy to detect glaucoma or non-glaucoma eyes. Three learning rates have been tested: $1e-3$, $1e-4$ and $1e-5$. Except the $1e-5$ learning rate (that we have chosen), the other learning rates lead to overfitting in the model.

The model was tried for 5 to 50 epochs with elements as mentioned above. The best result was achieved for 50 epochs. The loss fiction result was 0.04, the accuracy value was 98.16%. The result for feeding 20 unseen normal and glaucoma cases was 90%. The result indicates that our model learned to predict binary classification based on the dataset. Some of the results for the test dataset are shown in Fig. 3.

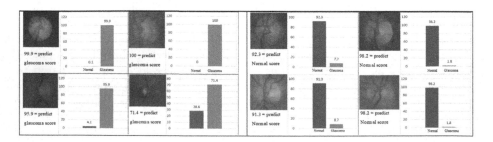

Fig. 3. Detected glaucoma *(left)* and normal cases *(right)* on test ODCRs in the RIM-ONE dataset with the proposed model based on NASNet

All results are shown in Table 1. "Test ACC" refers to the accuracy of twenty images randomly selected from RIM-ONE, which were unknown for the proposed

Table 1. Glaucoma detection results for different deep learning methods; – indicates that a result is not provided because of overfitting

Results in comparison with each other				
Classifier	Best epoch	Train ACC (%)	Train loss	Test ACC (%)
MNN	–	97.25	0.10	50.00
CNN	–	64.31	0.65	50.00
VGG	–	88.77	0.27	50.00
InceptionResNet	10	82.56	0.41	85.00
Xception	20	79.14	0.43	90.00
Proposed model	**50**	**98.16**	**0.04**	**90.00**

system. When checking the twenty test DFIs, an ophthalmologist was able to detect 70% of them correctly based on the given low resolution fundus images provided on RIM-ONE as test set. Expectedly, our proposed method can detect with eighteen images correctly out of twenty. This method has got 90% accuracy and you can see the results of the proposed method in the highlighted row in Table 1.

3   Conclusions

In this paper we propose a method based on the NASNet model that was trained accurately on 75% of the RIM-ONE V2 dataset and gained the least loss score for 50 epochs training. It was evaluated on a test dataset which included 20 unseen images. It was successful in classifying glaucoma and suspected glaucoma versus normal with 90% accuracy.

Totally, six models were trained where three of them (MNN, CNN, and VGG19) had an overfitting problem. Also, three other models (InceptionResNet, Xception, and proposed method) were deployed to corroborate the performance of the transfer learning models; results were compared to each other. Contributions of this paper are as follows:

1. We propose a strategy of using transfer learning techniques for detecting glaucoma. Transfer learning is an opportunity to use and test this method for the detection of healthy versus glaucoma fundus images.
2. Transfer learning models, CNN, and MNN were applied to investigate results in up to one hundred epochs. Moreover, the comparison of results indicates that the proposed method based on NASNet is an eminent method which is applicable to categorize data accurately (with 90% accuracy).
3. In this paper, the study was done on a publicly available dataset (RIM-ONE). This dataset allows us to evaluate images and extract different features locally or in the cloud. Reliable results are achieved despite the low quality and the small size of fundus images.

Overall, this research points toward an appropriate path for glaucoma detection using deep learning. In future work, we plan to provide a refined statistical analysis for the performance of the proposed model.

References

1. Sharma, P., Sample, P.A., Zangwill, L.M., Schuman, J.S.: Diagnostic tools for glaucoma detection and management. Surv. Ophthalmol. **53**(6), S17–S32 (2008)
2. Pascolini, D., Mariotti, S.P.: Global estimates of visual impairment: 2010. Br. J. Ophthalmol. **96**(5), 614–618 (2012)
3. Glaucoma New Zealand. www.glaucoma.org.nz. Accessed 5 Sep 2018
4. Gaasterland, D.E., Blackwell, B., Dally, L.G., Caprioli, J., Katz, L.J., Ederer, F.: Advanced glaucoma intervention study investigators: the advanced glaucoma intervention study (AGIS): 10. variability among academic glaucoma subspecialists in assessing optic disc notching. Trans. Am. Ophthalmol. Soc. **99**, 177 (2001)
5. Medeiros, F.A., Zangwill, L.M., Bowd, C., Sample, P.A., Weinreb, R.N.: Use of progressive glaucomatous optic disk change as the reference standard for evaluation of diagnostic tests in glaucoma. Am. J. Ophthalmol. **139**(6), 1010–1018 (2005)
6. Gordon, M.O., et al.: The ocular hypertension treatment study: Baseline factors that predict the onset of primary open-angle glaucoma. Arch. Ophthalmol. **120**(6), 714–720 (2002)
7. European glaucoma prevention study group and others: reproducibility of evaluation of optic disc change for glaucoma with stereo optic disc photographs. Ophthalmology **110**(2), 340–344 (2003)
8. Fang, L., Cunefare, D., Wang, C., Guymer, R.H., Li, S., Farsiu, S.: Automatic segmentation of nine retinal layer boundaries in OCT images of non-exudative AMD patients using deep learning and graph search. Biomed. Opt. Express **8**(5), 2732–2744 (2017)
9. Chen, X., Xu, Y., Wong, D.W.K., Wong, T.Y., Liu, J.: Glaucoma detection based on deep convolutional neural network. In: Proceedings of Engineering Medicine Biology Society, pp. 715–718 (2015)
10. Deng, J., Dong, W., Socher, R., Li, L.J., Li, K., Fei-Fei, L.: Imagenet: a large-scale hierarchical image database. In: Proceedings of Computer Vision Pattern Recognition, pp. 248–255 (2009)
11. Wahab, H., Haider, S.R., Khitran, S., ul Huda, N., Akram, M.U.: Bright region and vessel density based robust optic disc segmentation. In: Proceedings of IEEE International Conference Image Theory Tools Applications, pp. 1–6, October 2014
12. Norouzifard, M., Abdollahi Dehkordi, A., Naderi Dehkordi, M., GholamHosseini, H., Klette, R.: Unsupervised optic cup and optic disk segmentation for glaucoma detection by ICICA. In: Proceedings of Pervasive Systems Algorithms Networks. IEEE (2018)
13. Fumero, F., Alayon, S., Sanchez, J., Sigut, J., Gonzalez-Hernandez, M.: Rim-one: an open retinal image database for optic nerve evaluation. In: Proceedings of IEEE International Symposium Computer-based Medical Systems (2011). https://doi.org/10.1109/CBMS.2011.5999143
14. LeCun, Y., et al.: Learning algorithms for classification: a comparison on handwritten digit recognition. In: Neural Networks: The Statistical Mechanics Perspective, pp. 261–276 (1995)

15. Zeiler, M.D., Fergus, R.: Visualizing and understanding convolutional networks. In: Fleet, D., Pajdla, T., Schiele, B., Tuytelaars, T. (eds.) ECCV 2014. LNCS, vol. 8689, pp. 818–833. Springer, Cham (2014). https://doi.org/10.1007/978-3-319-10590-1_53
16. Tan, J.H., Acharya, U.R., Bhandary, S.V., Chua, K.C., Sivaprasad, S.: Segmentation of optic disc, fovea and retinal vasculature using a single convolutional neural network. J. Comput. Sci. **20**, 70–79 (2017)
17. Simonyan, K., Zisserman, A.: Very deep convolutional networks for large-scale image recognition. arXiv preprint arXiv:1409.1556 (2014)
18. Szegedy, C., Ioffe, S., Vanhoucke, V., Alemi, A.A.: Inception-v4, inception-resnet and the impact of residual connections on learning. In: Proceedings of AAAI Conference Artificial Intelligence, pp. 4278–4284 (2017)
19. Chollet, F.: Xception: Deep learning with depthwise separable convolutions. arXiv preprint, arXiv:1610.02357 (2016)
20. Gajarsky, T., Purwins, H.: An Xception residual recurrent neural network for audio event detection and tagging. In: Proceedings Sound Music Computing Conference (2018)
21. Choi, J.Y., Yoo, T.K., Seo, J.G., Kwak, J., Um, T.T., Rim, T.H.: Multi-categorical deep learning neural network to classify retinal images: a pilot study employing small database. PloS One **12**(11), e0187336 (2017)
22. Zoph, B., Vasudevan, V., Shlens, J., Le, Q.V.: Learning transferable architectures for scalable image recognition. arXiv preprint arXiv:1707.07012, 2(6) (2017)

Analysis of Voice Styles Using i-Vector Features

Wen-Hung Liao$^{(\boxtimes)}$, Wen-Tsung Kao, and Yi-Chieh Wu

Department of Computer Science, National Chengchi University, Taipei, Taiwan
whliao@nccu.edu.tw

Abstract. Many adjectives have been used to describe voice characteristics, yet it is challenging to define sound style precisely using quantitative measure. In this paper, we attempt to tackle the voice style classification problem based on techniques designed for speaker recognition. Specifically, we employ i-vector, a widely adopted feature in speaker identification, and support vector machine (SVM), for style classification. In order to verify the reliability of i-vector, we conduct pilot study, including noise sensitivity, minimum voice duration, and mimicry style test. In this study, we define eight voice styles and collect appropriate voice data to process and verify our hypothesis through the experiment. The results indicate that i-vector can indeed be utilized to classify voice styles that are commonly perceived in daily life.

Keywords: Voice styles classification · Machine learning ·
Support vector machine · i-vector

1 Introduction

Voice is the most common means for human to human communication. A speaker can evoke different emotions in their audience by a variety of demonstrative combination which includes terms selection, tone, speaking pace, vocal cords engaging level, and so on. Generally speaking, sound characteristics are not as rich as visual cues. It usually takes longer to accumulate enough vocal features for people to recognize voice types. In daily life, we are accustomed to use adjectives such as husky, high pitched, or "like that well-known announcer" to describe a person's voice style. Precise quantitative measures to define and classify voice styles, nonetheless, remain challenging. It is difficult for average users to label the style of a speech unless given some guidance or suggestion. Additionally, a specific style (e.g., childlike voice) may have many variants whose acoustic features differ. Defining appropriate classes that cover enough scenarios is itself a difficult task.

Eskenazi grouped speaking styles into several categories as follows [1]:

1. Voice qualities: It consists of features in frequency domain mostly.
2. Speaking rate: It refers to the speed of speech. That is, features in time domain primarily.

© Springer Nature Singapore Pte Ltd. 2019
C.-Y. Chang et al. (Eds.): ICS 2018, CCIS 1013, pp. 636–645, 2019.
https://doi.org/10.1007/978-981-13-9190-3_70

3. Dimensions of speaking styles: A qualitative three-dimensional space has been proposed to group the style terms, including intelligible, familiar, and strata intensity.
4. Specific tasks and styles: Different kinds of situation could represent speaking styles indirectly, such newscasts, sports, concerts, professional, interview, and so on.

Actually, the analysis of speaker's voice styles has already been requested and applied in human resources market [2]. However, these commercial applications or related psychological research [3] are more interested in prosodic features in the time domain. Acoustic features have been studied in speech recognition problems for a long time. Bou-Ghazale *et al.* [4] compared recognition performance of several acoustic approaches in various conditions such as noise level, mood, etc. It was concluded that a linear prediction features as well as M-MFCC or ExpoLog attain stable recognition results in all predefined conditions. We wonder if features in the frequency domain could represent voice styles as well. Specifically, we wish to identify the features that are associated with the perception of certain voice characteristics by formulating it as a speaker identification problem and examine appropriate methods of representation in this respect.

In our study, we define eight common styles which include, (1) calming, (2) childlike, (3) silvery, and (4) articulate for female voices; (5) husky, (6) excited, (7) energetic, and (8) articulate for male voices. We conduct pilot studies using different acoustic features and clustering techniques to perform preliminary analysis. Our findings suggest that features such as i-vectors [5] are more suitable for voice styles than for speaker identification in case a speaker attempts to mimic other's voice intentionally. Through experimental analysis, we validate that the adopted i-vector features are robust and effective for the classification of voice styles.

The rest of this paper is organized as follows. In Sect. 2 we review related work in speaker identification. Section 3 describes several pilot tests to ensure the robustness of i-vector features. The proposed classification scheme is also discussed. Section 4 presents and analyzes the experimental results. Section 5 concludes this paper with a short summary.

2   Related Work

Unlike speech recognition, the content of the speech should not be a factor (i.e., text-independent) when speaker identification is concerned. The following review enumerates and compares several well-known speaker modeling methods.

2.1   Gaussian Mixture Model

Reynolds *et al.* [6] introduced Gaussian Mixture Model method to model speaker-dependent spectral shapes. Both clear and telephone speech models could attain robust text-independent speaker identification accuracy. However, the modeling result of GMM is a high-dimensional vector which requires a large amount of speaker training data. In other words, it suffers from curse of dimensionality.

2.2 Universal Background Model

In most practical situations, it is difficult to collect a large amount of voice data from the target speaker we wish to detect. Therefore, a stable speaker recognition model is not always obtained by using above method. Reynolds *et al.* proposed the GMM-UBM method [7], which is to collect the voice of other non-target population as a universal background data to train a GMM model. Then we can adapt the target speaker model by only a small amount of training data and maximum a posteriori estimation from UBM. One notable issue of this method is that the recognition result greatly depends on the quality of recording caused by equipment or ambient noise.

2.3 Joint Factor Analysis

In Kenny's work, factor analysis is introduced to reduce the dimensionality of GMM vector [8]. This approach assumes that GMM vector consists of the following factors, (1) speaker-dependent (2) channel-dependent (3) others. Their results show that this method can effectively improve the accuracy of speaker recognition. Since it is difficult to make factors attributed completely to speaker-dependent and channel-dependent, the recognition performance still depends greatly on the recording quality.

2.4 i-Vector

Dehak *et al.* merge speaker and channel factors based on Joint Factor Analysis, which is named as Total Variability Matrix [5]. The simplified equation is shown in Eq. 1,

$$M = m + Tw \tag{1}$$

where M denotes the super vector of GMM, m is universal background model, T is total variability matrix, and w is a mapped vector using T. Dehak *et al.* refer to w as the i-vector. Nowadays, i-vector has been one of the state-of-the-art features for speaker recognition.

3 Voice Style Classification Using i-Vector

In order to develop the classification of voice styles as mentioned above, the following three stages have been devised:

1. Define common voice styles by selecting representative candidates.
2. Match the i-vector of the input voice with those extracted from the representative candidates.
3. If we can find a candidate whose acoustic features are similar to those of the input, they are deemed to have the same voice style.

As a matter of fact, step 2 is a speaker identification problem. However, many factors may interfere with the matching result during the speaker identification pipeline, such as ambient noise, different recording quality, and duration of the speech. In this section, we conducted several pilot studies to examine how these factors will affect the performance of identification. We then present the experimental design for style classification task.

3.1 Pilot Study

The voice data employed in our pilot study consists of the recordings of 15 female and 15 male announcers from local radio programs. Each data contains two minutes of speech (without background music) in length. Figure 1 depicts the workflow which is applied to the pilot tests. We employ support vector machine [9] to train classifiers for speaker identification, which is associated with voice style recognition in this study.

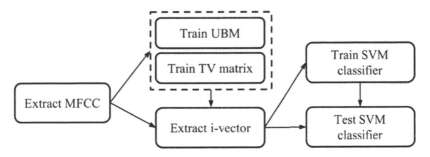

Fig. 1. Workflow of pilot study (speaker identification using i-vectors)

3.1.1 Minimum Voice Duration

Since it takes some time for human to perceive and identify a specific voice style, we assume that machine also needs to process a voice segment for certain duration to obtain correct classification result. Clearly, 1 s of audio is not enough for human or machine to make any sensible judgement. Yet what is the minimum duration of audio required for the training phase? Similarly, what is the minimum duration of audio required for the test phase? These are the questions that we would like to answer with this pilot study.

(a) *Minimum test data duration:* Each announcer's recording is divided equally into training and test data. Therefore, training/test recording duration of each announcer is 60 s. We further divide test recording into 30-s, 20-s, 10-s, 5-s, 3-s, 2-s, and 1-s segments. After that, we run the speaker identification process as indicated in Fig. 1. For each time duration, we repeat the process ten times and compute the average accuracy. Table 1 lists the results of this experiment, which suggests that 10-s audio recording could be used as minimum test data duration if high accuracy is to be maintained.

(b) *Minimum training data duration:* In this experiment, we fix the length of test audio to 10 s, and investigate the minimum duration required for training samples. Training audio is divided into 30-s, 10-s, 5-s, and 1-s segments, respectively. We then perform speaker identification and repeat the process 10 times to obtain average accuracy. Table 2 lists the experimental results for training samples of different durations. The results suggest that 60-s audio recording duration is required if we intend to maintain a high recognition rate.

Table 1. Experimental results for different test data durations.

Training audio (seconds)	Test audio (seconds)	Accuracy
60	30	100%
	20	100%
	10	**100%**
	5	96.67%
	3	90.56%
	2	83.89%
	1	60.56%

Table 2. Experimental results for different training data durations.

Training audio (seconds)	Test audio (seconds)	Accuracy
60	10	**100%**
30		96.19%
10		95.14%
5		89.47%
1		61.74%

To sum up, training audio of 60-s duration and test data of 10-s duration will be employed in all the subsequent experiments unless specified otherwise.

3.1.2 Performance Under Different Noise Levels

According to [5], if we have trained a total variability matrix well, then i-vector will represent the characteristics of the speaker reliably regardless of noise. We design this experiment to evaluate the performance of speaker identification using i-vector under different noise levels. We take one 60-s recording for training, and six 10-s recording files for testing, of each announcer. Based on the original volume, we add 1%, 2%, 4% white noise respectively. In addition, we apply filter to reduce noise for the 1% white noise recording for comparison. Each experiment is repeated 10 times to obtain average accuracy, as summarized in Table 3. The results reveal the strong influence of noise in the performance of the classifier. The effect of de-noising filter is prominent. Consequently, preprocessing such as de-noising is strongly recommended in practical situations.

3.1.3 Mimicry Style Test

The mimicry style test is designed to respond to the following question: if a voice actor is asked to mimic a certain style, will the i-vector based classifier report a result according to the 'style' or 'speaker identity'? Toward this objective, we collected the audio of two voice actresses with their original voice (denoted as Female #1 and #2 respectively), as well as their voice-over characters. For Female #1, two characters whose style is identified as childlike are gathered (denoted as Char. #A and #B); for Female #2, one character whose style is energetic (young boy voice) are gathered.

Table 3. Average accuracy with different levels of noise added.

Noise level (based on original volume)	Accuracy
1%	83.33%
2%	68.81%
4%	56.09%
Applying de-noising filter to 1% noisy audio	93.33%

The voice-over recordings are employed as test data, while the original voice recordings are regarded as training data. Two additional male husky voices and another two female childlike voices are also added to the training set.

The experiment is repeated 10 times to obtain average accuracy, as shown in Table 4. The results in Table 4 clearly indicate that mimicry style attain higher probability over original voice (i.e., speaker identity), suggesting that speaker identification can become ineffective if one tries to mimic other person's voice style. In other words, i-vector features may be more representative of the voice style than the intrinsic properties of the speaker's voice.

Table 4. Results of mimicry style test.

Audio source	Childlike style	Husky style	Female #1	Female #2
Char. #A of Female #1	**57.09%**	7.44%	25.05%	10.41%
Char. #B-1 of Female #1	**78.18%**	4.43%	12.34%	5.03%
Char. #B-2 of Female #1	**76.98%**	7.93%	11%	4.07%
Char. #B-3 of Female #1	**71.66%**	6.42%	12.53%	9.38%
Char. #B-4 of Female #1	**85.63%**	6.51%	3.59%	4.25%
Char. #B-5 of Female #1	**68.34%**	8.39%	12.12%	11.14%
Char. #B-6 of Female #1	**81.85%**	2.19%	8.25%	7.69%
Char. #B-7 of Female #1	**80.92%**	5.53%	4.4%	9.14%
Char. −1 of Female #2	4.14%	**66.17%**	10.61%	19.05%
Char. −2 of Female #2	5.12%	**44.86%**	19.1%	30.91%

3.2 Voice Style Classification

The experimental results of previous pilot studies demonstrate the stability of i-vector in the speaker identification task. The mimicry style test results also expose the limitations of i-vector features. To formally address the voice style classification problem, we need to define the categories of styles that are commonly perceived and possess high degree of consensus among a large group of audience. This is achieved by gathering data from public media. The initially collected audio files have to be checked to ensure that no excessive background music exists. We then perform hierarchical clustering to observe if meaningful groups which correspond to known voice styles have formed. After several iterations, we come up with eight voice types. With this result as guidance, we proceed to collect more audio files and perform the style classification task according to Fig. 1, the only difference being that the label for the audio is now 'voice style' instead of 'speaker identity'. Details are discussed in the following.

3.2.1 Dataset
We collect test audio from several sources, including local radio stations [10, 11], Youtube video and TV programs. We specifically search for the audio of celebrities or program hosts whose voices are distinctly recognizable. According to our pilot study, training data has to be at least 60 s in length. The length of test data, however, can vary. In order to perform cross-validation by randomly switching training samples and test data, the duration of all the audio segments employed in this experiment is set to 60 s. Additionally, we add computer-generated audio, including Google TTS [12] and Baidu TTS [13] voices as test samples.

3.2.2 Voice Styles
Our preliminary studies using hierarchical clustering show eight consistently perceived voice styles listed below: (1) Calming, (2) Childlike, (3) Silvery, (4) Articulate-female, (5) Husky (6) Excited (7) Energetic (8) Articulate-male.

Detailed information regarding the training and test audio are listed in Table 5 and Table 6, respectively.

Table 5. Detailed information of training data.

Voice style	#1	From	#2	From
Calming	Host	E-classical [10]	Host	E-classical [10]
Childlike	Talent	Youtube	Talent	Youtube
Silvery	Host	E-classical [10]	Youtuber	Youtube
Articulate-female	Host	E-classical [10]	Host	E-classical [10]
Husky	Host	E-books	Voice-over	E-books
Excited	Announcer	Youtube	Host	Youtube
Energetic	Host	Youtube	Youtuber	Youtube
Articulate-male	Host	E-classical [10]	Announcer	PBS [11]

4   Experimental Results

First of all, we train the classifier according to Fig. 1 and achieve 100% accuracy over all ten trials. The trained model is then tested with test audio listed in Table 6. The classification results are provided in Table 7. Note that we include the prediction probability of the SVM in the test results. As a result, we can examine the top-1 to top-8 cases in more detail. The Top-1 accuracy for all test samples is 67.5%, and Top-2 accuracy reaches 100%, indicating that our proposed approach is indeed effective.

Table 6. Detailed information of test data.

Voice style	Representer	From
Calming	Google TTS	[12]
Calming	Baidu TTS	[13]
Childlike	Talent	Youtube
Articulate-female	Singer	E-classical [10]
Articulate-female	Guest	E-classical [10]
Husky	Pianist	E-classical [10]
Articulate-male	Host	E-classical [10]
Articulate-male	Violinist	E-classical [10]

Table 7. Average prediction probability of voice style classification.

Test voice source	Expected class	Predicted class					
		Top-1		Top-2		Top-3	
Female #1	Childlike	Excited	45.62%	**Childlike**	16.38%	Calming	15.2%
Female #2	Articulate	**Articulate (F)**	39.99%	Calming	23.2%	Articulate (M)	11.4%
Female #3	Articulate	**Articulate (F)**	55.24%	Husky	22.49%	Energetic	7.19%
Male #1	Articulate	**Articulate (M)**	33.2%	Articulate (F)	17.99%	Calming	16.03%
Male #2	Husky	Articulate (M)	36.41%	**Husky**	24.53%	Calming	18.49%
Male #3	Articulate	**Articulate (M)**	69.17%	Excited	9.59%	Silvery	4.51%
Google TTS	Calming	**Calming**	32.1%	Silvery	25.67%	Articulate (F)	14.56%
Baidu TTS	Calming	Silvery	38.76%	**Calming**	21.39%	Excited	11.75%

To probe further into the 'misclassification' cases, we list the 8 prediction probabilities for the test audio in Table 8. Female #1 is known to have childlike voices. The 'Excited' class, however, gets the highest probability (45.62% vs. 16.38%). After listening to the audio file, we suspect that it could be due to the sampling process (10 s out 60 s) as well as the interference of background noise.

For Male #2, the prediction probabilities of 'Articulate' and 'Husky' do not differ significantly (36.41% vs. 25.53%). In fact, we have observed conflicting opinions in the labeling of this audio. Thus, the prediction matches that of human listener.

An interesting result arises when we present the Google TTS voices and Baidu TTS voices to our classifier. Our original label for these two audios is 'Calming'. However, the Baidu TTS voice possesses more 'Silvery' property than 'Calming', probably a desirable quality in computer-synthesized voices.

Table 8. Analysis of erroneous cases.

Test voice source	Calming	Childlike	Silvery	Articulate-female	Husky	Excited	Energetic	Articulate-male
Female #1	15.2%	**16.38%**	5.28%	4.87%	0.6%	45.62%	10.31%	1.75%
	Top-3	*Top-2				Top-1		
Male #2	17.68%	3.17%	2.06%	2%	**25.07%**	6.31%	6.59%	37.13%
	Top-3				*Top-2			Top-1
Baidu TTS	**21.6%**	9.72%	38.47%	2.59%	5.41%	11.83%	7.16%	3.23%
	*Top-2		Top-1			Top-3		

5 Conclusion

In this paper, we formulate the voice style classification problem as a speaker identification task and propose to employ i-vector features to address the problem. We conduct several pilot studies to validate the stability of the i-vector features. We then define and evaluate eight common styles for voice style classification. The results suggest that the adopted i-vector features are robust and effective for the classification of voice styles.

References

1. Maxine, E.: Trends in speaking styles research. In: Third European Conference on Speech Communication and Technology (1993)
2. Cox, D.: Is your voice trustworthy, engaging or soothing to strangers? (2015). https://www.theguardian.com/science/blog/2015/apr/16/is-your-voice-trustworthy-engaging-or-soothing-to-strangers
3. Chattopadhyay, A., Dahl, D.W., Ritchie, R.J., Shahin, K.N.: Hearing voices: the impact of announcer speech characteristics on consumer response to broadcast advertising. J. Consum. Psychol. **13**(3), 198–204 (2003)
4. Bou-Ghazale, S.E., Hansen, J.H.: A comparative study of traditional and newly proposed features for recognition of speech under stress. IEEE Trans. Speech Audio Process. **8**(4), 429–442 (2000)
5. Dehak, N., Kenny, P.J., Dehak, R., Dumouchel, P., Ouellet, P.: Front-end factor analysis for speaker verification. IEEE Trans. Audio Speech Lang. Process. **19**(4), 788–798 (2011)
6. Reynolds, D.A., Rose, R.C.: Robust text-independent speaker identification using Gaussian mixture speaker models. IEEE Trans. Speech Audio Process. **3**(1), 72–83 (1995)
7. Reynolds, D.A., Quatieri, T.F., Dunn, R.B.: Speaker verification using adapted Gaussian mixture models. Digit. Signal Process. **10**(1–3), 19–41 (2000)
8. Kenny, P.: Joint factor analysis of speaker and session variability: theory and algorithms. CRIM, Montreal, (Report) CRIM-06/08-13, 14, 28-29 (2005)

9. Chang, C.C., Lin, C.J.: LIBSVM: a library for support vector machines. ACM Trans. Intell. Syst. Technol. (TIST) **2**(3), 27 (2011)
10. E-classical Radio. https://www.e-classical.com.tw/index.html
11. Police Broadcasting Service. https://www.pbs.gov.tw/cht/index.php
12. Google TTS. https://translate.google.com.tw/
13. Baidu TTS. https://fanyi.baidu.com/#auto/zh/

Applying Deep Convolutional Neural Network to Cursive Chinese Calligraphy Recognition

Liang Jung and Wen-Hung Liao[(✉)] [iD]

Department of Computer Science, National Chengchi University, Taipei, Taiwan
whliao@nccu.edu.tw

Abstract. Calligraphy is one of the most important cultural art as well as writing tool in ancient China. Various writing styles have evolved over time in Calligraphy text, including Regular script, Clerical script, Semi-cursive script, Cursive script, and Seal script. In this study, we consider the cursive Chinese calligraphy recognition task as a variant of handwritten text recognition. We apply deep convolutional network approach to this recognition problem and achieve 84.6%, 92.6%, 93.7%, 96.7% average top1, top3, top5, top10 accuracy for 395 characters and 83.8%, 91.8%, 94%, 96.1% average top1, top3, top5, top10 accuracy for 632 characters. Our investigation indicates that text recognition tasks can be tackled by deep learning based approach even only when a limited number of training samples are available.

Keywords: Chinese calligraphy · Cursive style · Deep learning ·
Text recognition

1 Introduction

Chinese calligraphy is a traditional skill in Chinese culture, serving to convey the thoughts of Chinese literati. It is one of the most important cultural art as well as writing tool in ancient China. Various styles of Calligraphy have surfaced over the long history of China. The five most recognized types are: Regular script, Clerical script, Semi-cursive script, Cursive script, and Seal script. Of these styles, regular, clerical and seal scripts exhibit fixed structures and are easier to process with computer vision algorithms.

Recently, we have seen immense progress in the recognition of handwritten text using machine learning approaches [1]. However, automatic classification of text from historical documents remains a challenging task. Calligraphy text of the same type can vary significantly with the calligraphers, especially for the Cursive script. The difference between Cursive script and Regular script, as well as the diversity of Cursive scripts, make the recognition task even more difficult and time-consuming for historical workers who translate or digitalize the ancient Chinese documents. The call for automatic Cursive script Chinese Calligraphy recognition system has therefore arisen.

In this work, we consider the classification task for Cursive Chinese Calligraphy Text as a special case of handwritten text classification task. We first collected 4149 images of 395 different Chinese characters extracted from historical documents. We transform our dataset into two collections based on the consideration of variants:

© Springer Nature Singapore Pte Ltd. 2019
C.-Y. Chang et al. (Eds.): ICS 2018, CCIS 1013, pp. 646–653, 2019.
https://doi.org/10.1007/978-981-13-9190-3_71

(1) 2796 images of 395 different characters if variants are excluded, and (2) 4149 images of 632 different characters if variants are regarded as different characters. We then apply convolutional neural network to the text classification task. The efficacy of the proposed method is evaluated using top1, top5 and top10 classification accuracy.

The rest of this paper is organized as follows. In Sect. 2, we briefly review past researches regarding handwritten Chinese characters and cursive Chinese calligraphy character recognition. We then introduce our proposed CNN network structure and the flowchart for cursive Chinese calligraphy character recognition in Sect. 3. Afterwards, we demonstrate the dataset and explain our experiments design as well as results and failure analysis in Sect. 4. Finally, we conclude our results and discuss further developments of this research in Sect. 5.

2 Related Work

2.1 Handwritten Text Recognition

Since calligraphy also belongs to the handwritten family, we surveyed past studies related to handwritten text recognition task. In 2015, Zhang et al. proposed a deep convolutional network approach for handwritten Chinese character recognition [2]. In their work, they experimented M5, M6-, M6, M6+, M7-1, M7-2, M9 and M11 network architecture with CASIA HWDB1.1 dataset [3] for training and evaluation. The M11 model gives the best result of 97.3% top1 accuracy and 99.6% top5 accuracy for the 200-class classification task. Their models are also proved to be capable of dealing with low resolution text [4]. However, the CASIA HWDB1.1 dataset contains 300 images for each character, whereas our Cursive Chinese Calligraphy Text Dataset contains at most 37 images for a character class. We wish to find out if deep convolutional network works for text classification task even if we have very few training samples. Furthermore, the structure of Cursive Chinese Calligraphy Text is significantly different from regular handwritten text, and we wish to investigate if CNN also works in this kind of circumstance.

2.2 Cursive Chinese Calligraphy Text Recognition

There are very few existing works that concern Cursive Chinese text recognition. Actually, we only found one authored by Chen [5]. In Chen's work, the recognition task is achieved by calculating distances among a set of feature combinations and measures. Although his approach produced a decent result of 94.5% recognition rate, the details about both the feature combination and distance measure were not provided. In addition, Chen mentioned that their dataset contains 55 calligraphy images from five different authors. Details regarding the test data were not provided either.

3   The Proposed Approach

In this section, we introduce our data processing pipeline and our proposed network architecture. The system flow of a deep learning based OCR system is illustrated in Fig. 1. In this work, we assume that the segmentation module is robust or can be extracted manually by human, and focus only on the character recognition task. We briefly introduce the image preprocessing procedure in Sect. 3.1. We then explain our network design concept and architecture. Finally, implementation details and system environments are presented.

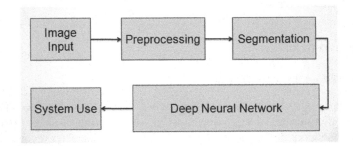

Fig. 1. System flow of deep learning based character recognition engine.

Fig. 2. Proposed convolutional network architecture adapted from M11 [2].

3.1   Preprocessing

First, each character image resized to 128 × 128. Then we normalize each image by dividing its standard deviation then subtracting its mean.

3.2   Network Architecture

In this work, we adapt the M11 network architectures from [2] to perform the recognition task. Since cursive style already simplifies the original structure of the text, we remove one of the fully connected layers to reduce computational complexity. Our network consists of 4 × 2 convolutional layers with max-pooling, followed by two fully connected layers. For each layer except the top layer, we apply ReLU for activation. For the top layer, we apply soft-max for activation function. The details are given in Fig. 2. Since we do not have many training samples for each character class, we also apply the Siamese convolutional neural network [6] architecture proposed by Koch et al. as a comparison. The architecture of Siamese convolutional neural network is shown in Fig. 3.

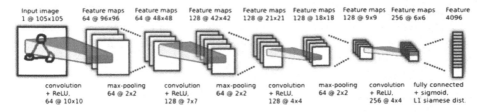

Fig. 3. The Siamese convolutional neural network proposed by Koch *et al.* [6].

3.3 Implementation Details and Environment

Our code is written on Python3.5.2 with numpy 1.14.2 [7], Pillow 5.1.0, tensorflow-gpu 1.8.0 [8], and keras 2.1.5 [9]. We use a computer running Ubuntu 16.04 with GTX 1080ti graphic card for training and evaluation process.

4   Experimental Results

In this section, we describe the details of our dataset, experiment design and evaluation metrics. We first introduce our cursive Chinese calligraphy dataset in Sect. 4.1. We then provide the experimental procedure and evaluation result of the Siamese convolutional neural network in Sect. 4.2.1. Afterwards, we explain the experimental flow and evaluation result of our proposed approach. Finally, we examine some failure cases to understand the limitation of the proposed neural network model.

Fig. 4. Cursive Chinese calligraphy images in our dataset. (a) Example of a pair of images that are structurally similar and are not considered as variants. (b) Example of a pair of images that are variants of the same character.

4.1   Dataset

Our dataset consists of two versions: 2796 images of 395 different characters (see Fig. 4(a)) if variants are excluded, and 4149 images of 632 different characters if variants are counted as different character (see Fig. 4(b)). All the images are collected through the internet [10]. Each character contains 1 to 37 images, which clearly lead to imbalanced data problem. Thus, we apply image augmentation for each character so that each character contains at least 20 samples. The parameters used for augmentation are as follows: rotations within 15°, horizontal shift within 5 pixels and vertical shift within 5 pixels. The final number of images after augmentation is 8479 for 395 characters and 13874 for 632 characters.

4.2 Model Evaluation

4.2.1 Siamese Convolutional Neural Network

Most deep learning frameworks call for a large amount of high-quality labeled data during the training stage. Issues have arisen when there are limited training samples at hand, which leads to the research field of one (or few) shot learning scheme. In 2015, Koch *et al.* [6] proposed the Siamese Convolutional Neural Network, which incorporates Convolutional Layers to the Siamese Neural Network [11]. They applied the Siamese Convolutional Neural Network to the classification of Omniglot dataset [12], in which each class contains only 20 samples only, and eventually achieved 92.0% one-shot accuracy. Since we encounter the same problem in this research, i.e., there are very few samples for each character in our dataset, we attempt to apply the Siamese Convolutional Neural Network to our cursive Chinese calligraphy recognition task.

For the evaluation of Siamese convolution neural network on our classification task, we first split the images of each character into three subsets: training, validation and evaluation, with the ratio 0.64/0.16/0.2. We trained the network for 200000 iterations. For each iteration, we generate 64 pairs of training data from the training images, where half of them are labeled '1', which indicates the pair of images are from the same class, and the other half labeled '0'.

The image selection process is as follows. Firstly, we randomly pick three images of one character in the training set, use the first two images to form a '1' pair. Secondly, we randomly select a character that is different from the one mentioned above. Then we randomly pick an image of the character and pair it with the third image of the first character picked to form a '0' pair. Afterwards, we evaluate the model by the following procedure. We perform 395 times of prediction. In each task, we randomly pick two images of a character in the test set, and then pop the character out. We then randomly take one image from all other characters to form a testing batch. After that, we put the test batch into the network. The output will be a 395×1 matrix, where each column indicates the probability that its label is '1'. Since we always put our ground truth at the 0th position, we need only to check if the probability of position 0 is in the top k. If it happens to be true, we add 1 to the top-k accuracy. The last step is to divide the top-k accuracy by 395 to get the true top-k accuracy.

For the experiments we conduct in this research with the aforementioned dataset, the results are 22.7%, 31.9% and 35.9% average top1, top5 and top10 accuracy for 395 characters' classification, respectively. The result suggests that the Siamese approach might not be appropriate for cursive Chinese calligraphy character recognition.

4.2.2 Our Proposed Model

We run the training and evaluation process for 10 times and then average the top1, top5 and top10 accuracy of each evaluation result. For each trial, we randomly split images in each character into training and testing subsets using 80:20 ratio. Then we shuffle the training and testing set to rearrange their order. In the training phase, we train the model for 100 epochs. Finally, we average the top1, top3, top5, top10 accuracy for the 395 characters' classification and 632 characters' classification task. The results are 84.6%, 93.7%, 96.7% average top1, top5, top10 accuracy for the 395 characters' classification, and 83.8%, 94.0%, 96.1% average top1, top5, top10 accuracy for 632 characters, respectively, as shown in Table 1.

Table 1. Classification result of 395 characters and 632 characters. Accuracy is the averaged among the 10 trials and rounded to first decimal place.

	Siamese-395 characters	Ours-395 characters	Ours-632 characters
Top1 accuracy	22.7%	**84.6%**	83.8%
Top5 accuracy	31.9%	93.7%	**94.0%**
Top10 accuracy	35.9%	**96.7%**	96.1%

4.3   Failure Case Investigation

As we examine the misclassification case, we speculated that the "feature resolution" of our model might be insufficient for characters that are structurally similar. Figure 5 demonstrates an example of two images that are structurally similar but are different characters. Additional preprocessing might be necessary to address this type of problem.

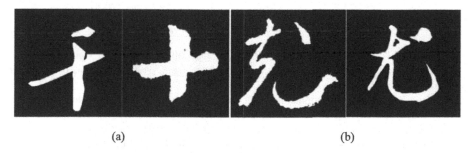

(a)   (b)

Fig. 5. Misclassified examples of two structurally similar images that are actually different characters. (a) Left: 干, right: 十. (b) Left: 充, right: 尤

5   Conclusion and Future Work

In this work, we apply deep convolutional neural network to cursive Chinese calligraphy text recognition task. Our model gives an 84.6%, 93.7%, 96.7% average top1, top5, top10 accuracy for the classification of 395 characters and 83.8%, 94%, 96.1% average top1, top5, top10 accuracy for 632 characters. As a proof of concept, our approach shows that (1) CNN is suitable for cursive Chinese calligraphy text recognition task, and (2) The number of training samples for text classification task might not necessarily be large to achieve satisfactory results.

For future work, we will continue to improve the performance of cursive calligraphy classification by obtaining more training samples from historical documents. Specifically, we will continue to investigate if (1) the network architecture and convolution kernels can be further simplified as text input is binary, and (2) the input image can be transformed by applying thinning algorithms (refer Fig. 6) as long as the structure is retained to reduce the influence of stroke width for text recognition. We have observed that if thinning is applied, the accuracy for our M11-like architecture dropped. But for the Siamese Convolutional Neural Network, despite the drop of the top1 accuracy, the top5 and top10 accuracy increased. We will therefore study the effect of thinning (or similar input simplification methods) to the accuracy of text classification task.

Fig. 6. Applying Zhang-Suen thinning algorithm [13] on cursive Chinese calligraphy characters.

References

1. Zhang, X.-Y., Bengio, Y., Liu, C.-L.: Online and offline handwritten Chinese character recognition: a comprehensive study and new benchmark. Pattern Recogn. **61**, 348–360 (2017)
2. Zhang, Y.: Deep convolutional network for handwritten Chinese character recognition. Computer Science Department, Stanford University (2015)
3. Liu, C.-L., et al.: CASIA online and offline Chinese handwriting databases. In: International Conference on Document Analysis and Recognition (ICDAR). IEEE (2011)
4. Huang, Y.-F.: Recognition of low resolution text using deep learning approach. MS thesis. National Chengchi University. https://hdl.handle.net/11296/pz3mh8
5. Chen, Y.-Z.: Segmentation and recognition of Chinese characters in cursive script in calligraphy documents. MS thesis. National Chao Tung University (2001). https://hdl.handle.net/11296/3x5597
6. Koch, G., Zemel, R., Salakhutdinov, R.: Siamese neural networks for one-shot image recognition. In: ICML Deep Learning Workshop, vol. 2 (2015)
7. NumPy Developers: NumPy. NumPy Numpy. Scipy Developers (2013)
8. Abadi, M., et al.: Tensorflow: a system for large-scale machine learning. In: OSDI, vol. 16 (2016)
9. Chollet, F.: Keras (2015)
10. Shufa. https://shufa.supfree.net/dity.asp

11. Bromley, J., et al.: Signature verification using a "siamese" time delay neural network. In: Advances in Neural Information Processing Systems (1994)
12. Lake, B.M., Salakhutdinov, R., Tenenbaum, J.B.: Human-level concept learning through probabilistic program induction. Science **350**(6266), 1332–1338 (2015)
13. Zhang, T.Y., Suen, C.Y.: A fast parallel algorithm for thinning digital patterns.". Commun. ACM **27**(3), 236–239 (1984)

Grassmannian Clustering for Multivariate Time Sequences

Beom-Seok Oh[1(✉)], Andrew Beng Jin Teoh[2], Kar-Ann Toh[2], and Zhiping Lin[1]

[1] School of EEE, Nanyang Technological University, Singapore, Singapore
`bsoh@ntu.edu.sg`
[2] School of EEE, Yonsei University, Seoul, Republic of Korea

Abstract. In this paper, we streamline the Grassmann multivariate time sequence (MTS) clustering for state-space dynamical modelling into three umbrella approaches: (i) Intrinsic approach where clustering is entirely constrained within the manifold, (ii) Extrinsic approach where Grassmann manifold is flattened via local diffeomorphisms or embedded into Reproducing Kernel Hilbert Spaces via Grassmann kernels, (iii) Semi-intrinsic approach where clustering algorithm is performed on Grassmann manifolds via Karcher mean. Consequently, 11 Grassmann clustering algorithms are derived and demonstrated through a comprehensive comparative study on human motion gesture derived MTS data.

Keywords: Mutivariate time sequence · Clustering · Grassmann manifold

1 Introduction

A time sequence (time series) records the changing state of a system over time, which can be loosely divided into univariate and multivariate time sequences. Multivariate time sequence (MTS) is defined as a set of p-dimensional time sequences of data with n equal time stamps, denoted as $\mathbf{y}(t) \in \mathbb{R}^p, p > 1$ and $t = 1, \cdots, n$, hence univariate time series is a special case of MTS where $p = 1$. The MTS is usually represented as a matrix $\mathbf{Y} \in \mathbb{R}^{p \times n}$. MTS appears ubiquitously in various applications [1–4].

Time sequence clustering is a fundamental subject in time sequence analysis. A large collection of methods have been developed to cluster different types of univariate time sequence data [2,3]. Putting their differences aside, it is far to say that in spirit they all attempt to devise the similarity/dissimilarity measures of two time sequences, which is assumed, either implicitly or explicitly, residing in a vector space. Some well-known instances are Euclidean distance, correlation measures etc [2]. Once the similarity measure is determined, general-purpose clustering algorithms can be adapted.

However, these clustering methods are largely improper for matrix-representation MTS which suggested that MTS does not lie on a vector space.

© Springer Nature Singapore Pte Ltd. 2019
C.-Y. Chang et al. (Eds.): ICS 2018, CCIS 1013, pp. 654–664, 2019.
https://doi.org/10.1007/978-981-13-9190-3_72

Moreover, MTS possess two unique properties namely joint temporal dynamics and correlation [5,6]. The former captures the temporal evolution while the latter represents the relationship between multiple sequences. An important school of thought that responses to this challenge is by using a linear subspace representation [4,5]. In this approach, firstly, each MTS is represented by a state-space dynamical model, such as autoregressive and moving average (ARMA) model [7]. Model parameters are learned and transformed into an orthonormal matrix, which can be viewed as a linear subspace structure. Secondly, a distance between the dynamical models (linear subspaces) is defined such as Martin distance, Frobenius distance etc [5,8] and computed over all the models estimated in the first stage. Finally, the clustering is carried out based on these distances.

This state-space approach has addressed all the requirements of MTS data clustering in principle and found successful in many applications related to MTS [5] or spatial-temporal data stream [9–14]. However, the major limitation is inflexibility in adopting large collection of general-purpose clustering algorithms in literature due to its linear subspace structure. For instance, the means computation in k-means algorithm is unclear for such a structure. Linear subspace representation is indeed residing on a special kind of differential manifold called Grassmann manifold. A set of linear subspaces can thus be perceived as points on the Grassmann manifold [14]. In this regard, linear subspace matching problem for clustering can be recast as a specific learning problem on the Grassmann manifold, coined as Grassmann MTS clustering.

In this paper, we streamline the realizations of Grassmann MTS clustering (see also [15]) for state-space dynamical modelling. Specifically, we classify them into three umbrella approaches: (i) *Intrinsic approach* where clustering is entirely constrained within the manifold where geodesic distances defined on Grassmann manifold are adopted directly. (ii) *Extrinsic approach* where the Grassmann manifold is firstly flattened via local diffeomorphisms or embedded into reproducing kernel Hilbert spaces (RKHS) via Grassmann kernels so that ordinary clustering can be carried out. (iii) *Semi-intrinsic approach* where clustering algorithm is performed on Grassmann manifolds via Karcher mean. Despite treatment of linear subspaces as points on Grassmann manifold for learning and clustering were reported in [10,11,13,14], they were not catered to MTS but more to image set or spatial-temporal data. Moreover, a systematic summarization and comparison remained absent.

The contribution of this paper is three-folded: (i) We outline three umbrella approaches for Grassmann MTS clustering and deliberate their respective characteristics, merits and demerits. (ii) We demonstrate 11 Grassmann clustering algorithms derived from these three approaches. (iii) We conduct a comprehensive comparative study based on human motion gesture derived MTS data.

2   Preliminary

2.1   State-Space Dynamical Model

The ARMA is well-known dynamical model for modelling MTS, $\mathbf{y}(t) \in \mathbb{R}^p$ [14]:

$$
\begin{aligned}
\mathbf{y}(t) &= \mathbf{C}\mathbf{z}(t) + \mathbf{w}(t) & \mathbf{w}(t) &\sim \mathrm{N}(\mathbf{0,R}) \\
\mathbf{z}(t+1) &= \mathbf{A}\mathbf{z}(t) + \mathbf{v}(t) & \mathbf{v}(t) &\sim \mathrm{N}(\mathbf{0,Q})
\end{aligned}
\tag{1}
$$

where $\mathbf{z} \in \mathbb{R}^d$ is the hidden state vector, $\mathbf{A} \in \mathbb{R}^{d \times d}$ the transition matrix, and $\mathbf{C} \in \mathbb{R}^{p \times d}$ the measurement matrix. $\mathbf{w}$ and $\mathbf{v}$ are noise component modeled as normal probability distribution with zero mean and covariance $\mathbf{R} \in \mathbb{R}^{p \times p}$ and $\mathbf{Q} \in \mathbb{R}^{d \times d}$, respectively.

In this model, the measurement matrix $\mathbf{C}$ encodes structural correlation detail while the transition matrix $\mathbf{A}$ captures temporal dynamic of MTS. The model parameters, $M = \{\mathbf{A}, \mathbf{C}\}$ can be learned via a closed-form solution proposed in [5]. For comparison of two models, the most commonly used similarity measure is based on subspace angles between column subspaces of the extended observability matrices $\mathbf{O}_m^T$ given as [5]:

$$
\mathbf{O}_m^T = \left[\mathbf{C}^T, (\mathbf{CA})^T, \left(\mathbf{CA}^2\right)^T, \cdots, \left(\mathbf{CA}^{m-1}\right)^T \right] \in \mathbb{R}^{q \times d}
\tag{2}
$$

where $q = mp$. The column space of $\mathbf{O}_m^T$ is a d-dimensional subspace of $\mathbb{R}^q$, where d is the dimension of the state-space $\mathbf{z}$. d is usually of the order of 5–10 and $m = d$ [14].

2.2   Grassmann Manifold

A Grassmann manifold $\mathcal{G}_{r,s}$ is a collection of all r-dimensional linear subspaces of a Euclidean space in $\mathbb{R}^s$ where the topology of Grassmann manifolds exhibits nonlinear structure. A linear subspace can be perceived as a point in a Grassmann manifold which may be specified by an $s \times s$ orthogonal matrix $\mathbf{X} = \mathbf{X}^T$ of rank r. Formally, the Grassmann manifold is defined as a particular subset of the symmetric matrices Sym_s [16]: $\mathcal{G}_{r,s} = \{\mathbf{X} \in Sym_s | \mathbf{X}^T = \mathbf{X}, rank(\mathbf{X}) = r\}$

Accordingly, a linear dynamical system can be identified as a point on the Grassmann manifold corresponding to the column space of the extended observability matrix [14]. The similarity/dissmilarity measurement of two points on a manifold is carried forward to the geodesic distance specified by that manifold as shown in Fig. 1(a) and (b). The geodesic distance between two points on the manifold is defined as the length of the shortest curve connecting the two points [17].

In our context, to represent the subspace spanned by the columns of extended observability matrices $\mathbf{O}_m^T$ defined in (2), an orthonormal basis can be computed by Gram-Schmidt orthonormalization or thin singular value decomposition (thinSVD) [10]. That is, a linear subspace that corresponds to (2) is operationally stored as a thin-tall orthonormal matrix $\mathbf{U} \in \mathbb{R}^{q \times d}$ for computation.

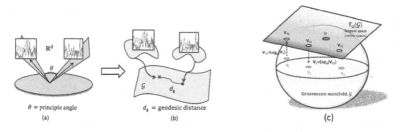

Fig. 1. (a) State-space dynamical models can be described in $\mathbb{R}^d$ by linear subspaces. (b) Linear subspaces in $\mathbb{R}^d$ can be represented as points on the Grassmann manifold. (c) The relation of Grassmann manifold and its tangent space in which $\mathbf{U}$ is chosen as Karcher mean.

A canonical distance between two subspaces is called principle angle [11]. Let $\mathbf{U}$ and $\mathbf{V}$ be two orthonormal matrices of size q by d, the principle angle $0 \leq \theta_1 \leq \cdots \leq \theta_d \leq \pi/2$ between two subspaces $span(\mathbf{U})$ and $span(\mathbf{V})$ defined recursively by $cos\theta_k = \max\limits_{u_k \in span(\mathbf{U})} \max\limits_{v_k \in span(\mathbf{V})} u_k^T v_k$ subject to $u_k^T u_k = 1, v_k^T v_k = 1, u_k^T u_j = 0$ and $v_k^T v_j = 0$, where $j = 1, \cdots, k-1$. The cosine of the principal angle is the first canonical correlation [11]. The k-th principal angle and canonical correlation are defined recursively.

The principal angles [11] and Procrustes distance metric [14] are common choices for the geodesic distance which can be respectively defined as follows:

$$\text{Principal angles: } d_g^2 (\mathbf{U}, \mathbf{V}) = \sum_i \theta_i^2. \tag{3}$$

$$\text{Procrustes distance: } d_p^2 (\mathbf{U}, \mathbf{V}) = tr \left(\mathbf{I} - \mathbf{A}^T \mathbf{A} \right) \text{ where } \mathbf{A} = \mathbf{U}^T \mathbf{V}. \tag{4}$$

3   Grassmann Clustering for MTS Data

Since the similarity/dissimilarity measurement and learning constitute the central components for data clustering, we hence recast a MTS clustering problem via linear dynamical modeling as a learning problem on the Grassmann manifold. Depend to the nature of the adapted clustering algorithm; learning problem in clustering can be reduced to a simple and more natural point-to-point matching problem via geodesic distance. In general, the clustering problem on Grassmann manifold can be streamlined into three categories namely, *intrinsic approach*, *extrinsic approach* and *semi-intrinsic approach*, which will be elaborated in the following subsections.

3.1   Intrisic Grassmann Clustering

The intrinsic approach is entirely constrained within the manifold itself [14]. Consequently, the existing clustering algorithms are irrelevant without substantial alteration in accordance to the manifold geometric characteristics, if not design afresh [18]. For example, clustering by Gaussian mixture model (GMM) [2] is inapplicable as Grassmann manifold does not define Gaussian density function. k-means is another negative instance as ordinary mean computation is not applicable to Grassmann manifold. Therefore, the simplest form in its kind is through a direct replacement of dissimilarity measure with geodesic distances in a chosen clustering algorithm. In this regard, spectral clustering (SC) [12,19] is deemed suitable in this context.

SC formulates the clustering problem as an eigenvector-decomposition problem of the Graph-Laplacian matrix. For a set of points $\{\mathbf{U}_i \in \mathbb{R}^{q \times d} | i = 1, \cdots, n\}$ on the Grassmannian manifold, an affinity matrix $\mathbf{A} \in \mathbb{R}^{n \times n}$ is first constructed by computing the similarity scores for all pair of $\mathbf{U}_i$. Here, we apply geodesic distances in (3) and (4) instead of usual distance measures used in vector space. Affinity matrix $\mathbf{A}$ can be constructed in different ways such as a fully connected graph (FC), a m-nearest neighbors (mNN) graph etc [19]. $\mathbf{A}$ is next converted to normalized Laplacian matrix, $\mathbf{L}_{norm}$ and then follows the identical steps given in the ordinary SC as shown in Algorithm 1.

Algorithm 1. Grassmann spectral clustering

1: **Input:** n points $\{\mathbf{U}_i\}_{i=1}^n$ on the Grassmann manifold, number of clusters K

2: Compute the affinity matrix $\mathbf{A}_{(i,j)} = \exp\left(\frac{-d^2(\mathbf{U}_i, \mathbf{U}_j)}{\sigma^2}\right)$ where $i \neq j$, $\mathbf{A}_{(i,i)} = 0$ and $d(\mathbf{U}_i, \mathbf{U}_j)$ is a similarity measurement function such as distance defined in (3), (4) and σ is a spread factor.

3: Compute the lowest K eigenvectors of normalized Laplacian matrix $\mathbf{L}_{norm} = \mathbf{D}^{-\frac{1}{2}}(\mathbf{D} - \mathbf{A})\mathbf{D}^{-\frac{1}{2}}$ where $\mathbf{D}_{(i,i)} = \Sigma_{j=1}^n \mathbf{A}_{(i,j)}$.

4: Normalize the rows of $\mathbf{V} \in \mathbb{R}^{n \times K}$ which consists of K eigenvectors, to have unit length by $\mathbf{Z}_{(i,j)} = \mathbf{V}_{(i,j)}/(\Sigma_j \mathbf{V}_{(i,j)}^2)^{\frac{1}{2}}$.

5: Every row of $\mathbf{V}$ be the corresponding point in the Euclidean space, the new set of points become $\{\mathbf{z}_i\}_{i=1}^n$ where $\forall \mathbf{z} \in \mathbb{R}^K$.

6: **Output:** Clusters $\{C_1, \cdots, C_K\}$ with $C_k = \{i | \mathbf{z}_i \in C_k\}$ obtained by the k-means clustering on $\{\mathbf{z}_i\}_{i=1}^n$

3.2   Extrisic Grassmann Clustering

Extrinsic method attempts to embed the points on the manifold into an Euclidean space [10] or to RKHS via kernel mapping and then performs clustering on Euclidean space or on the feature space [11].

A differential manifold such as Grassmann manifold $\mathcal{G}$ enables us to analyze derivatives of curves on the manifold. The derivative of a curve $\alpha(t)$ at a point $\mathbf{U} \in \mathcal{G}$ being a vector $\alpha'(t)$ lying in the vector space $T_{\mathbf{U}}\mathcal{G}$ is called a tangent space to $\mathcal{G}$ at $\mathbf{U}$. While it is not always true, in a generic situation for every point $\mathbf{U}$ in $\mathcal{G}$, there is a unique geodesic starting from $\mathbf{U}$ in every direction, giving us the exponential map $Exp_{\mathbf{U}} : T_{\mathbf{U}}\mathcal{G} \to \mathcal{G}$ such that $d(\mathbf{U}, Exp_{\mathbf{U}}(\mathbf{V}_T)) = \|\mathbf{V}_T\|_{\mathbf{U}}$ for every $\mathbf{V}_T$ in $T_{\mathbf{U}}\mathcal{G}$. As such, another distance measure on $\mathcal{G}$ known as tangent norm $d_T(\mathbf{U}, \mathbf{V})$ between $\mathbf{U}, \mathbf{V} \in \mathcal{G}$, can be written as [9]:

$$d_T^2(\mathbf{U}, \mathbf{V}) = \langle \mathbf{V}, \mathbf{V} \rangle_{\mathbf{U}} = \|Log_{\mathbf{U}}(\mathbf{V})\|_F^2, \tag{5}$$

where $\langle, \rangle$ is the inner product and $\| \cdot \|$ is the Frobenius norm.

The inverse map to $Exp_{\mathbf{U}}(\mathbf{V})$, the logarithm is defined only in a certain neighborhood of $\mathbf{U}$ and is denoted by $Log_{\mathbf{U}}$ [10]. The relation of Grassmann manifold and its tangent space and the forward and reverse mapping are illustrated in Fig. 1(c). This is essentially equivalent to flattening the manifold via local diffeomorphisms, i.e., the manifold is locally embedded into an Euclidean space [14]. Therefore, by mapping the point sets on the Grassmann manifold via $Log_{\mathbf{U}}(\cdot)$ to the tangent space, MTS clustering can be performed by using a general clustering algorithm designed for Euclidean space.

The reverse and forward mapping functions, $Log_{\mathbf{U}}(\cdot)$ and $Exp_{\mathbf{U}}(\cdot)$ can be computed by using Algorithms 2 and 3 respectively [10]. However, the manifold mapping may leads to some problems. The exponential map $Exp_{\mathbf{U}}(\cdot)$ is onto but only one-to-one in a neighborhood of $\mathbf{U}$. The $Log_{\mathbf{U}}(\cdot)$ is restrictively defined only around a small neighborhood of $\mathbf{U}$. It is impossible to define global coordinates which make the whole manifold resembles Euclidean space [16].

Algorithm 2. Manifold to tangent space mapping, $Log_{\mathbf{U}}(\cdot)$

1: **Input:** A to-be-mapped point on $\mathcal{G}$, $\mathbf{V} \in \mathbb{R}^{q \times d}$ and $\mathbf{U} \in \mathbb{R}^{q \times d}$
2: $\mathbf{R}\Sigma\mathbf{S}^T = thinSVD((\mathbf{I} - \mathbf{V}\mathbf{V}^T)\mathbf{U}(\mathbf{V}^T\mathbf{U})^{-1})$
3: $\Omega = \tan^{-1}(\Sigma)$
4: **Output:** $\mathbf{V}_T = vec(\mathbf{R}\Omega\mathbf{S}^T)$ ▷ $vec(\cdot)$ is a vectorization process

---

Algorithm 3. Tangent space to manifold mapping, $Exp_{\mathbf{U}}(\cdot)$

1: **Input:** A to-be-mapped point on $T_{\mathbf{U}}\mathcal{G}$, $\mathbf{V}_T \in \mathbb{R}^{q \times d}$ and $\mathbf{U} \in \mathbb{R}^{q \times d}$
2: $\mathbf{R}\Sigma\mathbf{S}^T = thinSVD(devec(\mathbf{V}_T))$ ▷ $devec(\cdot)$ denotes de-vectorization process.
3: **Output:** $\mathbf{V} = \mathbf{U}\mathbf{S}\cos\Sigma + \mathbf{R}\sin\Sigma$, where $\mathbf{V} \in \mathbb{R}^{q \times d}$

Another major path is to map $\mathbf{U} \in \mathcal{G}$ to a feature vector $\phi(\mathbf{U})$ in a Hilbert space through the kernel learning method [11]. A kernel function $k : (\mathcal{G} \times \mathcal{G}) \to \mathbb{R}$ is used to define the inner product on Hilbert space, thus forming a RKHS. According to Mercer's theorem, however, only positive definite and symmetric kernels delineate valid RKHS. A few Grassmann kernel functions have been devised such as projection kernel, $k_F = \|\mathbf{U}_t^T\mathbf{U}_j\|_F$, which derived from Frobenius norm and canonical correlation kernel [13].

By and large, a major advantage of being able to compute positive definite kernels on the Grassmann manifold is that it permits to utilize clustering methods that can be kernelized, such as k-means, spectral clustering etc. while still accounting for the geometry of manifolds. However, we are also restricted to use kernel-based clustering methods only. Furthermore, this approach also unavoidably inherited theoretical/technical challenges found in kernel learning paradigm such as unscalable for big data, ambiguity in choosing kernel functions and the associated parameters etc [16].

3.3 Semi-intrinsic Grassmann Clustering

A number of celebrated clustering algorithms, e.g., k-means and mean shift [18] and their variants, compute the distance as well as the means iteratively from the given data. On Grassmann manifold, the mean computation is not straightforward and requires a specific defined measure known as Karcher mean [20]. The Karcher mean (minimiser of squared distances between points and the mean on manifold) is itself an iterative algorithm to calculate the mean of a set of points on the manifold. Hence, semi-intrinsic method performs MTS clustering on Grassmann manifold using Karcher mean by iteratively moving from manifold to tangent spaces and vice versa. A typical instance of this approach applies in k-means and mean shift clustering on Grassmann manifold can be found in [14] and [18], respectively.

Since this approach is effectively carried out on Grassmann manifold, geodesic distances such as (3), (4) and (5) are used for similarity/dissimilarity measures. Semi-intrinsic approach differs from the intrinsic approach in such a way that it performs clustering on manifold based on Karcher mean as well as geodesic distance while mean computation is undefined for intrinsic approach. However, the cost of Karcher mean computation may offset the efficiency of a clustering algorithm.

4   Experiments and Discussions

In this section, we evaluate and compare various combinations of Grassmann clustering techniques outlined in Sect. 3 by using human motion capture derived MTS from CMU MOCAP database [21]. The motion capture encompasses recording human motion through tracking the 41 markers' movement taped on human actors. The movement sequence is thus represented by a series of 3-dimensional coordinates.

As shown in Table 1, we select 216 samples that correspond to nine gestures (clusters). Particularly, 41 marker positions (x, y, z) with first 120 time stamps stored in C3D format is utilized. Each sample of C3D is thus represented by a matrix $\mathbf{Y} \in \mathbb{R}^{123 \times 120}$. We model two types of MTS aforementioned with linear dynamical system (LDS) depicted in (1) and complex-valued LDS (CLDS) proposed by [6] with order number $d = 5$ and $m = d$. CLDS encodes hidden variables using complex number, which was demonstrated able to capture the dynamics and correlation characteristic of MTS much better compare to that of the LDS. Average clustering accuracy (%), which is obtained over 30 iterations, is used as performance indicator for comparison [22].

Table 2 enumerates the best clustering accuracy and CPU time of the 11 combinations. Note that we apply three well known clustering algorithms, i.e., k-means, spectral clustering (SC) and kernel SC (KSC) in this study. For extrinsic tangent space method, we only apply SC with Euclidean distance for affinity matrix construction but any general purpose clustering algorithm can be directly adopted in principle. Out of the 11 algorithms, semi-intrinsic k-means with tangent norm (TN) and extrinsic projection kernel (PK) were reported in [13] and [14], respectively.

Table 1. Experimental data description

Cluster no.	Gesture	Num. of samples	Taken from subjects	Cluster no.	Gesture	Num. of samples	Taken from subjects
1	Forward walking	46	#7, #8, #35	6	Golf swing	11	#63, #64
2	Forward running	22	#9, #35	7	Story	30	#138
3	Jumping	30	#118	8	Marching	10	#138
4	Salsa dancing	30	#60, #61	9	Walking with arm out	12	#132
5	Picking up something	25	#64, #115	-	-	-	-

Table 2. 11 combinations of the Grassmann clustering techniques used in evaluation

Methods	Clustering	Similarity measure/kernel function	Graph types
Intrinsic (4 methods)	SC^1	Principal angle (PA), procrustes distance (PD)	FC, mNN^2
Extrinsic (4 methods: tangent space 2	SC^1	Euclidean distance (ED)^3	FC, mNN^2
methods, Grassmann kernel 2 methods)	KSC^1	PK, Canonical correlation kernel (CCK)	FC
Semi-intrinsic^{4,5} (3 methods)	k-means	Tangent norm (TN), PA, PD	-

4.1 Results and Discussion

Table 3 tabulates the clustering accuracy (%) and the CPU processing speed (sec.) performances for C3D data set. The best performing parameters that associate to each technique are included. Note that ED applies to extrinsic tangent space SC while TN used in semi-intrinsic k-means. This experiment is conducted using a PC of 3.4 GHz clocks with 8G memory and a Matlab platform.

4.2 Summary

Table 4 provides a summary of three umbrella approaches for Grassmann MTS clustering in terms of merits and demerits which can serve as a reference for future research.

Table 3. Clustering performances of the 11 combinations on C3D data

| | Accuracy (%) | | | | | | CPU processing speed (sec.) | | | | | |
| | LDS | | | CLDS | | | LDS | | | CLDS | | |
	TN/ED	PA	PD	ED	PA	PD	TN/ED	PA	PD	ED	PA	PD
k-means	68.3	69.0	73.0	71.5	69.0	73.9	387.4	324.3	321.7	387.4	320.2	320.5
FC-SC	66.1	66.1	68.7	77.8	77.8	72.7	18.4	2.4	2.5	18.7	2.6	2.7
	($\sigma=2$)	($\sigma=2$)	($\sigma=2$)	($\sigma=1$)	($\sigma=1$)	($\sigma=1$)						
mNN-SC	68.0	68.0	69.0	82.0	81.9	81.0	18.0	2.2	2.4	18.5	2.5	2.5
	($\sigma=10^3$, $m=6$)	($\sigma=0.1$, $m=6$)	($\sigma=50$, $m=6$)	($\sigma=20$, $m=8$)	($\sigma=3$, $m=8$)	($\forall\sigma$, $m=7$)						
PK-KSC	72.2			73.6			1.7			1.8		
CCK-KSC	65.7			85.6			60.5			60.5		

Table 4. Merits and demerits of three umbrella Grassmann MTS clustering algorithms

Approaches	Merits	Demerits
Intrinsic	Exploit the true manifold geometric characteristics	Inflexible, the existing algorithms have to be substantially modified, if not design afresh.
Ex-Tangent space	Can adopt any common-purpose clustering algorithm in principal	Problematic if the mapping point is too far away from reference point, eg. Karcher mean
Ex-Kernel embedding	Fast and give reasonably good performance	Inflexible, limited to kernel based clustering methods, inherit open problems of kernel learning methods
Semi-intrinsic	Enable to exploit true manifold geometric characteristics without major alteration on the existing algorithms	Slow. Require forward and reverse mappings between manifold and tangent space iteratively

4.3   Summary

Table 4 provides a summary of three umbrella approaches for Grassmann MTS clustering in terms of merits and demerits which can serve as a reference for future research.

We first observe that the CLDS produces better accuracies than that of the LDS. For k-means, we notice that the adopted Procrustes distance consistently outperforms tangent norm used in [14]. This implies the chosen of geodesic distance is crucial for the algorithm. Table 3 also reveals that both manifold flattening and kernel embedding extrinsic methods have comparable performance but outperformed semi-intrinsic method marginally. However, intrinsic methods do better than extrinsic approaches despite of the small margin. It is interesting to notice that Procrustes distance is the best measure compared with that of tangent norm and principal angle in the experiments.

In terms of computational efficiency, semi-intrinsic approach is of several order magnitude slower than the rest due to iterative computation of Karcher mean. It is not a surprise to see that the intrinsic method is speedy as it does not go through additional processing such as reverse mapping or iterative Karcher mean computation. However, extrinsic kernel method can be efficient depends to the adopted kernel function, such as Projection kernel used in the experiment.

5 Conclusions

In this paper, we streamlined three umbrella approaches for Grassmann MTS clustering that based on state-space dynamical modelling. 11 algorithms were derived and studied extensively on a motion capture MTS data. We deliberated the characteristic, merits and demerits of each approaches based on the experimental results, which might be useful to serve as a reference for future research.

References

1. Hallac, D., Vare, S., Boyd, S., Leskovec, J.: Toeplitz inverse covariance-based clustering of multivariate time series data. In: ACM SIGKDD, pp. 215–223 (2017)
2. Liao, T.W.: Clustering of time series data—a survey. Pattern Recogn. **38**(11), 1857–1874 (2005)
3. Silva, J.A., Faria, E.R., Barros, R.C., et al.: Data stream clustering: a survey. ACM Comput. Surv. **46**(1), 13 (2013)
4. Veeraraghavan, A., Roy-Chowdhury, A.K., et al.: Matching shape sequences in video with applications in human movement analysis. IEEE TPAMI **27**(12), 1896–1909 (2005)
5. Boets, J., Cock, K.D., Espinoza, M., Moor, B.D.: Clustering time series, subspace identification and cepstral distances. Commun. Inf. Sys. **5**(1), 69–96 (2005)
6. Li, L., Prakash, B.A: Time series clustering: complex is simpler! In: ICML, pp. 185–192 (2011)
7. Harvey, A.C.: Time Series Models. The MIT Press, Cambridge (1993)
8. Kremer, H., Günnemann, S., Held, A., Seidl, T.: Mining of temporal coherent subspace clusters in multivariate time series databases. In: Tan, P.-N., Chawla, S., Ho, C.K., Bailey, J. (eds.) PAKDD 2012. LNCS (LNAI), vol. 7301, pp. 444–455. Springer, Heidelberg (2012). https://doi.org/10.1007/978-3-642-30217-6_37
9. Aggarwal, G., Chowdhury, A.K.R., Chellappa, R.: A System identification approach for video-based face recognition. In: ICPR, vol. 4, pp. 175–178 (2004)
10. Begelfor, E., Werman, M.: Affine invariance revisited. In: IEEE CVPR, vol. 2, pp. 2087–2094 (2006)
11. Hamm, J.: Subspace-based learning with Grassmann kernels. Ph.D. thesis, University of Pennsylvania (2008)
12. Hayat, M., Bennamoun, M., El-Sallam, A.A.: Clustering of video-patches on Grassmannian manifold for facial expression recognition from 3D videos. In: IEEE Workshop on Applications of Computer Vision, pp. 83–88 (2013)
13. Shirazi, S., Harandi, M.T., et al.: Clustering on Grassmann manifolds via kernel embedding with application to action analysis. In: IEEE ICIP, pp. 781–784 (2012)

14. Turaga, P., Veeraraghavan, A., Srivastava, A., Chellappa, R.: Statistical computations on Grassmann and Stiefel manifolds for image and video-based recognition. IEEE TPAMI **33**(11), 2273–2286 (2011)
15. Gruber, P., Theis, F.J.: Grassmann clustering. In: 14th European Signal Processing Conference, pp. 1–5 (2006)
16. Caseiro, R., Martins, P., Henriques, J.F., Leite, F.S., Batista, J.: Rolling Riemannian manifolds to solve the multi-class classification problem. In: IEEE CVPR, pp. 41–48 (2013)
17. Edelman, A., Arias, T.A., Smith, S.T.: The geometry of algorithms with orthogonality constraints. SIAM J. Mat. Anal. App. **20**(2), 303–353 (1998)
18. Cetingul, H.E., Vidal, R.: Intrinsic mean shift for clustering on Stiefel and Grassmann manifolds. In: IEEE CVPR, pp. 1896–1902 (2009)
19. Ng, A.Y., Jordan, M.I., Weiss, Y.: On spectral clustering: analysis and an algorithm. In: NIPS, pp. 849–856 (2002)
20. Karcher, H.: Riemannian center of mass and mollifier smoothing. Commun. Pure Appl. Math. **30**(5), 509–541 (1977)
21. MOCAP database. http://mocap.cs.cmu.edu
22. Nie, F., Xu, D., Tsang, I.W., Zhang, C.: Spectral embedded clustering. In: International Joint Conference on Artificial Intelligence, pp. 1181–1186 (2009)

Inflammatory Cells Detection in H&E Staining Histology Images Using Deep Convolutional Neural Network with Distance Transformation

Chao-Ting Li[✉], Pau-Choo Chung, Hung-Wen Tsai,
Nan-Haw Chow, and Kuo-Sheng Cheng

National Cheng Kung University (NCKU), Tainan, Taiwan
chting658@gmail.com

Abstract. Inflammatory cells such as lymphocytes and neutrophils are crucial indicators in diagnosing acute inflammation from liver histology images. However, there are several challenges in detecting the inflammatory cells. The inflammatory cells have large variation and also appear similar to other cells. In an often occasion, the inflammatory cells may overlap each other. It is also unavoidable to see the clustery noise in the background. To conquer the above-mentioned problems, this paper proposes a procedure, which implements the detection-then-classification by combining the distance transformation with deep convolutional neural networks for detecting an accurate position of each cell. Then a precise image patch can be extracted for a deep convolutional neural network for classification of the cells into nuclei, lymphocyte, neutrophils and impurity (e.g. Kupffer cell). The experimental results show that the proposed approach can effectively detect the inflammatory cells from H&E Staining liver histopathological images, with an accuracy of 93.7% in inflammatory cells classification.

Keywords: Dual morphological grayscale reconstruction ·
Distance transform · Convolutional neural network · Cell detection

1 Introduction

Analysis of histopathology image for computer-assisted is very popular in modern pathology. In computer-assisted diagnosis method, automatic cell detection is one of the essential steps. Recent studies show that different types of cells (e.g. nucleus, lymphocytes, neutrophils) play different role in tumor grading and disease diagnosis. Particularly, accurately classifying inflammatory cells (e.g. lymphocytes, neutrophils) play a critical step to better characterize acute inflammation diseases. For example, the gathering of lymphocytes around the portal vein demonstrates as on indicator of inflammatory caused by Hepatitis. Similarly, gathering of neutrophils, a major type of immune cells, may be regard as a phenomenon of cell necrosis, inflammation or bacterial infection. It is also reported that the locations and number of inflammatory cells determine whether there is acute inflammation.

© Springer Nature Singapore Pte Ltd. 2019
C.-Y. Chang et al. (Eds.): ICS 2018, CCIS 1013, pp. 665–672, 2019.
https://doi.org/10.1007/978-981-13-9190-3_73

However, there still have some challenges in automatic cell detection on histopathology image. For example, (1) large variation in the shape of cells, (2) crowed cells and overlapped cells, and (3) cluster and noise background.

Several methods for automatic cell detection based on image processing [7, 8] were proposed. Recently, CNN classifiers demonstrate the advantages of automatically learning the feature, and therefore many CNN-based methods are proposed [3–5, 12]. These methods implement the CNN as a two-class (e.g. cells, background) classifier to detect cells in patch-wise by sliding window. Wang et al. [3] proposed a cell detection method with sliding window based deep convolutional neural networks, to detect and classify different subtypes of cells.

In addition to the methods mentioned above, there are studies on neutrophil classification in the blood [9, 10]. Due to the image modality, these methods are not applicable to H&E Staining biopsy image. Thus, Wang et al. [6] proposed an automated method for Identifying Neutrophils in H&E Staining Histology Images. This method segments cells by iterative edge labeling, and identify neutrophils based on the segmentation results by considering also the context of each candidate cell. However, the researches for identifying neutrophils on the H&E straining are relatively unexplored. The reason is that neutrophils have large variation in shape, such as multiple lobes in nucleus per cell. The lobes of some neutrophils are perfectly well separated (e.g. Fig. 2(a) and (b)), but some may be crowed together and therefore are misidentified as lymphocytes (e.g. Fig. 2(c) and (d)). All these problems make the separating of individual cells a challenge, which in turn will degrade the performance in cell detection and classification.

In this paper, an automatic method which combines the dual morphological operation, the distance transformation and a deep convolution neural network is designed for inflammatory cells detection. As shown in Fig. 1, the cells in the H&E strained histopathology images reveal to be darker compared to the background, and therefore color intensity can be used to separate them from the background. But there existing many noises. Thus, our approach begins with an image enhancement by dual stage morphological gray reconstruction, which removes the noise in the background. Then, the cell detection is conducted by finding the center of each cell based on distance transformation. It is shown that by distance transformation the clumping and overlapping cells can be well separated by finding the peak in the distance transformation. Finally, a DCNN classifier is applied to classify the detected cells into four types (nucleus, lymphocyte, neutrophil and impurity).

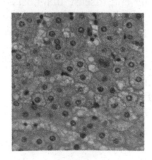

Fig. 1.

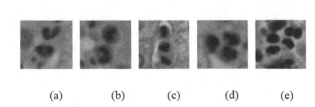

(a)   (b)   (c)   (d)   (e)

Fig. 2. (a)–(d) neutrophils (e) lymphocytes

2 Methodology

The method begins with an image enhancement. Followed is the cell detection, which finds the positions of the cells in biopsy image. Then, a convolution neural network is used to accurately classify these detected cells into nuclei, lymphocyte, neutrophil and impurity.

2.1 Detection of Clustered Cells

Image Enhancement: A liver biopsy image may contain many elements such as nuclei, lymphocyte, neutrophil and impurity as shown in Figs. 1, 2. Each of them plays a different role in liver disease diagnosis. Therefore, the detection and classification of types of the cells for statistic measurement is critical to assisted pathology image diagnosis. However, the cells may be located close to or far away from the tissue cutting/acquisition plane. The cells close to the cutting plane will be well-focused to show clear images. On the other hand, those away from the cutting plane will show smear images with unclear edges. As mentioned above, it is essential to segment all of cells from clutter background of the image correctly. To solve the problems mentioned above, a dual morphological grayscale reconstruction method proposed by Huang et al. [1] is used to eliminate clutter and irrelevancies in the background.

The first stage of the dual morphological grayscale reconstruction method adopts the same operation procedure as the morphological grayscale reconstruction [11], which starts with eroding the original image. The eroded image and the original image are considered as marker image and mask image respectively, and then, the marker image operates a series of conditional dilation with the original image as the mask image. In the second stage, the resultant image obtained from the first stage is dilated to produce a marker image, and the resultant image before dilation will be consider as mask image. After that, a series of conditional erosion is applied for the marker image with the resultant image as the mask image. The result of first stage and second stage are shown in Fig. 3(c) and (d), from which we can see that the first stage removes many small light blemishes and the second stage removes small dark ones. By so doing, this method removes cluster in the background while preserving the overall shapes of objects.

Resolving Overlapping Cell: It is common to see clumping immune cells in inflammatory areas. In this section, the clumping cells are detected by finding the peaks, which are the centers of cells. A simple approach to detect the peaks is H-maxima transform after distance transform (DT). H-maxima transform is widely used in local maxima detection. Implementation details are as following. First, we get a binary image after taking the threshold of the dual gray reconstruction result (shown in Fig. 3(e)). Second, the distance transform converts the binary image into a distance map measured using Euclidean distance, where every foreground pixel has a value corresponding to the distance from the background shown in Fig. 3(f). Then, the local maxima of DT are extracted by H-maxima transform which is to suppress undesired maxima and find regional maxima. Let A denote the distance map of clustered cells. The H-maxima transform is performed by

$$H(A, h) = A - R^{\epsilon}(A - h),$$

where h is a given depth, R and ϵ are reconstruction and dilation operators. The more details of the H-maxima operation procedure can be found in [10]. After H-maxima, we can obtain marker images, namely, the positions of the cells (shown in Fig. 3(h)) with a thresholding operation. As shown in Fig. 3(h), this approach well separates the overlapping cells. A demonstration of the overall process is illustrated in Fig. 3.

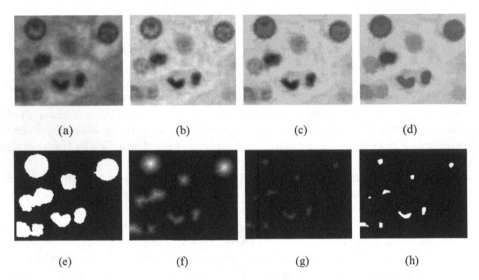

(a)   (b)   (c)   (d)

(e)   (f)   (g)   (h)

Fig. 3. The results of cell detection for liver biopsy images. (a) original image, (b) red channel, (c) and (d) are the results from dual morphological grayscale reconstruction, (e) binary, (f) distance transform, (g) H-maxima, (h) result (Color figure online)

2.2   CNN for Classification

With the above operations, various types of cells will be extracted. Some of them are not relevant for diagnosis, for example, the kupffer cells which would not be referred in disease diagnosis. These cells will be regarded as impurity in this paper. Thus, the extracted cells will be classified into one of four possible classes: nuclei, lymphocyte, neutrophil or impurity. In this paper, a convolution neural network, which takes each cell patch as the input, is trained for this propose. The cell patches are acquired from biopsy image with the detected cell positions as the centroid coordinates. The overall procedure is shown in Fig. 4.

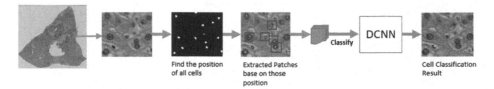

Find the position of all cells

Extracted Patches base on those position

Classify

DCNN

Cell Classification Result

Fig. 4. Cell classification model

CNN Architecture: In our method, the inputs of CNN are 80*80 image patches centered on the detected cell positions. The CNN consists of 8 layers: 4 convolutional (C) layers, 2 max-pooling (MP) layers, and 2 fully connected (FC) layers. In the output layer, the four-way *softmax* function is used as activation function, the *ReLU* function is used in the convolutional layers and prior to the output layer is a fully connected layer. The detailed configuration of our CNN is summarized as follows: Input (32*32*3) - C (32*32*32) - C (32*32*32) - MP (16*16*32) - C (16*16*64) - C (16*16*64) - MP (8*8*64) - FC (128) - FC (4).

CNN Training: Given four sets of training data: the nuclei, the lymphocyte, the neutrophil and the impurity patches, the DCNN is trained through the following minimization

$$\underset{w1,...wL}{\operatorname{argmin}} \frac{1}{N} \sum_{i=1}^{N} L(f(x_i; w_1, \ldots w_l), y_i), \tag{1}$$

where L is the loss function, f(.) is the output for DCNN, w_l denotes the weights for the l-th layer, and x_i, y_i are the input images and labels, relatively. The optimization of (1) is performed via backpropagation and Adam methods.

3 Experiments

Our dataset is obtained from National Cheng Kung University Hospital. All the ground truth is labeled by doctors. Each whole slide liver pathology image in the dataset is roughly 70000*50000 pixels. The four types of cells, which are nucleus, lymphocytes, neutrophils and impurities, are collected for our cell classification. In a total, we have 4522 patches for training and 518 for testing.

Among the 518 testing patches, there are 144 nuclei patches, 152 lymphocyte patches, 118 neutrophils patches and 104 impurities patches. We show the cell detection and classification result in Fig. 5 with red point for nuclei, green point for lymphocytes, and blue ones for neutrophils. Moreover, neutrophils and lymphocytes detection and classification result are shown in Fig. 6. According to the quantitative evaluation, the overall accuracy of our cell classification method on the testing data is 88.61%. Inflammatory cells classification can achieve 93.7% accuracy on the lymphocytes and neutrophils data. The results indicate that the method can classify the inflammatory cells (e.g. lymphocytes and neutrophils) with a good performance.

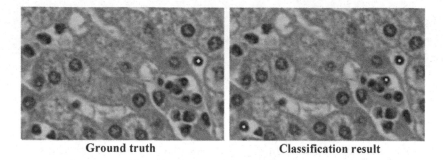

Ground truth   **Classification result**

Fig. 5. The propose method results

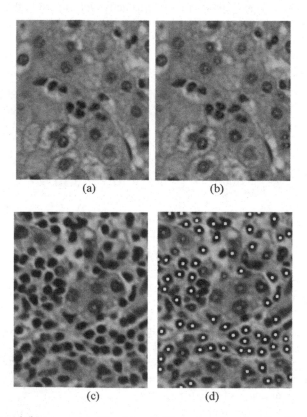

(a)   (b)

(c)   (d)

Fig. 6. (a) and (b) are neutrophils; (c) and (d) are lymphocytes classification results

4   Conclusion

This paper presents a procedure consisting of dual morphology reconstruction, distance transformation, and convolutional neural networks for the detection and classification of the four types of cells, namely, the nuclei, the lymphocyte, the neutrophil and the impurity cells. The dual morphology reconstruction uses two stages of morphological operations, the dilation centered first followed by erosion centered operation, to remove noises. Then the distance transformation is used and each of the peaks in DT is extracted to be the position of each individual cell. Finally, a well-situated patch taken from the position of each individual cell is supplied as the input of the deep convolutional neural network for classification. With the designed approach, the position of each individual cell can be identified and a patch of more precisely representing a cell can be supplied to the DCNN for classification. The results show that the approach can accurately detect the inflammatory cells in H&E staining liver histology tissue images.

Acknowledgments. This work was supported by Ministry of Science and Technology (MOST), Taiwan, under grant number MOST 107-2634-F-006-004.

References

1. Huang, P.W., Lai, Y.H.: Effective segmentation and classification for HCC biopsy images. Pattern Recogn. **43**(4), 1550–1563 (2010)
2. Cheng, J., Rajapakse, J.C.: Segmentation of clustered nuclei with shape markers and marking function. IEEE Trans. Biomed. Eng. **56**(3), 741–748 (2009)
3. Wang, S., Yao, J., Xu, Z., Huang, J.: Subtype cell detection with an accelerated deep convolution neural network. In: Ourselin, S., Joskowicz, L., Sabuncu, M.R., Unal, G., Wells, W. (eds.) MICCAI 2016. LNCS, vol. 9901, pp. 640–648. Springer, Cham (2016). https://doi.org/10.1007/978-3-319-46723-8_74
4. Pan, H., Xu, Z., Huang, J.: An effective approach for robust lung cancer cell detection. In: Wu, G., Coupé, P., Zhan, Y., Munsell, B., Rueckert, D. (eds.) Patch-MI 2015. LNCS, vol. 9467, pp. 87–94. Springer, Cham (2015). https://doi.org/10.1007/978-3-319-28194-0_11
5. Cireşan, D.C., Giusti, A., Gambardella, L.M., Schmidhuber, J.: Mitosis detection in breast cancer histology images with deep neural networks. In: Mori, K., Sakuma, I., Sato, Y., Barillot, C., Navab, N. (eds.) MICCAI 2013. LNCS, vol. 8150, pp. 411–418. Springer, Heidelberg (2013). https://doi.org/10.1007/978-3-642-40763-5_51
6. Wang, J., MacKenzie, J.D., Ramachandran, R., Chen, D.Z.: Identifying neutrophils in H&E staining histology tissue images. In: Golland, P., Hata, N., Barillot, C., Hornegger, J., Howe, R. (eds.) MICCAI 2014. LNCS, vol. 8673, pp. 73–80. Springer, Cham (2014). https://doi.org/10.1007/978-3-319-10404-1_10
7. Fatakdawala, H., et al.: Expectation–Maximization-driven Geodesic Active Contour with Overlap Resolution (EMaGACOR): application to lymphocyte segmentation on breast cancer histopathology. IEEE Trans. Biomed. Eng. **57**(7), 1676–1689 (2010)
8. Al-Kofahi, Y., Lassoued, W., Lee, W., Roysam, B.: Improved automatic detection and segmentation of cell nuclei in histopathology images. IEEE Trans. Biomed. Eng. **57**(4), 841–852 (2010)
9. Hiremath, P., Bannigidad, P., Geeta, S.: Automated identification and classification of white blood cells (leukocytes) in digital microscopic images. IJCA, Special Issue on RTIPPR **2**, 59–63 (2010)
10. Huang, D.C., Hung, K.D., Chan, Y.K.: A computer assisted method for leukocyte nucleus segmentation and recognition in blood smear images. J. Syst. Softw. **85**, 2104–2118 (2012)

11. Vincent, L.: Morphological grayscale reconstruction in image analysis: applications and efficient algorithms. IEEE Trans. Image Process. **2**, 176–201 (1993)
12. Garcia, E., Hermoza, R., Castanon, C.B., Cano, L., Castillo, M., Castanneda, C.: Automatic lymphocyte detection on gastric cancer IHC images using deep learning. In: IEEE 30th International Symposium on Computer-Based Medical Systems (CBMS), pp. 200–204 (2017)

Machine Learning Techniques
for Recognizing IoT Devices

Yu Chien Lin[✉] and Farn Wang

Department of Electrical Engineering, National Taiwan University,
Taipei, Taiwan, ROC
{r07943154, farn}@ntu.edu.tw

Abstract. Now Internet of Things is growing fast and presents huge opportunities for the industry, the users, and the hackers. IoT service providers may
face challenges from IoT devices which are developed with software and
hardware originally designed for mobile computing and traditional computer
environments. Thus the first line of security defense of IoT service providers is
identification of IoT devices and try to analyze their behaviors before allowing
them to use the service. In this work, we propose to use machine learning
techniques to identify the IoT devices. We also report experiment to explain the
performance and potential of our techniques.

Keywords: IoT · Internet of Things · Security · Scan · Devices · Tool

1 Introduction

As the technology of Internet of Things (IoT) is getting mature, in the next few years,
people are expecting explosive growth of the industry. There could soon be billions of
IoT devices globally [MWWHFMHL15]. As the total market value can soon reach
trillions of US dollars, many new paradigms of services can be invented and widely
spread. However, such a trend presents not only huge opportunities but also significant
risk [LYZYZZ17]. Specifically, IoT devices may collect sensitive user data and make
transmission and analysis. If those collected data are carelessly or maliciously transmitted to third parties, the data can be distributed out of control in the internet. At the
moment, many IoT services and devices are implemented with inappropriate security
technology. For example, many companies directly employ open-source modules
originally developed as solutions for mobile computing, stand-alone computers, or
even client-server computing and may not consider the security breaches in IoT services. In such situations, security breaches can be in algorithms (either in the client or
in the server sides), in the compiler-generated machine code, in middleware packages,

The work is supported by (1) project "*IoT Testing Service Platform*" by the Cybersecurity
Technology Institute, Institute for Information Industry, 2018, (2) project "*Coverage Testing
Technology based on Game Theory*" by Research Center for Information Technology Innovation,
Academia Sinica, 2018, and (3) project "*Cloud Client-Server Computing of Intelligent Test Service*"
(MOST 107-2221-E-002-037-MY3) by Ministry of Science and Technology.

C.-Y. Chang et al. (Eds.): ICS 2018, CCIS 1013, pp. 673–680, 2019.
https://doi.org/10.1007/978-981-13-9190-3_74

in the operating system, and in the communication protocol stacks. Hackers, computer viri, and malware are relentlessly exploring all such breaches.

Moreover, with the explosive growth of the IoT service market, new groups of customers and engineers will be attracted to the industry. On one hand, more people will certainly bring in new energy and bring about explosive growth to the market. On the other hand, new people will also expose the IoT services to new threats. For example, it has been reported that many IoT devices are not appropriately protected with passwords. In fact, many times, the managers and engineers just leave the password to the default ones set by the device manufacturers. As a result, the hackers and virus may easily capture such IoT devices and organize them in botnet for distributed denial of service (DDoS) attack.

To protect an IoT service, the first defensive line is the identification of the IoT devices. If we can identify the types, the models, the manufacturers of an IoT devices, a lot of analysis can then be applied and some preventive measures can be employed to elevate the security level of the service. For example, if we can identify the manufacturer and the model of a device, we can then use the manual of the manufacturer to monitor if the behavior of the device is not specified in the manual and may have been kidnapped.

At the moment, there are some technical and regulatory challenges in identifying the IoT devices. In the technical aspect, usually the device may not reveal its identity. Thus usually engineers rely on experiences to tell the models and manufacturers of IoT devices. It is also conceivable to implement an ad-hoc procedure that mimics the experience and expertise of the field engineers to identify the devices. At the moment, there is no general solution to identify the devices.

In the regulatory aspect, to forbid hacking and crawling the IoT devices, many countries disallow certain protrusive measures for identifying the IoT devices, including repetitive trials of the combinations of user accounts and passwords. Our goal is developing and experimenting a highly automatic general solution for identifying IoT devices by checking their message packets. There are two challenges.

1. *Valid scenarios for collecting messages from IoT devices.* In general, there could be difficulties in collecting the messages from IoT devices. Thus we need carefully find an application setting that allows for examination of those messages but is still a valid use case for the IoT service providers. We choose the setting of security measures of IoT service providers. We then assume that the service provider can collect messages from the IoT devices from the access points and analyze those messages to identify the devices.
2. *General solutions for automatic identification.* The message patterns of IoT devices of different manufacturers and models may exhibit diversity in their responses and handshaking protocols. Especially now the IoT protocols are not highly standardized. In fact, there are several IoT standards in the market now. Thus even for human engineers, identifying the IoT devices can be a messy and ad-hoc task. Tools like *shodan*[1] [BBDM14, GE15, Goldman13, Simon16] also works with many prewritten parsing rules and very often missed device identity information.

---

[1] https://danielmiessler.com/study/shodan/.

In general, it is believed that such a task that shows some fuzzy rules can be solved effectively with machine learning technology. In this work, experiment to see how this empirical knowledge can be effectively implemented with machine learning technology for IoT device identification.

In fact, there has been work in using machine learning technology in this aspect [MBSGOTE17]. However, their approach is for general settings while ours is for IoT service security. Especially, their approach uses queries to third-party IP analysis via internet and is not completely based on machine learning and not self-reliant. Thus one research question is whether it is feasible to only use machine learning technology for packet analysis to achieve the same accuracy.

In the remainder of this paper, respectively in Sects. 2 and 3, we first review related work and then briefly explain the background knowledge for the benefit of readers. Then in Sect. 3, we explain the software architecture and procedures of our implementation. Section 4 introduces our machine learning approach. Sections 5 and 6 are respectively the experiment report and the conclusion.

2   Related Work

There are work in device identification based on traffic patterns and radio pattern analysis [BBGO08, TDH03]. Similar techniques have also been used to analyze the message patterns and fight against botnet and malware [BSRB15, GPZL08, SLWL08].

There are also many wireless network scan tools in the internet. In low-level of the communication protocol stack, a popular tool is *network mapper* (NMAP)[2] developed by Lyon in 1997 for scanning specified features like packets, hosts, services, and operating systems.

For upper-layers, shodan is a popular tool [Goldman14]. Especially, in the darknet, people have utilized shodan to scan and discover equipments and services in the network. Conceptually, shodan can be viewed as a network search engine, just like Internet Explorer (Microsoft), Chrome (Google), and Firefox. But the above three search engines can only talk to network services in HTTP communication protocols.

Fig. 1.   Output example of Shodan

---

[2] https://nmap.org/.

Shodan is not subject to this constraint. Its core function is crawling network devices in the IP address range and keywords specified by the users and reporting their MAC addresses, ISP names, host names, communication ports, and service types. The most used keywords include webcam, Linksys, cisco, netgear, SCADA, and etc. The basic technique is to analyze the banners returned from the devices. Figure 1 is a typical output screen of shodan. Shodan can detect the connection types and encryption algorithms. But it is for full-scale scanning and uses database which is updated slowly. Usually, shodan does not scan all the ports and cannot recognize non-IoT hosts, including airboxes, mobile devices, and embedded systems. In comparison, our tool is especially designed for small environment like homes and offices. In such small spaces, usually database updates can be fast and efficient and scanning all ports is usually feasible. In our experiment, our tool can reach 99% successful recognition in scanning security vulnerability.

The only similar work to ours is [MBSGOTE17] which also uses machine learning to identify IoT devices. They used XGBoost engine to learn the models while we use a simpler approach of decision trees since usually the feature variables are not many. One thing interesting is that they did not use feature variables related to protocols. Instead, they query third-party modules, Alexa Traffic Rank[3] and GeoIP[4], to get features of the IPs. In that way, there solution is less self-sufficient than ours. In our work, all features are purely extracted from the packets and no query to third-party for features is needed in our technique. However, our accuracy is similar to theirs, roughly 99%.

3   NMAP-Based Packet Collection

Our solution architecture is shown in Fig. 2. We use low-level scanner NMAP to collect message packets from the IoT devices in specified IP ranges. We assume that our system is to be deployed for the security of the IoT service. Thus it is reasonable that the service provider would allow the installation of our tool in their access points (AP). After collecting the packets, the AP sends them (or extracted features to save the bandwidth) to our server for analysis. Then our server classifies the IoT devices using a pre-trained model.

We have also implemented a web program in the model-view-controller (MVC) [Reenskaug07] object-oriented software architecture that is commonly adopted and allows the managers read the scanning report from a browser and make various analysis.

In this section, we explain how we use NMAP to intercept the message packets from IoT devices. Basically, our procedure is a loop that iteratively and combinatorially sends a request to the target host connected to each port, then records the response, and then prepares for further exploration. This is in fact similar to most packet scanners. Our implementation is built on Transmission Control Protocol (TCP) and User-Data Protocol (UDP), two protocols in TCP/IP. Our scanning algorithm works on top of TCP and UDP. In these two protocols, every IP has ports ranging from 0 to 65535. The

---

[3] https://www.iplocation.net/alexa-traffic-rank.

[4] http://www.geoip.co.uk/.

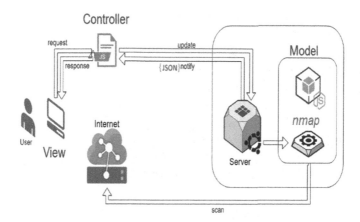

Fig. 2. Proposed architecture

first 1024 TCP ports are called well-known ports and are used by standard services, e.g., FTP, HTTP, SMTP, DNS, and etc. Port numbers bigger than 1023 are often used by other service development and application program communication. On one hand, if the port scanning is malicious, usually the scanner may use measures to prevent from being discovered. On the other hand, if the network managers can also use security procedure to detect whether a machine has sent out connection requests to vast number of ports. In such situation, the managers may issue a warning and block the machine.

To prevent from being blocked, an intruder may operate in the strobe or stealth mode while scanning the ports. In strobe mode, the scanner limits the ports to a small range instead of scanning all ports.

In the stealth mode, the scanner slow down the scanning rate so as to lower the possibility of reaching the internal threshold of scanning frequency set in the security procedure of the device managers. The scanner may also use different TCP flag settings and different TCP packets to collect different types of responses. Basically, the scanners try to use a diversified request types to find those operating ports. For example, SYN scanning can tell which ports are listening and which ports do not rely on response types. FIN scanning can get responses from closed port. Open and listening ports do not respond to FIN scanning. Thus port scanner can use SYN scanning and FIN scanning to decide which ports are open.

4   Machine Learning for IoT Device Identification

We first identified 23 binary features (in Table 1) from TCP/IP packets according to the suggestion in [Reenskaug07]. We then investigated their correlation with device types, device models, and device manufacturers.

Table 1. Features from packets

Types	Features
Link layer protocol (2)	*ARP, LLC*
Network layer protocol (4)	*IP, ICMP, ICMPv6, EAPoL*
Transport layer protocol (2)	*TCP, UDP*
Application layer protocol (8)	*HTTP, HTTPS, DHCP, BOOTP, SSDP, DNS, MDNS, NTP*
IP options (2)	*Padding, RouterAlert*
Packet contents (2)	*Size (int), Raw data*
IP address (1)	*Destination IP counter (int)*
Port class (2)	*Source (int), destination (int)*

Then we deleted those features that do not have strong correlation with the prediction labels. Then we use the flow in Fig. 3 to train a decision tree model and to predict the identification of an IoT device. In the training case, we collect the packets, with labels of the device identities. Then we extract features from the packets and use the features with labels as the training examples. The outcome of the training is a predicting model. Since we use decision trees in this work, the models are all decision trees.

In the predicting case, we extract the features from the packets without knowledge of their device identities, then feed the features to the predicting model, and then the model returns the types, models, and manufacturers of the IoT devices.

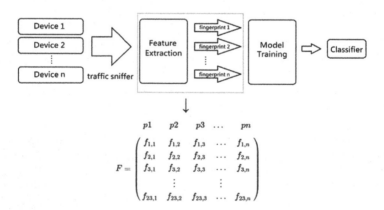

$$F = \begin{matrix} & p1 & p2 & p3 & \cdots & pn \\ & f_{1,1} & f_{1,2} & f_{1,3} & \cdots & f_{1,n} \\ & f_{2,1} & f_{2,2} & f_{2,3} & \cdots & f_{2,n} \\ & f_{3,1} & f_{3,2} & f_{3,3} & \cdots & f_{3,n} \\ & \vdots & & \vdots & & \\ & f_{23,1} & f_{23,2} & f_{23,3} & \cdots & f_{23,n} \end{matrix}$$

Fig. 3. Feature extraction process

5   Experiment

We have implemented our ideas in a tool called Intelligent IoT Fingerprinting (IIoTF) with Python, NMAP, Firebase[5], and Scapy[6]. Basically, packets collected with NMAP are further analyzed with the help of Scapy. Then we built an experiment platoform with two access points (AP) and seven IoT devices. The platform is shown in Fig. 4.

The seven IoT devices include airboxes, a smart phone, an IP camera, a desktop personal computer, and two laptops. The manufacturers include IOTECH, Microsoft, ASUSTek, Raspberry Pi Foundation, Espressif, TP-Link, and Xiaomi Communications. Then we collected 50000 responses from the IoT devices. 35000 packets were used for training while 15000 were used for prediction tests.

In the prediction tests, IIoTF is capable of reaching 99% accuracy which is comparable to the precision of [MBSGOTE17] which uses Alexa Traffic Rank and GeoIP to help analyzing the IP. In comparison, our IIoTF reaches similar accuracy without querying to third-party services. In summary, our

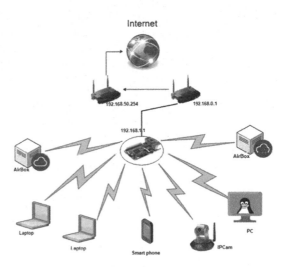

Fig. 4. Experiment configuration

experiment shows that it is feasible to identify IoT devices purely based on machine learning technology. This result pretty much answers the first research question and also shows the potential of our technology for operating environment where Internet connection are less than stable and affordable.

6   Conclusion

Automated device identification is important in engineering and has a long history. We focus on the recent explosively growing market of IoT services and propose to use machine learning technology for automatic IoT device identification. Our technology improves previous work [MBSGOTE17] since we do not rely on queries to third-party analysis services. Experiment report shows that our technology can reach similar accuracy. In the near future, it would be interesting to see how we can extend our prediction model for more devices and more IoT service settings.

---

[5] https://en.wikipedia.org/wiki/Firebase.
[6] https://en.wikipedia.org/wiki/Scapy.

References

[BBDM14]   Bodenheim, R., Butts, J., Dunlap, S., Mullins, B.: Evaluation of the ability of the shodan search engine to identify internet-facing industrial control devices. Int. J. Crit. Infrastruct. Prot. **7**(2), 114–123 (2014)

[BBGO08]   Brik, V., Banerjee, S., Gruteser, M., Oh, S.: Wireless device identification with radiometric signatures. In: ACM Conference on Mobile Computing and Networking (2008)

[BSRB15]   Bekerman, D., Shapira, B., Rokach, L., Bar, A.: Unknown malware detection using network traffic classification. In: IEEE Conference on Communications and Network Security (CNS) (2015)

[GE15]   Genge, B., Enăchescu, C.: ShoVAT: Shodan-based vulnerability assessment tool for Internet- facing services. Secur. Commun. Netw. **9**(15), 2696–2714 (2015)

[Goldman13]   Goldman, D.: Shodan: The Scariest Search Engine on the Internet, February 2014. http://money.cnn.com/2013/04/08/technology/security/shodan/

[GPZL08]   Gu, G., Perdisci, R., Zhang, J., Lee, W.: BotMiner: clustering analysis of network traffic for protocol-and-structure-independent botnet detection. In: USENIX Security Symposium (2008)

[LYZYZZ17]   Lin, J., Yu, W., Zhang, N., Yang, X., Zhang, H., Zhao, W.: A survey on internet of things: architecture, enabling technologies, security and privacy, and applications. IEEE Internet Things J. **4**(5), 1125–1142 (2017)

[MWWHFMHL15]   Meunier, F., et al.: The 'Internet of Things' Is Now: Connecting the Real Economy, 10 April 2015. www.morganstanley.com/what-we-do/research

[MBSGOTE17]   Meidan, Y., et al.: ProfilloT: a machine learning approach for IoT device identification based on network traffic analysis. In: ACM Symposium on Applied Computing (SAC) (2017)

[Reenskaug07]   Reenskaug, T.: The orginal MVC reports. Department of Informatics, University of Oslo. http://heim.ifi.uio.no/~trygver/2007/MVC_Originals.pdf

[SLWL08]   Strayer, W.T., Lapsely, D., Walsh, R., Livadas, C.: Botnet detection based on network behavior. In: Lee, W., Wang, C., Dagon, D. (eds) Botnet Detection. Advances in Information Security, vol. 36, pp. 1–24. Springer, Boston (2008). https://doi.org/10.1007/978-0-387-68768-1_1

[Simon16]   Simon, K.: Vulnerability analysis using google and shodan. In: Foresti, S., Persiano, G. (eds) Cryptology and Network Security. CANS 2016. LNCS, vol. 10052. Springer, Cham (2016). https://doi.org/10.1007/978-3-319-48965-0_51

[TDH03]   Talbot, K.I., Duley, P.R., Hyatt, D.H.: Specific emitter identification and verification. Technol. Rev., 113 (2003)

Scale Invariant Multi-view Depth Estimation Network with cGAN Refinement

Chia-Hung Yeh[1,2(✉)], Yao-Pao Huang[2], and Mei-Juan Chen[3]

[1] Department of Electrical Engineering, National Taiwan Normal University,
Taipei, Taiwan
chyeh@ntnu.edu.tw
[2] Department of Electrical Engineering, National Sun Yat-sen University,
Kaohsiung, Taiwan
[3] Department of Electrical Engineering, National Dong Hwa University,
Hualien, Taiwan

Abstract. In this paper we propose a deep learning based depth estimation method for monocular RGB sequences. We train a pair of encoder-decoder network to resolve depth information form image pairs and relative camera poses. To solve scale ambiguous of monocular sequences, a conditional generative adversarial network is applied. Experimental results show that the proposed method can overcome the problem of scale ambiguous and therefore is more suitable for a variety of applications.

Keywords: Multi-view depth estimation · Deep learning ·
Conditional generative adversarial network

1 Introduction

Depth estimation from image is a long-standing task in computer vision and robotics. Stereo cameras are widely used for gathering depth information. Depth can be easily estimated with triangulation when the relative distance of the two cameras is known. Although stereo systems achieve impressive results, monocular systems are much more widely used in daily application such as cell phones and web cams. Therefore, building a depth estimation system for monocular data is much more meaningful.

The task of depth estimation and camera pose estimation is highly related. Tradition 3D reconstruction algorithm usually starts with camera pose estimation, Structure from Motion (SfM) methods [1] have been widely used to estimate depth with correspondence feature motion between images. However, it requires a sufficient motion baseline of the camera. When it comes to indoor scenes, Structure from Motion usually fails due to the lack of enough feature movement. State-of-the-art Simultaneous Localization and Mapping (SLAM) methods such as ORB-SLAM [2] and LSD-SLAM [3] can give monocular camera pose estimation in real-time. However, pose estimation with monocular sequences have the problem of scale ambiguous, the recorded sequence can be either large object with large camera movement or small object with small camera movement. Recently, Convolutional Neural Network (CNN) has become a popular algorithm on depth estimation. Benefits from learning of the known objects' size, it can

C.-Y. Chang et al. (Eds.): ICS 2018, CCIS 1013, pp. 681–687, 2019.
https://doi.org/10.1007/978-981-13-9190-3_75

minimize the influence of the scale ambiguous. However, to generalize to unknow scenes, the training database needs to be very large, which makes the training procedure very long and model hard to converge. Some CNN method such as MVDepthNet [4] utilize known camera poses to reduce the problem complexity, but while the input camera pose usually comes from monocular slam system, the scale ambiguous problem still exists.

In this paper, we introduce a depth estimation network based on the concept of MVDepthNet. The multi-view network is used for initial depth estimation, and a conditional generative adversarial network is concatenated to resolve the scale ambiguous. The experimental results show that the proposed method performs better when no information of the scene is known, which make our approach more applicable to all situations.

2   Related Works

Traditional methods such as REMODE [5] searches correspondences between two images to update the robust probabilistic model, the model is then used for depth estimation. Recently, machine learning based method has been a popular solution for depth estimation, especially on monocular systems since machine learning is the best way to resolve scale ambiguous. Multi-view systems are known to be more generalized to unknow data. DeMoN [6] is one of the state-of-the-art learning-based method which takes two images as input. DeMoN's network consists of three parts: bootstrap net, iterative net and refinement net. The bootstrap net first estimates optical flow with a pair of images, the optical flow is then concatenated with input image pair for iterative net to estimate depth and camera ego-motion. Refinement net further improves the output depth map. MVDepthNet takes image-pose pairs as input to estimate depth information. The input poses are used to construct image matching cost for the network, which reduces the complexity of the problem. However, the application of MVDepthNet is also limited by the need of camera pose, where high accurate camera pose is hard to obtain in general, especially when only monocular RGB sequence is available. Lore et al. [7] use generative adversarial network for single image depth estimation. Singe image depth estimation has been a painful topic for supervised learning since the network needs to extract depth information base on the understating of the size of the leaned object. Generative adversarial training helps generalizing through datasets, therefore not only reduces the needed amount of training data, but also reduces the network size.

3   Network Architecture

The overall network architecture is shown in Fig. 1. In this paper, we propose a method which combines multi-view depth extraction and single image depth estimation. The proposed method can be separated into two parts: the multi-view net and the refinement net. The multi-view net is a pair of encoder and decoder which gives an initial guess of the depth. The refinement net is a Conditional Generative Adversarial Network which resolves scale ambiguous and provide refined depth map.

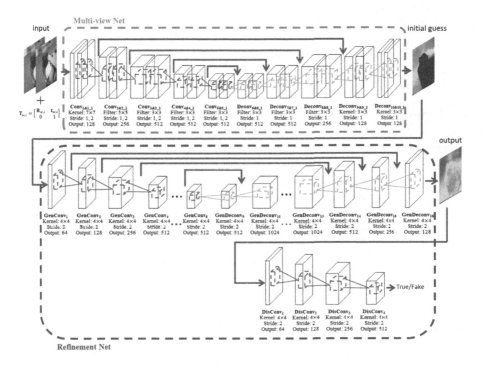

Fig. 1. Network architecture

3.1 Multi-view Net

The multi-view net takes image pair and camera motion as input. The motion input $\mathbf{T}_{w,i}$ is the $\mathbb{SE}(3)$ pose of the second frame in the first frame coordinates. Where $\mathbf{T}_{w,i} \in \mathbb{SE}(3)$ consists of a rotation matrix $\mathbf{R}_{w,i}$ and a translation vector $\mathbf{t}_{w,i}$. The $\mathbf{T}_{w,i}$ matrix can be easily transformed from quaternion, which is a widely used camera pose format of public dataset such as TUM RGB-D [8] or SUN3D [9]:

$$\mathbf{T}_{w,i} = \begin{bmatrix} \mathbf{R}_{w,i} & \mathbf{t}_{w,i} \\ 0 & 1 \end{bmatrix}, \tag{1}$$

We follow the architecture of MVDepthNet to build the multi-view net, which is an U-Net [10] like encoder-decoder pair with skip connection between encoder and decoder layers. The encoder consists of 10 convolution layers which alternate between stride 1 and stride 2, decoder consists of 10 convolution layers with all stride 1. The first two convolution layers use kernel size of 7, followed by two layers using kernel size of 5, all the rest layers use kernel size of 3.

3.2   Refinement Net

The refinement net is a conditional generative adversarial network which takes the initial guess of depth map as input. The generator of the refinement net also uses U-Net like architecture, which consists of 8 convolution layers of encoder and 8 convolution layers of decoder. The discriminator consists of 4 convolution layers, where an additional convolution layer is applied after the last layer to map the output to a 1-dimensional output.

4   Experiments

The experiments are done with the TUM RGB-D dataset, which provides RGB images and depth maps with ground truth camera pose tracked by eight high speed tracking cameras. The training procedure can be separated into two steps. First, the multi-view network is trained using ground truth camera pose as input to learn the relationship between view difference and depth information. Then, ORB-SLAM is applied to get camera poses with scale ambiguous simulating general application scenarios. The initial guesses are obtained with multi-view net using ORB-SLAM estimated camera pose as input. The refinement network is then trained with the initial guesses and learn to resolve the scale ambiguous using ground truth depth map as target. All data sets are separated into 2 to 1 for training and testing.

4.1   Error Metrics

Three measurements are used to evaluate the performance of the proposed method following DeMoN. The scale invariant error metric of [11] is adopted as

$$\text{sc} - \text{inv} = \sqrt{\frac{1}{n}\sum_i z_i^2 - \frac{1}{n^2}\left(\sum_i z_i\right)^2}, \tag{2}$$

Where $z_i = \log d_i - \log \widehat{d}_i$, d_i is the estimated depth value and $\widehat{d}_i$ is the ground truth depth value. L1-rel computes the depth error relative to ground truth depth, which increases the importance of close objects. L1-inv indicates the overall error of the depth map.

$$\text{L1} - \text{rel} = \frac{1}{n}\sum_i \frac{\left|d_i - \widehat{d}_i\right|}{\widehat{d}_i}, \tag{3}$$

$$\text{L1} - \text{inv} = \frac{1}{n}\sum_i \left|\frac{1}{d_i} - \frac{1}{\widehat{d}_i}\right|. \tag{4}$$

4.2 Results Comparison

The experimental results are shown in Table 1, we also provide the evaluation of multi-view net using ground truth camera poses as input as a high-level standard. The experimental results show that when the multi-view net takes non-ground truth camera poses as input, the error of the initial guess increases due to scale ambiguous. However, with the refinement net applied, the errors are significantly reduced and refined depth map is provided. Visualized comparison of depth map is shown in Fig. 2, the top row is the initial guess of the multi-view network, the second row is the output of the proposed method and the third row is ground truth depth map provide by the TUM data set.

Table 1. Evaluation of proposed method on the TUM RGB-D dataset

		Initial guess with GT	Initial guess	Refined depth
fr1 360	L1-rel	0.338651	0.484963	**0.364850**
	L1-inv	0.260986	0.488331	**0.226362**
	sc-inv	0.154147	0.264602	**0.177945**
fr2 xyz	L1-rel	0.496342	0.534264	**0.522433**
	L1-inv	0.373054	0.448495	**0.245257**
	sc-inv	0.162668	0.183056	**0.168893**
fr2 desk	L1-rel	0.420410	0.604840	**0.487680**
	L1-inv	0.248974	0.545204	**0.331853**
	Sc-inv	0.140869	0.255147	**0.206974**
fr3 loh	L1-rel	0.267545	**0.460359**	0.468598
	L1-inv	0.174589	0.429565	**0.308055**
	sc-inv	0.110857	0.228805	**0.193362**

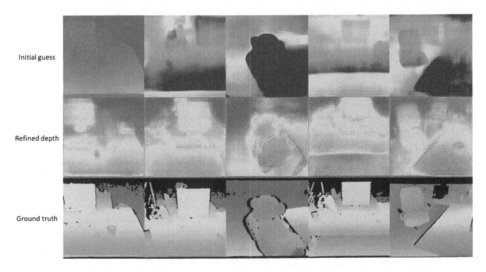

Initial guess

Refined depth

Ground truth

Fig. 2. Visualized depth estimation result on TUM RGB-D data set

5   Conclusion and Future Work

In this paper, we propose a deep learning based method to estimate depth information from monocular sequences. The proposed method is a combination of multi-view and single view system, which is suitable for a variety of situations. We focus our work on making the proposed method to work in situations that only video sequence is available while no other information is known. The experimental results show that the proposed method can recover from the error caused by the lack of information and therefore make the proposed method more applicable to all situations.

For the future work, more data set can be added to train the refinement net for further improvement on making the model more generalize. Also, more data set can be added for evaluations. SUN3D is a public data set which also provides RGB-D image pairs with camera ego-motion, which would be a good choice for augmenting training data.

Acknowledgments. The authors would like to thank the Ministry of Science and Technology, Taiwan, R.O.C. for financially supporting this research under grants MOST 107-2218-E-003-003-, MOST 107-2218-E-110-004-, MOST 105-2221-E-110-094-MY3 and MOST 106-2221-E-110-083-MY2.

References

1. Wu, C.: Towards linear-time incremental structure from motion. In: Proceedings of International Conference on 3D Vision, pp. 127–134, June 2013
2. Mur-Artal, R., Tardós, J.D.: ORB-SLAM2: an open-source SLAM system for monocular, stereo and RGB-D cameras. IEEE Trans. Rob. 33(5), 1255–1262 (2017)
3. Engel, J., Schöps, T., Cremers, D.: LSD-SLAM: large-scale direct monocular SLAM. In: Fleet, D., Pajdla, T., Schiele, B., Tuytelaars, T. (eds.) Computer Vision – ECCV 2014. LNCS, vol. 8690, pp. 834–849. Springer, Cham (2014). https://doi.org/10.1007/978-3-319-10605-2_54
4. Wang, K., Shen, S.: MVDepthNet: real-time multiview depth estimation neural network. arXiv:1807.08563 (2018)
5. Pizzoli, M., Forster, C., Scaramuzza, D.: REMODE: probabilistic, monocular dense reconstruction in real time. In: Proceedings of IEEE International Conference on Robotics and Automation, pp. 2609–2616, May 2014
6. Ummenhofer, B., et al.: Demon: depth and motion network for learning monocular stereo. In: Proceedings of IEEE Conference on Computer Vision and Pattern Recognition, vol. 5, pp. 6, July 2017
7. Gwn Lore, K., Reddy, K., Giering, M., Bernal, E.A.: Generative adversarial networks for depth map estimation from RGB video. In: Proceedings of IEEE Conference on Computer Vision and Pattern Recognition Workshops, pp. 1177–1185 (2018)
8. Sturm, J., Engelhard, N., Endres, F., Burgard, W., Cremers, D.: A benchmark for the evaluation of RGB-D SLAM systems. In: Proceedings of IEEE International Conference on Intelligent Robots and Systems, pp. 573–580, October 2012
9. Xiao, J., Owens, A., Torralba, A.: SUN3D: a database of big spaces reconstructed using SfM and object labels. In: Proceedings of IEEE International Conference on Computer Vision, pp. 1625–1632 (2013)

10. Ronneberger, O., Fischer, P., Brox, T.: U-net: convolutional networks for biomedical image segmentation. In: Navab, N., Hornegger, J., Wells, W., Frangi, A. (eds.) Medical Image Computing and Computer-Assisted Intervention – MICCAI 2015, vol. 9351, pp. 234–241. Springer, Cham (2015). https://doi.org/10.1007/978-3-319-24574-4_28
11. Eigen, D., Puhrsch, C., Fergus, R.: Depth map prediction from a single image using a multi-scale deep network. In: Advances in Neural Information Processing Systems, pp. 2366–2374 (2014)

Tracking of Load Handling Forklift Trucks and of Pedestrians in Warehouses

Syeda Fouzia[1]([✉]), Mark Bell[2], and Reinhard Klette[1]

[1] School of Engineering, Computer, and Mathematical Sciences,
Auckland University of Technology, Auckland, New Zealand
syeda.fouzia@aut.ac.nz
[2] Crown Equipment Ltd., Auckland, New Zealand

Abstract. Trajectory computation for forklifts and pedestrians is of relevance for warehousing applications such as pedestrian safety and process optimization. We recorded a novel dataset with a varying range of forklift models and pedestrians, busy with loading or unloading in warehouses. We have videos with frequently occluded trucks in aisles and besides racks, some with busy pedestrian activity, such as in docking areas. Robust target localisation is very essential for seamless tracking results. For localising forklift trucks/pedestrians, we trained a deep-learning based, faster region-based convolution neural network (faster RCNN) on our own recorded data. We used detection from the model output to configure a Kalman filter to estimate the trajectories in the image plane. We also improved the forklift trajectory based on computing pixel saliency maps for the region of interest detected by faster RCNN. Our analysis shows that with robust target detection (fewer false positives and false negatives) from our trained network and Kalman-filter-based state correction, tracking results are close to ground truth.

1 Introduction

Tracking is often preceded by interest object localisation in single or multiple frames. The representation of a *region of interest* (ROI) is based on object shape or an appearance model and which unique features are suitable to encode object representation. Many tracking algorithms use a combination of features to represent application-specific objects of interest. Accuracy of ROI detection (which is a forklift truck or a pedestrian in our case) and frame-to-frame data association to the same track is vital for building a robust tracker. For tracking, there are two options, *detection with recognition* or *detection without recognition*, where recognition means classification into object categories.

For environments with complex backgrounds as in case of warehousing (changing object scales and view angles, background clutter and occlusions), obtaining robust detection results is challenging. It limits most trackers to use only prediction information for *track* (or *trajectory*) prediction for objects of interest. Missing detection and false positives are very common for these methods. The resulting track association problem (between detection and target) is

© Springer Nature Singapore Pte Ltd. 2019
C.-Y. Chang et al. (Eds.): ICS 2018, CCIS 1013, pp. 688–697, 2019.
https://doi.org/10.1007/978-981-13-9190-3_76

Fig. 1. Capture of cameras 1–4. Shots show busy docking areas with pedestrians present, forklifts moving down the aisles, background clutter, and varying truck models

challenging. Since multiple scales and models of the same truck has to be dealt with, detectors based only on shape, appearance, motion, colour or any other cue, may not be sufficient for encoding target object features.

For our work, we recorded video data using four monocular uncalibrated cameras installed in a real production warehouse. Figure 1 depicts the capture from each camera. These cameras are fixed at four different key locations in our warehouse to capture activities in warehousing. We conduct experiments for tracking objects in single-truck scenario sequences as well as in multiple-pedestrian and multiple-truck sequences.

For single target tracking, we localise a forklift bounding box by training a *faster RCNN* (i.e. a special deep learning framework). We employ transfer learning with a pretrained AlexNet model [19]. Detection results are used to initialize a Kalman filter, used for the prediction of an object's future location. Based on localisation coordinate feedback from the faster-RCNN trained network, the Kalman filter corrects the predicted trajectory. We also improve the trajectory results by using a *saliency map* of the ROI (as detected by faster-RCNN). Using a ROI saliency map [14], the Kalman filter performs state correction for every frame. The resulting trajectory is improved and close to ground truth trajectory. Multiple-target tracking is discussed in Sect. 4.

The paper is structured as follows. Section 2 outlines related work in tracking by domain detection. Section 3 describes the algorithm, model training and implementation, with dataset details. In Sect. 4, qualitative results with three different kinds of forklift scenarios are shown for single and multiple target tracking. Section 5 outlines the quantitative evaluation for the tracking approach taken. Section 6 concludes the paper.

2   Related Work

Tracking by detection approaches are driven by recent progress in object detection. Such methods involve the application of a detection algorithm individually in each frame and the association of those detections across multiple frames for corresponding track formations. These trackers are generally more robust than background-based trackers, where a ROI can be detected by building a background representation and then finding objects due to deviations from the model for each incoming frame [17]. Tracking methods involving static cameras commonly rely on background subtraction as detection method. Some image segmentation algorithms are also used to partition the image into clusters or segments. In data-association-based tracking approaches, detection responses are linked to trajectories with global optimization (based on size or similar appearance) [1]. A combination of object detectors and Kalman filtering resulted in tracking techniques that are more time efficient and robust [6]. These methods employ probabilistic methods covering single or multiple object state estimation [16], taking object measurement and process noise uncertainties into consideration for state estimation and correction.

To deal with occluded and challenging tracking environments, further detection approaches have been explored. They rely on a correct detection output from the object detector. In some cases, 3D information or trained detectors are used for individual object parts or for application-specific motion models [7]. Learning object view angles from a set of training examples by means of supervised learning is also used to detect and classify ROIs [15]. With the recent advancement in computational resources, many methods used for ROI detection are employing deep learning techniques. Either they make use of sliding window approaches or region proposal methods, to generate object/region hypotheses, and then generate objectness scores by classifiers. These methods prove to be very robust to occlusions and varying scales of objects.

3   Our Tracking Model

We define a truck's previous state at instant k as $x_k = (x_k, v_{xk}, a_{xk}, y_k, v_{ky}, a_{ky})$; x_k and y_k are the centroid coordinates for a forklift truck, v_k is the velocity of the window center, and a_k is the acceleration. The main steps of the algorithm are as follows:

(1) For the previous frame, find the *bounding box* for the detected forklift truck using faster-RCNN. A pretrained AlexNet model is retrained with forklift training images involving varying truck models, colours and view angles. We use frames from our pre-recorded data.

(2) We calculate the *centroid* of the bounding box for the truck. Using detected centroid from each frame, we initialize a *track*. A track is a structure representing a detected object in the video. The purpose of the structure is to maintain the state of a tracked object.

(3) Initialize a Kalman filter to predict the centroid of the corresponding track in the current frame based on the previous initialized state [6].

(4) The predicted centroid-location, estimated by Kalman filter, is corrected using the corresponding detected centroid for the truck in the current frame.

(5) Estimating the trajectory for the collection of frames, showing the path followed by the truck centroid based on Kalman parameters adjustment and experimentation.

ROI Saliency-Map-Based Trajectory Improvement. To improve the forklift trajectory, we incorporated further improvement steps. We refined the location of a centroid computed by faster-RCNN bounding box criterion, based on

ROI pixel saliency map [8,14]. Visual saliency maps are able to mark salient pixels in the images and have good results with occluded objects in warehouse scenes. It is computationally fast. It took 0.5 s or less time per frame to compute a saliency map.

A centroid computed from faster-RCNN bounding box center criterion, seemed to be less stable. We used improved centroid computation, using the most salient region of the ROI. The points recomputed for trajectory correction by the Kalman filter were more consistent and accurate with respect to ground-truth centroid points. The improvement steps are as follows:

(1) We compute a pixel saliency map for the detected ROI from faster-RCNN [14].
(2) We threshold the ROI based on a maximum-saliency area into a *binary threshold saliency map*.
(3) We calculate the centroid of the corresponding threshold area.
(4) This time, the predicted centroid-location estimate by the Kalman filter, is corrected using the corresponding detected centroid points, from a binary threshold area.

Object Detection Using Faster-RCNN. Recent methods for object detection are employing deep learning techniques. *Faster-RCNN* [11] is an extension of the fast-RCNN [18] object detection technique. Both techniques use a convolutional neural network (CNN). RCNN [12] and fast-RCNN use a region proposal computation as a preprocessing step before running the CNN. Region proposal algorithms include edge boxes [13] or selective search, which are independent of the CNN. In the case of fast-RCNN, the use of such algorithms becomes the processing bottleneck compared to the CNN. Faster-RCNN resolves this issue by implementing the region-proposal mechanism using the CNN, thus making the region proposal a part of the CNN training and prediction steps. Faster-RCNN proposes a *regional proposal network* (RPN) which shares the fully convolution layers with a fast R-CNN object detection framework. RPN is a fully convolution neural network, which predicts both object proposals and objectness scores. It takes an image (of any size) as input and outputs a set of rectangular object proposals. The proposals and scores are fed into a fast-RCNN network for model training. The RPN, implemented as a fully-convolutional neural network can be trained end-to-end by back-propagation and stochastic gradient descent (SGD).

The faster-RCNN algorithm reduces the time of computation, enabling a cost-free region proposal generation. It has good object detection performance with high *mean average precision* (mAP) at ILSVRC 2015 and the COCO 2015 competition.

Dataset. We formulated and annotated a dataset for warehouses images for forklift trucks category. In our experiments we use a subset from our dataset, including 3,077 training images with manually labelled ground truth bounding boxes for forklift trucks and pedestrians defining 8,242 ROIs. We resize images to 600 × 600 pixel size and then annotate with corresponding label categories. We use faster-RCNN detections both for single and multiple object tracking trials. Each image contains 1–7 labeled instances of a forklift truck or pedestrian. Matlab $R2017a$ is used in model training. We used GeForce GTX 1080 Titanium GPU with compute capability 6.1 and 12 GB memory.

Faster-RCNN Training and Evaluation. We use a *transfer learning* app-roach. Transfer learning involves retraining few layers of a pre-trained deep learn-ing model for novel category classification tasks. We selected the AlexNet deep learning model. It is a 25 layered architecture pre-trained on 1,000 image cat-egories. We re-trained the last three layers of the model with our own forklift truck recorded data.

Training has four main phases. In the first two steps, we train the region proposal and detection networks separately as used in faster-RCNN. In the last two steps, we combine the networks from the first two steps. A single network is created for detection [11]. Training steps have different convergence rates, so we specify independent training options for each step. The *learning rate* for the first two steps is set higher compared to last two phases i.e. $1e^{-5}$ Since the last two steps are fine-tuning steps, the network weights can be modified more slowly than in the first two steps ($1e^{-6}$). During model training, image patches are extracted from training data. The two vital training parameters, the *positive overlap range* and the *negative overlap range*, control which image patches are used for training. We specify positive training samples as those samples that overlap with ground-truth boxes by 60% to 100%, as measured by the *bounding-box-intersection-over-union measure*. Negative training sample used overlap by 0% to 30%. The best values for these parameters are chosen by testing the trained detector on a *validation data set* (set separate from training and testing dataset).

To fully evaluate the detector, we tested it on a testing warehouse dataset (we used 600 images at multiple scales). We used the *average precision* evaluation measure over all the detection results. This is the ratio of true-positive instances of forklift trucks to all positive instances for the object, based on the ground truth. It provides a single number that incorporates the ability of the model to make correct classifications (Precision) and the ability of the detector to find all relevant objects of interest (Recall).

We achieved true positive = 367, false positive = 33, true negative = 83, false negative = 17, thus Precision = 91.75, Recall = 95.5, and f1 = 93.7. We obtained a running time for the detection as 5 frames per second on GPU.

4   Qualitative Results

Single Forklift Tracking. We obtained tracking trajectories that are close to manually estimated ground truth trajectories (based on calculating the accurate centroids of forklift trucks in each frame).

Scenario 1 shows a forklift truck moving straight down the aisle. There are not much curves or twists in the path; the truck is assumed to be moving with constant velocity. The faster-RCNN results are shown in Fig. 2, left. For trajec-tory, refer to Fig. 2, right: Left image shows the overlaid faster-RCNN detections along with tracking points; right image shows the final (estimated) trajectory. We improved the scenario 1 trajectory based on ROI saliency map thresholding; see Fig. 5, right. It shows the heat map for the overlaid saliency map on original images. Compare the estimated trajectories in Figs. 2, right, and 3. Figure 3 depicts the trajectory correction based on *ROI saliency thresholding*.

Fig. 2. Scenario 1. *Left.* Faster RCNN detection results. *Right.* Estimated trajectory

Fig. 3. *Left.* Saliency map with detected centroid in red. *Middle.* Trajectory estimated by Kalman. *Right.* Ground truth trajectory

Scenario 2 shows a forklift truck moving up the aisle from the left. Figure 4, left, depicts the faster-RCNN detection output. There was a missing detection for the forklift truck in a couple of consecutive frames in this scenario. The Kalman filter robustly predicted the path followed by the truck when the missing detection arises, based on motion statistics. For trajectory, refer to Fig. 4, right. The left image shows the overlaid faster-RCNN detection along with tracking points. The right image shows the estimated trajectory.

Fig. 4. Scenario 2. *Left.* Faster RCNN detection results. *Right.* Estimated trajectory

Scenario 3 has a truck moving from the right, occluded for a few frames behind the racks in the aisle, and then moving up to the left. Our trained forklift faster-RCNN model gives an accurate detection for the occluded truck. Refer to

694   S. Fouzia et al.

Fig. 5. *Left.* Scenario 3 trajectory. *Right.* Heat map for pixel saliency overlaid on frames

Fig. 6. Multiple target tracking. *Left to right.* Frames 35, 54, 88, and 121. Colored lines show track history of bounding box centroids for each tracked target

Fig. 5, left. Left image shows the overlaid faster-RCNN detection along with tracking points. The right image shows the estimated trajectory.

Multiple Target Tracking. For multiple forklift and pedestrian tracking, a detection association method is used. In every upcoming frame, new RCNN detections are assigned to corresponding tracks from the previous frame using the Hungarian algorithm [9]. The assignment cost is minimized and calculated based on the Euclidean distance d between the centroids of each pair of bounding boxes [4]:

$$d = ||p_c(j) - p_c(i)||_2 \tag{1}$$

where $p_c(i)$ and $p_c(j)$ are centroids of boxes i and j, respectively. A maximum distance threshold is used to rate the assignment such that matches are discarded if $d > d_{max}$.

With new detections being assigned to existing tracks, the track is updated by estimating the state using the new observation. If a track is not assigned, i.e. a new detection in the current frame, the new bounding box is predicted by the Kalman filter. Matches between new detections in two consecutive frames create a new track. In case of false detections, showing up for a few frames, or no detections associated to a track for threshold track age, the track is deleted.

Refer to Fig. 6. Forklift tracks shown in yellow and pedestrians with red bounding boxes. Forklift tracks 3 and 11, and pedestrian tracks 4, 15, and 6 remain consistent with no ID switching in the sequence we tested (of 840 frames). We have seen a few cases of track-ID switching. Colored lines show the track history of bounding box centroids, for each tracked target.

5   Quantitative Evaluation

Tracking performance can be mainly evaluated using two important evaluation measures, i.e. multiple object tracking accuracy (MOTA) and multiple object tracking precision (MOTP). MOTA takes into account all configuration errors made by the tracker i.e. false-positives, misses, number of mismatches, averaged over all frames:

$$\text{MOTA} = 1 - \frac{\sum_t (FN_t + FP_t + IDSW_t)}{\sum_t GT_t} \tag{2}$$

where FN_t is the number of false-negatives or misses, FP_t is the number of false-positives, and IDSW is the number of ID mismatches/switches, where t is the frame index and GT is the number of ground truth objects.

The multiple object tracking precision (MOTP) is the average dissimilarity between all true-positives and their corresponding ground truth targets:

$$\text{MOTP} = \frac{\sum_{t,i} d_{t,i}}{\sum_t c_t} \tag{3}$$

where c_t denotes the total number of matches in frame t and $d_{t,i}$ is the bounding box overlap of target i with its assigned ground truth object.

Table 1. *Left.* Single-object tracking. *Right.* Comparison of tracking results on TUD crossing sequence of [10] also showing our method. Last column shows our results for forklift-pedestrian sequence

				Sequence:TUD Crossing			
Quantitative evaluation			Measure	[2]	[22]	Ours	Results
Metrics	Saliency-based Kalman-track	Non-saliency-based Kalman-track	MOTP	73.1	71.9	72.3	81.3 ↑
			MOTA	61.3	33.7	51.2	85.1↑
			FAF	0.1	1.3	1.1	1.6
MOTP	78.76↑	52.1	MT	38.5	12.2	61.2↑	65.3↑
Miss rate	12.08 ↓	20.86	ML	15.4	44	41	43.1
FP rate	19.17	19.86	FP	14	7762	4033	513
Local-error	12.52 ↓	38.76	FN	401	325	156	1056
MOTA	67.36↑	56.88	ID SW	12	442	331	254
			Fragment	27	823	693	317

Table 1, left, outlines the evaluation for single forklift tracking using sequence scenarios as discussed before. It outlines the improvement we achieved by incorporating ROI saliency maps in our tracking framework. Corrections for bounding box centroids based on ROI saliency map resulted in lesser localisation errors and targets missed due to threshold distance. Eventually, MOTP and MOTA are enhanced accordingly. We used a singe object track as a special case of MOT with the CLEAR MOT measure [3].

We benchmarked our pedestrian/truck tracking framework and tested it on the TUD crossing public dataset [2]. TUD crossing is an outdoor sequence with

201 frames [10]. Table 1, right, outlines the methods we compared and the MOT evaluation results [5].

Since for the forklift-pedestrian category, no public benchmarks are available for evaluation, a ground truth for our dataset sequence was formulated and we evaluated tracking results for multiple forklift-pedestrian objects accordingly. We obtained very fair results for multiple-object tracking; see Table 1, right.

6 Conclusion

Our tracking framework may be extended by using an improved data association criterion. To lessen the number of track ID switches, further improvement modules need to be incorporated. The Kalman filter's linearity limitation is another bottleneck; an extended or unscented Kalman filter might be worth to be tested. Calculated pedestrian and truck trajectories also lead to further analysis tasks for pedestrian safety in warehousing.

References

1. Andriluka, M., Roth, S., Schiele, B.: People tracking by detection and people detection by tracking. In: Proceedings of Computer Vision Pattern Recognition, pp. 1–8 (2008)
2. Milan, A., Leal-Taix, L., Reid, I., Roth, S., Schindler, K.: MOT16: a benchmark for multi-object tracking. arXiv:1603.00831 (2016)
3. Bernardin, K., Stiefelhagen, R.: Evaluating multiple object tracking performance: the CLEAR MOT metrics. J. Image Video Process. **2008**, 1 (2008)
4. Cane, T., Ferryman, J.: Saliency-based detection for maritime object tracking. In: Proceedings of IEEE Conference on Computer Vision Pattern Recognition Workshops, pp. 18–25 (2016)
5. Schulter, S., Vernaza, P., Choi, W., Chandraker, M.: Deep network flow for multi-object tracking. In: Proceedings of IEEE Conference on Computer Vision Pattern Recognition, pp. 2730–2739 (2017)
6. Han, Z., Ye, Q., Jiao, J.: Online feature evaluation for object tracking using Kalman filter. In: Proceedings of IEEE International Conference on Pattern Recognition, pp. 1–4 (2008)
7. Luo, W., et al.: Multiple object tracking: a literature review. arXiv:1409.7618 (2014)
8. Yousefhussien, M.A., Browning, N.A., Kanan, C.: Online tracking using saliency. In: Proceedings of IEEE Applications Computer Vision, pp. 1–10 (2016)
9. Kuhn, H.W.: The Hungarian method for the assignment problem. Nav. Res. Logist. Q. **2**(1–2), 83–97 (1955)
10. Multi-object tracking benchmark. motchallenge.net
11. Ren, S., He, K., Girshick, R., Sun, J.: Faster R-CNN: towards real-time object detection with region proposal networks. In: Proceedings of Advances Neural Information Processing Systems, pp. 91–99 (2015)
12. Girshick, R., Donahue, J., Darrell, T., Malik, J.: Rich feature hierarchies for accurate object detection and semantic segmentation. In: Proceedings of IEEE Conference on Computer Vision Pattern Recognition, pp. 580–587 (2014)

13. Zitnick, C.L., Dollar, P.: Edge boxes: locating object proposals from edges. In: Proceedings of European Conference on Computer Vision, pp. 391–405 (2014)
14. Harel, J., Koch, C., Perona, P.: Graph-based visual saliency. In: Proceedings of Advances Neural Information Processing, pp. 545–552 (2007)
15. Papageorgiou, C., Oren, M., Poggio T.: A general framework for object detection. In: IEEE International Conference on Computer Vision, pp. 555–562 (1998)
16. Broida, T.J., Chellappa, R.: Estimation of object motion parameters from noisy images. IEEE Trans. Pattern Anal. Mach. Intell. $1(1)$, 90–99 (1986)
17. Shi, J., Malik, J.: Normalized cuts and image segmentation. IEEE Trans. Pattern Anal. Mach. Intell. $22(8)$, 888–905 (2000)
18. Girshick, R.: Fast R-CNN. In: Proceedings of International Conference on Computer Vision, pp. 1440–1448 (2015)
19. Krizhevsky, A., Sutskever, I., Hinton, G.E.: Classification with deep convolutional neural networks. In: Proceedings of Advances Neural Information Processing Systems, pp. 1097–1105 (2012)

UAV Path Planning and Collaborative Searching for Air Pollution Source Using the Particle Swarm Optimization

Yerra Prathyusha and Chung-Nan Lee[✉]

Department of Computer Science and Engineering,
National Sun Yat-Sen University, Kaohsiung, Taiwan
Prathyusha.yerra99@gmail.com,
cnlee@mail.cse.nsysu.edu.tw

Abstract. The air pollution has become a major ecological issue. The surpassed pollution levels can be controlled by searching the pollution source. An environmental monitoring unmanned aerial vehicles (UAVs) can address this issue. The challenge here is how UAVs collaboratively navigate towards pollution source under realistic pollution distribution. In this paper, we proposed a novel methodology by using the collaborative intelligence learned from Golden shiners schooling fish. We adopted shiners collective intelligence with the particle swarm optimization (PSO). We used a Gaussian plume model for depicting the pollution distribution. Furthermore, our proposed method incorporates path planning and collision-avoidance for UAV group navigation. For path planning, we simulated obstacle rich 3D environment. The proposed methodology generates collision-free paths successfully. For group navigation of UAVs, the simulated environment includes a Gaussian plume model which considers several atmospheric constraints like temperature, wind speed, etc. The UAVs can successfully reach the pollution source with accuracy using the proposed methodology. Moreover, we can construct the unknown distribution by plotting the sensed pollution values by UAVs.

Keywords: UAV · Swarm intelligence · Path planning ·
Navigation algorithm · Particle swarm optimization (PSO)

1 Introduction

Over the past decades, environmental awareness is becoming a vital issue in our societies. Owing to the industrialization of the countries and increased consumption of fossil fuels, the air pollution in the environment surpassed above the safety levels. Especially industrialization leads to pollution dispersion through plumes in the environment. It is required to find the pollution sources and monitor the exceeded levels of pollution concentration to control in the lower atmosphere. There are different systems developed, from satellite-based observing systems [1] to the classic local stations in cities [2]. Most of the existing systems are collecting data at ground level or uniting information from the total air column as in the case of satellite systems. The monitoring of pollution dispersion in different layers of the atmosphere has also become crucial.

© Springer Nature Singapore Pte Ltd. 2019
C.-Y. Chang et al. (Eds.): ICS 2018, CCIS 1013, pp. 698–709, 2019.
https://doi.org/10.1007/978-981-13-9190-3_77

Some of the literature have pollution monitoring methodologies in different areas. An example of UAVs autonomously detecting pollution source in the environment by swarm intelligence can be found in [3]. In this literature, for depicting the pollution source the Gaussian distribution is used. However, the paper hasn't mentioned which swarm intelligence it is incorporating. In [4] chemotactic heuristics and PSO are used for UAV navigation for pollution mapping. In their work they simulated a 2D environment with single UAV for pollution mapping and Gaussian distribution is used as a pollution function. Currently, a lot of new studies are happening in the area of group of coordinating UAVs. This field is still in its infant stage, a lot of new strategies and applications are being explored.

UAVs are airplanes without onboard pilots which can be controlled remotely or can fly independently based on pre-programmed flight strategies [5]. In the last few years, the research in UAVs has grown tremendously. They are used in the military and civil tasks [6]. In our study of the collective intelligence of UAVs, we are motivated by swarms in nature, such as a flock of birds, a colony of ants and schooling fish [7, 8]. One of the types of schooling fish is Golden Shiners. Their natural preference for darkness always ends them up in a shady area. These animals individually execute minimal sensing and control and achieve complex navigation performance. For pollution source searching, the group of UAVs must collaboratively navigate in the environment. Moreover, the UAVs are constrained with minimal knowledge with respect to sensing, message broadcasting as they can send and receive messages within the communication range. Under these constraints, the UAVs should be able to compute an emergent solution. We can instill the characteristics of Golden shiner schooling fish for group in which their preference to shady area can be associated to UAVs preference to the most polluted zones in order to find the pollution source. As with larger 3D search space and minimal UAVs it is best to apply swarm intelligence optimization technique called PSO for this task.

Overview

In this paper, for pollution source searching in the earth's atmosphere, a group of environmental sensing UAVs are used. A 3D simulator is designed for depicting UAV navigation environment. To estimate the pollution dispersion in the environment, several real constraints has to be taken like wind speed, temperatures, pressure, etc. Henceforth we used the Gaussian plume model to represent the real world pollution dispersion from a plume. Moreover, as the UAVs travel in 3D space, the path planning has to be done in the obstacle-rich environment. Hence we designed a methodology which adopts PSO successfully to generate feasible best cost paths. Therefore, a group of UAVs with minimal knowledge navigate towards pollution source using swarm intelligence technique called PSO inculcating Golden shiners schooling strategy.

2   Related Work

2.1   Particle Swarm Optimization

Particle swarm optimization (PSO) is an optimization algorithm in swarm intelligence. PSO is inspired by collective social behavior of animals. It is a simple and very powerful optimization algorithm used in different fields of science and engineering for various applications. The search space is the set of all possible solutions to the optimization problem. PSO computes an optimal solution under given cost function with multiple conditions [9–13].

2.2 Swarm Robotics

Swarm robotics are inspired by social insect's behavior which achieves the emergent behavior by working as group. Robots have minimum sensing and communication capabilities, hence to accomplish tasks they require cooperation. Recently a collective robot swarm navigation platform, called Shinerbot, was designed and built based on the behavior of the Golden Shiner Fish on a 2-dimensional platform where each robot has minimal knowledge about environment [14, 15].

Relatively less work has done in 3 dimensional group navigation of UAVs for pollution sources searching. The navigation of UAVs path planning approached are discussed in some different papers [16–18].

2.3 Gaussian Distribution

The probability density of the Gaussian distribution is

$$f\left(x|\mu, \sigma^2\right) = \frac{1}{\sqrt{2\pi\sigma^2}} e^{-\frac{(x-\mu)^2}{2\sigma^2}} \tag{1}$$

Where μ is the mean of the distribution, σ is the standard deviation and σ^2 is variance.

2.4 Gaussian Plume Model

This is one of the models used to depict the three-dimensional plume dispersion from a stack chimney. The height of the stack is h. The effective plume rise and pollution dispersion depends on several real atmospheric parameters [20, 21].

3 Proposed Methodology

3.1 Path Planning Algorithm

The goal is to send a group of UAV to the pollution region and then spread out to find the air pollutant. Since the scenario would be urban area, it will have obstacles of various sizes. The UAV has to compute an optimal path by avoiding collisions with the obstacles.

This algorithm is used to optimally navigate a UAV from a given location (source S) to a target location (destination-D) by optimizing vectors along the path to reduce the cost of journey by a UAV. Figure 1 shows the environment through which UAV has to navigate.

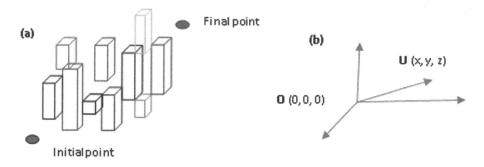

Fig. 1. (a) UAV navigation environment and (b) Position vector.

- UAV's position vector(r): Represents three-dimensional position of a UAV U (x, y, z) with respect to the reference origin (O).

$$r = \overrightarrow{OU} \tag{2}$$

- UAV's velocity vector: Illustrates the speed and direction in which a UAV flies.

Solution Concept

The path from initial point to the final point is the combination of all waypoints along the path. Hence we need to optimize the locations of waypoints along the path. The challenge here is to find optimal waypoints in the 3 dimensional obstacle rich environment. The resultant cost of the path is to be minimal and should avoid obstacles along the path. The brief flow of path planning is illustrated in the above flowchart (Fig. 2).

3.2   UAV Navigation Algorithm for Searching of Pollution Source

Finding a pollution source in three-dimensional environment is highly challenging. Sending a single UAV and finding the pollution source may not be feasible. Hence in this paper we used multiple UAVs to locate multiple pollution sources. We proposed a methodology where group of coordinating UAVs collaboratively explore pollution source using the golden shiners strategy. Shiners are associated as UAVs and their natural preference to darker areas can be associated as UAVs preference towards the pollution zone. Shiners sense light intensity at their locations whereas UAVs can sense pollutants at their respective positions. The shiners movement is based on social and environmental factors. The environmental factor for Golden shiners is the function of light intensity whereas for UAV navigation it is a function of pollution distribution. Regarding social factor a shiner senses the location of its neighbors and prefers its swimming direction such that it will stay together with the neighbors. Where as in the UAV navigation we make sure that UAVs stay with the group.

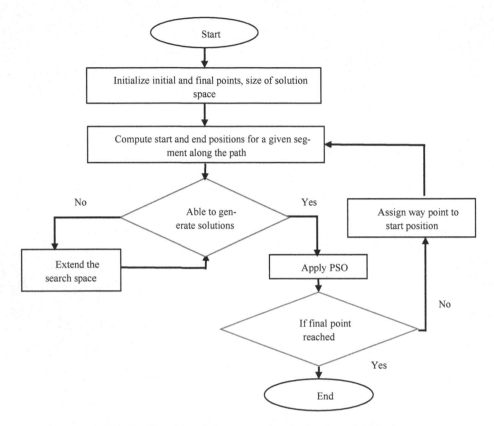

Fig. 2. Flowchart of the proposed path planning algorithm.

- The movement of the UAV with respect to environmental factor is achieved using the PSO technique in which the cost function includes the pollution distribution function. Shiners social factor with UAV communication is achieved by updating velocity vector towards the group along with collision-avoidance.

The following procedure explains how we are instilling shiners features.

The navigation of a UAV is administered by an environmental factor and a social factor. The environmental factor involves pollution sensing at a given location by a UAV. Neighboring UAVs determine the social factor.

- **Step 1**: Every UAV is associated with a unique id. All the UAVs are assumed to move with a constant velocity. The size of the group is initialized. Let it be s. The pollution threshold is initialized. Minimum distance between pollution sources has to be initialized. Every UAV has a status about searching. Once a UAV enters pollution searching phase then it is turned on or else no. Initially all UAVs are distributed with in a given space by avoiding collisions and maintaining minimum distance. The coordinates are specified by three numbers. The distance between two UAVs is calculated using Euclidean distance. In three-dimensional space, let the positions of two UAVs be U_1 (a, b, c) and U_2 (x, y, z) the distance between them is calculated using Eq. (3).

$$d = \sqrt{(x-a)^2 + (y-b)^2 + (z-c)^2}$$ (3)

- **Step 2:** We divide the searching environment into zones. Initially UAVs start navigating in the environment starting from first zone with random vectors. Each UAV can broadcast message to every other UAV regarding sensed information. Every UAV senses environment every t seconds. Once a UAV finds a pollution value above threshold then the UAV collaborates with the nearest s-1 neighboring UAVs and start searching for the pollution source using the PSO technique. All the UAVs in the group enter into searching phase by turning on searching phase. All the other UAVs still search in the zone till a fixed number of iterations and shift to the new zone. Then the search for other pollution sources in the environment continues zone after zone. Thus teams of UAVs are formed for searching different pollution sources. In every iteration if a UAV belongs to a group then the local and global best of the group are updated accordingly. Thus multiple pollution sources are computed using multiple UAV groups.

Problem Definition

The cost function F is the sum of the concentration of pollutants ($CO2$, $SO2$...) and the breach function.

$$F = P + \sum_{i=1}^{M} B_i(Y)$$ (4)

Where P is the pollution function which evaluates the pollution at a given location. The function $B_i(Y)$ is the breach function which is related to constraints like boundaries and obstacles. When the computed position of UAV may be at obstacle, then the corresponding penalty of breach function is assigned negative infinity. The problem here is to find the three dimensional coordinates of a maximum cost function which is the pollution source at which the concentration of pollutants is high.

How Particle Swarm Optimization Technique is Used

The PSO is used to obtain an optimal solution using a group of particles where every particle is known minimal knowledge and sensing of the environment. In this paper, we apply the PSO technique for finding the pollution source. Here in this pollution searching the group of UAVs are associated as a swarm of elements in the PSO. Swarm size is the number of coordinating UAVs involved in searching. A maximum number of iterations is the parameter to determine the number of time instances. Velocity vector at time instance (t + 1) for a particle i is updated using particle swarm optimization as follows

$$V_i(t+1) = \omega * V(t) + c_1 * r * (B_i(t) - P_i(t)) + c_2 * r * (G_i(t) - P_i(t))$$ (5)

Where $B_i(t), G_i(t)$ are personal and global best positions at time t. $V_i(t), P_i(t)$ are velocity and position vectors at t. ω is inertia coefficient. c_1 is personal coefficient, c_2 is social acceleration coefficient and r is a random real number between 0 and 1. The following diagram shows the brief view of pollution searching (Fig. 3).

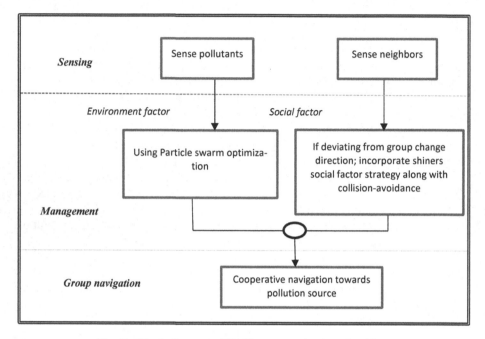

Fig. 3. Block diagram of UAV group navigation algorithm.

4   Simulations

4.1   Path Planning Simulation in 3D Environment

As the UAVs fly in 3 dimensional world, we simulated the 3 dimensional environment 1000 m × 1000 m × 1000 m with obstacles. PSO parameters: swarm size: 25, Number of iterations: 200, c1 = 2, c2 = 2, ω = 0.1, Initial point as (0.0, 0.0, 0.0) and final point as (1000.0, 1000.0, 250.0). We considered three cases for path planning with respect to height. Let N be the number of obstacles in the environment. The position of obstacles (x_i^o, y_i^o) are generated using uniform distribution in the environment. Let l_i^o be length, b_i^o be breadth and h_i^o be height of obstacle generated using uniform distribution. The length and breadth are in the range (25, 75) and height varies according to the following three cases.

- Case 1: h_i^o in the range (250, 300)
- Case 2: h_i^o in the range (25, 250)
- Case 3: h_i^o in the range (250, 300). Included one obstacle at (450, 450) of size 100 by 100 with height 300. d = 200 for all the cases.

From Fig. 4(b), one can observe that the path is crossing over the obstacle at right top most corner (blue color) which is because the last but one way point is (947, 947, 236) and the obstacle is at position (960, 940, 224) which is shorter than way point. As the graph is illustrated in 2d we can see the path is passing over obstacles. In Fig. 4(c) the path is excluding the manually entered obstacle at the diagonal. Hence we can state that in the 3 dimensional environment we are able to generate feasible using the proposed methodology.

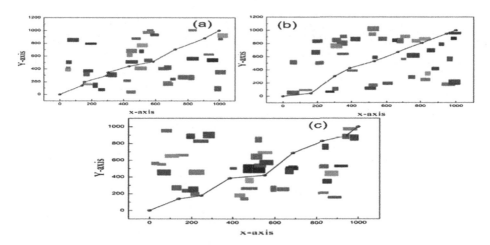

Fig. 4. 3-dimensional path planning for (a) case 1, (b) case 2 and (c) case3 (all figures are shown in 2D view of 3d path planning). (Color figure online)

4.2   UAV Navigation with Multiple Pollution Sources in the Environment

In the current simulation the environment is a 3 dimensional space with dimensions $1000 \times 1000 \times 250$. The environment is divided into 4 zones of equal dimensions $500 \times 500 \times 250$

1. Number of UAVs: 18, group size: 6, Threshold: 1 g/m^3, decision parameters $t = 5$, constant velocity: 15 m/s.
2. PSO parameters: swarm size: 6, Number of iterations: 400, $c_1 = 2, c_2 = 2, \omega = 1$.
3. Three pollution sources in the environment are placed. Out of which two distributions follow the Gaussian distribution with means (900, 100, 50) and (600, 900, 150) with x, y and z respectively. The sample size 75 in three-dimensions. The third pollution source is associated as the Gaussian plume dispersion. The stack is assumed as located at (0.0, 50.0, 0.0) with height 150 m.

As the searching is zone by zone. We start from bottom left and then follow anti clockwise fashion. Initially all the UAVs are distributed in the space $500 \times 500 \times 250$ which is first zone with minimum distance between UAVs as 50 m and maximum distance as 200 m.

From Fig. 5(a) we can observe that all UAVs are in the first zone distributed within an area. From Fig. 5(b) we can see some of the UAVs are in the pollution dispersion area. After 100 iterations we navigate the remaining non searching pollution phase UAVs to the second zone and continue further searching. In Fig. 5(d) we can see that all the UAVs are in the searching phase with three different pollution sources. The individual groups involve in searching for the pollution source. Thus we are able to successfully navigate to multiple pollution sources in the environment by dividing as groups of coordinating UAVs.

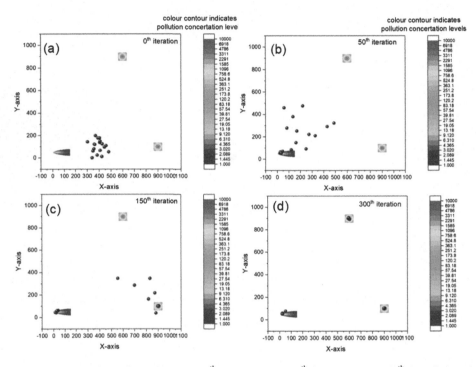

Fig. 5. The position of UAVs at (a) 0th iteration, (b) 50th iteration, (c) 150th iteration and (d) 300th iteration with three pollution sources.

4.3   Evaluation of Pollution Distribution Using Sensed Information by a Swarm of UAVs

As the distribution of pollution may not be known beforehand in the environment. We must be able to generate the distribution using UAVs tracked information during their navigation. Figure 6(a) is the distribution using the Gaussian plume model. The PSO parameters are swarm of size 50, $\omega = 1$, $c_1 = 2$ and $c_2 = 2$. The threshold of pollution concentration is set to 1 mg/s. Figure 6(b) is the plot of sensed values of UAVs every half meter which resembles the original plume distribution. Hence we can say that our proposed methodology is able to compute the pollution distribution in the environment.

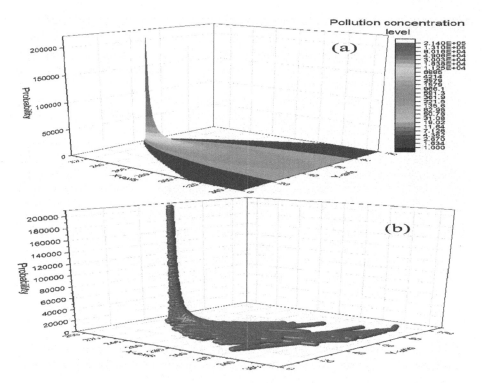

Fig. 6. (a) The Gaussian plume distribution of pollution source (b) The plot of UAVs sensed pollution values.

5 Conclusions

In this paper, we proposed a methodology to find the pollution source in the earth's atmosphere by using the Golden shiners schooling strategy with communication. We adopted PSO technique for collaborative navigation. The novelty of our approach is we used the Gaussian plume model for depicting environmental pollution function in the UAV search environment. The simulations done for UAV team navigation are able to successfully track the pollution source with accuracy by collaboratively sensing the environment and broadcasting messages with in the communication range. We are able to successfully find multiple pollution sources in the environment with teams of UAVs using the PSO technique. Moreover we are able to track the distribution of pollution dispersion under unknown pollution dispersion. As path planning is a key feature for UAV navigation in the obstacle rich environment. The challenge of path planning of 3 dimensional obstacle rich environment is achieved by the proposed methodology using PSO. We simulated for different scenarios with respect to different number of obstacles, segment spacing parameter t and we are able to successfully compute the collision-free paths. As a future work we would like to simulate a real city for path planning environment.

References

1. Hutchinson, K.D.: Applications of MODIS satellite data and products for monitoring air quality in the state of Texas. Atmos. Environ. **37**, 2403–2412 (2003). https://doi.org/10.1016/s1352-2310(03)00128-6
2. Lopez-Pena, F., Varela, G., Paz-Lopez, A., Duro, R.J., Castano, F.J.G.: Public transportation based dynamic urban pollution monitoring system. Sens. Transducers **8**(2010), 13–25 (2010)
3. Varela, G., Caamano, P., Orjales, F., Deibe, A., Lopez-Pena, F., Duro, R.J.: Swarm intelligence based approach for real time UAV team coordination in search operations. In: Third World Congress on Nature and Biologically Inspired Computing, pp. 365–370 (2011). https://doi.org/10.1109/nabic.2011.6089619
4. Alvear, O., Zema, N.R., Natalizio, E., Calafate, C.T.: Using UAV-based systems to monitor air pollution in areas with poor accessibility. J. Adv. Transp. **2017**, 1–14 (2017). https://doi.org/10.1155/2017/8204353
5. Newcome, L.R.: Unmanned aviation: a brief history of unmanned aerial vehicle. Am. Inst. Aeronaut. Astronaut. (2004). https://doi.org/10.2514/4.868894
6. Samad, T., Bay, J.S., Godbole, D.: Network-centric systems for military operations in urban terrain: The role of UAVs. Proc. IEEE **95**(2007), 92–107 (2007). https://doi.org/10.1109/jproc.2006.887327
7. Kapur, R.: Review of nature inspired algorithms in cloud computing. In: International Conference on ICCCA, 2015, pp. 589–594 (2015). https://doi.org/10.1109/ccaa.2015.7148476
8. Berdahl, A., Torney, C.J., Ioannou, C.C., Faria, J.J., Couzin, I.D.: Emergent sensing of complex environments by mobile animal groups. Science **339**(2013), 574–576 (2013). https://doi.org/10.1126/science.1225883
9. Kennedy, J., Eberhart, R.C.: Particle swarm optimization. In: Proceedings of IEEE International Conference on Neural Networks IV 1995, pp. 1942–1948 (1995). https://doi.org/10.1109/icnn.1995.488968
10. Shi, Y., Eberhart, R.C.: A modified particle swarm optimizer. In: Proceedings of IEEE International Conference on Evolutionary Computation, pp. 69–73 (1998). https://doi.org/10.1109/icec.1998.699146
11. Kennedy, J., Eberhart, R.C.: Swarm Intelligence. Morgan Kaufmann, San Francisco (2001). ISBN 1-55860-595-9
12. Shi, Y., Eberhart, R.C.: Parameter selection in particle swarm optimization. In: Porto, V.W., Saravanan, N., Waagen, D., Eiben, A.E. (eds.) EP 1998. LNCS, vol. 1447, pp. 591–600. Springer, Heidelberg (1998). https://doi.org/10.1007/BFb0040810
13. Eberhart, R., Kennedy, J.: A new optimizer using particle swarm theory. In: Proceedings of the Sixth International Symposium on Micro Machine and Human Science, pp. 39–43 (1995). https://doi.org/10.1109/mhs.1995.494215
14. Luo, E., Fang, X.H, Ng, Y., Gao, G.X.: Shinerbot: bio-inspired collective robot swarm navigation platform. In: Proceedings of the 29th International Technical Meeting of the Satellite Division of the Institute of Navigation, pp. 1091–1095 (2016)
15. Liang, H., Gao, G.: Navigating robot swarms using collective intelligence learned from golden shiner fish. In: Proceedings of Collective Intelligence Conference, 2014 arXiv:1407.0008 [cs.NE] (2014)
16. Salamat, B., Tonello, A.M.: Stochastic trajectory generation using particle swarm optimization for quadrotor unmanned aerial vehicles (UAVs). Aerospace **4**, 1–19 (2017). https://doi.org/10.3390/aerospace4020027

17. Zhang, B., Duan, H.: Three-dimensional path planning for uninhabited combat aerial vehicle based on predator-prey pigeon-inspired optimization. IEEE/ACM Trans. Comput. Biol. Bioinf. **14**, 97–107 (2017). https://doi.org/10.1109/tcbb.2015.2443789

18. Cekmez, U., Ozsiginan, M., Sahingoz, O.K.: Multi colony ant optimization for UAV path planning with obstacle avoidance. In: International Conference on Unmanned Aircraft Systems, pp. 47–52 (2016). https://doi.org/10.1109/icuas.2016.7502621

19. https://en.wikipedia.org/wiki/Normal_distribution

20. Turner, D.B.: Workbook of Atmospheric Dispersion Estimates EPA, Research Triangle Park, NC (1970)

21. Bruscaa, S., Famosob, F., Lanzafameb, R., Maurob, S., Marino, A.C.G., Monforteb, P.: Theoretical and experimental study of Gaussian plume model in small scale system. In: 71st Conference of the Italian Thermal Machines Engineering Association 101, pp. 58–65 (2016). https://doi.org/10.1016/j.egypro.2016.11.008

Software Engineering and Programming Languages

A Framework for Design Pattern Testing

Nien Lin Hsueh[✉]

Department of Information Engineering and Computer Science,
Feng Chia University, Taichung, Taiwan
nlhsueh@mail.fcu.edu.tw

Abstract. In the current trend, design pattern has been widely used for improving software quality. However, using design patterns is not easy, developers need to understand their complex structure and behavior, and have to apply them in the correctly. Therefore, several approaches are proposed to check the violence of pattern application in a system. We argue only static checking to patter structure is not enough, dynamic testing to test the patterns' semantics is necessary. In this paper, we propose a test model for design patterns. We explore the potential error point of each design pattern thoroughly, and encapsulate their testing methods into a package called "test pattern for design pattern (TP4DP)". Just like the design pattern, our proposed TP4DP includes the sample code of executable test cases which facilitate their application practically.

1 Introduction

In the current trend, design pattern has been widely used for improving software quality. In the academic research, design patterns is one of important research area and applied in different areas [7,14,16], many design pattern detection approaches are proposed [8,17,19], some work discuss pattern quality metrics [2,9,10], design pattern formalization and specification [12,23], and its benefits [11,13,20,21].

However, using design patterns is not easy, developers need to understand their complex structure and behavior, and have to apply them in the right way. Based on my teaching experience and some research reports, we know some patterns are applied in the wrong way [15,18]. Therefore, several approaches are proposed to check the violence of pattern application in a system [3,22]. We think only static checking to pattern structure is not enough, dynamic testing to test the patterns' semantics is necessary.

In this paper, we propose a test model for design patterns. We explore the potential error point of each design pattern thoroughly, and encapsulate their testing methods into a package called "test pattern for design pattern (TP4DP)". Just like the design pattern, our proposed TP4DP includes the sample code of executable test cases which facilitate their application practically.

This research was supported by the National Science Council, Taiwan R.O.C., under grants MOST 106-2221-E-035-MY2.

C.-Y. Chang et al. (Eds.): ICS 2018, CCIS 1013, pp. 713–720, 2019.
https://doi.org/10.1007/978-981-13-9190-3_78

For example, when we apply *Singleton* pattern, we should conduct the following tests: creating two objects and check if they have the same references. Another example is *Strategy*, when we applied strategy a with this paper, and replace it by another algorithm b, they should have the same behavior, that is, the same output. The following code shows the testing context (Fig. 1):

```
class TestStrategyDesignPattern {
    void testSameResult() {
        Context c = new Context();
        Strategy a = new StrategyA();
        c.setStrategy(a);
        int resultA  = c.doIt();
        Strategy b = new StrategyB();
        c.setStrategy(b);
        int restultB = c.doIt();
        assertEquals(a, b); // should have same result
    }
}
```

We use JUnit-like approach to test the Strategy-applied system. Different design pattern has different properties, therefore the test methods are also different. In this paper we will explore possible approach for them.

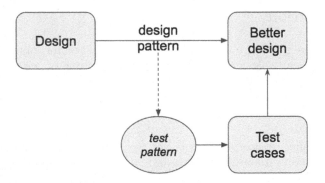

Fig. 1. The concept of *test pattern*

1.1   Paper Outline

The remainder of this paper is structured as follows: In Sect. 2, we describe the related work to this research. Section 3 introduces the details of our approach by two design pattern examples. Section 4 summarizes our approach and future work.

2   Related Work

2.1   Pattern Testing

Chu and Hsueh proposed test refactoring development [5]. Test-first strategy and code refactoring are the important practices of Extreme Programming for rapid development and quality support. The test-first strategy emphasizes that test cases are designed before system implementation to keep the correctness of artifacts during software development; whereas refactoring is the removal of "bad smell" code for improving quality without changing its semantics. However, the test-first strategy may conflict with code refactoring in the sense that the original test cases may be broken or inefficient for testing programs, which are revised by code refactoring. In general, the developers revise the test cases manually since it is not complicated. However, when the developers perform a pattern-based refactoring to improve the quality, the effort of revising the test cases is much more than that in simple code refactoring (see Fig. 2). To address this problem, the composition relationship and the mapping rules between code refactoring and test case refactoring are identified, which infer a test case revision guideline in pattern-based refactoring. A four-phase approach to guide the construction of the test case refactoring for design patterns is developed.

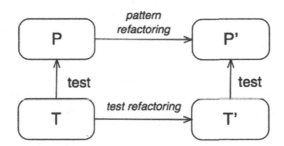

Fig. 2. Pattern based test case refactoring

To understand the application context for a pattern in a system, Lin proposed a *Design Pattern Unit Test (DPUT)* approach, which utilizes java Annotation skill to record the pattern utilization and verifies with the expection in the DPUT. This research also design a software framework to help developers design the DPUP in a specification basis. The code is implemented as an Eclipsed plug-in which can automatically transform DPUT into class diagram for better understanding. For the system maintainers they can find out the errors in the earlier phases.

2.2   Pattern Evaluation

Huston [10] provides an analysis method to examine whether design patterns are compatible with design quality metrics. Each pattern solution has a non-pattern solution that provides a simple solution if that pattern is not adopted. The comparison of the metric score returned for a non-pattern solution against that for a pattern solution is employed for examining the compatibility. For example, the *Mediator* design pattern is compatible with the coupling factor metric (COF) if the pattern is intended to promote loose coupling, and the COF degree of a design with *Mediator* is significantly less than that of design without the pattern. The research results display little pattern-metric conflicts, that is, using design patterns can reduce high metric scores, which might otherwise cause low-quality alarm.

Hsueh et al. [9] improves Huston's approach and propose a general approach to verify if a design pattern is well-design. The approach is based on the object oriented quality model. They decompose a design pattern into functional requirement and non-functional requirement parts, both of them have related structure to realize the requirements. A *quality focus* is also defined to formally identify the intent of the design pattern. If the quality focus is not consistent with the structures, the design pattern will be seen as a conflicting design.

In other efforts, there have been attempts to quantify differences between using patterns and non-pattern versions in different contexts, such as game development [1] or a software engineering course [4]. Ampatzoglou and Chatzigeogiou use a qualitative and a quantitative approach to evaluate the benefits of using patterns in game development [1]. They perform the evaluation on two real open-source games under the versions of implementation with pattern and without pattern. The results of experiments show that the application of patterns can reduce complexity and coupling, as well as increase the cohesion of the software. Chatzigeorgiou et al. [4] assign each student team attended the software engineering course to deliver a software application with and without patterns for assessing students' comprehension and the benefits of patterns. In addition to collecting problems from students' reports, they also ask students to provide the measured values with 7 metrics for comparing the non-pattern and the pattern versions. The experiment reveals some points related to the efficient learning of design patterns in a software engineering course.

3   Our Approach

To design the test model for pattern testing, we have to consider the following issues:

- Correctness and Precision. Correctness considers if all faults can be explored by the proposed test cases, and Precision considers if the test can explore the faults in an efficient way. Our test model should satisfy correctness and precision.
- Coverage. In general we have many coverage strategies for testing, for example statement coverage or branch coverage. When we test we should enlarge the coverage as we can. Therefore we should care about the normal cases, boundary cases and exception cases. When we utilize this concept to testing a pattern-applied system, what are the boundary cases and exception cases?

- Generalization. Gamma et al. classified patterns into creational patterns, structural patterns and behavioral patterns [6]. Patterns in the same group may have same testing issues and methods. We can modularize our testing programs by class generalization.

Potential Pattern Violation (PPV). To test the pattern-applied application more efficiently, we propose the concept of *Potential Pattern Violation (PPV)*. Each pattern has different potential violation that may happen in the application.

Test Pattern for Design Pattern (TP4DP). One of the benefits of design pattern is it is well structured and contains executable code for programmers. Our TP4DP follows the same concept. A test pattern has the following sections:

- Pattern name: the pattern under test;
- Potential pattern violation: the possible issues when applying the pattern;
- Testing guideline: the guideline to test the pattern;
- Demo code: same code to test the pattern.

3.1   Testing *"Singleton"* Pattern

Pattern Name: Singleton. The intent of the singleton is to ensure a class has only one instance, and provide a global point of access to it.

Potential Pattern Violation. There are two PPV in the Singleton pattern:

- PPV1: When we create two objects from the same class, they refer to different objects.
- PPV2: The original object constructor is not set to be private.

Testing Guideline. Create two objects of the same Singleton class, check if there are equal by using the operator "==".

Demo Code. Here is the demo code for the class *Radio*

```
1  class TestRadio {
2      void testRadioSingletonPPE1 () {
3          Radio r1 = Radio. instance ();
4          Radio r2 = Radio. instance ();
5          assertTrue (r1==r2): "Singleton is violated";
6      }
7  }
```

To test the PPV2, we use static testing to check if the constructor is declared as **private**. The example below is the one that doesn't pass the PPV2 checking.

```
1  class Radio {
2      static Radio instance ;
3      static Radio getInstance () {
4          if ( instance == null)
5              instance = new Radio();
6          }
7      return instance ;
8      }
9  }
```

3.2   Testing "*Observer*" Pattern

Pattern Name: Observer. The intent of observer is to "define a one-to-many dependency between objects so that when one object changes state, all its dependent are notified and updated automatically." To achieve this aim, the pattern encapsulate the core (or common or engine) components in a Subject abstraction, and the variable (or optional or user interface) components in an Observer hierarchy.

The Observer object should register to the subject initially. When the subject changes state, the registers (observers) will get notified and react to the message. Note that all observers implement the same interface (called Observer) such that the Subject can communicate with them.

Potential Pattern Violation. When we implement this pattern, we may make error when we have single or many observers registering to the subject, especially on the extreme case- the first and the last observer and when no observer registers to the subject.

- PPV1: When *subject* changes state, the *observer* object does not get notified;
- PPV1.1: The first register does not get notified;
- PPV1.2: The last register does not get notified;
- PPV2: No objects register to the subject. The system behaves abnormally when the subject object changes state.
- PPV3: The Subject is coupled not only to the Observer base class but also its subclasses (static review).

Guideline. To test PPV1, we should create some observers and register to the subject, and then change state to cause the event trigger. Check if the observer update its view or state. In most cases the observers update its state by changing GUI view and is difficult to check by program, in this case we can check by our direct observation (by eyes). Note that we should be careful to see the first and last observer to meet the PPV1.1 and PPV1.2.

To test PPV2, we change the state of the subject before the observers register the subject, and then check if any abnormality occur. PPV3 needs a static verification to check if the Subject class navigate the concrete observer class. The design pattern checking tool (such as *pattern4*) can identify what is the *Observer* class, and then we verify if the *Subject* navigates (refers to) any *Observer* implementation classes.

Demo code. To test PPV1, we create some observers and check if the first and last observer will get the notification.

```
1  class TestObserver {
2    void testObserverPPV1() {
3      Subject s = new Subject();
4      Observer obs1 = new XObserver();
5      Observer obs2 = new YObserver();
6      Observer obs3 = new YObserver();
7      s.addObserver(obs1);
8      s.addObserver(obs2);
9      s.addObserver(obs3);
10     s.changeState();
11   }
12   void testObserverPPV2() {
13     Subject s = new Subject();
14     s.changeState();
15   }
16 }
```

4 Conclusion

In this paper we propose an idea of pattern test for guiding the programs with patterns applied. We believe a program is error-prone when they are designed in delicate and complex structure. Design patterns are good for flexible design but not easy to understand and apply. For pattern beginners we need a guideline, framework or tool to help them. We demonstrate two examples of *Singleton* and *Observer* to illustrate our ideas. In the future we will explore more design patterns and develop a framework for the pattern test.

References

1. Ampatzoglou, A., Chatzigeorgiou, A.: Evaluation of object-oriented design patterns in game development. Inf. Softw. Technol. **49**(5), 445–454 (2007)
2. Ampatzoglou, A., Chatzigeorgiou, A., Charalampidou, S., Avgeriou, P.: The effect of gof design patterns on stability: a case study. IEEE Trans. Software Eng. **41**(8), 781–802 (2015)
3. Blewitt, A., Bundy, A., Stark, I.: Automatic verification of java design patterns. In: Proceedings 16th Annual International Conference on Automated Software Engineering (ASE 2001), pp. 324–327. IEEE (2001)
4. Chatzigeorgiou, A., Tsantalis, N., Deligiannis, I.: An empirical study on students' ability to comprehend design patterns. Comput. Educ. **51**(3), 1007–1016 (2008)
5. Chu, P.-H., Hsueh, N.-L., Chen, H.-H., Liu, C.-H.: A test case refactoring approach for pattern-based software development. Software Qual. J. **20**(1), 43–75 (2012)
6. Gamma, E., Helm, R., Johnson, R., Vlissides, J.: Design Patterns: Elements of Reusable Object-Oriented Software. Pearson Education, Boston (1994)
7. Graves, A.R., Czarnecki, C.: Design patterns for behavior-based robotics. IEEE Trans. Syst. Man Cybern. Part A Syst. Hum. **30**(1), 36–41 (2000)
8. Heuzeroth, D., Holl, T., Hogstrom, G., Lowe, W.: Automatic design pattern detection. In: 11th IEEE International Workshop on Program Comprehension, pp. 94–103. IEEE (2003)

9. Hsueh, N.-L., Chu, P.-H., Chu, W.: A quantitative approach for evaluating the quality of design patterns. J. Syst. Softw. **81**(8), 1430–1439 (2008)
10. Huston, B.: The effects of design pattern application on metric scores. J. Syst. Softw. **58**(3), 261–269 (2001)
11. Izurieta, C., Bieman, J.M.: A multiple case study of design pattern decay, grime, and rot in evolving software systems. Software Qual. J. **21**(2), 289–323 (2013)
12. Khwaja, S., Alshayeb, M.: Survey on software design-pattern specification languages. ACM Comput. Surv. **49**(1), 21 (2016)
13. Ng, T.H., Cheung, S.C., Chan, W.K., Yu, Y.-T.: Do maintainers utilize deployed design patterns effectively? In: Proceedings of the 29th international conference on Software Engineering, pp. 168–177. IEEE Computer Society (2007)
14. Oduor, M., Alahäivälä, T., Oinas-Kukkonen, H.: Persuasive software design patterns for social influence. Pers. Ubiquit. Comput. **18**(7), 1689–1704 (2014)
15. Prechelt, L., Unger-Lamprecht, B., Philippsen, M., Tichy, W.F.: Two controlled experiments assessing the usefulness of design pattern documentation in program maintenance. IEEE Trans. Software Eng. **28**(6), 595–606 (2002)
16. Sahin, C., et al.: Initial explorations on design pattern energy usage. In: 2012 First International Workshop on Green and Sustainable Software (GREENS), pp. 55–61. IEEE (2012)
17. Tsantalis, N., Chatzigeorgiou, A., Stephanides, G., Halkidis, S.T.: Design pattern detection using similarity scoring. IEEE Trans. Software Eng. **32**(11), 896–909 (2006)
18. Wendorff, P.: Assessment of design patterns during software reengineering: lessons learned from a large commercial project. In: 2001 Fifth European Conference on Software Maintenance and Reengineering, pp. 77–84. IEEE (2001)
19. Zanoni, M., Fontana, F.A., Stella, F.: On applying machine learning techniques for design pattern detection. J. Syst. Softw. **103**, 102–117 (2015)
20. Zhang, C., Budgen, D.: What do we know about the effectiveness of software design patterns? IEEE Trans. Software Eng. **38**(5), 1213–1231 (2012)
21. Zhang, C., Budgen, D.: A survey of experienced user perceptions about software design patterns. Inf. Softw. Technol. **55**(5), 822–835 (2013)
22. Zhao, C., Kong, J., Zhang, K.: Design pattern evolution and verification using graph transformation. In: 40th Annual Hawaii International Conference on System Sciences HICSS 2007, p. 290a. IEEE (2007)
23. Zhu, H.: On the theoretical foundation of meta-modelling in graphically extended BNF and first order logic. In: 2010 4th IEEE International Symposium on Theoretical Aspects of Software Engineering (TASE), pp. 95–104. IEEE (2010)

Supporting Java Array Data Type in Constraint-Based Test Case Generation for Black-Box Method-Level Unit Testing

Chien-Lung Wang and Nai-Wei Lin[✉]

National Chung Cheng University, Chiayi County 621, Taiwan, R.O.C.
jack04387@gmail.com, naiwei@cs.ccu.edu.tw

Abstract. Test case generation for arrays is more sophisticated than scalars. It involves the generation of both the size of an array and the values of the array elements. This issue is more challenging in black-box testing than in white-box testing because the specification usually does not describe how arrays are processed in the program. This paper proposes a constraint-based approach to generate test cases for Java arrays in black-box method-level unit testing. The constraint-based framework in this paper uses Object Constraint Language as the specification language. The constraint-based specification is then converted into a constraint-based test model, called constraint logic graph. A constraint logic graph is a succinct representation of the disjunctive normal form of the specification. Test case generation is formulated as a set of constraint satisfaction problems generated from the constraint logic graph. These constraint satisfaction problems are then solved using the constraint logic programming to generate the test cases.

Keywords: Constraint-based testing · Black-box testing ·
Method-level unit testing · Test case generation · Array data type

1 Introduction

Many software testing techniques have been developed during last several decades. However, most of these software testing techniques are still performed manually at present. The automation of the software testing activity should be able to significantly reduce the cost of the software testing activity. Automatic software testing consists of the automatic generation of test cases and the automatic execution of test cases. The automatic execution of test cases is already quite mature. For example, the collection of xUnit testing frameworks is widely used now [1]. On the other hand, the automatic generation of test cases is still very immature. There are two types of techniques for generating test cases: black-box testing and white-box testing [2]. In black-box testing, both test input and expected output of a test case are derived from the specification of the software behaviors.

Ideally, software testing ensures the correctness of all software behaviors. In practice, verifying all software behaviors is usually impossible because of a large or infinite amount of behaviors. To reduce the amount of behaviors to test, equivalence class

© Springer Nature Singapore Pte Ltd. 2019
C.-Y. Chang et al. (Eds.): ICS 2018, CCIS 1013, pp. 721–731, 2019.
https://doi.org/10.1007/978-981-13-9190-3_79

partitioning, test coverage criteria management, and boundary value analysis are usually performed [2]. The constraint-based approach [3–5] reduces the test case generation problem to a constraint satisfaction problem.

A constraint-based test case generator consists of three components: constraint modeling, constraint generation, and constraint solving, as shown in Fig. 1. In constraint-based black-box testing, the software specification is usually defined in a constraint-based specification language such as Object Constraint Language (OCL). The constraint-based specification is first converted into a constraint-based test model, called a constraint logic graph (CLG), which graphically and succinctly represents the software behaviors in the same way as a logic expression in disjunctive normal form. Equivalence class partitioning is performed by systematically enumerate the complete paths in the constraint logic graph. The conjunction of constraints on a complete path refers to a conjunctive clause in the disjunctive normal form and corresponds to an equivalence class of behaviors. Complete paths will be enumerated until the set of equivalence classes satisfies a specific test coverage criterion. Boundary value analysis is then performed for each complete path to generate a set of variants that correspond to test cases occurring at the boundaries of an equivalence class. Each of these variants corresponds to a constraint satisfaction problem and can be solved using constraint logic programming (CLP). Each solution of a constraint satisfaction problem corresponds to a test case. This paper uses the constraint logic programming system ECLiPSe [6] to solve constraints.

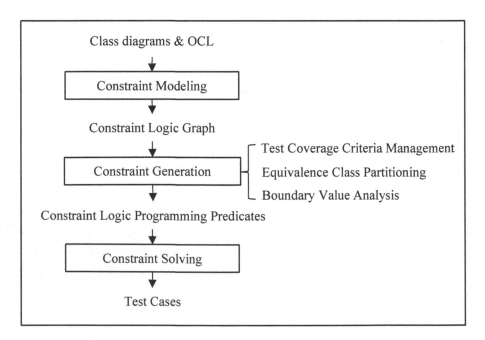

Fig. 1. The architecture of a constraint-based test case generator.

Test case generation for arrays is more sophisticated than scalars. It involves the generation of both the size of an array and the values of the array elements. This issue is more challenging in black-box testing than in white-box testing because the specification usually does not describe how arrays are processed in the program. However, for techniques like test-driven development where the test cases are designed before code implementation, only black-box testing can be applied. This paper proposes a constraint-based approach to generate test cases for Java arrays in black-box method-level unit testing.

The remainder of this paper is given as follows. Section 2 describes the constraint modeling component. Section 3 details the constraint generation component. Section 4 illustrates the constraint solving component. Section 5 gives a primitive evaluation. Finally, Sect. 6 concludes this paper.

2   Constraint Modeling

The constraint modeling component parses an OCL Specification and converts it into a CLG. This component is implemented using the compiler generator ANTLR [7]. The following example would be used as a running example for this paper. Consider a class Sort with a method `sort()`. The following is the OCL specification for the method `sort()`.

```
package runningExample
context Sort::sort():Integer[]
pre SizeErrorException: size@pre>0
post:
  if(size@pre>1) then
  let arrayIndex : Array(Integer) =
      RandomIndexArray{1..size@pre} in
    Sequence{1..size@pre-1}->iterate(it: Integer;
      acc: Boolean = true |
      acc and arrayData[it]<=arrayData[it+1]) and
      Sequence{1..size@pre}->iterate(it: Integer;
        acc: Boolean = true |
        acc and arrayDa-
        ta[it]=data@pre[arrayIndex[it]]) and re-
        sult=arrayData
  else
    result=data@pre
  endif
endpackage
```

The condition `pre` specifies that the method `sort()` should be invoked with the size of the array being greater than 0. The condition `post` specifies that if the size of the array being greater than 1, after the invocation, the array should be sorted in increasing order.

The constraint modeling component first reads in the OCL specification and constructs its corresponding abstract syntax tree. It then converts the abstract syntax tree into a CLG. To handle Java array data types, three representation mappings are established between class diagrams and Java programs, as shown in the Table 1.

Table 1. Three array representation mappings between class diagrams and Java programs.

Class diagram	Java type
int[N]	int[N]
int[0..*]	int[]
ArrayList	ArrayList

CLGs are directed graphs. Each CLG consists of four types of nodes: the start node, the end node, constraint nodes, and connection nodes. The start node is denoted as a black dot and represents the beginning of the CLG. The start node has a unique outgoing edge and no incoming edges. The end node is denoted as a black dot with a surrounding circle and represents the end of the CLG. The constraint node is denoted as a rectangle and represents a constraint, which may in the form of Boolean expressions, relational expressions, logical expressions, or method invocations. A direct edge connecting two constraint nodes implies the conjunction of the two corresponding constraints, as shown in Fig. 2. The connection node is denoted as a diamond and is used to spawn multiple outgoing edges and/or merge multiple incoming edges. The connection of two paths by two connection nodes implies the disjunction of the two corresponding conjunctions of constraints, as shown in Fig. 3.

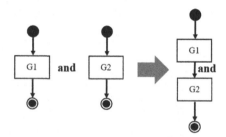

Fig. 2. The conjunction of constraints.

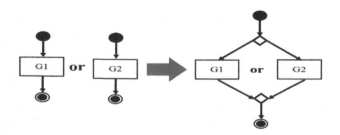

Fig. 3. The disjunction of constraints.

If a constraint node contains logical expressions, namely, and operators or or operators, the constraint modeling component will transform the CLG according to the test coverage criterion. Our system supports test coverage criteria such as decision coverage, decision/condition coverage, and multiple condition coverage.

The constraint modeling component traverses the abstract syntax tree in depth-first order and constructs the CLG correspondingly. For example, for the OCL if construct at the left-hand side of Fig. 4, the corresponding CLG is shown at the right-hand side of Fig. 4, the disjunction of the conjunction of C1 and C2 and the conjunction of !C1 and C3. For the OCL iterate construct at the up side of Fig. 5, the corresponding CLG is shown at the down side of Fig. 5. For the method `sort()` in the running example, the corresponding CLG is shown in Fig. 6.

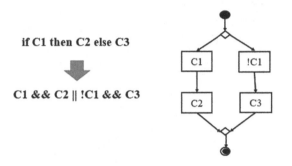

Fig. 4. The CLG for an OCL if construct.

`Set{1..c-> size()}-> iterate(index:Integer; C1 | C2).`

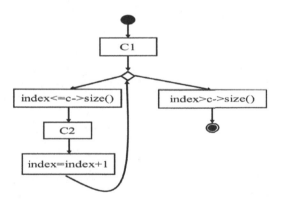

Fig. 5. The CLG for an OCL iterate construct.

3 Constraint Generation

The constraint generation component generates the conjunction of constraints for a complete path on the CLG. It will perform equivalence class partitioning, test coverage criteria management, and boundary value analysis. It first performs equivalence class partitioning by enumerating the complete paths of CLG in breadth-first order. For the running example, the constraint generation component will enumerate the following paths in order:

[8] -> [9]
[7] -> [24] -> [25]
[7] -> [10] -> [11] -> [12] -> [13] -> [17] -> [18] -> [19] -> [20] -> [23]
...

These paths will be enumerated and the conjunction of constraints on the paths will be solved until the feasible paths satisfies the specific test coverage criterion. In the

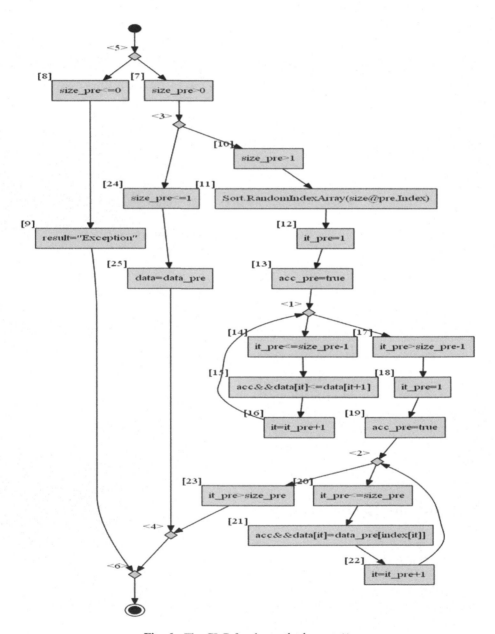

Fig. 6. The CLG for the method sort().

handling of array data types, in addition to the values of the array elements, we also need to consider the size of the array. For an array of unspecified size, we usually generate test cases for arrays of size 0, 1, and 4, respectively. For an array of size n, we usually generate test cases for arrays of size 0, 1, i, $n-1$, n, respectively, where $1 < i < n - 1$.

4 Constraint Solving

The constraint solving component transforms the constraints on a complete path into a constraint logic programming predicate. The constraint logic programming system ECLiPSe is then used to solve the constraint logic programming predicate. If the constraint logic programming predicate is solvable, then the complete path is feasible, the solution is a test case, and the path is used to update the test coverage. The constraint generation and solving continues until the specific test coverage is satisfied. The suite of test cases generated is then used to generate the test script.

```
:- lib(ic).
:- lib(timeout).
sortSort([Data_pre,Size_pre],[],[Data,Size],[],
         [Result],[]):-
Size_pre#=4, Size_pre#>0, Size_pre#>1,
randomIndexArray(Size_pre,ArrayIndex),
It#=1,
Acc=true,
It#=<(Size_pre-1),
Acc,
Index253#=It,
dcl_1dInt_array(ArrayData,Size_pre),
findelement(ArrayData,Element253,Index253),
Index254#=It+1,
findelement(ArrayData,Element254,Index254),
Element253#=Element254,
It_2#=(It+1),
...
It_9#=(It_8+1),
It_9#>Size_pre,
Result=ArrayData,Data=Data_pre,Size=Size_pre,Size#>=0.

testSort(Obj_pre,Arg_pre,Obj,Arg,Result,Exception):-
[Size_pre]:: -32768..32767,
[Size]:: -32768..32767,
Size_pre#=4,
dcl_1dInt_array(Data_pre, Size_pre),
  length(Data,Size_pre),
```

```
List1_pre=Data_pre,
Obj_pre1=[List1_pre,Size_pre],
Obj1=[List1,Size],
sortSort(Obj_pre1,Arg_pre1,Obj1,Arg1,Result1,Exception),
length(List1,Size),
labeling_1dInt_array(Data_pre),
msort(Data_pre,List2_pre),
Obj_pre2=[List2_pre,Size_pre],
Obj2=[List2,Size],
sortSort(Obj_pre2,Arg_pre2,Obj2,Arg2,Result2,Exception),
length(List2,Size),
reverse(List2_pre,List3_pre),
Obj_pre3=[List3_pre,Size_pre],
Obj3=[List3,Size],
sortSort(Obj_pre3,Arg_pre3,Obj3,Arg3,Result3,Exception),
length(List3,Size),
Obj_pre=[List1_pre,List2_pre,List3_pre,Size_pre],
List=[List1,List2,List3],
Obj=[List,Size],
Result=[Result1,Result2,Result3,Size].
```

To use ECLiPSe, the array access `Data[it]` is converted to the following predicate invocation: `Findelement(Element,Data,It)`. For the running example, the constraint solving component will generate a test case for an array of size 4 with elements: {28042, 18601, 30470, 1424}. The resultant test script is as follows:

```
import junit.framework.TestCase;
import java.util.ArrayList;
import java.util.Arrays;

public class TestSort extends TestCase {
   Sort objSort = null;
   Sort objSortPost = null;

  public void testsort() {
    try {
      int[] objArray = {28042, 18601, 30470, 1424};
      objSort = new Sort(objArray);
      int[] objArrayPost={1424, 18601, 28042, 30470};
      objSortPost = new Sort(objArrayPost);
      objSort.sort();
```

```
        String expect = objSortPost.toString();
        String real=objSort.toString();
        Boolean result=expect.equals(real);
        assertTrue(result);
    } catch (ArraySizeException e) {
        assertFalse(false);
    }
  }
}
```

5 Evaluation

This section uses the PIT Mutation Testing [8] to verify the quality of the test cases. Given a program passed the suite of test cases, the PIT Mutation Testing generates a collection of mutants, each of which is a program version formed by performing a single syntactic modification (or inserting an error) called a mutator in the program. Table 2 shows some types of mutators of the PIT Mutation Testing using the example statement, if(array[j-1] > array[j]), in Bubble Sort. This collection of mutants is then tested by the suite of test cases. The mutation score is the ratio of the number of mutants whose error is detected by the suite of test cases to the total number of mutants.

Table 2. Some mutator types generated in PIT Mutation Testing.

Mutator types	Mutants
Math mutator	if(array[j +1] > array[j])
Inline constant mutator	if(array[j − 0] > array[j])
Conditionals boundary mutator	if(array[j − 1] >= array[j])
Negate conditionals mutator	if(array[j − 1] <= array[j])
Remove conditionals mutator	if(true), if(false)

To observe whether the order of elements in the input array matters, we generate a suite of test cases consisting of the 24 permutations of an array of size 4. We use 5 common sorting methods as benchmarks, as shown in the Table 3. The Line Coverage field represents the number of code lines covered. The Mutation Score field represents the score obtained by using all the test cases together. The Max score field represents the maximum score of using one of the 24 test cases. The Min Score field represents the minimum score of using one of the 23 test cases of test data besides the sorted array. The Sorted Score field represents the score obtained from the test case of the already sorted array. The Average Score field represents the average mutation scores of all the test cases.

Table 3. The mutation scores for a suite of test cases consisting of the 24 permutations of an array of size 4.

Sort	Line coverage	Mutation score	Max score	Min score	Sorted score	Average score
Bubble sort	8/8	25/29	25/29	23/29	13/29	24/29
Insertion sort	7/7	21/23	21/23	19/23	10/23	20/23
Selection sort	11/11	18/22	18/22	17/22	11/22	18/22
Merge sort	25/25	47/48	46/48	34/48	24/48	42/48
Quick sort	21/21	33/37	31/37	22/37	25/37	27/37

The Mutation Score fields are not 100% because the mutant (`array[i] > array[i+1]`) generated from (`array[i] >= array[i+1]`) is not detected as an error. The table shows that for sorting programs for arrays of size 4, using one test case on average (the Average Score) has almost the same score as using the full suite of test cases. We also generate a suite of test cases consisting of 24 random permutations of an array of size 7. This result shows that, in general, the size of the array does not affect the quality of the test cases for sorting.

In summary, we can generally generate three test cases for arrays of size larger than 3. Namely, one is the sorted array, one is the reverse of the sorted array, and one is any other random array.

6 Related Work

Braione et al. [9] proposed a white-box test case generator for complex structured inputs by using symbolic execution to generate path conditions that precisely describe the relationship between program paths and input data structures, and converting the path conditions into the fitness functions of search-based test generation problem. Our black-box approach can complement their white-box approach, in particular, for test-driven development.

7 Conclusion

Test case generation for collections like arrays, linked lists, and so on is more sophisticated than scalars. This issue is more challenging in black-box testing than in white-box testing because the specification does not describe how collections will be processed in the program. This paper proposes a constraint-based approach to generate test cases for Java arrays in black-box method-level unit testing. This approach will generate three test cases for arrays of size larger than 3. Namely, one is the sorted array, one is the reverse of the sorted array, and one is another random array.

Acknowledgments. This paper was partially supported by Ministry of Science and Technology of R.O.C. under grant number 106-2221-E-194-023.

References

1. Beck, K., Gamma, E.: JUnit. http://junit.org. Accessed 10 Oct 2018
2. Bezier, B.: Software Testing Techniques, 2nd edn. Van Nostrand, New York (1990)
3. Chang, C.-K., Lin, N.-W.: A constraint-based framework for test case generation in method-level black-box unit testing. J. Inform. Sci. Eng. **32**(2), 365–387 (2016)
4. DeMillo, R.A., Offutt, A.J.: Constraint-based automatic test data generation. IEEE Trans. Softw. Eng. **17**(9), 900–910 (1991)
5. Gotlieb, A., Botella, B., Rueher, M.: Automatic test data generation using constraint solving techniques. In: International Symposium on Software Testing and Analysis, pp. 53–62 (1998)
6. Apt, K.R., Wallace, M.G.: Constraint Logic Programming Using ECLiPSe. Cambridge University Press, Cambridge (2007)
7. Parr, T.: The Definitive ANTLR 4 Reference. 2nd edn. Pragmatic Bookshelf (2013)
8. PIT Mutation Testing. http://pitest.org. Accessed 10 Oct 2018
9. Braione, P., Denaro, G., Mattavelli, A., Pezze, M.: SUSHI: a test generator programs with complex structured inputs. In: International Conference on Software Engineering, pp. 21–24 (2018)

Cost-Driven Cloud Service Recommendation for Building E-Commerce Websites

Chia-Ying Wang, Shang-Pin Ma$^{(\boxtimes)}$ ⓘ, and Shou-Hong Dai

Department of Computer Science and Engineering,
National Taiwan Ocean University, Keelung, Taiwan
chiaying@ittw.tw, albert@ntou.edu.tw,
xanxusver.v.r@gmail.com

Abstract. With the evolution of software engineering technology, using cloud services to replace self-built information systems has been proven an economical and reliable way. However, how to help e-commerce service system builders to choose suitable compositions of cloud services that meet their needs is still a challenge. In the past decade, a number of academic studies have explored the selection strategies and algorithms for cloud services, however, most efforts are not able to consider multiple types of cloud services simultaneously to provide composite cloud service solutions. To address the above issue, this study proposes a cost-driven recommendation method, called ECSSR (E-Commerce Service Suite Recommendation). ECSSR takes the user budget as the core factor and simultaneously considers the user's preferences for the service types. A prototype system, referred to as ECClouder, is also designed and implemented to realize the features of ECSSR. ECClouder is able to collect the user's requirements, convert application-level requirements into infrastructure-level requirements, and produce appropriate cloud service solutions. The case study show that ECClouder can effectively help users to find cloud service solutions that are reasonably priced and meet their needs.

Keywords: Cloud service selection · Cloud service composition ·
Cloud service recommendation

1 Introduction

In recent years, EC (e-commerce) industry has become increasing mature, and e-commerce services in various fields have continued to flourish. With the evolution of software engineering technology, using cloud services to replace self-built information systems has become an economical and reliable way. However, how to help e-commerce service system builders to choose cloud services that meet their needs is still a challenge. Nowadays, the majority of the Taiwanese e-commerce system builders tend to adopt the "bundled" service solutions, which leads to rigid setup options and uncompetitive pricing. In addition, the websites provided by the bundled solutions tend to be very similar, both aesthetically and functionally. If an e-commerce builder wants to establish its own infrastructure using cloud services, it would have to consider a multitude of service components, such as IaaS (Infrastructure as a Service), database,

© Springer Nature Singapore Pte Ltd. 2019
C.-Y. Chang et al. (Eds.): ICS 2018, CCIS 1013, pp. 732–742, 2019.
https://doi.org/10.1007/978-981-13-9190-3_80

DNS (Domain Name System), payment, and logistics. Due to the varying services and characteristics, finding appropriate cloud service compositions is both time-consuming and difficult. Even if e-commerce builders spend a lot of time to conduct analysis and comparison, it is still not easy to find suitable cloud service compositions. Furthermore, most e-commerce companies do not fully understand which services can best optimize their business, so that it is possible to lead to the shortage of memory or network flow, or ballooning cost. In the past decade, a number of academic studies have explored the selection strategies and algorithms for cloud services, however, multiple issues still need to be addressed:

- Most methods do not consider multiple types of cloud services simultaneously.
- Most methods do not identify the linkages between different attributes for the same or different service types.
- Most ordinary users are hard to formulate detailed specifications for cloud services that will be applied; however, most methods neglect this issue.

To overcome the above difficulties, this study proposes a cost-driven recommendation method, referred to as ECSSR (E-Commerce Service Suite Recommendation). To retrieve appropriate cloud service compositions (also called service suite in this study) with multiple service types, ECSSR takes the user budget (cost) as the core factor and considers the user's preferences for the service categories. For the service compositions of the same price, ECSSR conducts expert judgement analysis through the Analytic Hierarchy Process (AHP) method. A prototype system, called ECClouder, is also designed and implemented to realize the features of ECSSR. ECClouder is able to collect the user's requirements, convert application-level requirements into infrastructure-level requirements, and produce appropriate cloud service solutions. Finally, we have applied the proposed approach to a real case.

The remainder of this paper is organized as follows: Sect. 2 outlines background knowledge and related work. In Sect. 3, we describe the proposed ECSSR approach in depth. Section 4 presents a case study that applied ECSSR. Section 5 draws a number of conclusions.

2 Background and Related Work

This study adopted AHP (Analytic Hierarchy Process, AHP) [1] and WSM (Weighted Sum Model, WSM) [2] for the analysis and optimization of cloud service selection. AHP is a layered, systematic approach of analysis, specialized in solving complex, multi-factorial problems with high accuracy. When analyzing conflicting results, it uses consistency indicator to address the conflicts. Since the method is modelled in a layered, multifactorial structure, it provides high reliability and practicality when being used to analyze the expert judgement of various cloud services; WSM is a multi-criteria algorithm, specialized in applying information into a standardized, weighted algorithm, ultimately providing a uniformed, comparable expression.

In recent years, there have been many studies focus on the selection methods and algorithms of cloud services. Many studies applied AHP to objectively select cloud services [3–9] and proving the effectiveness of AHP. In addition, Tajvidi et al. used

AHP and Fuzzy AHP for the detailed indicator evaluation [10]. Multiple research efforts adopted the WSM algorithm to process indicators and service types [11–13], further proving the effectiveness and practicality of WSM. Qu et al. proposed an approach to separate the objective and subjective indicators to increase the accuracy and the precision [14]. Ghosh et al. proposed an algorithm of measuring the trust degrees for cloud services [15] and highlighted the importance of SLA (service-level agreement) [16]. Uchibayashi et al. proposed a scheme that uses Cloud Ontology for easing the cloud service selection [17]. Gaurav presented the Ranked Voting method to rate the best services for users [18] based on user preferences.

3 E-Commerce Service Suite Recommendation (ECSSR)

In this section, we fully discuss the research methods, including the system roles and processes, system architecture and core methods.

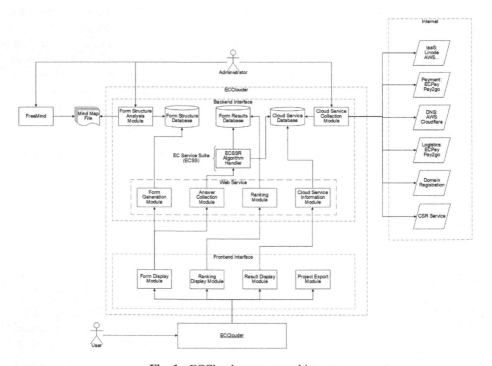

Fig. 1. ECClouder system architecture.

3.1 System Roles and Process

In this study, we defined three system roles: domain experts, advanced users and ordinary users. Domain experts are familiar with the cloud service-related knowledge and data, and are responsible for the maintenance of domain ontology that is represented by the Mind Map [19]. The rationale of using Mind Map is that it is able to visualize the ontology appropriately and easy to use. Advanced users have adequate knowledge and are able to define the user demands and requirements. Ordinary users are not familiar to domain knowledge of cloud services and not capable of specifying appropriate detailed infrastructure-level requirements. For ordinary users, ECSSR elicits application-level user requirements by asking a requirement form and convert the application-level requirements into infrastructure-level ones. For both ordinary users and advanced users, ECSSR recommends them several cloud service composition solutions by using the proposed ECSSR algorithm and saves the recommended plans into database for further use (to share or review of recommended service compositions).

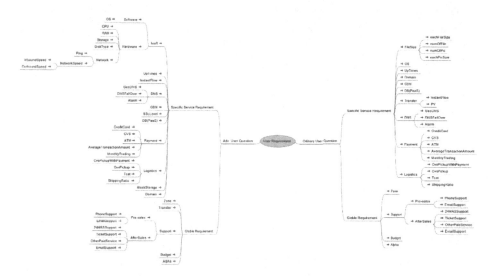

Fig. 2. Example of a whole ontology in ECCSSR.

3.2   System Architecture

Figure 1 is the ECClouder system architecture, a web application including four core modules and their associations. As mentioned, domain experts are expected to define the domain ontology in Mind Map by using the FreeMind[1] software and exporting the corresponding XML file. Figure 2 is an example of a whole ontology (A resizable figure is available at https://dashboard.ecclouder.com/ontology/f1.png). As mentioned, there two kinds of users in ECSSR so that the ontology is divided into two corresponding parts. For the part of ordinary users, application-specific properties were defined, including properties of each file size, number of files, and estimated page views (please refer to Table 1 to see the example of indicators for specifying ordinary user requirements). Ordinary users only need to have the basic knowledge of the characteristics of the applications. The part of advanced users defines the indicators used in the specifications of cloud services as well as the conversion rules between application-level and infrastructure-level indicators. (Please refer to Table 2 to see the example of conversion rules).

---

[1] https://sourceforge.net/projects/freemind/.

736   C.-Y. Wang et al.

Table 1. Example of indicators for specifying ordinary user requirements.

Parameter	Description	Unit
eachFileSize	Each file size	KB
numOfFile	Number of files	N/A
numOfPIc	Number of pictures	N/A
eachPicSize	Each picture size	MB
PV	Page view	PV
Zone	Multi-zone	Y,N
OS	Operating system	WindowsLinux
Domain	Domain name	Y,N
CDN	Content delivery network	Y,N
Budget	Budget	USD/Mo
DB (PaaS)	DB (PaaS)	Y,N
GeoDNS	GeoDNS	Y,N
CVS	Convenience store payment	Y,N
ATM	ATM payment	Y,N
CreditCard	CreditCard payment	Y,N
UpTimes	UpTimes	%
24HRSupport	24 h support	Y,N
DNSFailover	DNS failover	Y,N
Alarm	DNS alarm	Y,N
CvsPickup	Convenience store pickup	Y,N
Tcat	Tcat logistic	Y,N
MonthlyTrading	Monthly trading	N/A
Shippingratio	Shipping ratio	%
CvsPickupWithPayment	Convenience store pickup with payment	Y,N
OtherPaidService	Other paid service	Y,N
AverageTransactionA mount	Average transaction amount	N/A
InstantFlow	Instant flow	PV
PhoneSupport	Phone support	Y,N
EmaillSupport	Email support	Y,N
Ticketsupport	Ticket support	Y,N
Alpha	Tolerance	N/A

The Form Structure Analysis module is able to generate forms based on the expert-defined domain ontology. The Cloud Service module crawls the cloud service providers' information (currently by using jsoup[2]) and save the information to the database. Currently, we have collected data of (1) IaaS services, such as Linode, AWS, Vultr, CONOHA, and DigitalOcean; (2) payment services, such as ECPay and Paytogo; (3) database services, such as CONOHA and AWS; and (4) DNS services, such as loudflare, DNSimple, and DynDNS. ECClouder Web Services, providing services in

---

[2] https://jsoup.org/.

REST style, are responsible for receiving inputs in frontend and returning required backend data. The ECSSR Algorithm Handler module is responsible for performing the proposed ECSSR and PCS algorithms.

In summary, ECClouder is online website that links multiple RESTful services to provide required functionality to ordinary and advanced users based on the domain ontology represented by Mind Map and provided by domain experts.

Table 2. Example of conversion rules between application-level and infrastructure-level indicators.

Parameter	Description	Conversion rules
CPU	Number of core/threads	eachFileSize/2*numOfFile/100
RAM	Memory capacity	1C/1G OR CPU*2 (GB)
Disk	Disk capacity	(eachFileSize *numOfFile/512+nu mOfPic*eachPicSize)*10
DiskType	Disk type	If(numOfFile*eachFileSize +numOfPic*eachPicSize<=2GB & (numOfPic<2000)) HDD
Transfer	Transfer	(eachFileSize+eachPicSize)/2*30 MB*PV or Higher
InstantFlow	Instant flow	InstantFlow
Ping	Response time	<200 ms
BlockStorage	Block Storage	numOfPic > 2000 or eachPicSize > 4MB
In bound Speed	Inbound speed	100 Mbps
Outbound Speed	Outbound Speed	100 Mbps
SSLLevel	SSLLevel	DV
UpTimes	UpTimes	UpTimes
OS	Operating system	Windows, Linux
PhoneSupport	Phone support	PhoneSuppoit
EmailSupport	Email support	EmailSupport
Budget	Budget	Budget
24HRSupport	24 h support	2 4HR Support
TicketSupport	Ticket support	Ticket support
OtherPaidServlce	Other paid seivice	OtherPaidService
GeoDNS	GeoDNS	If(Zone=Y)Y
DNSFailover	DNS Failover	DNSFailover
Alarm	DNS Alarm	Alarm
DB(PaaS)	DB(PaaS)	If(Z one=Y‖DB (Paa S)=Y)Y
CDN	Content delivery network	If(CDN=Y‖Z one=Y)Y
Domain	Domain name	Domain

(continued)

Table 2. (*continued*)

Parameter	Description	Conversion rules
CreditCard	CreditCard payment	CreditCard
CVS	Convenience store payment	CVS
ATM	ATM payment	ATM
CvsPickup	Convenience store pickup	CvsPickup
CvsPickupWithPayment	Convenience store pickup with payment	CvsPickupWithPayment
Tcat	Tcat logistic	Teat
AverageTransactionAmount	Average transaction amount	AverageTransactiouAmount
Mo nt hlyTrading	Monthly trading	MontlilyTrading
ShippingRatio	Shipping ratio	ShippingRatio
Alpha	Tolerance	Alpha

3.3   ECSSR (EC Service Suite Recommender)

Here we describe the EC Service Suite Recommender (ECSSR) algorithm and Plan Composition Scoring (PCS) algorithm in depth.

ECSSR Algorithm
The proposed ECSSR algorithm include seven main steps, as follows:

1. The user inputs the application-level (for ordinary users) or infrastructure-level (for advanced users) requirements, budget B and the tolerance range α ranging from zero to one.
2. ECSSR uses the budget B and the tolerance range α to calculate the maximum budget, $B_{max} = B * (1 + \alpha)$, then asks the user to give preference ratings (from 1 to N; N means the number of service types) for all service types.
3. ECSSR allocates budget based on the order of user preferences; in other words, the more important service type is allocated in higher priority.
4. Based on the application-level or converted infrastructure-level requirements, ECSSR calculates the sum of all the lowest priced plans from each service type to obtain P_{min}. If P_{min} is larger than B_{max}, ECSSR prompts the user to adjust the requirements and/or the budget, and backs to step one. Note that ECSSR always confirms all candidate plan of service compositions satisfy the user requirements.
5. ECSSR then calculates the sum of the average prices of all service types to obtain P_{avg}. ECSSR sets the service composition of P_{avg} to the baseline, the composition mostly close to B_{max} to the upper line, and the composition of P_{min} to the bottom line. All candidate service compositions are ranked by the cost from high to low.

6. ECSSR calculates the scores of each the service plan combinations by the PCS algorithm (detailed algorithm description is shown below).
7. ECSSR returns the ranked list of service compositions to the user.

PCS Algorithm

The basic concept of the Plan Composition Scoring (PCS) algorithm is that the best service composition is the baseline while the worse service compositions are the upper line and the bottom line. Note that even worse service compositions also satisfy the user requirements. By following the above concept, ECSSR give an *Initial Service Score (ISS)* for each service type of each service composition: *ISS* in the baseline is zero, *ISS* in the upper/bottom line is one, and others are between zero and one according to the position of the involving service in the list. For example, if there are five services in the service type IaaS between the upper line and the baseline, the score of the first service (in upper line) is 1, the second service is 0.25, the third service is 0.5, the forth service is 0.75, and the five service (in baseline) is 0. By using this way, ECSSR gathers all scores of all service types for each service composition, and sums all scores to obtain the *Initial Composition Score (ICS)*. For example, for a service composition, if its *ISS* of IaaS is 0.25, *ISS* of payment is 0.5, *ISS* of DNS is 0.33, and *ISS* of database is 0, its aggregated *ICS* is 1.08. ECSSR also converts the *ICS* to *FCS* *(Final Composition Score)* by using the Eq. (1). For the above example, the FCS of the service composition is 73, a medium to high score. Note that the design of *FCS* gives each cloud service composition a reasonable score to let best candidate composition be with score 100 and worse candidate be with score 0.

$$FCS(k) = (N-ICS(k))/N * 100 \tag{1}$$

where k indicates the kth cloud service composition and N means the number of service types.

For the cases of service *compositions* with equal price, ECSSR conducts expert judgement analysis through the Analytic Hierarchy Process (AHP) method to obtain weights for all service types, and multiplies the *ISS* scores of each service type by its corresponding weight to by following the Weighted Sum Model (WSM) method. The adjusted scores are used to determine the ranks of these compositions with equal price.

4   Case Study

In this section, we present a real case in Taiwan, *Food E-Commerce Website*, to illustrate the functionality and characteristics of ECClouder. In this case, *User A* is the owner of a food supplier who wants to establish an online food supply website. The website requires displaying a large number of high-quality pictures and allows consumers to pick-up goods at convenience store with online payment or on-site payment to speed up the transaction process. Meanwhile, *User A* occasionally wants to hold online food auctions to boost exposure and popularity, therefore the website needs to be hosted in a server that can handle influx of traffic. Because *User A* is not familiar with server management, he/she requires 24/7 supporting services for the cloud IaaS services. In addition, sine *User A* has registered a domain name, he/she does not need to apply a new domain name. Finally, *User A* actually use our system, ECClouder[3], to seek for appropriate cloud service compositions.

We expected that this case study could demonstrate the following features:

1. The differences between ordinary users and advanced users.
2. The conversion of application-level requirements into infrastructure-level requirements.
3. The characteristics of the proposed cost-driven algorithm.

Firstly, *User A* gives preference ratings to all service types. Ratings given by the *Expert B* are used on the specific cases through AHP algorithm to derive weighted results (Please see https://dashboard.ecclouder.com/example/t3.png for the preference setting). Next, *User A*'s requirements are converted into infrastructure-level requirements (please see https://dashboard.ecclouder.com/example/t4.png).

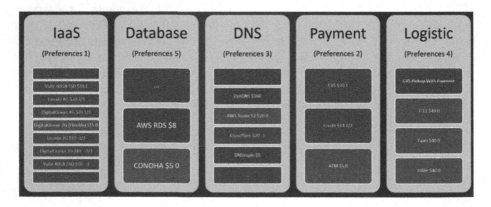

Fig. 3. Illustrations of candidate cloud service compositions for the food e-commerce website.

ECSSR performs initial filtering based on budget, eliminating unsuitable compositions that are not able to meet requirements or the given tolerable budget. In Fig. 3, we can see that the blue section is the most ideal service composition plans for *User A* (the baseline), while gray sections are other candidate plans between baseline and upper/bottom lines. Table 3 shows returned top-4 service compositions with final scores in this example. It can be observed that the highest ranked plan of service composition well fits *User A*'s requirements. ECSSR's core concept is to match the services with the budget first, so it is able to find the best composition from the viewpoints of both service cost and user budget. Besides, when facing service compositions with equal price, ECSSR integrates the domain expert's ratings through the AHP method to calculate weighted values for each service type and adjust the ranks accordingly.

---

[3] http://dashboard.ecclouder.com/.

Table 3. Final ranked cloud service compositions with scores.

Case A

Solution	IaaS	Database	DNS	Payment	Logistic	Price	Final score	Ranking
D	DigitalOcean 2G (Flexible) $15 0	CONOHA $5 0	AWS $20 0	ATM $5 0	711 & Fami & Hilife $40 0	85	100	**1**
E	DigitalOcean 4G $20 1/3	CONOHA $5 0	AWS $20 0	ATM $5 0	711 & Faun & Hilife $40 0	90	91.6666667	**2**
A	Linode 2G $10 −1/3	CONOHA $5 0	AWS $20 0	ATM $5 0	711 & Fami & Hilife $40 0	80	91.6666667	**2**
B	DigitalOcean 2G $10 −2/3	CONOHA $5 0	AWS $20 0	ATM $5 0	711 & Fami & Hilife $40 0	80	83.3333333	**4**

5 Conclusion

This research proposes an ECSSR (EC Service Suite Recommender) algorithm, to provide different types of users appropriate cloud service compositions based on their specific needs and requirements and help the users to build their e-commerce websites. This study also designs and realizes the ECClouder system, allowing users to get recommendations of cloud service compositions without manual searching and comparison of various cloud service plans. Besides, we have applied the proposed approach to an actual case study. The results of the case study show that ECSSR can effectively enable users to find the best or near-optimal cloud service composition with the most reasonable cost.

In the future, we plan to devise a systematic update method for obtaining up-to-date information in a more efficient and effective way.

Acknowledgments. This research was sponsored by Ministry of Science and Technology in Taiwan under the grant MOST 105-2221-E-019-054-MY3.

References

1. Saaty, T.L.: Decision Making for Leaders-The Analytic Hierarchy Process for Decisions in a Complex World. RWS Publications, Pittsburgh (1990)
2. Goh, C.H., Tung, Y.-C.A., Cheng, C.H.: A revised weighted sum decision model for robot selection. Comput. Ind. Eng. **30**, 193–199 (1996)
3. Sun, L., Dong, H., Hussain, F.K., Hussain, O.K., Chang, E.: Cloud service selection state-of-the-art and future research directions. J. Netw. Comput. Appl. **45**, 134–150 (2014)
4. Karim, R., Ding, C., Miri, A.: An end-to-end QoS mapping approach for cloud service selection. In: IEEE Ninth World Congress on Services (2013)
5. Lee, S., Seo, K.-K.: A hybrid multi-criteria decision-making model for a cloud service selection problem using BSC, fuzzy delphi method and fuzzy AHP. Wirel. Pers. Commun. **86**, 57–75 (2016)

6. Garg, S.K., Versteeg, S., Buyya, R.: SMICloud: a framework for comparing and ranking of cloud services. In: Fourth IEEE International Conference on Utility and Cloud Computing (2011)
7. Menzel, M., Ranjan, R.: CloudGenius: decision support for web server cloud migration. ACM (2012)
8. Lo, C.-C., Chen, D.-Y., Tsai, C.-F., Chao, K.-M.: Service Selection based on fuzzy TOPSIS method. In: 2010 IEEE 24th International Conference on Advanced Information Networking and Applications Workshops (WAINA) (2010)
9. Zhang, X., Dou, W.: Preference-aware QoS evaluation for cloud web service composition based on artificial neural networks. In: Wang, F.L., Gong, Z., Luo, X., Lei, J. (eds.) WISM 2010, vol. 6318, pp. 410–417. Springer, Heidelberg (2010). https://doi.org/10.1007/978-3-642-16515-3_51
10. Tajvidi, M., Ranjan, R., Kolodziej, J., Wang, L.: Fuzzy cloud service selection framework. In: IEEE 3rd International Conference on Cloud Networking (CloudNet) (2014)
11. Chen, G., Bai, X., Huang, X., Li, M., Zhou, L.: Evaluating services on the cloud using ontology QoS model. In: 2011 IEEE 6th International Symposium on Service Oriented System Engineering (SOSE) (2011)
12. Oh, S.H., La, H.J., Kim, S.D.: A reusability evaluation suite for cloud services. In: 2011 IEEE 8th International Conference on e-Business Engineering (ICEBE) (2011)
13. Govil, S.B., Thyagarajan, K., Srinivasan, K., Chaurasiya, V.K., Das, S.: An approach to identify the optimal cloud in cloud federation. J. Cloud Comput. Serv. Sci. 1(1), 35–44 (2012)
14. Qu, L., Wang, Y., Orgun, M.A., Liu, L., Liu, H., Bouguettaya, A.: CCCloud: context-aware and credible cloud service selection based on subjective assessment and objective assessment. IEEE Trans. Serv. Comput. 8(3), 369–383 (2015)
15. Ghosh, N., Ghosh, S.K., Das, S.K.: SelCSP: a framework to facilitate selection of cloud service providers. IEEE Trans. Cloud Comput. 3, 66–79 (2015)
16. Khurana, R., Bawa, R.K.: QoS based cloud service selection paradigms. In: 2016 6th International Conference - Cloud System and Big Data Engineering (Confluence) (2016)
17. Uchibayashi, T., Apduhan, B., Shiratori, N.: Towards a cloud ontology clustering mechanism to enhance IaaS service discovery and selection. In: Gervasi, O., et al. (eds.) ICCSA 2015. LNCS, vol. 9155, pp. 545–556. Springer, Cham (2015)
18. Baranwal, G., Vidyarthi, D.P.: A framework for selection of best cloud service provider using ranked voting method. In: 2014 IEEE International Advance Computing Conference (IACC) (2014)
19. Roussey, C., Pinet, F., Kang, M.A., Corcho, O.: An introduction to ontologies and ontology engineering. In: Falquet, G., Métral, C., Teller, J., Tweed, C. (eds.) Ontologies in Urban Development Projects. Advanced Information and Knowledge Processing, vol. 1, pp. 9–38. Springer, London (2011). https://doi.org/10.1007/978-0-85729-724-2

Healthcare and Bioinformatics

A Computer-Aided-Grading System of Breast Carcinoma: Pleomorphism, and Mitotic Count

Chien-Chaun Ko[1]([✉]), Chi-Yang Chen[1], and Jun-Hong Lin[2]

[1] Department of Computer Science and Information Engineering,
ChiaYi, Taiwan, R.O.C.
kocc@mail.ncyu.edu.tw, b1089451@gmail.com
[2] Department of General Surgeon, DaLin TsuiChi Hospital,
ChiaYi, Taiwan, R.O.C.

Abstract. Breast cancer has become the third leading cause of death for women in Taiwan. For clinical pathologists, the grading criteria: Nottingham Modification of the Bloom-Richardson (NBR) System based on histological pathology is a gold standard to assess the lesion severity of the invasive ductal carcinoma. The grading indices for the disease based on NBR include tubular formation, pleomorphism, and mitotic count. Because the manual grading is measured depending on qualitative analysis, it usually causes a big workload due to its various variability. The major goal of this work is to extend our previous work and propose a computer-aided-diagnosis system to assess quantitatively the severity of the breast carcinoma. To this end, it first analyzes the H&E stained slide images of the breast specimen using a series of image processing operations to extract feature parameters related to morphometry of mammary tissue, and hyperplasia degrees of nucleus, and mitotic count of nuclei based on histology and cytology, and choosing important features with feature selection, and identify the scores using support vector machine finally. Experimental results reveal that the proposed system not only can obtain satisfactory performance, but also provide histological grade and prognosis information for clinical pathologists to improve the efficiency of diagnosis.

Keywords: Histopathology · Pleomorphism · Mitotic count ·
Expectation Maximization · Watershed transform · Feature selection ·
Receiver operating curve · K-Folds validation · Support vector machine ·
One-Against-All

1 Introduction

Clinically, tubule formation, pleomorphism, and mitotic count are important indices in histological grades, and can be determined in terms of Nottingham Modification of the Scarff-Bloom-Richardson (NBR) grading system which can predict patient's prognosis. Each index of NBR evaluated is given a score of (from score 1 to score 3) in terms of degrees of cell aggressiveness, respectively. It also can denotes different carcinoma pattern. The NBR grading can be categorized into three grades (from 1 to 3) by adding these three individual scores together to obtain the final grade for the tissue specimen. The summed scores ranging from 1 to 3, 4 to 6, and 7 to 9 are assigned low grade

© Springer Nature Singapore Pte Ltd. 2019
C.-Y. Chang et al. (Eds.): ICS 2018, CCIS 1013, pp. 745–757, 2019.
https://doi.org/10.1007/978-981-13-9190-3_81

carcinoma (grade 1), intermediate grade carcinoma (grade 2), and high grade (grade 3) carcinoma, respectively. A low grade (i.e., lower score) whose cell is identified as poorly differentiated and slower-growing carcinoma. The grading results can thus be used to evaluate the degrees of cell hyperplasia or differentiation, and interpret whether the cells have invaded other organ or not [1]. Therefore, clinicians can use this information to help guide the treatment or prognosis options for patients. In general, histopathological diagnoses/grading of breast carcinoma depends on manual identification based on histology and cytology on the tissue sections acquired from biopsy aspiration or surgery. However, the manual grading of the disease is a subjective and qualitative assessment, and may lead to inconsistency result.

Recently, automated histopathological image analysis has become a significant research topic in medical imaging. Therefore, there are several studies focusing on H&E prostate biopsy using image processing, extracting features related to carcinoma, and classifying the grades using the Gleason score [2, 3], but fewer studies explore the NBR grading of breast carcinoma. Moreover, these proposed methods were performed on biopsy images under a high magnification so that higher computational complexity is inevitable. To resolve this problem, developing a computer-aided diagnosis system which can efficiently determine the grades of breast carcinoma for clinical diagnosis, has become a big challenge. In the previous work, we not only proposed a fully automatic segmentation method to detect region of interest for grading [4, 5], but also focused on the grading index measurements of pleomorphism and mitotic count.

Our work aims to produce a more versatile histopathological computer-aided-diagnosis system suing image processing technologies and machine learning. In this study, high and low magnification (from object lens X10, to X40) histology-slide images of breast tissue specimens fetched from a microscope and CCD camera were first selected carefully as our experimental samples. For low power images, a series of image processing operations including contrast enhancement, Expectation Maximization clustering, and Watershed operation were applied to detect the nuclei of interest. Next, the shape and texture features combined with a tree-based SVM classifier based on One-Against-all voting strategy were performed to evaluate the severity of pleomorphism. For high power images, the nuclei of interest related to the analyses of mitotic count of nuclei were segmented using Expectation-Maximization algorithm and ellipse fitting. Next, feature parameters including morphology, intensity, and texture features were measured for the following classification stage. Finally, the feature parameters extracted from abnormal cell and the mammary duct were trained and validated based on support vector machine (SVM) after feature selection stage in order to choose a better classification model based on receiver operating characteristic curve analysis.

2   Materials and Methods

If images acquiring from patient's breast tissues via mammogram or ultrasound were clinically identified as suspicious breast carcinoma, their tissue specimens would be further collected by a clinician who performed aspiration biopsy or excision of breast tissue. A series of stages to create histopathological specimens including fixation, dehydration clearing, embedding, sectioning, H&E staining, and cover slipping on a whole slide were conducted by an experienced pathologist.

2.1 Image Acquisition

Digital images for our experiments were finally fetched via a CCD camera mounted on an Olympus BX50 microscope with $10\times/40\times$ (depending on the index assessed) magnification. These images create the specimen for the scoring of tubule formation, pleomorphism, and mitotic count. All images evaluated were acquired on the area with the worst nuclei differentiation for a core biopsy sample; that is, entire classification based on region of interest (ROI) of a specimen. Original images fetched contain a resolution of 1524×1012 pixels with RGB colors per pixel, but these images would be further transformed into a resolution of 512×512 pixels in order to reduce processing complexity. A data set composed of 210 images was chosen as our experimental samples. This data set include 90 tubular formation images, 80 pleomorphism images, and 40 mitotic count images. The score of each ROI was manually measured by an expert pathologist as ground truth for comparison.

High degrees of epithelial pleomorphism may exhibit poor differentiation and worse prognosis. If nuclei has regular shape and size, it may be identified as a low degree of pleomorphism and give a score 1, medium degree of pleomorphism may give a score 2, and high degree of pleomorphism may give a score 3, respectively. In continuous 10 high power field, measuring the mitotic count can predict the cell proliferation and prognosis. For low proliferation, one may give a score 1, but medium and high degrees of proliferation may give a score 2 and 3, respectively.

In order to mimic the pathologist's identification on grading, we propose a computer-aided system to assess individual scoring index using quantitative measures. It first detect a complete ROIs at the lesion area to detect the interesting nuclei, measure or evaluate these features corresponding to the scoring of the index, and give a score of the index based on a robust classifier.

In a normal breast tissue, gland units (including cytoplasm, lumen and nuclei) are served as foreground, but stroma and lymphocyte cells or mucin are referred to as background. In fact, a gland may not have a specific shape or size especially for a malignant tissue; it can be oval, round, and can be either small or large in size. Hence, we can't detect a gland or nuclei using a simple segmentation model. In the past few years, a tubular formation scoring of breast carcinoma was proposed by us [5]. In this study, we extend the previous research, and focus on the scorings of pleomorphism and mitotic count, respectively. The detailed flow charts for the segmentation of these two scoring indices are illustrated as below (see Figs. 1 and 2):

Two original H&E stained images for measuring scores of pleomorphism and mitotic are delineated in Fig. 3(a) and (b), respectively.

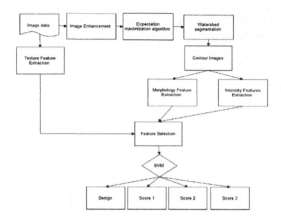

Fig. 1. Flowchart for the scoring of pleomorphism

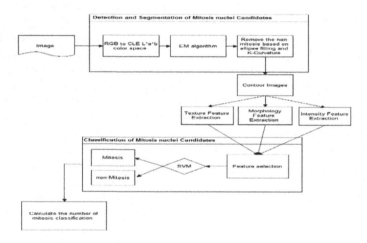

Fig. 2. Flowchart for the scoring of mitotic count

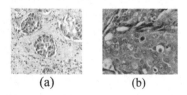

(a)   (b)

Fig. 3. Original images of (a) pleomorphism, (b) mitotic count.

2.2   Segmentation

Segmentation of Pleomorphism

If one wants to evaluate the severity of the pleomorphism, examining the variations of the epithelial cells on a microscope such as morphology and areas is a necessary procedure to identify the pathology of nucleus. The shape of each nucleus may approximate to a round shape for a normal nucleus but without inappropriate proliferation. Once a nucleus generates irregular shape or larger area due to poor proliferation, inappropriate cell proliferation is inevitable. In order to identify the abnormal cells caused by pleomorphism, segmentation of nucleus is an initial step for identification of these cells. Here, a contrast enhancement using Sigmoid filter on the H component of HSV color space is used to improve the contrast of the original image [14]:

$$O(i,j) = I(i,j) + I(i,j) * C * \frac{1}{1 + e^{-I(i,j)}}, \tag{1}$$

where O(i, j) is the output image, I(I,j) is the unprocessed input image, and C is a factor. Figure 4(a) is the resulting image after performing contrast enhancement on Fig. 3(a). Then, a clustering based on Expectation Maximization (E-M clustering) on the feature set {L, *a, *b, R, G, B} from 20 training samples and classified as 5 groups for different materials (delineated with different colors), as shown in Fig. 4(b). The E-M clustering calculate the likelihood function and must perform the following two steps in introducing features:

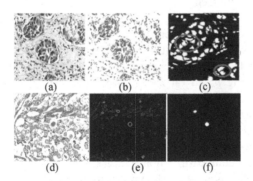

| (a) | (b) | (c) |
| (d) | (e) | (f) |

Fig. 4. (a) Result after enhancement with Sigmod filter, (b) E-M clustering as 5 groups, (c) Final segmentation result of pleomorphism, (d) Candidate cells after EM clustering as 5 groups, (e) Remained cells after ellipse fitting, (g) Final detected mitotic cells.

E step:

$$E[z_{ij}] = \frac{e^{\frac{-1}{2\sigma^2}(x_i - u_j)^2}}{\sum\limits_{n=1}^{k} e^{\frac{-1}{2\sigma^2}(x_i - u_j)^2}} \tag{2}$$

M step:

$$P(x_n|\Theta) = \sum_{k=1}^{K} P(x_n, k|\Theta) = P(k|\Theta)$$

$$\sum_{k=1}^{K} = (P(x_n, k|\Theta)) = \sum_{k=1}^{K} c_k P(x_n|k, \Theta) \tag{3}$$

where μi is its variance, and σi standard deviation. As shown in Fig. 4(b), these objects contain nucleus with different intensities (delineated with yellow and blue colors), cytoplasm with different intensities (delineated with green and violet colors), and background with noise and fat (delineated with white color). Among them, only nuclei with different intensities were selected as our interesting objects (i.e. candidate nuclei). However, some pixels inside the nucleus actually may be preserved as holes inside the nucleus which may affect the segmentation after E-M clustering. A hole-filling algorithm based on morphology hole-filling approach was adopted to create a complete cell structure with smooth contour. Finally, a watershed algorithm based on distance was performed to separate out overlapping nuclei due to imperfect segmentation operations. This approach first measures the distances of the overlapping nuclei away from the center of the overlapping nucleus on the image after the hole-filling operation and form as a distance image. Then, operations including morphological erosion and local minimum detection were performed on the distant image to separate out the overlapping nuclei (see Fig. 4(c)).

Segmentation of Mitotic Cells
In order assess the severity of the cells, pathologist often calculate the mitotic number of cell with 40X object magnification under a microscope. In terms of histopathology, mitotic cell may shows as deep blue and irregular morphology. These information usually are adopted to identify the mitotic nuclei. In order to identify the mitotic nucleus, E-M clustering based on the feature set f = {r, g, b, L, a*, b*} was first utilized to separate as 5 groups from the original image like the E-M clustering in the previous stage (See Fig. 4(d)). Among them, only pixels with deep blue was chosen as candidate mitotic cells. Hence, some objects that are small in size may be filtered out with area. Nevertheless, some pixels that do not belong to actual mitotic cell may be retained due to similar color distribution but dissimilar shape after clustering. In terms of histopathology, nucleus may be shown as elliptic or circular in shape. In order to exclude these objects with different shapes, the contours of all objects are detected based on morphologic contour detection:

$$I_{result} = I_{binary} - I_{binary} \ominus S \tag{4}$$

where I_{binary} is the binary image after clustering and area removal, S is structuring element for mathematical morphology. A Minimum Ellipse Fitting proposed by Andrew Fitzgibbon *et al.* was applied to detect the actual nucleus from the candidate cells in the previous stage caused by debris (see Fig. 4(e)). In addition, the mitotic cells may be shown as irregular morphology during cellular proliferation or differentiation (i.e. interphase). In order to remove the non-mitotic cells, K-curvature was measured on every candidate cells and designed to identify the actual mitotic cells correctly. As shown in Fig. 4(f), the actual mitotic cells are detected finally.

2.3   Feature Extraction

The scorings of pleomorphism and mitotic are evaluated over the whole tumor, and depends on the degree of cell inappropriate proliferation or differentiation; In order to give a score or assign a grade on the histological image according to the scoring criterion, it is necessary to design a robust classifier based on the measured features from the candidate object of interest. The extracted features associated with the grading of the histological pathology contain morphology feature, intensity feature, and textural feature. They can be measured using various statistic, or probability models. The relationship between the features and the scoring index is evaluated to select better features and reduce the feature dimension.

Features of Pleomorphism

Morphology Feature
In this stage, ten quantitative features associated with pleomorphism are measured for classification including: average nucleus area, maximum nucleus area, minimum circularity, average form factor, average roundness, average elliptic-normalized circumference, average long axis to short axis ratio, average extend, and average solidity, etc.,. In addition, eleven quantitative features associated with mitotic count are measured for classification including: average nucleus area, nucleus perimeter, maximum nucleus area, minimum circularity, average form factor, average roundness, average elliptic-normalized circumference, average length of short axis, average length of long axis, average extend, and average solidity, and long axis to short axis ratio (LSR) etc.,.

Intensity Feature
Extracting intensity feature can assess the intensity variations of nucleus, because inappropriate differentiation may cause apparent intensity variation of nucleus. Four intensity features for pleomorphism and mitotic count are measured including: average, standard deviation, minimum, and maximum values from intensity variations.

Textural Feature
Texture is one of important features in identifying lesions or carcinoma cells. Various texture descriptions have been developed such as Gabor filter, local binary, Ranklet, and GLCM, etc. Among them, GLCM is one of the most commonly used approach. It can reflect the orientation, neighboring spacing or variation range. In this stage, the computed textural features for an image patch include first-order statistics, second-order statistics, and Gabor filter features. Grey-level co-occurrence matrix (GLCM) is a second-order statistic feature usually used to analyze the texture of ROI for classification due to its capability in describing orientation, intensity variation that consider spatial relationship of neighboring pixels [9]. The texture variations can thus be measured by using some specific statistic model, and probability model based on

GLCM $C\varphi$,d (i, j). To this end, a normalized co-occurrence matrix $P\varphi$,d (i, j) is first measured from GLCM $C\varphi$,d (i,j):

$$P_{\emptyset,d}(i,j) = \frac{C_{\emptyset,d}(i,j)}{\sum_{i,j} C_{\emptyset,d}(i,j)} \tag{5}$$

where i is the intensity of the desired pixel, $C\varphi$,d (i,j) is the number of frequencies that pixel pairs with intensities z_i and z_j (in our case intensities = 256) occur in the window described by a specified distance d, and a specified orientation φ. Once the GLCM is determined, a number of features related to texture descriptions can thus be measured from the normalized GLCM which includes energy, entropy, contrast, homogeneity, correlation, and variance, etc. In our experiments, we initially set d = 1, φ = 0, 45, 90, and 135 degrees, respectively. Moreover, we chose only the average of these four degrees as our orientation for clarity.ly, a total of 21 features for pleomorphism of cells and a total of 20 features for mitotic count of cells are initially used for scoring or classification. Therefore, the feature vector of a tissue image I is denoted by {F(I)}x, x = 1..., N, where N = 21 for pleomorphism of cells, N = 20 for mitotic count of cells.

2.4   Feature Selection

However, the features used may contain not only a number of inefficient features, but the features affecting the scoring accuracy. In order to resolve the problem, removing these non-significant features is necessary. In this stage, four search schemes for feature selection including best-first-search, genetic-search, greedy-step-wise search, and linear-forward-selection are gradually tested and chosen on the samples based on correlation measures [10]. If the measure for a specific feature is greater than a specific threshold, the tested feature is chosen, and preserved temporarily. In practice, a specific feature will be selected finally as an available feature if it is selected by at least three search schemes; otherwise, the feature will be further removed. These reserved feature $\varphi(x_i)$ form a feature subset for classification. Let x_i denote a feature subset or vector associated with the cancer region, and is formed by the preserved features. Finally, only maximum and minimum area, average LSR, average Extent, average intensity, minimum intensity, correlation, and homogeneity for GLCM are preserved for classification of pleomorphism. And nucleus area, roundness, LSR, extent, solidity, minimum intensity, and Entropy for GLCM are preserved for classification of mitotic count.

2.5   Multi-class Classification

Recently, support vector machine (SVM) has become a powerful classifier especially for two-class classification. This classifier also has various types depending on the kernel functions used, and can be applied to classify multi-classes based on multi SVM using a voting strategy [11]. If SVM is used to classify multi-classes, it must combine several binary SVMs. Basically it has two types from its constructing methods such as One-Against-One (OAO) and One-Against-All (OAA). Here, OAO based on voting strategy is designed to identify as N classes with different kernel functions $K(x_i, x_j)$ based on SVM that are applied to assess the degrees of pleomorphism and mitotic count on the segmented images. We trained a n-classifier (n = 4, in our experiments, scores from 0 ∼ 3), one for each feature subset x depending on the scores measured. A decision function or hyperplane g(x) = sgn{f(x)} for a two-class classifying function f(x) is denoted as

$$f(x) = \omega^T \emptyset(x_i) + b$$

$$= \sum_{i=1}^{n} \alpha_i y_i \emptyset(x_i) \emptyset(x_i) + b \tag{6}$$

where w^T denotes either of two classes w1, and w2, b is its bias value. In our cases, the features of the input space is a nonlinear function in a two-dimensional space. Therefore, a radial based function (RBF) with Gaussian kernel is adopted in our classification. One input the feature vector into the designed OAO SVM classifier. Using the classifying function f(x) one can efficiently predict the class as y = sign {f (x)}. Finally, a robust classifier will be selected depending on the area under curve measured from the receiver operating characteristic (ROC) curve analysis via validation stage and testing stage on the samples.

3   Experimental Results and Discussion

3.1   Dataset for Scoring

A clinician fetched breast tissue of patients via core biopsy or breast excision. These samples were conducted with H&E stained, and the experimental images were acquired by a pathologist carefully under a microscope. A total of fifty gland images containing 81 glands and 85 lm area was selected to evaluate the performance of the gland segmentation.

3.2   Performance Evaluation of Pleomorphism

In earlier work, we have obtained satisfactory segmentation results on tubule formation assessment based on measure indices proposed by Madabhushu et al. [12, 14]. In this paper, the segmentation results for all sample images such as pleomorphism and mitosis were compared with classifications by an experienced pathologist who manually delineated the boundary of each interesting object (i.e. pleomorphism and mitotic nucleus in our case) $P = \{p_1, p_2, \ldots, p_\gamma\}$ as ground truth. And, the corresponding contours detected by the proposed method are denoted as $Q = \{q_1, q_2, \ldots, q_\gamma\}$. Indicator for evaluation of segmentation performance such as boundary error and area error of pleomorphism of epithelial cell and mitotic cell are measured. The error rate was measured using true positive rate (TPR), false negative rate (FNR), and false positive rate (FPR) which are averaged over all the test images, but boundary errors were measured using Hausdorff distance (H.D) and Mean absolute distance (MAD) [12]. In order to assess the segmentation, fifty histology images containing 4190 epithelial cells were chosen to validate the segmentation performance. The performance evaluation of the pleomorphism and mitotic segmentation is shown in Table 1, respectively.

Table 1. Segmentation performance comparison with manual delineation by a pathologist

Error index for evaluation	Boundary error (pixels)		Area error (%)		
Components of breast tissue	HD	MAD	TPR	FPR	FPR
Pleomorphism of epithelial cell	20.07	3.79	86.7	13.3	0.013
Mitotic cell	21.12	3.05	89.86	10.14	0.016

The segmentation results using our approach for pleomorphism cell detection were compared to the method proposed by Dalle *et al.* [14] which shows under segmentation in many nuclei as shown in Fig. 5. We also compared the segmentation result of mitotic count with the method proposed by Christoph *et al.* [13] which shows over segmentation, as shown in Fig. 6.

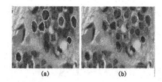

Fig. 5. The segmentation of pleomorphism, (a) Dalle's method (blue contours); (b) Our proposed method (red contours) (Color figure online)

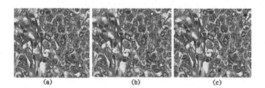

Fig. 6. Segmentation of mitosis, (a) original mitosis delineated by a pathologist; (yellow regions); (b) detected mitosis by Chistoph's method (yellow regions); (c) detected mitosis by our method (black regions) (Color figure online)

3.3   Performance Evaluation of Scoring

The ground truth for pleomorphism or mitosis score of each image was determined by an experienced pathologist. The features chosen by the feature selection method were input to the proposed SVM classifier with four-classes. Then, a k-folds (k = 5) image-based cross validation was performed on all sample images. All experimental samples for the scoring of pleomorphism consist of 80 images (50 training samples, 30 testing samples), but the sample images of mitotic count consists of 40 images and 151 nuclei (53 mitotic nuclei, and 98 non-mitotic nuclei). The kernel function for our SVM classifier adopted is a radial-basis-kernel. Kernel parameters used with $\sigma = 0.001$ and $C = 312.5$ can obtain optimal classification results. The classification evaluation can be categorized as four classes: benign (score 0), score 1, score2, and score 3, respectively.

The confusion matrix for our samples of pleomorphism and mitosis is shown in Table 2. Table 2 shows the identification accuracy of mitosis. Pathologist can count the number of the nucleus having mitosis in order to measure the scores.

Table 2. Confusion matrix for scoring evaluations of plemorphism

Methodology	Classification scores	Accuracy
Proposed method	Score 1 vs. Score 2	87.5%
	Score 2 vs. Score 3	82.5%
	Score 1 vs. Score 3	85%
	Score 0 vs. Score 1	90%
	Score 0 vs. Score 2	85%
	Score 0 vs. Score 3	85%

Experimental results reveal that the proposed scoring system of pleomorphism can obtain satisfactory accuracy in different score comparisons. This is because that the proposed scoring system utilizes better segmentation methods to detect nuclei of interest. In addition, feature selection combined with an optimal classifier is an essential key to improve the scoring performance. Especially, we calculate the overall accuracy as the average accuracy of the pleomorphism scoring for our method. The average accuracy measure in all classification problems reaches 88.75% (see proposed method 2) (Tables 3 and 4).

Table 3. Performance evaluation comparison based on classification using different approaches

Methodology	Accuracy	Sensitivity	Specificity
Proposed method 1 (Feature selection using SVM)	87.5%	85%	90%
Proposed method 2 (Feature selection using correlation)	88.75%	86.7%	93.6%

Table 4. Performance evaluation comparison based on classification on mitosis and non-mitosis

Prediction	Prediction class		
Ground truth	Mitosis	Non-mitosis	Total
Actual class Mitosis	50	6	56
Non-mitosis	3	92	95
Total	53	98	161

Above all, we compare the classification accuracy of the mitosis proposed by us with traditional method proposed by Christoph et al. [13]. Experimental result also reveal that the proposed methd1 can obtain better accuracy (88.81%) in comparison with Christoph's method, as shown in Table 5; that is, method 1 can obtain the best accuracy. If one can measure the number of mitotic cells from images within 10 power fields, the severity of the mitosis aggressiveness (mitosis rate) can thus be determined.

Table 5. Classification accuracies of mitosis with different methods

Methodology	Accuracy	Sensitivity	Specificity	ROC area
Proposed method 1 (Feature selection using correlation + SVM(RBF))	88.81%	94.44%	93.8%	0.907
Proposed method 2 (Feature selection using SVM + SVM(RBF))	88.19%	94.33%	93.8%	0.902
Proposed method 3 (Feature selection using SVM +SVM(Linear))	82.7%	80.8%	80.8%	0.83
Christoph's method [13]	85%	68%	75%	0.84

The evaluation criterion depends on the number of mitotic cells within 10 high power filed and described as follows:

$$\begin{cases} scor1\,1 & number\ of\ the\ mitotic\ cells < 9 \\ score\,2 & 10 < number\ of\ the\ mitotic\ cells < 19 \\ score\,3 & number\ of\ the\ mitotic\ cells > 19 \end{cases} \tag{8}$$

4   Conclusion

In this paper, we extend our previous research and propose a computer-aided scoring system based on SVM classifier with RBF kernel function, which can assess the degrees of pleomorphism and mitosis due to cell aggressiveness of breast carcinoma. The proposed system is demonstrated to be capable of mimicking a pathologist's decision for NBR grading of breast carcinoma in breast carcinoma grading, and improves the shortcomings of qualitative grading by an experienced pathologist. Although it can obtain better performance in comparison with other reporter works, we expect to increase much more image samples or some efficient features for testing in order to further improve the accuracy of the classifier. Besides, how to apply new AI identification tool such as deep learning for scoring is another developing goal in the near future in order to create a robust grading system of breast carcinoma. Especially, how to resolve insufficient samples problem with state of the art such as Data Augmentation or Generative Adversarial Networks (GAN) is a trend in order to improve the performance in the near future.

Acknowledgment. This work was supported by a grant from Ministry of Science and Technology, R.O.C under a contract MOST 105-2221-E-415-020-MY2.

References

1. Fitzgibbons, P.L., Conolly, J.L., Page, D.L.: Updated protocol for the examination of specimens from patients with carcinomas of the breast. A basis for checklist. Arch. Pathol. Lab. Med. **124**, 1026–1033 (2000)
2. Lin, W.C., Li, C.C., Christudass, C.S., Epstein, J.I., Veltri, R.W.: Curvelet-based classification of prostate cancer histological images of prostate cancer images of critical Gleason scores. In: 2015 IEEE 12th International Symposium on Biomedical Imaging (ISBI), pp. 1020–1023 (2015). https://doi.org/10.1109/ISBI.2015.7164044
3. Peng, Y., et al.: Computer-aided identification of prostatic adenocarcinoma: segmentation of glandular structures. J. Pathol. Inf. **2**, 33 (2011)
4. Ko, C.C., Lin, C.H., Liao, K.S., Chen, C.Y.: A fully automatic method to mammary gland segmentation. In: International Computer Symposium, Taiwan (2014)
5. Ko, C.C., Cheng, C.Y., Lin, C.H.: A computer-aided grading system of breast carcinoma: scoring of tubule formation. In: Advanced Information Networking Annual (2015)
6. Paschos, G.: Perceptually uniform color spaces for color texture analysis: an empirical evaluation. IEEE Trans. Image Process. **10**(6), 932–937 (2001)
7. Pena, J., Lozano, J., Larranga, P.: An empirical comparison of four initialization methods for the k-means algorithm. Pattern Recogn. Lett. **20**, 1027–1040 (1999)
8. Chen, P., Zheng, C.X., Wang, H.J.: Robust color image segmentation based on mean shift and marker-controlled watershed algorithm. In: Proceeding of Second International Conference on Machine Learning and Cybernetics, Xian, China, pp. 2572–2576, January 2003
9. Haralick, M., Shanmugan, K., Dinstein, I.: Textural features for image classification. IEEE Trans. SMC **3**, 610–621 (1973)
10. Liu, H., Motoda, H.: Computational Methods of Feature Selection. Chapman & Hall/CRC Press, Boca Raton (2007)
11. Chang, C.C., Lin, C.J.: LIBSVM:a library for support vector machines. ACM Trans. Intell. Syst. Technol. **2**, 27:1–27:27 (2011)
12. Madabhushu, A., Metaxas, D.N.: Combining low-, high-level and empirical domain knowledge for automated segmentation of ultrasonic breast lesions. IEEE Trans. Med. Imaging **22**(2), 155–169 (2003)
13. Sommer, C., Fiaschi, L., Hamprecht, F.A., Gerlich, D.W.: Learning-based mitotic cell detection in histopathological images. In: Proceedings of IEEE International Conference on Pattern Recognition (ICPR), pp. 2306–2309 (2012)
14. Hassan, N., Akamatsu, N.: A new approach for contrast using Sigmoid function. Int. J. Arab Inf. Technol. **1**(2), 21–26 (2004)
15. Fitzgibbon, A., Pilu, M., Fisher, R.B.: Direct least square fitting of ellipses. IEEE Trans. Pattern Anal. Mach. Intell. **21**(5), 476–480 (1999)

Cateye: A Hint-Enabled Search Engine Framework for Biomedical Classification Systems

Chia-Jung Yang[1,2] and Jung-Hsien Chiang[1(✉)]

[1] Department of Computer Science and Information Engineering,
National Cheng Kung University, Tainan City, Taiwan
jchiang@mail.ncku.edu.tw
[2] Department of Radiology, Taitung Mackay Memorial Hospital,
Taitung City, Taiwan

Abstract. Objective: In this paper, we propose Cateye, a Python-based search engine framework tailored for searching in biomedical classification systems such as ICD-10, DSM-5, MeSH, and SNOMED CT. Many biomedical classification systems have coarse-grained and fine-grained structures to handle different levels of information. The general-purpose search engines, which are designed for document retrieval face three major problems: too strict terminology, not efficient search, and uncertainty regarding when to stop searching. These disadvantages make it painful for searching in classification systems.

Materials and Methods: We used the ICD-10 coding systems as our sample materials. We designed a hint bar that gets displayed together with search results and helps the user to formulate correct queries. A hint is a suggestion of a search term that can best divide the search space into two.

Results: The case studies show that our hint mechanism performs at least one step deeper per search step in most cases, while the searching may be slow or even fail if the users compose the query arbitrarily.

Conclusion: The source code for Cateye for searching the classification systems associated with coarse-grained and fine-grained architecture is available at https://github.com/jeroyang/cateye.

Keywords: Information retrieval · Disease classification ·
Natural language processing

1 Introduction

"What is the best search term to narrow down the search space?"

Many classification systems or controlled vocabularies used in the biomedical fields have a hierarchical structure that represents the granulation information. For example, the International Statistical Classification of Diseases and Related Health Problems 10th Revision (ICD-10) [1], Diagnostic and Statistical Manual of Mental Disorders, Fifth Edition (DSM-5) [2], Medical Subject Headings (MeSH) [3], and Systematized Nomenclature of Medicine Clinical Terms (SNOMED CT) [4, 5] contain disease

© Springer Nature Singapore Pte Ltd. 2019
C.-Y. Chang et al. (Eds.): ICS 2018, CCIS 1013, pp. 758–763, 2019.
https://doi.org/10.1007/978-981-13-9190-3_82

names classified as belonging to classes ranging from coarse granularity to fine granularity. In ICD-10, *S52.122S Displaced fracture of head of left radius, sequela* is a particular condition that has a series of ancestors representing a more coarse-grained disease, as shown in Fig. 1. While using this type of classification systems, annotators tend to find the possible most fine-grained class. Annotators need to be familiar with classification systems and require a top-to-bottom exploration process to identify the most suitable class. To accelerate this search process, we developed a search engine architecture that empowers annotators to locate fine-grained classes in the shortest possible times by providing several hints that recommends the most information-rich search terms. In this paper, we introduce our Python-based framework that can generally be applied to any classification system or controlled vocabularies adapted from [6]. We examined the assessments of usability of the test case of ICD-10 with system usability scale and observed that users were satisfied with the interface design (see details in [6]). The source code can be download at https://github.com/jeroyang/cateye. The demo website is at http://icd10.name.

	Code	Disease name
Coarse-grained	S52	Fracture of forearm 前臂骨折
	S52.1	Fracture of upper end of radius 橈骨上端骨折
	S52.12	Fracture of head of radius 橈骨頭骨折
	S52.122	Displaced fracture of head of left radius 左側橈骨頭移位性骨折
Fine-grained	S52.122S	Displaced fracture of head of left radius, sequela 左側橈骨頭移位性骨折之後遺症

Fig. 1. Hierarchical structure of the ICD-10 classification system from coarse-grained to fine-grained classes.

2   Methods and Materials

A hint is a suggestion of an additional search term which will divide the current search results best into two.

There are three major problems on searching in a classification system or a controlled vocabulary:

1. Too strict terminology: Biomedical classification systems or controlled vocabularies usually use a small set of vocabulary and do not provide satisfactory synonyms. Thus, to search in the classification system is frustrating because one may never find the result if he/she cannot use the same terminology used in the system.
2. Not efficient searching: To search in classification systems requires repeatedly typing, checking results, and building the query by guessing.

3. Uncertainty to stop searching: An annotator tries to find the possible most fine-grained class but there is no feedback from the search engine to prompt the stop of search.

We tackle these three problems with one design; hint bar in the search engine. The hint bar gets displayed together with the search results and displays suggestions of valuable search terms.

Let Θ be a collection of classification systems or controlled vocabularies, and θ represents a single class or term in Θ. We tokenize the name of θ and call the tokens $H = \{h_1, h_2 \ldots h_m\}$. Further, we lemmatize H into lemma $\Lambda = \{\lambda_1, \lambda_2 \ldots \lambda_m\}$. We build the inverted index of Λ for search as an ordinary information retrieval system and used H to generate hints.

Let $\Theta_q = \{\theta_1, \theta_2 \ldots \theta_n\}$ be the search results of an arbitrary query q. We calculate the hint score β for each θ using the following formula:

$$\beta_h = 1 - \left| \frac{|\{h_j : \theta_j \in \Theta_q\}|}{1 + |\Theta_q|} - 0.5 \right| \tag{1}$$

The top-k hints with highest β will be shown into the hint bar as displayed in Fig. 2.

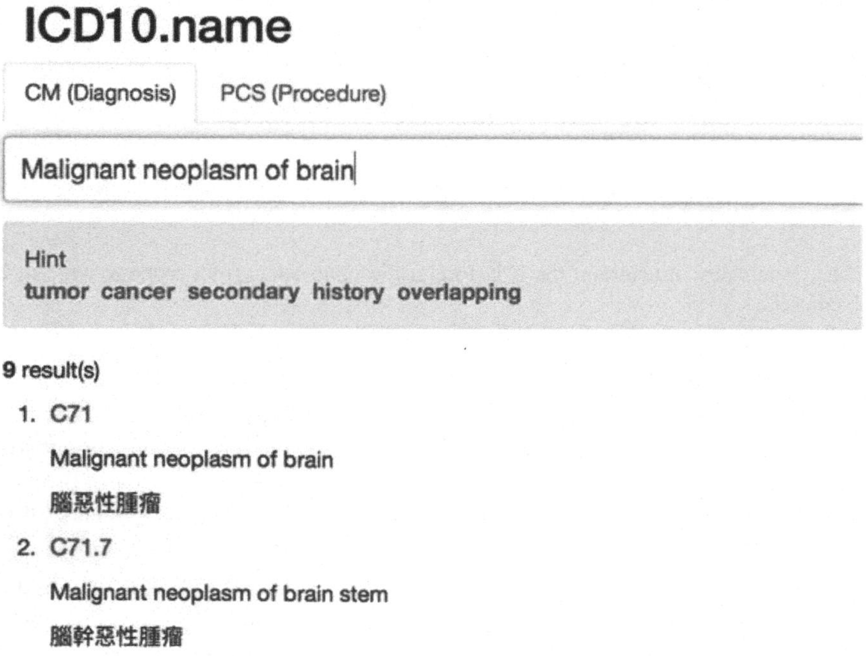

ICD10.name

CM (Diagnosis)   PCS (Procedure)

Malignant neoplasm of brain|

Hint
tumor cancer secondary history overlapping

9 result(s)

1. C71

   Malignant neoplasm of brain

   腦惡性腫瘤

2. C71.7

   Malignant neoplasm of brain stem

   腦幹惡性腫瘤

Fig. 2. Hint bar provides the suggestion of the search terms which can rapidly narrow down the search results.

We also implement two additional features in the system to improve its usability:

1. Spelling correction as discussed in [7] fixes the spelling errors automatically based on the shortest edit distance.
2. Search term fallback gradually eliminates the most non-specific search term in the query when the query generates zero results, to pull the user back to a broader query which can yield some results.

We use the ICD-10 coding systems and the Chinese translation provided by the National Health Insurance Administration of Taiwan as our sample materials. ICD-10 is composed of two parts: the first is the ICD-10 Clinical Modification (ICD-10-CM) that encodes the diseases and the second is the ICD-10 Procedure Coding System (ICD-10-PCS) that encodes the procedures.

3 Results

We examine our system using test cases in [8]. We randomly selected five cases with their clinical information and diagnoses and determined the most fine-grained class for each disorder. Table 1 shows the diagnoses and their formal ICD-10 classifications. The depth of code is the number of counts of the letters after decimal point plus one. This represents the level of fine-grained of the code in the coding system. In general, deeper codes require more step to search. The count of the saved steps is calculated by subtracting the depth of code by the search steps.

Table 1. Test results of the cases randomly selected from Radiopaedia.org.

Case	Diagnosis	ICD-10 code	ICD-10 name	Depth of code	Search steps	Saved steps
1	Bipartite patella	M22.91	Unspecified disorder of patella, right knee	3	3	0
2	Ulcerative colitis	K51.818	Other ulcerative colitis with other complication	4	3	1
3	Langerhans cell histiocytosis	C96.6	Unifocal Langerhans cell histiocytosis	2	1	1
4	Glioblastoma	C71.1	Malignant neoplasm of frontal lobe	2	3	−1
5	Talar osteochondral defect	S92.145A	Nondisplaced dome fracture of left talus, initial encounter for closed fracture	5	5	0

In Case 2, one step was saved because ulcerative colitis is a specific disease that does not have many sub-classes. Similarly, in Case 3, one step was saved because Langerhans cell histiocytosis is a very rare disease that does not have sub-classes as indicated in ICD-10. In Case 4, one search step is wasted because glioblastoma is not classified in ICD-10; thus, we use a more general term such as brain tumor to start the search. Case 5 reached the upper limit of the depth of code. This is one of the worst cases in ICD-10 classification. Also, it takes five steps to identify the specific ICD-10 code.

Generally speaking, Cateye makes one step deeper per search iteration. Even in the worst case, the fallback mechanism helps the user to identify a new start point for the following search process.

4   Discussion

The information needs for searching in classification systems is different from that in ordinary documents. For ordinary document searching such as searching in Google, we construct the query to fit our information needs mainly by guess. The goal of the ordinary document search is to find some non-specific satisfactory results. In contrast, we highly depend on the feedback of the search engine when we search in a classification system, and the goal of the search is to find a specific class which is as fine-grained as possible. To the best of our knowledge, no search engine framework with this capability is available in public.

The hint bar helps users standardize their terminologies. Users avoid incorrect spelling or missing vocabularies by clicking on the hint instead of typing the suggestion when using our system. The hints in the hint bar tend to divide the search results into two and are highly efficient in narrowing the results. Moreover, the increasingly smaller search results indicate the time of termination of the search process.

5   Conclusion

We propose Cateye, a Python-based search engine framework, specialized for searching in biomedical classification systems associated with coarse-grained and fine-grained architecture. The design of the hint bar, spelling correction, and fallback mechanism available in Cateye enhances searching in the biomedical classification systems.

References

1. WHO: International Classification of Diseases (ICD) 10
2. DSM-5: diagnostic and statistical manual of mental disorders fifth edition DMS-5. Am. Psychiatr. Assoc. (2013). https://doi.org/10.1017/cbo9781107415324.004
3. Nelson, S.J., Johnston, W.D., Humphreys, B.L.: Medical subject headings. Relationships in Medical Subject Headings (MeSH). In: Relationships in the Organization of Knowledge (2001)

4. Price, C., Spackman, K.: SNOMED Clinical Terms® (SNOMED CT®). BJHCIM Br. J. Healthc. Comput. Inf. Manag. (2000). https://doi.org/10.1038/5947
5. Donnelly, K.: SNOMED-CT: the advanced terminology and coding system for eHealth. Stud. Health Technol. Inform. **121**, 279 (2006)
6. Chung, C., Yang, C.-J., Lin, H.-C.: UX process to machine learning: for ICD-10 search assistant. In: Taiwan Computer Human Interaction (TAICHI), Tainan (2017)
7. Wagner, R.A., Fischer, M.J.: The String-to-String Correction Problem. J. ACM **21**, 168–173 (1974). https://doi.org/10.1145/321796.321811
8. Gaillard, F.: Radiopaedia.org, the Wiki-based collaborative Radiology resource (2014)

Wearable Ear Recognition Smartglasses Based on Arc Mask Superposition Operator Ear Detection and Coherent Point Drift Feature Extraction

Wen-Shan Lin[1] and Chian C. Ho[2(✉)]

[1] Graduate School of Vocation and Technological Education,
National Yunlin University of Science and Technology,
Douliou, Yunlin County 64002, Taiwan
[2] Department of Electrical Engineering,
National Yunlin University of Science and Technology,
Douliou, Yunlin County 64002, Taiwan
futureho@yuntech.edu.tw

Abstract. On the wearable smartglasses device, this paper proposes a simple but practical 2D ear detection algorithm based on Arc Mask Superposition Operator (AMSO) and luminance density verification. In detail, in the first half phase of the proposed ear detection algorithm, a few ear candidates are extracted by AMSO followed by multilayer mosaic enhancement and orthogonal projection histogram analysis. Then, in the second half phase, the most likely ear candidate can be effectively verified by a straightforward comparison of luminance density. Experimental results show that the proposed ear detection algorithm without any detection false positive can achieve better hit rate and faster response performance than conventional AdaBoost-based ear detection algorithm. Afterward, Coherent Point Drift feature extraction algorithm on Android smartglasses device is also introduced. Implementation results show the real-time performance of the wearable ear recognition smartglasses is feasible for diverse biometric applications.

Keywords: Ear detection · Ear recognition · Wearable smartglasses

1 Introduction

With the ever-increasing demand of anti-terrorism and public security worldwide, biometric technologies have been drawing more and more attention in industrial and academic fields. Among a variety of biometric technologies and applications, fingerprint and iris features must be captured by extremely high-resolution camera within very close distance. So face and ear features are more convenient and noninvasive for biometric recognition than fingerprint and iris features. Especially, ear feature is invariant to facial expression, cosmetics disguise, eyeglasses interference, and age range. Also, ear recognition is the best alternative to face recognition or in combination

© Springer Nature Singapore Pte Ltd. 2019
C.-Y. Chang et al. (Eds.): ICS 2018, CCIS 1013, pp. 764–777, 2019.
https://doi.org/10.1007/978-981-13-9190-3_83

with face recognition while the face target is deflected and the ear contour is rotated to appear frontally and wholly [1–3]. In fact, face recognition applications are carried out under non-frontal pose more often, and ear feature should not be ignored in the meanwhile. Also, ear feature is even more unique from person to person than face feature, that is, ear recognition offers richer biometric performance than face recognition [4].

Figure 1 illustrates the flowchart of typical ear recognition system. In typical ear recognition system, the ear detection stage is the fundamentally prerequisite and exceptionally difficult in typical ear recognition system because the ear color is not different from its neighboring face skin color at all and the ear contour itself is not outstanding enough to be located. Therefore, how to highlight the ear contour (i.e. the inner and outer edges of the ear) exclusively from the lateral portrait is the first and key step to the ear detection stage. This is what the paper is focusing on and improving on.

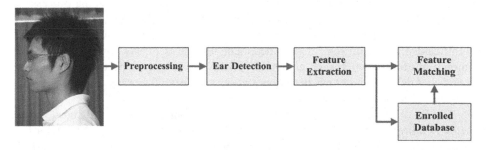

Fig. 1. Flowchart of typical ear recognition system.

Besides, similar to typical face recognition system, the feature extraction stage of typical ear recognition system in Fig. 1 can also apply well-known feature extraction algorithms, like Principal Component Analysis (PCA) and Linear Discriminant Analysis (LDA), seamlessly. This paper adopts and improves Coherent Point Drift (CPD) at the feature extraction stage because of its nature of non-rigid registration of point sets.

The paper is organized as follows. Section 2 reviews the pros and cons of conventional ear detection algorithms. Section 3 clarifies the proposed Arc Mask Superposition Operator (AMSO) ear detection algorithm and CPD feature extraction algorithm in detail. Section 4 illustrates the experimental results about the ear detection rate comparisons and the ear recognition rate. Section 5 refines the implementation methodology of the proposed ear recognition algorithms onto wearable smartglasses. Finally, Sect. 6 gives conclusions and future work.

2 Conventional Ear Detection Algorithms

In general, there are three main categories of ear detection algorithms in the past years. The first category depends upon the contour information. At first, it looks for the largest skin color area in the lateral portrait and regards the area as the lateral face region.

Next, the upper-rear quarter of the lateral face region is cropped and converted into the gradient edge image through Canny operator. Finally, the elliptic contour sets of the human ear can be detected by Randomized Hough Transform within the upper-rear quarter of the lateral face region [5, 6]. The detection rate of these contour-based ear detection algorithms is immune to illumination variation and feasible for real-time embedded applications like wearable smartglasses because of its low computational complexity. But, in fact, the ear without effective contour enhancement preprocessing cannot easily be differentiated from the neighboring lateral face or hair regions because the contour density and intensity of the ear are not more outstanding than its neighboring lateral face or hair regions.

As for the second category of ear detection algorithms, it is AdaBoost with Haar-like features. AdaBoost algorithm with Haar-like features is popularly used for comprehensive pattern detection applications, like face detection, gesture detection, character detection, and license plate detection. AdaBoost algorithm with Haar-like features can also perform well on the ear detection once the elaborate ear training process for the ear pattern is qualified [7–9]. However, the hit rate and false alarm rate of AdaBoost algorithm are usually a dilemma. In particular, the false alarm rate of the ear detection significantly rises with the hit rate increment regardless of any cascade stages, any amount of training patterns, or any ratio of positive training examples to negative ones. Besides, AdaBoost-based ear detection algorithms are too complex to be feasible for real-time embedded applications like wearable smartglasses.

Finally, the third category of ear detection algorithms depends on 3D head model. After building up the 3D head model exactly, it extracts the ear valley regions as candidates through the surface curvature estimation, and selects the most probable candidate as the final detected result through the ear contour shape [3, 10, 11]. However, exact 3D head model is usually computationally expensive and memory-consuming. Especially when high-definition and high-cost 3D image capturing and modeling equipment is unavailable, the inaccuracy of 3D head model will deeply deteriorates the detection rate of those 3D-based ear detection algorithms.

3 Proposed Ear Recognition

In view of the pros and cons comparison between those conventional ear detection algorithms above, this paper proposes the contour-based Arc Mask Superposition Operator (AMSO), multilayer mosaic enhancement, and orthogonal projection histogram analysis for pre-stage ear candidate extraction, and adopts luminance density comparison for post-stage ear candidate verification. Thus the proposed ear detection algorithm is not only better than those conventional contour-based ear detection algorithms but also simpler than those conventional AdaBoost and 3D-based ear detection algorithms. The proposed ear detection algorithm makes itself achieve many aspects of advantages, such as computational simplicity, illumination immunity, ear-like differentiation, reliable hit rate, no false alarm rate, and no complex equipment requirement. More details about the proposed ear detection algorithm are illustrated in Fig. 2 and described in the subsequent sections.

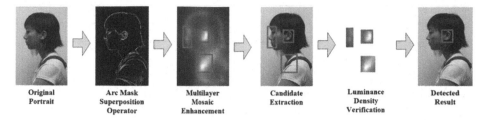

Original Portrait	Arc Mask Superposition Operator	Multilayer Mosaic Enhancement	Candidate Extraction	Luminance Density Verification	Detected Result

Fig. 2. Flowchart of proposed ear detection algorithm.

3.1 Arc Mask Superposition Operator

Because the ear contour is actually composed of diverse arc edges, the inner and outer edges of the human ear cannot be differentiated by any directional straight mask operators, which are shown in Figs. 3 and 4. In addition, although the contour shape of the human ear in the lateral portrait somewhat resembles an ellipse, conventional Hough-based ellipse detection algorithms always catch something elliptic but other than the ear, like the head contour or the eye socket. Therefore this paper proposes the AMSO method featuring 4-directional arc mask operators shown as Fig. 5 to emphasize both the elliptic edge of the ear outer contour and the arc edges inside the ear. Figure 6(a)–(d) shows the gradient images of the portrait are highlighted by 4-directional arc mask operators, respectively. It is obvious that 4-directional arc mask operators can make the ear contour much bolder than any directional straight mask

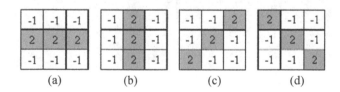

(a)   (b)   (c)   (d)

Fig. 3. Straight mask operators of (a) horizontal, (b) vertical, (c) reverse diagonal, and (d) diagonal types.

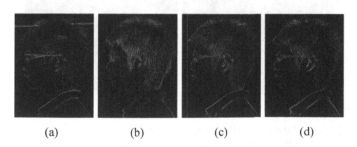

(a)   (b)   (c)   (d)

Fig. 4. The gradient images of the portrait highlighted by straight mask operators of (a) horizontal, (b) vertical, (c) reverse diagonal, and (d) diagonal types.

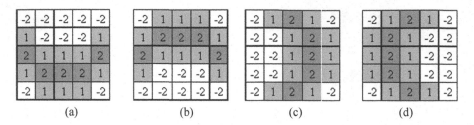

Fig. 5. Arc mask operators of (a) upward, (b) downward, (c) leftward, and (d) rightward types.

operators. In spite of many arc edges outside the ear region being also emphasized in this stage, most of them can then be weakened by mathematical morphological operators of horizontal or vertical ellipse, which is shown in Fig. 7. Eventually, four gradient images preprocessed by 4-directional arc mask operators and elliptic morphological operators are superposed and binarized into the resulting contour image as shown in Fig. 8. According to a great deal of experimental results like Fig. 8, it is verified that the proposed AMSO method can work well on differentiation of the ear contour under various complex conditions, e.g. illumination difference, ear dimension, accessorized glasses, on-plane rotation, and clothes stripes. The detailed flowchart of the proposed AMSO stage is depicted in Fig. 9.

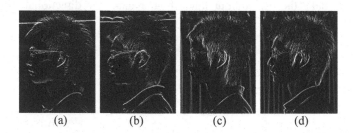

Fig. 6. The gradient images of the portrait highlighted by straight mask operators of (a) horizontal, (b) vertical, (c) reverse diagonal, and (d) diagonal types.

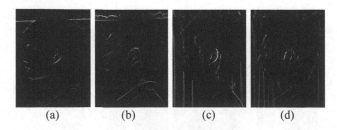

Fig. 7. The gradient images of the portrait highlighted by straight mask operators of (a) horizontal, (b) vertical, (c) reverse diagonal, and (d) diagonal types.

Fig. 8. The resulting contour image of the lateral portrait highlighted by proposed AMSO.

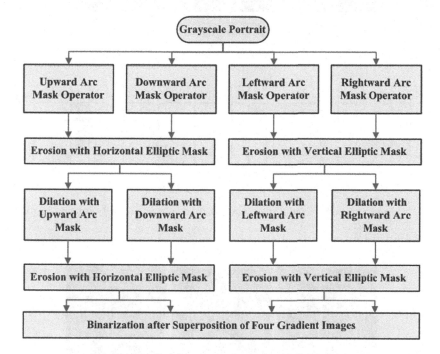

Fig. 9. Detailed flowchart of proposed AMSO stage.

On the other hand, this paper also pays attention on the design issue of the arc mask operators of AMSO. Figure 10 shows the resulting contour images of some other examples of portraits highlighted by the proposed arc mask operators of Fig. 5. But, if a thinner type of arc mask operators shown in Fig. 11 is applied, the resulting contour images with thinner edges, even broken edges, are generated as shown in Fig. 12. In addition, a sharper type of arc mask operators shown in Fig. 13 is applied, the resulting contour images is generated as shown in Fig. 14. In Fig. 14, the contour images are similar to Fig. 10, but are filled up with interference noise across the face and hair regions. Thus it is proven that the type of the arc mask operators in Fig. 5 is the

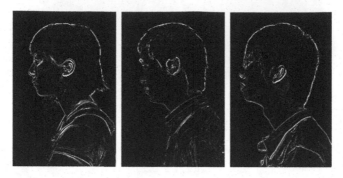

Fig. 10. The resulting contour images of other examples highlighted by the arc mask operators of Fig. 5.

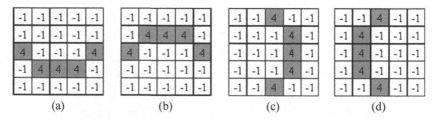

Fig. 11. Thinner arc mask operators of (a) upward, (b) downward, (c) leftward, and (d) rightward types.

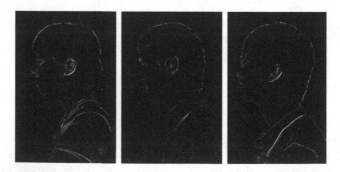

Fig. 12. The resulting contour images of the lateral portraits highlighted by the thinner arc mask operators.

preferable one for the proposed AMSO method. Anyway, there is a constraint for these arc mask operators. The elements in each column of the arc mask operators of upward and downward types are necessarily summed to zero, and so are those in each row of the arc mask operators of leftward and rightward types.

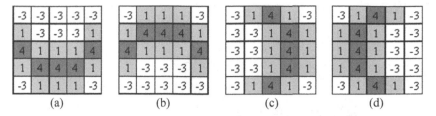

Fig. 13. Sharper arc mask operators of (a) upward, (b) downward, (c) leftward, and (d) rightward types.

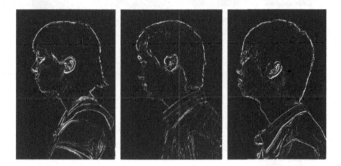

Fig. 14. The resulting contour images of the portraits highlighted by the sharper arc mask operators.

3.2 Multilayer Mosaic Enhancement

Although the AMSO stage can remarkably raise the intensity and density of the ear contour in the resulting image, this paper further adopts a secondary preprocessing method, multilayer mosaic enhancement, to highlight the entire ear region more densely than other arc-shape objects in the portrait. Based on the inherent characteristic of single-layer mosaic window enhancing the entire area of the highest edge density best, this paper puts mosaic window effect of various block sizes on the resulting image of the prior stage circularly and iteratively. After superposition of multi-block-size mosaic images, the entire ear region is spotlighted with stronger candidate differentiation. The detailed flowchart of the multilayer mosaic enhancement stage in the proposed ear detection algorithm is illustrated in Fig. 15.

3.3 Orthogonal Projection Histogram Analysis for Candidate Extraction

In the proposed ear detection algorithm shown in Fig. 2, the candidate extraction stage can intuitively perform orthogonal projection histogram analysis on the resulting image of the multilayer mosaic enhancement stage. Here, in order to raise the efficiency and precision of the orthogonal projection histogram analysis for locating extremes, a rough smooth criterion for curves of the orthogonal projection histogram is used. Figure 16 shows the detailed flowchart of this stage in the proposed ear detection algorithm. After this stage, one or a few ear-like candidates will be extracted.

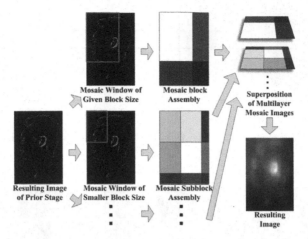

Fig. 15. Detailed flowchart of the multilayer mosaic enhancement stage.

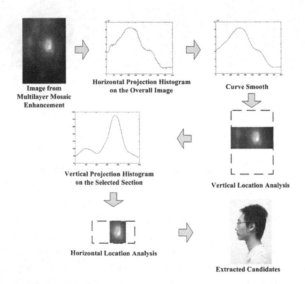

Fig. 16. Detailed flowchart of the candidate extraction stage.

3.4   Luminance Density Verification

However, in case of the number of the extracted candidates is more than one like the complicated conditions in Fig. 17, this paper adopts a straightforward comparison method of luminance density verification to pick out the brightest candidate as the final detected result, which is illustrated in Fig. 17. The function of luminance density verification is to evaluate and compare the luminance density of the extracted candidates. The luminance density of the extracted candidate region is defined as the ratio of all pixel intensity summation to the area size.

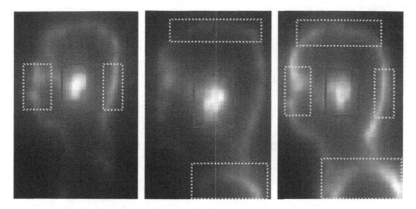

Fig. 17. Complicated conditions of more than one ear candidate extraction.

3.5   Ear Feature Extraction

After successfully acquiring the resulting image of the proposed ear detection algorithm, the ear feature can then be cropped, extracted, and matched by some workable ear recognition freeware, e.g. Coherent Point Drift for Biometric Identification: Ear Recognition [13, 14]. It is originally a PCA-based algorithm, but this paper transforms PCA-based Coherent Point Drift into ASMO-based one to conform to our proposed ASMO ear detection algorithm. Thereby, the feature extraction and feature matching stages of the ear recognition system as shown in Fig. 1 can proceed smoothly.

4   Experimental Results

In the experiment on biometric detection and recognition, Intel OpenCV open source library is popularly used in many literatures as well as in this paper. This paper utilizes the example of AdaBoost in Intel OpenCV open source library without any modification for the comparison experiment. The training parameters for AdaBoost ear detection algorithm is listed in Table 1. Here, 828 positive examples and 10451 negative examples (about 1:13) are involved into the training process of AdaBoost ear detection algorithm.

In addition, in our self-built portrait database, there are totally 94 photos (94 persons) with identical resolution of 600 × 900. Figure 18 displays our self-built portrait database summarily. Various complex conditions are taken into consideration in the photos of the portrait database in Fig. 18, like illumination difference, ear dimension, accessorized glasses, on-plane rotation, and clothes stripes. But, occlusion and expression variation issues are not taken into consideration here.

Figure 19 demonstrates the detection rate comparison between the proposed ear detection algorithm, original AdaBoost ear detection algorithm of 3-stage training, and original AdaBoost ear detection algorithm of 4-stage training, in term of hit rate, miss rate, and false positive rate. Here, false positive rate is defined as the ratio of false positives in the hit cases to the hit cases. It is obvious that the proposed ear detection

Table 1. Training parameters for AdaBoost ear detection algorithm.

```
-npos 828
-nneg 10451
-nstages 4
-mem 1200
-nonsym
-maxfalsealarm 0.05
-mode All
-w 20
-h 30
```

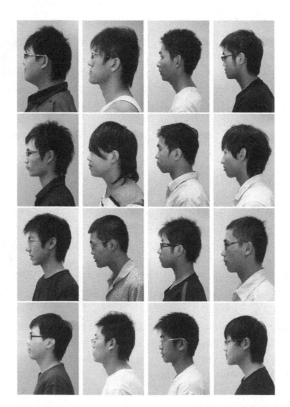

Fig. 18. Self-built portrait database with visible ears.

algorithm featuring AMSO methods, multilayer mosaic enhancement, orthogonal projection histogram analysis, and luminance density verification can achieve a 100% detection hit rate and a 0% false positive rate. The proposed ear detection algorithm is really superior to conventional AdaBoost ear detection algorithm with Haar-like features. On the other hand, Fig. 20 exhibits the subjective detection results of the proposed ear detection algorithm.

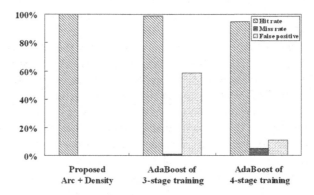

Fig. 19. Detection rate comparison between the proposed ear detection algorithm and two original AdaBoost ear detection algorithms.

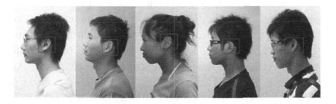

Fig. 20. Subjective detection results of the proposed ear detection algorithm.

5 Smartglasses Implementation

If biometric technologies is further integrated and ported onto the wearable smartglasses device, biometric technologies can be used anywhere and anytime, and can be ubiquitously applied to anti-terrorism security, roadside inspection, banking authentication, community patrol, port examination, airport customs, military weapon, hooligan filtering and high-mountain administration. Especially the ear recognition technology is eager to be implemented into the wearable smartglasses device so that the wearable ear recognition device can work more conveniently and closely to the human ear. Because Epson Moverio BT-200 smartglasses platform with a built-in auto-focus camera and Linux-based Android embedded operating system with plentiful open-source and free-royalty libraries [12] are very useful to realize the implementation of wearable ear recognition device. It is well known that Android embedded platform is one of the best choices for real-time embedded implementation. Thus this paper also expects to implement the proposed ear detection algorithm onto Android smartglasses device.

However, the execution performance of the RISC processor on the wearable smartglasses device is usually quite slower than that of the CISC processor on the personal computer platform. At this moment, the optimization methodology of the proposed ear detection implementation onto Android embedded platform is crucial.

Through a series of well-suited Java software development kit, it is actually easy and quick to finish the Android embedded implementation of the proposed ear detection algorithm featuring AMSO methods, multilayer mosaic enhancement, orthogonal projection histogram analysis, and luminance density verification. Originally, the execution time of the embedded version takes as long as 1861 ms. This paper makes good use of 8 Java optimization skills as follows to improve the execution efficiency. (1) Avoiding creating object instances to reduce memory allocation, (2) slicing up multidimensional arrays into parallel single one-dimension arrays, (3) using native method in C/C++ code that is running faster than Java programming, (4) avoiding floating-point operations because embedded processor cannot support, (5) changing to compare the loop condition with 0 because Java Virtual Machine's fine tuning, (6) avoiding internal method calls inside the loop condition, (7) moving the method call out of the loop as more as possible, and (8) declaring constants as static final type. As a result, the execution time is decreased from 1861 ms to 951 ms.

Furthermore, this paper studies on how to simplify the architecture of the proposed ear detection algorithm without sacrificing the detection performance. In this simplified architecture, the elliptic morphological operator of the proposed AMSO stage only performs the erosion operation once. More importantly, the resulting contour image of the proposed AMSO stage is downsampled prior to the multilayer mosaic enhancement stage. It will significantly reduce a lot of execution time of the multilayer mosaic enhancement stage and reduces the overall execution time to 72 ms. According to the implementation result on Android smartglasses device, the detection performance of the simplified architecture of the proposed ear detection is hardly different from the complete architecture of that. So it is believed that the wearable ear recognition device can achieve the real-time biometric performance in the near future, with the on-going technical advancement on processor capability and optimization methodology.

6 Conclusions

Wearable ear recognition device can be accomplished only if good ear detection system is attained. In this paper, a 2D contour-based algorithm that is immune to illumination difference, ear dimension, accessorized glasses, on-plane rotation, and clothes stripes is proposed. The proposed ear detection algorithm is simple but practical, and is suitable for wearable smartglasses implementation. Besides, high-definition 3D camera and high-cascaded AdaBoost classifier are unnecessary. Linking with certain ear database, wearable ear detection technology can be applied to anti-terrorism security, roadside inspection, banking authentication, community patrol, port examination, airport customs, military weapon, hooligan filtering and high-mountain administration.

Acknowledgments. This work was supported in part by Ministry of Science and Technology, Taiwan, under Grant MOST 106-2221-E-224-053.

References

1. Pflug, A., Busch, C.: Ear biometrics: a survey of detection, feature extraction and recognition methods. IET Biometrics **1**(2), 114–129 (2012)
2. Hezil, N., Boukrouche, A.: Multimodal biometric recognition using human ear and palmprint. IET Biometrics **6**(5), 351–359 (2017)
3. Yan, P., Bowyer, K.W.: Biometric recognition using 3D ear shape. IEEE Trans. Pattern Anal. Mach. Intell. **29**(8), 1297–1308 (2007)
4. Chang, K., Bowyer, K.W.: Comparison and combination of ear and face images in appearance-based biometrics. IEEE Trans. Pattern Anal. Mach. Intell. **25**, 1160–1165 (2003)
5. Ziedan, I.E., Farouk, H., Mohamed, S.: Human ear recognition using voting of statistical and geometrical techniques. In: Proceedings of International Conference on Advanced Control Circuits Systems (ACCS) Systems and International Conference on New Paradigms in Electronics and Information Technology (PEIT), pp. 105–111, Alexandria (2017)
6. Deepak, R., Nayak, A.V., Manikantan, K.: Ear detection using active contour model. In: Proceedings of International Conference on Emerging Trends in Engineering, Technology and Science (ICETETS), pp. 1–7, Pudukkottai (2016)
7. Islam, S.M.S., Bennamoun, M., Davies, R.: Fast and fully automatic ear detection using cascaded AdaBoost. In Proceedings of IEEE Workshop on Applications of Computer Vision (WACV), pp. 1–6 (2008)
8. Yuan, L., Zhang, F.: Ear detection based on improved AdaBoost algorithm, In: 2009 International Conference on Machine Learning and Cybernetics, pp. 2414–2417, Baoding (2009)
9. Abaza, A., Hebert, C., Harrison, M.A.F.: Fast learning ear detection for real-time surveillance. In: Proceedings of IEEE International Conference on Biometrics: Theory, Applications and Systems (BTAS), Sep 2010, pp. 1–6 (2010)
10. Maity, S., Abdel-Mottaleb, M.: 3D ear segmentation and classification through indexing. IEEE Trans. Inf. Forensics Secur. **10**(2), 423–435 (2015)
11. Zhang, L., Li, L., Li, H., Yang, M.: 3D ear identification using block-wise statistics-based features and LC-KSVD. IEEE Trans. Multimedia **18**(8), 1531–1541 (2016)
12. Epson, Moverio BT-200 Technical Information for Application Developer. https://tech.moverio.epson.com/en/life/bt-200/pdf/bt200_tiw1405ce.pdf
13. Coherent Point Drift for Biometric Identification: Ear Recognition. http://wareseeker.com/Graphic-Apps/coherent-point-drift-for-biometric-identification-ear-recognition.zip/36e1acea6
14. Myronenko, A., Song, X.: Point set registration: coherent point drift. In: IEEE Transactions on Pattern Analysis and Machine Intelligence, Dec 2010, vol. 32, no. 12, pp. 2262–2275 (2010)

Automatic Finger Tendon Segmentation from Ultrasound Images Using Deep Learning

Chan-Pang Kuok[1], Bo-Siang Tsai[1], Tai-Hua Yang[2], Fong-Chin Su[2], I-Ming Jou[3], and Yung-Nien Sun[1,4(✉)]

[1] Department of Computer Science and Information Engineering, National Cheng Kung University, Tainan, Taiwan
ynsun@mail.ncku.edu.tw
[2] Department of Biomedical Engineering, National Cheng Kung University, Tainan, Taiwan
[3] Department of Orthopedics, E-Da Hospital, Kaohsiung, Taiwan
[4] MOST AI Biomedical Research Center, Tainan, Taiwan

Abstract. Ultrasound imaging is the most commonly applied method for the diagnosis and surgery of a trigger finger. However, the ultrasound images are noisy and the boundaries of tissues are usually very unclear and fuzzy. Therefore, an automatic computer assisted tool for the tissues segmentation is desired and developed. The segmentation results of the conventional methods were satisfactory but they usually depended on the prior knowledge. Recently, the deep-learning convolutional neural network (CNN) shows amazing performance on image processing and it can process the image end-to-end. In this study, we propose a finger tendon segmentation CNN which overcomes the requirement of prior knowledge and gives promising results on ultrasound images. The evaluation result is remarkable high with DSC 0.884 on 380 testing images and the prediction time is fast by 0.027 s per image. This work, to our best of knowledge, is the first deep learning finger tendon segmentation method from transverse ultrasound images.

Keywords: Segmentation · Finger tendon · Ultrasound images · Deep learning

1 Introduction

Trigger finger is a common finger disease. In the diagnosis and surgery, ultrasound imaging is widely applied to observe the clinical condition of the finger tissues. Trigger finger happens when there is a difference of diameter of a flexor tendon and its retinacular sheath [1]. It causes pain, clicking, catching, and loss of motion on the affected finger, and the treatment generally includes medication, splinting, rehabilitation, corticosteroid injection, or surgical pulley release [1].

Figure 1 shows a transverse ultrasound image at the A1 pulley of the right middle finger. The hand is upwards and the ultrasound probe is placed on the top, an arrow notes the elliptical tendon. It can be observed that the image is noisy, and the boundary of the tendon is very unclear and fuzzy. Thus a computer assisted tool to segment the tissue is very desirable.

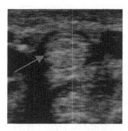

Fig. 1 An ultrasound image of a finger at A1 pulley.

There are numerous conventional methods for the segmentation of ultrasound images. Chuang *et al.* [2] proposed a method to segment the finger tissues by using adaptive texture-based active shape model. Martins *et al.* [3] proposed a method to segment the finger extensor tendon by using active contours framework with prior knowledge and phase symmetry preprocessing. Although the conventional methods can get satisfactory results, however, they need an aggressive initialization or prior knowledge; these increase the complexity of the methods.

In recently years, the deep learning convolutional neural network (CNN) shows amazing performance on image processing tasks. Mishra *et al.* [4] proposed a pipelined network of a CNN followed by clustering to segment the vessel in liver ultrasound images. For Intra Vascular UltraSound (IVUS) images, Yang *et al.* [5] proposed the IVUS-Net which was a Fully Convolutional Network (FCN) architecture network, followed by a post-processing contour extraction step to segment the interior and exterior regions of human arteries. Liu *et al.* [6] developed a deep adversarial neural network for the segmentation of the nerve structure of brachial plexus on ultrasound images.

In this study, we propose a finger tendon segmentation CNN for transverse ultrasound images which is based on the Fully Convolutional DenseNet (FC-DenseNet) [7]. The network is trained and tested end-to-end, the results are promising and the testing time is fast. This work, to our best knowledge, is the first deep learning study on finger tendon segmentation from transverse ultrasound images.

2 Data Material and Method

2.1 Data Material

The transverse ultrasound images on the right middle finger that contains the A1 pulley of a health person are captured at National Cheng Kung University Hospital, Taiwan. There are nine repeats acquisitions at different times and about 100–200 images are obtained at each round, total 1215 images in 9 groups are prepared for this study. The images are captured by Siemens ACUSON S2000 Ultrasound System and a 18-5.5 MHz linear 18L6 HD transducer is used. The original image size is 620×230 pixels with 0.07×0.07 mm^2 pixel spacing, a 192×192 pixel size ROI of tendon is cropped out from each image and becomes the input data of this study. The tendon on each image is annotated by Dr. T.H. Yang and becomes the segmentation ground truth.

2.2   Method

We propose a finger tendon segmentation CNN which is based on the structure of FC-DenseNet [7]. The network is an encoder-decoder structure with skip connections between the downsampling and upsampling sides. A principal component which is called the dense block [8] applied in the network is shown below and the proposed segmentation network is presented as follows.

Dense Block. DenseNet [8] is an efficient structure to observe and use feature maps at different layers and give more accurate classification results together with training convenience. A dense block which includes convolution layers is the key component of the network. Figure 2 shows a dense block with 3 layers, in each layer a successive processes of batch normalization, ReLU and n × n filter convolution are included and the circle with letter 'c' means concatenation. So the output feature map of a layer will concatenate to the input of itself. A growth rate, k is designed which is the output feature map channel number of a layer, and k is the same for all layers of a block. For example, if k = 4, the output feature map channel number of the dense block at Fig. 2 is 12.

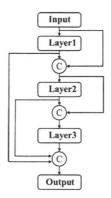

Fig. 2 A dense block example.

Finger Tendon Segmentation Network. Figure 3 shows the proposed segmentation network, the input is the finger tendon ultrasound image and the output is the segmentation result. The channel number of the output feature map and the dimension are shown in the figure, the transition down includes a successive processes of batch normalization, ReLU, 1 × 1 filter size convolution and 2 × 2 max pooling with stride 2, and the transition up includes a successive processes of batch normalization, ReLU and 3 × 3 transposed convolution with stride 2. Similar to [9], we apply the increasing growth rate in the network, the growth rate of the dense block on the top level is 8, and it becomes twice after each downsampling and become half after each upsampling, and there are 6 layers on each dense block of the network.

In the network flow, the input image is convoluted to become a feature map and then passed to a dense block. The output of the dense block is concatenated with its input

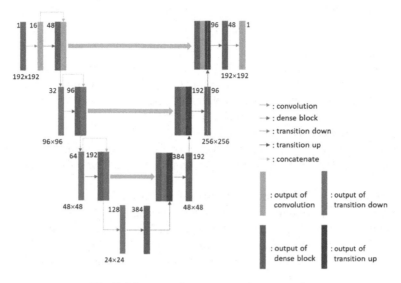

Fig. 3 Finger tendon segmentation network.

and then downsampled by the transition down. The downsampled result is passed to a dense block and the same operation repeats three times in this network. The last dense block output is upsampled by the transition up. The result is concatenated with the corresponding feature maps from the downsampling side and then passed to a dense block. The dense block output is upsampled and the same operation repeats three times in this network. Finally, the last dense block output is convoluted to generate the segmentation result.

Training and Testing. There are 9 groups, total 1215 images used in this study, we randomly select 6 groups of them as the training data and the remaining 3 groups as the testing. So there are 835 images for training and 380 for testing. Data augmentation of rotation, flipping, cropping, gamma and noise adding are applied on the training. The network is trained by RMSProp optimizer for minimizing the Dice loss [10], the mini-batch size is 4. Similar to [11], the network parameter are initialized by using the Gaussian distribution, the initial learning rate is 0.0005 and a polynomial decay [12] is applied. The training stops after 100 epochs, and the training time is about 8 h. When testing, the input is the finger tendon ultrasound image and the output is the segmentation result.

3 Experimental Results

3.1 Segmentation Evaluation

Dice coefficient similarity (DSC) is applied to evaluation the segmentation performance of the proposed method, and the definition of DSC is shown as

$$DSC = \frac{2|A \cap B|}{|A| + |B|},$$

(1)

where A is the ground truth and B is the segmentation result. For comparison, a U-net [13] with similar structure is built. The number of parameters of the proposed network is about 4.14 million and the U-net is about 4.81 million. After testing 380 images, the DSC of the proposed method is 0.884 ± 0.052 and the U-net is 0.851 ± 0.142. The proposed method has about 3% improvement when compared to the U-net with similar parameter amount, and the standard deviation of the proposed one is also smaller, this imply that the proposed method can give more stable and promising segmentation results.

Figure 4 shows the visualization results of the methods, where the input images, results of U-net and proposed method are shown from left to right columns. The ground truth is shown in red color and the result is cyan. Both of the methods can get good fitting results on sample 1. The results from both methods on sample 2 are fitting, although there is an unclear dark region on the left side of the tendon in the image. The U-net result is over segmented on sample 3 and the proposed method is fitting. For the fuzzy contour of the tendon on sample 4, the U-net and the proposed results are largely and slightly over segmented on the right side of the tendon respectively.

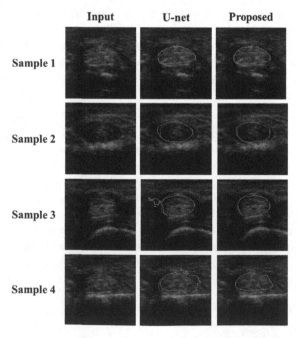

Fig. 4 Segmentation results.

3.2 Computation Performance

The system runs on a PC with Intel i7 CPU, 32G RAM memory and an NVIDIA GTX1080Ti display card is equipped. The network is implemented in Python with TensorFlow framework. The training time is about 8 h and the testing time is about 0.027 s per image.

4 Conclusion

In this study, an efficient and promising finger tendon segmentation CNN for ultrasound images is proposed. The method overcomes the prior knowledge requirement of conventional methods, the network is trained and tested end-to-end. The segmentation performance is remarkable and stable, and the prediction time is fast. In the future, more ultrasound image data will be investigated and different tissues related to the trigger finger disease will be attempted.

Acknowledgments. This work was supported by Ministry of Science and Technology, Taiwan under grant MOST 107-2634-F-006-005. It was carried out at the AI Biomedical Research Center, Tainan, Taiwan.

References

1. Makkouk, A.H., Oetgen, M.E., Swigart, C.R., Dodds, S.D.: Trigger finger: etiology, evaluation, and treatment. Curr. Rev. Musculoskelet. Med. **1**(2), 92–96 (2008)
2. Chuang, B.I., et al.: A medical imaging analysis system for trigger finger using an adaptive texture-based active shape model (ATASM) in ultrasound images. PloS One **12**(10), e0187042 (2017)
3. Martins, N., Sultan, S., Veiga, D., Ferreira, M., Teixeira, F., Coimbra, M.: A new active contours approach for finger extensor tendon segmentation in ultrasound images using prior knowledge and phase symmetry. IEEE J. Biomed. Health Inform. **22**(4), 1261–1268 (2018)
4. Mishra, D., Chaudhury, S., Sarkar, M., Manohar, S., Soin, A.S.: Segmentation of vascular regions in ultrasound images: a deep learning approach. In: Proceedings of IEEE International Symposium on Circuits and Systems (ISCAS), pp. 1–5, May 2018
5. Yang, J., Tong, L., Faraji, M., Basu, A.: IVUS-Net: an intravascular ultrasound segmentation network. arXiv preprint arXiv:1806.03583 (2018)
6. Liu, C., Liu, F., Wang, L., Ma, L., Lu, Z.M.: Segmentation of nerve on ultrasound images using deep adversarial network. Int. J. Innov. Comput. Inform. Control **14**(1), 53–64 (2018)
7. Jégou, S., Drozdzal, M., Vazquez, D., Romero, A., Bengio, Y.: The one hundred layers tiramisu: fully convolutional densenets for semantic segmentation. In: IEEE Conference on Computer Vision and Pattern Recognition Workshops (CVPRW), pp. 1175–1183, July 2017
8. Huang, G., Liu, Z., Van Der Maaten, L., Weinberger, K.Q.: Densely connected convolutional networks. In: Proceedings of CVPR, vol. 1, no. 2, p. 3, July 2017
9. Huang, G., Liu, S., van der Maaten, L., Weinberger, K.Q.: CondenseNet: an efficient DenseNet using learned group convolutions. In: Proceedings of CVPR, pp. 2752–2761 (2017)

10. Milletari, F., Navab, N., Ahmadi, S.-A.: V-net: fully convolutional neural networks for volumetric medical image segmentation. In: Proceedings of 2016 Fourth International Conference on 3D Vision (3DV), pp. 565–571 (2016)
11. He, K., Zhang, X., Ren, S., Sun, J.: Delving deep into rectifiers: surpassing human-level performance on ImageNet classification. In: Proceedings of the IEEE International Conference on Computer Vision, pp. 1026–1034 (2015)
12. Chen, L.C., Papandreou, G., Schroff, F., Adam, H.: Rethinking atrous convolution for semantic image segmentation. arXiv preprint arXiv:1706.05587 (2017)
13. Ronneberger, O., Fischer, P., Brox, T.: U-net: convolutional networks for biomedical image segmentation. In: Navab, N., Hornegger, J., Wells, W., Frangi, A. (eds.) MICCAI 2015. LNCS, vol. 9351, pp. 234–241. Springer, Cham (2015). https://doi.org/10.1007/978-3-319-24574-4_28

Two-Dimensional TRUS Image and Three-Dimensional MRI Prostate Image Fusion System

Chuan-Yu Chang[1(✉)], Chih-An Wang[1], and Yuh-Shyan Tsai[2]

[1] Department of Computer Science and Information Engineering,
National Yunlin University of Science and Technology, Douliu, Taiwan
chuanyu@yuntech.edu.tw
[2] Department of Urology, National Cheng Kung University Hospital,
Tainan, Taiwan

Abstract. In the diagnosis of prostate disease, urologists examine the presence of fibrosis or tumors in the prostate tissue of patients by magnetic resonance imaging (MRI) and transrectal ultrasonography (TRUS). In general, urologists will imagine the location of fibrosis or tumors in 3D space. To resolve this a fusion algorithm for three-dimensional (3D) prostate magnetic resonance imaging (MRI) and 2D TRUS was developed. Fiducial registration error was employed in this study to evaluate the registration error of the upper half contour. Experiments showed that the proposed method achieved good fusion results. The system can further guide urologists in the performance of TRUS for tissue biopsy or high intensity focused ultrasound (HIFU).

Keywords: Prostate segmentation · Iterative closest point · Image fusion · 3D registration

1 Introduction

The prostate is an exocrine gland in the male reproductive system, with its primary function being the secretion and storage of prostatic fluid. It is located in the bottom of the pelvic cavity and surrounded by vital organs. Therefore, if the prostate contracts a disease, the organs around it will likely to also be infected, leading to urinary tract obstruction or urethritis, and, if the situation worsens, hematuria or urinary incontinence [1]. Urologists usually perform digital rectal examination (DRE) for preliminary diagnosis of prostate diseases. The diagnosis of DRE may vary between urologists. Urologists make subjective judgments based on their fingertips and clinical experience; therefore, the diagnostic accuracy of DRE varies [2]. The transrectal ultrasonography (TRUS) is the most commonly used imaging technology in the diagnosis of prostate diseases. However, conventional TRUS has a low signal-to-noise ratio, resulting in poor image quality.

In this paper, a fusion algorithm for three-dimensional (3D) prostate magnetic resonance imaging (MRI) and 2D TRUS was developed. The system can guide

© Springer Nature Singapore Pte Ltd. 2019
C.-Y. Chang et al. (Eds.): ICS 2018, CCIS 1013, pp. 785–792, 2019.
https://doi.org/10.1007/978-981-13-9190-3_85

urologists in the performance of TRUS for tissue biopsy or high intensity focused ultrasound (HIFU).

All the medical images used in this study were collected from the National Cheng Kung University Hospital. In the developed system, the experienced urologist manually outlines the prostate boundaries in TRUS and MRI images as references for modeling. The findings of this study showed that the subsequent image registration results could help physicians determine patient conditions, thereby improving diagnostic accuracy and precision in performing radiotherapy or electrotherapy.

2 Proposed Method

In this paper, a 2D TRUS and 3D MRI images fusion system was developed. There are three main processes namely TRUS prostate contour position transformation, iterative closest point registration, and 3D fusion in the proposed method. Figure 1 shows the flowchart of the proposed fusion system.

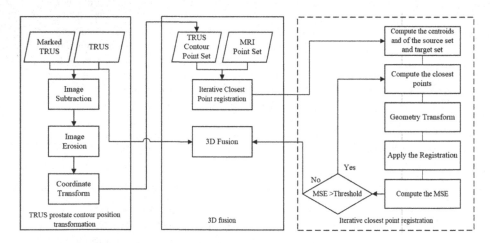

Fig. 1. Flowchart of the proposed system

Step 1: TRUS prostate contour position transformation

Image processing techniques, specifically image subtraction and image erosion, are applied on the boundary of the prostate marked by physicians in the TRUS images. Through this, the actual location of the prostate boundary is identified and converted into point sets (3D coordinates) for use in the next step.

Step 2: Iterative closest point registration

To compute the alignment of points in the 2D TRUS and 3D MRI images, the centroid alignment (i.e., aligning the centroid of the point sets in corresponding TRUS and MRI images) is performed, followed by computation of the rotation alignment of the two point sets.

Step 3: 3D fusion

Fusion processing is conducted by overlaying the image registration results obtained in Step 2 with the patient's TRUS images, thereby enabling the urologist to perform diagnosis in a 3D environment.

2.1 Data Preprocessing

1. Establishment of the 3D MRI model

In this paper, the software application ITK-SNAP was chosen for urologists to manually mark out the prostate in MRI images. The marked cross-sectional images were then layered to form a 3D model, and interpolation was subsequently performed to smooth the model's exterior surface. Interpolation performed computation by varying intervals, namely 3, 5, and 7 voxels. Figure 2 shows the interpolated 3D prostates by 3, 5, and 7 voxels. The model generated using 7 voxels interval was chosen in this paper.

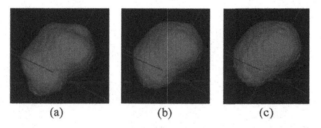

(a)   (b)   (c)

Fig. 2. The resulting model of interpolate by (a) 3voxels, (b) 5 voxels, and (c) 7 voxels.

2. Prostate boundaries outlined by urologists in the TRUS

An experienced urologist manually marked out the prostate boundary from the raw TRUS images. Figure 3 shows the outlined prostate boundaries of TRUS with image field of 126° or 140°.

2.2 Registration of 2D TRUS and 3D MRI Images

The main anatomical planes of the human body, including transverse plane, coronal plane and sagittal plane. In this paper, both TRUS and MRI images were captured from the transverse plane, which means that the upper and lower sides (marked as the "top" and "bottom" in Fig. 4) of such images correspond to the front and back sides, respectively, of the human body. Since the instruments for obtaining TRUS and MRI are different, the obtained images existed horizontal tilt. As illustrated in Fig. 4, the TRUS image exhibits a tilt of 40° to the vertical plane.

The proposed method first performed centroid alignment and then computation for iterative closest point registration. In the process of rigid registration, the system followed the upper-half contour of the TRUS prostate image for alignment. Because the

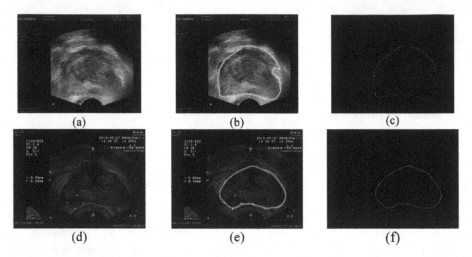

Fig. 3. The origin TRUS with image field of (a) 140° and (d) 126°, the outlined boundaries by an experienced urologist with image field of (b) 140° and (e) 126°, the extracted boundaries (c) 140° and (f) 126°.

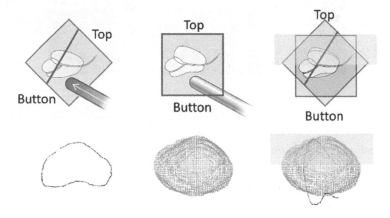

Fig. 4. The schematic diagram of image fusion with MRI and TRUS

point sets in both the TRUS and MRI images largely retained their original orientations, the amount of rotation possible was limited. The yellow-colored areas in Fig. 4 denote the portions of contour involved in the attempted alignment.

The program used in this study to perform image fusion was the Visualization Toolkit (VTK) [3]. Furthermore, the iterative closest point method first proposed by Besl and McKay [4] was employed for alignment of the prostate 3D point sets and partial prostate segmentation contour point sets. Figure 5 presents a flowchart of the iterative closest point method [5].

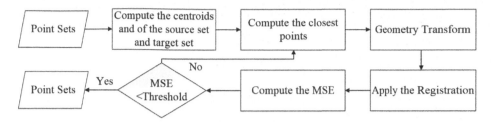

Fig. 5. The flowchart of the iterative closest point

2.3   Image Fusion

Before image fusion, the translation offset, rotation matrix, and scale matrix should be obtained in advance. The translation offset, rotation matrix, and scale matrix are defined as follows:

The centroids of the source set (μ_x) and target set (μ_p) are defined as:

$$\mu_x = \frac{\sum_{i=1}^{N_x} x_i}{N_x} \tag{1}$$

$$\mu_p = \frac{\sum_{i=1}^{N_p} p_i}{N_p} \tag{2}$$

where N_x is the total number of data points in the source set, and N_p is the total number of data points in the target set.

The translation offset between these two centroids can be expressed as:

$$T = \mu_x - \mu_p \tag{3}$$

The orthogonal matrix corresponding to a rotation by the unit quaternion $z = q_0 + q_1 i + q_2 j + q_3 k$ with ($|z| = 1$) when post-multiplying with a column vector is given by

$$R(q_R) = \begin{bmatrix} q_0^2 + q_1^2 - q_2^2 - q_3^2 & 2(q_1 q_2 - q_0 q_3) & 2(q_1 q_3 + q_0 q_2) \\ 2(q_1 q_2 + q_0 q_3) & q_0^2 - q_1^2 + q_2^2 - q_3^2 & 2(q_2 q_3 - q_0 q_1) \\ 2(q_1 q_3 - q_0 q_2) & 2(q_2 q_3 + q_0 q_1) & q_0^2 - q_1^2 - q_2^2 + q_3^2 \end{bmatrix} \tag{4}$$

The scale factor between two point sets can be calculated by:

$$S = \left(\sum_{i=1}^{N_x} \left\| r'_{x,i} \right\|^2 \bigg/ \sum_{i=1}^{N_p} \left\| r'_{p,i} \right\|^2 \right)^{1/2} \tag{5}$$

where $r'_{x,i}$ and $r'_{p,i}$ are the centralized distance of the source set and target set, respectively, expressed as:

$$r'_{x,i} = r_{x,i} - \mu_x \tag{6}$$

$$r'_{p,i} = r_{p,i} - \mu_p \tag{7}$$

Coordinates of the prostate contour in the TRUS image are subsequently aligned by applying these parameters. Figure 6 illustrates the schematic diagram of prostate image fusion.

Fig. 6. Schematic diagram of prostate image fusion

3   Experiment Results

The TRUS and MRI images used for experiments were obtained from Department of Urology, National Cheng Kung University Hospital, Taiwan. A total of 15 cases were collected in this paper. Because of the different types of probe used in the hospital, the TRUS images had an image field of either 126° or 140°. Therefore, samples of different image fields were processed separately. Figures 7 and 8 illustrate the fusion results of images with image fields of 140° and 126°, respectively.

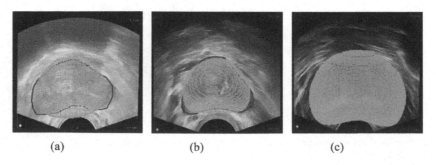

(a)   (b)   (c)

Fig. 7. The fusion results (a)–(c) by image field of 140°

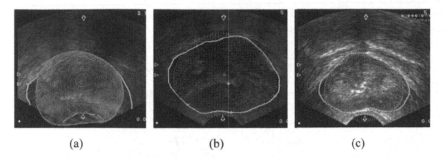

| (a) | (b) | (c) |

Fig. 8. The fusion results (a)–(c) by image field of 126°

This experiment measures the percentage overlap of the upper half contour of 2D TRUS with the registered 3D MRI contour. This value indicated how much the contour had been distorted, thereby providing urologists with a clearer understanding of the TRUS images at their disposal. Figure 9 shows the schematic diagram of contour registration, in which red contour is the boundary of TRUS prostate and blue contour is the registered 3D MRI boundary. $H_{prostate}$ denotes the height of the red contour of TRUS prostate. H_{point} is the height of the overlapped contour between TRUS prostate and the MRI prostate model.

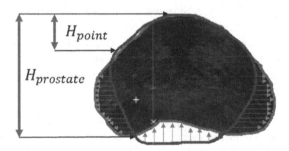

Fig. 9. Schematic diagram of fiducial registration (Color figure online)

Fiducial registration error (FRE) defined as Eq. (8) is an alignment measurement that is the mean distance between corresponding fiducial points after a registration has been effected.

$$\text{FRE}_{\text{point}} = \frac{1}{N_{\text{point}}} \sum_{i=1}^{N_{\text{point}}} \text{Distance}(\text{point}(n), \text{closest\_point}(n)) \qquad (8)$$

where N_{point} is the number of fiducial coordinate points in the source set (red contour). Distance (.,.) denotes the Euclidean distance between two points. In which, point(n) and closest_point(n) denote the nth fiducial point in the source set and the target set, respectively. Table 1 listed the FRE of TRUS image field of 126° and 140° under different fiducial point ratios. From Table 1, $FRE_{point\ (140°)}$ and $FRE_{point\ (126°)}$ obtained the smallest registration errors in the N_{point} of the 40% and 50%, respectively.

Table 1. FRE_{point} for image field of 126° and 140°

N_{point}	$FRE_{point\ (140°)}$	$FRE_{point\ (126°)}$
10%	2.9314	5.4834
20%	3.4182	5.4084
30%	3.0779	4.3179
40%	2.5806	3.4840
50%	2.6306	3.1963
60%	3.0789	3.8563
70%	3.9613	4.9086
80%	5.1117	5.8859
90%	5.2171	6.1714
100%	5.0742	5.8414

4   Conclusions

The MRI–TRUS fusion images would aid urologists in gaining a better understanding of patients' conditions, thereby improving the quality of their treatment. This paper proposed a system for image fusion based on the fiducial registration. The 3D MRI model is registered with the upper contour of 2D TRUS images. The minimum registration error of the upper half contour was achieved when 40%–50% fiducial coordinate points was used. If sufficient case data becomes available, more detailed and comprehensive feature data can be obtained.

Acknowledgment. This work was financially supported by the "Intelligent Recognition Industry Service Center" from The Featured Areas Research Center Program within the framework of the Higher Education Sprout Project by the Ministry of Education (MOE) in Taiwan.

References

1. Prostate disease. https://www.betterhealth.vic.gov.au/health/ConditionsAndTreatments/prostate-disease
2. Digital Rectal Exam vs. PSA Test For Prostate Cancer. https://www.disabledworld.com/health/cancer/prostate/rectal-examination.php. http://www.webmd.com/urinary-incontinence-oab/picture-of-the-prostate
3. VTK - The Visualization Toolkit. https://www.vtk.org/
4. Besl, P.J., McKay, N.D.: A method for registration of 3-D shapes. IEEE Trans. Pattern Anal. Mach. Intell. **14**, 239–256 (1992). https://doi.org/10.1109/34.121791
5. Horn, B.K.P.: Closed-form solution of absolute orientation using unit quaternions. J. Opt. Soc. Am. A **4**, 629–642 (1987). https://doi.org/10.1364/JOSAA.4.000629

Author Index

Abdul-Rahman, Anmar 627

Bao, Bing-Kun 215
Barnett, George 131
Bell, Mark 688

Cao, Yunbo 280
Chang, Arthur 260, 270
Chang, Chia-Hao 115
Chang, Ching-Lueh 457
Chang, Ching-Lung 391
Chang, Chuan-Yu 163, 406, 785
Chang, Jyh-Biau 82
Chang, Tin 406
Chang, Yu-Chien 349
Chang, Yue-Shan 302
Chao, Shu-Jung 3
Chapman, Jon W. 131
Chen, Bo-Xian 449
Chen, Chia-Mei 76
Chen, Chia-Yen 178
Chen, Ching-Ju 532
Chen, Chi-Yang 745
Chen, Chu-Song 141
Chen, Gen-Huey 495
Chen, Keyang 168
Chen, Kuan-Chung 82
Chen, Li-Hsuan 524
Chen, Mei-Juan 681
Chen, Ming-Te 543
Chen, Pei-Yin 95
Chen, Szu-Ying 207
Chen, Tzung-Her 580
Chen, Vivien Yi-Chun 358
Chen, Wei-Ting 95
Chen, Yen Hung 440
Chen, Yu-Sheng 260, 270
Chenbunyanon, Chaitawat 190
Cheng, Hui-Jun 321
Cheng, Kuo-Sheng 665
Cheng, Wai-Khuen 385
Chi, Po-Wen 559

Chiang, Jung-Hsien 758
Chiao, Hsin-Ta 302
Chien, Po-Chuan 440
Chiu, I-Hsuan 238, 250
Chiu, Jih-Ching 3, 49, 62
Chou, Chien 227
Chow, Nan-Haw 665
Chu, Chao-Ting 476, 485
Chuang, Yung-Yu 207
Chung, Pau-Choo 665
Chung, Tzu-Hsuan 406

Dai, Shou-Hong 732
Dharmadi, Richard 163

Fan, Chao 291
Fan, Chun-I 590
Fan, Hsiang-Shian 567
Fang, Shi-Mai 270
Fang, Wen-Pinn 349
Feng, Tian-Zheng 368
Fouzia, Syeda 688
Fu, Ru-Hong 368

GholamHosseini, Hamid 627

Han, Mei 280, 291
Han, Ping-Hsuan 115
He, Jian-Wen 503
Ho, Cheng Ssu 186
Ho, Cheng-Yuan 238, 250
Ho, Chian C. 106, 764
Ho, Chian-Cheng 476, 485
Hong, Tzung-Pei 157
Hsia, Shih-Chang 20, 28
Hsieh, Sun-Yuan 524
Hsu, Chan-Hung 495
Hsu, Chung-Chian 260, 270
Hsu, Ping-Kun 599
Hsu, Ruei-Hau 590
Hsueh, Nien Lin 713
Hu, Qinghua 291

Huang, Chao-Yang 543
Huang, Chih-Yang 440
Huang, Chuen-Min 310
Huang, Guan-Jen 62
Huang, Kuo-Si 425
Huang, Ming-Hsiang 330
Huang, Wen-Chi 349
Huang, Yao-Pao 681
Huang, Ya-Yung 376
Huang, Yi-Chin 35
Hung, Chung-Wen 532
Hung, Chung-Yuan 376
Hung, Siang-Huai 425
Hung, Yi-Ping 115

Jan, Yao-Fu 115
Jhu, Yu-Chen 399
Ji, Puzhao 168
Jian, Guo-Zhang 150
Jiang, Ji-Han 190
Jiang, Xin-Yan 20
Jiang, Yan-Ru 550
Jou, I-Ming 778
Jung, Liang 646
Juniarta Dwiyantoro, Alvin Prayuda 163

Kang, Li-Wei 368
Kao, Mong-Jen 468, 507
Kao, Peng-Yuan 115
Kao, Wen-Tsung 636
Karati, Arijit 590
Klette, Reinhard 627, 688
Ko, Chien-Chaun 745
Ku, Keng-Chu 495
Kuo, Wen-Chung 608
Kuok, Chan-Pang 778

Lai, Chien-Hung 543
Lai, Chun-Ming 131
Lai, Gu-Hsin 76
Lai, Jun-Jie 406
Lai, Xin-Hong 406
Lai, Yung-Ling 503
Lee, Chuan-Min 516
Lee, Chung-Nan 698
Lee, D. T. 468, 507
Lee, Tsung-Lin 49
Lei, Chin-Laung 618
Li, Chao-Ting 665

Li, Chun-Hsien 115
Li, Jia-Long 260
Li, Wei-Ting 532
Li, Xiang-Xuan 28
Li, Yueh-Lin 49, 62
Liao, Wen-Hung 636, 646
Lin, Bo-Chen 95
Lin, Chien-Chou 399
Lin, Ching-Chi 495
Lin, Chun-Yuan 321
Lin, En-Wei 406
Lin, Han-Yu 550
Lin, Iuon-Chang 599
Lin, Jerry Chao-Lee 358
Lin, Jim-Min 358
Lin, Jun-Hong 745
Lin, Jun-Yi 415
Lin, Mu-Ting 599
Lin, Nai-Wei 721
Lin, Wen-Shan 106, 764
Lin, Yu Chien 673
Lin, Yu-Pin 608
Lin, Zhiping 654
Liu, Hao-Yu 543
Lo, Chien Shun 186
Lu, Wei 524
Lu, Yi-Xuan 3

Ma, Shang-Pin 732
Mao, Chun-Chien 321
Muchtar, Kahlil 163
Munggaran, Muhammad Rizky 163

Nemati, Ali 627
Norouzifard, Mohammad 627
Nugraha, Indra 163

Oh, Beom-Seok 654

Pai, Kung-Jui 433
Prathyusha, Yerra 698
Pu, Jiansu 168, 280, 291

Rahman, Faris 163
Rao, Yunbo 168, 291

Shen, Day-Fann 197
Shieh, Ce-Kuen 82
Shyu, Shyong Jian 460

Song, Jiali   168
Su, Fong-Chin   778
Su, Ja-Hwung   157
Sun, Wei-Ting   302
Sun, Yung-Nien   778

Tan, Teik-Boon   385
Teoh, Andrew Beng Jin   654
Toh, Kar-Ann   654
Tsai, Bo-Siang   778
Tsai, Cheng-Hung   35
Tsai, Hung-Wen   665
Tsai, Meng-Han   618
Tsai, Yi-Lin   391
Tsai, Ying Zhen   460
Tsai, Yuh-Shyan   785
Tseng, Kuo-Tsung   449
Tsoi, Kin-Wa   207
Tu, Cheng-Hao   141
Tu, Hai-Lun   468
Tu, Tai-Yuan   580

Wang, Bo-Yung   28
Wang, Chia-Ying   732
Wang, Chien-Lung   721
Wang, Chih-An   785
Wang, Chih-Hung   580
Wang, Chuin-Mu   150
Wang, Chun-Yu   82
Wang, Farn   673
Wang, Ming-Hung   559, 618
Wang, Qing   280
Wang, Shag-Kai   20
Wang, Shyue-Liang   157
Wang, Wen-Fong   406, 415
Wang, Wen-Shiang   543
Wei, Lirui   280, 291

Wen, Dan-Wei (Marian)   76
Weng, Chi-Yao   567
Wu, Chia-Hung   550
Wu, Hsien-Huang   376
Wu, Qi-Hon   197
Wu, S. Felix   131
Wu, Yi-Chieh   636

Xin, Zhige   131
Xu, Changsheng   215
Xu, Haotian   178

Yan, Ming-Yi   330
Yang, Chang-Biau   425, 449
Yang, Cheng-Hsing   567
Yang, Chia-Jung   758
Yang, Ching-Yu   406
Yang, Huei-Fang   141
Yang, Ji-min   580
Yang, Shu-Kai   227
Yang, Tai-Hua   778
Yang, Wei-Chieh   618
Yang, Wuu   330
Yang, Yu-Chiao   157
Yap, Jia-Hong   82
Ye, Yong-Bin   3
Yeh, Chia-Hung   681
Yen, Li-Hsing   338
Yu, Hung-I   507
Yuan, Shyan-Ming   302
Yu-Chiang, Li   415

Zeng, Bo-jyun   376
Zhang, Jin   215
Zhang, Yuwei   280, 291
Zheng, Wei-Sheng   338

Printed in the United States
By Bookmasters